Standard Encyclopedia of

Pressed Glass

THIRD EDITION

1860 – 1930

Identification & Values

Bill Edwards

&

Mike Carwile

COLLECTOR BOOKS

A Division of Schroeder Publishing Co., Inc.

Front cover: Helmet butter dish, very rare, blue, $750.00; Memphis butter dish, vaseline, $3,000.00; Jumbo butter dish with knife rack, rare, crystal, $500.00.

Back cover: Bee butter dish, rare, vaseline, $350.00.

Cover Design: Beth Summers
Book Design: Terri Hunter

COLLECTOR BOOKS
P.O. Box 3009
Paducah, KY 42002-3009

www.collectorbooks.com

Bill Edwards
620 W. 2nd St.
Madison, IN 47250

Mike Carwile
180 Cheyenne Dr.
Lynchburg, VA 24502
carwile@centralva.net

The current values in this book should be used only as a guide. They are not intended to set prices, which vary from one section of the country to another. Auction prices as well as dealer prices vary greatly and are affected by condition as well as demand. Neither the authors nor the publisher assumes responsibility for any losses that might be incurred as a result of consulting this guide.

Contents

Dedication

To Steve and Radka Sandeman, and the late John Gregory for all their help in rescuing this edition when we so badly needed photos. The Sandemans have always been a great help, and in the short time we were privileged to know John, we considered his friendship special.

Acknowledgments

A work of this magnitude just couldn't be accomplished without the help of many people who contributed time, information, and photos of their glass, and we are very pleased to thank them for their aid:

A very special thanks to those who permitted us to photograph their collections or show their photos. These include Don and Becky Hamlet, Fred and Shirley Seay, Marian S. Fahrback, Eugene Serbus, Herman and Evelyn Wallace, Bill and Phyllis Burch, Ronald and Becky Lee, Don and Dorene Ashbridge, Rick and Bonnie Boldt, Richard and Merri Houghton, and Emma H. Crane.

In addition, we want to thank all the others who helped. These include Jack and Carolyn Carwile, Ruth H. Johnson, Emily J. Claybrook, Barry Mays, Wildwood Antique Market, Lou's Antiques, Bob and Pat Davis, Estate Specialist, Granny's Antiques, Trevillian Auction Company, Consign It Shop, Peddler Antiques, Back Street Antiques, Roanoke Antique Mall, Green Market Antiques, Walnut Avenue Antiques, Olde Liberty Antique Mall, Snoopers Antique Mall, Old Fort Antique Mall, Blue Ridge Antique Center, West Piedmont Regional Antique Mall, Cambria Emporium, Christiansburg Antique Mall, John's Antiques, Fox Den Antiques, The Silent Woman Antiques, Lexington Antique Mall, Rolling Hills Antique Mall, Valley View Antique Mall, Standardsville Antique Mall, Midlothian Antique Center, Kaleidoscope — The Glass Lady, Stuart's Draft Antique Mall, Antiquer's Mall, Green House Shop, Country Shops of Culpepper, Minute Man Antique Mall, Shackleford's Antiques, Chippenham Antique Center, Stage Coach Antique Mall, Riverbend Auction Company, Green Valley Auction Incorporated, Old Garage Antiques, Miller's Antique Mall of Lebanon, Martha W. Cope, Gene Reno, Don Watley, Singletree Antiques, and Ronald E. Noble.

And finally, we want to acknowledge all those who read the second edition and offered their help with photos or information for the current edition, especially Steve and Radka Sandeman who shared so much of their glass, as well as James Edward Dial, Ted Friesner, Janet Goetz, Alan Sedgwick, James S. Wilkins, Alice Miller, Gary and Sharon Vandevander, Norman E. Archer, Larry Enriques, Gerald Reed, Joseph Brooks Jr., John Sherwood, Joyce Power, Mr. and Mrs. Lloyd Howard, Stephen Stewart, Bill Holmeide, Frank Smith, Gregory Fergeson, Maggie Ramey, Mary Bland, William and Patsy Roberts, Virginia Radcliffe, and Anthony E. Vossman.

Introduction

American pressed glass had its beginning in 1821 when J. P. Bakewell received a patent to produce glass furniture knobs. Before that time glass was blown, financially often beyond the reach of most, simple in design by necessity, and limited in availability. With the Bakewell patent, others quickly followed and within a few years, pressed tableware was being produced in vast amounts and in shapes previously unheard of. America's pressed glass industry was on its way.

Other makers and other patents soon followed but in the 1860s urgent military need for available lead forced the glass industry into a bind that lasted until William Leighton Sr., developed a soda-lime formula for Hobbs, Brockunier, eliminating the need for lead in glass production. Finally, glass could be pressed easily and was thinner and more adaptable to detailing, permitting patterns never possible before. Within a decade pressed glass was at its zenith and companies still bound to old ways of flint glass began to pass from the scene, replaced by a wave of vital new concerns. Plants sprouted where there was a supply of natural gas in western Pennsylvania, Ohio, West Virginia, Maryland, and Indiana. Hundreds of patterns and dozens of shapes with elaborate geometric, animal, fruit, and fauna designs poured into the marketplace in crystal and sparkling colors.

By the 1890s problems in the glass industry had mounted; labor disputes, depletion of some of the gas supply, a national depression, all forced a rethinking of production methods. Soon combines like that of U. S. Glass (fifteen companies joining together) and National (nineteen companies) were organized. Impact on the marketplace was rewarding, with increased production, reworked moulds, and re-issued patterns, all allowing full mileage from every glass pour. New patterns and treatments were offering cased, ivory (custard), and opalescent glass treatments that remain very collectible today.

By early 1900, production again suffered. The number of quality producers dwindled due to fires, financial failures, or various other reasons. The answer was new blood with new ideas, and companies like Northwood, Fenton, Millersburg, Imperial, and Cambridge brought iridized, gilded, enameled, and stained wares to intrigue new interest from buyers.

By the end of the 1920s with a national depression looming, a loss of quality began. This, coupled with a trend toward reproduction of early pressed items and the arrival of full-machine moulding, changed the industry forever. Sixty years of quality hand-pressed glass seemed doomed as Depression glass became the norm, and for all intent, the golden age of American pressed glass ended.

Pattern Attribution

Researchers and writers of books about American glass patterns are often criticized for their conclusions, but the reader should be aware of all the pitfalls in placing a pattern or group of patterns with a single maker.

Glass companies opened and closed with some regularity; they moved to other locations at will; combines like U.S. Glass and National absorbed companies, controlling their production, often moving moulds from one member-factory to another; and finally blanks were sold to other concerns to be stained, gilded, or decorated, with these concerns then advertising and selling the glass as their own, and never giving credit to the glassmaker.

All of these things have clouded the history of glass and so mistakes were often made in the identification of a pattern's true maker. Granted, in the last decade, research has gained ground, and while all of us do our best to be as accurate as possible, some mistakes do occur, and some patterns linked to one maker also may have been made by others. So we hope the reader won't judge too quickly. Every year more facts are learned, more company catalogs appear, more company glass ads surface, and more general information is confirmed or discounted.

As we've said in previous editions, we use several methods for attribution that include identifying glass shards, comparing with other patterns for similarity, and researching old glass catalogs and advertisements. In addition we take a long look at those researchers who have gone before us and compare one writer's ideas with another's.

We hope readers will add their knowledge to the mix and let us know when they have information that runs contrary to ours. We happily correct our mistakes whenever we know about them and that is why we produce succeeding editions of all our books. So if you question our conclusions, share your knowledge with us so that we can improve our books with each new edition.

Shapes

Berry Set – has one large bowl (usually 8" – 9") and six individual small bowls.

Bread Plate – may be round or oblong. Usually larger than a regular plate.

Cake Stand – a flat plate shape on a stem. Can also be found without the stem and are "plates" not stands.

Carafe – a water bottle that doesn't come with a stopper.

Celery Vase – a tall holder for stalks of celery. May be flat based or on a stem.

Compote – a stemmed vessel, usually meant to hold fruit (large) or jelly (small), or just be decorative.

Cruet – a stoppered bottle that holds liquids such as oil.

Decanter – a bottle to hold spirits. Can have many shapes but comes with its own stopper. Depending on the type of spirits, it can be found with wine glasses, goblets, clarets, or champagne glasses.

Ice Cream Set – like the berry set, this one is shallow and has the edges of the bowl turned up and slightly inward.

Jam Jar – a receptacle for jam. Has a lid that is slotted for its own spoon. Also known as a mustard jar when holding mustard or horseradish.

Nappy – a one-handled piece, meant to hold mints, jam, nuts, etc.

Pickle Dish – a long, narrow flat dish used to hold pickles.

Punch Set – consists of a punch bowl, a standard or base and matching cups (often twelve, but may be as few as six); and occasionally a large underplate.

Salt Dip – a small flat salt holder that is usually put at each place setting. Can be a master salt or individual salt dip.

Sandwich Tray – a large plate, usually with a center handle.

Shakers – usually means salt and pepper shakers although there is a larger shape that is a sugar shaker.

Syrup – a handled container for syrup. Has a metal lid and pouring spout.

Table Set – usually has four parts; covered butter dish, a covered sugar holder, a creamer, and a spooner (spoonholder).

Toothpick Holder – just what the name implies. A small receptacle, handled or not, to hold toothpicks.

Water Set – consists of a water pitcher and six matching tumblers. The pitcher may be a squat design, a tall tankard, a pedestal based one, or a standard shape (usually has a collar base). Tumblers can be of standard size, tall (called lemonade tumblers), or squat.

Glass Companies

Adams and Company, Pittsburgh, Pennsylvania, c. 1851 – 1891. Joined U. S. Glass Co. in 1891 as Factory A.

Aetna Glass and Manufacturing Co., Bellaire, Ohio, 1880 – 1891.

American Flint Glass Works, Wheeling, West Virginia, 1840s.

Anchor Hocking Glass Co., c. 1904 to present. Began as Hocking Glass Co., and in 1906 Ohio Flint Glass Co. merged with it.

Atterbury and Company, Pittsburgh, Pennsylvania, 1850s.

Bakewell, Pears and Company, Pittsburgh, Pennsylvania. Began as Bakewell, Payn and Page Co. (Pittsburgh), 1808. Still operating in the 1870s.

Beatty, Alexander J. and Sons, Steubenville, Ohio, 1879. Moved to Tiffin, Ohio, and joined U. S. Glass in 1892 as Factory R.

Beatty-Brady Glass Co., Steubenville, Ohio, 1850; Dunkirk, Indiana, 1898. Joined National Glass in 1899.

Beaumont Glass Co., Martins Ferry, Ohio, 1895. In 1905 joined Hocking Glass Co., which became Anchor Hocking Glass Co.

Beaver Falls Cooperative Glass Co., Beaver Falls, Pennsylvania, 1879. Became Beaver Falls Glass Co., 1887.

Bellaire Goblet Co., Bellaire, Ohio, 1879; Findlay, Ohio, 1888. Joined U. S. Glass in 1891 as Factory M.

Belmont Glass Co., Bellaire, Ohio, 1866; still operating in 1888.

Boston and Sandwich Glass Co., Sandwich, Massachusetts, 1825 – 1889.

Boston Silver Glass Co., East Cambridge, Massachusetts, 1857 – 1870s.

Brilliant Glass Works, Brilliant, Ohio, 1880. Moved to LaGrange in 1880 and merged with Novelty Glass Works, 1889.

Bryce, McKee and Co., Pittsburgh, Pennsylvania, 1850. Became Bryce, Walker and Co. in 1854.

Bryce, Walker and Co., Pittsburgh, Pennsylvania, 1855; became Bryce Brothers in 1882.

Bryce Brothers, Pittsburgh, Pennsylvania, 1882. Moved to Hammondsville, Pennsylvania, 1889; joined U. S. Glass in 1891 as Factory B. Moved to Mt. Pleasant, Pennsylvania, in 1896 and was still operating in 1952.

Bryce, Higbee and Co. (Homestead Glass Works), Pittsburgh, Pennsylvania, 1879. Became J. B. Higbee Glass Co. c. 1900 at Bridgeville, Pennsylvania, and was still operating in 1911.

Buckeye Glass Co., Wheeling, West Virginia, 1849; moved to Bowling Green, Ohio, in 1888. Closed c. 1903. See Excelsior Glass Works for their other factory.

Cambridge Glass Co. (National Glass Co.), Cambridge, Ohio, 1901; closed 1958.

Campbell, Jones and Co., Pittsburgh, Pennsylvania, 1865. Became Jones, Cavitt and Co., 1883.

Canton Glass Co., Canton, Ohio, c. 1883; Marion, Indiana, 1883; joined National Glass in 1899.

Central Glass Co., Wheeling, West Virginia, 1863; joined U. S. Glass in 1891 as Factory O; became Central Glass Works later.

Central Glass Co., Summitsville, Indiana. Joined National Glass in 1899; survived and was still operating in 1924.

Challinor, Taylor and Co. (Challinor, Hogan Glass Co.), Pittsburgh, Pennsylvania, 1866; Tarentum, Pennsylvania, 1884. Joined U. S. Glass as Factory C in 1891.

Columbia Glass Co., Findlay, Ohio, 1886; joined U. S. Glass in 1891 as Factory J.

Cooperative Flint Glass Co., Beaver Falls, Pennsylvania, 1879 – 1937.

Crystal Glass Co., Pittsburgh, Pennsylvania, 1879; Bridgeport, Ohio, 1882. Burned in 1884. Moved to Bowling Green, Ohio, 1888. Joined National Glass Co. in 1899; reorganized by 1906; closed in 1908.

Cumberland Glass Co., Cumberland, Maryland. Joined National Glass Co. in 1899.

Curling, R. B. and Sons (Curling, Price and Co.), Pittsburgh, Pennsylvania, 1827; became Dithridge and Sons, 1860.

Dalzell, Gilmore, and Leighton Glass Co. (Dalzell Brothers and Gilmore), Brilliant, Ohio, 1883; went to Wellsburg, West Virginia, in 1888; joined National Glass, 1899.

Dithridge and Co. (Ft. Pitt Glassworks), Pittsburgh, Pennsylvania, 1860. To Martins Ferry, Ohio, in 1881; New Brighton, Pennsylvania, in 1887 and became Dithridge and Sons.

Doyle and Company, Pittsburgh, Pennsylvania, 1866. Joined U. S. Glass, 1891 as Factory P.

Dugan Glass Co. (Indiana Glass Co.), Indiana, Pennsylvania, 1892. Dugan/Diamond became Diamond Glass Company, 1913 – 1931.

Duncan, George and Sons, Pittsburgh, Pennsylvania, 1874. Became George A. Duncan and Sons and George Duncan's Sons; joined U. S. Glass in 1891 as Factory D. Became Duncan and Miller Glass Co. in 1903.

Eagle Glass and Mfg. Co., Wellsburgh, West Virginia.

East Liverpool Glass Co., East Liverpool, Ohio, 1882 – 1883. In 1889 Specialty Glass Co. started there.

Elson Glass Works, Pittsburgh, Pennsylvania, c. 1870s.

Evansville Glass Co., Evansville, Indiana, 1905

Excelsior Glass Works (Buckeye Glass Co.), Wheeling, West Virginia, 1849; moved to Martins Ferry, Ohio, 1879. Burned in 1894.

Fairmont Glass Co. joined National Glass in 1899.

Fenton Art Glass Co., Martins Ferry, Ohio, and Williamston, West Virginia, 1906 to present.

Findlay Flint Glass Co., Findlay, Ohio, 1889; failed shortly thereafter.

Fostoria Glass Co., Fostoria, Ohio, 1887; Roundsville, West Virginia, 1891. Added factory at Miles, Ohio, in 1910. Still producing.

Franklin Flint Glass Co., Philadelphia, Pennsylvania, 1861. Operated by Gillinder and Sons.

Gillinder and Sons, Philadelphia, Pennsylvania, 1861. Moved to Greensburg, Pennsylvania, in 1888. Joined U. S. Glass as Factory G in 1891.

Greensburg Glass Co., Greensburg, Pennsylvania, 1889; joined National Glass in 1899.

Heisey, A. H. Glass Co., Newark, Ohio, 1895; still operating in 1953.

Higbee, J. B. Glass Co., Bridgeville, Pennsylvania, 1900; still operating in 1911.

Hobbs, Brockunier and Co. (Hobbs, J. H. Glass Co.), Wheeling, West Virginia, 1863. Joined U. S. Glass as Factory H in 1891; dismantled shortly thereafter.

Imperial Glass Co., Bellaire, Ohio, 1901 – 1984.

Indiana Glass Co., Dunkirk, Indiana, 1897.

Indiana Tumbler and Goblet Co., Greentown, Indiana, 1853. Joined National Glass in 1899; burned in 1903.

Jefferson Glass Co., Steubenville, Ohio, 1901; to Follansbee, West Virginia, in 1907; still operating in 1920s.

Jenkins Glass Co., Greentown, Indiana, 1894.

Jones, Cavitt and Co., Pittsburgh, Pennsylvania, 1884.

Kemple, John E. Glass Co., Kenova, West Virginia; East Palestine, Ohio, 1945 – 1970. Reproduced McKee patterns from old moulds.

Keystone Tumbler Works, Rochester, Pennsylvania, 1897; joined National Glass in 1899.

King, Son and Co., Pittsburgh, Pennsylvania, 1864 as Johann, King and Co.; became King Glass Co., c. 1879.

King Glass Co., Pittsburgh, Pennsylvania, c. 1879; became U. S. Glass Factory K in 1891.

Kokomo Glass Co., Kokomo, Indiana, 1899.

LaBelle Glass Co., Bridgeport, Ohio, 1872; burned in 1887; sold in 1888 to Muhleman Glass Works, LaBelle, Ohio.

Lancaster Glass Co., Lancaster, Ohio, c. 1915.

Libbey, Wh. H. and Sons, Co., Toledo, Ohio, c. 1899.

McKee and Brothers, Pittsburgh, Pennsylvania, c. 1853; moved to Jeannette, Pennsylvania, 1889; joined National Glass in 1899. Was McKee Glass Co. by 1904.

Millersburg Glass Co., Millersburg, Ohio, 1909 – 1912.

Model Flint Glass Co., Findlay, Ohio, 1888; to Albany, Indiana, between 1891 and 1894. Joined National Glass in 1899; failed c. 1903.

National Glass Co., Pittsburgh, Ohio, 1898 – 1905.

New England Glass Co. (New England Glass Works), Cambridge, Massachusetts, 1817. Became W. L. Libbey and Sons in 1880.

Nickel Plate Glass Co., Fostoria, Ohio, 1888. Joined U. S. Glass as Factory N in 1891.

Iowa City Flint Glass Co., Iowa City, Iowa, 1880 – 1882.

Northwood Glass Co., Indiana, Pennsylvania (became part of Dugan Glass Co., c. 1896). Joined National Glass in 1899. Became Harry Northwood Glass Co. in 1910 at Wheeling, West Virginia. Failed c. 1923.

Novelty Glass Co., LaGrange, Ohio, 1880. Moved to Brilliant, Ohio, 1882. Joined U. S. Glass in 1891 as Factory T. Moved to Fostoria, Ohio, in 1892 and burned in 1893.

Ohio Flint Glass Co., Lancaster, Ohio; joined National Glass in 1899.

Pittsburgh Glass Works, Pittsburgh, Pennsylvania, 1798 – 1852. Became James B. Lyon Glass Co. Associated with O'Hara Glass Co., Pittsburgh. Joined U. S. Glass in 1891.

Portland Glass Co., Portland, Maine, 1864.

Richards and Hartley Flint Glass Co., Pittsburgh, Pennsylvania, 1866; Tarentum, Pennsylvania, 1884. Joined U. S. Glass in 1891.

Ripley and Co., Pittsburgh, Pennsylvania, 1866; became U. S. Glass Factory F in 1891.

Riverside Glass Co., Wellsburg, West Virginia, 1879; joined National Glass in 1899.

Robinson Glass Co., Zanesville, Ohio, 1893; joined National Glass in 1899; burned in 1906.

Rochester Tumbler Co., Rochester, Pennsylvania, 1872; joined National Glass in 1899.

Royal Glass Co., Marietta, Ohio, joined National Glass in 1899.

Specialty Glass Co., East Liverpool, Ohio, 1889 – c. 1898.

Steiner Glass Co., Buckhannon, West Virginia, 1870s.

Tarentum Glass Co., Tarentum, Pennsylvania, was operating in 1894; still operating in 1915.

Thompson Glass Co., Uniontown, Pennsylvania, 1889 to 1898.

Union Flint Glass Works, Pittsburgh, Pennsylvania, 1854. Moved to Bellaire, Ohio, in 1880; Martins Ferry, Ohio, in 1880; sold to Dithridge Flint Glass Works in 1882. New plant at Martins Ferry; to Ellwood, Pennsylvania, in 1895. Became Northwood Co. in 1896.

Westmoreland Glass Co. (Westmoreland Specialty Co.), Grapeville, Pennsylvania, 1889.

West Virginia Glass Co., Martins Ferry, Ohio, 1861; joined National Glass in 1899.

Windsor Glass Co., Pittsburgh, Pennsylvania, 1887.

Explanation to Our Readers

Photos in our books are from a variety of sources, and most come from readers like you. For this reason, the color of photo background will vary; when these photos have the backgrounds removed, some variations in the coloring of the glass will occur from item to item. We want the reader to understand why these variations happen, and we feel it is a small price to pay for sharing patterns from our readers with other collectors.

Bill Edwards & Mike Carwile

Decoration Definitions

ENAMELING: A hand-painted design used to add emphasis to the pattern of the glass.

ENGRAVING: Glass design is cut into the piece by a copper wheel and differs from ETCHING (frosting) which is done using a pattern sheet and either acid or sand.

FLASHING: Often confused with staining, flashing is actually a thin layer of glass applied to the original glass, often altering the color.

FROSTED: A clouding of the glass by treating it to an acid etching or by abrasion from a rough agent such as sand.

GILDING: A light application of gold decoration, often seen on edges, as a banding, or decorating the design of a glass item.

GOOFUS: A special treatment that combines gilding and enameling to cover the entire pattern. Added to the backs of bowls or plates and to the underside of lamp bases, it was sealed but can be removed by wear or scraping.

STAINING: A thin coat of paint that is applied to glass, usually in a heat-application treatment. Colors are primarily ruby, lemon, amber, or pink (this color is also called Maiden's Blush or cranberry).

American Table Glass Factories

We are including this list of table glass factories that was composed in 1985 by the late William Heacock and he states: "These are factory listings, not company listings. Frequently a single factory would go through a number of different owners or reorganizations."

We hope the information will be helpful in some way to collectors of glass and will add to all the information about pressed glass factories in this country. We are happy to share Mr. Heacock's efforts with readers. Since I helped Mr. Heacock assemble portions of this listing, I feel our use of it is completely justified.

Bill Edwards

Adams and Company, Pittsburgh, Pennsylvania (1851 – 1935) (originally known as Adams, Macklin & Co.). Joined USG in 1891. Making percolator tops in 1935. Patterns: Liberty Bell (1876), King's Crown (1890), Moon & Star (Palace), possibly Horseshoe (Good Luck).

Aetna Glass and Manufacturing Co., Bellaire, Ohio (1880 – 1889). Patterns: Adonis Swirl (formerly Gonterman Swirl), Hobnail-In-Square, Jumbo covered figural fruit bowl, possibly Butterfly Handles (journal quote), Goddess of Liberty epergne, Aetna's No. 300.

American Glass Company, Anderson, Indiana (1889 – 1890). Started by former Buckeye manager John F. Miller, this new factory was a manufacturer of opalescent, decorated, cut, and engraved tableware, lamps, etc. in the style of Buckeye, Northwood, etc. The factory was closed about a year after it began operations in mid-1889. It then became the Hoosier Glass Co., a manufacturer of prescription ware.

Atterbury and Company, Pittsburgh, Pennsylvania (1858 – 1902?). Patterns: Basket Weave (pitcher has snake handle), Ceres (Medallion), Atterbury Lily, many milk glass covered animal dishes, possibly Raindrop, Atterbury Waffle.

Bakewell, Pears and Co., Pittsburgh, Pennsylvania (1807 – 1880?) (had four different names) 1880 last patent. Patterns: Argus (Thumbprint), Bakewell Cherry, Arabesque, Icicle, Ashburton, Bakewell Victoria.

A.J. Beatty & Sons, Steubenville, Ohio (1850? – 1890); Tiffin, Ohio (1890 – 1891) joined USG. The Steubenville factory was also absorbed by U.S. Glass but never operated. Mr. A.J. Beatty also involved in Brilliant and Federal Glass factories, among others. Patterns: Beatty Rib, D&B with V-Ornament, Beatty Waffle, Over-all Hobnail, Orinoco. A July 1888 journal lists their No. 87 new opalescent line, as well as No. 79 crystal set, plain or engraved.

Beatty-Brady Glass Co., Dunkirk, Indiana (1898 – 1907); Indiana Glass Co. (1907 – present). Patterns: Loop and Jewel, Shrine, Late Butterfly, Flower Medallion, Narcissus Spray, Rocket, Rayed Flower, Bethlehem Star, Star Band, Whirled Sunburst in Circle, Double Pinwheel, Nogi, Togo, Gibson Girl.

Beaumont Glass Co., Martins Ferry, Ohio (1898 – 1902); Grafton, West Virginia (1903 – 1906); Morgantown, West Virginia (1913 – recent). Grafton factory became Tygart Valley Glass Co. Percy Beaumont went to Union Stopper Co., Morgantown, West Virginia, in 1906, and then opened his own lamp shade factory in that town about 1913. Patterns: Decorated only until 1899 (X-Ray, Esther); Flora, Beaumont's Columbia, Widmer, Acorn salt & pepper, Seaweed cruet, Inside Ribbing.

Bellaire Goblet Co., Bellaire, Ohio (1876 – 1888); Findlay, Ohio (1888 – 1891), joined USG–M. Factory manager, John Robinson, opened Robinson Glass Co. at Zanesville, Ohio. Patterns: Queen's Necklace, Gargoyle goblet, Bellaire, Daisy & Cube, Log and Star, Pig & Boxcar match holder, Bellaire Basketweave, Corset toothpick, Turtle salt, and many other novelty design goblets.

Belmont Glass Company, Bellaire, Ohio (1866 – 1890); Belmont Glass Works (listed under this name in 1888). The firm reportedly chipped molds for Crystal, Gillinder, and Fostoria. Patterns: Dewberry (early), Royal (figured woman's head), Belmont #100 (Daisy & Button on pedestal stem), No. 444 line released July 1888, described as a full line in both plain and engraved.

Boston and Sandwich Glass Co., Sandwich, Massachusetts (1825 – 1888). Patterns: A variety of lacy glass in early years, much opal ware and art ware in later years.

Brilliant Glass Works, Brilliant, Ohio (1880 – 1882). Factory burned in 1882, rebuilt and leased to Dalzell Bros. & Gilmore (1883 – 1884). Purchased by Central in 1884, operated by them as second factory until late 1886. Sold again in 1888 by new firm which moved equipment and molds to Greensburg, Pennsylvania, in 1889. Reopened as prescription ware factory in 1894, burned down in 1895. Patterns: see Greensburg Glass Co. A July 1888 journal states Brilliant was offering Winona and Melrose, and a new line Aurora. Some of these molds also used later at Huntington, also possibly at Royal Glass Co., Marietta, Ohio.

Bryce Brothers, Pittsburgh, Pennsylvania (1850 – 1835). Had three other names, joined USG in 1891 as Factory B, closed during Depression. Patterns: Harp, Diamond Point, Tulip with Sawtooth, Strawberry, Thistle, Jacob's Ladder, Atlas, Panelled Daisy, Ribbon Candy, Wooden Pail, Roman Rosette, Pleating, Diamond Quilted (No. 1108), Argent, Derby, Pittsburgh, Wheat & Barley, Rose in Snow. Bryce Bros., Mt. Pleasant, Pennsylvania (1896 – present) became part of Lenox Corp. in 1965. Patterns: specialized in production of stemware.

Buckeye Glass Company, Martins Ferry, Ohio (1879 – 1896). Harry Northwood worked there in 1887. Factory burned down in February 1896. Patterns: Acorn, Reverse Swirl (Opalescent, Speckled). Trade journal of 6/28/88 reports the firm released seven new lines in "common crystal" and "opalescent, with glass feet." The latter could be the controversial Northwood Hobnail, which was listed by BB in 1890.

Cambridge Glass Co., The, Cambridge, Ohio (1901 – 1957). Originally built by newly formed National Glass Company but opened as an independent concern. Purchased by A.J. Bennett in 1910. Patterns: Star-of-Bethlehem, Cambridge Ribbon, Marjorie, Chelsea, Bordered Ellipse, Alexis, Big X pitcher, Stratford, and many others.

Campbell, Jones & Co., Pittsburgh, Pennsylvania (1863 – 1886); Jones, Cavitt & Co., Ltd. (1886 – 1891). Factory burned down in January 1891. Revi incorrectly indicates factory closed in 1895. Some molds acquired by U.S. Glass. Patterns: Currant, Rose Sprig, Panelled Dewdrop, Dewdrop with Star, Argyle, Button and Oval Medallion (Russian), Barley.

Canton Glass Co., Canton, Ohio (1883 – 1903?), joined National Canton Glass Co., Marion, Indiana (1898 – recent), branch plant which also joined National, listed in 1899 ads.

Patterns: Jumbo, Hercules figural stem lamp, Kingfisher toothpick, acquired Paden City molds in the 1950s, some National molds during takeover (re-organized in 1904 in Marion as an independent). Later patterns include many from National: Kingfisher toothpick, Domino shakers, Eagle & Leaf vase.

Central Glass Co., Wheeling, West Virginia (1863 – 1939), joined USG–O Central Glass Co., Summitville, Indiana (1898 – 1900), joined National in 1899. The West Virginia firm began as Osterling & Henderson Co. and was closed down by USG in 1893, reopened as an independent in 1896. Moved to Indiana in 1898 to be closed after National merger. West Virginia factory opened again as a new company sometime after 1900, carrying same old name. Patterns: U.S. Coin, Log Cabin, Open Plaid, Cabbage Rose, Leaflets (with reclining cat finial), Wheat in Shield, Picture Window. Patterns from Indiana unknown. Main design from last Wheeling firm was their Krys-Tol line of Chippendale pattern, many etched stem lines.

Challinor, Taylor & Co., Tarentum, Pennsylvania (1866 – 1893). Earlier known as Challinor, Hogan Glass Co., at Pittsburgh. Joined USG as Factory C, burned down in 1893. Patterns: Oval Panel, Flower & Panel, Blockade, Hobnail with Bars, Double Fan, Opaque Scroll, Sanborn, Majestic Crown, Scroll with Star, Flying Swan.

Columbia Glass Company, Findlay, Ohio (1886 – 1892), joined USG in 1891. Patterns: Heavy Gothic, Broken Column, Henrietta, Radiant, Puss in Slipper, Dog Vase, Double Eye Hobnail, Bamboo Beauty, Shell on Ribs, Old Columbia, Banquet, Pointed Jewel, Climax.

Co-Operative Flint Glass Co., Ltd., Beaver Falls, Pennsylvania (1879 – 1937), earlier called Beaver Falls Co-Operative Glass Co. Patterns: Co-Op's Columbia, Eulalia (Currier & Ives), Madoline, Jewelled Moon and Star, Co-Op's Rex (Fancy Cut toy set), Sunk Daisy, Ivy-in-Snow, Sheaf and Block, Art Navo, Famous, Magna, Dewberry.

Crystal Glass Co., Pittsburgh, Pennsylvania (1868 – 1890). Other companies used this name or similar names, including the rebuilt La Belle Glass Works in 1888. Patterns: Frosted Eagle, Polar Bear, Pinafore (Actress?), a swan pattern of unknown description.

Crystal Glass Co., Bridgeport, Ohio (1888 – 1908). A reopened La Belle Glass Works, operated by Ed Muhlemann (later of Imperial Glass Co.), joined National in 1900, closed in 1908, probably never reopened. Patterns: Beaded Swirl and Lens, Big Button, Clematis (Flower and Pleat), Block and Lattice, Bullseye & Arrowhead.

Dalzell Brothers & Gilmore (1884 – 1888), Wellsburgh, West Virginia; Dalzell, Gilmore & Leighton Co. (1888 – 1902), Findlay, Ohio, joined National in 1900, closed in 1902. Patterns: Onyx ware, Klondike pattern, Dalzell's Columbia, Bringing Home the Cows, Bicycle Girl, Retort, Deer and Oak Tree, Eye Winker, Paragon, Double Fan, Wellsburg, Magnolia, Racing Deer pitcher, Serrated Teardrop, Plume and Fan, Bulging Bars wine, Three Birds pitcher, Quaker Lady, Teardrop & Cracked Ice, Ivanhoe.

Dithridge and Co., Pittsburgh, Pennsylvania (circa 1850 – 1903), started as R.B. Curling Co., ended as part of Pittsburgh Lamp, Brass and Glass Co. Patterns: Versaille, Astoria, Roses & Ruffles, mostly opal table and novelty lines, lamps, syrups, shakers, etc.

Doyle and Co., Pittsburgh, Pennsylvania (circa 1866 – 1891), USG–P Atterbury designed for them in 1870. Patterns: Red Block, Picket Band, Stippled Grape & Festoon, Grape & Festoon with Shield, Panelled Forget-Me-Not, Hobnail with Thumbprint Base, Doyle's Shell.

Dugan Glass Co., The, Indiana, Pennsylvania (1904 – 1913), Diamond Glass-Ware Company (1913 – 1931). Formerly The Northwood Co., which merged into National (1890 – 1904). Patterns: Many carried over from former owners; Maple Leaf, Inverted Fan & Feather, Shell, Beaded Ovals in Sand, Argonaut Shell, Circled Scroll, Quilted Phlox.

Dugan Glass Company, Lonaconing, Maryland (1914 – 1915); Lonaconing Glass Company, Lonaconing, Maryland (1915 – 1916?). Started by Thomas Dugan after he left Indiana, Pennsylvania, in Nov. 1914, leaving five months later due to friction. The name was then changed to Lonaconing Glass Co. Patterns: Reissued old molds from some National factories, including Melrose (Brilliant/Greensburg), Circular Saw (Riverside), Cadmus (Beaumont), and National Prism (a pattern advertised by National in 1903).

George Duncan & Sons, Pittsburgh, Pennsylvania (1874 – 1892), USG-D Factory began as Ripley & Co. in 1866 but name changed in 1874 when Mr. Ripley established new firm by this name elsewhere in Pittsburgh. Factory burned in 1892. Patterns: Many also by USG, molds may have been relocated to other factories after factory burned down: Swirled Column, Three Face, Squared Shell and Tassel, Berkeley, Swag Block, Snail, Double Snail, Zippered Block, Maltese Cross, Late Block, Gonterman.

George Duncan's Sons & Co., Washington, Pennsylvania (1894 – 1900), Duncan & Miller Glass Co. (1900 – 1955). Patterns: Flowered Scroll, Grated Diamond & Sunburst, Starred Loop, Teepee, Quartered Block, Quartered Diamonds, Button Arches, King Arthur, Sunflower Patch, many others.

Eagle Glass & Mfg. Co., The, Wellsburg, West Virginia (1890s – still in business in 1913). Patterns: Maker of mostly novelties, lamps, vanity items, salt shakers, toothpicks, etc., mostly in milk glass (decorated).

East Liverpool Glass Co., East Liverpool, Ohio (1882 – 1883), burned after opening, patterns preserved by local library. Patterns: East Liverpool (K4, 69), reportedly Beaded Swirl & Disc (Pet Sal), probably based on this same library (however the latter is proven U.S. Glass).

Elson Glass Co., The, Martins Ferry, Ohio (1882 – 1894), West Virginia Glass Mfg. Co. (1894 – 1900), joined National. Patterns: Elson Block IOU, a variant of Daisy & Button, West Virginia Optic, "Pandora" (trade journal listing), Scroll with Cane Band, Gem, Opalescent Fern, Polka Dot.

Evansville Glass Co., Evansville, Indiana (1903 – 1908?). Trade journals of 1904 indicate six new lines of tableware were displayed. Only Fernette pattern attributed to date. Firm also operated a separate bottle factory. Last trade notice found is from early 1907. Molds probably sold to other firms.

Federal Glass Co., Columbus, Ohio (1901 – 1978). Patterns: Got molds from National, USG, Co-Op, McKee, etc. Beaded Triangle pitcher, D & B with V-ornament pitcher, Stars & Stripes (Jenkins), Kansas (USG), Boxed Star (Jenkins), Peacock Feather (USG).

Fenton Art Glass Co., The, Williamstown, West Virginia (1907 – present). Patterns: Butterfly and Berry, Honeycomb with Clover, Waterlily with Cattails, Orange Tree.

Findlay Flint Glass Co., The, Findlay, Ohio (1888 – 1891). Patterns: Findlay #19, Pillar, Findlay's Dot, Spur Hobnail, Drawers toothpick holder, Elephant Head mustard with lid, Squash caster set, Pichereau ink well, Butterfly toothpick.

Fostoria Glass Company, Fostoria, Ohio (1887 – 1891); Moundsville, West Virginia (1891 – 1986). Diverse manufacturer of pressed and blown glass tableware, lamps, decorated opal specialties, blown stemware, cut glass, etched and engraved ware, and much, much more. Acquired by Lancaster – Colony. Factory closed in 1986. Some molds moved to Indiana Glass Co. Patterns: Cameo (Apple and Grape in Scroll), Diamond Window, Captain Kidd (Red Block copy), Brazillian, Fostoria's Atlanta, Lorraine, Victoria, Hartford, Alexis (these five names used by other firms); and many others.

Gillinder & Sons (1861 – 1891). Philadelphia and Greensburg, Pennsylvania, factories originally called Franklin Flint Glass Co., Philadelphia, Pennsylvania (second factory at Greensburg, Pennsylvania joined in 1891, as factory G). Patterns: Classic, Westward Ho, Ruffles, Barred Star, Daisy & Button with Thin Bars.

Greensburg Glass Co., Greensburg, Pennsylvania (1889 – 1892); Greensburg Glass Co., Ltd. (1893 – 1898); Greensburg Glass Co. (1901 – 1937), sold to L.E. Smith, started by Brilliant Glass Co., re-organized with new management and new patterns in 1893. Closed in late 1898, joined National Glass in 1900, factory sold in 1901. Operated until L.E. Smith Glass Co. took over and operated as a second factory location. Patterns: Aurora, Florida (Sunken Primrose), Melrose, Murano, Tacoma, Corona (molds on last two moved to McKee in 1902).

A.H. Heisey Glass Co., Newark, Ohio (1895 – 1957). Patterns: Ring Band, Winged Scroll, Locket on Chain, Greek Key, Punty Band, Plain Band, Fandango, Fancy Loop, Pineapple with Fan, Continental, Kalonyal, Touraine.

Bryce, Higbee & Co., Homestead, Pennsylvania (1879 – 1906); J.B. Higbee & Co., Bridgeville, Pennsylvania (1907 – 1916). Patterns: Cut Log (Ethol), New Era, Flora, Sheraton, Sprig, Grand, Homestead, Drum toy set, Panelled Thistle, Hawaiian Lei, Style, Perkins, Alfa.

Hobbs, Brockunier & Co., Wheeling, West Virginia (1845 – 1891), joined USG. Hobbs Glass Co. (reorganized under John Hobbs in August 1888), started as Barnes, Hobbs & Co., a "partnership limit on the old firm" expired on 12/31/1887. Patterns: Leaf & Flower, Viking, Goat's Head, Blackberry, Hobnail, Mario, Hobb's Block, Hexagon Block, Wheeling Peachblow (Coral), Daisy & Button.

Huntington Glass Company, The, Huntington, West Virginia (1891 – 1897). Started up by old New Brighton stockholders, bought molds from Greensburg Glass Co. in 1894. President Addison Thompson moved to new factory at Marietta, Ohio (see Royal Glass Co.). Patterns: Pearl, Huntington, others from Greensburg molds (Aurora, Winona, Brilliant).

Imperial Glass Company, The, Bellaire, Ohio (1902 – 1984). Listed in October 1902 trade journals as independent with 56 pots, 16 more than Fostoria Glass. Patterns: Octagon, File, Nu-Cut pressed ware, carnival glass tableware.

Indiana Glass Co. (see Beatty-Brady Glass Co.)

Indiana Tumbler & Goblet Co., Greentown, Indiana (1894 – 1903). Joined National in 1901, burned down in 1903. Patterns: Austrian, Holly Amber, Dewey, Teardrop & Tassle, Herringbone Buttress, Cactus, Cord Drapery, Leaf Bracket, Pleat Band (all known as Greentown glass).

Jefferson Glass Company, Steubenville, Ohio (1901 – 1907); Follansbee, West Virginia (1907 – 1933). Several owners and reorganizations. Ads for firm still appeared as late as 1936, possibly selling remaining stock of bankrupt firm. Patterns: Tokyo, Ribbed Thumbprint, Chippendale, Ribbed Drape, Jefferson Optic, Follansbee, Jefferson Colonial, Diamond with Peg, some Button Arches, Dolly Madison, Swag with Brackets, concentrated on lighting ware after 1910.

King, Son & Co., Pittsburgh, Pennsylvania (1864 – 1880); King Glass Company, The (1880 – 1835), joined USG-K, joined U.S. Glass in 1891. Closed during the Depression after Pittsburgh flood. Patterns: Panelled Grape Band, Bleeding Heart, Frosted Ribbon, King's No. 500, Double Arch King's Centennial Thumbprint, Picket, Jumbo wall match holder.

Kokomo Glass Co., The, Kokomo, Indiana (1901 – 1905); D.C. Jenkins Glass Co. (1906 – 1932). Patterns: Panelled Grape, Sunburst, Grape Jug, Cherry with Thumbprint, Thistlebow.

La Belle Glass Co., Bridgeport, Ohio (1872 – 1888), Harry Northwood here from 1884 to 1888. Factory closed April 1888 due to exaggerated reconstruction costs of burned and rebuilt factory. Sold in September 1888 to Capt. Ed Muhleman, becoming Crystal Glass Works. Patterns: Queen Anne, Actress, Bamboo, a copy of Hobbs Hobnail, opalescent sets.

Lancaster Glass Co., The, Lancaster, Ohio (1908 – 1937). A new firm established by Lucien Martin (formerly at Hobbs, Fostoria, National, and Hocking Glass Co.) at the closed Ohio Flint Glass Co. plant. Factory absorbed by Hocking Glass Corp. in 1937. Patterns: Rustic Rose, Stippled Fans, Pogo Stick, Panelled Oak, Carnation, reissued McKee's Kansas and Beaded Triangle, also made many unnamed patterns (FGM catalog).

Lonaconing Glass Co., Lonaconing, Maryland (1915 – 1919?) see Dugan Glass Co., Lonaconing, Maryland.

McKee & Bros., Pittsburgh, Pennsylvania (1864 – 1888); McKee & Bros., Jeannette, Pennsylvania (1888 – 1900); National Glass Company, McKee & Bros., Jeannette, Pennsylvania (1900 – 1904); McKee-Jeannette Glass Co., Jeannette, Pennsylvania (1904 – 1910); McKee Glass Company, Jeannette, Pennsylvania (March 1910 – 1952). Patterns: Belleflower, Excelsior, Eugenie, Barberry, Panelled Hexagons, Comet, Yale, Dragon, Germanic, Champion, Carltec, Britannic, Heart Band, Lenox, Lone Star, Sunbeam, Majestic, Tappan toy set, Sultan toy set, Wild Rose with Bowknot, Geneva, imitation cut "tec" patterns, Prescut lines.

Millersburg Glass Co., Millersburg, Ohio (1909 – 1912), became Radium Glass Co., then sold to Jefferson Glass Co. in 1913. Some molds sent to Jefferson's Canadian factory. Patterns: Ohio Star, Country Kitchen, Hobstar & Feather, Millersburg Flute, carnival glass novelties.

Model Flint Glass Co., Findlay, Ohio (1888 – 1894); Model Flint Glass Co., Albany, Indiana (1894 – 1900); National Glass Co., Model Flint Glass Works (1900 – 1902). Patterns: Bevelled Star, Heck, Wreath & Shell, Shepherd's Plaid, Model's Peerless, Midway, Twist toy set.

National Glass Company, The (1900 – 1904). Announced in fall 1899, nineteen factories joined. Some burned down, others were closed by National. In 1904 the merger accepted defeat and leased or sold the remaining factories, as well as the one built by them at Cambridge. In 1908 the parent company went into receivership.

Member factories:
1. **Beatty-Brady Glass Works**, Dunkirk, Indiana.
2. **Canton Glass Works**, Marion, Indiana.
3. Central Glass Works, Summitville, Indiana.
4. Crystal Glass Works, Bridgeport, Ohio.
5. **Cumberland Glass Works**, Cumberland, Maryland.
6. Dalzell, Gilmore & Leighton Works, Findlay, Ohio.
7. **Fairmount Glass Works**, Fairmount, West Virginia.
8. Greensburg Glass Works, Greensburg, Pennsylvania.
9. **Indiana Tumbler & Goblet Works**, Greentown, Indiana.
10. Keystone Glass Works, Rochester, Pennsylvania.
11. **Model Flint Glass Works**, Albany, Indiana.
12. **McKee & Bros. Glass Works**, Jeannette, Pennsylvania.
13. **The Northwood Glass Works**, Indiana, Pennsylvania.
14. **Ohio Flint Glass Works**, Lancaster, Ohio.
15. **Riverside Glass Works**, Wellsburg, West Virginia.
16. Robinson Glass Works, Zanesville, Ohio.
17. **Rochester Glass Works**, Rochester, Pennsylvania.
18. **Royal Glass Works**, Marietta, Ohio.
19. West Virginia Glass Works, Martins Ferry, Ohio.

All in boldface were still in operation in 1902. The numbers on each factory were used in a special advertisement coding for ordering patterns. The Greentown and Marietta factories burned shortly afterward. The Cambridge Factory was built the following year, but opened as an independent concern. Patterns and factory numbers: S-Repeat (13), The Prize (12), Reward (15), Delos (6), Vulcan (12), Cord Drapery (8), Hobble Skirt (15), and many others.

New Brighton Glass Company, New Brighton, Pennsylvania (1888 – 1891), went bankrupt in early 1891. Stockholders started up a new factory at Huntington Glass. Local New Brighton investors reopened abandoned factory as a maker of prescription ware, but factory failed soon after. Patterns: A Paradise pattern is mentioned in trade journals, also colored tableware (research pending).

New England Glass Co., East Cambridge, Massachusetts (1818 – 1888); W.L. Libbey & Son Co., Toledo, Ohio (1888 – present), now known as The Libbey Glass Co. Patterns:

Maize, Washington Centennial, Huber, Mitre Diamond, Union, Vernon, Reeded, Philadelphia.

New Martinsville Glass Mfg. Co., New Martinsville, West Virginia (1900 – present), now called Viking Glass Co. Patterns: NM Carnation, Japanese Iris (Rebecca), NM Lorraine, Frontier, Florene, Leaf & Star, reissued many Higbee molds when Ira Clark came to NMG from Higbee.

Nickel Plate Glass Co., The, Fostoria, Ohio (1888 – 1891), USG-N, started up in June 1888. Patterns: Frosted Circle, Richmond, Akron Block, Fluted Ribbon, Fostoria pattern, N.P. Thumbprint.

Northwood Glass Works, The, Martins Ferry, Ohio (1888 – 1890); Northwood Glass Co., The, Elwood City, Pennsylvania (1890 – 1895); The Northwood Co., Indiana, Pennsylvania (1896 – 1904), joined National; H. Northwood & Co., Wheeling, West Virginia (October 1902 – 1924). Patterns: Royal Ivy, Royal Oak, Leaf Umbrella, Quilted Phlox, Louis XV, Alaska, Fluted Scrolls, Wild Bouquet, Maple Leaf, Inverted Fan & Feather, Peacock at the Fountain, Singing Birds, Argonaut Shell, S-Repeat, Crystal Queen. Many of these patterns were continued in production by National and Dugan/Diamond.

O'Hara Glass Co., Ltd., Pittsburgh, Pennsylvania (1848 – 1891). USG-L, originally called J.B. Lyons, joined U.S. Glass in 1891. Patterns: O'Hara Diamond (Sawtooth & Star), Cordova, Prism Column, Pennsylvania Hand, Daisy in Diamond.

Ohio Flint Glass Co., Dunkirk, Indiana (1893 – 1899); Lancaster, Ohio (1899 – 1908). Firm began in Bowling Green, Ohio, at a leased factory while new one built at Dunkirk. A fire destroyed factory in Indiana, so another new plant was built at Lancaster. The brand new factory was almost immediately absorbed by National Glass and was expanded. Managers operated independently after National became holding company in 1904. Closing in 1908, the factory reopened later that year as a new tableware firm, the Lancaster Glass Co. Then later absorbed by Hocking Glass Corp. in 1937 (see Lancaster Glass). Patterns: Belle, Ada, Chippendale (Jefferson and Central also made this), other Krys-Tol line patterns (Kenneth and Gloria).

Paden City Glass Mfg. Co., Paden City, West Virginia (1916 – 1951), started up with many Higbee molds. After closing, many molds went to Canton Glass, Marion, Indiana, and to Viking Glass Co., New Martinsville. Patterns: Tree, Higbee Pineapple (#206), Estelle (Higbee Colonial), Inna, Etta, Webb, later DG era patterns like Penny Line, Crow's Foot, Gadroon, Largo, etc.

Pittsburgh Lamp, Brass & Glass Co., Pittsburgh, Pennsylvania (12/1901 – 1926). Three manufacturers (Dithridge, Kopp Lamp & Glass, Pittsburgh Lamp & Brass) which made mostly lamps, but some tableware in opal and satin colors in early years. Became Kopp Glass Inc., with remaining factory in Swissvale by 1926. Patterns: continued lines of Dithridge and Kopp's famous ruby "red satin" (possibly Open-Heart Arches).

Portland Glass Co., The, Portland, Maine (1864 – 1874). Patterns: Three of Life, Loop & Dart with Round Ornament. Has been unfortunately credited with many other lines which were made much later by other firms.

Richards & Hartley Glass Co., Tarentum, Pennsylvania (1866 – 1893?), became Factory E of U.S. Glass in 1891, factory sold to Tarentum Glass Co. in 1894. Patterns: Loop & Dart with Diamond Ornaments, Hanover, Thousand Eye, Hartley, Russian, Three Panel, D&B with Crossbars, Oval Loop, Oregon, Clover, Bar & Diamond.

Ripley & Co., Pittsburgh, Pennsylvania (1874 – after 1902), USG-F (see also George Duncan & Sons for earlier firm by this name). Joined USG in 1891, closing date uncertain. Patterns: Scalloped Swirl (York Herringbone), Mascotte, Nail, Roanoke, Teardrop & Thumbprint, Dakota.

Ripley & Co., Connellsville, Pennsylvania (1910 – 1918), office in Pittsburgh, Pennsylvania. Made tableware until about 1915, factory became Capstan Glass Co. in 1918 (jars and bottles). Patterns: Iverna and others.

Riverside Glass Co., Wellsburg, West Virginia (1879 – 1907), joined National but re-emerged as an independent. Closed in 1907, reopened later as Crescent Glass Co., a manufacturer of automobile lenses and blown tumblers. Patterns: Empress, Esther, Croesus, X-Ray, Victoria, America, Double Daisy (Riverside's Chrysanthemum?), Box-in-Box.

Robinson Glass Co., Zanesville, Ohio (1896 – 1900). Started by former Columbia manager, John D. Robinson. Joined National and immediately closed. Molds moved to Ohio Flint and later Cambridge factory. Patterns: Vera (Faggot), Monroe, Zanesville.

Royal Glass Company, Marietta, Ohio (1898 – 1903). Started up by Huntington Glass president Addison Thompson, joined National Glass in 1900. Factory reportedly burned down in 1903. Patterns: a No. 314 "figured" pattern is mentioned in trade journals for 1902, another "imitation cut" pattern in 1901. Probably continued production of some Brilliant/Greensburg/Huntington molds.

L.E. Smith Glass Co., Mt. Pleasant, Pennsylvania (1908 – present). Originally a gold and silver decorating company, started making glass by 1912. Mr. Smith severed his connection with firm in 1912, moving over to Westmoreland Specialty Co. Oddly, no factory name change ever occurred. By 1929, firm was operating Greensburg factory as a subsidiary. Mt. Pleasant factory still in operation today, a division of Libbey-Owens. Patterns: Decorated Rock Crystal and Chippendale with gold, early patterns unknown, much Depression tableware in color.

Tarentum Glass Company, Tarentum, Pennsylvania (1894 – 1918). A new concern reopening old Richards & Hartley factory with entirely new lines, burned in 1918. Patterns: Manhattan, Albany, Atlanta (Royal Crystal), Columbia (Heart with Thumbprint), Hartford, Peerless (Frost Crystal), Virginia, Victoria, Portland, Georgia, many of these with names used by other factories.

Thompson Glass Co., Ltd., Uniontown, Pennsylvania (1889 – 1895). Acquired by National in 1901, reopened briefly by George Fry, brother of H.C. Fry, of Patterson-Fry Specialty Co., a glass decorating firm. Patterns: The Summit, Tile, Truncated Cube, Bow Tie.

Tygart Valley Glass Co., Grafton, West Virginia (1906 – 1926). A reorganized Beaumont Glass Co., originally continued production of tableware, stationers' goods. By 1918 made bottles, jars, and tumblers. Factory burned in 1926 and company moved to Washington, Pennsylvania.

United States Glass Co., Pittsburgh, Pennsylvania (1891 – 1963). A consolidation of factories. Most were closed by the time the Great Depression ended, with only the Glassport and Tiffin factories remaining in operation until 1963. The Glassport factory was destroyed by a tornado and the Tiffin factory became Tiffin Art Glass Co. (dismantled in 1985).

Member factories:
A. Adams & Co., Pittsburgh, Pennsylvania
B. Bryce Bros., Pittsburgh, Pennsylvania
C. Challinor, Taylor & Co., Ltd., Tarentum, Pennsylvania
D. George Duncan & Sons, Pittsburgh, Pennsylvania
E. Richards & Hartley, Tarentum, Pennsylvania
F. Ripley & Co., Pittsburgh, Pennsylvania
G. Gillinder & Sons, Greensburgh, Pennsylvania
H. Hobbs Glass Co., Wheeling, West Virginia
J. Columbia Glass Co., Findlay, Ohio
K. King Glass Co., Pittsburgh, Pennsylvania
L. O'Hara Glass Co., Pittsburgh, Pennsylvania
M. Bellaire Goblet Co., Findlay, Ohio
N. Nickel Plate Glass Co., Fostoria, Ohio
O. Central Glass Co., Wheeling, West Virginia
P. Doyle & Co., Pittsburgh, Pennsylvania
R. A.J. Beatty & Sons, Tiffin, Ohio
S. A.J. Beatty & Sons, Steubenville, Ohio (non-operating)
T. Novelty Glass Co., Fostoria, Ohio

New factories built: Glassport, Pennsylvania, and Gas City, Indiana.

Valley Glass Co., Beaver Falls, Pennsylvania (1889 only), formerly Whitla Glass Co. Patterns: Probably Monkey, opal glass novelties, and condiments.

Westmoreland Specialty Co. (1892 – 1923); Westmoreland Glass Co., Grapeville, Pennsylvania (1923 – 1985). Began in 1889 to 1892 as The Specialty Glass Co., East Liverpool, Ohio. Grapeville factory closed in 1985. Patterns: Pillow & Sunburst, Late Swan, Westmoreland's No. 15 (Cut Log copy), Shell & Jewel, Late Westmoreland, High Hob, Flute & Crown, English Hobnail, Cane Medallion, Indian Sunset, Wellington, Flickering Flame.

West Virginia Glass Co., The (see Elson Glass Company).

Whitla Glass Company, Beaver Falls, Pennsylvania (1887 – 1890). Closed January 1890 by bankruptcy, became Valley Glass Company. Patterns: Started by John Whitla who also started New Brighton Glass Co.

Patterns

Acorn

Acorn Band

Actress

Ada

Adams Apollo Lamp

Acorn

Dated about 1870, this pattern's maker is unknown, but shapes include a pitcher, goblet, table set, celery vase, egg cup, covered compote, and an open compote. Some researchers credit Boston and Sandwich Glass for this pattern.

Acorn Band

There are some variations in this pattern made by the Portland Glass Company. A similar design accredited to Boston and Sandwich Glass is called Panelled Acorn Band. Shapes include a table set, celery vase, egg cup, compotes, flat or footed sauces, goblet, wine, water pitcher, covered compote, covered bowls, open bowl, and stemmed dessert.

Actress

This collection of similar designs is attributed to Addams & Company and known as Pinafore, Theatrical, or Goddess of Liberty as well as Jenny Lind or Annie. Shapes include many size bowls, a table set, cake stand, candlesticks, celery vase, cheese dish, covered compotes both high and low, goblet, jam jar, pickle dish, water set, milk pitcher, platter, relishes, salt, and dresser tray. All subjects deal with the theater or actors.

Ada

Made by Cambridge Glass Company and Ohio Flint Glass, Ada dates to 1898 and was made in more than 100 shapes that include a table set, water set, berry set, cruet, shakers, compotes, pickle dish, celery vase and dish, goblet, wine, and syrup. The design is well balanced and interesting.

Adams Apollo Lamp

From the Adams Glass Company of Pittsburgh in the 1880s, this lamp is 11⅞" tall and can be found in crystal, blue, amber, and canary. It is distinguished by the Maltese cross-like decoration around the base.

Adonis

Made by McKee & Brothers in 1897, Adonis is also known as Washboard or Pleat and Tuck. In addition to clear, examples in canary and blue glass are known. Shapes are berry sets (beaded rim), table sets, cake plate, cake stand, celery vase, covered or open compotes, jelly compote, plates in both 10" and 11" sizes, relish tray, shakers, and syrup.

Adonis

African Shield

African Shield

Made by the Sowerby Glass Company of England, this pattern is well known to carnival glass collectors. Its only shape seems to be the squat vase shape shown that is 2⅞" tall and has a top diameter of 3½". Originally a wire flower holder fit into the top of the vase.

Alabama

Alabama

From U. S. Glass in 1890 and the first of the States series, Alabama is also called Beaded Bulls-Eye and Drape by some collectors. It is found in clear, green, or ruby in table sets, tall celery vase, both covered and open compotes, covered honey dish (rare), nappy, water set, syrup, and three sizes of relish dishes.

Alaska (Northwood)

Alaska (Northwood)

Made in both crystal and opalescent glass, beginning in 1897 through 1912, this well-known pattern is found in berry sets, water sets, table sets, a rose bowl, a jewelry tray, as well as several novelty pieces. Besides the opalescent colors, clear or emerald green glass are known and are often decorated with enamel flowers.

Aldine

This pattern is also known as Beaded Ellipse and is credited to McKee in 1900 (some references also credit it to Cambridge as their #2519 and to Imperial as their #261 in 1910). It is found in crystal with some rare items found in chocolate glass. Shapes include a table set, covered bowl, water set, wine, pickle dish, and a celery dish. Thanks to Alan and Lorraine Pickup for sharing this rare chocolate creamer with us.

Aldine

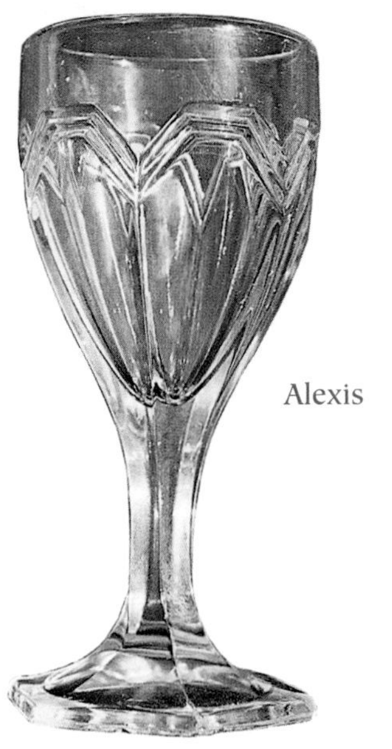
Alexis

Almond

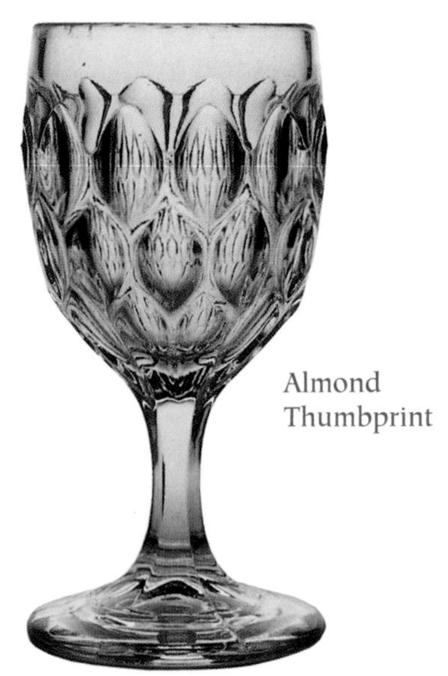
Almond Thumbprint

Amarylis

Alexis

This was first shown as Fostoria's #1630 Alexis pattern (1909 – 1925) and then in only the goblet shape from D.C. Jenkins as their #23 goblet. Shapes from Fostoria are many and include bowls, a table set, tall celery vase, celery tray, catsup, champagne, claret, cocktail, cordial, ice bowl and plate, custard (two styles), decanter, egg cup, finger bowl, goblet, relish jar, ice tea set with plates, water set (three size pitchers), mayonnaise plate and bowl, syrup, nasturtium vase, nut bowl, olive tray, cruets (three sizes), pickle tray, tankard pitcher, salt shakers, sherbets (high or low), sugar sifter, sweet pea vase, toothpick holder, water bottle, wine, whiskey tumbler, and a wine tumbler. The toothpick holder was reproduced in 1980 for founders of the Fostoria Glass Society of America.

Almond (U. S. Glass)

Listed as their #5601, this U. S. Glass Company pattern is found in a wine decanter with matching tray and stemmed wines. It is shown in clear and was also available with gold trim and may have been made in emerald green glass. The design should not be confused with Diamond Thumbprint which is sometimes called simply Almond, which was made by Bryce, Bakewell, and also U. S. Glass in 1891. It is also known as Mirror and Fan.

Almond Thumbprint

This is attributed to Bryce, Bakewell (1865), Bakewell, Pears (1868), and then U.S. Glass in 1891. Shapes include a table set, champagne, celery vase, high or low covered compotes (5", 7", 10"), a cordial, cruet (two styles), decanter goblet, punch set, water set, salt dip (master or individual), covered sweetmeat, and a wine. It is found in crystal, milk glass, or blue.

Amarylis (Northwood)

Primarily a bowl pattern that was designed for a goofus treatment, some pieces are plain crystal and show the design well. The example shown is an 8" bowl with scalloped edges. This is a Northwood pattern and some pieces are so marked. We suspect plates and possibly smaller bowls were made but haven't seen them. It is also known as Tiger Lily.

Amazon

Made by U. S. Glass in both clear and ruby stained glass, this pattern is also called Sawtooth Band by some collectors. Shapes are many and include a banana stand, both oval and round covered bowls, table set, celery vase that may be flat or footed, child's toy table set, champagne, claret, goblet, wine, both open and covered compotes, water set, egg cup, syrup, vase, and master and individual salt dips. Covered bowls have "lion" handles and finials.

Amazon

Amberette

Also known as Panelled Daisy and Button or Ellrose (without the amber stain), this pattern was first made by George Duncan and Sons in 1885 and then by U. S. Glass in 1892. Shapes include covered or open bowls in two sizes with flat or collared bases, finger bowl, table set, butter pat, cake stand, celery tray or vase, compotes, cruet, gas shade, olive dish, pickle dish, milk pitcher, water set, bread or dinner plates, sauces, and salt shaker.

Amberette

American Beauty

Mistakenly called a Northwood pattern, this is actually Cooperative Flint's La France, made in 1909; some collectors also call this pattern Rose and Sunbursts. Shapes include a table set, water set, berry set, and jelly compote (shown). The pattern is pictured in a 1909 Butler Brothers ad next to Northwood's Gold Rose pattern, which likely explains the mistaken identity in years past.

American Beauty

Angel's Crown

In the 1890s Dalzell, Gilmore & Leighton made a series of jelly tumblers and jars in Finlay, Ohio, and this jar is one of the designs attributed to them. It has a winged angel sitting on top of a crown with the usual interior paneling found on most of these pieces. The idea was to turn the jelly out into a saucer so that the interior design was moulded into the jelly mound. Many companies made similar wares.

Angel's Crown

Angelus

Angular

Apple Tree

Applied Filigree

Appomattox

Angelus
Apparently the moulds for the Huntington line from Huntington Glass Company (1892 – 1896) were retooled to form this Angelus line of glass (according to Heacock). Shapes include a table set, celery vase, pickle dish, waste bowl, water set, and a wine. Montgomery Ward advertised both lines from 1892 to 1896 with the Angelus examples not showing the diamond-point filling that the Huntington line had.

Angular
Made in the 1880s (maker unknown), this rather plain design depends on the handles for its name. Shapes we've been able to verify are a table set, water set, and covered compote. Surely some of the pieces in this design were etched but we haven't seen them.

Apple Tree
Apple Tree was made by the Fenton Art Glass Company in 1912 as their #1561 pattern and is found mostly in carnival glass in water sets. In other types of glass only the vase whimsey (sometimes with a straight top and sometimes like the spittoon top shown) is known. Colors for this vase shape are crystal, Royal Blue, Moonstone (semi-opaque white), Milk Glass, Ebony, and Jade Green opaque.

Applied Filigree
We wanted to show at least one example of this form of glass decoration. It is a decorative threading that is applied to the glass item much like cake decoration is added. Here we have a footed tankard pitcher in amber glass with clear filigree. We suspect this pitcher is English but have no proof. These items were more decorative than useful.

Appomattox
Found on many dressers in the early 1920s, these mirrors were made in a host of designs and materials. The example shows a back that imitates Jasperware while the handle is a fine, pressed glass wand that would please any lady.

Aquarium
Made by U. S. Glass after 1891 and possibly as late as 1909, this favorite of collectors is reported in the water pitcher shape only, in clear, amber, and emerald green. The pattern is very realistic with fine mould work and is well worth the search.

Aquarius Lamp
Made in 1893 and reported in six sizes, this fine lamp can be found in crystal, amber, blue, and the vaseline shown. The maker is unknown to us at this time and we have little other information about it.

Arcadia Lace
Made in 1927 by Jenkins Glass, this nice pattern was advertised in water sets, table sets, berry sets, celery vase, both 6" and 11" plates, 8" pickle dish, covered candy dish, nappy, rose bowl, and 6" or 10" vases that are either flared or cupped. This is Jenkins #202 pattern.

Arch and Forget-Me-Not Bands
Found only in clear glass, this familiar pattern dates to the 1880s but the maker seems to be unknown at this time. Shapes are a berry set, table set, and water set, as well as a covered jam jar.

Arched Fleur-de-Lis
This is a Bryce, Higbee pattern found in crystal or ruby stained glass like the mug shown. Other shapes include a table set, water set, shakers, a vase, banana stand, cake stand, 7" bowl, jelly compote, handled olive dish, square plate, relish, sauce, toothpick holder, and a wine. Most often seen is the pedestal-based vase shape.

Aquarium

Aquarius Lamp

Arch and Forget-Me-Not Bands

Arcadia Lace

Arched Fleur-de-Lis

Arched Grape

Arched Ovals

Argent

Argus (Thumbprint)

Army Hat

Arched Grape

This pattern is from Boston and Sandwich Glass (1870s) and is also attributed to Burlington Glass of Canada. Finials are clusters of grapes and leaves, and shapes include a table set, celery vase, champagne, covered compote, goblet, water set, wine, and flat and footed sauces.

Arched Ovals

Sometimes called Optic or Concaved Almond, this U. S. Glass pattern was their #15091, made in 1905, in clear, ruby stained, emerald green, or rose-flashed, some pieces with gold trim. Shapes include a berry set, table set, water set, cake stand, celery vase, covered and open compotes, goblet, mug, plate, relish, shakers, syrup, sauce, toothpick holder, and wine glass.

Argent

One of the many patterns from U. S. Glass (Bryce) in 1891, Argent is also known as Rope Bands or Clear Panels with Cord. Shapes known in crystal are a table set, water set, compote, celery vase, cake stand, and platter. Both the sugar and the compote shape can be found in either open or covered pieces.

Argus (Thumbprint)

Made by Bakewell, Pears and Company in 1870, by King, Son & Company in 1875, and McKee & Brothers in 1865, and also known as Concave Ashburton, Argus has been reproduced by Imperial Glass and Fostoria for the Henry Ford Museum (pieces are marked HFM). Shapes known are ale glass, beer glass, bitters bottle, bowls (open or covered), table set, celery vase, champagne, high or low covered compotes, open compote, cordial, decanter, egg cup, jelly glass, goblet, honey dish, oil lamp in two sizes, mug, paperweight, pickle jar, water set, punch set, salt dips, and wine.

Army Hat

Since the last edition we've learned that this novelty miniature hat is actually a powder jar made by the Paden City Glass Company in the 1920s. It features a military hat, complete with bill and insignia. It is 1" tall and measures 3½" in diameter.

Arrowhead

Also called Anderson, this pattern's maker is unknown. Production was in the 1895 – 1905 era and both crystal and canary are known (other colors are also a possibility). Shapes include a table set, pickle dish, compote, celery dish, but certainly other shapes probably exist. The design is a good one.

Arrowhead-in-Oval

From Higbee Glass in 1890 and produced for many years, this pattern was first called Madora. Shapes include a 7" plate, sherbet, handled basket, cake stand, celery, toy table set, stemmed rose bowl, table set, punch set, and water set.

Art

Sometimes called Job's Tears or Teardrops and Diamond Block, Art was made by Adams & Company in the 1870s and then as a U. S. Glass product in the 1890s, in both clear and ruby stained. Shapes are a 10" fruit basket, berry set, table set, cake stand, both covered and open compotes in several sizes, cracker jar, cruet, banana dish, goblet, mug, water set, relish, and wine.

Artichoke

This is Fostoria's pattern #205, made in 1891 in clear or with acid finish, and with limited production in opalescent treatment. Shapes include a bobeche, bowls, table set, cake stand, celery vase, covered compote in two sizes, open compotes in two sizes, cruet, finger bowl, oil lamp, both bulbous and tankard pitchers, shakers, syrup, water tray, flat or footed sauces, and vase.

Ashburton

This pattern was made by New England Glass in 1869; Bakewell, Pears in 1875; Bryce, Richards in 1854; and U.S. Glass after 1891. Shards are reported at Burlington in Canada also, and Boston & Sandwich is also reported to have made this pattern. Colors are crystal, amber, amethyst, aqua, canary, green, and milk glass. Shapes are many and include an ale glass, bitters bottle (shown), carafe, bowl, table set, celery vase, champagne, claret, open compote, cordial, decanter, egg cup, goblet, lamp, mug, water set, sauce, vase, wine. Many shapes have several variations and some pieces are engraved.

Arrowhead

Arrowhead-in-Oval

Art

Artichoke

Ashburton

Ashman

Atlanta

Ashman

There appears to be much confusion about this pattern, with some collectors calling it Cross Bar or Crossroads, but it isn't the same as either of these. Ashman is reported to be from Adams & Company in 1886. All pieces of Ashman are square in shape and are found in clear, amber, or blue. Shapes include a bread tray, bowl, table set, cake stand, open or covered compotes, goblet, water set, relish, water tray, wine, and pickle jar.

Atlanta

From the Westmoreland Company and advertised as their #228 in 1908, this pattern is found in table sets, jelly compote, goblet, salt shakers, celery vase, berry set, syrup, wine, toothpick holder, and lamp shade (electric or gas sizes). The primary design seems to be the hobstar in an oval, bordered by a wreath of leaves. Also made by Federal in 1914.

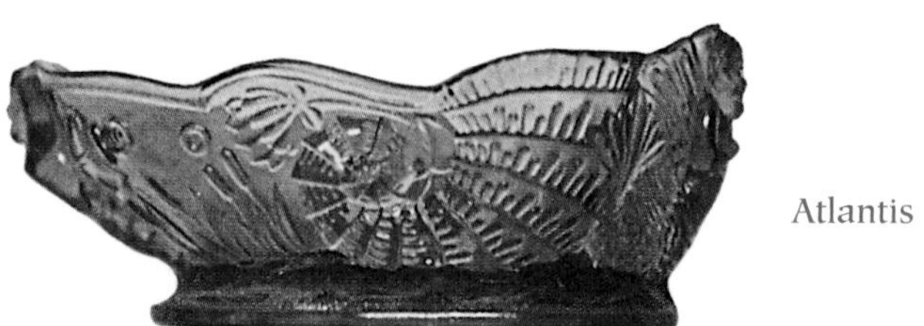

Atlantis

Atlantis

Shown is a very strange bowl shape, approximately 6" long and 2¾" wide. The coloring is a fine blue and the design is one of two Neptune-like figures at each end with a cornucopia and drifting seaweed on the sides. We believe this may have been an open master salt but can't confirm its use or maker at this time. Also known in amber.

Atlas

Atlas

This is not the same Atlas pattern as that from Bryce, and later U.S. Glass; it is attributed to Atterbury in the 1870s. It is a well-designed compote with a toga-draped figure holding up the bowl. The treatment is opal or milk glass opaque. We hope readers can shed more light on this pattern for us.

Atlas (Bryce)

Also known as Cannon Ball, Bullet, Knobby Bottom, or Orbed Feet, this pattern is attributed to Bryce Brothers (1889) and U.S. Glass (1891), and is found in crystal, etched crystal, or ruby stain. Shapes include covered and open bowls (5", 6", 7", 8"), finger bowl, table set, hotel table set, cake stand (8", 9", 10"), celery vase, covered or open compotes (5", 7", 8"), cordial, goblet, jam jar, mug, milk pitcher, water set, salt shakers (single, master), sauce (flat or footed), syrup, toothpick holder, water set, wine, and whiskey tumbler.

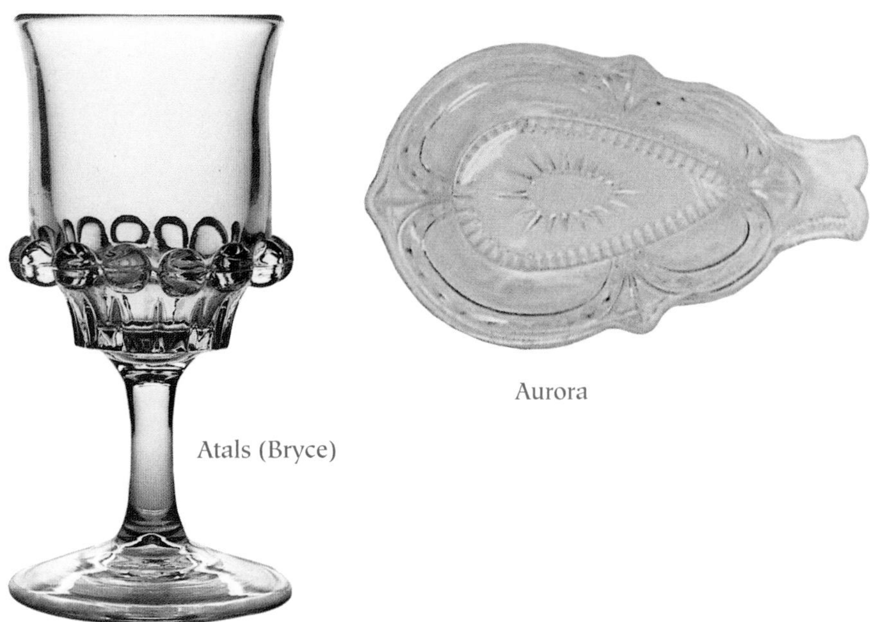

Atals (Bryce)

Aurora

Aurora

Aurora was made by Brilliant Glass and then Greensburg Glass (1888) and is also called Diamond Horseshoe by some collectors. Shapes include a table set, cake stand, compotes, cordial, wine, salt shaker, pickle dish, and bread plate. The design is often difficult to distinguish from one shape to another.

Austrian

This pattern, also called Finecut Medallion or Western, was first made at the Indiana Tumbler and Goblet Company (Greentown) and in 1897 at Indiana Glass in Dunkirk, Indiana, and Federal Glass in 1914. Austrian can be found in clear, amber, canary, green, chocolate glass, Nile Green opaque, and cobalt blue. Shapes include a banana stand, berry set, table set, child's table set, child's mug, compotes, cordial, goblet, nappy, water set, punch set, shakers, wine, and both a rose bowl and vase in three sizes.

Austrian

Azmoor

This was Ohio Flint Glass pattern #45, first advertised in 1904. The glass is fine and the design bold and impressive. Shapes are many and include a table set, punch set, 8½" oval relish, handled nappy, small deep bowl, cruet, tumbler, and a water pitcher. The design was pictured as shown here or with the center pinwheel pattern reversed. We want to thank Jean C. Loomis for sharing this photo and for her fine book called *Krys-tol! Krys-tol! Krys-tol!*

Azmoor

Aztec

Aztec Sunburst

Aztec

Aztec was part of McKee & Brothers' (1903 – 1927) "tec" grouping of patterns and found in crystal or ruby stained glass. Shapes include a table set, berry set, celery bowl, pickle dish, water set, punch set, water bottle, cordial, goblet, claret, champagne glass, wine, and rose bowl. The punch set production was continued by McKee-Jeannette until 1950.

Aztec Sunburst

This pattern, also called Sunburst, was made by McKee in 1910 and found in bowls, a table set, celery vase, shakers, a quart pitcher, half gallon pitcher, 8" saucer, cracker bowl, rose bowl, compote (7", 8", 9"), salver, handled nappy, pickle dish, celery tray, berry, creamer and open sugar, tall compote, vase, sweet pea vase, tall cake plate, and the tall footed rose bowl shown. This pattern has been reproduced in colors.

Baby Animals

Baby Animals

Showing a cat in a basket and a baby bear on a drum, this mug is found in two sizes (the large size has a flower in the base). It was more than likely made in the 1890s and the small size has been reproduced in colors by Mosser Glass and in carnival glass in 1977.

Baby Face

Baby Face

Baby Face was made by McKee and Brothers in 1880 (Geo. Duncan made a similar pattern called Three Face), and found in both clear and frosted glass. Shapes include a table set, celery dip bowl, celery vase, champagne, covered compote in four sizes, open compote in two sizes, cordial, goblet, water pitcher, and wine.

Balky Mule

Balky Mule

Actually, these water trays, found in 9½" and 12¼" sizes, are part of the Currier and Ives pattern made by the Bellaire Goblet Company in 1889. The only similarity to the parent design is the banding on the outer rim of the tray.

Ball and Swirl

The mug shown was made by Beatty & Sons, as well as McKee Brothers (1894). Other shapes include a table set, shakers, a celery vase, 6" plate, cordial set, syrup, footed jelly, cake stand, and candlesticks. Colors are clear, ruby stain, opaque white, and marigold carnival glass.

Ball and Swirl

Baltimore Pear

Baltimore Pear was from Adams and Company in 1874, then U. S. Glass in 1891, and is also known as Maryland, Gipsy, or Twin Pear. Shapes include covered or open bowls, bread plate, table set, cake plate, cake stand, celery vase, covered or open compotes, goblet, honey dish, pickle tray, water set, milk pitcher, plates, sauce, relish tray, and water tray. It has been reproduced.

Baltimore Pear

Bamboo Beauty

From U. S. Glass in 1891, this seldom-seen pattern was made in a rare table set, berry set, and water set. Factory ads show the table set with two sizes of trays that do not match, so perhaps these weren't meant to be part of the pattern. Only clear pieces of Bamboo Beauty have been seen by us, and some appear to have once had gold trim at the top.

Bamboo Beauty

Band

Perhaps this should be called "Dugan's Band" to distinguish it from another pattern with this name. Dugan/Diamond's pattern is well known to carnival glass collectors and is found in the violet basket shape, here shown in the original handled holder. Made from a tumbler mould, only the edges have been rolled to fit in the metal holder.

Band

Band and Diamond Swirl

This 6" vase shape was from U. S. Glass, made in 1898, and shown in one of their ads as part of a vase assortment. It was their #16048 pattern and can be found in clear, amber, or emerald green with gold trim.

Band and Diamond Swirl

Banded Buckle

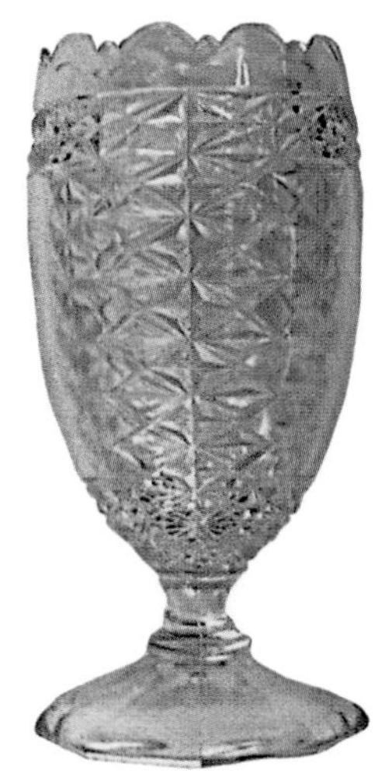
Banded Diamond Point

Banded Buckle

First a product of the Sandwich Glass Company and later made by other factories after 1870, Banded Buckle is known in flint and non-flint glass. Shapes are table sets, berry sets, egg cup, goblet, water set, footed salt dip, high and low open compotes, wine, and cordial. A similar pattern called Buckle without the banding is known.

Banded Diamond Point

Similar to so many other allover diamond patterns, this one has a serrated edge, and the design is ringed at the bottom and banded at the top. Shapes reported are a table set, berry set, and the goblet shown. Other shapes may certainly exist. The maker was Columbia in 1889 and then U.S. Glass in 1891.

Banded Diamond with Peg

Banded Diamond with Peg

This is a variant of the regular Diamond with Peg pattern, made first by McKee Glass in 1894 and then by Jefferson Glass after 1900. In 1913 Jefferson began marking their items "Krys-tol." Shapes known are a table set, toothpick holder, berry set, and water set. Pieces can be found in both clear and ruby stained. The example shown is a tumbler.

Banded Finecut

Banded Finecut

We've learned little about this pattern and the shapes seem to be limited to the one-handled nappy shown, a goblet, and a wine. We'd certainly like to hear from readers who know of other shapes. The example shown has a beautiful wheel-cut design in the base that adds greatly to the overall pattern.

Banded Fleur-de-lis

Banded Fleur-de-lis

Originally called Imperial's #5, this pattern is well known to carnival glass collectors by that name. It is shown in crystal in a 1909 Imperial catalog in a berry set (flat or footed), cake stand, jelly compote, egg cup, water set, milk pitcher, syrup, shakers, celery vase, table set, and the footed cake stand shown. Only a celery vase and bowls are reported in carnival glass.

Banded Raindrops

Found in crystal, amber, opalescent blue, and milk glass, this pattern is also called Candlewick; the maker is unknown. Shapes include a table set, water set, covered compote, cup and saucer, goblet, 7½" and 9" plates, square relish dish, shakers, sauce, and wine.

Banded Star

This pattern was made by King, Son & Company in 1880. Shapes include a table set, water set, celery vase, sauces, high or low covered compotes, individual creamer and sugar, and pickle dish.

Banner

This collectible butter dish was made by Bryce Brothers for the 1876 Centennial and later as a U. S. Glass novelty. (A rare flag shield bread tray with Miss Liberty's head was made in 1891 that is similar in design.) It is found in clear, blue, and amber. No other shapes have appeared to date, but others may certainly have been made.

Bar and Block

Also known as Nickel Plate's Richmond or Akron Block and reissued by U. S. Glass in 1891, there are many variations of this pattern, all listed under the same name(s). The pitcher shown is always called Bar and Block and other shapes include a table set, tumbler, celery vase, finger bowl, shakers, mustard jar with lid, and wine.

Bar and Diamond

Made by Richards and Hartley (U.S. Glass in 1891) and also known as Kokomo, Richards and Hartley Swirl, or Zippered Swirl, this pattern is found in both clear or ruby stained glass. Shapes include compotes, a sugar shaker, decanter, shakers in two styles, cruet, tray, toy table set, hand lamp, wine, celery vase, and a full table set. On some pieces the swirl is reversed.

Banded Raindrops

Banded Star

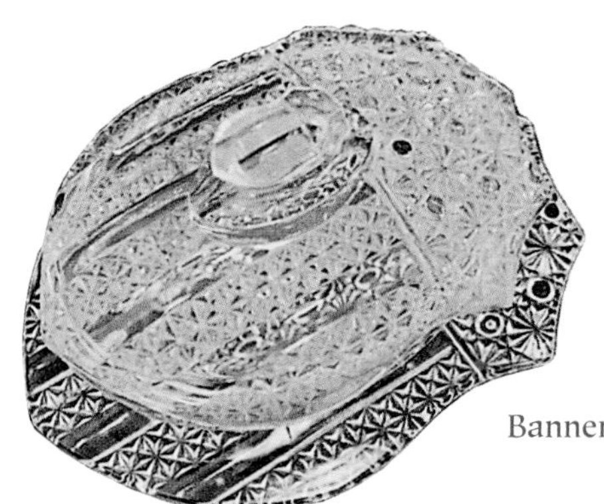

Banner

Bar and Block

Bar and Diamond

Barberry

Barley

Barrelled Thumbprint

Barry Plate

Basket Epergne

Barberry

Barberry was reported to have been made by Boston and Sandwich Glass in the 1860s and then by McKee Glass in the 1880s. Shapes include a table set, wine, cordial, celery vase, cake plate, egg cup, goblet, footed sauce, syrup, sauce, covered bowls, covered compote, bowls (open), 6" plate, tumbler (footed), pitcher, and a cup plate. The design is a very good one and quite collectible.

Barley

Also called Indian Tree or Sprig, this pattern's maker is unknown, but may be Campbell, Jones & Company of Pittsburgh in the late 1870s. It can be found in clear and rare colors that include amber. Shapes include round or oval bowls, a table set, cake stands, celery vase, covered or open compotes on high or low stands, cordial, vegetable dishes, honey dish, jam jar, pickle caster, pickle dish, water set, plates, platter, flat relish dish, relish wheelbarrow in two sizes, sauce, bread tray, and wine.

Barrelled Thumbprint

The original name was Challinor's Thumbprint made by Challinor, Taylor, Ltd., of Tarentum, Pennsylvania, in 1882. Shapes reported are a table set, water set, berry set, celery vase, goblet, pickle dish, salt shakers, water bottle, wine, and nappy in 4", 4½", 6", and 8" sizes.

Barry Plate

Apparently this was made to honor the work of St. Bernard dogs in their Swiss rescue missions (the named dog, "Barry," saved 40 people before being killed himself). The plate has a frosted center and is 10" in diameter. The maker and date of production are not known.

Basket Epergne

In the late 1800s affluent homes centered their dining room table with elaborate pieces like the one shown here, a tall standard with a shallow bowl on top and stems that held six small baskets. Handles and arms or stems are hand applied. The bowl usually held grapes or fruit while the baskets held mints or nuts.

Basketweave

Made around the mid-1880s, this pattern is found in crystal, amber, canary, apple green, blue, and some items in milk glass. Shapes include berry sets, waste and finger bowls, a table set, covered or opened compotes (both high and low), a cordial, egg cup (double or single), goblet, mug, milk pitcher, pickle dish, water set, cake plate, footed or flat salt dip, sauce, saucer, syrup, water tray, and a wine. Now credited to Chicago Glass Company.

Beacon #410 Innovation

This pattern is from the McKee Glass Company in the mid-1920s and features the vase shown, two sizes of square vases, a sugar and creamer set, handled basket, fernery, oval orange bowl, fruit compote, 12" footed tray, several footed bowl shapes, and several flat novelty bowls. It was advertised in clear, jade, or opalescent glass, and we've heard of the handled basket in carnival glass.

Bead and Scroll

From Riverside Glass, this well-known pattern is found in clear, blue, frosted, ruby stained, cobalt, emerald, and amber glass, many times with gold trim. Shapes are a water set, goblet, jelly compote, toothpick holder, table set, berry set, salt shakers, berry set, and a rare child's toy table set.

Bead Column

While the maker of this pattern is listed as unknown by most writers, one does venture a guess that this is a D.C. Jenkins Glass Company pattern. We do know it was made in the 1905 – 1910 period and can be found in a table set as well as a water set. I believe it may well have been made in a relish dish and a celery vase, too.

Beaded Arch Panels

Attributed to Burlington Glass Works of Canada in 1890, this pattern is also known as Archaic Gothic or simply Beaded Arch. Shapes are a table set, goblet, and handled mug. Pieces are found in clear or cobalt blue.

Basketweave

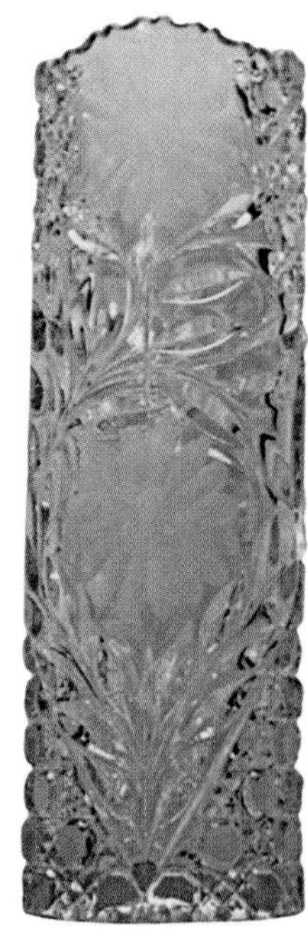

Beacon #410 Innovation

Bead and Scroll

Bead Column

Beaded Arch Panels

Beaded Band

Beaded Beauty

Beaded Chain

Beaded Coarse Bars

Beaded Comet Band

Beaded Band

Attributed to Burlington in 1884, this very nice pattern is found in crystal and occasionally in colored glass (rare). Shapes we know about are a table set, water set, covered compote, goblet, syrup jug, spoonholder, relish, wine, and spouted syrup that bears a patent date of June 29, 1884.

Beaded Beauty

Typical of many items that were meant to be ruby stained, this ball-stemmed beauty with beaded top (four small beads and one large one) has a very superior engraved floral design. It was probably sold as both an open vessel or one with a lid (there is a lid rim inside). It measures just over 6" tall and has a top diameter of 7¼". We've taken the liberty of giving it a name. Made by Paden City Glass as their #555 line.

Beaded Chain

Also known as Looped Cord, this easy-to-recognize pattern can be found in a table set, celery vase, plate, sauce, relish, water set, and the goblet shown. The maker is in question at this time but the pattern dates to the late 1870s. Additional information on this pattern would be greatly appreciated.

Beaded Coarse Bars

Found in table sets, water carafe, mug, goblet, pickle dish, and salt shakers, this ribbed pattern is much like so many others made in the 1890 – 1910 era of pressed glass. The maker is presumed to be U. S. Glass but we have no confirmation of this, and certainly other shapes may exist.

Beaded Comet Band

Also known as Ways' Beaded Swirl, this pattern was made at Albany, Indiana, by Model Flint Glass in 1893. It is found in crystal and ruby stained glass and is also known in carnival glass (rare) as Beads and Bars. Crystal shapes include a berry set, 10" plate, table set, cruet, and pickle dish, but the carnival examples are a nut bowl (from the spooner) and a rose bowl.

Beaded Grape

Beaded Grape was made by U. S. Glass Company in 1899 and possibly Burlington Glass in Canada in 1910, in clear, emerald green, and gold trimmed. It is also known as California. Shapes include a table set, cake stand, cordial, compotes, toothpick holder, 6" vase, wine, round or square bowls, round or square water sets, pickle dish, sauces, shakers, berry set, and bread plate.

Beaded Grape Medallion

This pattern is credited to the Boston Silver Glass Company in 1869 (shards have been found at Boston and Sandwich Glass) and was made in clear crystal. Shapes include a flat bowl, a table set, cake stand, caster set, celery vase, champagne, covered high or low compotes, open compote, cordial, oval bowl, egg cup, goblets, honey dish, pickle dish, pitcher, 6" plate, relish dish, salt dip, master salt dip, sauce, and a wine.

Beaded Medallion

This well-known pattern, also known as Beaded Mirror, was made by Sandwich Glass in the early 1870s. It can be found in a water set, table set, jelly compote, egg cup, open salt, relish, sauce, and possibly a goblet. Apparently found in clear glass only.

Beaded Panel and Sunburst

Beaded Panel and Sunburst was made by Heisey (their #1235) in 1898 and some believe by U. S. Glass earlier in clear or color stained. Shapes include a table set, hotel creamer and sugar, bowls, berry bowls, nappy, celery vase, celery tray, toothpick holder, plate, cruets in three sizes, pickle tray, spoon tray, salt dip, shakers (three shapes), punch set, water set, carafe, wine, whiskey tumbler, water sets in two sizes, compotes in five sizes, cake stand, and oil jug.

Beaded Shell

Called simply Shell by opalescent glass collectors and Beaded Shell by carnival glass people, this pattern was also made in crystal, colored glass, and decorated glass. The Dugan Glass, Company is the maker. Shapes include a berry set, table set, water set, mug, cruet, shakers, toothpick holder, a cruet set, and compotes. Shown is a green master berry bowl with gilded beading.

Beaded Grape

Beaded Grape Medallion

Beaded Medallion

Beaded Panel and Sunburst

Beaded Shell

Beaded Stars and Swag

Beaded Swag

Beaded Swirl and Ball

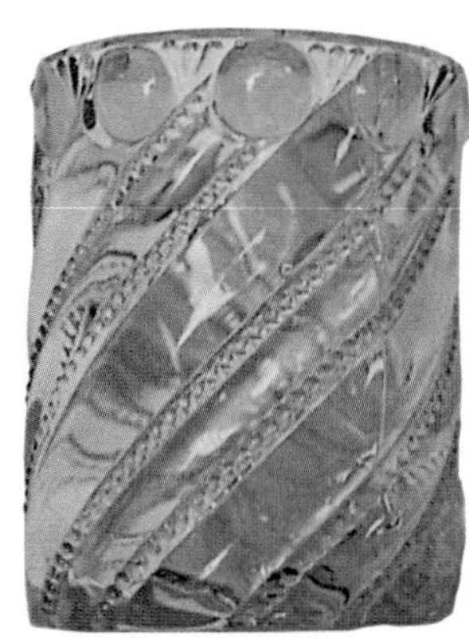
Beaded Swirl and Lens

Beaded Tulip

Beaumont's Columbia

Beaded Stars and Swag

This pattern is from the Fenton Glass Company and found in opalescent as well as carnival glass, crystal, and even custard glass. Production dates to 1907 and there is a similar pattern from the same maker called Beaded Moon and Stars. Shapes are plates, bowls, rose bowls, and the banana bowl shape shown.

Beaded Swag

Beaded Swag was made by Heisey (their #1295 pattern) about 1899 in clear, green, ruby stained, custard, and opalescent glass. The mug shown was a popular souvenir item and is often found with lettering. Besides the mug shape, a cup and saucer are known.

Beaded Swirl and Ball

Beaded Swirl and Ball is also known as Westmoreland's Puritan and was originally made by Leerdam of Holland. Westmoreland's mug, made in the 1905 – 1910 era, can be found in crystal, emerald green, cobalt blue, amethyst, and dark brown, all with gold trim. Other shapes in this pattern are a wine glass and an egg cup. The mug is found in both 4 oz. and 8 oz. sizes.

Beaded Swirl and Lens

This very attractive pattern can be distinguished by its "lens." The maker is unknown to us at this time but a table set, water set, berry set, and possibly other shapes can be found. This is not the same pattern as Beaded Swirl and Disc by U. S. Glass.

Beaded Tulip

Beaded Tulip was shown in McKee & Brothers' 1894 catalog in clear, blue, emerald green, and amber. Shapes include an oval 9½" bowl, table set, cake stand, champagne, covered or open compotes, cordial, oblong ice cream dish, goblet, jam jar, pickle dish, milk pitcher, water set, bread or dinner plates, relish, sauce (flat or footed), water tray, wine tray, and wine glass.

Beaumont's Columbia

The Beaumont Glass Company made this, their #100, in 1898. It is found in crystal, vaseline with gold trim, ruby, or amber stain. Shapes include a table set, water set, berry set, cruet, syrup, high standard compote, plates (8" and 10"), celery tray (also used for cruet set), jelly compote, toothpick holder, vase, celery vase, and salt dips.

Bee Butter Dish

While this Bryce Brothers' pattern is known as a bee pattern and a butter dish, it is advertised in a U.S. Glass catalog (Bryce was the factory B of U.S. Glass) as a "Fly pickle dish" so it may have been resurrected from earlier production and given a second life as a covered pickle dish. It certainly looks more like a fly than a bee, and is found in clear, vaseline, amber, or blue.

Begging Dog

Credited to the Iowa City Glass Works, this mug closely resembles their Dog mug and was made about 1881. Colors are clear, amethyst, and possibly cobalt blue. The mug is 2⅜" tall and has a diameter of 2".

Belladonna

Belladonna was made by the Northwood Glass Company as their #31 pattern and shown in a 1906 catalog. It is found in crystal, green, and ruby stained, shapes include a table set, berry set, water set, and toothpick holder (shown). The design is very plain except for the ring of beading with notching on each side.

Bellflower

First attributed to Boston & Sandwich Company in the 1840s and then Bryce, McKee Glass Company, this pattern is found in variations that include Single Vine with Fine Rib, Double Vine with Fine Rib, both Single and Double Vine with Course Rib, and Cut Bellflowers. Colors are clear, amber, vaseline, blue, green, milk glass, opaque blue, sapphire blue, and opalescent. The many shapes include bowls, table set, cake stands, celery vase, caster set, open or covered compotes, wines, cordials, goblets, celery vase, plates, water set, mug, pickle dish, lamps, decanter, syrup, milk pitcher, and a covered sweetmeat. Many shapes have wide variations and various sizes.

Belmont #100

This pattern was also called Belmont's Daisy and Button and was made with a daisy and button as part of the design in 1886. Shapes include a table set, a celery vase (on the cover of our second edition), and the plate shown, but other shapes probably were made. Some crystal pieces are engraved and all pieces are made in plain crystal, as well as the beautiful vaseline glass.

Bee Butter Dish

Begging Dog

Bellflower

Belladonna

Belmont #100

Belmont Diamond

Berry

Berry Cluster

Berry Spray

Berlin

Belmont Diamond

From the Belmont Glass Company in 1897, this pattern that resembles both Blockade (from Belmont) and King's Curtain can be found in round bowls, oval bowls, and the cruet shape. The cruet dates to 1885 and was thought the only shape in this pattern for many years.

Berlin

Berlin, also called Reeded Waffle, was made by Adams and Company in 1874 and U.S. Glass in 1891. Shapes include a table set, water set, cruet, wine, cracker jar, ice bowl, and a goblet. Berlin is found in crystal, ruby stained or amber stained glass. We mistakenly labeled this piece as Open Plaid in the first book, and we are happy to make a correction.

Berry

We certainly wish we had more information about this pattern. It was obviously made in a table set and we suspect there have to be other shapes such as a celery vase, goblets, or wines. In design it somewhat resembles the Fairfax Strawberry pattern but isn't the same. We'd certainly appreciate any information from readers about this design.

Berry Cluster

Found in a table set (with open or covered sugar), celery vase, water set, goblet, and perhaps other shapes, this realistic pattern is easily identified by the curved twig ring and the clusters of berries and leaves that stand out greatly. We believe this pattern dates to the 1890s but can't identify the maker.

Berry Spray

This short-stemmed wine from the Indiana Tumbler and Goblet Company at Greentown seems to be found only in clear glass. Shards were found at the factory and only the one shape is reported. The design is a spray of well-stippled leaves and two clusters of fruit without tendrils. Production was in the 1890s.

Bethlehem Star

A pattern from Indiana Glass Company and made in 1910, Bethlehem Star is found in a table set, water set, celery vase, covered compote (4½", 5", 8"), cruet, goblet, relish, sauce, wine, and jelly compote. Only clear has been reported.

Bevelled Buttons

From U. S. Glass, this was originally Duncan #320 made in 1891. Shapes include a table set, pickle jar, sauce, bowls, celery vase, and open compotes made in three sizes (7", 8" and 9"). While only crystal pieces are known, some are gold decorated.

Bevelled Diamond and Star

The shapes in this pattern made by Tarentum Glass Company in 1898 in both clear and ruby stained glass include a table set, shakers, water set, syrup, cruet, and bread plate. The pattern is a strong one that covers only the lower portion of the piece, permitting the upper area to be engraved on some pieces.

Bicycle Girl

Known only in the tankard pitcher shape and made in the 1880s, this very fine pattern's maker is Dalzell, Gilmore and Leighton Glass. The design shows a young girl in the dress of the late 1800s, riding a bicycle through a leafy bower. The mould work is excellent.

Big Basketweave

First made by Dugan (1910) and then by Diamond Glass (1913), this well-known vase pattern is mostly found in carnival glass, in vases and handled baskets (in two sizes), and bowl exteriors. In crystal we have seen vases and baskets in clear and vases in celeste blue glass.

Biliken Flute

The title seems to be generic but this wine glass shown is always called Biliken Flute. Other shapes known include a table set, pickle dish with tab handle, and a goblet. We do not know the maker and suspect more than one factory in more than one timeframe made versions of this simple design. Thanks to the late John Gregory for sharing this and many of the wines shown in this book.

Bethlehem Star

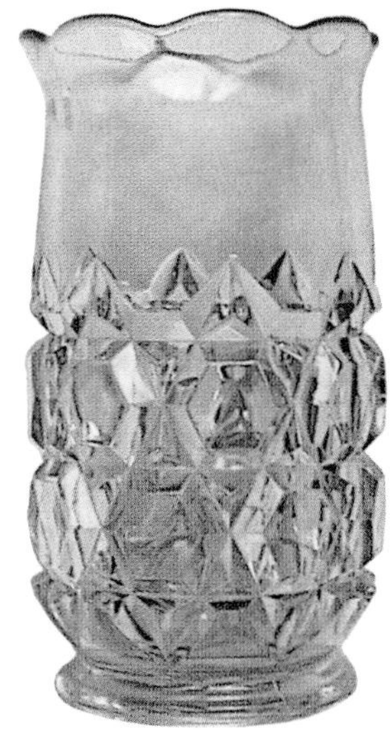

Bevelled Buttons

Bevelled Diamond and Star

Bicycle Girl

Big Basketweave

Biliken Flute

Bird and Cherry

Birch Leaf

Bird and Harp

Bird and Strawberry

Bird Basket

Bird in Nest with Flowers

Birch Leaf

The maker of this pattern is unknown. It was made in the 1870s in crystal or milk glass and shapes include a table set, covered or open compotes, goblet, wine, egg cup, master salt dip, pickle dish, and celery vase. Shown is a syrup jug with the original top fitting.

Bird and Cherry

We have no information about this piece other that it was shown in Metz as a holder for a mustard jar (the insert is missing on this one). It is found in crystal and the canary example shown (we suspect it was also made in other colors that may include blue or amber but can't be sure). We welcome additional information on this item.

Bird and Harp

Found in three sizes, this mug was made by McKee & Brothers Glass Company about 1880. It is found in clear and purple slag glass. The design is interesting with a harp on each side of the handle and a bird nesting on a bough.

Bird and Strawberry

From Indiana Glass Company in the 1910 – 1920 era and found in clear or with blue-green-red staining, this well-known pattern was made into a table set, water set, berry set, various odd bowls (5", 9" 10"), cake stand, celery tray, celery vase, hat (made from tumbler and very rare), cup, goblet, chop plate, sandwich plate, relish dish, and wine.

Bird Basket

Credited to Bryce Brothers in 1886, this novelty toothpick or match holder is a real find. It is shown in amber but also came in clear or blue.

Bird in Nest with Flowers

This mug was made by Challinor & Taylor Ltd. in the 1880s. It is 3⅜" tall and has a top diameter of 3⅛". It was made in crystal and the purple slag shown. There is a variant with a starred bottom rather than the normal cat on the base.

Bird on a Branch

From a line of mug patterns first made by Bryce and then U. S. Glass, this one has two robin-like birds on opposite sides and an owl opposite the handle. Between the birds are branches and leaves. The mug's handle is knobbed and the base notched-and-prismed.

Birds at Fountain

The maker of this pattern seems to be unknown, but it dates to the early 1880s and was made in clear or milk glass. Shapes are few and include a small bowl, flat sauce, goblet, miniature mug, cake stand, covered compote, and table set.

Birds in Swamp

Like so many novelty goblets, this one shows a designer's imagination. It has a threaded background, tree branches, leaves, and two birds nesting. Perhaps the threading is meant to be the woven nest but it's hard to tell. The maker isn't known to us but we believe the goblet dates to the 1880s.

Blackberry (Hobbs)

Blackberry was made in 1870 by Hobbs, Brockunier in crystal or opal ware (Hobbs called this treatment porcelain) with the pattern #3829. Shapes are many and include celery, tall celery, champagne, high and low compotes, high and low covered compotes, egg cups (single or double), goblet, nappy, syrup, water set, table set, relish, salt dip, wine, and oil lamps (8½", 9½", 11½"). Shown is the complete table set.

Blazing Cornucopia

Also known as Paisley or Golden Jewel by some collectors, this is a U. S. Glass pattern made in 1913. Found in clear and painted (purple, pink, or olive green), and gold trimmed glass. Shapes include a table set, water set, berry set, cruet, goblet, wine, cup, pickle dish, jelly compote, nappy, olive dish, celery tray, and toothpick holder.

Bird on a Branch

Birds at Fountain

Birds in Swamp

Blazing Cornucopia

Blackberry (Hobbs)

Bleeding Heart

Blockade

Block and Bar

Block and Circle

Block and Jewel

Bleeding Heart

First made by King & Son in the 1870s and then by U. S. Glass in 1898 in crystal or opaque glass, Bleeding Heart is an available pattern in oval or round covered bowls (5", 7", 8", 9"), waste bowl, table set, cake stand in three sizes, oval or round compotes, covered compotes (7", 8", 9"), egg cup, goblet, jelly dish, honey dish, mug, pickle tray, water set, plate, oval platter, relish tray, and master and individual salts. Shards were found at Iowa City Flint Glass Company.

Blockade

Made by U. S. Glass (Challinor #309) in 1891 and often called Diamond Block with Fan, the pattern is a cousin of Red Block. Shapes include a table set, water set, finger bowl, celery vase, open compote in 4", 6", 7", 8" sizes, covered compote in three sizes, goblet, square dish in 7" 8", 9" sizes, and nappy in two sizes.

Block and Bar

This mysterious pattern was made in the 1860s – 1870s. We know of only the creamer shown, a water pitcher, a sugar, and a goblet. Both crystal and vaseline examples exist. We welcome any additional information from readers.

Block and Circle

Block and Circle was originally named Mellor and produced by Gillinder in 1880. Shapes include a table set, celery vase, 6" covered sweetmeat, open compote in three sizes, berry set, water set, goblet, oval dish, miniature lamp, and beer mug.

Block and Jewel

This is very similar to a pattern called Milton, but it has a round jewel in the square rather than a diamond prism design. The maker is unknown at this time but we suspect this pattern was made by Bellaire Goblet or Dalzell, Gilmore & Leighton at Finlay, Ohio. The only shape reported is the stemmed wine shown.

Block and Panel

We've heard of this pattern in a table set, celery vase (shown), salt shakers, and goblet. It was more than likely made in several other shapes, but we have no record of these and the maker seems to be unknown at this time.

Block and Pillar

Found on salt and pepper shakers and on this vase shape, we suspect this pattern may well be found on table sets, water sets, and other table pieces. The pattern is a simple one, adaptable to nearly any shape and was made in the 1890s. The vase shown is 8" tall and has traces of gold trim around the flared rim.

Block and Triple Bars

We have very little information about this pattern except to say it was made in a table set as well as a goblet. Probably additional items exist, and the goblet has a fan added at the top of the design.

Blocked Thumbprint Band

Besides the mug shape shown, this Duncan & Miller pattern is found in a cruet, toothpick holder, wine, and shot glass in both clear and ruby stained glass. The pattern was made in 1904 and continued for nearly a decade.

Blooms and Blossoms

From the Northwood Company, this pattern can be found in carnival (rarely), opalescent, ruby stain, gilding, enameled, clear, vaseline, or emerald green glass. Shapes include a one-handled nappy, bowls, and plates. This pattern dates to 1905 and is also called Mikado, Flower and Bud, and Lightning Flower by some collectors.

Bohemian Drape

We are confident this very fine covered jar with matching bowl was a product of the 1880s or 1890s. The jar is 9" tall and the bowl has a 10" diameter. The glass is an outstanding vaseline and the lid has a brass berry and leaf finial. Any information readers can share about this piece would be greatly appreciated. Thanks to the Sandemans for sharing it with us.

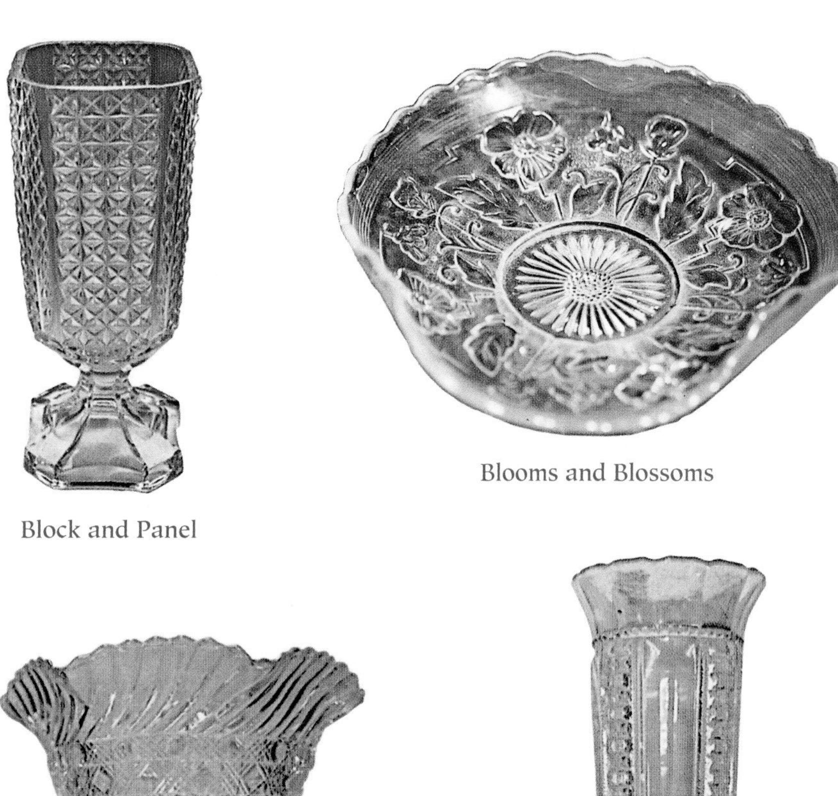

Block and Panel

Blooms and Blossoms

Block and Triple Bars

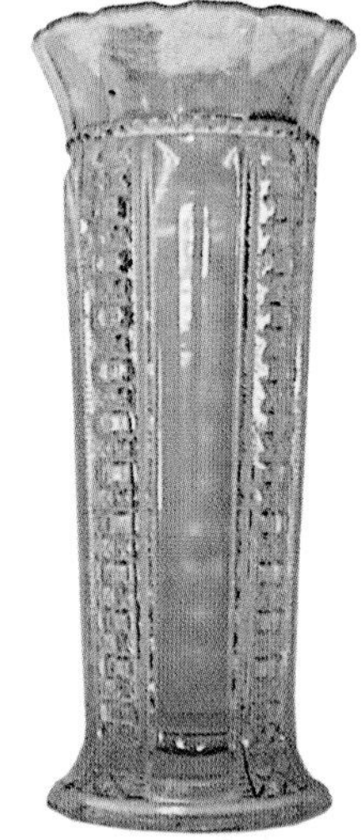

Block and Pillar

Blocked Thumbprint Band

Bohemian Drape

Bosc Pear

Bow Tie

Box Pleat

Boy and Girl Face

Boy with Begging Dog

Branched Tree

Bosc Pear

From Indiana Glass in 1913, this was their #150 pattern. Its shapes include a berry set, four-piece table set, and a water set, as well as a scarce celery vase. Found in crystal, gilded crystal, and purple flashed fruit.

Bow Tie

This was Thompson Glass's pattern #18 in 1889. Shapes include bowls in four sizes, a table set, butter pat, cake stand, celery vase, high or low compotes in several sizes, goblet, jam jar, orange bowl, water set, milk pitcher in two sizes, water set with three sizes of pitchers, punch bowl, relish dish, flat and footed sauces, and both master and individual salt dips.

Box Pleat

Made by Adams & Company in 1875 and sometimes called O'Hara's Crystal Wedding, this pattern can be found in a table set, compote, water set, celery vase, and cake stand. Most pieces have feet.

Boy and Girl Face

Found with a matching saucer that is called Acorn, this cup was a product of the Columbia Glass Company of Findlay, Ohio, in the late 1880s and then U.S. Glass after 1891. The cup shows a boy on one side, a girl on the other, while the saucer has a vining of acorns. Both pieces were made in clear, blue, or amber.

Boy with Begging Dog

Collectors feel this mug was made in the 1890s and may be a companion piece to the Deer & Cow and Heron & Peacock mugs since the three mugs make a graduated size grouping and because of similar shape. Colors are clear, blue, opaque blue, and milk glass. One side shows the boy and begging dog while the other shows a boy in a kneeling position with a food bowl.

Branched Tree

Branched Tree was from Dalzell, Gilmore, and Leighton in the 1890s and found in crystal, amber, and blue glass. Shapes include a table set, water set, celery vase, covered compote, and goblet. The unimaginative design isn't easy to mistake.

Brass Nailhead

We've heard this mug is found in flint opalescent glass but the example here is not opalescent. In addition, our example is marked "France," so the pattern is probably not compatible with the lacy saucer that has been linked with it. The mug is 1¾" and is distinguished by the two spiked collars that span it.

Brass Nailhead

Brazen Shield

Brazen Shield was from Central Glass as their #98, then Cambridge Glass in 1905, and finally from Indiana Glass. Shapes include a table set, water set, berry set, pickle dish, salt shakers, goblet, wine, and the jelly compote shown.

Brazen Shield

Brazilian

Advertised as Fostoria's #600 pattern in 1898, Brazilian is also known as Cane Shield. Shapes include a table set, toothpick holder, salt shaker, pickle jar, vase, sauce, handled olive, water set, finger bowl, compote, carafe, celery tray, celery vase, cracker jar in three sizes, berry set, cruet, sherbet, and rose bowl.

Brinkerhoff Inkwell

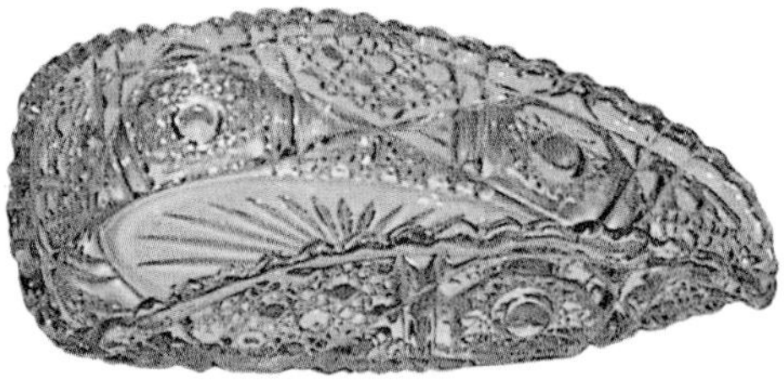

Brazilian

Bringing Home the Cows

This was made by the Dalzell, Gilmore, and Leighton Glass Company in 1890 in clear only. Shapes include a four-piece table set and the water pitcher shown. Neither matching tumblers have been reported nor the usual accompanying table items.

Brinkerhoff Inkwell

This neat little inkwell with the large plume pen was made in 1872 by A. W. Brinkerhoff Company. It is marked "Pat'd–May 7th–1872." The design is a simple one with a wide band at the top and convex columns at the base.

Bringing Home the Cows

Britannic

Britannic Floral

Broken Arches

Broken Pillar and Reed

Broken Column

Britannic

Made by McKee Glass Company in 1894, this well-balanced pattern can be found in clear, amber, and ruby stained glass. Shapes include a fruit basket, banana stand, cologne, carafe, oval bowl (7", 8", 9"), round bowl, rose bowl, square bowl, table set, cake stand (large or small), caster set, celery tray, celery vase, covered compote, open compote (5", 6", 7", 8½", 10"), cruet, custard cup, olive dish, pickle dish, goblet, honey jar, cracker jar, lamp (two types and sizes), mug, shakers, sauce, syrup, toothpick holder, ice cream tray, vase, wine.

Britannic Floral

If you examine the Britannic pattern shown above, you will see the primary design of this piece is the same with added leaf and floral patterning below it. Here we show a creamer but certainly other shapes must exist. Britannic was made by McKee in 1894 and this variant may be also but we have no proof.

Broken Arches

Made by Imperial Glass in 1914 in carnival glass and crystal and bearing a catalog designation of Snap-14, this well-done geometric pattern is found on punch sets and an 8½" bowl. The bowl is ruffled and the punch bowl may be either ruffled or just round with serrated edges.

Broken Column

Also called Irish Column or Notched Rib, this was first a Columbia Glass pattern in 1891 and U. S. Glass the following year. Sometimes found with gilding, shapes are a table set, water set, banana dish, 13½" long handled basket, cake stand, celery tray, covered compote, open compote, cruet, finger bowl, goblet, pickle caster, 8" plate, shakers, sauce, syrup, water bottle, and wine. Some pieces have ruby trim.

Broken Pillar and Reed

Also known as Kismet, this was Model Flint's #909 pattern. It can be found in crystal, blue, amber, green, gold flash, Maiden's Blush, and opalescent colors. Pieces include a bonbon, 8" bowl, table set, cake stand, celery vase and celery tray, cologne, compote, custard cup, soap dish, jelly compote, pickle tray, squat pitcher, plate, shakers, syrup, tankard water set, tray, and toothpick holder.

Bryce Fashion

This pattern was made in the 1880s and found in crystal, amber, amethyst, blue, vaseline, ruby stained glass, and a rare blue example that is ruby stained. It is also known as Daisy & Button with Red Dots in stained glass. Shapes include the toothpick holder shown, a creamer formed from a cup shape, and a creamer formed from the toothpick holder mould.

Bryce Fashion Butter Dish

Shown as a U.S. Glass product from their factory B (Bryce Brothers) in 1891, this very unusual butter dish seems to have no matching pieces and must have been one of the several single butter dish designs like Lorne. It is known in crystal and here we show the vaseline version.

Bryce Hobnail

Bryce Hobnail, also called Panelled Hobnail, was first made by Bryce Brothers in the 1880s and then as part of U.S. Glass after 1891. Shapes include bowls, a table set, wine, mug, open or covered compotes, celery vase, pickle dish, and a goblet. Colors are clear, canary, blue, or milk glass.

Bryce Panel

From U. S. Glass in the 1880s, Bryce Panel shapes include a syrup, table set, and the celery vase shown. The design is minimal and one wonders why a second pattern wasn't used. It is found in clear and clear with gold trim.

Bryce Ribbon Candy

Bryce made this pattern in 1885 and U. S. Glass as their #15010 pattern in 1898. It is also called just Ribbon Candy. Shapes include covered or open oval bowls (4", 5", 6", 8"), table set, cake plate, cake stand, child's table set, celery vase, claret, covered compote, cruet, cordial, cup and saucer, honey dish, lamp, pickle dish, water set, milk pitcher, 6", 7", 8", 9" 10" plates, bread plate, relish, shakers, sauce, syrup, and wine.

Bryce Fashion

Bryce Fashion Butter Dish

Bryce Hobnail

Bryce Panel

Bryce Ribbon Candy

Buckingham

Buckle and Diamond

Buckle with English Hobnail

Buckle with Star

Bullet Emblem

Bull's-Eye and Daisy

Buckingham

This was advertised as U. S. Glass design #15106 in 1907 and produced at the Glassport factory. Shapes include a table set, water set, berry set, and a sauce which can be found with advertising and is also shown as such on page 278.

Buckle and Diamond

Made by McKee and Brothers Glass in 1880, this unusual pattern's shapes include a table set, water set, bowls, and goblet. The design is one of a band of opposing forms that include ovals, diamonds, and scrolls, some clear and some with finecut file.

Buckle with English Hobnail

This very well-done pattern can be found in a table set, berry set, shakers, pickle dish, and celery vase. The maker escapes us and certainly other shapes may exist. Shown is the spooner shape.

Buckle with Star

Buckle with Star was made in 1880 by Bryce, Walker and then by U. S. Glass in 1891 at the Bryce factory ("B") in clear only. Shapes include covered bowls in four sizes, table set, cake stand, celery vase, cologne bottle, covered and open compotes, goblet, honey dish, mug, mustard jar, water set, relish tray, master salt, flat or footed sauces, syrup, wine, and handled tumbler.

Bullet Emblem

Also called Shield and made by U. S. Glass Company in 1898 as a Spanish-American War commemorative, pieces were originally decorated in red, white, and blue with the bullet finial in silver. Shapes are a table set consisting of covered butter dish, covered sugar bowl, creamer, and spooner.

Bull's-Eye and Daisy

Originally called Newport, this is a U. S. Glass pattern made in Glassport in 1909. Besides clear, it can be found in emerald green as well as decorated bull's-eyes. Shapes are table sets, water sets, syrup, toothpick holder, shakers, and wine. Some pieces may also be found with ruby staining.

Bull's-Eye and Fan

Made by U. S. Glass in 1905, this was their #15090 pattern. It is also known as Daisies in Oval Panels by some collectors. Shapes are a table set, water set, goblet, berry set, mug, toothpick holder, and cake stand. It was made in crystal, crystal with colored bull's-eye, blue, or green glass. Some pieces are gilded.

Butterfly

Known as Big Butterfly by some carnival glass collectors where only the tumbler is known (rare), this U. S. Glass pattern (#6406) is found in crystal in a table set, water set (scarce), celery vase, pickle dish, mustard jar, salt shakers, relish dish, and bowls. Handles on some pieces are frosted.

Butterfly (Frosted)

Made by Aetna Glass in 1883, this pattern is also known as Butterfly Handles. Shapes include a table set, covered compote, celery vase, shakers, and probably other shapes. The frosting occurs on both the lid and the bowl of the compote shown.

Butterfly (Plain)

Like the frosted compote shown above, this one is also from the Aetna Company in about 1883, a line that is also called Butterfly Handles by some. Shapes include a table set, covered compote, celery vase, shakers, and water set.

Butterfly and Berry

Besides the carnival glass pieces and the amberina vase whimsey (pulled from a tumbler) we showed in the last edition of this book, we are pleased to show pieces of the first reported berry set in this pattern in crystal. It was made by Fenton in 1911 and was one of the company's major patterns for two decades. It has been reproduced, mainly in carnival glass.

Butterfly and Thistle

We haven't been able to learn the maker of this very attractive design, but it is a shame to see it only on the 9" bowl shape. The pattern is deep and well balanced with a touch of whimsey about it. Four butterflies hover around four thistle stalks that seem to grow out of a file-centered star.

Bull's-Eye and Fan

Butterfly (Plain)

Butterfly (Frosted)

Butterfly

Butterfly and Berry

Butterfly and Thistle

Butterfly with Spray

Button Arches

Button Panel

Buzz-Star

Buttressed Loop

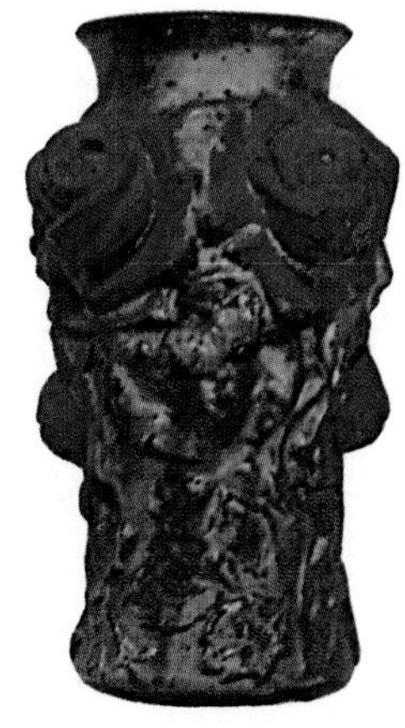

Cabbage Rose

Butterfly with Spray

Also known as Acme and made by Bryce, Higbee and Company in 1885, shapes include a mug in two sizes, table set, celery vase, covered compotes in high or low standard, and water set. Covered pieces have butterfly handles and finials; this pattern should not be confused with the Butterfly and Fan goblet that is part of the Japanese or Grace pattern.

Button Arches

Also known as Red Top or Scalloped Daisy, this is a pattern made by Duncan & Miller and U. S. Glass and dates to 1897. It can be found in crystal or ruby stained pieces that were used as souvenir glass, often with a frosted band. It can also be found in clambroth coloring. There are many shapes which include a water set, toothpick holder, table set, compote, syrup, cruet, cup, shakers, and wine.

Button Panel

In their advertising, this was Duncan's #44 pattern, made in 1900. It can be found in crystal, ruby stained glass, and gold decorated glass in a toothpick holder, berry set, table set, cruet, toy (child's) table set, shakers, pickle dish, and celery vase.

Buttressed Loop

From Adams and Company as their #16 in 1874, this uncomplicated pattern can be found in crystal, green, blue, amber, and canary glass. Shapes include a compote, covered bowl, and table set.

Buzz-Star

Buzz-Star is also known as Whirligig and was made by U. S. Glass as #15101 in 1907 at the Bryce factory. Shapes include a table set, water set, toy table set (called Whirligig by collectors), berry set, pickle dish, goblet, wine, toy punch set, and salt dip.

Cabbage Rose

Not to be confused with the famous Central Glass pattern of 1870, this design is from the goofus period, found in vases in 5", 7", and 10" sizes. The roses, like the poppies in another goofus pattern we show, are puffed out and very artistic but appear too gaudy in the painted pieces. Still, these vases are collectible.

Cabbage Rose (Central)

Cabbage Rose was made by Central Glass as their #140 in 1870 and is found in crystal. Mosser Glass reproduced the goblet and spooner in amber, clear, green, amethyst, and blue in 1963. Shapes include a bitters bottle, handled basket, oval or round bowls (covered or open in several sizes), a table set, cake plate, cake stand (six sizes), celery vase, champagne, covered compote (eight sizes and high or low shapes), open compotes (four sizes), cordial, egg cup, goblets, mug, pickle dish, milk pitcher, water set, sauce, relish dish, master salt, and a wine (shown).

Cable and Thumbprint Match Holder

Shown in Jay Glickman and Terry Fedosky's *Yellow-Green Vaseline* book, this match or toothpick holder has a hexagonal base and may well be from England or Europe. It is a product of the 1860s we believe.

Cabbage Rose (Central)

Cable and Thumbprint Match Holder

Cactus

Far different from the Greentown pattern with the same name, this Millersburg design is on bowls only as an exterior intaglio pattern. It is found on both carnival glass and crystal and was made from 1909 to 1912 only when the factory was sold to Jefferson Glass. Millersburg crystal is clear, sparkling, and top quality in every instance. It is very collectible.

Cambridge #2351

Also found in carnival glass in a few shapes, this geometric pattern was made in crystal in a table set, berry set, water set, 7" vase, oil bottle, half-gallon jug, cologne bottle, orange bowl, punch set, spoon tray, whiskey set with tray, handled olive, sweet pea vase, shakers, toothpick holder, wine, footed jelly, sherbet, celery tray, celery vase, 7" large compote, and a small punch bowl that stands 9" tall. Production dates to 1906.

Cactus

Cambridge #2351

Cambridge #2658

This was a specialty pattern from Cambridge in 1910 and found on a creamer, mug, or tumbler shape. Colors are clear, ruby stained, enameled crystal, and carnival glass (mug or tumbler only). The design is much like others in the era of ruby stained souvenir items where the top portion is unpatterned for lettering.

Cambridge #2658

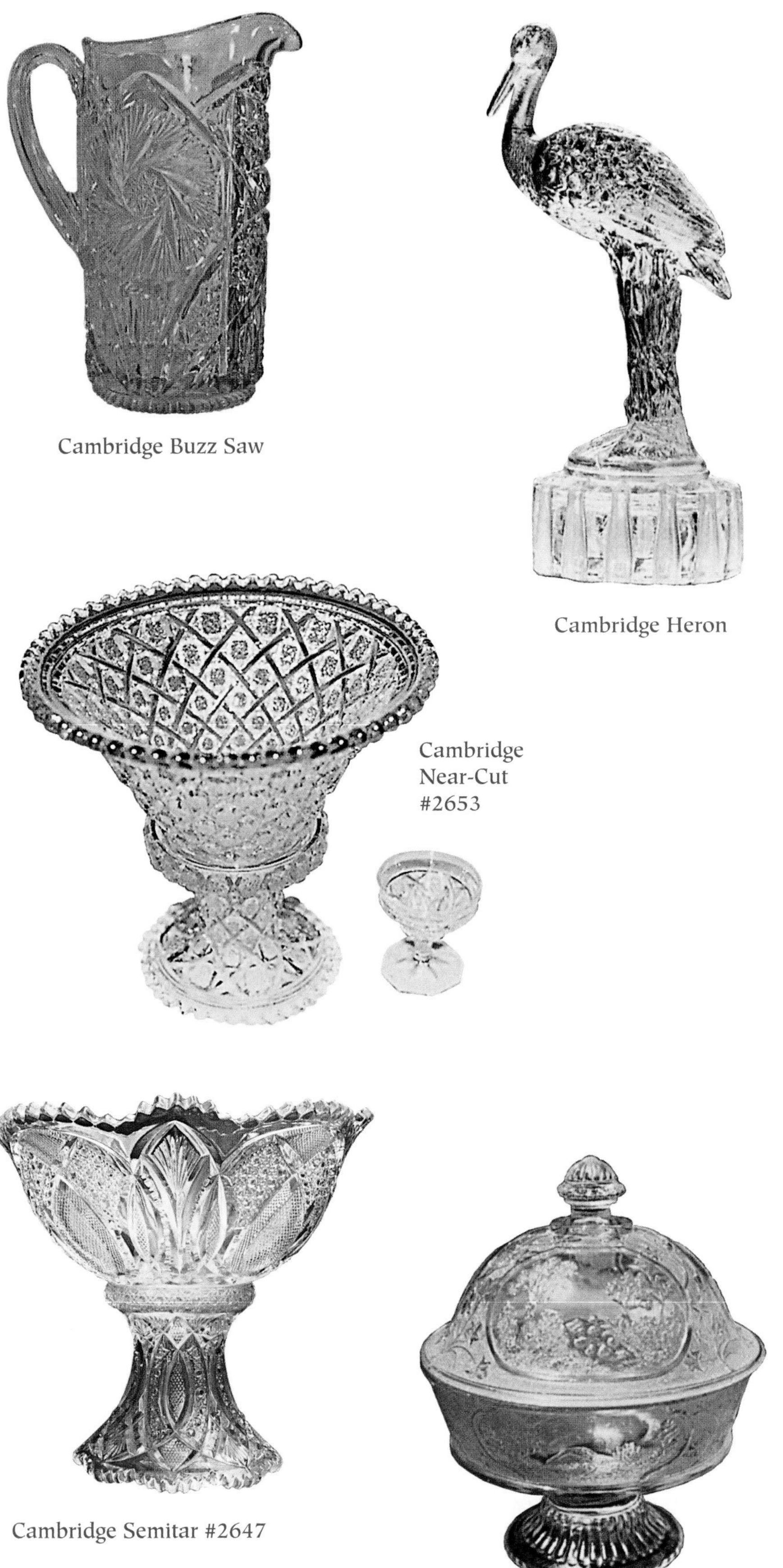
Cambridge Buzz Saw

Cambridge Heron

Cambridge Near-Cut #2653

Cambridge Semitar #2647

Canadian

Cambridge Buzz Saw

Advertised by Cambridge as their #2699 Buzz Saw pattern, shapes include a squat handled basket, cruet, olive nappy, sherbet, rose bowl, 5" and 7" nut bowls, 5", 6", 7", 8", 9" bowls, celery tray, water set, berry set, table set, milk pitcher in two sizes, celery vase, syrup, cologne, and salt shakers. It is also called Double Star.

Cambridge Heron

Shown in old Cambridge ads in 9", 12", 16", and a massive 20" example, this figural flower holder or frog is known in both clear crystal and a pale green glass that is the color of old Coca-Cola bottles. These pieces fit inside various sized bowls and held flowers. Imagine the size of bowl that held the larger herons!

Cambridge Near-Cut #2653

This pattern is shown in Cambridge Company catalogs and marked "Near-Cut." Shapes include a pickle tray, ice cream tray, celery tray, 5" individual square ice cream dish, water set, goblet, footed jelly compote, tall handled celery, double handled cracker jar with lid, quart squat pitcher, punch bowl with base, handled custard cup, and footed sherbet. It is also known as Cambridge Ribbon.

Cambridge Semitar #2647

From the Cambridge Glass Company, this very fine pattern's shapes include a table set, water set (squat or tankard), water carafe, cruet, whiskey tumbler, jelly compote, footed bonbon, shakers, pickle tray, celery tray, spoon tray, 6", 7", 8" plates, various bowls, small punch set (sometimes with advertising), large punch set, and a 9" bowl advertised as a "special deep bowl."

Canadian

Canadian has been attributed to the Burlington Glass Works of Ontario in the 1870s. Shapes include covered or open bowls, table set, cake stand, covered and open compotes (high or low) in several sizes, goblet, jam jar, mug, milk pitcher, water set, bread plate, dinner plates in five sizes, sauce, and wine.

Cane

Cane was first a product of Gillinder & Sons and then McKee Glass Company in 1884. Colored crystal (amber, apple green, blue, and vaseline) as well as clear were made in this well-designed pattern. Shapes include a berry set, table set, water set, oval bowl, finger bowl, waste bowl, celery vase, compote, cordial, goblet, honey dish, match holder in a kettle shape, pickle dish, milk pitcher, small plate, relish, shakers, slipper tray, and wine.

Cane

Cane Horseshoe

Cane Horseshoe

Cane Horseshoe was made in clear and gold trimmed by U. S. Glass as their #15118 in 1909 and also called Paragon. Shapes include a cruet, salt shakers, cake stand, berry set, water set, table set, celery tray, and compote.

Cane Insert

Sometimes called Arched Cane and Fan, this is a Tarentum Glass Company pattern made in 1898 in crystal or emerald green. Shapes include a table set, carafe (shown), cake stand, celery vase (rare), berry set, goblet, hair receiver, mug, and water set. Some pieces have gold trim.

Cane Insert

Cane Pinwheel

This pattern is actually a part of Cambridge Glass Company's #2699 Buzz-Saw pattern but has several different design forms. Shapes of this variation include a table set, quart pitcher, squat quart pitcher, cruet, syrup, cologne bottle, celery tray, berry set, and odd bowls.

Cannonball Pinwheel

Advertised as U. S. Glass pattern #15094 in 1906, this pattern was later made by Federal Glass in 1910. Other names for it are Caldonia or Pinwheel, and shapes include a 10" cherry tray, square olive, 7½" pickle dish, tall handled sugar, sherbet, nappy, shakers, milk pitcher, celery vase, water set, table set, berry set, cup, wine, goblet, jelly compote, 6" square plate, and 9" fruit plate.

Cane Pinwheel

Cannonball Pinwheel

Capital

Caprice

Carltec

Cardinal

Carnation (Lancaster)

Capital

Made by Westmoreland in the early 1900s, this pattern is called Estate by carnival glass collectors. In crystal it can be found with gold trim or color flashed. Shapes include a mug (shown), toothpick holder, puff box, creamer and sugar, and perfume bottle.

Caprice

This well-known Cambridge pattern was made in dozens of shapes over a long time span. Shapes include several sizes of plates, a cup and saucer, shakers, bitters bottle, oil bottle, ashtrays, cigarette holders, table set pieces, ice bucket, decanter, wine, goblet, tall and short sherbets, footed tumblers, condiment and salad sets, bridge sets, and bowls of all shapes and sizes.

Cardinal

Also called Blue Jay or Cardinal Bird, this pattern is attributed to the Ohio Flint Glass Company in 1875. Found only in clear, shapes include a table set, cake stand, berry set, goblet, honey dish, water set, and flat or footed sauce in two sizes. The honey dish is found either open or with a cover.

Carltec

This is one of the "tec" patterns from McKee and Brothers Glass. It was made in 1894 and re-issued in 1917. There are many shapes, including a table set (two shapes in creamers), water set, berry set, various bowls, handled basket, rose bowl, spoon tray, pickle dish, celery bowl, olive tray, bonbon, handled compote, 11" plate, and two preserve dishes. Bowls can be square or round.

Carnation (Lancaster)

Made by the Lancaster Glass Company in 1911 and differing greatly from the New Martinsville Carnation design, this pattern can be found in crystal and decorated crystal. Shapes include a table set, water set, berry set, goblet, pickle dish, and possibly a milk pitcher.

Carnation (New Martinsville)

Far different from the Lancaster pattern with the same name shown elsewhere, this one was made by New Martinsville Glass in 1904 or 1905. It is found in crystal mostly but can be found in rare ruby stained pieces, often with gilding like the tumbler shown here. Shapes include a toothpick holder, a water set, wine, goblet, and a pickle dish but certainly other shapes may exist.

Carnation (New Martinsville)

Carnation with Elk

This 11" plate (the carnation is also known on bowls and smaller plates with flower centers) is a rare item and is mostly found with goofus treatment (this one was stripped). Carolyn McKinley in her goofus glass book calls this "Carnation cake plate with Elk" and lists a 13" size too. We suspect this pattern was created in the early 1900s and would appreciate any information readers may share about it.

Carnation with Elk

Cathedral

Originally called Orion by Bryce Brothers in 1885, this pattern was made by U. S. Glass after 1891. Some collectors know it as Waffle and Fine Cut. Found in amber, amethyst, blue, vaseline, clear, and clear with ruby stain, shapes include 5", 6", 7", 8" bowls, table set, cake stand, celery vase, covered compote, open compote, cruet, goblet, lamp, mug, water set, relish tray, salt boat, and sauce, flat or footed.

Cathedral

Cat in a Tangle

This whimsical mug dates to the 1880s and can be found in both clear and amber colors. The design is of a cat caught in a tangle of flowers and vines that seem to have a life of their own. The mug is 2" tall and has a diameter of 1¾".

Cat in a Tangle

Cat's Eye

This pattern, also called Thumbprint on Spearhead, is shown in several references as older glass, but John Gregory tells us it was first made as Breton by Paden City Glass in 1930 and later by Canton Glass. If that is true, then this isn't old glass. Shapes include a table set, pickle dish, bowls, and the wine goblet shown.

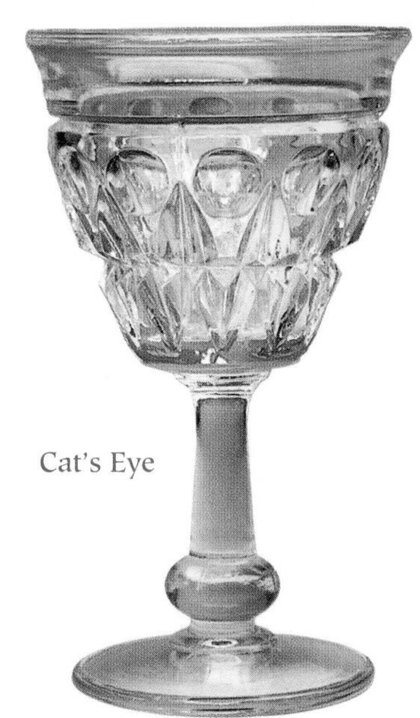

Cat's Eye

Cat's-Eye and Fan

Cat up a Tree with Dog

Center Medallion

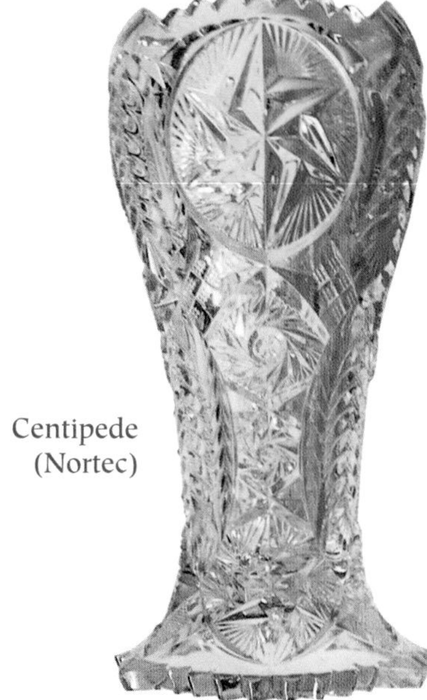
Centipede (Nortec)

Chain

Chain and Shield

Cat's-Eye and Fan

A pattern from George Duncan & Sons in 1878, this design is found in a table set, berry set, compote, sauce, and large footed bowl. Other shapes certainly may exist but haven't yet been found by us. It was originally called Roman.

Cat up a Tree with Dog

What a sense of humor glass designers had and the tall tankard pitcher shown typifies that humor. Here we have a cat clinging to the tree trunk while the dog is trying to bring the feline down. Even the abstract dog and cat are funny. We know of no other shapes in this pattern but they may certainly exist.

Center Medallion

Credited to LaBelle Glass Company of Bridgeport, Ohio, this little-discussed pattern is found in a table set, water pitcher, pedestal or flat berry dishes in three sizes, covered compotes in at least two sizes, and a flat serving dish with a lid. The factory burned in 1887 and production is believed to have been in the years just before the fire. It is found in crystal or etched crystal.

Centipede (Nortec)

Nortec, part of McKee's vast "tec" series of patterns produced from 1901 to 1930, was produced in 1903. It can be found in a berry set, table set, plates (8" – 10"), punch bowl with base, custard cup, tall compote, bonbon, nappy, celery tray, shakers, brush holder, card tray, horseradish with lid, 9" vase (shown), cruet, water set, and syrup. Several shapes, especially the vase, have been reproduced in colors not originally made. It is commonly called Centipede.

Chain

Made in the 1870s, the pattern's manufacturer is unknown. Only clear pieces have been found in a table set with stemmed pieces, covered compote, cordial, wine, and berry set. The design is very much like Chain with Star.

Chain and Shield

Attributed to Portland Glass Company and made in the late 1870s, this very interesting pattern's shapes include a table set, water set, goblet, 7" and 11" plates, sauce, wine, celery vase, and oval platter.

Chain with Star

Although first from Bryce as their #79 pattern, this is perhaps one of the better known patterns from U.S. Glass in 1890. Shapes include a table set, cake stand, cake plate, pickle dish, plate, sauce, oval bowls, a berry set, relish dish, wine glass, and salt shakers.

Chandelier

From O'Hara Glass Company (1888) and then U. S. Glass (1891), shapes are numerous and include high or low banana stands, bowls in 6", 7", and 8" sizes, finger bowl, stemmed fruit bowl, violet bowl, table set, cake stand, caster set, celery vase, covered and open compotes in high and low standards, goblet, ink well (marked "Davis Automatic – May 8, 1889"), pitchers in half-pint, pint, quart, and half-gallon sizes, shakers, master salt, sauce, sponge dish, water tray, tumbler, and rare wine.

Chatelaine

Perhaps one of Imperial Glass Company's better water set patterns, it is well-known in purple carnival glass which brings a premium price. In crystal, the pieces are nearly as scarce and are always in demand. No other shapes are known.

Cherry

This pattern was made by Bakewell, Pears & Company in about 1870 in crystal and opaque opalescent glass. Shapes include a rare plate, goblet, champagne, berry set, table set, stemmed wine, open or covered compotes, and novelty bowls in several shapes.

Cherry and Cable

Also known as Panelled Cherry and mistakenly called Cherry Thumb-prints, this Northwood pattern is well-known to collectors and was made in crystal and carnival glass and is currently being reproduced in opalescent glass and decorated glass. Shapes include a table set, water set, berry set, sauce, syrup, and compotes with or without lids. The pattern was first made in the early 1900s.

Chain with Star

Chandelier

Chatelaine

Cherry and Cable

Cherry

Cherry and Fig

Cherry Lattice

Cherry with Thumbprints

Chestnut Oak

Chick and Pugs

Cherry and Fig

Cherry and Fig was made by Dalzell, Gilmore, & Leighton. Shapes include a table set, water set, berry set, covered or open compotes, pickle dish, goblet, celery vase, and wine.

Cherry Lattice

Made by the Northwood Glass Company in 1907, this seems to be a short-lived design, found only on decorated crystal (reproduction pieces in carnival glass were made in the 1970s). Shapes made are a table set, berry set, water set, and compote.

Cherry with Thumbprints

From Jenkins in the 1920s, this very nice pattern can be found in a water set, berry set, sauce, stemmed wine, toothpick holder, syrup, lemonade tumbler, mug, covered bowls, and the covered bean pot shown. Besides plain crystal, this pattern can be found with decoration.

Chestnut Oak

This very realistic design, also called Old Acorn by some collectors, was made in the late 1800s (maker unknown). Shapes include a table set, flat celery dish, covered compote, open compote, egg cup, goblet, water set, and flat sauce; sugar may be covered or open and creamer may be flat or pedestal based.

Chick and Pugs

Chick and Pugs was from Bryce Brothers in the 1880s and then U.S. Glass after 1891. It was made in clear, amber, canary, blue, and amethyst glass and is small for a mug being 2" tall and having a diameter of 1⅞". It has the same shape as other mugs from Bryce that include Feeding Deer and Dog, and Robin in Tree.

Chicken Foot Stem

What a super piece of glass this is and so imaginative. The goblet has a chicken done in the crystalography technique while the stem is a chicken leg with the foot holding up the bowl! We'd certainly appreciate hearing from anyone with additional information on this piece.

Chippendale (Ohio Flint)

Chippendale was first made by Ohio Flint Glass in 1906, then by Jefferson Glass in 1907, then Central Glass in 1919, and finally by George Davidson (England) in 1933. Shapes are many and include a table set, berry set, odd bowls, water set, vase, salts, mustard jar, candlesticks, sherbet, compotes, dresser set (tray, pin tray, cologne, puff box, hair receiver, pomade, ring holder), and dozens of other shapes. Jefferson made some ruby stained pieces and in 1912 Westmoreland made a similar pattern (their #1700 Colonial) called Keystone Colonial, which has been reproduced. Most Chippendale pieces from America are marked "Krys-tol" and a few say "Chippendale Krys-tol."

Chrysanthemum Leaf

Chrysanthemum Leaf was made by Boston and Sandwich Glass in the 1880s and later by National Glass after 1900. It is found in crystal and chocolate glass. Shapes include a table set, berry set, toothpick holder, carafe, compote, cracker jar, cruet, water set, salt shakers, sauce, and syrup. Crystal pieces are often gold trimmed.

Chrysanthemum Sprig

Originally called Pagoda, this pattern from the Northwood Company is better known as Chrysanthemum Sprig by collectors. It is found in custard glass (Ivory), turquoise opaque, often with gilding and decorated enameling. Shapes include a berry set (oval), a table set, water set, celery vase, compote, cruet, toothpick holder, and a condiment set, consisting of a tray, cruet, and salt and pepper shakers.

Chicken Foot Stem

Chrysanthemum Leaf

Chippendale (Ohio Flint)

Chrysanthemum Sprig

Circular Saw

Classic

Church Windows

Classic Intaglio

Church Windows

From U. S. Glass as their #15082 in 1903, this pattern is also known as Tulip Petals or Columbia. It was made in clear or decorated crystal in table sets, cake stand, celery vase, covered jelly compote, sardine dish, goblet, water set, and bowl. The example shown has gold trim.

Circular Saw

This pattern is also known as Rosetta and credited to Beaumont Glass, but it was shown in 1905 national ads as being made at the Riverside Glass Works, so we question the Beaumont attribution. It was found in crystal and rose stain, and the shapes include a table set, berry set, breakfast set (creamer and sugar), cruet, punch set, and water set.

Classic

From Gillinder & Sons in 1875, this well-known pattern can be found either with a collar base or twig footed. Pieces are clear or with acid finish, but rare milk glass is known. Shapes include covered or open bowls, table set, celery vase, covered or open compotes, goblet, jam jar, milk pitcher, water pitcher, five plates with different subjects, sauces, and sweetmeat jar.

Classic Intaglio

Recent evidence from Siegmar Geiselberger indicates these salt holders with intaglio (incised) designs are from the Czechoslovakian firm of Heinrich Hoffman in 1927. The round one has a Cupid and Psyche design and the 2½" long rectangular one shows Diana on a chariot.

Classic Medallion

The maker of this fine pattern seems to be a mystery, but it dates to the 1870s and 1880s. Some collectors call this pattern Cameo. Shapes include flat or footed bowls, table set, celery vase, covered or open compotes, goblet, water pitcher (if tumblers were made, we haven't been able to verify them), and sauce.

Clear Diagonal Band

Made in 1880 by Ripley and Company, Pittsburgh (they joined U. S. Glass in 1891 as Factory F), this pattern was later made by a Canadian company. Shapes are a table set, water set, platter, goblet, salt shaker, berry set (flat or footed), celery vase, low or high compote, and marmalade jar. It is typical of early, less decorated patterns.

Clear Lion Head

Also known as Atlanta by some collectors, this is a Fostoria pattern from 1895, found in a berry set, shakers, toothpick holder, cake stand, jam jar, pickle dish, table set, toy table set, and sauce. Shown is a spoonholder that is etched GETTYSBURG–1863, obviously a souvenir piece.

Clear Ribbon

Clear Ribbon was made by George Duncan and Sons in the 1880s in crystal or ruby stained crystal. Shapes include a table set, compote, celery vase, footed sauce, bread tray, pickle dish, goblet, and water set. The raised ribbons are separated by threaded sections, giving this pattern its name (and not to be confused with the Ribbon pattern that is found in clear or frosted).

Clio

Also known as Daisy Button and Almond Band, this is a Challinor, Taylor, Ltd. pattern first made in 1885 in clear crystal, green, canary, and blue glass. The company was a part of U. S. Glass. Shapes cataloged are a table set, water set, covered compote, goblet, celery vase, and plates in both 7" and 10" sizes. The plate has no panels or thumbprints.

Classic Medallion

Clio

Clear Ribbon

Clear Lion Head

Clear Diagonal Band

Coachman's Cape

Clover (Richards & Hartley)

Coarse Zig Zag

Coin and Dewdrop

Colonial Lady

Clover (Richards & Hartley)

Clover was first made by Richards & Hartley Glass in the 1880s and then by U.S. Glass in 1891. Shapes include a table set, berry set, sauce, 6" bowl, 11" bowl, and various compotes. It can be found in crystal, emerald green, and stained glass in amber or ruby. It is often confused with another U.S. Glass pattern called Panelled Daisy and Button.

Coachman's Cape

This was made by the Bellaire Goblet Company (1880s) and U.S. Glass in 1891 in clear crystal. The only shapes reported are a goblet and the stemmed wine, courtesy of John Gregory. Since a number of patterns were also made in cordials, this one may show up in that shape also.

Coarse Zig Zag

From Bryce, Higbee and Company in 1905, this pattern is often found in malls and shops, especially in small pieces like a creamer. It was made in a table set, water set, wine, plate, salt shakers, and berry set, in clear crystal only.

Coin and Dewdrop

We've looked for other shapes in this attractive pattern and surely there must be some, but to date we can only substantiate the goblet shown. On a stippled background, the rings or circles seem to float like bubbles in champagne. We'd be happy to hear about other shapes in this pattern.

Colonial Lady

This is a line of silver or gold decorated items from Westmoreland designated their #1700 line. It was made in 1912 and had many pieces, including a table set, 6" and 9" vases, cruet, and salt shakers. The metallic designs may vary from shape to shape and indeed, other glassmakers like Dugan/Diamond made this filigree work also.

Colonial Stairsteps

Reported in opalescent glass with a Northwood trademark (we haven't seen it), this pattern is found in only a few shapes that include a table set and the toothpick holder shown. Pieces are known in both crystal and blue opalescent.

Colonis

U. S. Glass pattern #15145 from 1913, Colonis is found in a berry set, table set, pickle dish, water set, milk pitcher, cake stand, cordial, celery vase, syrup, egg cup, oval dish, and tray. Can be found decorated in gold, blue, or rose.

Colorado

Made by U. S. Glass as one of the States series, Colorado dates to 1897 and was made in clear crystal, ruby or amethyst stain, green, or cobalt blue, all with or without decoration. Rare pieces are also known in clambroth. The variety of shapes include tri-cornered bowls, table set, water set, footed cheese dish, cup, sauce, 12" vase, toothpick holder, sauce, shakers, and a smaller open individual sugar with handles.

Columbia

Several patterns are called by this name but this is Imperial's design, well-known to carnival glass collectors. It was made in 1909 and can be found in a compote, rose bowl, footed plate, and vase shapes, all from the same mould.

Columbia #100

This pattern was made by Beaumont Glass in 1900 and is sometimes called Beaumont's Columbia. It is found in clear or vaseline (either of which can also be engraved). Shapes are many and include a table set, water set, toothpick holder, and celery vase (shown). Note that there is also gilding around the middle of the piece and this is typical.

Colonial Stairsteps

Colonis

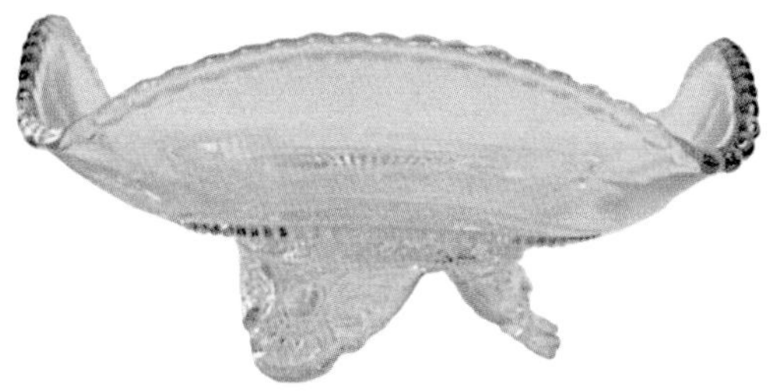

Colorado

Columbia

Columbia #100

Columbian Coin

Column Block

Columned Thumbprints

Consolidated Shell

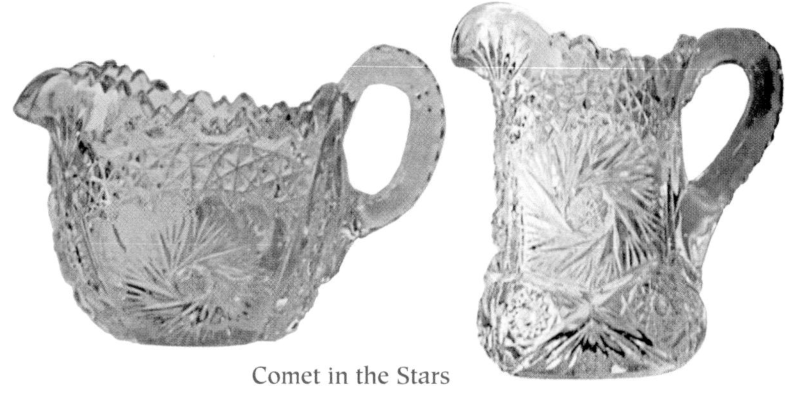
Comet in the Stars

Columbian Coin

Columbian Coin was made by U. S. Glass in 1891 after the government stopped the use of U. S. coins for design. It is found in clear, frosted, and bronze or ruby stained glass and has been widely reproduced. The many shapes include a table set, water set, berry set, cake stand, covered and open compotes, goblet, toothpick holder, pickle jar (shown), ale glass, covered or open bowls, celery tray or vase, champagne claret, cruet, epergne, beer mug, milk pitcher, shakers, syrup, waste bowl, water tray, and wine.

Column Block

This was an O'Hara Glass Company pattern first made in the 1880s that was also called Panel & Star. It is found in both crystal and vaseline glass and shapes include a table set, salt shaker, toothpick holder, pitcher, celery vase, pickle dish, and a jelly compote.

Columned Thumbprints

A Westmoreland pattern made in 1905, Columned Thumbprints can be found in a table set, celery vase, syrup, shakers, cruet, toothpick holder, berry set, water set, and cup. The glass is quite thick and sparkling on pieces we've seen.

Comet in the Stars

Made by U. S. Glass as their #15150 in 1914, this pattern can be found in table sets, bowls of all sorts, water set, handled relish, celery vase, and the celery tray shown. The design shows differently from piece to piece and may be a bit hard to recognize, but basically contains a large whirling star, smaller hobstars, and sections of fan. No colors have been reported, but examples with gold trim are known.

Consolidated Shell

We showed this Consolidated Lamp & Shade Company pattern in our fourth opalescent glass book in Rubina Verde, but here is an example in a beautiful decorated satin glass with blue and gold. This wonderful piece stands 5" tall and had a center width of 5½".

Co-op Columbia

This was a pattern from Cooperative Flint Glass Company in the early 1900s found in clear, decorated, and gold trimmed. Shapes include a table set, shakers, goblet, pickle dish, relish tray, bowls, and wine.

Co-op's Royal

Co-op's Royal, made by the Co-operative Flint Glass Company in 1890s, can be found in crystal and ruby stained glass. Shapes include a table set, goblet, celery vase, pickle dish, bowls, shakers, water set, toothpick holder (shown), and a wine.

Coral Gables

We found very little information about this pattern, except that most writers agree there are both goblets and a wine (shown here from the collection of John Gregory). Mollie McCain shows a drawing of a cruet so that shape may exist. We welcome any information about this pattern.

Cord Drapery

First made at Greentown, Indiana, by National in 1899 and later at the Indiana Glass Company after 1907, this pattern is found in clear, amber, blue, green, opal, and chocolate glass. Shapes include oval and round bowls, table set, cake stand, covered and open compote, cruet, mug, pickle dish, shakers, syrup, toothpick holder, water tray, wine, and sauces.

Cornflower

Heacock attributes this to the Dugan Company from shards found in the Helman digs. It is seen in a tall water set, a decanter, and matching wine glass. It was part of Dugan's Filagree line that included the Dugan Maple Leaf pattern, Waving Quill, and Diamonds and Clubs. These pieces were gilded and are found in blue, green, amethyst, and ruby glass.

Co-op Columbia

Co-op's Royal

Cord Drapery

Coral Gables

Cornflower

Cornucopia

Cornucopia – Jeannette

Cornucopia

Cornucopia was made by Dalzell, Gilmore & Leighton Company in 1885. The pitcher has a fruit-filled cornucopia on one side and may have either cherries and figs, blackberries and grapes, or strawberries and currants on the other. Shapes include a table set, water set, cake stand, celery vase, covered compote, goblet, mug, berry set, wine, cordial, and small lamps that may have come along at a later date. Some shapes such as the goblet have been reproduced.

Cornucopia – Jeannette

Intended to be sold in pairs, this Cornucopia vase was from the Jeannette Glass Company in the 1920s. It can be found in other types of glass as well that include carnival glass, and was made through the Depression era and into the 1940s in milk glass.

Cosmos

Cosmos Drape

Cosmos

Cosmos, also called Seamless Daisy, was made by Consolidated Lamp and Glass in 1898 in clear, opaque, and cased colors. Shapes include a table set, condiment set, water set, lemonade set, shakers, syrup, perfume, various trays, pickle caster, and several sizes of lamps. Some clear pieces as well as opaque ones have enameling.

Cosmos and Cane

From the U.S. Glass Company and primarily known in carnival glass, this is a rare crystal handled basket shape. We suspect other shapes in crystal were made, and these may include a water set, a jelly compote, and bowls, but we have no proof. These shapes as well as others were all found in iridized glass.

Cosmos and Cane

Cosmos Drape

Oil lamps are really in a field all their own but some are included in this book to give collectors a taste of their importance in the collecting field. The one shown here is from the 1890s and is known as Cosmos Drape. It, like others, came in more than one size. Some were gilded or decorated in one way or another. It is also known as Rosa and is found in green and crystal.

Cosmos Variant
Made by the Diamond Glass Company and primarily found in carnival glass, this pattern is one we are happy to show in rare uniridized glass in a super emerald green. We suspect a clear example was made also and since both bowls and plates exist in carnival glass, surely both shapes were made in clear or green uniridized glass.

Cottage
Cottage was first issued by Adams & Company in 1874, then by U. S. Glass after 1891, with the goblet made by the Bellaire Goblet Company in 1889. Clear, amber, blue, emerald, and ruby stained are the original colors. Shapes include a banana stand, berry set, finger bowl, fruit bowl, waste bowl, table set, cake stand, celery vase, champagne, claret, covered and open compotes, cruet, cup, goblet, mug, pickle dish, water set, milk pitcher, plate (many sizes), relish, shakers, syrup, water tray, and wine.

Country Kitchen
From Millersburg Glass, this pattern is best known in carnival glass. Shapes include a berry set, ice cream set, plates in 5", 7", 9", and 11", and a table set. Some bowls and plates have advertising on them and there is a variant in flint opalescent glass (rare), and a sister pattern called Potpourri that is known in compotes, salvers, and a scarce milk pitcher.

Covered Fish Dish
Attributed to Atterbury & Company of Pittsburgh in the 1870s, this 8" novelty item is known in crystal, blue, or canary. We are told these dishes were used to serve relish or candies and were quite popular from 1870 to 1900. We are very grateful to the Sandemans for this photo and all the others they've contributed to us.

Crab Claw
Made by the Imperial Glass Company of Bellaire, Ohio, in 1909, this pattern is also known as Blaze and can be found in carnival glass as well as crystal. Shapes reported are an 11½" plate, 7" rose bowl, 8" and 9" master berry bowls, and 5" individual berry bowl that may be flared, ruffled, or round. It has been reproduced.

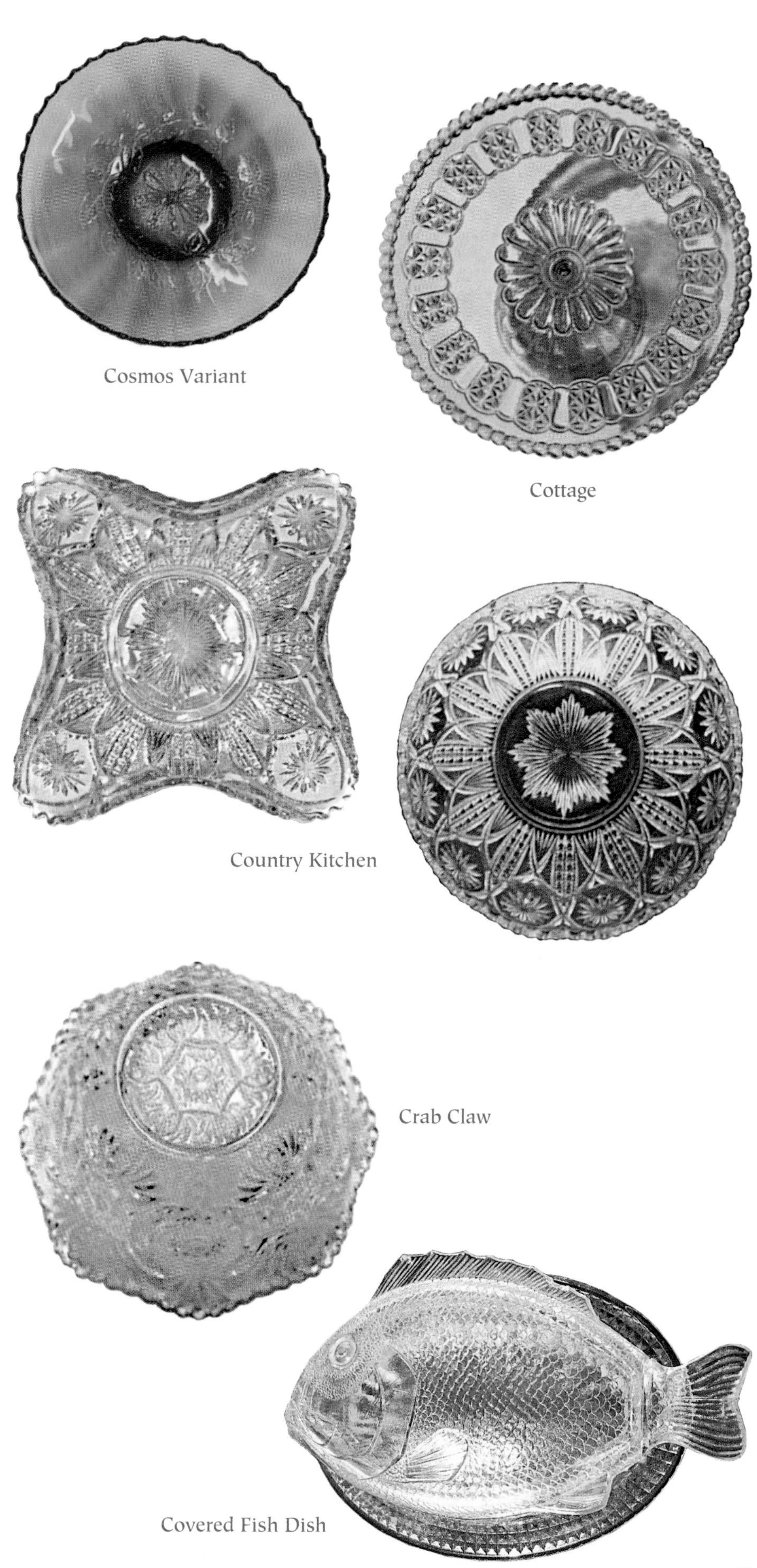

Cosmos Variant

Cottage

Country Kitchen

Crab Claw

Covered Fish Dish

Crab Claw Variant

Cradled Prisms

Cranesbill

Crate

Crested Hobnail

Croesus

Crab Claw Variant

Made by the Imperial Glass Company as their #409 pattern and found in carnival glass as well as crystal, this pattern is known in a tall, flat based water pitcher and tumblers. Date of production was 1906 and the water set is still shown in the 1909 factory catalog.

Cradled Prisms

Made by Challinor, Taylor Glass Company in the 1880s, this very interesting pattern can be found in a basic table set of covered butter, covered sugar, creamer, spooner, and goblet shape. Just why so few shapes seem to have been made is a mystery, and we'd be very interested in hearing of any others.

Cranesbill

We do not know the maker of this nice pattern but evidence supports an 1890 origin of the few items found. Shapes include a table set, berry set, and water set. Shown is the pedestal water pitcher. The top rim is distinctive with its file edge.

Crate

Aside from being told this novelty paperweight was a product of Vallerysthal Glass in 1908, we know nothing about it, except to point out the great detail work on the wood look and even the individual nails. Any information on this piece would be appreciated.

Crested Hobnail

This very nice child's mug, shown with a twist handle, is credited to Columbia Glass by one reference and to Bellaire Glass by another. Our research shows Columbia made a similar mug with a plain handle while Bellaire is the maker of the rope or twist handled version. The mug is found in clear, amber, or blue and stands about 3" tall.

Croesus

Croesus was first made by Riverside Glass in 1897 and then McKee and Brothers in 1901, in clear, green, or amethyst with gold trim. Shapes are many and include covered flat or footed bowls, open bowls, table set, cake stand, celery vase, covered or open compotes, condiment set, pickle dish, cruet, water set, toothpick holder, and condiment tray.

Cross Bands

Information on this pattern is nearly non-existent, except for the few shapes reported that include a creamer, covered sugar, a spooner, and a covered butter dish. The maker is also unknown, but the date of production seems to be in the late 1870s. The design is similar to Two Band but has the cross pattern breaking up the diamond banding.

Cross Bands

Crossed Block

Also known as Roman Cross, shapes include a table set, goblet, oval bowl, pickle dish, and goblet. The pattern was first advertised in 1890, but the maker isn't known at this time. Only clear crystal seems to be found.

Crossed Block

Crossed Shield

From Fostoria, this was their #1303, made in the 1890s. Shapes include a table set, water set, berry set, four sizes of compotes that include a jelly compote, goblet, wine, cordial, celery vase, and pickle dish.

Crossed Shield

Crown Salt

Shown in old ads under this name, this heavy salt dip was made by Bakewell, Pears in 1872. The design is simple but distinctive and could be used with many table pieces. Clear crystal is the only treatment we know.

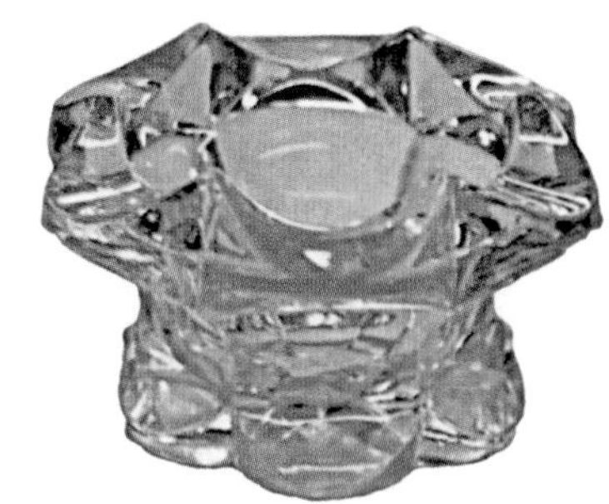
Crown Salt

Crucifix

Made by both Imperial and Cambridge in slightly different configurations, this very collectible candlestick was also made in carnival glass by the Imperial Company, and these are rare and expensive. The example shown is also from Imperial and is very well done. It is 9½" tall and of very heavy crystal.

Crucifix

Crystal Queen

Generally credited to the Northwood Glass Company in 1897 (some pieces are also credited to Cambridge Glass in 1904), shapes include a table set, water set, berry set, milk pitcher, compotes in two sizes, vases, handled basket, pickle dish, and celery vase. There are 125 shapes listed as being made but all seem to be scarce. Shown is a master berry bowl.

Crystal Queen

Crystal Rock

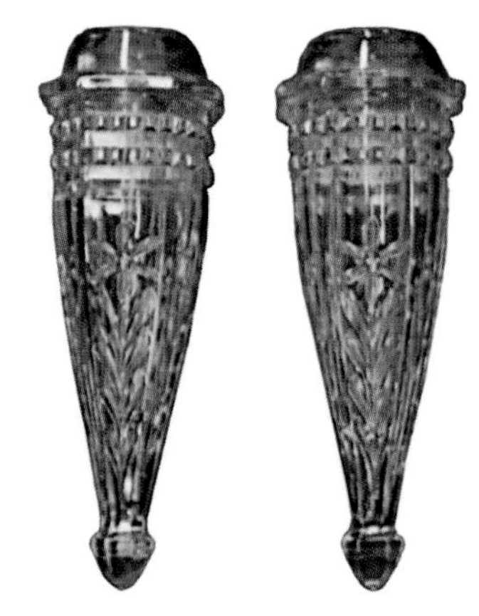
Crystal Star

Crystal Rock

From U. S. Glass about 1905, this pattern is found in clear and decorated glass. Shapes include a table set, water set, and berry set, all shown in a 1905 U. S. Glass ad.

Crystal Star

These very pretty vaseline auto vases were made at the end of our timespan for this book. They were made in 1929, are about 7¾" long, and have an engraved pattern of star-like flowers, stems, and leaves below a series of notching and ball bordering. As auto vases go, these are better than most and deserve attention.

Crystal Wedding

Cupid and Venus

Crystal Wedding

Also called Crystal Anniversary, this prolific pattern was made by Adams Glass in the early 1880s and was a part of U. S. Glass. There are many shapes, including a water set, table set, vase, shaker, salt dip, pickle dish, cruet, open compote, covered compote (high and low in three sizes), banana stand, shakers, claret, celery vase, cake stand, and goblet. Westmoreland later reproduced this pattern, especially in the compote shapes, so look for glass clarity when buying.

Cupid and Venus

Also known as Guardian Angel, this was a Richards & Hartley Glass pattern in 1875, reissued by U. S. Glass in 1891. Made in clear, amber (limited), and vaseline (limited), in shapes that include a berry set, table set, cake stand, celery vase, covered or open compotes, cordial, cruet, goblet, jam jar, three sizes in mugs, pickle caster, water set, bread plate, relish, and wine glass.

Cupids

Cupids

Also known as Cupid Hunt, this is a beautiful dome-based piece, animated around the entire bowl with figures. Anyone having additional or contrary information about this pattern, its maker, and date of production is urged to write us.

Curled Leaf

Also known as King's #198 or Vine Band, this mug can be found in clear, cobalt blue, canary, or light amethyst. In addition other shapes are known that include a water pitcher. The makers were King Glass Company in the 1880s and then U.S. Glass after 1891. The mug can also be found (rarely) with a mustard lid, indicating it was a promotional item.

Curled Leaf

Currant

Made by Campbell, Jones & Company in 1871. Shapes include oval bowls, table set, cake stand (three sizes), celery vase, covered high and low compotes, open compote, cordial, egg cup, goblet, honey dish, jam jar, water set, milk pitcher, plates, relish dish, salt, sauces, and wine.

Currant

Currier and Ives

Currier and Ives, from the Bellaire Goblet Company in Findlay, Ohio, in 1889, can be found in clear and rarely in amber, blue, cobalt blue, and vaseline. Shapes include a table set, canoe-shaped bowl, covered or open compote, cordial, cup and saucer, decanter, goblets, oil lamp, mug, pickle dish, milk pitcher, water set, bread plate, dinner plate, relishes, shakers, salt dip, sauce, syrup, wine, and the water tray ("Balky Mule") made in 9½" and 12¼" sizes.

Currier and Ives

Curtain Tie-Back

This was made in the 1860s by an unknown glasshouse, and originally produced in both flat or footed pieces. Shapes include square bowls, table set, celery vase, celery tray, covered compote, goblet, plate, pickle dish, water set, relish, shakers, sauce, water tray, and wine.

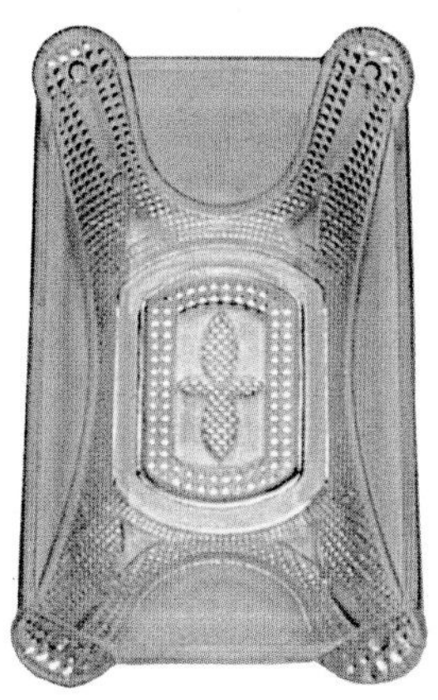

Curtain Tie-Back

Curved Star

Cut Block

Dahlia

Cut Log

Curved Star

This pattern is a puzzle since evidence points to several glass companies. First we find it in carnival glass where it accompanies the U.S. Glass version of the Headdress pattern and it is also shown in catalogs of Brockwitz of Germany. Finally, catalogs from Iittala-Karhula in Finland show versions of this design and Eda of Sweden also shows it! Apparently moulds traveled freely in Europe with this pattern. Shown is a 14" stemmed cake stand but bowls, compotes, a vase, a large epergne, butter dish, rose bowl, and a celery vase are known. The pattern is also known as Cathedral by some collectors.

Cut Block

This pasttern was made by the A.H. Heisey Company as their #1200 pattern and can be found in clear and ruby stained glass. Shapes include a table set, cruet, individual sugar and creamer, pickle dish, celery vase, and a syrup. The pattern dates to 1896.

Cut Log

Originally called Ethol, this Greensburg Glass Company pattern is also known as Cat's Eye and Block. Shapes found are a table set, water set, berry sets, large and small cake stand, celery vase, covered compote 6" and 8", open compote on low and high stems in 7", 8", and 10" sizes, goblet, mug, nappy, 16½" vase, and stemmed wine. Cut Log was made in 1885.

Dahlia

Dahlia was made by Bryce Brothers in 1885. Colors include apple green, blue, vaseline, and clear. Shapes include oval bowls, table set, cake stands, covered or open compotes, cordial, egg cup (double or single), mugs, goblet, pickle dish, water set, milk pitcher, bread plate, dinner plate, platter with either fan or grape handles, jam jar, relish, salt dips, syrup, sauce, and wine.

Dahlia (Goofus Pattern)

Known by this name to goofus glass collectors, it is actually the #131 pattern from Indiana Glass (Canton Glass also made a Dahlia pattern in the 1880s). Shapes we've seen are the 11" plate shown, 4", 9", and 10" bowls. These pieces were designated by factory ads as decorated ware. The design is well done and the glass clear and sparkling under the goofus.

Dahlia (Goofus Pattern)

Daisy and Button (Hobbs)

While many companies had a try at this pattern, the Hobbs, Brockunier Company's #101 was the best known, found in crystal, Old Gold, sapphire, marine green, canary, ruby, and amberina. There were many shapes, including a bar bottle, finger bowl, round or square bowls, star-shaped bowls, table set (three shapes), caster set, canoe, hanging canoe, flared celery dish, shoe celery dish, cheese dish, cologne, ice bowl with drainer, match safe, molasses cans, pickle yacht, pickle jar, plates, shades, water set (three sizes), ice cream tray, toothpick holder, and whiskey tumbler.

Daisy and Button (Hobbs)

Daisy and Button Caster Set

Daisy and Button Basket

Like the other pieces shown in this very popular and extensive pattern, this one (shown in vaseline) is one of the many novelty items. Here is a bowl that has been fitted into a metal frame that is often called a "bride's basket." The metal frame has its own interesting floral and leaf design that adds to the attraction.

Daisy and Button Caster Set

Also part of Hobbs #101 line in the Daisy and Button design, this caster set is exactly as it was assembled. The holder is crystal, and the bottles are found in various Hobbs colors that include canary, amber, blue, and marine green. Two shapes of bottles are known with this being the bulbous set (the other is cylinder shaped).

Daisy and Button Basket

Daisy and Button Shoe

Daisy and Button Slipper

Daisy and Button Variant

Daisy and Button Wheelbarrow

Daisy and Button with Crossbars

Daisy and Button Shoe

Made by Hobbs in 1884 as part of their large Daisy and Button pattern line, this shoe was actually a novelty celery dish. It can be found in either a plain or figured sole and measures nearly 12" in length. Colors are crystal, canary, Old Gold, ruby, amberina, sapphire, and Marine green.

Daisy and Button Slipper

Made by Geo. Duncan & Sons, this slipper dates to 1886 and was patented by John E. Miller. It is very similar to a D & B slipper produced by Bryce Brothers but with a higher heel. We show a crystal one in our Commemorative and Advertising section.

Daisy and Button Variant

The owners of this butter dish believe it to be a U.S. Glass pattern (Bryce Brothers factory B), but we haven't been able to verify this in any of our Bryce references. We would appreciate any additional information readers may have about this pattern, its maker, or the additional shapes known.

Daisy and Button Wheelbarrow

Almost everyone had a try at a Daisy and Button pattern so we can't identify the maker of this unusual novelty piece, but we can ascertain that it is old. Like the Sietz Bath piece or the slippers, hats, canoes, or boats in this pattern, this one could be used on the table or just admired. It is on vaseline glass and has a brass wheel and pinnings.

Daisy and Button with Crossbars

This was originally a Richards & Hartley pattern (#99) called Mikado that was reissued by U.S. Glass in 1891. It is also known as Daisy and Thumbprint and Crossbar. It is found in clear, dark amber, canary, and blue. Shapes include a catsup bottle, finger bowl, oval bowls (6", 8", 9"), waste bowl, table set, celery vase, high or low compotes (open or covered), cordial, cruet, goblet, pickle jar, oil lamp, mug (two sizes), pickle dish, water set, milk pitcher, plate, shakers, sauce, syrup, toothpick holder, water tray, and wine.

Daisy and Button with Narcissus

Also known as Clear Lily, this is a pattern made by the Indiana Glass Company of Dunkirk, Indiana, in 1910. Shapes found are a table set, water set, decanter, goblet, compote, shakers, celery tray, water tray, wine, celery vase, sauce, and bowl. This is a quality pattern that is very collectible.

Daisy and Button with Thumbprint

Made first by Adams and Company in 1885 and then by U.S. Glass in the 1890s, this pattern is found in table sets, water sets, berry sets, square bowls, covered or open compotes, cake stand, celery vase, goblet, and wine. Besides the crystal pieces, blue or amber items are known.

Daisy and Button with V Ornament

Originally Beatty's #555 and #558 and also known as Daisy with V Ornament, this well-known pattern is available in clear, amber, blue, and vaseline. The pattern was later reissued by both Federal and U. S. Glass. Shapes include an octagonal bowl, berry set, finger bowl, table set, celery vase, goblet, match holder, mug in four sizes, pickle caster, pickle jar, water set, milk pitcher, plate in four sizes, gas shade, sherbet, toothpick holder, sauce, water tray, and wine.

Daisy and Plume

Also called Daisy and Palm this well-known Northwood pattern (later made by Dugan/Diamond) can be found in crystal, carnival glass, and opalescent glass. Shapes are a stemmed rose bowl, footed rose bowl, compote, and stemmed compote. The footed pieces have three square feet.

Daisy and Plume (Dugan)

Here is the Dugan version of this pattern that was also made by Northwood. All Dugan pieces are found with three square legs and may be shaped into rose bowls, open bowls, or compotes. The example shown is opened into a bowl shape with three-in-one edging, a typical Dugan edge treatment. Daisy and Plume is found in opalescent, carnival, goofus, and crystal glass.

Daisy and Button with Narcissus

Daisy and Button with Thumbprint

Daisy and Button with V Ornament

Daisy and Plume

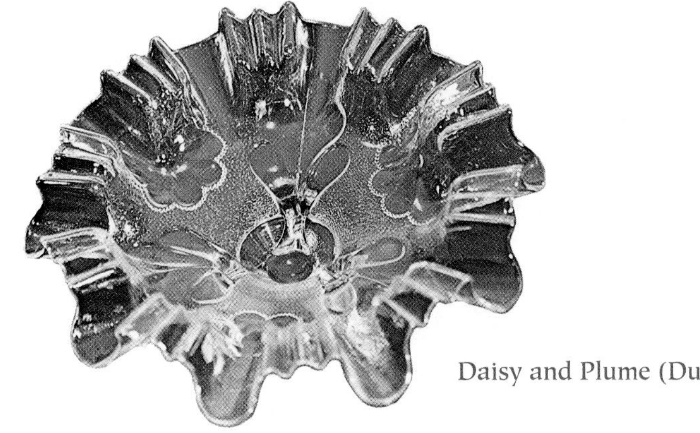

Daisy and Plume (Dugan)

Daisy and Scroll

Daisy Banded Crystal Wedding

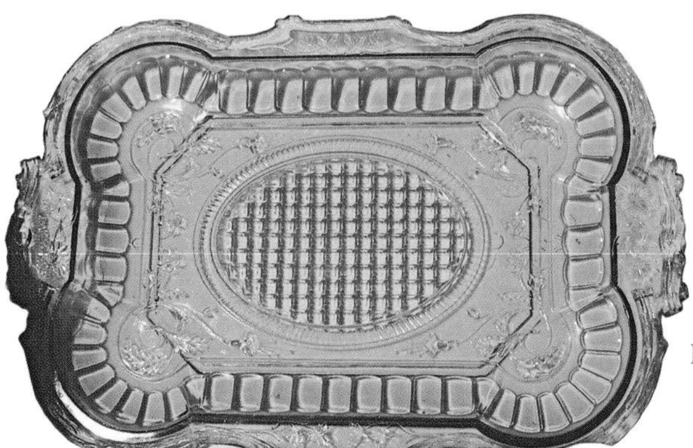

Daisy and Tree Limb

Daisy Band

Daisy and Scroll

Made by U. S. Glass as pattern #15104 in 1907, Daisy and Scroll is also known to collectors as Buzz Saw in Parentheses or U. S. Victoria. Some of the shapes known are a table set, berry set, water set, shakers, and syrup. It can be found plain or decorated with gold.

Daisy and Tree Limb

Believed to be an Atterbury pattern by some and dating to 1881, this very fine pattern is somewhat of a mystery. Belknap refers to it in milk glass. The tray shown is in a beautiful amber glass and is 14" long and 9½" wide. The handles and rim have branches, with daisies on the handles and additional flora in the inner scrolling.

Daisy Band

Daisy Band was made by Columbia Glass in the 1880s and U.S. Glass after 1891, and is found in clear, amber, and blue glass. Shapes are the handled cup and matching saucer. Some collectors call this pattern Hob-in-Square but an Aetna Glass pattern in opalescent glass is known by this name, so Daisy Band is the correct name.

Daisy Banded Crystal Wedding

Like the standard Crystal Wedding pattern shown elsewhere, this one was made by Adams & Company and then by U. S. Glass in 1891. Original production included clear, acid finish, and ruby stained pieces (some amber stain is known as are blue and vaseline). Here we have a mould change that added a band of daisy-like flowers around the lid, compote bowl, and the stem.

Daisy Band Variant

This variant is like the regular Daisy Band except it is taller, has a small rim around the top, and has three rows of square thumbprints rather than the normal two. Both were made by Columbia in the 1880s and then by U.S. Glass in 1891.

Daisy Band Variant

Daisy Basket

Made by Imperial in both crystal and carnival glass, this was their #699, first produced in 1917. It was reproduced in carnival glass in the 1960s with the IG trademark. In size, these baskets average 10" in height and have top diameter of 5" – 6". Production of the old pieces ended in 1930.

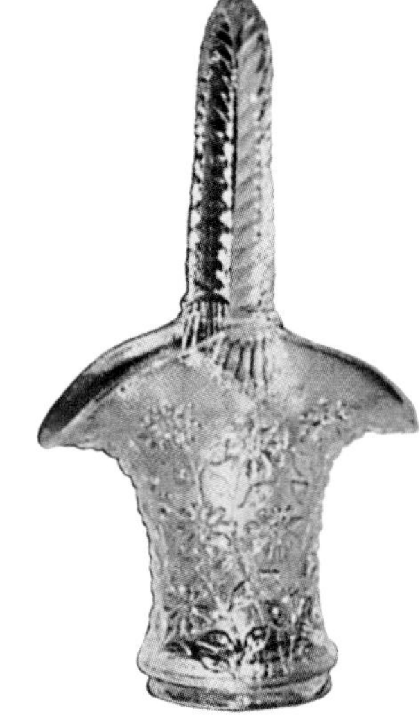

Daisy Basket

Daisy-in-Square

Shapes in this pattern made by U. S. Glass in 1891 (Duncan #330) include a table set, water set, berry set, milk pitcher, celery vase, pickle tray, syrup, shakers, sauce, and the pedestal based vase shown. Some items were gold trimmed.

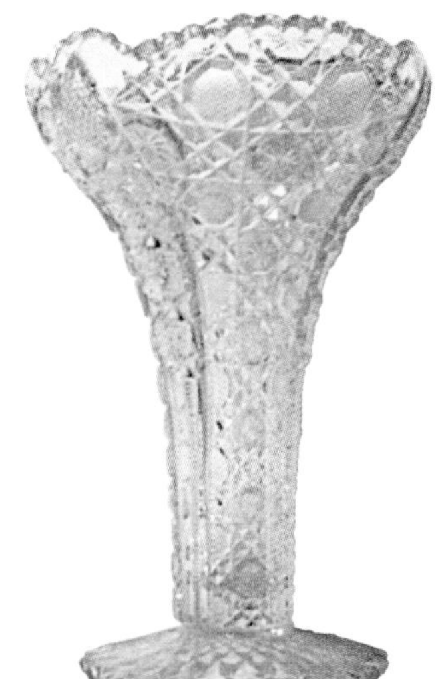

Daisy-in-Square

Daisy Medallion

Also known as Sunburst Medallion, this pattern can be found in table sets, water sets, berry sets, compote, goblet, and cake stand. The design is soft and delicate, and the maker has not been determined at this time.

Daisy Medallion

Daisy Pleat

We've learned almost nothing about this pattern except some call it Daisy Pleat (it may well have another name). We've seen only the mug shape which has a diagonal banding with a flower in a square, a section of pleating, and a spray of stem and leaves. We would appreciate any information on this pattern.

Daisy Pleat

Daisy Swag

We believe this pattern is English but have no proof other than its component parts. The feet are reeded just like the handle and the creamer's top is ruffled in a typical English manner. We suspect Davidson may be the maker and are sure it was made in crystal as well as the vaseline shown. We'd really appreciate any information readers can offer on it.

Daisy Swag

Dakota

Dalton

Dart

Dalzell Swan

Darwin

Dakota

Dakota is also known as Baby Thumbprint or Thumbprint Band, and was first made by Ripley & Company in 1885 and then as a U. S. Glass State pattern in 1898 in clear, ruby stained, or cobalt glass. Shapes include a cake basket (flat or footed), cologne bottle, sauce bottle, betty set, waste bowl, table set, cake stand in several sizes, celery tray, celery vase, open and covered compotes in five sizes, cruet, cruet set, goblet, honey dish, mug, water set, milk pitcher (pitchers are tankard or bulbous), plates, sauces, water tray, and wine tray.

Dalton

Dalton has been attributed to Tarentum Glass in 1904. Shapes include a table set, water set, cup, goblet, 10½" plate, miniature rose bowl, toothpick holder, and two-piece breakfast set consisting of a creamer and sugar (open).

Dalzell Swan

We've heard this piece called Swimming Swan or Floating Swan, but since we are convinced it was made by Dalzell, Gilmore & Leighton (the shape is like others from that company), we are giving it their name. The stance of the bird resembles Millersburg's Nesting Swan bowls also, with the arched neck and wings raised in a strong pose. Anyone who can shed some light on this pattern is urged to contact us.

Dart

While we are confident this pattern was made in the 1880s, the maker remains unknown to us. Found only in clear, shapes are a table set, bowls, jelly compote, goblet, water set, and sauce. A covered compote in two sizes is also known.

Darwin

Also called Monkey Head, this is either a toothpick or a match holder. It was made by Richards and Hartley Glass in 1880s and was named after the death of Charles Darwin in 1882. It is found in clear or amber.

Davidson Tulip Vase

This stemmed vase has every indication that it is of English origin and resembles several patterns from the George Davidson Company of Gateshead, England. We believe it was made in crystal as well as the vaseline shown and may have been made in other colors as well.

Decorated Three Face

Like the other Three Face pieces made by George Duncan & Sons and later by U.S. Glass in 1891, this piece has the added Duncan style decoration that is called Frosted Sunflower Band. Notice that the stem is also frosted on this piece and the top is scalloped. We believe this piece was made at U.S. Glass, despite the Duncan characteristics.

Deer Alert

More realistic than many of the "deer" patterns, this one has fine foliage and a realistic deer with wide rack, looking alertly over its shoulder. The pitcher seems to be the only shape reported, and it is a tankard on a short pedestal base. All deer pieces are very collectible and this one is no exception. We do not know the maker, but it may be Dalzell.

Deer and Castle

Made in Europe in the late 1880s and early 1900s, this stained and then cut-back glass was very popular in its time. It came in all shapes and several colors that include ruby, cobalt blue, amber, and emerald green. Subjects were just as varied with the very popular Deer and Castle design. Shapes include water sets, vases, ewers, bowls, compotes, and lighting lustres. Reproductions abound.

Deer and Cow

Shaped like the Boy with Begging Dog mug shown on page 42, this 1880s mug is 2" tall and has a diameter of 1⅞". It is found in clear, blue, blue opaque, or milk glass. It shows a deer on one side and the head of a cow or steer on the other, and the mould work is outstanding.

Davidson Tulip Vase

Decorated Three Face

Deer and Cow

Deer Alert

Deer and Castle

Deer and Dog

Deer and Oak Tree

Deer and Pine Tree

Delaware

Despot

Deer and Dog

The American maker is unknown, but shards were found in Canada's Burlington Glass Works. Pieces are clear or acid finished, and shapes include a table set, celery vase, champagne, cheese dish, covered compote (high or low) in two sizes, cordial, goblet, marmalade jar, mug, water pitcher, flat or footed sauces, and wine. Some collectors feel LaBelle Glass first made this pattern.

Deer and Oak Tree

From Dalzell, Gilmore, and Leighton and then Indiana Tumbler and Goblet (Greentown) in the 1880s, this superior deer pattern is known in crystal or chocolate glass in the water pitcher shape and a mug shape. All pieces are very collectible.

Deer and Pine Tree

Credited to both McKee & Brothers (mug) and Belmont Glass and also called McKee's Band Diamond or Deer and Doe, this pattern was made in a waste bowl, table set, cake stand, celery vase, covered or open compotes (7", 8", 9"), jam jar, goblet, pickle dish, milk pitcher, water pitcher, sauce, oblong dishes (7", 8", 9"), and a water tray. The mugs are found in two sizes and colors include clear, amber, apple green, blue, or canary. Colored pieces may be found with or without gilt.

Delaware

Similar to the Bohemian pattern and also known as New Century or Four Petal Flower, Delaware is U.S. Glass pattern #15065, made in 1899. Treatments include crystal, emerald green, custard, ruby stain, and milk glass. Shapes include a berry set, table set, water set, cruet, celery vase, shakers, custard cup, breakfast creamer and sugar, toothpick holder, banana bowl, basket in silver holder, finger bowl, fruit bowl, pin tray, compote, pomade box, puff box, gas or electric shade, and a stemmed claret.

Despot

This very plain, little-known wine goblet with the inside ribbing isn't much to write home about. The pattern is also called Inside Optic and the maker is unknown, at least to us. Alice Hulett Metz says it was made in the 1890s.

Dew and Raindrop

From Kokomo Glass in 1905 and found in crystal or ruby flashed crystal, Dew and Raindrop can be found in a table set, berry set, goblet, mug, water set, salt shakers, sauce, sherbet, and wine.

Dewdrop

Also known as Hobnail, this Columbia Glass pattern, later reissued by U. S. Glass in 1891, was advertised in the same set as Double-Eye Hobnail. Shapes include a table set, shakers, handled cake tray that is shown, sugar shaker, caster set, wine, and syrup.

Dewdrop in Points

Shapes in this 1880 Greensburg Glass Company pattern include a table set, covered or open compote, pickle dish, goblet, water set, plate, sauce, and bread plate. The pattern is fairly easy to find.

Dewdrop with Star

From Campbell, Jones and Company, Pittsburgh, this simple pattern was first made in 1877 and extended over several years. Shapes are a table set, cake stand, cheese dish, compotes on both high or low standards, pickle dish, water set, plates (several sizes from 4" to 11"), sauce (flat or footed). Dewdrop with Star has been reproduced in both crystal and colors.

Dewey

Dewey is also known as Flower Flange and was made by Indiana Tumbler & Goblet Company in 1898 in clear, canary, amber, blue, green, and chocolate glass. Shapes include a berry set, table set, cruet, mug, parfait glass, water set, plate, shakers, sauce, trays in two sizes, and breakfast set. Note: Later made by U. S. Glass until 1904 after the Greentown plant closed. Other scarce colors include opaque white and Nile green. Some pieces were reproduced by Imperial.

Dew and Raindrop

Dewdrop

Dewey

Dewdrop in Points

Dewdrop with Star

Diagonal Band

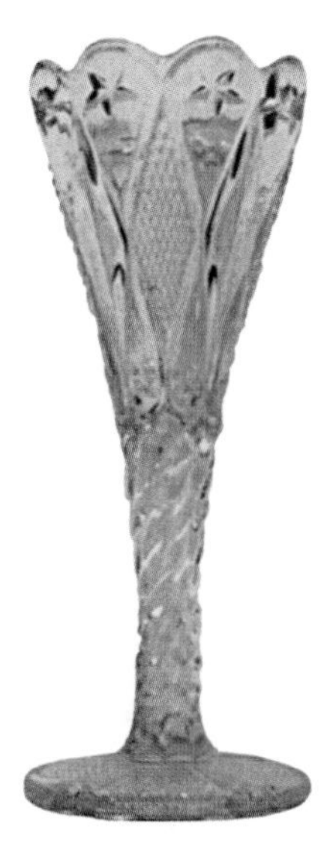

Diamond

Diamond and Fan (Millersburg)

Diamond and Sunburst (U.S. Glass)

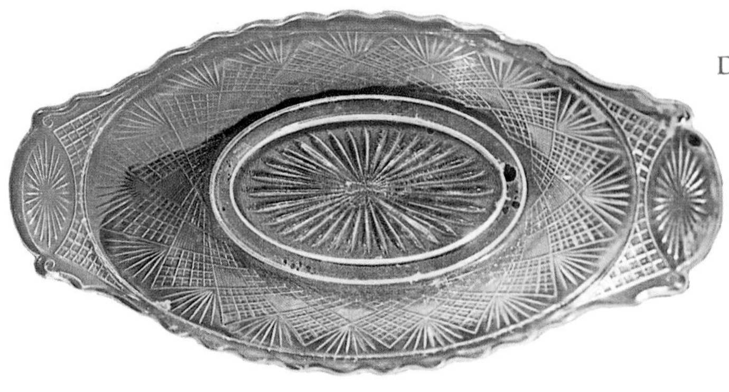

Diamond and Sunburst (Portland)

Diagonal Band

This is McKee's Jewel pattern found in crystal or apple green glass. Shapes are a table set, water set, goblet, covered compote, bread plate, relish, flat sauce, and wine.

Diamond

Diamond is reported to be from the Ohio Flint Glass Company in 1897 and was shown in their ads. Shapes include the vase shown, table set, water set, berry set, compote, pickle dish, goblet, pickle jar, toothpick holder, and wine. Some collectors have confused this pattern with Buckingham, a U. S. Glass pattern, but close examination will show the differences.

Diamond and Fan (Millersburg)

The only shape reported is the bowl with the exterior pattern. In carnival glass it is found with the famous Nesting Swan interior. Here we have one of three crystal bowls known with a plain interior. The bowl has an 8¼" diameter.

Diamond and Sunburst (Portland)

From Portland Glass in 1865, this pattern is much like others with a similar name. It can be found in a table set, wine, pickle dish, celery dish, and perhaps other shapes.

Diamond and Sunburst (U.S. Glass)

Sometimes called Diamond and Sunburst Zippers, this U.S. Glass pattern was their #15018 made in 1893. It is found on table sets, a square bowl, water set, pickle dish, shakers, wine, goblet, and a celery vase. It was made in crystal and ruby stained glass.

Diamond Block

Diamond Block, an Imperial design found in crystal and carnival glass, comes with either a plain or serrated top. Shapes include a milk pitcher, juice tumbler, rose bowl, candlesticks, compote, pedestal based vase in two sizes, and the cylinder vase shown. The pedestal vase is either 8" or 9" tall, and the cylinder vase stands 12" tall.

Diamond Bridges

Diamond Bridges was made by U.S. Glass Company in 1897 as their #15040 pattern in crystal or emerald green glass. Shapes include a table set, water set, berry set, compotes, pickle dish, goblet, wine, and pickle jar.

Diamond Cut with Leaf

Credited to the Windsor Glass Company around 1890, this pattern can be found in a table set, goblet, cordial, wine, shakers, a plate, and the mug shown. Colors are clear, amber, canary, blue, and green. We suspect even more shapes were made and wouldn't be surprised to see a water set.

Diamond in Diamond

What an appropriate name for this pattern that is found in a table set, in compotes, water set, bowls, toothpick holder, pickle dish, goblet, and wine. The maker hasn't been confirmed and certainly other pieces may exist.

Diamond Point

This well-known vase was made by the Northwood Company. It is found mostly in carnival glass or opalescent glass but was obviously made in crystal. It is an allover pattern and usually bears the Northwood trademark. Sizes range from 7" to 13", depending on how much it was swung.

Diamond Point Band

From the U.S. Glass Company about 1896, this nice mug was made in clear, vaseline, green, or ruby stained. In addition, a goblet and a wine are reported so other shapes probably exist. The mug is 3¼" tall and has a 2½" diameter. The design is one of crosshatching in a band above a band of prisming.

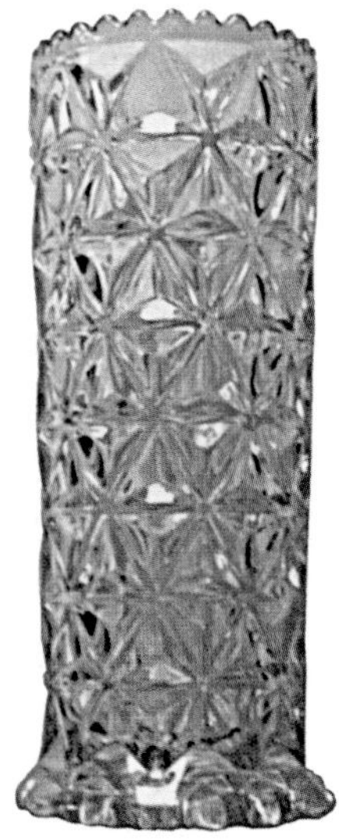

Diamond Block

Diamond Bridges

Diamond Cut with Leaf

Diamond Point Band

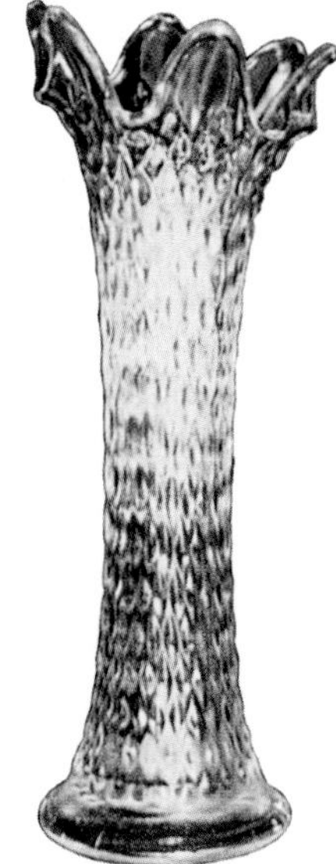

Diamond Point

Diamond in Diamond

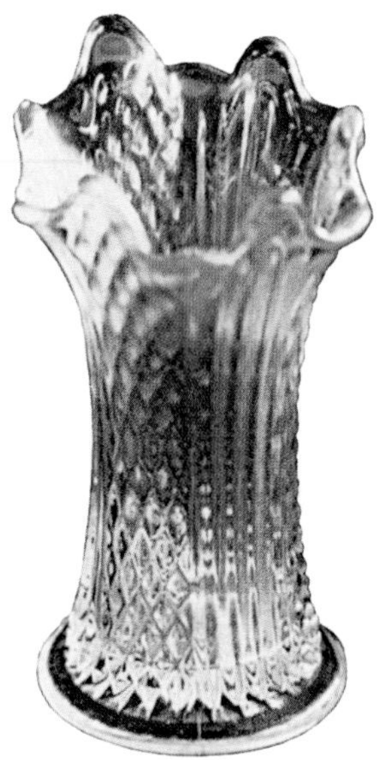

Diamond Point Columns

Diamond Point Discs

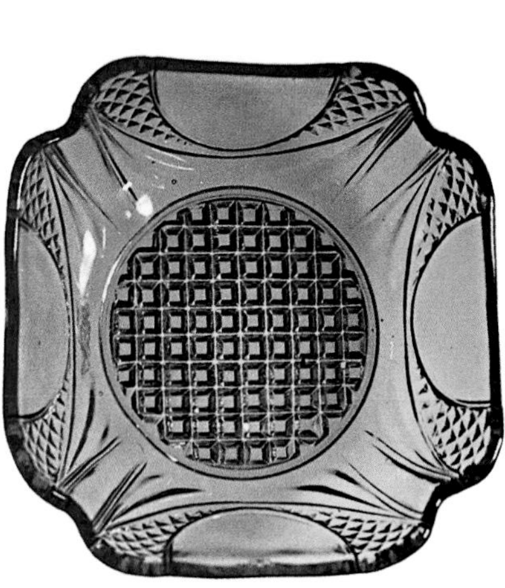

Diamond Point Loop

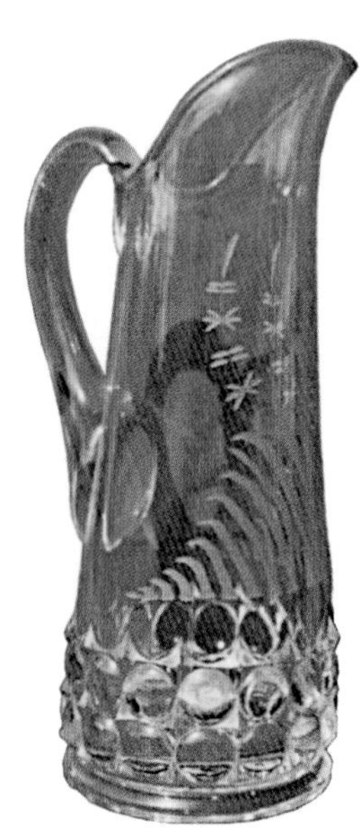

Diamond Point with Cannonballs

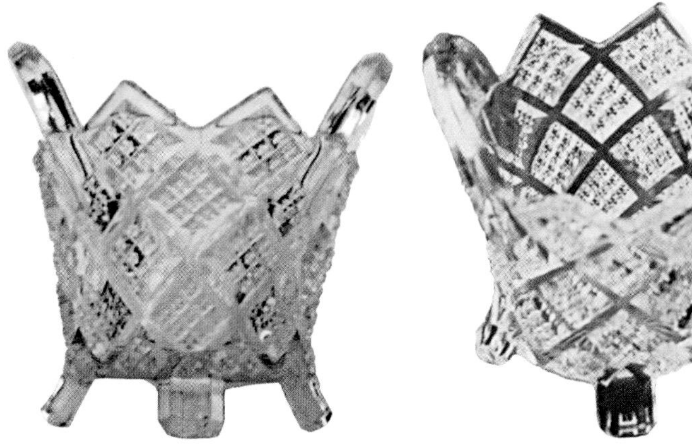

Diamond Points

Diamond Point Columns

This pattern was made by the Fenton Art Glass Company in 1911, mainly in carnival glass or opalescent glass. The example shown is almost crystal (there are tiny bits of iridization on the flames at the top of the vase). It is 7" tall but these were also swung to taller sizes and some were pulled into bowl shapes too.

Diamond Point Discs

Diamond Point Discs was made first by J.B. Higbee in 1905 and then at New Martinsville Glass as their #601. Shapes include a berry set, table set, shakers, cake stand, compote, celery vase, and individual salt dips.

Diamond Point Loop

From the 1890s (maker is unknown to us), this well-done pattern is found in a table set, celery vase, square plate, berry bowl, goblet, celery, and pickle dish. Made in crystal, amber, apple green, or blue. Some pieces are engraved.

Diamond Point with Cannonballs

We are using the owner's name for this fine tankard pitcher since the maker or name hasn't come to light. The only design is a series of spheres in three rows with a convex diamond separating each of them. The rest of the pitcher has a fanciful engraving and the handle is applied. We welcome any information from readers on this pattern.

Diamond Points

Credited to the Northwood Glass Company, this rare basket shape (a very rare footed rose bowl is also known) is found in carnival glass as well as crystal. All pieces are rare and the carnival pieces bring huge prices. If you will compare this piece to the Diamond Points Variant rose bowl shown on p. 83, you will see the differences. The variant piece is probably the York pattern from Fostoria.

Diamond Points Variant

This is the name given to the rare carnival rose bowl, but we are rather sure this pattern is really Fostoria's York pattern. In crystal, shapes reported are a table set, berry set, the rose bowl, 5½" banana bowl, custard cup, cruet, two styles of shakers, and syrup. Some items are gold trimmed, like the rose bowl shown.

Diamond Points Variant

Diamond Quilted

Diamond Quilted

This pattern, which dates to 1880 from an unknown maker, is found in crystal, amethyst, amber, blue, and vaseline. Shapes include an open oval bowl, a round bowl (6", 7"), champagne, high or low open or covered compotes, cordial, goblet, mug, table set, water set, sauce, salt (master or individual), water tray (round or clover shaped), 9" vase, and a wine. Shown is a seldom found milk pitcher.

Diamonds (Millersburg)

Shown is a rare Millersburg Diamonds tumbler in amethyst glass. This pattern has been seen on a crystal punch bowl base, a pitcher, and a tumbler, but anything other than a carnival piece is very rare.

Diamonds and Clubs

Diamonds (Millersburg)

Diamonds and Clubs

This is one of the better designs for vessels made by the Dugan/Diamond factory in Indiana, Pennsylvania, beginning in 1907, in opalescent glass, crystal, green, ruby, and blue glass, with the colors decorated. Shapes include a water set with tankard pitcher and wine decanter and matching wine glasses. In addition some of the water sets are known as Swastika because of an opalescent overlaid swastika pattern.

Diamond Spearhead

Made by Northwood as part of National Glass, this was the #22 design, found in many shapes in opalescent glass as well as clear crystal. Shapes include a table set, water set, goblet, berry set, toothpick holder, syrup, celery vase, shakers, mug, jelly compote, tankard creamer, tall compote, sugar shaker, water bottle, and rose bowl.

Diamond Spearhead

Diamond Strawberry

Diamond with Circle

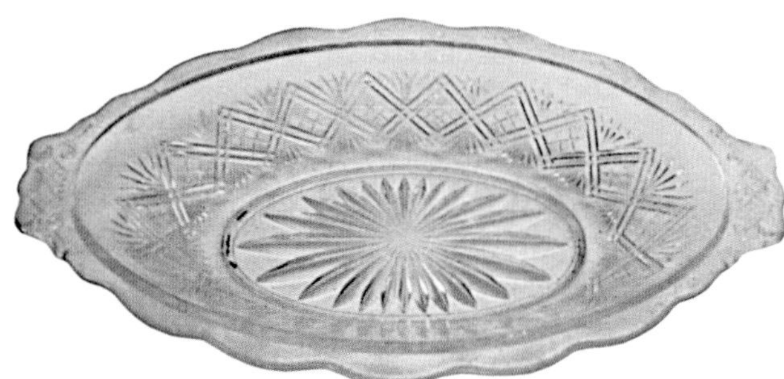

Diamond Sunburst

Diamond with Dual Fan

Diamond Swirl

Diamond Strawberry

Also called Strawberry and Fan Variant, this is Fostoria's #402 design made in 1900. Shown is the tumbler shape, but it was also made in squat pitcher and probably other shapes as well. The design is a good one, covering all the available space by being very organized.

Diamond Sunburst

Made by Bryce, Walker Company in 1894, this well-known pattern can be found in many shapes, including a table set, oval bread plate, master salt, pickle dish, sauce, cake stand, and celery vase. There are several variations, possibly made by other glass companies, but close examination will reveal the differences. Some have notched diamonds while others have differences in the crosshatching.

Diamond Swirl

Also known as Zippered Swirl and Diamond, this U. S. Glass pattern dates to 1895 and is found in clear or ruby stained glass. Shapes include a table set, salt shakers, water set, syrup, and toothpick holder, as well as an individual sugar and creamer.

Diamond with Circle

Not to be confused with the Diamond In Circle pattern, this 1880s design seems to be a companion pattern to the Upright Rabbit and Wolf patterns since they both have the bent twig handle. Colors reported are clear, amber, blue, and apple green. The maker is unknown to us.

Diamond with Dual Fan

We do not know the maker of this well-done pattern but shapes include a table set, water set, berry set, shakers, 10" plate, toothpick holder, pickle dish, goblet, and wine. Any information from readers would be appreciated.

Diamond with Fan

Diamond with Peg

Divided Hearts

Dog Cart

Dog Chasing Cat

Diamond with Fan

From the Imperial Glass Company, this pattern is their #538 and was made in 1909. Shapes known are a water set, berry set, pickle dish (oval), and table set. The glass is quite thick. Some pieces may be decorated with gilding.

Diamond with Peg

Diamond with Peg was first made by the McKee Glass Company in 1894 and then by the Jefferson Glass Company after 1913 and can occasionally be found with Jefferson's "Kry-stol" mark. It is found in clear or ruby stained glass that can often be decorated. Shapes include a table set, water set, berry set, toothpick holder, pickle dish, shakers, a goblet, wine, and celery vase. A sister pattern called Banded Diamond with Peg is shown on page 28.

Divided Hearts

Divided Hearts was made by the Boston & Sandwich Company in the 1860s. It is found on a table set, lamp, open compote, egg cup, footed salt, and goblet. The pedestal water pitcher is shown so water sets must exist.

Dog Cart

Dog Cart is also known as Boys in Cart and was part of a series (Frolic, Boys in a Cart, and Boys Falling Over Log) by Gillinder and Sons in the 1880s. The plates measure 10¾".

Dog Chasing Cat

First, we want to appologize for the mistaken Stippled Chain Variant attribution to this pattern in the first edition of this book. Several people informed us it is a George Davidson pattern from 1886 found in crystal or opaque white as their #5812 pattern. It can be found on a cream jug and sugar basins that can be open or covered as shown. We thank the readers for their input.

Dog Chasing Deer

Dog Chasing Deer

Dog Chasing Deer was another Bryce Brothers pattern from the 1880s and then a U.S. Glass after 1891. Colors reported are clear, frosted, amber, blue, and milk glass. The shape and handle are like those on Pointing Dog, Swan, and Bird on a Branch. This mug measures 3¾" tall and has a diameter of 3¼".

Dog Hunting

Dog Plate

Dog Hunting

Attributed to Greentown by some collectors (we are not convinced), this humorous pattern seems to be found only on the tankard water pitcher shown. The mould work is quite good and the shape of the pitcher is like that of some Deer Alert pitchers.

Dog Plate

Made by the Columbia Glass Company of Findlay, Ohio, in the late 1880s and sometimes called Findlay Dog, this is really one-half of a set that included a Cat Plate. Both are 6" in diameter and considered rare finds for collectors.

Dog Vase

Dog Vase

Attributed to the Columbia Glass Company in the 1880s, this rare pattern is shown in all three known colors. The very idea of a dog standing on its hind legs holding a daisy and button cornucopia vase calls for a special sort of humor that is as rare today as are these vases.

Dog with Collar

From the Iowa City Glass Company in the 1880s, this mug is found in clear as well as amethyst and is a retooled version of the Dog without Collar shown below. After the first moulds were used in 1881, someone decided to add the collar. The mug is 3⅜" tall.

Dog with Collar

Dog without Collar

Dog without Collar

Also from the Iowa City Glass Company in 1881, this mug is found in clear or amethyst and stands 3⅜" tall. It is the first version of this pattern before the collar was added to the dog.

Dog with Pail

Made by Belmont Glass in 1885, this novelty is either a toothpick holder or a match holder. It is scarce and desirable and would be a treasure for any collector of novelty glass items. This pattern was reproduced in several different types of glass and is also known as Dog wiht Hat.

Dog with Pail

Dolphin

Credited to Hobbs, Brockunier in 1880, this pattern is found either clear or with a frosted base. Shapes include a celery vase (shown), covered or open compotes in two sizes, covered oval bowls in two sizes, a covered pickle jar, pitcher (jug), a table set, and a master salt.

Dolphin and Herons

Called simply Dolphin by its maker, Model Flint Glass, this very fine item is usually found in small stemmed pieces called card trays in blue, white, and canary opalescent, but here we show the very rare vase shape in crystal. The stem of this piece is a dolphin holding the bowl in its mouth while herons are around the bowl of the vase.

Dolphin

Dolphin and Herons

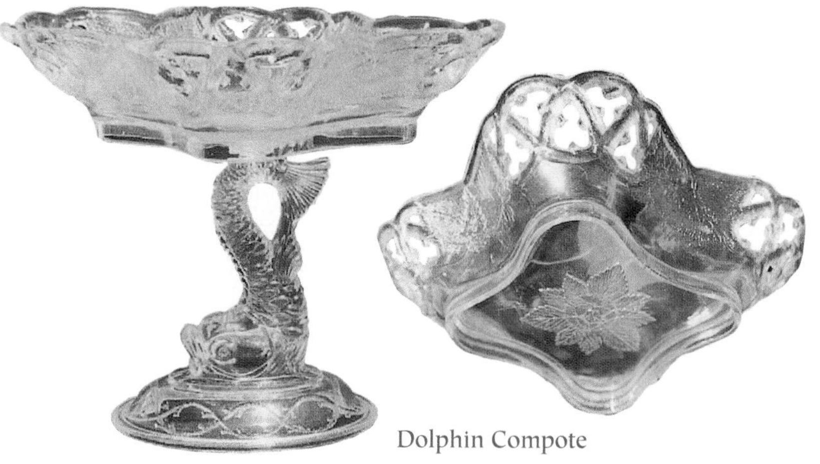
Dolphin Compote

Dolphin Match Holder

Dot

Double Beetle Band

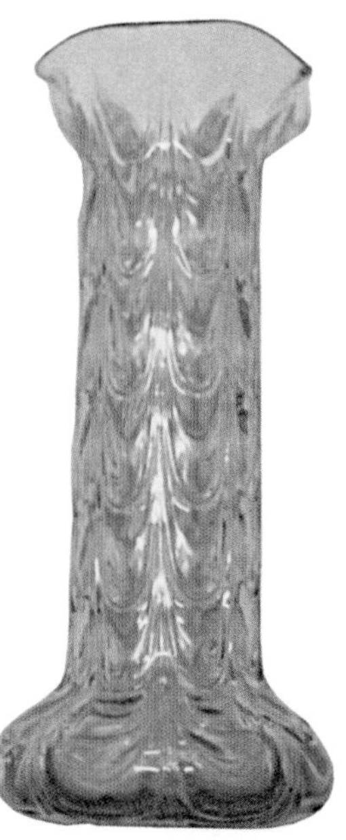
Double Drape

Dolphin Compote

Found in crystal, vaseline, and amber (other colors may exist as well), this two-piece compote with a dolphin base and separate bowl top sits on a scalloped platform. The top has piercing and a flower and leaf medallion. The base of the dolphin is domed and has an interwoven scroll effect. We believe this piece is English, but would appreciate any information about it.

Dolphin Match Holder

Credited to the Bellaire Glass Company by many collectors but not fully determined, this 4½" tall match holder can be found in crystal, amber, blue, or canary glass. Besides the dolphins around the stem, the design features the Stars and Bars pattern that is definitely a Bellaire pattern.

Dot

Credited to U. S. Glass in 1891, this confusing pattern is also wrongly called Raindrop, a pattern that does not have the banded top that cuts through the first row of dots. Shapes reported in the Dot pattern are table set, relish, and square berry set. Some pieces have gold trim.

Double Beetle Band

This pattern was made by the Columbia Glass Company in the 1880s in crystal, amber, blue, and yellow glass. Shapes include a table set, water set, goblet, flat or footed sauce, pickle dish, celery vase, and wine.

Double Drape

This nice vase is 13" tall. Each drapery loop is actually double, hence the name. The maker is unknown, but drapery pieces in carnival glass are well known and from more than one maker. This isn't like any of those designs so we must wait for more information on this piece. Anyone who knows more about this pattern is urged to contact us.

Double Pinwheel

Although originally called Juno by its maker, Indiana Glass, most collectors call this pattern Double Pinwheel. First made in 1915, shapes include a table set, berry creamer and sugar, water set, covered compote, open compotes (two sizes), condiment tray, toothpick holder, syrup, heart-shaped nappy (no handles), and the wine shown. The pattern has also been called Star Whorl by some collectors.

Double Relish

We do not have a name for this patterned double relish, made by Campbell, Jones and Company of Pittsburgh (became Jones, Cavitt and Company in 1883). Date attributed to the production of this piece is 1879, and we'd appreciate any additional information about this relish from readers.

Double Ribbon

First made by King Glass in 1870, this pattern later became a part of the U. S. Glass line in 1891. It can be found in either clear or frosted in a bread plate, footed sauce, compote, pickle dish, egg cup, shakers, a table set, water set, and covered compote.

Double Spear

From McKee and Brothers in the 1880s, this pattern's shapes include a table set, compote, celery vase, sauce, goblet, pickle dish and relish, and water set.

Double Vine

Virtually nothing seems to be known about this plate, with both maker and date of production a mystery. It is shown in Lee's *Early American Pressed Glass* (Plate 187) with text on page 645. The edging is identical to Columbia Glass's Dog Plate and Cat Plate, but we have no connecting proof.

Douglass

Found in crystal, ruby stained, or etched glass, this is a Cooperative Flint Glass pattern, made in water sets, berry sets, table sets (two styles of butter dish), toothpick holder, shakers, and punch set. Shown is one of the plain individual berry bowls but these are known with etched fleur-de-lis designs, too.

Double Relish

Double Pinwheel

Double Ribbon

Double Spear

Douglass

Double Vine

Dove

Doyle's Shell

Dragon

Drape

Drum

Dove

Made by the Canton Glass Company of Marion, Indiana, in 1919 (reproduced by Guernsey Glass in 1949 in azure blue), this 6" vase has a companion piece called Peacock (a card stand). Original colors seem to have been crystal, blue, and possibly amber. Canton Glass began in Canton, Ohio, in 1883, then moved to Beaver Falls, Pennsylvania, in 1890, and then to Marion in 1891 (in Hartford City, Indiana, after 1958).

Doyle's Shell

Also known as Knight, Cube and Fan, or U.S. Shell, this pattern was first from Doyle & Company in the 1880s, and then by U.S. Glass after 1891. It is found in clear, amber, ruby stain, and blue. Shapes include a table set, waste bowl, water tray, wine (shown), celery vase, and pickle dish. In addition there is a mug that varies slightly in design.

Dragon

This strange creature is a real find, especially on the plate shape shown, where it can be viewed to the best advantage. Other shapes include a table set, small compote, open sugar, and goblet. All pieces are considered rare, but the goblet is most often found.

Drape

Often found with gilding on the top banding, this mug was produced in the late 1880s or early 1890s we believe. It measures 3⅛" tall and has a diameter of 2¼". We do not know the maker or if other colors are known at this time but would be interested in hearing from anyone with more information on this pattern.

Drum

Drum was made by Bryce, Higbee & Company in the mid-1880s as a toy or child's table set in crystal or blue. The Drum set is considered rare. Before the set was made, a covered mustard was advertised, and a child's mug in three sizes is also known. The finials on the butter and the sugar are shaped like tiny cannons.

Drum and Eagle

Similar to the Drum pattern from Higbee, this very attractive child's mug is now recognized as a Westmoreland pattern. It is found in clear, ruby stained, or with gilt. It stands 2¼" tall and is also called Eagledrum by some collectors. Date of production was about 1909.

Duchesse

This seldom discussed pattern is shown in a U. S. Glass ad in a half-gallon pitcher, matching tumblers, water tray, and spill bowl, all numbered with a #137 engraving. Strangely, the engraving differs from the one shown on the pitcher we have here.

Dugan's Honeycomb

Made by the Dugan Glass Company of Indiana, Pennsylvania, primarily as a carnival glass pattern, this honeycombed item can also be found in opalescent glass and the "Japanese" treatment shown with silver glass graining. Shapes from the same mould are bowls, nut bowls, or the rose bowl. Colors in the Japanese treatment were blue, green, or amethyst glass.

Duncan #13

One of a line of simple, paneled utility pieces made by George Duncan and Sons around 1900, this mug shape is a bit harder to find than the tumblers in the same pattern. Also made were goblets, wine glass, and stemmed sherbet.

Duncan #40

This was from George Duncan and Sons in 1891 and is also known as Sunburst by some collectors. Shapes include a finger bowl, punch set, punch tray, table set, celery tray, open compotes in ten sizes, round or square nappy, water set, water pitcher with metal top, plate, shakers, gas shade, tankard pitcher, vases in six sizes, and individual sugar and creamer.

Duncan #98

Shown in Geo. Duncan and Sons ads as their #98 pattern, it was first made in 1887 and discontinued by 1890. Shapes known are table pieces such as a berry set (their name for a matched creamer and open sugar) or a jelly set (covered bowl with an underplate shown) that has a silver finial. Colors are crystal, amber, canary, or blue.

Drum and Eagle

Duchesse

Dugan's Honeycomb

Duncan #13

Duncan #40

Duncan #98

Duncan #904

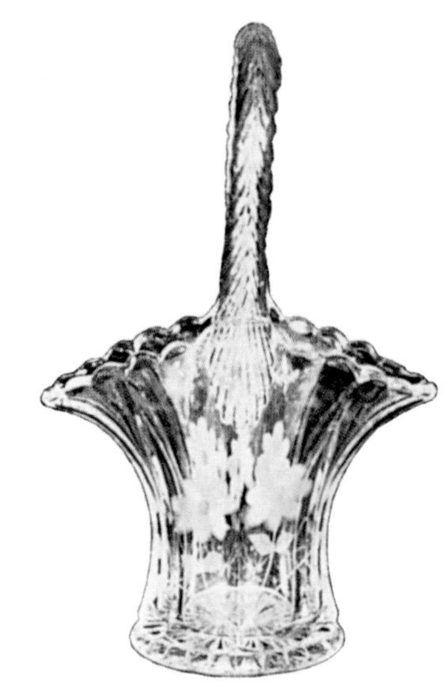

Duncan and Miller Basket

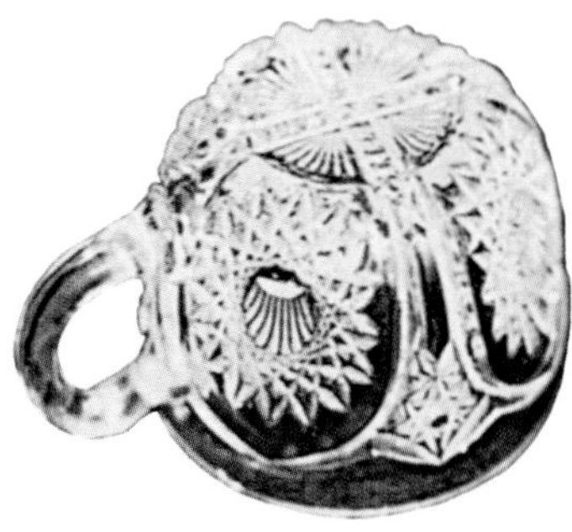

Duncan Homestead

Duncan's Clover

Duncan's Late Block

Duncan #904

Seldom discussed and similar to a host of other designs from George Duncan and Sons Glass Company, shapes in the #904 design include a table set, water set, cup, goblet, and various bowl shapes. The base spears are always the same length and are seamed in the center of each one.

Duncan and Miller Basket

Very much like a similar basket made by Westmoreland and shown on page 266 in this book (Westmoreland's #750), this handled basket has divided panels in front and back that the Westmoreland pattern does not. Etching varies, and both flowers and fruit are known.

Duncan Homestead

Made as Duncan #63, this pattern is found in many shapes. The key to the design is the seashell in the center of the hobstar. Shapes include a table set, punch set, toothpick holder, celery vase, syrup, cruet, two styles of shakers, finger bowl, individual salt dip, compotes, vases, berry set, individual creamer and sugar, and odd bowls in several sizes.

Duncan's Clover

This pattern was made by Duncan and Miller in 1904. It was made in crystal in an extended table service that includes a water set, table set, berry set, toothpick holder, wine, and finger bowl. It can be found with gilding as in the example shown.

Duncan's Late Block

Sometimes called Waffle Block, this was Duncan's #331 pattern, made for U. S. Glass in 1891, in crystal or ruby stained glass. There are many shapes, including a parlor lamp, syrup, celery boat, square bowl, tri-cornered bowl, punch set, mustard jar, square sauce, cruet, ice tub (shown), handled relish, jelly compote, sugar shaker, salt shaker, rose bowl, and table set.

Dutch Mill

Here is another mug from the 1880s which can be found in clear, as shown, and in blue or amethyst glass. It measures 2⅞" tall and has a 2¾" diameter. We do not know the maker of this mug, but a variation called Dutch Mill Variant is credited to George Davidson & Company.

Dutch Mill

Early American

From Westmoreland in 1917 and continued in production until the 1940s, this was their #555 design, made in both crystal and amber glass. Shapes include a table set, five-part relish dish, relish jar with lid, bowl, 8" plate, sherbet, cup and saucer, shakers, goblet, 9" vase, and nut dish. It is also called English Hob.

Early American

Early Excelsior

Early Excelsior was first made by Boston and Sandwich in the late 1850s, then by Ihmsen and Company and McKee Brothers in 1860 and is also called Giant Excelsior, Barrel Excelsior, or Flare Top Excelsior. Shapes include an ale glass, bar and bitters bottles, a water bottle, bowls, table set, candlesticks, champagne, claret, covered or open compote, cordial, decanter (quart or pint), egg cup (double or single), jelly, goblet, lamp, mug, pickle jar, milk pitcher, water set, master salt, spill holder, syrup, whiskey tumbler, vase, and a wine. Only crystal is known.

Early Excelsior

Early Panelled Grape Band

Information about this pattern is sketchy but some attribute it to Sandwich in the 1870s. Shapes include a table set, water set, berry set, compotes, pickle dish, open salt, goblet, wine, bread tray, egg cup, and celery vase. Some shapes seem to have more threaded banding than others.

Early Panelled Grape Band

Edgewood

From Fostoria, this well-known pattern dates to 1899 and can be found in a table set, salt shakers, toothpick holder, water carafe, syrup, cup, and sherbet. Originally known as #675, Edgewood may be decorated or gilded.

Edgewood

Egg in Sand

Egyptian

Electric

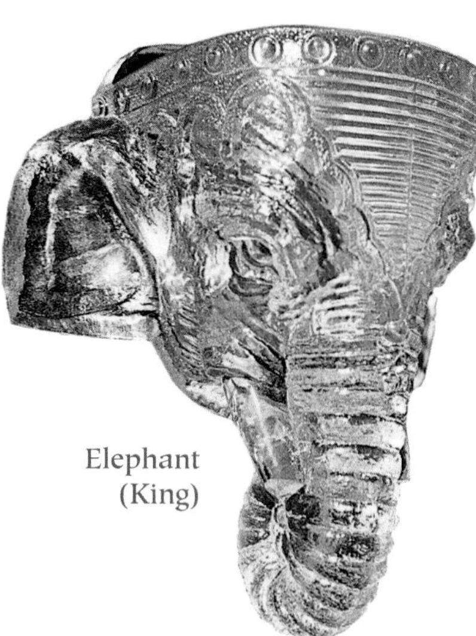
Elephant (King)

Elephant Head

Egg in Sand

Also known as Bean, this 1880s pattern, maker unknown, can be found in crystal, amber, or blue glass. Shapes include a table set, cake stand, covered jelly compote, swan center dish, goblet, jam jar, water set, milk pitcher, rectangular platter, relish, shakers, sauce, bread tray, water tray, and wine.

Egyptian

Egyptian, also called Parthenon, was made by Adams and Company in 1884. Shapes include bowls, table set, rare pyramid-shaped butter mould, celery vase, covered high or low compotes, open compote, goblet, honey dish, pickle dish, water pitcher, closed handle plate in three sizes, plate with pyramid handles, relish tray, flat or footed sauces, the Cleopatra platter, and a Salt Lake Temple platter.

Electric

Electric, from U. S. Glass in 1891 as their #15038, was made in crystal and ruby stained. Shapes include a table set, salt shakers, cracker jar, sauce, bread plate, pickle dish, relish dish, and toothpick holder.

Elephant (King)

Made by the King Glass Company in 1890, this rare wall pocket novelty match holder is an outstanding piece of glass, measuring 5" tall and 4½" across. It shows a circus elephant with a tasseled head cover and has to be the prize of any novelty collection.

Elephant Head

This super toothpick holder novelty was made by the Findlay Flint Glass Company of Findlay, Ohio, in 1890, but has been reproduced. It can be found in crystal, dark amber, blue, and opal (milk glass). The mould detail is outstanding and the features very realistic.

Elson Dewdrop #90

Made in 1887 by Elson Glass, this pattern has long been mistakenly attributed to the Northwood Company. It is found in crystal or flint opalescent glass in a table set, water set, berry set, mug, celery vase, and two-piece breakfast set (creamer and sugar).

Elson Dewdrop #90

Empress

Shown in Riverside Glass ads in crystal, gilded, green, blue, amethyst, and etched glass, this was the #492 pattern (oil lamps were numbered 493). Shapes include a berry set, table set, toothpick holder, water set, plate, footed pitcher, shakers, cruet, tray, celery vase, syrup (shown), pickle tray, covered or open compotes (four sizes), jelly compote, breakfast set, cake salver, small cake plate, master and individual salt dips, mustard pot, ice cream bowls (small and large), and lamps in five sizes.

Empress

English Colonial

Made by McKee as their #75 in 1900, this pattern is found in nearly 50 shapes! These include a table set, water set, berry set, cruet, syrup, toothpick holder, salt shakers, punch set, compote, wine, cordial, claret, sauce, decanter, plate, jelly compote, and relish.

English Colonial

English Daisy and Button

Bearing the Rd number 95625, the only shape we've found is this 9" dome-based bowl, but surely other shapes exist. Notice the Daisy and Button work is separated by fans with Daisy and Button centers. A very pretty pattern that is a real find for collectors.

English Daisy and Button

English Oval Candlesticks

These flint candlesticks stand 8½" tall and most collectors believe they are English. They have been found in crystal as well as the canary examples shown. The name is derived from the ovals that appear both on the base in a flower petal form and on the stem.

English Oval Candlesticks

English Zipper Flower

Esther

Essex

Etched Venice

Etched Mustard Pot

English Zipper Flower

While we feel confident this oval shallow bowl is English we can't say what company made it. It very much resembles products of the Geo. Davidson Company but it is possible that someone else like Greener & Company may be the true maker. We'd certainly appreciate any information about this pattern.

Essex

This was made by Fostoria Glass in 1905. Shapes include a table set, water set (two shapes in the pitchers), claret, toothpick holder, champagne, sauce, wine, berry set, cup, sugar shaker, syrup, celery vase, and sundae dish.

Esther

As we said in the first edition, this is a product of Riverside Glass in 1896 and is known as Tooth and Claw by some collectors. It is found in berry sets, table sets, tall compotes, a jelly compote, cruet, goblet, relish, shakers, syrup (rare), toothpick holder, jam jar, lamp, and a caster set. Colors are crystal, green, ruby, or amber stained glass. Here is the covered butter dish with the correct bottom.

Etched Mustard Pot

We believe this quality mustard pot, from the 1890s, with metal lid and a beautiful etching of leaves may be European but we can't be sure. The glass is a good quality and the etching outstanding.

Etched Venice

This pattern is like the enameled version from U.S. Glass (Adams factory) in 1891; but it is etched rather than enameled. It is shown on a beautiful vaseline glass with the matching water tray and would be a standout in any collection. Thanks to the Sandemans for sharing it with us.

Evangeline

Credited to the U. S. Glass Company in 1918, this pattern was advertised as #15131 and made in an extended table service that included a table set, water set, berry set, compote, wine, celery tray, handled jelly dish (shown), sauce, cake stand, and shakers. It is shown in some ads as an export item to Mexico and South America.

Evelyn

We've also heard this pattern called Thumballa. It was made by the Fostoria Glass Company, according to their former director of design, Marvin G. Yutzey. We've seen this pattern in both carnival and emerald green glass in the bowl or plate shapes but suspect it may have also been produced in crystal. Production seems to have been in the 1930s, and all pieces known have a ground base.

Eyewinker

Also known as Cannon Ball or Winking Eye, this Dalzell, Gilmore & Leighton pattern has been dated to 1889. It is found only in clear crystal and shapes include a banana dish, berry set, vegetable bowl, covered bowl, table set, cake stand in three sizes, celery vase, covered compote in nine sizes, open compote in nine sizes, cruet, honey dish, oil lamp, water set, milk pitcher, square plate in five sizes, round or square sauce, salt shakers, and syrup. It has been reproduced.

Faceted Flower Swirl

Also known as Faceted Flower, the swirl additive makes sense because the glass swirls. The maker is unknown to us, but the pattern dates to the 1880s. Shapes include a water set, table set, celery vase, water tray, cruet, toothpick holder, and pickle tray.

Fairfax Strawberry

Also known as simply Strawberry, this Bryce, Walker & Company pattern (shards were also found at the Boston & Sandwich site) dates to 1870. Originally made in clear and milk glass, shapes include an oval bowl, table set, celery vase, covered high or low compote, egg cup, goblet, honey dish, pickle tray, water set relish, master salt, sauce, syrup, and wine.

Evangeline

Evelyn

Eyewinker

Faceted Flower Swirl

Fairfax Strawberry

Falling Leaves

Famous

Fan Band

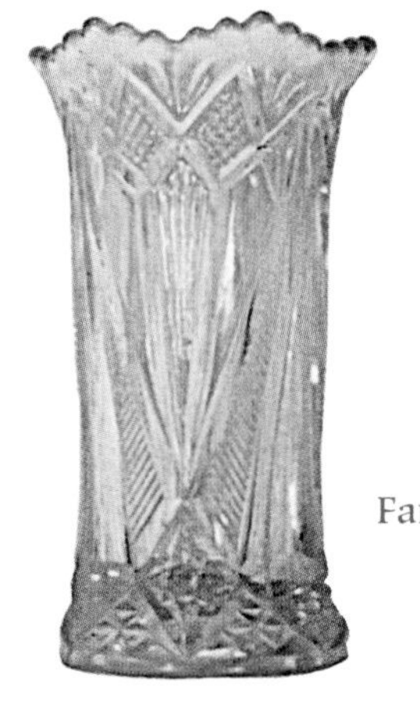
Fancy Cut

Fancy Loop

Falling Leaves

Actually this pattern should be called Federal's Vine. It was part of the Federal Glass line from 1910. Shapes include an oval bowl, table set, water set, berry set, milk pitcher, pickle dish, celery tray, pedestal one-quart pitcher, covered bowls in 5", 6", 7", 8" sizes, covered compotes in the same sizes, and milk pitchers in flat or pedestal bases.

Famous

Also known as Panelled Thumbprint or Thumbprint Panel, Famous was made by Cooperative Flint Glass Company in 1899. It can be found in an extended table service that includes a table set, toothpick holder, salt shaker, syrup (scarce), and the oil lamp shown. Other shapes probably exist and a water set is quite possible as well as a berry set.

Fan Band

Also called Bryce Yale or Scalloped Flower Band, this design was made by Bryce, Higbee and then U. S. Glass from 1885. Pieces may be engraved and shapes include a table set, water set, compote, tray, finger bowl, and wine.

Fancy Cut

Well known by toy set collectors, this is a Cooperative Flint Glass pattern made in 1905. It is also called Rex and the tiny water pitcher is found in carnival glass. Shapes include toy punch sets, water sets, berry sets, and table sets. The example shown is a vase whimsey and is previously unlisted. It has some variation from the smaller pieces in that the top is serrated and the design has fans above the diamonds.

Fancy Loop

Made by A. H. Heisey in 1897 as their #1205, this well-known pattern is a good one. Shapes include a table set, water set, spoon tray, punch set, shakers, toothpick holder, jelly compote, cracker jars, wine, goblet, celery vase, bonbon, champagne, claret, cruet, jelly dish, master or individual salt dips, sherry, bar tumbler, and vase.

Fandango

Fandango was made by A. H. Heisey Company as their #1201 in 1896 and is also known as Diamond Swag. Shapes include a table set, pickle tray, celery vase, nappy, cracker jar, tall cookie jar, rose bowls, cheese plate, tankard creamer, jelly compote, salver, banana stand, compotes in several sizes, toothpick holder, wine, assorted bowls, individual and hotel table pieces, berry set, water set, carafe, finger bowl, custard cup, mustard pot, bar bottle, syrups, cruets, butter pat, salt dip, horseradish jar, sugar shaker, salt shakers, and ice bowl with underplate.

Fan with Diamond

Sometimes called Shell, this McKee and Brothers pattern was first made in 1880 and is available on a water set, wine, table set, 9" x 6½" oval dish, egg cup, goblet, pickle dish, syrup, and high and low covered compotes. The design is typical of early non-flint glass patterns that were not too busy.

Fan with Split Diamond

Made by Westmoreland in 1890, shapes include a table set, water set, berry set, and mustard pot. The pieces are often found with gold trim. Interestingly enough, a covered piece called a mustard sugar was advertised in the 1890s and sold with mustard inside when Westmoreland's own mustard was packaged at the company.

Fan with Star

Made by Challinor, Taylor in 1880 as their #304 pattern and the next year by U. S. Glass, Fan and Star can be found in berry sets, table sets, celery vase, open 8" compote, goblet, water set, and 7" plate. It was made in slag glass, amber, blue, and canary as well as crystal.

Fandango

Fan with Split Diamond

Fan with Diamond

Fan with Star

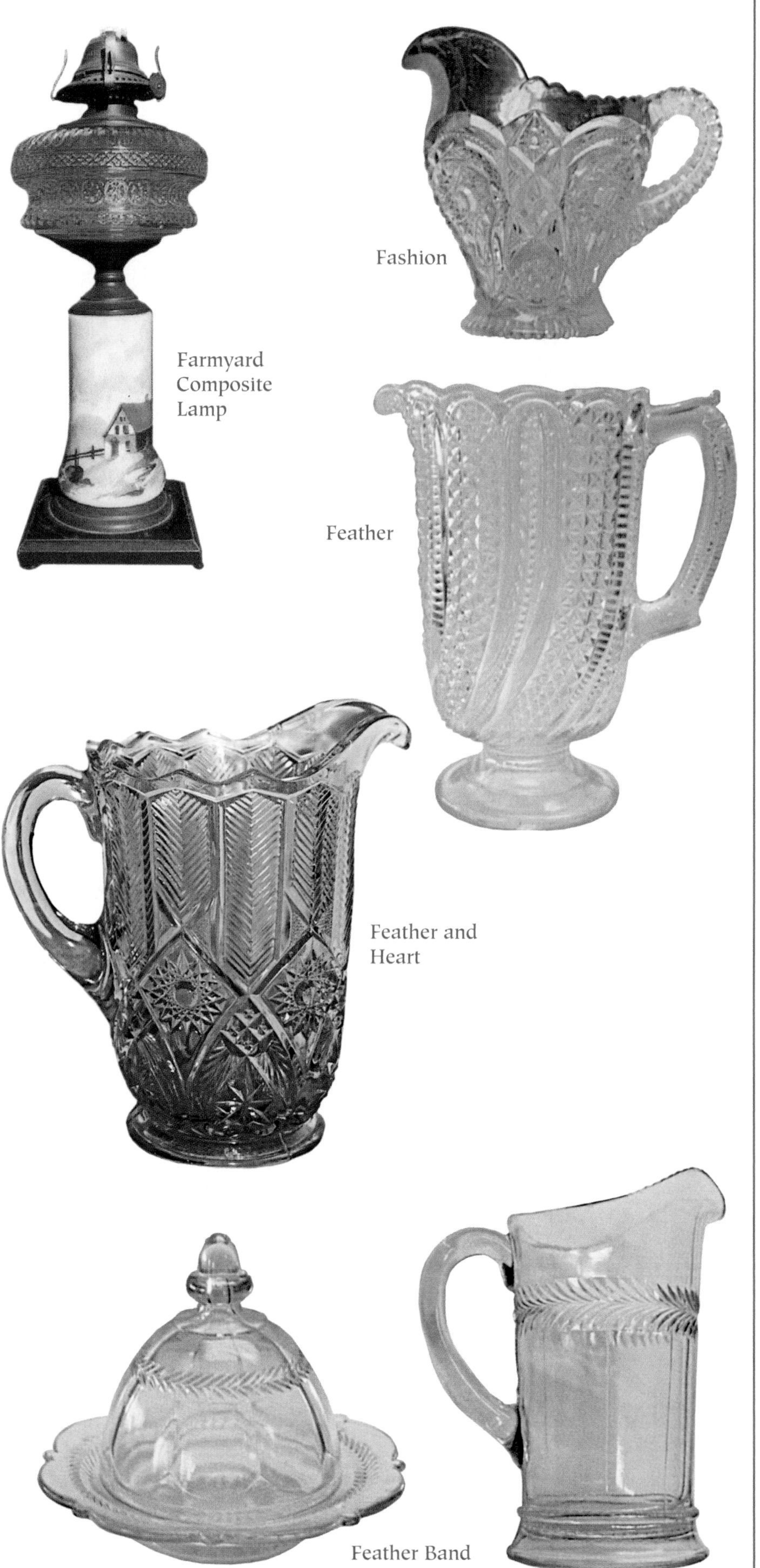

Farmyard Composite Lamp

Fashion

Feather

Feather and Heart

Feather Band

Farmyard Composite Lamp

We believe this nice lamp is from the Boston & Sandwich Glass Company and dates to the 1880s since it is very similar to other composite lamps from that firm. The design features a farm scene with a red-roofed barn. The font is a fine vaseline glass.

Fashion

From the Imperial Glass Company catalog of 1909, we know when this pattern was first made in crystal (it was one of the company's leaders in carnival glass, also). Shapes are a berry set, water set, table set, small covered butter, covered jelly compote, toothpick holder, sherbet, custard cup, 4", 5½", 6½", 8½", and 10" compotes, punch set, orange bowl with standard, 9", 10" and 12" bowls, 7" rose bowl, nappy, 11" plate, 8" salver, and 12" salver. It has been reproduced.

Feather

Here is a pattern with more names than any ought to have. It is also known as Indiana Swirl, Prince's Feather, Doric, Fine Cut and Feather, Swirl, and Feather Swirl. It was made by McKee and Brothers in 1896 in a wine, table set, water set, cake stand, 8" bowl, celery vase, cordial, goblet, 10" plate, and compote.

Feather and Heart

Made by Millersburg in 1910, and found only in a water pitcher and matching tumbler, this pattern is best known in carnival glass, but crystal pieces do exist (the pitchers are somewhat scare and the tumblers rare). The design is a good one and is often confused by beginning collectors with the Inverted Feather pattern made by Cambridge.

Feather Band

Made by the U. S. Glass Company in 1919, this pattern is advertised in an export catalog on that date, indicating it was shipped for sale to both Mexico and South America. Shapes known are a table set, water set, and berry set, but I suspect other shapes were made, especially pickle dish, celery vase, or set of shakers.

Feather Duster

Feather Duster is also known as Huckle or Rosette Medallion and #15043 from U. S. Glass, in clear or emerald green. Shapes include 5", 6", 7", 8" covered or open bowls, table set, cake stand (four sizes), high or low covered compotes (four sizes), open compotes (four sizes), saucer (four sizes), egg cup, mug, pickle dish, milk pitcher, water set, plates, platter, shakers, relish tray, sauces, water tray, and wine.

Feather Duster

Feathered Arrow

Feathered Arrow

Found in carnival glass (marigold), crystal, olive green glass, and rose glass, this unusual pattern is seen in bowls, a nut bowl, rose bowl, and a bowl with a returné rim. The pattern is all exterior and because of the color selection, we now feel this pattern was a product of the 1920s, so that would eliminate Millersburg as a possible maker.

Feathered Ovals

This pattern has been seen in both table sets and water sets (water pitcher shown), all with the same pedestal-type bases, but handle types differ from one piece to the next as do pouring spouts. It was from Cambridge (#2579) and later Federal.

Feathered Ovals

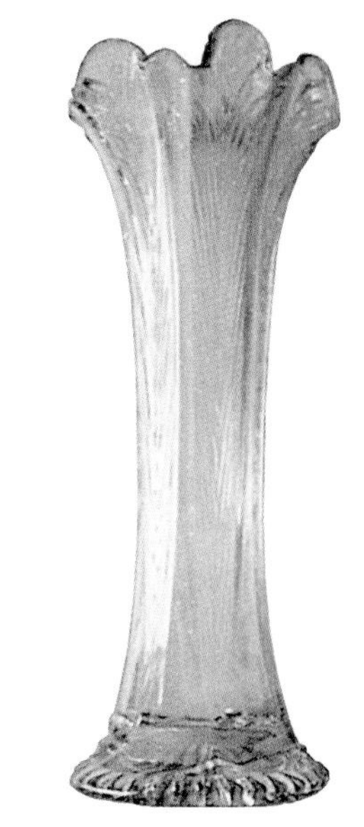

Feathers

Feathers

This is a vase shape made by the Northwood Glass Company in 1905. It is found in crystal, opalescent, carnival, and colored glass. The vase may stand as short as 9" or be pulled to 14'. Many pieces are marked with the Northwood trademark.

Federal #1910

Another pattern from Federal Glass in 1910, this geometric design was offered in more than 30 shapes that include vases in three shapes, cup, wine, mayonnaise set, goblet, water set, table set, berry set, celery vase, shakers, jelly compote, milk pitcher, celery tray, salad bowls, master compote, toothpick holder, and pin tray.

Federal #1910

Feeding Dog and Deer

Fern Garland

Fern Burst

Fenton Grape and Cable

Fernette

Feeding Dog and Deer

This well-done mug was made by Bryce Brothers in the 1880s and then by U.S. Glass after 1891. It is found in crystal, amber, blue, canary, and a lavender or pale amethyst. Shown is the Deer side.

Fenton's Grape and Cable

Fenton had a version of the Grape and Cable pattern that is nearly identical to Northwood's. It is found in carnival glass as well as crystal. Crystal shapes are a giant footed orange bowl (shown with frosted grapes, leaves, and collar leaf-ring) as well as a rare punch set with scroll feet.

Fern Burst

Also known as Palm Wreath and once thought to be from Millersburg, many collectors recently assigned it to Jefferson Glass. It is, however, shown in a 1906 Butler Brothers catalog beside a Westmoreland pattern called Atlanta. Shapes known to us are bowls, table set, compotes, goblet, and sauce. The design is a very good one, made on quality glass.

Fernette

Advertised under this name in a January 1, 1906, ad from the Evansville Glass Company of Evansville, Indiana, this seldom discussed pattern is a very good one, not easily forgotten. Shapes include a table set, berry set, water set, and toothpick holder.

Fern Garland

This pattern is from McKee Glass in the 1890s and is sometimes called Colonial with Garland. Shapes include the goblet shown, a table set, celery vase, water set, celery tray, violet vase, wine, shakers, and cup. Pieces may be ruby stained and all old pieces are marked "Prescut." Also found without the garland design, this plain version is called Old Colony.

Ferris Wheel

Sometimes called Lucile by carnival glass collectors where it is known in a water set, Ferris Wheel was made by Indiana Glass in 1910. Shapes known are a table set, water set, flat covered berry set, pedestal berry bowl, cruet, half-gallon jug, covered jelly compote, 6½" preserves, vase, and wine. Originally it was called Prosperity.

Festoon

Festoon was first advertised in Montgomery Ward's catalog in 1894 (the maker is unknown) as Frosted Glass Water Set. Shapes include a finger or waste bowl, round or rectangular bowls, table set, cake stand in two sizes, covered or open compotes, mug, pickle caster, pickle dish, and pickle jar, water set, relish tray, water tray, and plates in four sizes.

Field Thistle

From U.S. Glass in 1912, this pattern is found in crystal as well as carnival glass. Shapes include a berry set, table set, water set, nappy (shown), 9" plate, open compote, 6" plate, chop plate (11"), olive dish, and a caster set. Some pieces may have gilding.

File

From Imperial in 1909 as their #256, File is found in both crystal and carnival glass. Crystal shapes include a water set, table set, shakers, 7" vase (shown), berry set, oil bottle, grape plate, 8½" shallow bowl, 5½" and 7" rose bowls, 8" banana bowl, 4", 6", 8", and 10" plates, and pickle dish.

Filigree Metal Base Lamp

While we have no proof, this lamp has an English look about it and we believe it wasn't made in this country. The base is cast pot metal with a silver-look finish and the font is a beautiful swirl pattern in a strong vaseline that also has a British look. We welcome any information on this item.

Ferris Wheel

Festoon

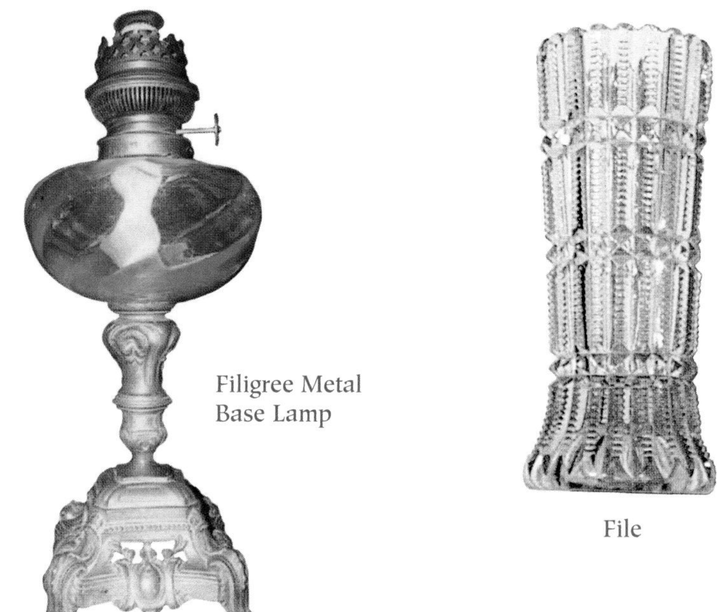

Filigree Metal Base Lamp

File

Field Thistle

Finecut

Finecut and Block

Finecut and Fan

Finecut and Panel

Finecut Heart

Finecut

Credited first to Bryce Brothers in the 1870s and then U.S. Glass after 1891, this well-designed pattern's shapes include a table set, finger bowl, sauce, tray, toothpick holder, compote, pickle dish, celery vase, celery dish, pickle jar, plates, and the relish boat shown. Colors are crystal, amber, blue, vaseline, and canary.

Finecut and Block

Finecut and Block is also known as King's #25 and attributed to King, Son & Company as well as Portland Glass and the Model Flint Glass Company (1890 – 91), and known in clear, clear with amber, blue, pink stained blocks, and all amber, blue, or canary. There are many shapes, including cologne and perfume bottles, many types of bowls, table set, cake stand (five sizes), celery tray, champagne, claret, compotes, cordial, custard and egg cups, goblets, lamp, mug, water set, milk pitcher, plates, soap dish, and wine.

Finecut and Fan

Made by Bryce, Higbee and Company in 1905, Finecut and Fan shapes include a child's toy table service, oval pickle dish, regular table set, sauce, and heart-shaped bowl. Some pieces may be gold trimmed.

Finecut and Panel

Finecut and Panel was made by Bryce Brothers, Richards & Hartley (1889), and then U.S. Glass as their #260 pattern in 1891. Colors are crystal, amber, blue, or canary. Shapes include a berry set, waste bowl, cake stand, table set, covered or open compotes, cordial, cup, goblet, pickle dish, dishes (7", 8", 9"), milk pitcher, water set, plates, oval platter, relish tray, bread tray, water tray, and a wine.

Finecut Heart

Found primarily as an exterior pattern on Millersburg's Primrose bowl in carnival glass, this very attractive crystal version is a rare find. It measures about 10" across the top and can be straight sided or ruffled. Millersburg has few equals with geometric patterns or glass quality.

Finecut Ovals

Made by Millersburg, this exterior bowl pattern is usually found in carnival glass paired with a Whirling Leaves interior pattern but here we find the only reported example of a crystal bowl. Please note the bowl has traces of gilt.

Finecut Shield and Inverted Thumbprint

The maker of this fine covered compote is unknown to the owner and to us, so we've taken the liberty of giving it a name. It has a twin thumbprint finial, thumbprints around the top of the cover, the bottom of the bowl, and on the base, while there are shields of finecut on both pieces and engraving. We would like to hear from anyone with information on this pattern.

Finecut Square with Daisy Button

We now know this pattern was really part of the Jumbo line from Canton Glass in 1884 (and probably Aetna Glass also). The design matches the square-based covered butter dish. We've seen this pitcher in both crystal and amber glass, as shown.

Finecut Umbrella

This very nice novelty piece may have been designed as a pickle dish but we can't be sure. It measures 9½" in length and has a very nice handle. The design fills veined areas that resemble the spars of an umbrella. The maker is unknown to us at this time, but we would appreciate any information on this piece readers may have to offer.

Fine Prisms and Diamonds

Found in carnival glass as well as crystal, this vase appears in 1912 Butler Brothers catalogs but the maker is not identified. They range in height from 11" to 15", have ruffled tops, and the pattern is a simple one of three rows of rope-like banding.

Finecut Ovals

Finecut Square with Daisy Button

Finecut Shield and Inverted Thumbprint

Finecut Umbrella

Fine Prisms and Diamonds

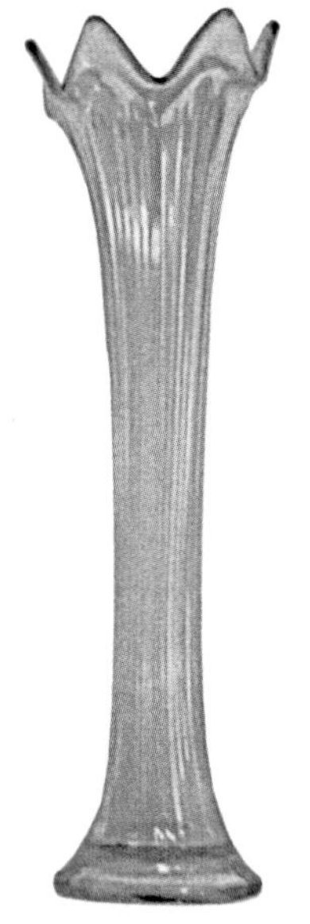

Fine Rib

Fish and Swans

Fishscale

Flamingo

Flattened Diamond and Sunburst

Fine Rib

Primarily known in carnival glass, this vase shape by the Fenton Art Glass Company dates to 1909 and is also found in crystal and rare opalescent pieces. The vases range in size from 7" to 15" tall.

Fish and Swans

Unlisted in previous references, this very unusual pattern is shown on a creamer, the only reported shape so far. It shows swans floating on waves while fish swim below! What imagination glassmakers in this era had, and what a joy it is to see their work. Anyone with knowledge of this pattern is urged to write us.

Fishscale

Fishscale was first made by Bryce and then reissued by U. S. Glass in 1891. Shapes include an ashtray (daisy and button slipper on fishscale tray), covered bowls, open bowls, table set, cake stand in four sizes, celery vase, both covered and open compotes in six sizes, goblet, finger lamp, mug, pickle scoop dish, water set, milk pitcher, square plate in four sizes, relish, shakers, flat or footed sauce, syrup, condiment tray, and round water tray.

Flamingo

Not to be confused with Frosted Stork, this well-done pattern, maker unknown, is found in table sets, pickle jar, and goblet. All pieces have the rings for finials or stems, and the goblet has a many-ringed stem. Shown is the covered pickle jar.

Flattened Diamond and Sunburst

Also known as Sunburst or Peerless, this 1870s pattern's maker is Model Flint Glass. It can be found in clear and amber glass, and shapes include a table set, sauce, celery vase, toy table set, cordial, water set, egg cup, goblet, pickle dish, double relish, cake stand, bread plate (motto), and 6", 7", 11" plates.

Flattened Hobnail

Flattened Hobnail is like many hobnail patterns, except it has no points on any hob. The maker isn't known to us, but the shapes include a table set, salt shakers, celery vase, goblet, toothpick holder, and possibly wine.

Fleur-de-Lis

Also known as Threaded Scribe, this lamp's maker is so far unknown, but the production dates to the 1920s. It was made in at least two sizes, and the example shown has slight traces of goofus treatment or gold trim.

Fleur-de-Lis and Drape

Also called Fleur-de-Lis and Tassel, this is a U. S. Glass pattern from 1891. It was made in a mustard pot, tray, shakers, cup and saucer, cruet, bowl, compote, finger bowl, tray, cordial, wine, water set, claret, and sauces in either flat or footed types. Besides clear, this pattern can be found in emerald green or milk glass.

Flora

From Beaumont Glass in 1898, this pattern is most often found in opalescent glass, but it is also known in crystal (shown) as well as emerald green. Shapes include a berry set, table set, water set, cruet, syrup, toothpick holder, a celery vase, a compote, and several novelty bowl shapes.

Floradora

Floradora is also called Bohemian and was made by the U.S. Glass Company as their #15063 pattern in 1899. It can be found in crystal, emerald green, rose-flashed, and frosted, often with decoration. Shapes include a table set, water set, berry set, tall straw jar, celery vase, pickle dish, goblet, wine, and a toothpick holder.

Flattened Hobnail

Fleur-de-Lis

Fleur-de-Lis and Drape

Flora

Floradora

Floral Oval

Floral Peacock

Florida

Flower and Panel (#23)

Florentine Candlestick

Floral Oval

Credited to both Higbee Glass and New Martinsville Glass as their #99 in 1910, Floral Oval is found in a table set, water set, square plate (shown), rectangular bowl, jelly compote, and wine. The design is quite busy and seems to vary from shape to shape.

Floral Peacock

We haven't a clue as to who made this very fine bowl or the date of manufacture, but it is a quality piece of glass. It is 10" wide and 5" deep with the peacock and flower sprays intaglio into the bowl's marie. The rest of the design is also intaglio around the bowl and consists of fans in a sunrise. Other pieces may exist, but we haven't seen them. Any information on this pattern would be appreciated.

Florentine Candlestick

Several glassmakers had similar candlesticks including Northwood and Dugan/Diamond, but the one shown was Fenton's #449 example. It can be found in both 8" and 10" sizes in colors that include crystal, vaseline, blue, green; carnival colors of marigold, red, blue, green, and white; opaque colors of black, yellow, or blue.

Florida

Florida was made by U. S. Glass as their #15056 in clear or emerald green and is also known as Green Herringbone or Panelled Herringbone. Shapes include a table set, covered or open compote and bowls, celery vase, mustard pot, pickle dish, water set, plates, relish trays, shakers, sauces, syrup, and wine.

Flower and Panel (#23)

Flower and Panel is also known as Stylized Flower. It was made by Challinor, Taylor & Company in 1885 and later by U.S. Glass in 1891, and is found in crystal, opalescent, amber, and mosaic (slag). Shapes include a covered butter dish (shown), creamer, sugar, spooner, as well as a pitcher.

Flower and Pleat

Credited to Crystal Glass in the early 1890s, this pattern is also known as Midwestern Pomona by some collectors. It is found in crystal, frosted crystal, ruby stained (rare), and color-washed glass. Shapes include a table set, toothpick holder, shakers, pickle dish, and probably others.

Flower Band

Flower Band is also called Bird Finial or Frosted Flower Band. The maker is unknown but the production is believed to be in 1870. Both clear and clear with frosted bands are known and shapes include a table set, celery boat, water set, custard cup, milk pitcher, flat or footed sauces, and covered compotes that can be either round or oval. The bird finial is outstanding.

Flower Fan

Called Snowflower by some collectors, this U. S. Glass pattern was their #35135 made in 1912 (Bryce). Shapes include a table set, water set, cruet, shakers, compote, cake stand, pickle dish, and vase. Some pieces are gold trimmed.

Flower Medallion

This pattern was made by Indiana Glass Company in 1919. Shapes include a table set, a water set, a berry set, a sauce dish, and a toothpick holder. Many pieces are found with gold trim and some are seen with ruby, green, or blue staining as well. This pattern has been reproduced by Indiana in the 1980s and 1990s. A few rare old tumblers in marigold carnival are known.

Flower Pot

Also called Potted Plant, this pattern appears to be from Bryce, Higbee, in clear or amber glass. Shapes include a table set, cake stand, covered or open compotes, goblet, milk pitcher, water set, shakers, flat or footed sauce, and "In God We Trust" bread tray.

Flower and Pleat

Flower Band

Flower Fan

Flower Medallion

Flower Pot

Flower with Cane

Flute

Flute and Cane

Flying Swan

Forks

Flower with Cane

Made by U. S. Glass as their #15141 and also known to collectors as Diamond Gold, this pattern dates to 1895. Shapes include a table set, water set, toothpick holder with fancy base, berry set, and custard cup. Pieces may be clear, gold trimmed, or ruby stained.

Flute

Virtually every company had a try at a flute or wide panel pattern. In carnival glass they were often secondary patterns used on the exterior to complement the primary interior pattern. Here is a typical example. Most shapes can be found, and these include table sets, water sets, berry sets, compotes, toothpick holders, goblets, shakers, punch sets, and vases.

Flute and Cane

Sometimes called Huckabee, this Imperial pattern is better known in carnival glass, but the crystal pieces, listed as #666, date to 1919 and can be found in a water set, berry set, 6" plate, table set, celery vase, compote, champagne, cordial, goblet, cup and saucer, milk pitcher, and handled bowl in either 5" or 7" sizes.

Flying Swan

Credited to the Westmoreland Specialty Glass Company, the piece shown is not the same pattern but is also called Flying Swan. The Westmoreland swan is found on opaque glass although it was made in other types of glass a decade earlier. We have no information on our Flying Swan handled sugar and welcome any information on this piece.

Forks

Shown in Cambridge ads as their #2696 line, the covered cracker jar shows up in Imperial's 1909 line as their #410. Just how Imperial got the mould is a mystery, but the factory catalog is hard to dispute, and we know patterns moved from one maker to another with some consistency.

Fostoria Clock Sets

We've grouped these two sets together since they are both from Fostoria and both were produced at about the same time (1920s – 1930s). Each set had a clock and a pair of candlesticks and each could be found in clear, vaseline, and possibly other colors.

Fostoria's Dandelion

This is Fostoria's #1819, made in 1911. Shapes include a berry set, toothpick holder, and stemmed sherbet. Certainly other shapes were made, and some traces of gold trim can be found on a few pieces.

Fostoria's Priscilla

Priscilla was made as Fostoria's #676 in clear or emerald green (with or without gilding) in 1898. Shapes include a water bottle, bowl, table set, cake stand, celery vase, covered or open compote, cruet, sherbet, egg cup, goblet, oil lamp, jam jar, pickle dish, water set, shakers in two sizes, salt dip in two styles, syrup, toothpick holder, and vase.

Four Pillars

First made by the Northwood Glass Company at the Indiana, Pennsylvania, plant and later by Dugan/Diamond Glass at the same location, Four Pillars is known in carnival glass, opalescent glass, and crystal. Some Northwood pieces have advertising on the base, and a few Dugan/Diamond pieces have their trademark.

Four-Seventy-Four

When we showed this pattern in the last book, we hadn't seen this beautiful pitcher in pale aqua glass. The pattern is from Imperial Glass and is found in crystal as well as carnival glass. Shapes include a berry set, table set, water set (two sizes of pitchers), punch set, milk pitcher, compote, vases (three sizes), sherbet, wine, goblet, and a cordial, as well as several condiment containers and a seldom-seen mug shape.

Fostoria Clock Sets

Fostoria's Dandelion

Fostoria's Priscilla

Four Pillars

Four-Seventy-Four

Four-Seventy-Four Variant

Fox and Crow

Framed Jewel

French Seltzer Bottle

Fringed Drape

Four-Seventy-Four Variant

Comparison with the standard Imperial Four-Seventy-Four pattern will reveal both designs were made from the same mould with the variant coming later than the regular design, after the mould had been retooled. Shapes in this variant include a table set and a water set. The mould change covered only the floral portion of the design, and it is difficult to imagine why such a change was made.

Fox and Crow

While one writer credits this pattern to the Indiana Tumbler and Goblet Glass Company of Greentown, Indiana, most of us label this pattern as maker unknown because Greentown information does not indicate it came from that factory. Only the water pitcher is known to us and production seems to have been in the 1890s.

Framed Jewel

Framed Jewel was from the Canton Glass Company as their #140 pattern, made in 1893, and is found in crystal and ruby stained crystal. Shapes include a table set, water set, goblet, toothpick holder, and wine. The design of overlapping optic and thumbprint with beaded edge is a bit difficult to see on most pieces.

French Seltzer Bottle

These bottles, made in the 1920s, are often etch lettered as the one we show. These held Vichy water and were an important part of the bar scene in this time.

Fringed Drape

Fringed Drape was made by McKee Glass Company in 1901 and frequently called Crescent by some collectors. Shapes include a table set, jelly compote, celery vase, celery tray, 6" deep bowl, 5" – 11" oval bowls, round bowl in four sizes, cordial, cruet, cup, pickle jar, pickle tray, sauce, shakers, syrup, handle for salad fork (rare and unique), flat vase in 10" and 14", and footed vase in 6", 8", and 9" sizes.

Frog and Leaf

From Co-operative Flint Glass Company of Beaver Falls, Pennsylvania, this match or toothpick holder was made in 1911. It shows a realistic frog holding a tulip-like flower that is the receptacle. It all sits on a dome base that is ribbed and is very well done indeed.

Frolicking Bears

This whimsical pattern was made by U. S. Glass Company in the early 1900s and is known mostly to carnival glass collectors in rare olive green pitchers and tumblers that bring astronomical prices. In crystal it is found in clear pitchers and tumblers but here we show a very rare item, a crystal piece with a sterling silver overlay. It is the only one reported in this technique so far.

Frost Crystal

Frost Crystal, from Tarentum Glass in 1906, was made in clear, gold trimmed, and ruby stained glass. Shapes include a table set, water set, celery boat, custard cup, shakers, bowls, plate, and the huge stemmed fruit bowl shown. The glass on this piece is very thick and heavy.

Frosted Block

Made by the Imperial Glass Company, beginning in 1913 and continuing for several years, this pattern was made in carnival glass, vaseline, opalescent, and several colors. Shapes include a table set, berry set, plate, rose bowl, pickle dish, square bowl, vase, compote, milk pitcher, water set, and many other shapes.

Frosted Chicken (Chick)

This pattern was made by Riverside Glass in 1883. It can be found in plain or engraved examples, and shapes include a table set, covered bowl on a low standard, celery vase, covered compote, goblet, jam jar, shakers, and sauce. Finials are chicks emerging from shells, but open pieces are determined by clear concave panels, separated by clear vertical convex panels.

Frolicking Bears

Frog and Leaf

Frosted Block

Frost Crystal

Frosted Chicken (Chick)

Frosted Circle

Frosted Eagle

Frosted Fleur-de-Lis

Frosted Fruit

Frosted Heron

Frosted Circle

Sometimes called Horn of Plenty, this is U. S. Glass pattern #15007 from Bryce Brothers in 1876. Shapes are a table set, covered or open bowls in two sizes, cake stand in three sizes, water set, celery vase, covered compote, and pickle jar.

Frosted Eagle

This pattern has been attributed to the Crystal Glass Company in 1883 by one writer, but there has been no confirmation of this. Found in clear or frosted, shapes include a covered bowl, table set, celery vase, covered compote with eagle finial, a water pitcher, and both master and individual salt dips. All covered pieces have eagle finials. The base is mismatched on the example shown.

Frosted Fleur-de-Lis

Frosted Fleur-de-Lis was first made by King, Son & Company in 1885 and then U.S. Glass in 1891. Shapes include a table set, water set, pickle dish, celery vase, goblet, wine, and small or large cake stand. It is also known as Stippled Fleur-de-lis and can be found in crystal, amber, blue, green, milk glass, and possibly ruby stain.

Frosted Fruit

Made by the Beatty-Brady Glass Company of Dunkirk, Indiana, in 1896 as a part of the National combine, this very attractive and well-executed pattern can be found in water sets, table sets, and berry sets. The design of basketweave and a series of fruits that include grapes, cherries, peaches, apples, etc., along with natural vines is a very appealing pattern. Pieces can be found either with a frosted finish or plain crystal. The factory designation for this pattern was #1/105.

Frosted Heron

Difficult to see since the pattern is entirely engraved, this Heron design is distinguished by the elongated pitcher spout, the squared handle that has a banding, and blossom design. The heron is posed with its head looking back over its body. No other pieces are known to us.

Frosted Leaf

Frosted Leaf is attributed to Boston and Sandwich Glass (1860) and then Portland Glass (1873 – 1874) in clear glass with machine ground frosted leaves. Some shapes were reproduced by Imperial in 1978 for the Smithsonian and are marked "S.I." Shapes in old glass include a celery vase, table set, champagne, open or covered compote, cordial, decanter (pint or quart), egg cup, goblet (lady's or gent's), oil lamp, water set, salt dips, sauce, and a wine.

Frosted Quail

The owner of this piece admits it may be part of the Frosted Pheasant line, but the birds are totally different and he thinks this is a quail (and we agree). It is possible the base on the piece shown is not correct. We understand a covered compote as well as a table set are known. All are rare.

Frosted Ring

Apparently this is another pattern from Boston Silver Company, dating to the 1870s and then made later by someone else. It seems to be a variant of the Beaded Mirror pattern, sometimes called Beaded Medallion. The finial of a well-done acorn is the same. The lid has rings of frosting, hence the name, and certainly other shapes exist.

Frosted Stork

Reported to have been made by Crystal Glass of Bridgeport, Ohio, in 1879, shards have also been found at Burlington of Canada. It is also called Flamingo or Frosted Crane. Shapes include berry set, finger bowls, ice bowl, oval bowl, table set, goblet, jam jar, pickle jar, water set, handled plate, oval platter (One-O-One border or Scenic border), relish tray, sauce, and a water tray. Shown is a stemmed celery vase. In addition, recent evidence suggests this pattern may have been also made at the Iowa City Flint Glass Works, especially items with the oval-and-bar border.

Frosted Quail

Frosted Leaf

Frosted Ring

Frosted Stork

Frosted Stork Platter

Fuchsia

Fruit Band

Garden of Eden

Galloway

Frosted Stork Platter

Like the companion ABC plate shown on page 283, this platter was made in two sizes. This one measures 12" x 8¼" and a larger water tray measures 15½" x 11". The design shows three storks amid tropical vegetation and varies from one size to the next. All pieces have a frosted center. It was from the Iowa City Flint Glass Company.

Fruit Band

Besides the small berry bowl shown, large berry bowl, and salt and pepper shakers, we haven't seen this pattern in other shapes. The design is a simple one, a band of various pieces of fruit, sometimes in a cluster, sometimes singly. Along the rim a border of piecrust rolls is the only other design.

Fuchsia

This pattern comes in clear glass only, as far as we know. Shapes include a table set, celery vase, cake stand, goblet, open compote, tumbler, 8" and 10" plates, and the mug shape shown.

Galloway

Galloway was from U. S. Glass as their #15086, and is also known as U. S. Mirror, Virginia, Woodrow, or Jefferson's #15601 (Jefferson also made this pattern in Canada in 1900 – 1925). U. S. production was 1904 – 1919. Found in clear with ruby stain or rose blush, shapes include a handled basket, water bottle, bowls in two shapes, table set, cake stands, celery vase, champagne, covered compotes, open compotes, cracker jar, cruet, custard cup, egg cup, goblet, mugs, casters, olive dish, pickle jar, milk pitcher, water set, salt dips, punch set shakers, syrup, toothpick holder, and water tray. It was made in many home, hotel, and individual pieces.

Garden of Eden

This pattern was made in the 1870s or early 1880s by an unknown firm (but may be Portland Glass) and is also known as Fish, Lotus, or Turtle. Shapes include a table set, cake stand, compote, egg cup, goblet (plain or serpent stem), honey dish, mug, pickle dish, water set, plate (Give Us This Day), round plate, relish (with or without handles), master salt, and sauce.

Garden Pink

Garden Pink was made at Indiana Glass in 1913 as their #167 pattern. Shapes include 4½", 5½", 7½" footed bowls, 9½" footed oval bowl, handled nappy, goblet, wine, jelly compote, water set, pickle dish, covered 8½" compote, cake stand (salver), and heart-shaped dish.

Garfield Drape

Also called Canadian Drape, this reported Adams and Company pattern is also suspected to be Canadian. Date of production may be 1881, following Garfield's death. Shapes include a berry set, table set, water set, milk pitcher, cake stand, covered compote (high and low), open compote, goblet in two sizes, honey dish, oil lamp, pickle dish, memorial bread plate, mourning plate, star center plate, and relish.

Garland of Roses

Reported in crystal, vaseline, chocolate glass, and opalescent glass, this pattern dates to the early 1900s and isn't often found. Shapes include a table set, celery vase, toothpick holder, footed bowl with flared rim, egg cup, and open footed salt dish.

Gem Star

Made by the West Virginia Glass Company in 1894, Gem Star can be found in an extended table service that includes a table set, water set, celery vase, berry set, and the cruet shown. The design is quite conservative as patterns go, and only the eight-pointed star with rays makes up any design there is.

German Band Cap

From Geo. Duncan & Sons, this novelty is 2⅜" across and 1¾" tall. It is found in crystal, blue, amber, and canary, but its intended use defies us. It hasn't been reproduced.

Garden Pink

Garland of Roses

Garfield Drape

German Band Cap

Gem Star

Gibson Cameo Plate

Gilded Lady Lamp

Gibson Girl

Girl with a Fan

Giraffe

Gibson Cameo Plate

This very nice plate was originally a goofus treatment. It measures 8½" in diameter and has the design on the exterior, showing the profile of the famous Gibson Girl while the rim is filled with scroll work. The maker is unknown, at least to us.

Gibson Girl

This was originally called Medallion and made by the National Glass Company in 1903. It is considered a rare pattern in all shapes which include a table set, water set, relish dish, 4" flat sauce, and 10" plate. No goblets or wines have been reported.

Gilded Lady Lamp

This lamp has a nicely done brass base with a detailed lady's head, titled to the right. It is similar to the figural based lamp some collectors call Jenny Lind. The font is a beautiful plain vaseline that has enameled flowers and leaves. We welcome further information about this lamp.

Giraffe

One of many novelty goblet patterns (maker is unknown) that are etched, this one is very popular with collectors and was part of a series dealing with African animals.

Girl with a Fan

This novelty goblet is one of several from the Bellaire Goblet Company of Findlay, Ohio. Production was around 1890 for this piece, and fragments have been unearthed at the factory site. The only color is clear.

Girl with Laden Apron

This fine pattern is attributed to Crystal Glass Company in 1880, but recent evidence points to Iowa City Flint Glass as the maker. The border of the plate has the same "one-hundred-one" sort of design as the Frosted Pheasant oval covered dish, so the maker must be the same. Any information on this piece would be appreciated.

Girl with Laden Apron

Globe and Star

Globe and Star

Probably from the 1890s, this pattern's shapes include a table set, covered compote, open compote (shown), cake stand, jelly compote, sauce, pickle dish, celery vase, goblet, and wine. It is found in crystal as well as amber, blue, and possibly other colors like canary.

Goat's Head

This rare pattern is attributed to Hobbs, Brockunier Glass Company in 1878 and found with frosting or completely clear. The only pieces we can confirm are a covered butter dish, creamer, spooner, half-gallon pitcher, oval bowl, covered compote, and sugar that can be either covered or open. The goat is found on the footed base extension as shown.

Goat's Head

Goddess of Hunt

Goddess of Hunt

This fine platter is actually part of the Psyche and Cupid line from Riverside Glass Works (1880). The treatment is called crystalography, first used by Washington Beck at Dithridge & Company. The piece is a handled rectangular tray with griffins and scroll on the sides and a center motif of the huntress with bow and arrows. It is also called Virginia Dare.

Golden Medallions

The owner of this superb water set believes it may be either from France or Belgium (I'd vote for France). It has a very un-American applied handle, and the shape is very different also. Besides the obvious gilding and the engraved grape-and-leaf patterns, there are the medallions with black enameling, gilt, and satin flowers. We'd like to hear from anyone with information on this pattern.

Golden Medallions

Golden Rule Plate

Gonterman Swirl

Goofus Grape

Gooseberry Variant

Goose Boy

Golden Rule Plate

With a center design like a feather fan and a row of ribbing, followed by the lettering: "DO UNTO OTHERS AS YOU WOULD HAVE THEM DO UNTO YOU," this nicely lettered piece would enhance any glass collection. The plate measures 9" in diameter and has a rolling beaded edge. The maker is unknown to us.

Gonterman Swirl

Called Adonis Swirl by its maker, Aetna Glass Company in 1888, this pattern and its companion patterns (Adonis Hobnail and Adonis Pineapple) are found in opalescent glass as well as the non-opal treatment shown with a frosted base. Tops are found in blue or amber and shapes include a berry set, table set, water set, cruet, celery vase, lamp shade, cologne bottle, finger bowl, toothpick holder (shown), and a shaker is suspected.

Goofus Grape

Somewhat like the Dugan/Diamond Grape Intaglio pattern, this one has doubled the vines, stems, leaves, and clusters of grapes so that they virtually cover every area of the bowl, with tendrils twining everywhere. We are confident that plates as well as the bowls are known and probably in more than one size. Any information on this pattern would be appreciated.

Gooseberry Variant

From the 1880s and found in clear, blue, milk glass, opaque blue, or opaque teal glass, this small mug (1⅞" tall and 1⅞" diameter) is very much in design like some of the Fenton berry patterns and may well have been the inspiration for them years later.

Goose Boy

Also called Boy with Goose (there is a similar compote showing a girl with goose), it is believed the maker of these pieces is the Portland Glass Company (1864 – 1873) of Portland, Maine. The stems and bases are frosted on the piece shown, but both boy and girl compotes are also found in clear.

Gordon

From the Burlington Glass Company of Canada (1875 – 1909), this well-done covered compote is known by this name to Canadian collectors. Other shapes probably exist. The design is mostly a series of bull's-eyes that ride on beading and the beading even extends in rows down the stem. Anyone have more information on this pattern?

Gothic Grape

Besides the very fine dresser set shown, we've seen this same pattern on a massive 9" vase shape. It was made in Europe in the early 1920s we believe, and here we show a spectacular perfume bottle, matching powder box, and a mirrored tray with glass grape and leaf handles. The leaves on all pieces are frosted while the grapes are clear.

Gothic Windows

Gothic Windows was made by Indiana Glass Company as their #166 in the 1920s in clear and gold trimmed glass. Shapes include a table set, water set, pickle dish, berry set, and both open and covered compotes.

Grand

Credited to both Bryce, Higbee in 1885 and Diamond Glass, Limited of Canada the same year, Grand can be found in clear or ruby stain and colors may exist. Shapes include a covered bowl (flat or footed), open footed bowls, table set, cake stand in two sizes, celery vase, covered or open compotes (high or low) in three sizes, cordial, decanter, goblet, mug, water set, plates, relish, and shakers.

Grape

While similar to another mug by King, Son & Company called Grapevine, this mug has a different handle and has no vines or leaves, only sparse clusters of grapes. Found only in clear glass, the Grape mug measures 2¾" tall and has a base diameter of 2".

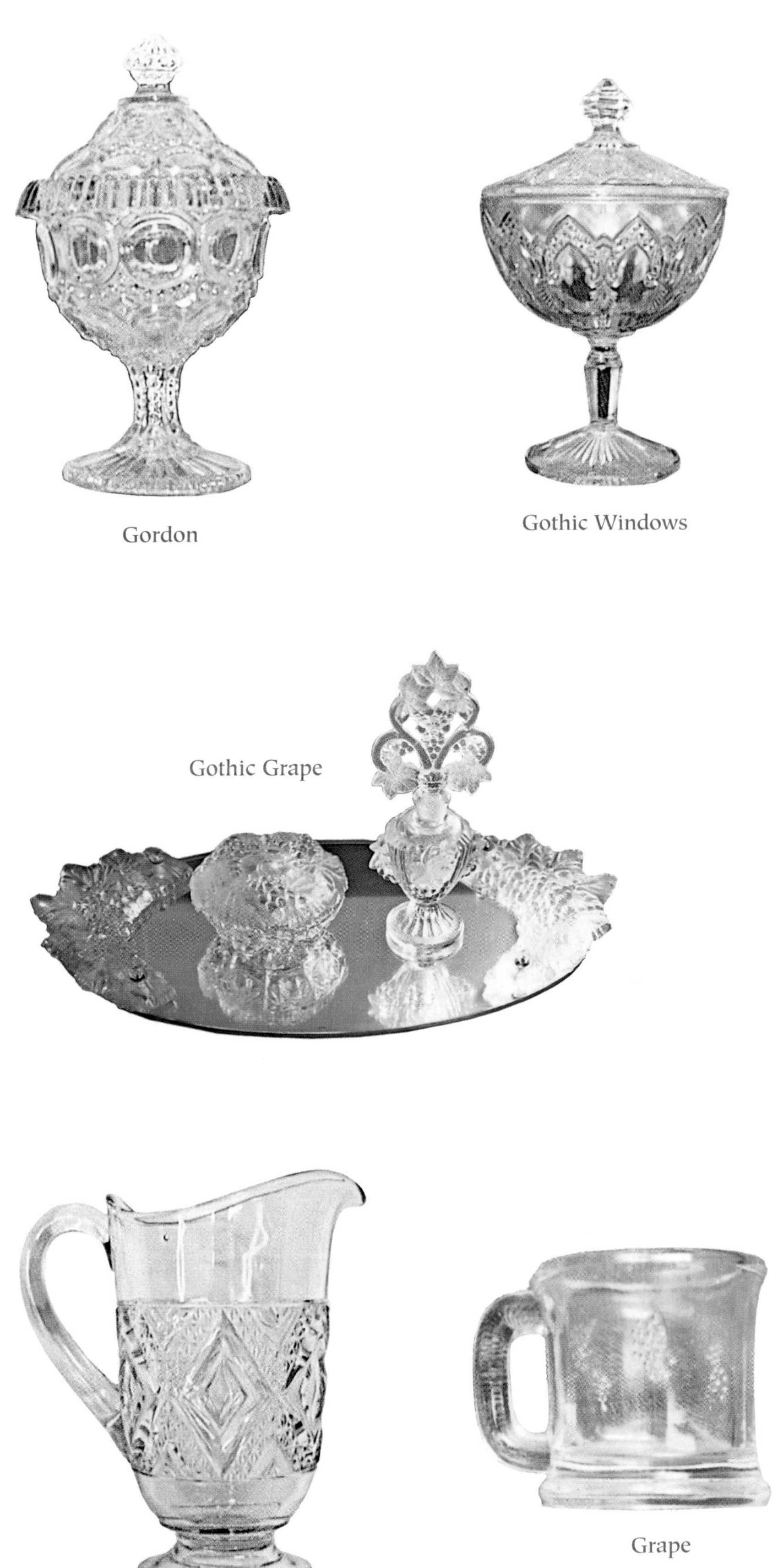

Gordon

Gothic Windows

Gothic Grape

Grand

Grape

Grape and Cable

Grape and Cable with Thumbprints

Grape and Festoon

Grape Band

Grape Bunch

Grape and Cable

Famous as a carnival glass pattern, this Northwood design can also be found in opalescent glass in a few shapes. In crystal, shapes known are the footed orange bowl, handled bonbon, plate, and covered sweetmeat on a stem. Pieces may be clear or decorated in gold and stain. Many pieces are marked, and all date to the 1905 – 1917 period of the factory's production. It has been reproduced.

Grape and Cable with Thumbprints

Usually lumped with Northwood's regular Grape and Cable, this variation with the added thumbprints on the base should be considered on its own. Shapes are found mostly in carnival glass and include a table set, water set (standard or tankard pitchers), covered cracker jar, berry set, whiskey set, tobacco jar, and whimsey hat shape. Recently a berry set in crystal surfaced and is the only one reported at this time. This pattern has been reproduced.

Grape and Festoon

First made by Boston & Sandwich Glass, then Doyle & Company, and finally U. S. Glass in 1891, this pattern is found with four variations (clear leaf, stippled leaf, veined leaf, or stippled grapes). Shapes include a 6" bowl, table set, celery vase, high or low covered compote, egg cup, goblet, 7½" lamp, pickle tray, milk pitcher, water pitcher, plate, relish tray, sauce, wine and master salt.

Grape Band

Grape Band was made by Bryce, Walker and Company around 1870 in clear crystal only. Shapes include a table set, compote, wine, egg cup, celery vase, cordial, goblet, 6" plate, master footed salt dip, pickle dish, high or low covered compotes, as well as a water set (pitcher on a pedestal base is shown).

Grape Bunch

We understand this pattern was made in the 1870s, either by Sandwich Glass or by Doyle and Company. Verified shapes are a wine, goblet, table set, water set, celery vase, and pickle dish. Shown is what we believe is the egg cup.

Grape on Crackle

Along with its companion vases showing roses or poppies on a crackle background, these 9" vases originally had a goofus treatment of gold, red, and green colors. They are advertised in Butler Brothers catalogs over many years, from 1906 to 1924, and were only part of the huge goofus invasion of the glass world during that time.

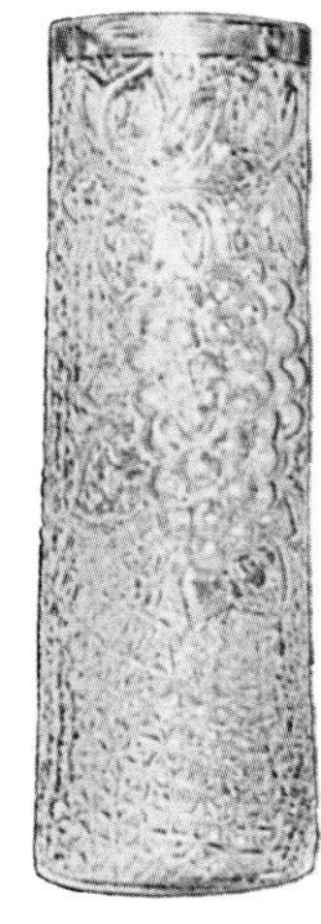
Grape on Crackle

Grapes with Overlapping Foliage

Grapes and Roses on Basketweave

Typical of many goofus glass vase patterns, this one is hourglass shaped. It has a cluster of grapes on the lower lattice and a rose above. This vase is 10" tall with an acid finish.

Grapes with Overlapping Foliage

This pattern was made by Hobbs, Brockunier primarily in opal (their porcelain treatment) but possibly in crystal, around 1870. Shapes include a celery vase, 4" nappy, 8" nappy, and a four-piece table set, as well as the pedestal-based water pitcher shown. Hobbs opal glass was a very dense milk glass that has a pinkish glow under ultraviolet light.

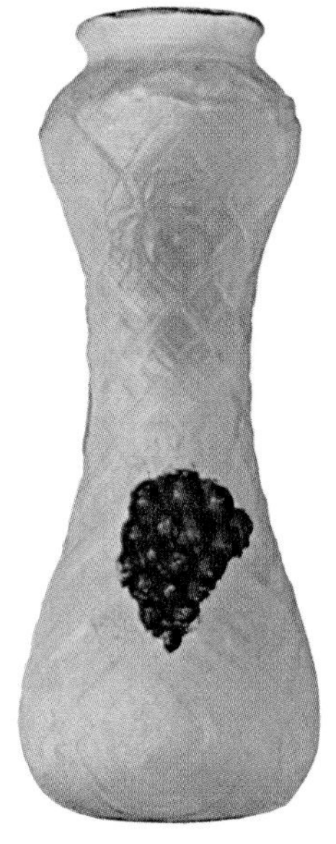
Grapes and Roses on Basketweave

Grapevine and Cherry Sprig

Grapevine and Cherry Sprig

Grapevine and Cherry Sprig was made by the Northwood Company in the early 1900s and found in a water set, square-footed bowl, and table set. Some pieces are etched, some with a goofus treatment. The design is very realistic and the quality of glass very fine. Pieces are scarce and desirable.

Grapevine Basket

This nice basket with a metal handle measures 8¾" long, 6¼" wide, and is 4¼" tall. It has a basketweave design with grapes, leaves, and grapevines on each side. We have no knowledge of the maker at this time.

Grapevine Basket

Grape without Vine

Grape with Thumbprint

Grape with Vine

Grasshopper with Insect

Grasshopper without Insect

Grape without Vine

Also known as Federal Grape, this was Federal Glass pattern #507. It can be found in a water set, table set, berry set, four sizes of covered compotes, four sizes of open compotes, four sizes of covered bowls, and four sizes of open utility bowls.

Grape with Thumbprint

Attributed to the Jenkins Glass Company after 1900, shapes include a table set, water set, toothpick holder, salt shaker, cup, covered compote, and bowls. It was made in crystal, milk glass, and possibly colored glass.

Grape with Vine

Found in clear, carnival, and goofus glass, this pattern is similar to the Jefferson Vintage bowl that is found in opalescent glass. Its shapes include a table set, covered compote, a plate, large and small bowls, sauce, honey dish, and a water set. The pattern dates to about 1900 and the maker hasn't been determined at this time.

Grasshopper with Insect

This pattern was made by Riverside in 1883 in clear, amber, blue, or vaseline glass. There are three variations: with insect, without insect, and with long spear. The example shown is with insect. Shapes include a covered bowl, open footed bowl (deep or shallow), table set, celery vase, covered compotes, jam jar, pickle dish, water set, footed 8", 9", and 10½" plates, salt dip, shakers, and flat or footed sauces.

Grasshopper without Insect

Also known as Locust or Long Spear (one of the variations) and just like the pattern shown elsewhere with the insect, this piece can be found in covered or open bowls, celery vase, table set, compotes, jam jar, pickle dish, pitcher, plates, shakers, salt dip, and flat or footed sauces.

Grated Diamond and Sunburst

As their #20, this George Duncan and Sons pattern can be found in a table set, salt shakers, punch set, toothpick holder, salt dip, water carafe, and several sizes of bowls. The pattern dates to 1895 and is often found with gold trim.

Greek Key and Scales

From the Northwood Company about 1906, this bowl pattern with a dome base was first made in opalescent glass, but is best known in carnival glass. In addition, as part of the extensive Northwood goofus line, this crystal treatment was made and probably predates the carnival treatment. In addition, there is a companion pattern called Greek Key and Ribs that can also be found in all three treatments.

Greentown Dolphin

One of the best known novelties from the Indiana Tumbler and Goblet Company of Greentown, Indiana, this animal piece is mostly known in chocolate glass but can also be found in Nile green, amber, cobalt blue, clear, emerald green, and the rare Golden Agate treatment. The dolphin's mouth may be sawtoothed, beaded, or smooth. It has been heavily reproduced.

Greentown Squirrel

We realize this pattern is usually just called Squirrel, but two other patterns are known by this name so we've made the addition. It was made by the Indiana Tumbler and Goblet Company (Greentown), only in a pitcher (can be flat or scalloped on the top), in crystal or chocolate glass.

Grogan

We've heard of only crystal examples reported in a table set, goblet, wine, and a celery vase (other shapes probably exist). This pattern's maker is unknown to us and we would certainly like to hear from anyone who has additional information.

Grated Diamond and Sunburst

Greek Key and Scales

Greentown Dolphin

Greentown Squirrel

Grogan

Grumpy Woman and Man

Hand

Hand and Torch

Hand Vase

Hanover

Grumpy Woman and Man

Also known as Captain Hook by some collectors, this toy mug (2" tall and 1⅞" in diameter) can be found in clear, frosted, or opaque blue and is reported in opalescent glass. Production dates to the 1880s we believe. Shown is the "old man" side.

Hand

From the O'Hara Glass Company (pattern #90) in 1880, finials on covered pieces are clinched hand holding a bar, while the primary designs are clear and diamond point panels. Shapes include bowls, table set, cake stand, celery vase, covered and open compotes, cordial, goblet, honey dish, jam jar, mug, pickle tray, water set, platter, syrup, water tray, and wine.

Hand and Torch

Attributed to Bakewell, Pears and Company of Pittsburgh, this open compote has the distinguishing hand and torch stem for which it was named. The bowl has been frosted and then engraved in a flower and leaf pattern, but it can also be found without engraving.

Hand Vase

Also called Cornucopia Vase by some collectors, these were shown in both the 1886 and 1890 company catalogs of George Duncan and Sons Glass. They were made in two sizes (at least), 7⅞" tall and 6" tall, and Fenton copied the larger size in the 1930s. Colors known are crystal, amber, canary, or blue, and some were made with etching on the hand.

Hanover

Also called Block with Stars, this was first a Richards and Hartley design in 1888 and then from U. S. Glass in 1891. Shapes include bowls, table set, cake stand, celery vase, cheese dish with cover, covered high or low compotes, cruet, goblet, mug in two sizes, water set, milk pitcher, plates, platter, puff box, sauce, and wine. Hanover is found in clear, amber, vaseline, or blue glass.

Harp Double Relish

Not the same pattern as the well-known Harp pattern by Bryce Brothers, this one is a very fancy scroll design with a center rolled handle of acanthus leaves. The maker is unknown to us, and we'd appreciate any information readers have about this pattern. It probably dates to the 1880s and is a beautiful double relish tray.

Harp Double Relish

Hartley

Also known as Daisy and Button with Oval Panels or Panelled Diamond Cut and Fan and made by Richards & Hartley in 1887 and then U. S. Glass in 1891, this well-known pattern is available in amber, blue, vaseline, clear, or etched clear. Shapes include a bread plate, table set, bowls in four sizes, cake plate, covered and open compotes, goblet, water set, milk pitcher, plate, relish tray, and wine.

Hartley

Hawaiian Lei

From Bryce, Higbee in 1913 (their #44629), this pattern was called Gala by the company. Shapes are many and include round or square plates, a table set, handled basket, sauce, cake stand, compote, one-handled nappy, rose bowl, twin relish dish, sherbet, tall jelly compote, oval pickle dish, vase, stemmed ice cream, wine, salver, claret, nut bowl, salad bowl, honey dish, goblet, celery tray, child's table set, water set (three sizes in pitchers), mayonnaise bowl, water stand, swing vase, and a handled toothpick holder.

Hawaiian Lei

Heart and Sand

Heart and Sand is also known as Vincent's Valentine and was made by New Martinsville Glass as their #724 pattern and found in clear, gold decorated, enameled, or ruby stained glass. Shapes include a table set, water set, berry set with 8", 7", and 4½" bowls, and toothpick holder.

Heart and Sand

Heart Band

Heart Band, from McKee Glass in 1897, can be found in crystal, ruby stained, green, and rarely carnival glass. Some pieces are gilded. Shapes include a table set, toothpick holder, shakers, celery vase, tumbler, and a mug. Often the ruby stained items were lettered as souvenir items.

Heart Band

Heart Plume

Heart Stem

Heart with Thumbprint

Heavy Finecut

Heavy Diamond

Heart Plume

Also known as Marlboro, this was U. S. Glass pattern #15105 from 1907. It was made in clear, rose flashed, and gold trimmed glass. Shapes include a table set, shakers, relish tray, water set, compote, pickle dish, syrup, and wine.

Heart Stem

The maker of this unusual pattern seems to be unknown but we are confident the design dates to the late 1880s or early 1890s. Shapes include a table set, celery with two handles, covered compote, goblet, salt shaker (rare), and handled sauce. Occasionally pieces of Heart Stem turn up with engraved designs.

Heart with Thumbprint

Sometimes called Tarentum's Hartford or Columbian, this Tarentum Glass Company pattern was made in 1898 in clear, ruby stain, emerald green, Nile green, cobalt blue, and custard. Many pieces were gold trimmed, and shapes include a banana boat in two sizes, barber bottle, cologne, berry set, table set, cake stand, carafe, card tray, celery vase, compote in two sizes, cruet, goblet, hair receiver, ice bucket, oil lamp, mustard jar, water set, plates, powder jar, punch set, rose bowls, syrups, condiment tray, vases, and wine.

Heavy Diamond

Shown in old Imperial Glass Company catalogs, this pattern is well known in carnival glass. Few collectors of crystal give it much consideration, but it is available in a beautiful pedestal vase, milk pitcher, creamer, sugar, compote, berry set, covered butter dish, and spooner. The diamond veining has a small diamond at each point of intersection, giving the pattern its unique look.

Heavy Finecut

This pattern was made by Geo. Duncan & Sons in 1883 and is found in crystal, canary, amber, and blue. Shapes include a molasses can, celery vase, celery boat, cheese plate and cover, cologne (five sizes), decanter, finger bowls (four variations), lamp, mustard, oil, bottle, pickle boat, pickle jar, water set, butter pat, plate (three sizes), salt, salver (three sizes), champagne, claret, cordial, goblet, wine, tray, and water bottle.

Heavy Jewel

Fostoria Glass made this pattern in 1900 in crystal only. Shapes reported are a table set, water set, and toothpick holder (rare). The sugar bowl may be open or with a lid. If anyone knows of other shapes in this pattern, we would appreciate hearing from them.

Heavy Leaf

The owner of this 9" bowl tells us this is the name of the pattern, but we have no knowledge of its maker or the date of production. We are confident there are other pieces, at least smaller bowls, but haven't seen them. We'd certainly like to hear from any reader who can tell us more about this pattern for it is a good one.

Heisey Pineapple and Fan

Like other Heisey patterns, this one is found in many shapes that include a table set, toothpick holder, custard cup, salt dip, shakers in two styles, oil bottle, molasses can, nut bowls, mug, hotel creamer and sugar, berry set, odd bowls, celery vase, nappy, pickle tray, celery tray, banana bowl, cheese plate, cake stand, salver, pickle jar, cracker jar in three sizes, compotes, and water set with five sizes of pitchers.

Heisey Pinwheel and Fan

Pinwheel and Fan was produced as Heisey's #350 pattern (there is a variant handled basket identified as #460). Shapes include a creamer, sugar, puff box, water set (with a three-pint pitcher), punch set, and 4", 5", and 8" bowls (called nappies by the maker). Colors are clear crystal and vaseline.

Heisey's #300 Colonial

#300 Colonial was first made by the Heisey Company in 1897. It was made in many shapes including a table set, water set (three sizes), berry set, milk pitcher, celery vase, breakfast set, cake stand, plate, syrup in three sizes, shakers (three styles), mustard jar, cruet (five sizes), honey dish, toothpick holder, punch set, goblet, cordial, wine, champagne, parfait, cocktail, sherbets, fruit bowls, compotes, nappy, loving cup with spoon, and oval trays.

Heavy Leaf

Heisey Pineapple and Fan

Heavy Jewel

Heisey's #300 Colonial

Heisey Pinwheel and Fan

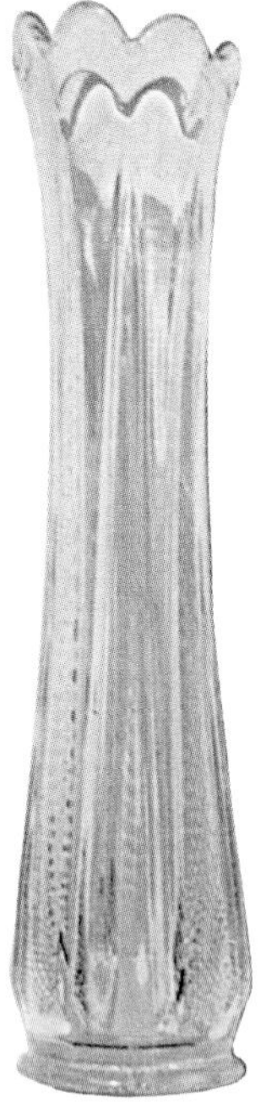
Heisey's #1250

Heisey's Old Sandwich

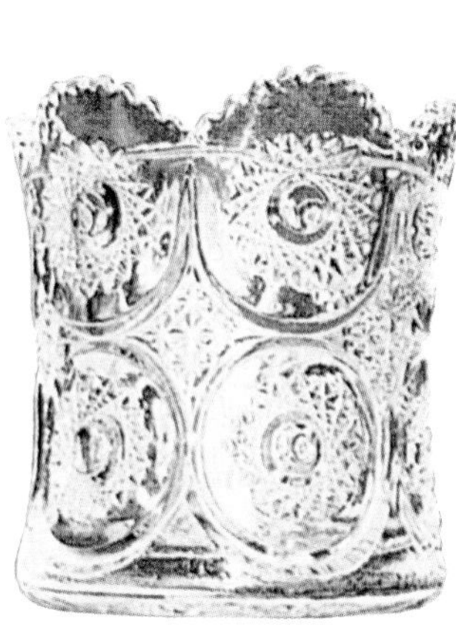
Heisey's Sunburst

Helmet Butter Dish

Henrietta

Heisey's #1250

This pattern is from 1897, and shapes include a table set, water set, shakers, bonbon, spoon tray, cruet, bowls, pickle jar, sauce, cracker jar, compotes, plates in two sizes, berry set, and the whimsey vase shown.

Heisey's Old Sandwich

Made at the very end of our timeframe, this Heisey pattern (their #1404) is found in crystal, amber, blue, pink, and green. Shapes include an ashtray, basket, mug (four sizes), oval or round bowls, candlesticks, catsup bottle, claret, champagne, 6" open compote, creamer (open or round, three sizes), cup and saucer, decanter, finger bowl, goblet, pitcher, ice pitcher, juice glass, cruet, parfait, pilsner, plate (three sizes), shakers, sherbet, sugar (round or oval), sundae, tumbler, and wine.

Heisey's Sunburst

Listed in catalogs as their #343 and produced from 1904 to 1920, this Heisey marked pattern has several variations from shape to shape, making it difficult to identify. Shapes include a table set, water set, berry set, shakers, pickle dish, cruet, milk pitcher, celery tray, celery vase, and wine. Pieces exceed 100 shapes in this pattern, with two types of creamers, pitchers, etc.

Helmet Butter Dish

Attributed to King, Son & Company of Pittsburgh, this novelty butter dish is a real collector's find and is considered a rarity. It was made in clear, amber, or blue glass, and we know of no matching pieces. Even damaged examples bring sizable prices, and perfect examples are very rare.

Henrietta

Henrietta was made by the Columbia Glass Company (#14) in 1889 and U. S. Glass in 1892 in clear, engraved, ruby stained, or emerald green. Shapes include a rectangular bowl, rose bowl, round bowls, table set, cake stand, caster set, celery vase or tray, compote, cracker jar, cruet, cup, bone dish, bonbon, olive dish, confection jar, lamp, mustard jar, pickle jar, bulbous or tankard water set, bread plate, breakfast creamer and sugar, salt dips, sauce, shades, syrup, and 5", 7", and 9" vases.

Hero

Hero is sometimes called Ruby Rosette and was made by the West Virginia Glass Company as their #700 in 1894. Shapes include a table set, shakers, cruet, berry set, mustard pot, celery vase, cake stand, goblet, oil lamp, hand lamp, and pickle jar.

Hero

Heron

We've learned very little about this pattern except its name and that it is believed to have been made in the 1880s. The design has the crystalography look about it, but we can't be sure. We'd appreciate any information available about this pattern from readers.

Heron

Heron and Peacock

From the late 1800s and similar to several other mugs, the Heron and Peacock mug is found in clear, blue, milk glass, opaque blue, and opalescent glass. It has been widely reproduced, first by Degenhart and then by others, so be sure of what you are buying.

Herringbone

Heron and Peacock

Herringbone

Dating to the early 1880s, Herringbone's maker isn't known to us. Shapes reported are a table set, stemmed celery vase, goblet, water set, flat sauce, wine, and open compote. The sugar bowl may be either open or with a lid. The design is a bit like one by the Cambridge Company called Inverted Feather.

Herringbone and Mums

Produced by the Jeannette Glass Company of Pennsylvania, this late pattern, made in 1928, is similar to the common Iris and Herringbone pattern. Herringbone and Mums, however, is scarce in crystal and only a rare tumbler is known in carnival glass. In crystal, we believe complete water sets were made, and possibly other shapes as well.

Herringbone and Mums

Hexagonal Block Band

Production of this pattern began about 1880, but the maker is unknown, at least to us. Shapes include a table set, water set, berry set, goblet, celery vase, pickle dish, and wine.

Hexagonal Block Band

Hexagonal Bull's-Eye

Hickman

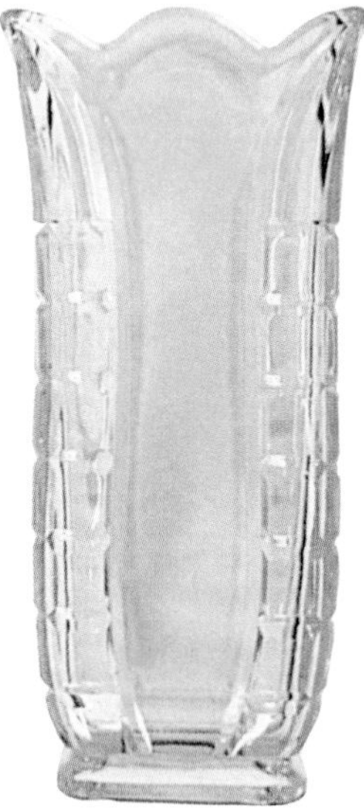

Hidalgo

Higbee Flute

Hinoto

Hexagonal Bull's-Eye

From Dalzell, Gilmore, and Leighton in 1890, this distinctive pattern is also known as Creased Hexagon Block or Double Red Block (when ruby stained). Shapes include a table set, celery vase, goblet, water set, sauce, and wine.

Hickman

Made by McKee and Brothers in 1897, Hickman can be found in bowls, jelly compote, three styles of salt shakers, sauce, toothpick holder, banana stand, pepper bottle, table set, celery, champagne, cologne, condiment set, cruet, covered and open compotes, punch set, toothpick holder, and many other shapes. It was made in clear, green, and two shades of amber.

Hidalgo

Also called Adams #5 or Frosted Waffle, this was first an Adams & Company pattern and then reissued in 1891 by U. S. Glass in clear, clear etched, clear with amber panels, or ruby stain. Shapes include a berry set, finger bowl, waste bowl, table set, high or low compotes in four sizes (covered), open compotes, cruet, cup, saucer, goblet, pickle dish, water set, milk pitcher, bread plate, master and individual salt dips, syrup, and water tray.

Higbee Flute

Marked Higbee, this Flute pattern is distinct by its wide, overhanging, arched top. It is found in a table set, goblet, wine, stemmed dessert, pickle dish, celery tray, and bowls.

Hinoto

Also known as Diamond Point with Panels and Banded Diamond Point, this Boston & Sandwich flint pattern was made in the late 1850s and into the 1860s, in clear and then in vaseline. Shapes include a celery vase, champagne, egg cup, goblet, master open salt, sweetmeat with cover, table set, tumbler (flat), whiskey tumbler (footed) that we show here, and a wine.

Hobbs Canoe

Found in two types (the one shown that sits and a hanging canoe), this is part of Hobbs #101 Daisy & Button line. It is found in Old Gold (amber), canary, clear, amberina, ruby, sapphire, or Marine green. Production dates to 1884.

Hobbs Canoe

Hobbs Hobnail

First made by Hobbs as their 323 pattern (and later by U.S. Glass after 1891 we understand), this pattern is found in crystal, Old Gold (amber), sapphire, green, canary, ruby rubina, ruby amber, ruby sapphire, ruby verde, canary opalescent, and many other opal treatments. Shapes include a bitters bottle, bowls (round or square) in three sizes, celery vase, pitchers (five sizes), syrup, cruet, pickle jar, table set, water tray, tumbler, water bottle, vase (two shapes), toy tumbler, and shakers. This pattern is also called Dew Drop.

Hobbs Hobnail

Hobbs Polka Dot

Hobbs Polka Dot was made in 1884 in crystal, Old Gold, sapphire, green, canary, cranberry, rubina, rubina verde, ruby amber, ruby sapphire, and opalescent colors. Shapes include pitchers (five sizes), covered cheese dish (shown), footed 8" bowl, cruet, water bottle, tumbler, sauce, deep sauce, oil bottle, celery vase, covered sugar (handled or without handles), champagne glass, a buttermilk tumbler, bar bottles, lemonade mug, shakers, custard cup, and a mustard pot.

Hobbs Polka Dot

Hobnail

This was made by many companies over many years in virtually every shape imaginable, but we do not intend to show all the variations here. The stemmed shakers shown are unique because of the ruby staining and the original tops. Some pieces are made in opalescent glass, some in carnival glass, some in colors, gold trimmed, or stained. Shapes include water sets, berry sets, lamps, table set, toothpick holders, goblets, trays, bone dishes, vases, and perfumes.

Hobnail

Hobnail Band

Hobnail-in-Square

Hobnail with Bars

Hobnail with Fan

Hobstar (Imperial's #282)

Hobnail Band

Dating to the early 1880s (maker is unknown at this time), this very recognizable pattern can be found in a table set, water set, sauce, plate, cup and saucer, coaster, celery tray, champagne, candlesticks, wine, goblet, custard cup, and syrup (shown).

Hobnail-in-Square

Made by the Aetna Glass and Mfg. Company in 1887, Hobnail-in-Square is best remembered for the opalescent pieces, but it was also made in crystal and colored glass. Crystal shapes reported are a water set, table set, celery vase, cake stand, and salt shakers. In recent years, this pattern has been reproduced by the Fenton Company in several treatments and is known as their Vesta pattern.

Hobnail with Bars

From the Brilliant Glass Works (1888) and then from U.S. Glass after 1891, this pattern is also known as Barred Hobnail or Winona. It is found in clear, vaseline, or opalescent glass and shapes include a table set, water set, sauce, goblet, shakers, and the stemmed cake stand shown. In addition, some items have been reported in an acid finish, and a mug is reported in clear and amber glass.

Hobnail with Fan

Hobnail and Fan was from Adams and Company as their #150 pattern in 1890 (Adams joined U. S. Glass in 1891). Shapes include a table set, water set, oblong dish, goblet, individual salt dip, sauce, tray, and wine.

Hobstar (Imperial's #282)

Hobstar was surely one of Imperial's most prominent patterns from 1909 in both crystal and carnival glass. The shapes are many and include 13" salver, rose bowls in 5½", 7", 9", plate in 5", 10½", fruit bowl, orange bowl, punch set, compotes in 10", 10½", 11", jelly compote, sherbet, sundae, wine, goblet, water set, water tray, syrup, milk jar with lid, celery vase, table set, cookie jar with lid, and large and small berry bowls that are round, crimped, or shallow. It has been reproduced.

Hobstar and Feather

Hobstar and Feather was one of the Millersburg Glass Company's best known carnival glass patterns, but a rather wide assortment was also made in crystal including a water set, table set, berry set, stemmed compote, stemmed rose bowl, squat mammoth pitcher, sherbet, plate (three sizes), pickle dish (three sizes), punch set, nut bowl, 11" master boat, lemonade set (rare), ice cream set, covered cracker jar, bridge set, banana boat (three sizes), applesauce boat, and a card tray. Both plain crystal and frosted as well as rare ruby stained pieces were made.

Hobstar and Tassel

This scarce pattern from the Imperial Glass Company is mostly seen in crystal, but a few rare items in carnival glass are known. The pattern dates to 1909. In crystal shapes include 7½" plate, 5" rose bowl, 5½" berry bowl, 7" crimped bowl, 7½" grape (ruffled) plate, 6½" ice cream bowl, 4" lily bowl, and 4" rose bowl. All items are from the same mould, and some crystal pieces have gilding.

Hobstar Band

Found in both crystal and carnival glass, this pattern's maker is undecided but many feel it may be U.S. Glass. Shapes known are a flat-based pitcher, a pedestal-based pitcher (sometimes with advertising), a tumbler that can be flared or straight, large bowls of various shapes, as well as a scarce handled celery vase.

Hobstar and Feather

Hobstar Band

Hobstar and Tassel

Hobstar Flower

Holland

Hollis

Holly

Holly Amber

Hobstar Flower

Illustrated in a 1909 Imperial catalog as their #404C, this 5½" compote is known to carnival glass collectors as Hobstar Flower. In crystal, besides the compote, there is a 10" shallow berry bowl, 11" orange bowl, 9" berry bowl, 10½" nut bowl, 13" fruit bowl, punch set, 9½" compote, 12" fruit bowl on a stand, and 9½" stemmed fruit bowl.

Holland

From McKee Glass in 1894 and also known as Oat Spray, this pattern's shapes include a table set, water set, berry set, open or covered compotes, pickle dish, toothpick holder, goblet, and stemmed wine.

Hollis

Found in a water set as well as the celery vase shown, this pattern was made in the early 1900s. The design is one of repeated diamonds and is similar to a pattern called Diamond Bar and Block. Probably other shapes exist, especially table pieces.

Holly

Shards of this pattern were found at Boston & Sandwich Glass Company and date of production is in the late 1860s and early 1870s. Shapes include covered bowls either flat or footed, table set, celery vase, cake stand, high or low covered compote, egg cup, goblet, pickle dish, water set, salt dip, sauce, syrup, and wine. Tumblers are either flat or footed.

Holly Amber

This famous pattern, created by the Indiana Tumbler and Goblet Company (Greentown), was made in clear (Holly Clear) and the treatment shown. Shapes include bowls, a table set, covered compotes, mugs, nappies, pickle tray, a water set, plates, shakers, syrup, and toothpick holders (shown). The pattern has been reproduced in several types of glass including carnival in the 1970s.

Honeycomb

Honeycomb and Hobstar

Honeycomb with Star

Honeycomb

Many companies including Bakewell, Pears made the Honeycomb pattern, but we haven't been able to verify the maker of the covered piece shown. Many shapes are known including table sets, bowls, compotes, celery vases, decanter, egg cup, vase, pickle dish, etc. Anyone who can pin down the piece we show here is asked to contact us.

Honeycomb and Hobstar

First made by Ohio Flint Glass in 1907 and called Gloria, this pattern is found in crystal and ruby stained glass (some with gilding). When Ohio Flint closed, the moulds went to Jefferson Glass (with the vase mould finding its way to Millersburg in 1909 where it was made in carnival glass). Shapes include a berry set, water set, table set, vase, water bottle, compote (two sizes), cruet, and several whimsied shapes.

Honeycomb with Star

Honeycomb with Star was made by Fostoria Glass in 1905. Shapes include a table set, water set, cake stand, sauce, compote, cruet, celery vase, pickle dish, and vase shape. The stars that are centered in some of the honeycomb sections are hard to see.

Horse

Horse and Cart

Horse, Cat, and Rabbit

Horsemint

Horse Inkwell

Horse

Apparently part of a series of early etched pieces (tumblers and goblets), this Horse pattern is found on the tumbler shape shown (on one side only) as well as on a goblet shape that is identical to that of other patterns that include Dog with Rabbit in its Mouth, Fern Circles, Dot Band with Cord and Tassel, and Forsythia Leaf. We believe these pieces all date to the 1870s but have no further information about them.

Horse and Cart

Credited to the Central Glass Company in the 1890s, this is another of those novelty pieces meant for either matches or toothpicks. This one has a horse and cart pulling a gigantic barrel with a tiny driver standing on one of the barrel staves.

Horse, Cat, and Rabbit

Goblets were an ideal shape for some of the whimsical patterns not found on other shapes, and this appears to be one of those. Just why the combination of a cat, a rabbit, and a horse, all on the same piece, is a mystery but this is a very collectible pattern for goblet collectors. It was made by Iowa City Flint Glass Company.

Horse Inkwell

The maker of this treasure is unknown to us, but it has to be one of the best items of its kind that we've seen. It is a double inkwell with a satin finished horse lying down between them. We'd appreciate any information readers can share on this piece.

Horsemint

After we showed this pattern in the first edition of this book, a reader was kind enough to write and point out that this pattern is from the Indiana Glass Company and was their #156 pattern made in crystal or ruby stained glass. Shapes include a table set, covered compote, goblet, heart-shaped bowl or nappy, pickle dish, footed vase, and a water set.

Horseshoe

Huber

Horseshoe Daisy

Horseshoe

Also known as Good Luck or Prayer Rug, this pattern was made by Adams and Company in 1881. Shapes include a table set, jam jar, plate, bowl, covered compote, wine (rare), sauce, platter, cake stand, celery vase, bread plate, master salt (rare), and relish. Covered pieces have a horseshoe finial.

Horseshoe Daisy

Known as their #717 in ads, this pattern was made by New Martinsville Glass. It can be found in several sizes of bowls, water set, and table set, and probably other items. Some items were decorated in gilding.

Huber

Also known as Falmouth, this is a product of Bakewell, Pears, produced 1870 – 1880s. Shapes include both low and tall covered compotes, celery vase, table set, water set, decanter, wine, goblet, three-pint jug, salt dip, egg cup (two varieties), bitters bottle, and stemmed champagne.

Hummingbird

Made in the 1880s, most researchers list this as "maker unknown." Hummingbird is also called Bird and Fern, Flying Robin, or Thunder Bird and was made in clear, amber, blue, or canary. Shapes include a waste bowl, table set, celery vase, open compote, goblet, water set, milk pitcher, flat or footed sauce, water tray, and wine.

Hummingbird

Hundred-Leaved Rose

Ibex

I-H-C

Illinois

Imperial Grape

Hundred-Leaved Rose

Also called Leaved Rose and made in the 1890s, this little-discussed pattern can be found in table sets, bowls, sauce, open and covered sugars, a water set (tumbler shown), and probably other shapes as well. It is known in both crystal and frosted crystal, but colors may exist.

Ibex

This is another of the etched goblets in the series of African wildlife. This one is very desirable and is considered quite rare by most collectors. Besides the Ibex, there are others that show a giraffe, an alligator, a lion, two tigers, two camels, two giraffes, an elephant, a leopard, and a monkey in a tree.

I-H-C

From the McKee Glass Company in 1894 and reported in crystal and green with gilding, this pattern's shapes include a table set, berry set, water set, compotes, sauce, pickle dish, celery vase, and the 7" bud vase shown.

Illinois

Also called Clarissa or Star of the East, this U. S. Glass design was their #15052 pattern made in 1898 in clear, emerald green, and with ruby stain. Shapes include a handled basket, bonbon, cruet, berry sets in round or square, finger bowl, table set, cake stand, candlesticks, celery tray and vase, cheese dish, jelly compote, olive dish, water jug, banquet lamp and shade, jam jar, pickle jar, water set (tankard or standard), plate, puff box, and straw holder.

Imperial Grape

Primarily a carnival glass pattern, this Imperial pattern is also found in milk glass, slag, crystal, and the beautiful teal crystal shown. Non-carnival shapes include a handled sandwich plate, decanter, stemmed wine, goblet, berry set, and a beautiful rose bowl.

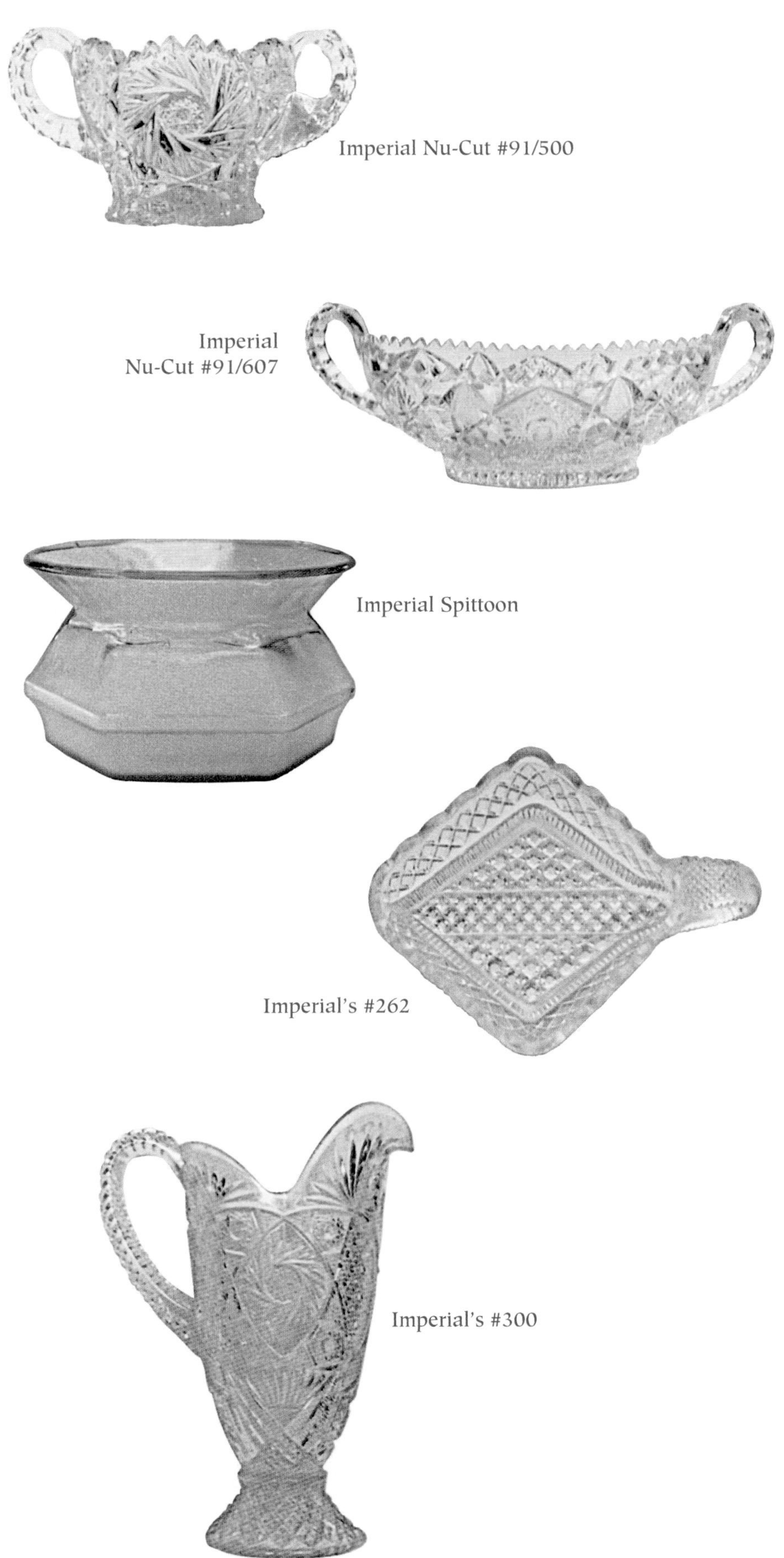
Imperial Nu-Cut #91/500

Imperial Nu-Cut #91/607

Imperial Spittoon

Imperial's #262

Imperial's #300

Imperial Nu-Cut #91/500

Much like other whirling star patterns, this Imperial one comes in a jelly compote, nappy, 6", 8", and 10¼" bowls, a 6½" vase, breakfast set (sugar and creamer), mayonnaise bowl, and plate (oval). It is sometimes gold trimmed.

Imperial Nu-Cut #91/607

Made in 1909 and shown in their catalog, this Imperial Glass pattern can be found in bowls of various sizes and the two-handled pickle dish shown. The design is mostly hobstars, separated by diamonds of file pattern.

Imperial Spittoon

Found mostly in carnival where it is called Hobnail Soda Gold, this man's spittoon by the Imperial Glass Company was also made in a pastel green glass as well as amber. Here is the crystal version which has the bumps or hobnails smoothed out, giving it a smooth appearance. These are scarce and quite collectible.

Imperial's #262

Shown in a 1909 Imperial Company catalog, this seems to be the only shape shown. It is a five-inch nappy the company calls an "olive nappy." It is a shallow, diamond-shaped piece with one knobby handle. Any additional information on this pattern would be appreciated.

Imperial's #300

We know very little about this pattern except that it was made by the Imperial Glass Company of Bellaire, Ohio, from 1905 to 1909. Shown is the 9" pitcher that, along with taller tumblers, was part of a lemonade set. There may well be other shapes in this pattern but as of now we haven't heard about them.

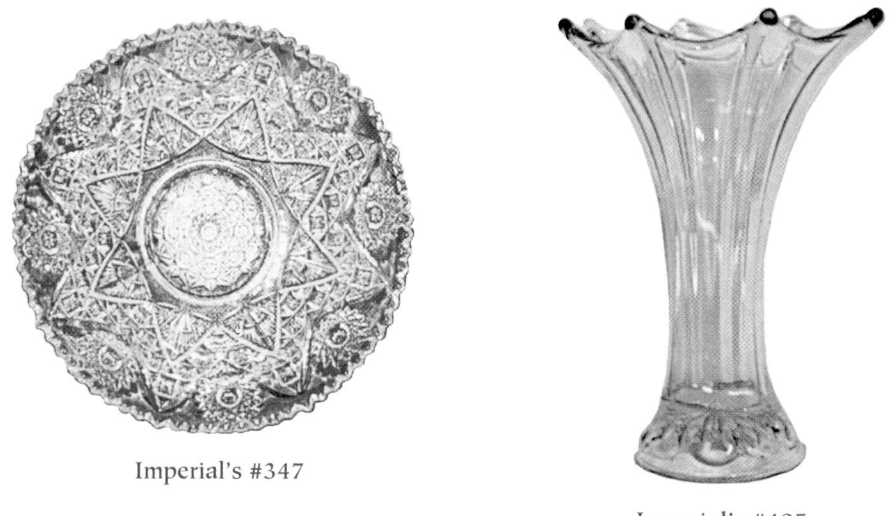

Imperial's #347

Imperial's #405

Imperial's #403½

Imperial's #737

Imperial's #750

Imperial's #347

Shown in the Imperial 1909 company catalog, this pattern is quite distinctive and very strong. It can be found on berry sets that are ruffled or flared as well as on ice cream sets. The glass is clear and sparkling and ranks among Imperial's best.

Imperials' #403½

Found in the 1909 Imperial catalog, this water set pattern has never been named (as far as we know). It is a very nice design with an applied rope handle and large icicles that seem to extend over a field of diamond cut. No other shapes are reported in either crystal or ruby stain or with gild.

Imperial's #405

Imperial made a series of vases in 1909 that were pretty much alike except for size and a few details in the base makeup. The example shown has a "star and thistle" design on the inside of the base. These vases came in 9" – 13" sizes and many were also used in carnival glass production.

Imperial's #737

Shown in Imperial assortments of various patterns once used in other types of glass such as carnival glass, this short stemmed 8½" bowl was called a salad bowl in the advertisement. It is typical of the company's geometric patterns that were designed to imitate cut glass, at a much lower cost.

Imperial's #750

Much like another pedestal bowl known as Fancy Flowers, also made by Imperial, this piece is considered a stemmed fruit bowl. The design is a good one with hobstars in ovals and swags that border sections of file. The glass is clear and sparkling.

Imperial's #3888

Shown in a 1909 factory catalog, this pattern can be found on a 7½" rose bowl (called a nut bowl in the catalog), 10" master bowl, 9" crimped berry bowl, and 4½" individual berry bowl. The primary design seems to resemble a maltese-like cross, separated by a hobstar in an oval.

Imperial's #4040

This outstanding geometric design was shown in the 1909 Imperial company catalog in two shapes only (the 9½" fruit bowl shown here and a 9½" compote from the same mould). The glass is very thick, measuring almost ¾", and weighing a hefty seven pounds. It has been reproduced.

Imperial's Basket

Like the Imperial Daisy Basket shown elsewhere, this novelty piece stands 10" tall to the top of the handle and was primarily a carnival glass pattern. It was also made in milk glass and clear glass. The pattern is a waffle-block type with a rope and fringe handle. Production began in 1914 and continued for several years.

Imperial's Bellaire (#0464)

Bellaire was shown in a late Imperial ad in a banquet size punch set (the bowl and base weigh 21 lbs!) and an 8½" deep salad bowl. The punch set is 15" tall and the bowl top measures 15" across. All pieces including the cups are marked "Nu-Cut." The design is unusual and combines raised diamonds, almond-like spears, a hobstar, and criss-cross sections.

Imperial's Pansy

Widely known in carnival glass and showing the exterior pattern which is called Scroll Embossed, this 1908 Imperial Glass pattern is a realistic one. Crystal pieces are a bit scarce but still bring less than their iridized counterparts.

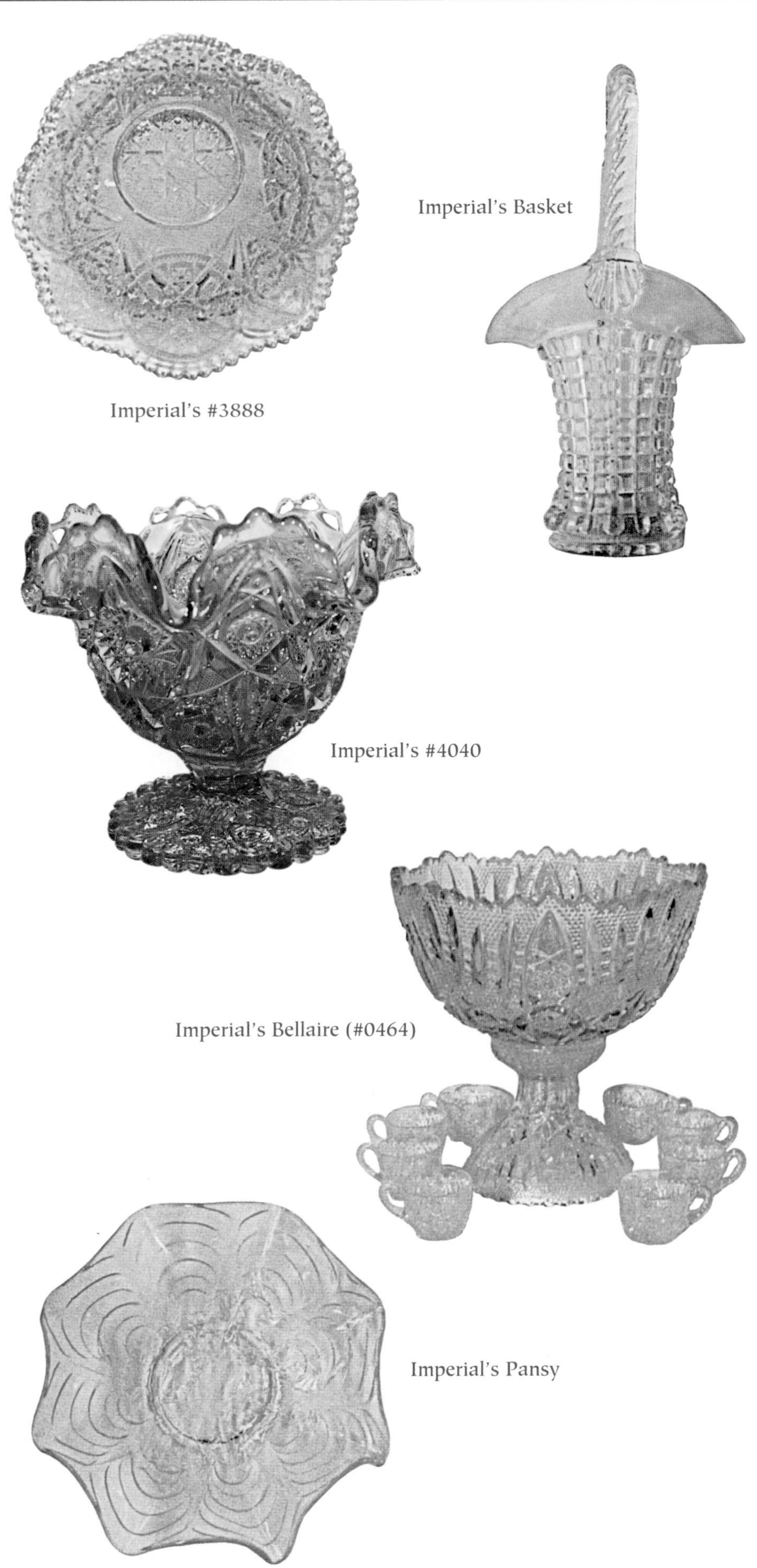

Imperial's Basket

Imperial's #3888

Imperial's #4040

Imperial's Bellaire (#0464)

Imperial's Pansy

Imperial's Wicker Basket (#428½)

Imperial's Thunderbolt

Indiana's #115

Indian Sunset

Indiana

Imperial's Thunderbolt

Advertised as Imperial's #4047 in 1909, this 13" bouquet vase is a fine example of the geometric pedestal vases being turned out by the company in Bellaire, Ohio. Imperial probably made more pedestal vases than anyone, and most of the designs are good ones.

Imperial's Wicker Basket (#428½)

Shown in a 1909 Imperial Glass Company catalog as their #428½ pattern, only the handled basket that held matching salt and pepper shakers seems to have been made. Finding the complete set is difficult but even the basket alone is worth owning.

Indian Sunset

Dating to 1905, this geometric pattern is quite similar to several others. Shapes include a table set, water set, berry set, celery tray, bonbon, salt shakers, and pickle dish. Some examples may be gold trimmed.

Indiana

Indiana was produced as U. S. Glass pattern #15029, in 1897, and found in clear, and rare ruby stained glass. Shapes include a perfume, carafe, catsup bottle, finger bowl, table set, celery tray, bowls in five sizes, celery vase, cruet, compote, oval bowl in three sizes, nappy, jelly dish, water set, shakers, sauce, syrup, oblong tray, and ice tub.

Indiana's #115

Made by the Indiana Glass Company of Dunkirk, Indiana, about 1915, this often-seen pattern can be found in the basic pieces: a table set, berry set, and water set. The most identifiable portion of the design would be the two plain almond ovals at each side of the whirling star circle.

Indiana's #123

This 1890s pattern by the Indiana Glass Company very closely resembles an Imperial pattern known as Octagon. Shapes of #123 include a table set, celery vase, cruet, covered compotes, 12" plate, celery tray, jelly compote, cake stands, goblet, wine, pitchers, tumbler, berry set, punch sets, covered compotes, toy table sets, water sets, and punch sets. Some collectors call this pattern Panelled Daisies and Finecut.

Indiana's #123

Indiana's #156

Indiana's #156

This is another Indiana Glass pattern from 1913. Shapes include a table set, water set, celery tray, pickle dish, goblet, nappy, 6½" vase, footed banana bowl, footed salad set, footed nut bowl, heart-shaped dish, 12" plate, cabarette bowl, jelly compote, 8" compote, and covered compotes in 6½" and 7½" sizes. Each piece has the X-file banding.

Indiana's #165

This was made by the Indiana Glass Company of Dunkirk, Indiana, in the early 1900s. Shapes include a table set, breakfast set, water set (three pitcher sizes), salts (two sizes), celery, olive, pickle dish, celery dish, berry set (two sizes), vase, footed jelly, footed sauce, handled compote, open compote (three sizes), syrup, berry creamer and sugar, water bottle, and several sizes in utility creamers and sugars.

Indiana's #165

Indiana Silver

From the Indiana Glass Company in Dunkirk, Indiana, about 1918, this is a silver overlay pattern. Shapes include a table set, berry set, goblet, sherbet, and footed rose bowl. The design has a modern look that fit into the Art Deco design of the time.

Innovation #407

This was another part of the McKee Innovation line (there were numbers 407, 408, 410, 411, 414, 415, 417, and others) that featured pressed patterns with wheel-cut flowers. Here is a 10" cylinder vase with a star band, but this same design came in a compote, bonbon, footed rose bowl, creamer and open sugar, nappy, celery tray, 8" bowl, fernery, basket, and a lamp with matching shade.

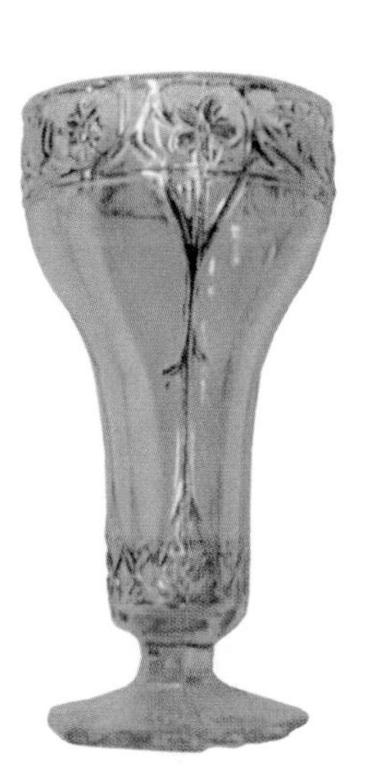

Indiana Silver

Innovation #407

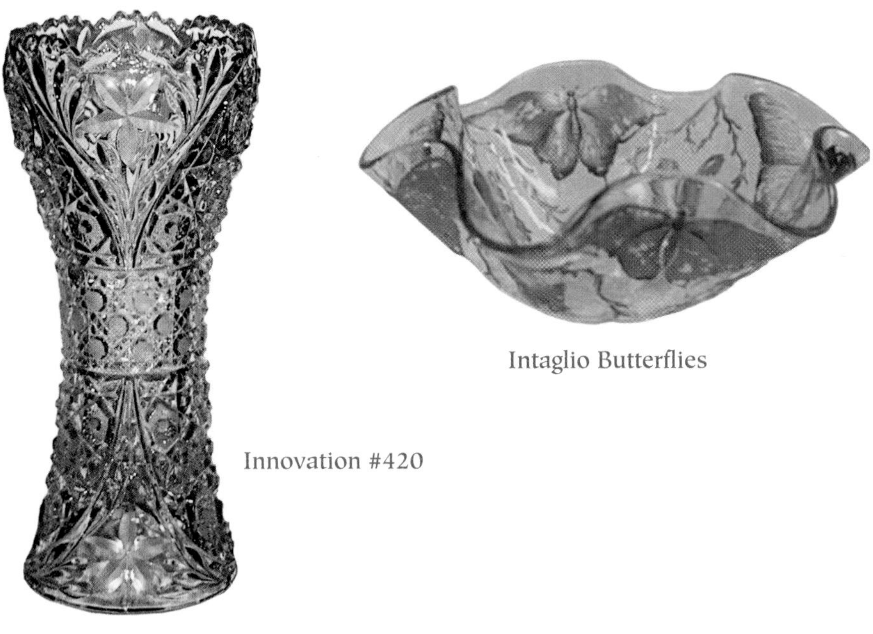

Intaglio Butterflies

Innovation #420

Inside Ribbing

Intaglio Sunflower

Inverted Eye

Innovation #420

This was one of the many patterns in a line McKee called Innovation that was made in 1917. Shapes include a creamer and open sugar, an 8" bowl, a stemmed trumpet vase, a 12" corset vase (shown), a 10" three-footed salad bowl, celery tray, 10" oval salad bowl, and a large stemmed compote with separate footed stand. All items are pressed with a wheel-cut flower in the design.

Inside Ribbing

Also called Pressed Optic, this is a Beaumont Glass pattern from 1900. It can be found in opalescent glass as well as clear, vaseline, emerald green, or blue glass. Pieces may be plain or decorated with enameling as shown. Shapes include a table set, berry set, celery vase, syrup, cruet, pickle dish, and a toothpick holder. This was Beaumont's #101 pattern.

Intaglio Butterflies

Made by the Dugan/Diamond Company beginning in 1905, this line was made for the goofus process and had many bowls, compotes, and sauces showing fruits, flowers, and butterflies. The patterns are exterior, intaglio ones, and only the designs were painted, unlike most goofus treatments.

Intaglio Sunflower

This was U. S. Glass pattern #15125, made in 1911 in clear and decorated crystal. Shapes include a table set, water set, toothpick holder, and tall straw holder with a lid. Has anyone seen this pattern in emerald green glass?

Inverted Eye

From National Glass Company in 1902, this was their #519 pattern. Shapes include a table set with either flat or pedestal base and a toothpick holder. We would be interested in hearing about other shapes in this pattern.

Inverted Feather

Made by Cambridge as their #2651, this pattern is found in carnival glass as well as crystal. Crystal pieces are known in punch sets, tall wine decanter, goblets, whiskey tumbler, covered cracker jar, footed sherbet, tall footed sherbet, and oil bottle. Not all shapes are made in carnival glass and most are considered rare.

Inverted Fern

Possibly made by Boston and Sandwich Glass (no proof is known) in the 1860s, this pattern is a well-known design. Shapes include a table set, egg cup, sauces, champagne, open compote, goblet, honey dish, 6" plate, water set, master salt dip, and a wine.

Inverted Peacock

From the Cambridge Glass Company in the early 1900s, this beautiful pattern was well advertised for several years in Butler Brothers catalogs with a matching tray, and there was also a similar fish set. The design combines both incised floral sprays and a well-designed peacock on a branch. Tumblers are just as impressive. It is Cambridge's #2837 pattern.

Inverted Strawberry

Inverted Strawberry was from Cambridge Glass in 1908 and can be found in carnival glass, clear, colors, and decorated glass. Shapes include a table set, toy table set, candlesticks, compote, footed creamer and sugar, footed bonbon, jelly compote, oil bottle, water set, wine, goblet, celery vase, berry set, custard cup, squat basket, stemmed sweet pea vase, rose bowl, covered powder jar, and footed fruit bowl. It has been reproduced.

Inverted Feather

Inverted Peacock

Inverted Fern

Inverted Strawberry

Inverted Thumbprint and Star

I.O.U.

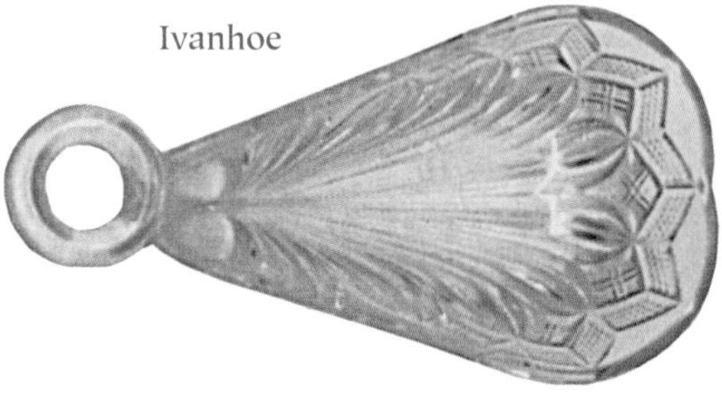

Ivanhoe

Iowa

Iverna

Inverted Thumbprint and Star

The maker of this pattern seems to be unknown, but the goblet is found in clear, canary, amber, blue, or apple green. The photo doesn't really show the design to its best advantage, but there is a star between each of the inverted thumbprints.

I.O.U.

From the West Virginia Glass Company (their #219 pattern) and dating to 1898, this pattern is scarce and very desirable. It was made in a complete table service that includes a table set, water set, berry set, celery vase, and pickle dish. Shown is the tumbler in vaseline, but crystal or emerald green is also known.

Iowa

Iowa was made by U.S. Glass (their #15069) as part of their States series, and is found in crystal and rose flashed as well as gilded. Shapes include a table set, water set, berry set, celery vase, pickle dish, goblet, cake stand, compote, and the wine shown which has gilding on the ribs.

Ivanhoe

From Dalzell, Gilmore, and Leighton in 1897, this pattern is often confused with Amboy (we did). Shapes include a table set, cake salver, celery vase, cracker jar, creamer, cup, jelly compote, nappy, 10" plate, relish, sauce, syrup, toothpick holder, spoon tray (shown), and a water set.

Iverna

Credited to Ripley in 1911 as their #303 (and later by Paden City), this pattern was also made by Imperial Glass after 1915, and since pieces are known with the "Krys-tol" mark some pieces had to be made by either Ohio Flint Glass or Jefferson Glass! Shapes include a berry set, table set, compote, footed fruit bowl, punch set, biscuit jar, vase, handled sherbet, pickle dish, celery tray, spoon tray, and handled jelly.

Jabot

We actually have very little knowledge about this pattern except on reference that is vague. We know it was made in table sets and water sets since we've seen pieces of each, but the maker escapes us at this time. We're sure it was made before 1910, however, and may even be earlier.

Jacob's Ladder

Jacob's Ladder was from Bryce, McKee & Company, then U. S. Glass in 1891, and then Diamond Glass of Canada (U. S. Glass #4778) and is also known as Imperial. Made in clear, amber, blue, canary, green, pink, and rarely, carnival glass. Shapes include a cologne bottle, caster set, covered or open bowls, celery vase, covered or open compotes, cruet, goblet, honey dish, jam jar, mug, water set, 6" plate, platter, relish dish, master salt, sauces, syrup, wine, and rose bowl.

Japanese

Japanese was made by George Duncan & Sons in 1880 and is known by several other names including Butterfly and Fan and Japanese Fan. Shapes include a bowl, table set, celery vase, covered or open compotes, goblet, pickle jar with lid, plate, water pitcher, and flat or footed sauce. Finials on Japanese pieces are square with a half-sphere on the top.

Japanese Iris

Another glass design that is primarily a goofus production item, this very regal and realistic iris can be found on a 7" pickle tray as shown as well as a 10" vase and a 6½" vase. Like many goofus designated patterns, the mould work is quite good, and the vase could certainly stand on its own merits.

Jefferson's Winged Scroll

This Jefferson version with three feather-like additions at the top of the design is very much like the Heisey #1280 pattern called Winged Scroll. Shown is a fancy perfume with a stopper that is part of a dresser set that also included a puff box and a hair receiver that was advertised in 1915. Jefferson pieces are usually marked "Krys-tol" and are known in ruby stain, custard, and clear.

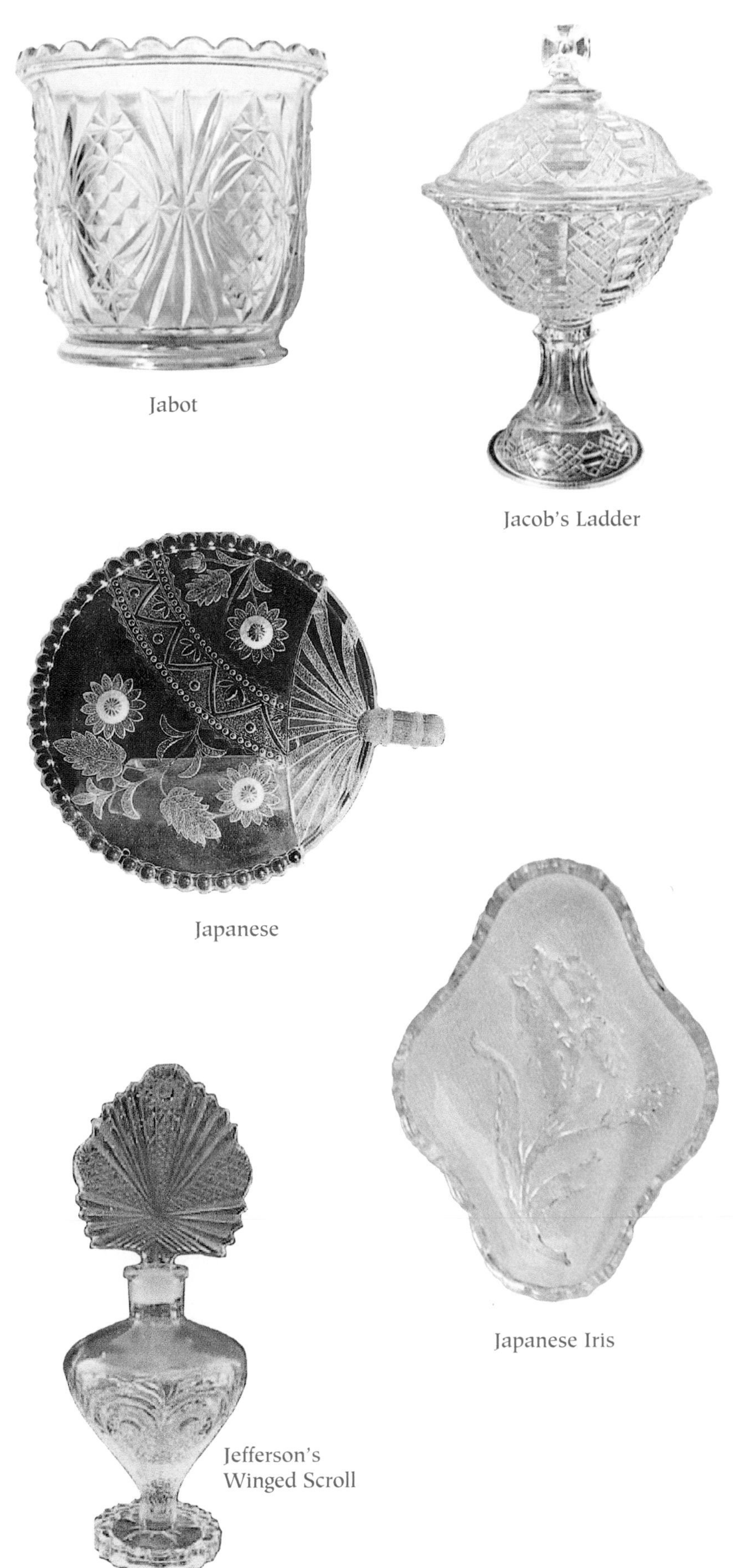

Jabot

Jacob's Ladder

Japanese

Japanese Iris

Jefferson's Winged Scroll

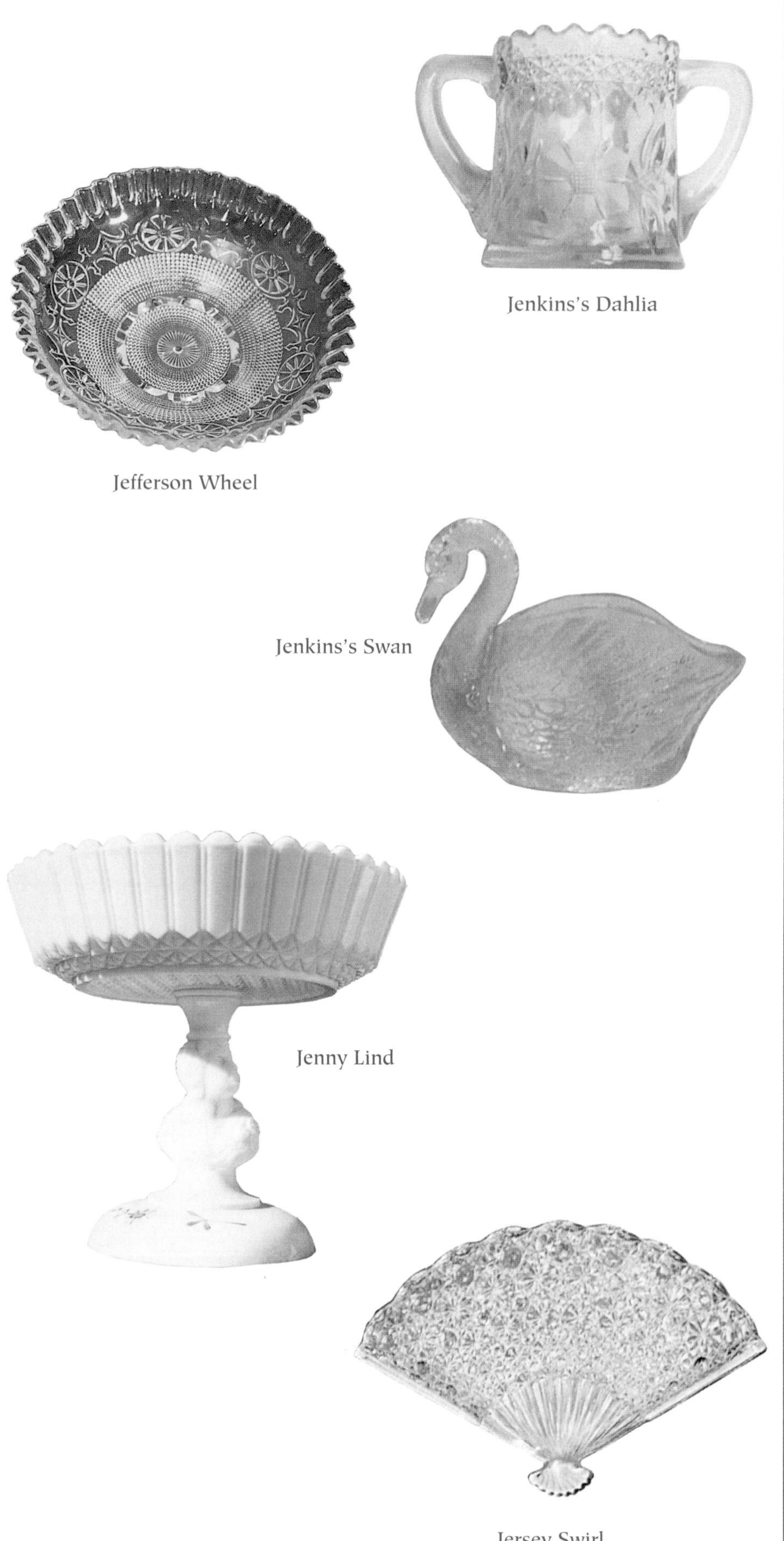
Jenkins's Dahlia

Jefferson Wheel

Jenkins's Swan

Jenny Lind

Jersey Swirl

Jefferson Wheel

Found primarily in opalescent glass, this Jefferson Glass pattern was their #260 design, made in 1905. As you can see, it was also made in crystal and has been reported in carnival glass for years without a single example known to date (we await proof).

Jenkins's Dahlia

This was made by the Jenkins Glass Company, a concern well-known for combinations of geometric and engraved pieces. This one called their Dahlia cutting is found in a table set, compote, and vase (other shapes are possible).

Jenkins's Swan

Just about every glass company had a try at these open Swan pieces. This one was from the Jenkins Glass Company in 1915. It was their #460 and advertised as a 12 oz. Swan dish. Many of these swan pieces were used to hold salt, relish, jelly, or even sugar, but the intended use of this one isn't known.

Jenny Lind

Numerous articles have been made to honor this singer, and the compote shown is one. It was made by Challinor and Taylor and is shown in the opal glass treatment with enameled flowers on the base. Others were made in crystal, frosted crystal, and in colors by various makers. Most date from the late 1880s to the 1890s.

Jersey Swirl

Also known as Windsor Swirl, Swirl and Diamonds, or Windsor, this pattern originated at the Windsor Glass Company in 1887, in clear, amber, blue, and canary glass. It has been widely reproduced in the 1960s and 1970s. Shapes in old glass include bowls, table set, cake stand, candlesticks, covered and open compotes, cruet, cup, dresser tray (fan shape), goblet, jam jar, pickle caster, water set, plates, syrup, and wine.

Jeweled Butterflies

From Indiana Glass of Dunkirk, Indiana, this was the factory's Mikado pattern, also known as Late Butterfly. Shapes include a table set, berry sugar and creamer, water set, handled nappy, cruet, shakers, and 5", 6", 7", and 8" bowls. We believe this pattern dates to 1907 or shortly after, and certainly other shapes may have been made.

Jeweled Heart

Dugan/Diamond produced this pattern for many years in carnival glass, opalescent glass, and crystal where the shapes are bowls, 9" rose bowl, salt shakers, berry set, cruet set (cruet, shakers, tray, and toothpick holder), water set, table set, syrup, and plate. Jewelled Heart is found in aqua glass, goofus, and gold decorated also, and can even be found with enamel work. It has been reproduced.

Jeweled Loop

Made in 1909 as their #261, this Imperial pattern can be found in a table set, celery vase, water set, goblet, jelly compote (low), 8" compote, berry set, pickle dish, and 11" celery tray. Some pieces have gold trim.

Jewel with Dewdrop

This was made by Cooperative Flint Glass and then reissued by U. S. Glass in 1907 as a States pattern called Kansas. Jewel with Dewdrop can be found in a berry set, table set, toothpick holder, wine, cake stand, celery vase, bread plate, covered compote, goblet, covered jelly jar, nappy, shakers, syrup, and preserve dish (oval). In addition, U. S. Glass added a small mug, and some of their production was color stained glass.

Jeweled Butterflies

Jeweled Heart

Jeweled Loop

Jewel with Dewdrop

Johnson Child's Mug

Jubilee

Jumbo

Kaleidoscope

Kayak

Johnson Child's Mug

This pattern is also called Dart and Ball, and we believe it may be a product of the King Glass Company but can't be sure. It is found in toy pieces that include a table set, mug, and goblet. Colors are clear (rare), cobalt, opal, and milk glass. The mug shown is named for the owner's family.

Jubilee

Jubilee, also known as Isis or Radiant Daisy and Button, was made by McKee Glass in 1894 in clear or ruby stained. Shapes include a table set, celery tray, high or low compotes, oblong 8" dish, goblet, pickle dish, water set, 9" plate, and wine.

Jumbo

Jumbo is attributed to Aetna Glass & Manufacturing Company of Bellaire, Ohio, and the Canton Glass Company of Canton, Ohio, in 1884 and can be found in clear, acid finish, amber, blue, or canary (colors are very rare). Shapes include a table set, covered compotes in 7", 8" 10", and 12" sizes, sauce dish, water pitcher, and the famous spoon rack. The three-bottle caster set, goblet, and elephant toothpick holder are not original to this set. The compote shown does not have the original base.

Kaleidoscope

Kaleidoscope can be found on marigold carnival bowls and in crystal on bowls, rose bowls, and water sets. The overall design is really a series of rings of pattern, none of which is all that distinctive, but taken together are pleasant enough. The maker is unknown to us, so any information about this pattern would be appreciated.

Kayak

From Imperial Glass, this unusual pattern is known in water sets, compotes, berry set, cake stand, and tray. The primary design is a divided oval that is then sectioned with diamonds of file and hobstar between the groups of oval.

Keg

What an imaginative design this is on this lamp. Like many other oil lamps we've seen, this one seems to have no previous identification, so we've taken the liberty of naming it. If anyone can give us information on this piece, we'd appreciate their input.

Kentucky

Kentucky was from U. S. Glass (their #15051) in 1897, and is found in clear or emerald green glass. The clear can be amber or ruby stained, and in rare instances, cobalt blue. Kentucky was retooled from the Millard pattern. Shapes include bowls, table set, cake stand (two sizes), celery tray (two sizes), celery vase, covered compotes (four sizes), open compote (four sizes), goblet, olive dish, water set, cruet, plates, shakers, sauces, syrup, toothpick holder, and wine.

Keyhole

More familiar to carnival glass collectors, this Dugan/Diamond pattern can also be found in opalescent glass, goofus, and crystal, like the bowl shown. The only shapes are large dome-based bowls that may be round, ruffled, or shaped like a banana bowl. Keyhole is an exterior pattern and in carnival glass has an interior design called Raindrops.

King's Block

Originally this was King's Glass pattern #312 and it continued as U. S. Glass design in 1891, in crystal or vaseline glass. Shapes include a table set, cruet, oval bowls, pickle tray, goblet, and wine.

King's Crown

This very familiar pattern is also called Excelsior or Ruby Thumbprint, and came from U. S. Glass (Adams factory) in 1891. Many shapes are known, including a table set, pickle caster, fruit basket, footed orange bowl, toothpick holder, square honey dish, cup and saucer, mustard jar, and individual salt dip. King's Crown is found in plain crystal, amber stained crystal, or ruby stained crystal. It has been reproduced.

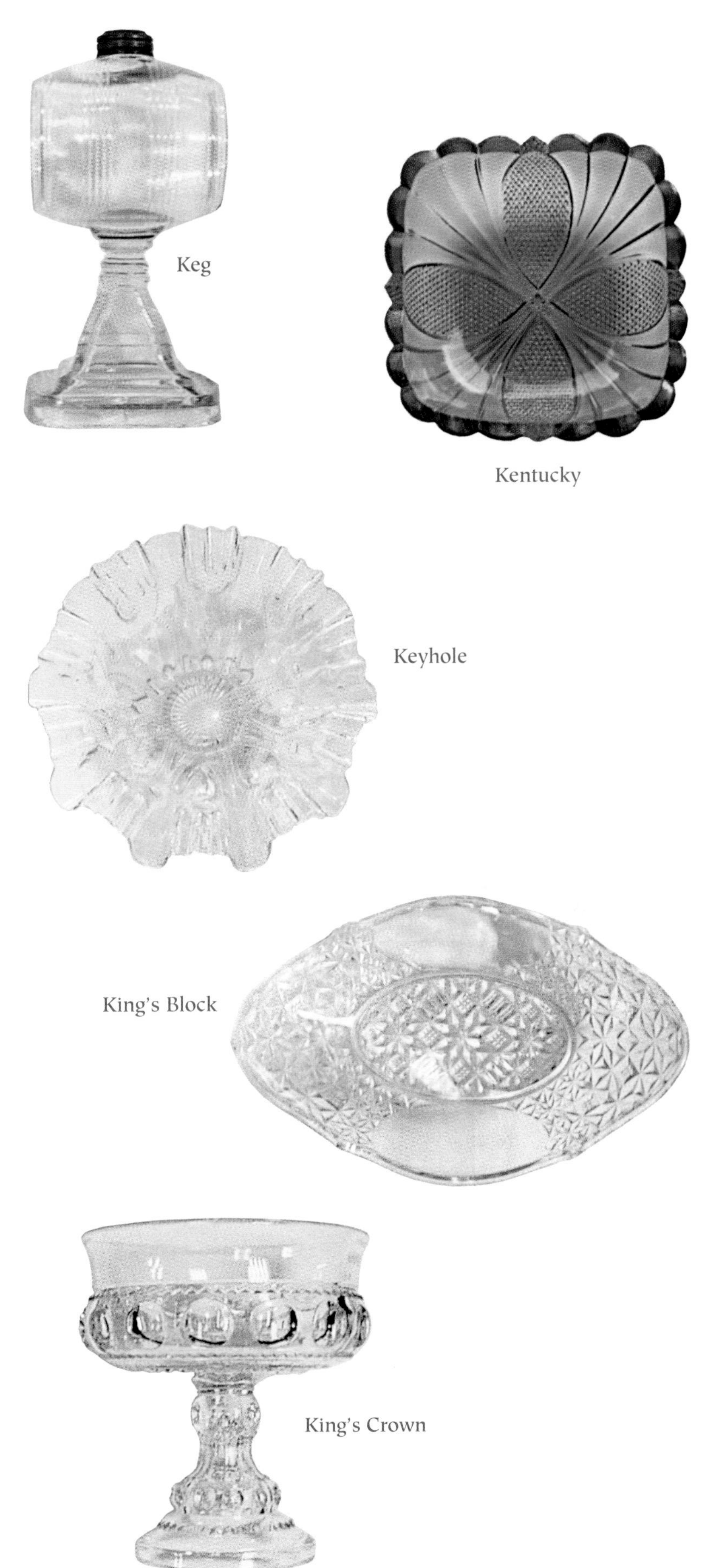

Keg

Kentucky

Keyhole

King's Block

King's Crown

King's Curtain

Klear-Kut #705

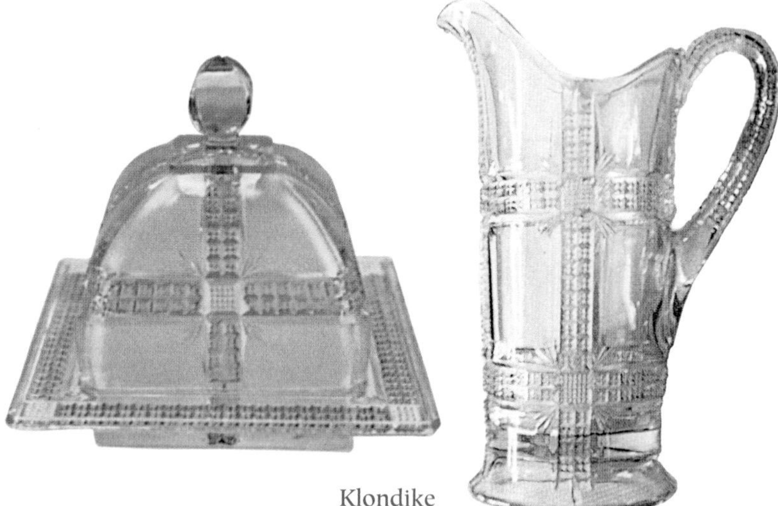

Klondike

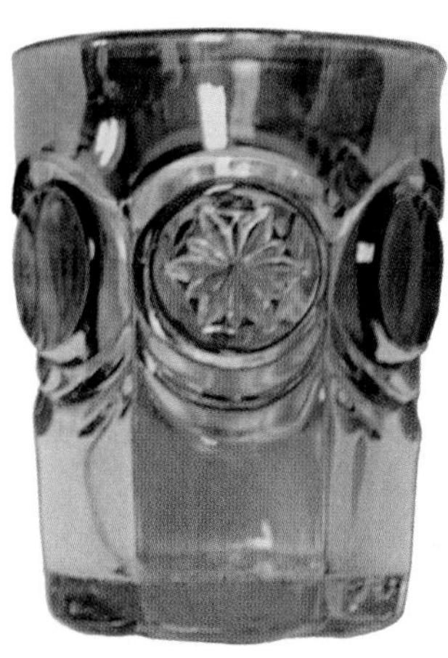

Knobby Bull's-Eye

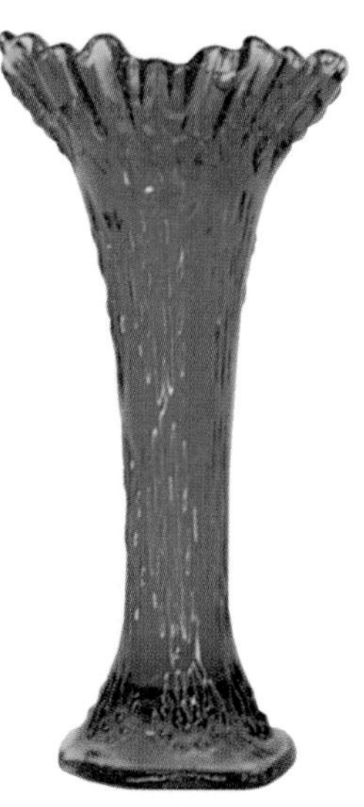

Knotted Beads

King's Curtain

Dating to the 1880s, the maker of this splendid pattern is unknown at this time. Shapes include a table set, water set, goblet, 7" plate, shakers, sauce, wine, cake stand, and bowl.

Klear-Kut #705

Made by the New Martinsville Glass Company and introduced as their Klear-Kut pattern in 1906, this design is found on a water set as well as a table set. Some pieces were given a gold-trimmed treatment.

Klondike

From Dalzell, Gilmore & Leighton in 1898, this pattern has many names which include Amberette, English Hobnail Cross, and Dalzell #75. It can be found in clear, clear with acid finish, and amber stain. Shapes include square bowls, table set, cake stand, champagne, oblong celery tray, condiment set, cruet, cup, goblet, water set (round or square pitcher), relish tray, shakers, syrup, toothpick holder, tray, wine, and vase in four sizes.

Knobby Bull's-Eye

Also known as Cromwell, this was a U. S. Glass pattern advertised as their #15155, made in 1915. Available in an extended table service that includes a table set, toothpick holder, berry set, two types of salt shaker, celery tray, wine, decanter, and stemmed compote. Both plain crystal and decorated crystal are known.

Knotted Beads

Made by Fenton Glass in 1911 and primarily a carnival glass vase pattern, Knotted Beads is sometimes found in crystal, and here we show an extremely rare red example with amberina edges and base. Red carnival pieces are also known. These vases range in size from 9" to 14" tall.

Kokomo

Made by Jenkins Glass as their #400 line in the 1920s, the ordinary pattern is like many others that rely on allover diamonds. Shapes reported in a Jenkins ad are a table set, water set, berry set, covered casserole, jam jar, jelly compote, nappy, covered compote, and pickle dish.

Krys-tol Colonial

This was first made by Ohio Flint Glass in 1906 as part of their Krys-tol line (Kenneth, Gloria, Chippendale). When the company closed in 1907, the moulds went to Jefferson and then in 1909 some were purchased by John Fenton for the Millersburg plant. The punch bowl shown became the exterior for Millersburg's famous Big Thistle punch bowl in carnival glass. In addition, Ohio Flint made other Colonial lines, including their famous 1776 Colonial.

La Belle Rose

Primarily a goofus pattern from 1910, this is a sister pattern of the Carnation design. It can be found on large plates, large bowls, and smaller bowls as well as a smaller saucer-size plate.

Lacy Daisy

Lacy Daisy was made by U. S. Glass in 1918 and is also known as Daisy. Shapes include a table set, jam jar, jelly compote, cruet, rose bowl, cake plate, puff box, service plates, three-legged bowls, individual salt, and toy table set. Rare staining of ruby or amber are reported.

Lacy Dewdrop

This is a Cooperative Flint Glass Company pattern dating to 1890 that is found in crystal, milk glass, and scarce iridized items. Shapes include a table set, berry set, mug, water set, sauce, covered berry set, and open or covered compotes.

Kokomo

Krys-tol Colonial

La Belle Rose

Lacy Daisy

Lacy Dewdrop

Lacy Medallion

Lacy Roman Rosette

Ladders

Ladder with Diamonds

Lacy Medallion

Also known as Jewel and very similar to the Colorado pattern, Lacy Medallion has no feet and is lettered. Date of production by U.S. Glass is 1905 according to McCain, and it is found in crystal, cobalt blue, ruby stain, green, clambroth, and a rare vaseline shown. Shapes include a mug, salt shaker, toothpick holder, wine, and a toy table set. The toothpick holder has been reproduced.

Lacy Roman Rosette

Sometimes called Early Roman Rosette, this pattern, known in clear and colors that include amber and blue, is from the lacy period of pressed glass and dates to just before the Civil War. Shapes are limited to a plate, honey dish, and bowl shape as far as we know, but certainly a table set may exist, as well as shakers, goblets, candlesticks, or covered pieces.

Ladders

From Tarentum Glass Company, this was their #292 pattern made in 1901. Shapes include a table set, water set, vase, celery vase, berry set, cup, and cruet. Pieces are often gold trimmed.

Ladder with Diamonds

Also called Fine Cut and Ribbed Bars, this was Duncan and Miller's #52 pattern made in 1901. Shapes include a table set, water set, celery vase, berry set, cruet, cup, goblet, 9¼" plate, toothpick holder, shakers, and vase. Some pieces are gold trimmed like the creamer shown.

Lady with Fan

Shown is a stemmed celery that was advertised with this name. It may well be a part of a pattern known as Girl with a Fan that was made by Bellaire Glass Company in 1886 in a goblet, but we can't be sure. Any information on this pattern would be appreciated.

Lady with Fan

Lamb

Credited to the Iowa City Flint Glass Works and made about 1881, the shape matches other mugs from that company. Found in clear, blue, turquoise, and the amethyst shown. It stands 3" tall and has a 2¾" diameter.

Lamb

Lantern

This candy holder is found in at least two sizes and was a favorite of children. Like many other pieces designed to hold candy, some pieces have been reproduced. Major manufacturers of the original pieces include Westmoreland, Victory Glass, J.H. Millstein, L.E. Smith, J.C. Crosetti, Eagle Glass, and Play Toy. Even Cambridge had a try at a few pieces. Lantern pieces are all thought to be old.

Lantern

The Last Supper Plate

Based on Leonardo da Vinci's famous painting, this popular plate with grape borders was from both Model Flint and the Indiana Glass Company where it was in production until 1960, a production period of nearly 50 years. It is 11" long x 7" wide. Old examples are easy to spot because of their clarity and the quality of the glass. It has been reproduced.

The Last Supper Plate

Late Honeycomb

We haven't been able to learn the maker of this pattern, seen in water sets and berry sets, but from the shape of the water pitcher, it is certain this pattern came along after 1915. The quality of the glass is good, however, and pieces are worth owning.

Late Honeycomb

Late Tomato Vine

Lattice and Daisy

Lattice

Lattice and Notches

Lattice-Edge

Late Tomato Vine

This water set is obviously late in the production of pressed crystal and may be from the Jeannette Company, but we have no documentation of this. The shape is much like other pieces from that factory. The design, however, is a nice one with the fruit, leaves, and vine covering much of the allotted space.

Lattice

Lattice is also called Diamond Bar and was made by King and Son in 1880 and then U. S. Glass in 1891. It is found in a table set, plate, platter, cake stand, celery vase, egg cup, water set, sauce, wine, cordial, salt shaker, and covered compote.

Lattice and Daisy

From the Dugan Glass Company in opalescent glass and then by the Diamond Glass Company (Dugan's successor) in carnival colors, here we show a previously unreported crystal tumbler. Perhaps there is a matching pitcher since it is known in carnival colors, but if so, we haven't heard of it. We are grateful to the Sandemans for sharing this find with us.

Lattice and Notches

Also known as Lattice and Lens, this pattern can be found in a table set, berry set, and goblet. Other shapes may certainly be available but haven't been reported to us at this time. The pattern dates to 1880 and the maker isn't known. Both plain crystal and gilded glass are known.

Lattice-Edge

Lattice-Edge was shown in U. S. Glass Company ads in several sizes and with some design variations, in crystal and milk glass. The only additional information under the picture of the piece we show was the lettering "OW," and we haven't any idea what it means. Date of production was probably in the early 1900s. Opal colors were white or turquoise, according to the ad.

Lattice Medallion with Buds

A variant of the regular Northwood pattern that is found on opalescent pieces, this crystal treatment (often with goofus) has added buds on the lattice work and omits the starburst design inside the medallions. Production must date to the 1908 – 1909 period.

Lattice Thumbprint

This has been attributed to the Central Glass Company as their #791, but beyond that we've been able to learn almost nothing about this pattern. Shapes are said to include both covered or open compotes, but surely other shapes exist. On the covered compote shown, there is gold trim on the finial. Anyone with information on this pattern is urged to contact us. Covered bowls are also reported.

Laverne

Also known as Star in Honeycomb, this Bryce Brothers pattern dates to the late 1880s. Shapes include oval or round bowls, table set, cake stand, celery vase, both covered or open compotes, goblet, pickle tray, water set, relish dish, flat or footed sauce, and wine.

Leaf and Dart

Credited to Richards and Hartley in 1875 and U.S. Glass in the 1890s, this pattern is a good one. Shapes include a table set, footed bowl, celery vase, covered or open compotes, cruet, egg cup, goblet, honey dish, finger lamp, milk pitcher, water set, relish tray, master salt, sauce, syrup, and a wine.

Leaf and Rib

The maker of this nice pattern is unknown at this time. Pieces are found in clear, amber, blue, and canary and shapes include a berry set, table set, water set, shakers, celery vase, and a pickle dish.

Lattice Medallion with Buds

Lattice Thumbprint

Laverne

Leaf and Rib

Leaf and Dart

Leaf and Star

Leaf Bracket

Leaf Mould (Northwood)

Leafy Scroll

Lenox

Leaf and Star

From New Martinsville Glass as their #711, this pattern is also known as Tobin. It dates to 1910 and is found in clear, ruby stained, and has been listed in rare carnival glass (I'm skeptical). Shapes include a banana boat, berry set, fruit bowl, nut bowl, celery vase and tray, jelly compote, cruet, dresser jar, goblet, hair receiver, humidor, plate, water set, toothpick holder, vase, and wine.

Leaf Bracket

Leaf Bracket was made by the Indiana Tumbler and Goblet Company (Greentown) in 1900 in crystal, opalescent, Nile green, or chocolate glass. Shapes include a table set, cruet, berry set, celery tray, shakers, toothpick holder, water set, and tri-cornered bowl.

Leaf Mould (Northwood)

Leaf Mould was made in 1891 as their #333 line and can be found in many treatments that include Spatter; Royal Silver; Opal Cased Spatter; satin finishes in lime, canary, red, white, and blue; opaque finishes in turquoise; special spatter treatments in Yellowine or Tortoise Shell. Shapes include a berry set, table set, water set, fairy lamp, toothpick holder, celery vase, sugar shaker, salt shaker, syrup, and cruet. The name refers to the mould pattern, not the design. Shown is a sugar shaker in Royal Silver, a cased treatment with silver and red spatter.

Leafy Scroll

Made by U. S. Glass, this was their #15034 pattern. Shapes include a table set, berry set, water set, goblet, wine, and toothpick holder. The company ad says "One of Our 1896 Patterns," so we know this is the date of original production.

Lenox

From McKee Glass in 1898 and apparently found in opal as well as crystal (the tankard pitcher shown has a touch of opal on the handle and a fine silver lip), Lenox shapes include a table set, water set, berry set, toothpick holder, breakfast set, mug, cruet, jelly compote, and individual salt dip.

Liberty

This pattern which is also known as Cornucopia by some collectors, was made by McKee & Brothers in 1892 and then by Cambridge Glass in 1903. Shapes include a berry set, table set, water set, water tray, goblet, wine (shown), champagne, and cordial. Some pieces are gilded.

Lighthouse and Sailboat

Lighthouse and Sailboat can be found in three sizes (2½" tall, 3⅛" tall, and 3⅝" tall) and in clear, amber, or blue. It has the same handle formation and shape as the Dutch Mill mug, but there are other differences. A lighthouse on one side and a sailboat on the other are ringed by a floral wreath.

Liberty

Lighthouse and Sailboat

Lily of the Valley

Lily of the Valley was made by Boston & Sandwich Glass (1870s) and King & Son (1870s), in crystal (shards found at Burlington Glass of Canada) and produced in two variations (hexagon base or with legs). Shapes include a berry set, table set, cake stand, celery tray, celery vase, covered or open compotes, a rare cordial, cruet, oval dish, egg cup, goblet, honey dish, pickle scoop, milk pitcher, water pitcher, relish, master salt (covered or open), tumbler (flat or footed), and a rare wine.

Lincoln Drape

This pattern was made by the Boston & Sandwich Company in 1865 – 1880, in clear, cobalt blue, opaque white (milk glass), or opaque green. The pattern is also known as Oval and Lincoln Drape and is found as we show it or with a tassel. Shapes include a table set, celery vase, covered or open compotes (two sizes), decanter, egg cup, goblets in two sizes, honey dish, oil lamp, water set, master salt, syrup, and wine.

Lincoln Drape

Lily of the Valley

Lindburgh

From Imperial Glass in the 1920s, this pattern is shown in one of their ads under this name. Shapes in crystal are a water set, berry set, table set, cake plate, 7" rose bowl, and low stemmed compotes in 7" and 8½" sizes. The ad says Lindburgh was made in crystal, pink, and green glass, indicating it was geared to compete in the Depression glass era.

Lindburgh

Lined Heart

Lion and Baboon

Lion and Cable

Lion and Baboon Lamp

Lion and Honeycomb

Lined Heart

Made in 1906 by the Jefferson Glass Company, this vase pattern was primarily an opalescent one, but examples in blue, green, or clear are known without the opalescence. Vases range in size from 7" to 14" tall.

Lion and Baboon

From the early 1880s (the maker is unknown), this unique pattern of slightly convex vertical panels becomes very distinguished with the addition of lion's head finials and baboon feet! All shapes are rare and include a table set, celery vase, oil lamp, milk pitcher, water pitcher, and reported toy table set.

Lion and Baboon Lamp

Not the same pattern as the Lion and Baboon shown above, this lamp came along a few years later we feel but was still made by the early 1900s. It can be found with at least two font designs and certainly may have been made in other colors but we have no evidence of this. We'd like to hear from readers about this piece.

Lion and Cable

Frequently called Tiny Lion and made by Richards & Hartley (pattern line #525) in the 1880s, this pattern is found in clear or acid finished. Shapes include a table set, celery vase, covered high or low compotes in three sizes, a goblet, jam jar, water set, milk pitcher, bread plate, shakers, and a sauce. All handled pieces have sprawled lions on them. It has been reproduced.

Lion and Honeycomb

We believe this fine covered compote with the sprawled lion finial may be English in origin but have no proof. The rest of the design is a fine incised honeycombing over the lid and the bowl, and the stem is prismed. We welcome any information on this pattern from readers.

Lion Head

Lion Head was possibly a pattern from Gillinder & Sons in 1877. Some stem variations are known between this pattern and Lion and a look-alike master salt is not original to these pieces. Shapes include a table set, toy table set, covered compote in four sizes, jam jar, and sauces in three sizes. It has been reproduced.

Little Fishes

This was the #1607 pattern from the Fenton Glass Company in 1915. It is well known to carnival glass collectors where it is found in small and large footed bowls and a plate shape. It is rare in crystal and found in 5½" footed bowls as shown and in the 10" size in either flat or footed bowls. No crystal plate has been reported at this time.

Little Owl

Little Owl was made by Bryce, Higbee as part of set called Menagerie that included a fish spooner, a bear sugar, a turtle butter, and the owl creamer shown. Pieces were made in clear, amber, or blue. The owl creamer shown stands 3¾" tall. The pitcher also shows evidence of having gold trim at one time.

Little Samuel

This piece showing the Little Samuel base is, of course, part of Hobbs, Brockunier's Tree of Life line. This line can be found in a number of glass treatments including clear, frosted, and on compotes (shown), epergnes, and as stems for lamps and candlesticks. The figure dates to 1877 and is a boy kneeling and praying with a Bible in hand. In some cases the foot of the piece is opal (opaque) or black.

Locket-on-Chain

A.H. Heisey's #160 pattern, also known as Stippled Beaded Shield, was made from 1896 to 1912. It is found in either crystal or ruby stain. The shapes include a berry set, table set, water set, cruet (rare), wine, toothpick holder (rare), and a pickle dish.

Lion Head

Little Fishes

Little Owl

Little Samuel

Locket-on-Chain

Loganberry and Grape

Log Cabin

The Lone Fisherman

Long Buttress

Long Fan with Acanthus Leaf

Loganberry and Grape

Loganberry and Grape was made by Dalzell, Gilmore & Leighton in the 1880s and is also known as Blackberry and Grape or Raspberry and Grape. Shapes include a table set, water set (from the same mould as Cherry and Fig), celery vase, and two styles of goblets.

Log Cabin

This was Central Glass Company's pattern #748 made in 1875. Shapes include covered bowls in two sizes, table set, covered compote, jam jar with lid, and flat rectangular sauce. Found primarily in clear, it was also made in amber, blue, and vaseline, but all colors are rare. It has been reproduced.

The Lone Fisherman

This covered cheese dish is part of the Actress line made by Adams and Company. The lid shows a scene from the play *The Lone Fisherman* and a scene from Shakespeare's *Comedy of Errors* with twin Dromios (gnomes). The base is frosted.

Long Buttress

Long Buttress was made by the Fostoria Company in 1904 as their #1229. Shapes include a table set, toothpick holder, shakers, salt dip, celery vase, pickle dish, syrup, pickle jar, various sizes in vases, water set, oblong pin tray, pomade, and individual creamer and sugar. Long Buttress is often mistaken for a similar pattern called Portland as well as New Martinsville's Placid pattern.

Long Fan with Acanthus Leaf

This pattern was made by the Greensburg Glass Company in 1886 and is also known as Bijou. Shapes include a table set, water set, berry set, pickle dish, salt shaker, and goblet. It is possible some pieces had gilding as traces of gold have been seen.

Long Maple Leaf

We do not know the maker of this pattern, but it dates to the 1880s and can be found in crystal as well as canary and possibly other colors. Shapes include a table set, water set, celery vase, pickle dish, compote, and various bowls.

"The Looking Glass"

If you look closely at the design around the rim of this oval platter, you will see where it gets its name. A young girl admires herself in the cheval glass while a chubby cherub looks on. The treatment is the same crystalography as the Goddess of Hunt (aka: Virginia Dare) shown on page 119, so there may well be a connection between the two patterns.

Loop

Loop, also known as O'Hara, was made by a number of companies that include Central Glass (1870), Challinor, Taylor (1875), and McKee (1875). There is some variation from one maker to another. Shapes include a bitters bottle, carafe, covered bowls, table set, cake stand, celery vase, covered and open compotes, several decanters, egg cup, goblets, oil lamp, water set, milk pitcher, plate syrup, salt dip, wine, and vases in three sizes.

Loop and Block

Loop and Block is also called Draped Red Block by some collectors. We've heard this pattern declared to be from Pioneer Glass as their #23 pattern and also from Thompson Glass. We are confident it was made in the early 1890s and is found in clear or ruby stained glass. Shapes include a table set, bowls, sauce, celery vase, decanter, goblet, wine, berry set, tray, jelly compote, and the tumbler shown.

Loop and Dart with Diamond Ornament

Shards of this pattern have been found at Boston & Sandwich Glass. The pattern dates to late 1860s and beyond. Shapes include an oval bowl, table set, celery vase, covered compote (high or low), high or low open compote, cordial, egg cup, goblet, water set, 6" plate, oval relish tray, master salt, sauce, and wine.

Long Maple Leaf

Loop

"The Looking Glass"

Loop and Block

Loop and Dart with Diamond Ornament

Loop and Jewel

Lorne

Loop with Dewdrop

Loop with Prism Band

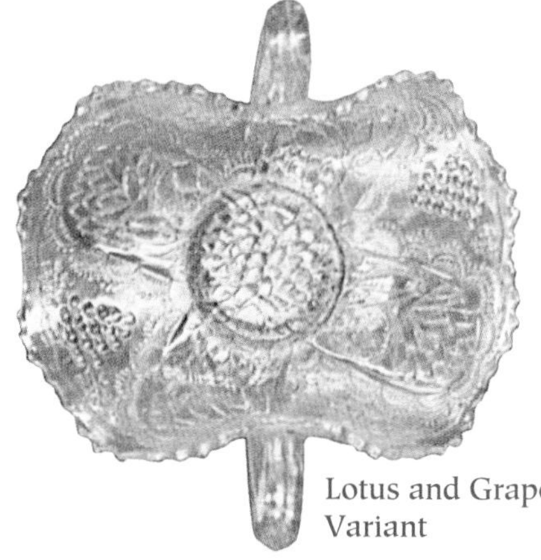
Lotus and Grape Variant

Loop and Jewel

Also called Jewel and Festoon, Queen's Necklace, or Venus, this pattern was made by Indiana Glass (1903) and as part of National Glass (1905 – 1915) in clear and rare milk glass and colors. Shapes include bowls (6", 7", 8"), table set, sherbet cup, flat square 5" dish, goblet, pickle dish, water set, square 5½" plate, relish tray, salt dip, salt shaker, sauces (flat or footed), syrup, berry sugar bowl, vase, and a wine.

Loop with Dewdrop

Loop with Dewdrop was made by U. S. Glass as their #15028 in 1892. Shapes include a table set, water set, berry set, cake stands, compotes, celery vase, mug, syrup, shakers, goblet, oval bread tray, wine, sauce, and bowls in four sizes.

Loop with Prism Band

The maker of this pattern is unknown to us, but we feel sure it was made in the 1890s. Shapes include a table set, a water set, and goblet, but certainly other pieces such as a celery vase, pickle tray, toothpick holder, and wine are strong possibilities. We hope to hear from anyone with additional knowledge of this pattern.

Lorne

Made by U. S. Glass (Bryce Brothers, Factory B), this pattern is shown in a company ad with a group of butter dishes that were not a part of table settings, so we can assume there are no matching pieces. Lorne is the company name.

Lotus and Grape Variant

Primarily a carnival glass pattern from the Fenton Glass Company in 1907, this is the variant with the petticoat lace trim (the standard Lotus and Grape pattern does not have this added design). In carnival, a footed bowl and bonbon are known, but only the latter has been reported in crystal.

Lozenges

Dating to the 1880s, maker unknown, this pattern is found in a table set, celery vase, and open compote (shown). Certainly other shapes may have been made, but we can document only those listed. Anyone having additional information on this pattern should contact us.

Lustre Rose

Lustre Rose was made by the Imperial Glass Company (their #489 pattern) in the 1915 – 1918 era and mostly known as a carnival glass pattern in nearly 20 shapes. In crystal, this lone 10" footed fernery bowl is the only piece of crystal we've spotted, but surely there were other shapes made. The pattern has been heavily reproduced over the years in iridized glass, beginning with Imperial's re-issues in the 1950s.

Magna

Made in 1898, this pattern's maker is unknown. Shapes include a table set, water set, berry set, milk pitcher, syrup, shakers, toothpick holder, celery vase, and pickle dish.

Magnet and Grape

Magnet and Grape was made in a frosted version by Boston and Sandwich Glass Company in flint glass in the 1860s and in the plain shown by Adams after 1870. In 1971 Imperial reproduced this pattern for the Metropolitan Museum of Art (marked "M.M.A."). Old shapes include a table set, bowl, champagne, celery vase, egg cup, goblet, master salt, berry set, wine, cordial, decanter, and goblet (two sizes).

Maize

Maize was made by the Libby and Sons Company in 1889 and has been found in crystal, opaque white, custard, decorated glass, and rare carnival glass. Shapes include a water set, table set, rose bowl, decanter, sugar shaker, bowls, shakers, carafe, finger bowl, celery bowl, and a condiment set. Shown is a 3⅞" tall tumbler.

Lozenges

Magna

Lustre Rose

Magnet and Grape

Maize

Maltese

Maltese and Ribbon

Manhattan

Maple Leaf

Maltese

From George Duncan and Sons Glass Company, this was their #1003 pattern, made in 1886 and discontinued in 1889. Made in crystal (some pieces are found in canary, amber, or blue), shapes include a handled basket, bowls, brandy decanter, celery boat, celery vase, open compotes (4", 4½", 7", 8"), covered compotes (6", 7", 8"), custard cup, goblet, finger bowl, nappies (4", 4½"), berry bowls (4", 4½", 7", 8", 9"), oil bottle, pickle dish, pickle jar, pitcher (two sizes), plate (four sizes), crumb plate (shown), salver, table set, tray (two sizes), and water bottle.

Maltese and Ribbon

Hobbs' #102 pattern, from 1886, can be found in crystal, amber stain, canary, and sapphire. Shapes include a finger bowl, round bowls (8", 9"), square bowls (7", 8"), celery vase, small bowls, oval bowls (7", 8", 9"), pickle dish, water set, half gallon pitcher, master salt, lamp shade (two sizes). The pattern has two variations and resembles Duncan's Maltese pattern.

Manhattan

Manhattan was made by U.S. Glass in 1898 in clear, gilded, and with ruby stain. It has been widely reproduced. Old shapes include a berry set (bowls in six sizes), table set, punch set (shown), cake stand, celery vase, compotes (two sizes), syrup, plates (four sizes), water bottle, covered cheese dish, biscuit jar, cruet (two sizes), goblet, ice bucket, olive dish, relish, straw holder, and toothpick holder. Rare pieces are found in carnival glass.

Maple Leaf

Maple Leaf, now known to be from Gillinder & Sons in 1888, is also called Leaf or Maple Leaf on Trunk and can be found in clear, amber, blue, canary, or frosted glass. Shapes include covered bowls, a table set, cake stand, celery vase, covered compote, cup plate, goblet, water set, milk pitcher, plates (one is the Grant "Let Us Have Peace" plate shown on page 289), oval platter, oval tray, oblong platter, and twin relish with leaf handles. The goblet was reproduced in 1938 and 1971 in original colors and amethyst glass.

Maple Leaf Variant

We try to avoid variants, but this piece is actually listed as a variant of the Gillinder and Sons pattern called Maple Leaf. The regular design dates to the 1880s and so must this one. Found in crystal, vaseline, blue, sapphire, or amber glass. Shapes for the variant are a 10" plate and 10½" platter (shown).

Marburg Ladle

This very attractive ladle with the wooden handle is marked "Patent–April 21, 1896." Other than that I can shed little light on this piece.

Mardi Gras

Held as a George Duncan and Sons pattern by many collectors, Mardi Gras was actually a later pattern of the Washington, Pennsylvania, plant of Duncan and Miller, in 1894. Shapes include a table set, champagne, wine, shakers, toothpick holder, cake stand, handled jelly, bowls, cordial, punch cup, bitters bottle, stemmed sherry, pickle dish, celery vase, and tumblers. It can be found in crystal or ruby stained crystal.

Marilyn

This pattern was made by the Millersburg Company in 1909 mostly in carnival glass. The water pitcher can be occasionally found in crystal but not the tumblers. No other shapes were made.

Marjorie

Marjorie was made by Cambridge Glass as #2631 and is known to carnival glass collectors as Sweetheart. Shapes include a table set, water set, berry set, punch set, cracker jar, cruet, syrup, pickle tray, card set, nappy with two handles, shakers, salt dip, toothpick holder, napkin ring, handled cookie jar, carafe, olive dish, knife rest, cloverleaf tray, squat pitcher, tall cracker jar, tea tumbler, rose bowl, and a rare spittoon shape.

Maple Leaf Variant

Marburg Ladle

Mardi Gras

Marilyn

Marjorie

Marquisette

Marsh Pink

Martec

Mary Ann

Maryland

Marquisette

Credited to Cooperative Flint Glass by Alice H. Metz, this pattern dates to the 1880s. Shapes include a table set, sauce, celery vase, covered compote, water set, goblet, wine, open compote, champagne, open sugar, and cordial.

Marsh Pink

Also known as Square Fuchsia, this pattern's maker is unknown, but the date of production is in the 1880s. Found in crystal and a rare amber, shapes include a table set, open or covered bowls, cake stand, covered compote, jam jar, water pitcher, covered jelly compote, pickle caster, 10" plate, wine, and flat or footed sauces.

Martec

Martec, another of the "tec" patterns from McKee Glass, was first advertised in 1906. Shapes include a table set, punch set, berry set, water set, lemonade set (tankard pitcher), oval jelly dish, jelly compote, high footed compote, plates (5", 8", 11"), stemmed dessert, celery tray, water bottle, syrup jug, cruet, pickle tray, shakers, 4" deep bowl, 8" deep bowl, and a breakfast (berry set) set of creamer and sugar.

Mary Ann

Found in both the vase shape (shown) or a three-handled loving cup with a flat top, this Dugan/Diamond pattern is found mostly in carnival glass where it was produced in marigold or amethyst glass. Here we show a green non-iridized example, and both the loving cup and the vase are known in crystal and satinized amber, as well as with silver decoration.

Maryland

Advertised as U. S. Glass pattern #15049 in clear or with ruby stain, Maryland was also known as Loop and Fan or Loop and Diamond. Shapes include a banana dish, bowls, table set, cake stand in three sizes, celery vase, celery tray, covered and open compotes in three sizes, cup, goblet, honey dish, olive, pickle dish, water set, milk pitcher, bread plate, shakers, toothpick holder, and wine.

Masonic

Masonic was also called Inverted Prisms and first attributed to Indiana Tumbler and Goblet, then McKee & Brothers in 1917 in crystal or emerald green (rare). Shapes include a table set, celery vase, cake stand, water set, oblong dish, square covered honey dish, sardine box (?), vase, tri-cornered nappy, and toothpick holder (may be plain or ruby stained).

Massachusetts

Also called Arched Diamond Points, Cane Variant, Geneva #2, or Star and Diamonds, this was U. S. Glass pattern #15054. It can be found in carnival glass on rare occasions, on emerald green or ruby stained glass, and with gold trim. Shapes include a table set, water set, berry set, basket, bar bottle, celery tray, champagne, cologne bottle, cordial, cruet, goblet, mug, gravy boat, olive dish, mustard jar, wine, whiskey, sherry, plate, relish, and vase in three sizes.

Mayflower

In carnival glass, this scarce pattern compliments the rare Grape Wreath interior pattern, but on crystal bowls only the Mayflower exterior is used, and it completely holds its own as a strong, well-balanced geometric design. The crystal from the Millersburg company is always clear and heavy, making it a favorite of collectors.

McHob

From McBeth, Evans Glass Company in 1928, this is listed as their "H" pattern and is shown in the pitcher and tumblers in three sizes. This firm began in 1899 in the optical lens business and graduated to lamp globes and chimneys before making glasswares, being absorbed by Corning Glass in 1937.

McKee's #1004

Called a globe vase in their ads, this 8" example is marked "PresCut." It is shown with similar vase shapes in various sizes, that are marked #1000, #1001, and #1005. Date of production is reported to be around 1915.

Masonic

Mayflower

Massachusetts

McHob

McKee's #1004

McKee's Tambour Art Clock

Medallion

Medallion Sunburst

Melon with Leaf

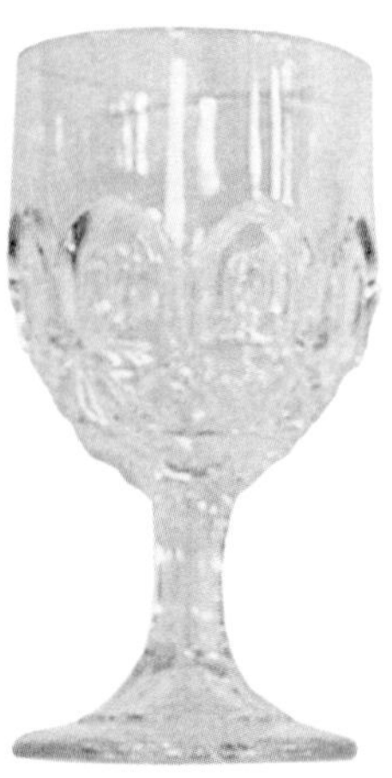

Melton

McKee's Tambour Art Clock

This clock, shown in a 1923 McKee Glass company catalog, was a real novelty in the glass world. Some novelties of this type from this period had matching candlesticks. The Tambour Art clock is found in crystal as well as the canary shown.

Medallion

Also known as Hearts and Spades or Spades, the pattern's maker is unknown but the pattern dates to 1885 – 1895. It can be found in clear, amber, apple green, blue, and canary. Shapes include caster bottles, waste bowl, table set, water set, cake stand, celery vase, open or covered compotes, egg cup, goblet, pickle dish, relish tray, sauce (flat or footed), water tray, and a wine. The covered butter has been reproduced by Imperial and is marked "IG."

Medallion Sunburst

Medallion Sunburst was made by Bryce, Higbee and Company in 1905 and is also known as Banquet. Shapes include a banana dish, round and square bowls, table set, cake stands, celery vase, celery tray, cruet, custard cup, jam jar, mug, mustard jar, olive dish, water set, milk pitcher, plates, relish tray, shakers, toothpick holder, 9½" vase, and wine.

Melon with Leaf

Attributed to Atterbury and Company of Pittsburgh in 1878, this well-done covered piece has been widely reproduced for the L.G. Wright Company. Original treatments are crystal, amber, canary, blue, milk glass, and blue opaque glass while new items (called Acorn candy boxes by Wright) were made in both satin and clear glass in amber, blue, green, amethyst, and milk glass.

Melton

Very little seems to be known about this pattern. The maker has not come to light, nor the date of production (we feel it is in the 1890s). Shapes known to us are a table set, goblet, and wine, but surely others exist and we'd be happy to hear from anyone who has more knowledge of this pattern.

Memphis

A well-known Northwood pattern made in crystal, carnival glass, and emerald with gilding, this pattern is also known as Doll's Eye by some collectors. It was made first in 1908, and crystal shapes include a water set, berry set, table set, fruit bowl with base, two sizes of punch sets, and decanter with matching wine glasses.

Mephistopheles

In demonology, Mephistopheles ranks next to Satan, and the piece shown is a figure with horns and a wild beard. Some believe this piece is European, and there is a similar mug with the same name. Collectors call the piece shown an ale glass, and the figure is frosted, while stripes of gilding run around the top.

Michigan

One of the U. S. Glass States series, this was their #15077. It is also known as Desplaines, Loop & Pillar, and Panelled Jewel. Shapes are a berry set, table set, toy table set, goblet, water set, salt shakers, toothpick holder, and wine. Some items have ruby stain, painted decoration, or even two stains.

Millard

Also called Fan and Flute, this was U. S. Glass pattern #15016, made in 1893 in clear, amber stained, or ruby stained glass. Shapes include a table set, syrup, celery vase, plate, toothpick holder, cruet, shakers, celery tray, bowls, cake stand, compote, cup, oblong dish, goblet, water set, flat or footed sauce, syrup, and wine.

Millersburg Cherry

Millersburg Cherry is better known in carnival glass where it is found on berry sets, ice cream sets, water sets, and table sets. It is occasionally found on rare pieces of crystal in a water pitcher, milk pitcher, and in a very rare emerald green jardiniere whimsy (pulled from a bowl).

Memphis

Mephistopheles

Michigan

Millard

Millersburg Cherry

Millersburg Tulip Compote

Minerva

Miniature Loving Cup

Minnesota

Mirror Image

Millersburg Tulip Compote

Found primarily on carnival glass where it is very rare, this graceful 9" beauty was also made in crystal, as shown, where only a few examples are also known. The base is octagonal as is the slender stem, and the bowl has eight wide panels. The glass is outstanding, all making this a real collector's find.

Minerva

Attributed to Adams in 1881 and Burlington Glass of Canada, this set of related designs is very collectible. Shapes include a table set, berry set, champagne, covered compotes (high or low), open compote, goblet, honey dish, jam jar, pickle dish, water set, milk pitcher, bread plate, dinner plate, platter, and flat or footed sauces.

Miniature Loving Cup

Shown often in the Butler Brothers catalogs, this miniature loving cup with three handles is not only gold trimmed but gold covered. A similar piece can also be found in carnival glass, but we feel this one is from a separate glassmaker. Any information on this piece would be appreciated.

Minnesota

As one of the many States patterns from U. S. Glass, this was sold in clear, ruby stained, gold trimmed, and rarely in carnival glass. Shapes include a berry set, table set, oval bowl, goblet, humidor, water set, syrup, toothpick holder, wine, mug, vase, banana stand, basket, bonbon, round or square compotes, hair receiver, cup mug, match safe, plate, and tray.

Mirror Image

While we still haven't learned the maker of this unusual pattern we've now been able to add this beautiful vase shape from Jean Hall to the pitcher we showed in the last edition. And we've learned there is a tumbler shape as well. Surely there are bowls too so we hope to hear from anyone having additional shapes in this pattern.

Missouri

Missouri was pattern #15058 from U. S. Glass in 1898, in clear or emerald green (plain or gold trimmed). Shapes include bowls, table set, cake stands (four sizes), open and covered compotes in four sizes, celery vase, sauces, cordial, cruet, covered dish, donut stand, goblet, mug, olive dish, pickle dish, milk pitcher, water set, relish dish, shakers, syrup, and wine.

Mitered Diamond

Also called Sunken Buttons or Pyramid, this pattern dates to the 1880s (maker hasn't been confirmed). Shapes include a table set, berry set, compote, wine, platter, shakers, cordial, and a sauce. It can be found in clear, canary, amber, and blue.

Mitted Hand

The only reference we can find on this bowl is Metz, Book I. It is 6" long and shows a gloved hand supporting a bowl of Daisy and Button patterning. We believe this dates to the late 1880s, and Metz calls it "An Indiana novelty glass product."

Model's Gem

Gem is also called Double Red Block or Hexagon Block and was made by Model Flint Glass in 1893 (Richards & Hartley made a version of Gem also). Shapes include table sets, water sets, berry sets, goblet, wine, mustard bowl, celery vase, pickle dish, oil lamp, and saucer. It is found in crystal and ruby stained crystal.

Monarch

This seldom discussed pattern from McKee (1901 – 1905) is part of their PresCut line. It is found in crystal in a 9" deep bowl, a punch bowl with stand, a cup, and the cruet shown. Other shapes probably exist but these are the only ones shown in the McKee catalog. It is possible this pattern was part of an assortment of several patterns that were packaged together.

Missouri

Mitered Diamond

Mitted Hand

Model's Gem

Monarch

Monkey and Vines

Moon and Star

Morning Glory

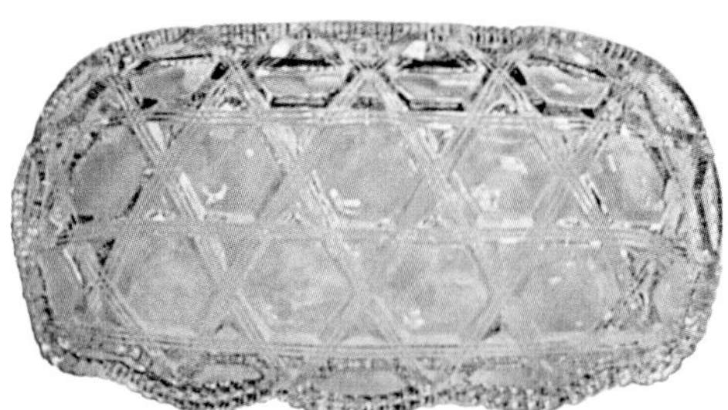
Mt. Vernon

Multiple Scroll

Mutt Jug

Monkey and Vines

Credited to Dithridge and Company Glass Works in 1879, this neat little mug (2½" tall with a 2½" diameter) seems to have been made only in clear glass with the crystalography process. One side shows a monkey looking at a turtle, and the other side shows the turtle biting the monkey's hand.

Moon and Star

From Adams & Company (1888), Cooperative Flint (1896), and U. S. Glass (1898), this well-known pattern has been widely reproduced. Original treatments were clear, clear frosted, and ruby stained. Shapes include a carafe, covered bowls, open bowls, waste bowl, table set, cake stand, celery vase, champagne, cheese dish, claret, covered or open compotes, egg cup, goblet, oil bottle, oil lamp, shakers, syrup, bread tray, water tray, wine, salt dip, and relish tray.

Morning Glory

This flint pattern, from the Boston & Sandwich Company in 1860, is rare in most shapes. Shapes include a table set, pitcher, goblet, footed tumbler, salt dip, wine, champagne, stemmed dessert, and an egg cup. The goblet and wine have been reproduced.

Mt. Vernon

From McKee Brothers in 1870, this pattern is also called Prism by some collectors. Shapes include a table set, goblet, pickle dish, relish dish, and rectangular bowls.

Mutiple Scroll

From the Canton Glass Company in the early 1890s, this well-done pattern is found in various shapes that include a table set, bowls, celery vase, pickle dish, wine, mug, and a square plate. Colors reported are clear, amber, or blue. This was Canton's #130 pattern.

Mutt Jug

The Mutt Jug was produced by New Martinsville Glass Company as their #46 (there was also a Jeff mug #36). As you can probably guess, the Mutt was a tall jug and the Jeff a squat one. No other shapes are found in this pattern.

Nail

Nail was made by U. S. Glass in 1892 as their #15002, in clear, engraved or ruby stained. It is sometimes called Recessed Pillar-Thumbprint Band. Shapes include a berry set, table set, cake stand, celery vase, covered or open compotes, cordial, goblet, water set, bread plate, dinner plate, sauce, and wine.

Nailhead

Bryce, Higbee and Company made Nailhead in the 1880s in clear, decorated glass, or aquamarine. Shapes include a goblet, berry set, table set, cake stand, celery vase, covered or open compotes, cordial, water set, bread tray, bread and dinner plates, sauce, and wine.

Narcissus Spray

Narcissus Spray was an Indiana Glass pattern made in 1915 and several years after. Besides clear glass, decorated pieces are known, and shapes include a berry set, table set, water set, and round or oval bowls.

Narrow Swirl

This tall narrow creamer was reportedly used as a container for mustard, honey, relish, and horseradish and had a metal lid. It is hard to imagine how such a lid fit, but we will accept the premise until we hear otherwise.

National

From an 1891 U. S. Glass (Ripley, Factory F) catalog, this unusual bread tray is a treasure. Shaped like a shield, it is similar in design to a U. S. Glass butter dish called Banner (shown on page 29), and the two pieces make a fine display. The National tray is a rare item.

National Star

National Star was made by the Riverside Glass Works (their #508) in 1900, in clear, gilded, ruby stain, ruby stain over vaseline, and vaseline glass. Shapes include a table set, a water set, a berry set, and a jelly compote.

Nail

Nailhead

Narcissus Spray

Narrow Swirl

National

National Star

Navarre

Near-Cut #2636

Near-Cut #2692

Nearcut Daisy

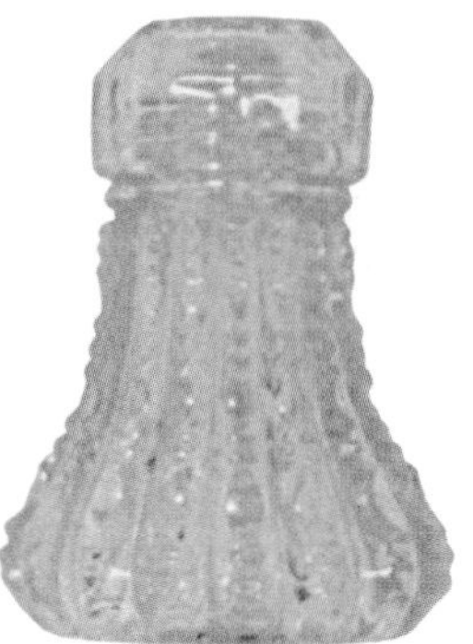
Nelly

Navarre

Known best by chocolate glass collectors, this pattern is from McKee and Brothers Glass in 1900. Only a table set, toothpick holder, and handled nappy are known to us, but other shapes may have been made, and we'd like to hear from anyone with additional information.

Near-Cut #2636

Made by Cambridge Glass in 1906, this near-cut pattern was, as the title states, their #2636. It can be found in a table set, bowls, water set, cruet, handled basket, wine, celery vase, salt shaker, berry set, and massive 8" vase.

Near-Cut #2692

Made in 1909, this very plain pattern was available in several shapes that included the oil cruet shown, a table set, water set, and a berry set. The design is a subtle wide panel with a narrow panel ridged between. It was also made by Cambridge.

Nearcut Daisy

Also known as Red Sunflower and made by the Cambridge Glass Company in 1910, this well-done pattern is found in bowls, a table set, water set, cruet, oil lamp, and a rose bowl. This was Cambridge's #2760 pattern, but in the 1930s the bowl shapes were made in Finland's Iittala-Karhula plant, and examples so marked are found in carnival glass.

Nelly

Made by McKee Glass Company in 1894 in clear only, this pattern can be found in a table set, celery vase, compote, berry set, sauce, cake stand, and salt shakers like the one shown, which has a glass top. Nelly is also called Sylvan or Florence by some collectors.

New England Pineapple

Also known as Loop and Jewel, Pineapple, or Sawtooth, this pattern is from either New England Glass or Boston & Sandwich (1850 – 1870). Shapes include a caster bottle, oil bottle, berry set, fruit bowl, table set, caster set, champagne, covered compotes, open compotes, cordial, cruet, decanter (pint or quart), egg cup, goblets, honey dish, mug, pickle dish, milk pitcher, water set, 6" plate, salts, flat or footed sauce, spillholder, sweetmeat, bar tumbler, whiskey tumbler, and wine.

New England Pineapple

New Jersey

New Hampshire

New Hampshire was from U. S. Glass as one of the States series patterns, #15084, made in 1903 in crystal, ruby stained, or gold trimmed glass. Shapes include a biscuit jar, carafe, square or round bowls, table set, cake stand, celery vase, covered or open compotes, breakfast set, cruet, custard cup, pickle dish, water set (bulbous or tankard), 8" plate, relish tray, shakers (three sizes), syrup, vase, toothpick holder, and wine.

New Hampshire

New Jersey

New Jersey was another of the States patterns from U. S. Glass (#15070) in 1900 and is also known as Loops and Drops. Shapes include a water carafe, bowls, cake stand, celery tray, celery vase, covered and open compotes, cruet, fruit bowl on stand, goblet, olive dish, pickle tray, water set (two types of pitchers), plates, salt shakers, gas shade, two shapes of syrups, toothpick holder, and wines.

New Martinsville #169

Many glass companies had a try at similar candlesticks, but this pair came from New Martinsville and are 7" tall. These were marketed shortly before the factory was destroyed in a fire caused by the Ohio River flooding that caused stored lime to heat and burn. The factory reopened nine months later.

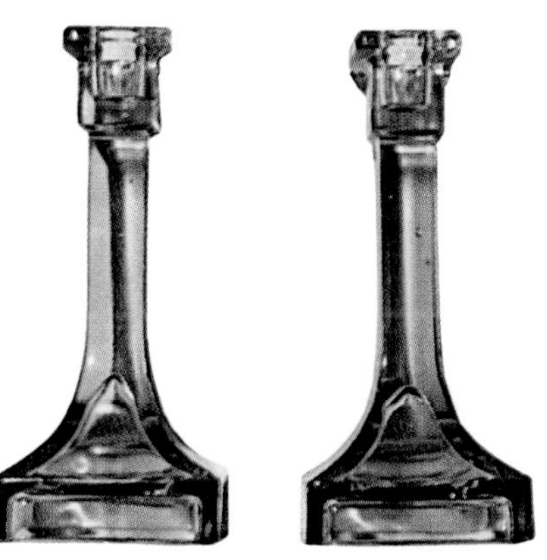

New Martinsville #169

Niagara

This pattern should be called U. S. Niagara to distinguish it from the Fostoria pattern with the same name. U. S. Glass made this design as their #15162 in 1919. Shapes include a table set, berry set, syrup, cruet, cracker jar, plate, compote, cup, mustard jar, and handled jelly. Some pieces were gold trimmed.

Niagara

#9 Book

Nogi

Nonpariel

Northern Star

North Star

#9 Book

Credited to Adams and Company (they joined U.S. Glass in 1891 as factory A), this book-shaped match holder is listed as their #9 pattern. It is one of the better novelties and would grace any collection of small or novelty items.

Nogi

This frequently found pattern, from Indiana Glass in 1906, is also called Pendant or Amulet. Its shapes include a table set, water set, goblet, pickle dish, plate, shakers, a 6" berry bowl, a vase, and a 6" compote. Nogi can be found in clear glass as well as ruby stain and gilded items. Production extended for several years.

Nonpariel

We are told this unique pattern is made in a table set, water set, and in bowls, but aside from the few table set pieces we've seen, we know little about it. The glass is well done, however, and the design interesting enough to catch your attention. We'd be happy to hear more about this pattern.

Northern Star

Made by the Fenton Art Glass Company of Williamstown, West Virginia, this pattern is found in carnival glass in small bowls, in opalescent glass in bowls and plates (three sizes), and in crystal in both bowls and plates. The design of a six-pointed star with file inside is an easy one to remember.

North Star

We've taken the liberty of naming this pattern from the Lancaster Glass Company in 1910, although it is also known as Stippled Fans. Shapes include the usual table set, water set, and berry set, but other shapes were probably produced. The water set pieces have been seen with gold trim.

Northwood Near-Cut #12

Rarely found in carnival glass in limited shapes, this 1906 Northwood pattern was made in crystal in a water set, table set, berry set, nappy (sometimes with advertising), compote, goblet, wine, salt shakers, celery vase, pickle dish, punch set, toothpick holder, and others (34 shapes are known).

Northwood Peach

Made by the Northwood Glass Company in 1912 and best known by carnival glass collectors, this well-done pattern really shows best as we show it here in crystal with ruby and gold trim. Shapes for both types of glass are a berry set, table set, and water set.

Northwood Strawberry

Well known by carnival glass collectors, this very realistic fruit pattern was made by Northwood in 1910 and can be found on bowls or plates. The exterior on the piece shown has a basketweave design but a fine ribbed exterior was also made. Besides crystal, Strawberry was made in carnival glass. Some crystal pieces were given a goofus treatment or were gilded and enameled.

Northwood Thin Rib

Found in many glass treatments including carnival glass, opalescent glass, opaque glass, clear crystal, colored crystal, and custard glass, this was a standard vase design from the factory. It was made in at least three base sizes and can be found in examples as short as 9" or as tall as 17". The piece shown is black amethyst glass with enameled floral sprays and dates to 1918.

Northwood Near-Cut #12

Northwood Peach

Northwood Strawberry

Northwood Thin Rib

Northwood Wildflower

Nu-Cut #537

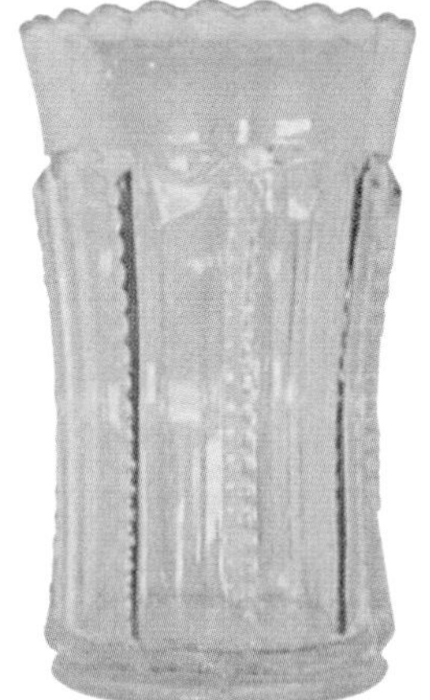

Notched Panel

Nu-Cut Star

Nursery Rhyme Bowl

Northwood Wildflower

Primarily known in carnival glass where it sometimes has an interior pattern called Blossomtime, this 6" compote with the screw-type stem can be found in crystal or emerald green glass as shown. Pieces are often found with the Northwood trademark, and some of the crystal or green pieces show traces of goofus paint or gilding.

Notched Panel

Made by Tarentum Glass in 1902, in clear or ruby stained glass, Notched Panel can be found in a table set, toothpick holder, shakers, berry set, relish, and square bowls.

Nu-Cut #537

As part of Imperial Glass Company's 1914 Nu-Cut line, this #537 compote, 4½" tall, was apparently made in very limited amounts, especially in carnival glass where it is found only in marigold. Shapes in #537 also include bowls, but only in crystal.

Nu-Cut Star

Nu-Cut Star was listed in catalogs as Imperial's #91/555 and found in a table set, mayonnaise set (bowl and under plate), 6½" bowl, jelly compote, handled nappy, pickle tray, and nut bowl. The threaded hub on the compote's stem is typically Imperial in design.

Nursery Rhyme Bowl

Different in design than the other plates with this motif, this one shows an outer ring of grapes, characters from children's stories, and an inner design of more grapes. The maker is unknown to us, and we'd like to hear from any reader with additional information on this item.

Octagon

Octagon was made by the Imperial Glass Company as their #505 pattern and is known best in carnival glass. Shapes in crystal include a water set, table set, stemmed vase, toothpick holder, shakers, berry set, decanter, wine, cordial, compote in two sizes, goblet, nappy, sherbet, milk pitcher, punch set, and plate. A similar design was made by Indiana Glass (Indiana's #123) that is often confused with Octagon.

O'Hara's Crystal Wedding

This pattern, also known as Box Pleat, was made by Adams & Company in 1875. Shapes include a table set, water set, cake stand, and celery vase. All pieces have three rolled feet and handles are applied.

O'Hara's Diamond

This pattern was from O'Hara Glass in 1885 and then U.S. Glass after 1891 as their #15001 pattern. It was made in crystal and ruby stained glass. Shapes include a table set, banana stand, shakers, plain tray, cup and saucer, finger bowl, bowls, sauce, toothpick holder, pickle dish, and a water set. Some pieces were souvenir decorated items.

Ohio Star

Made by Millersburg Glass in 1909 (and later at Jefferson's Canadian factory), this pattern is best known in carnival glass, but a wide assortment of shapes were made in crystal. These include a table set, water set, berry set, assorted bowl shapes and sizes, water pitchers (three sizes), tumblers (three sizes), compotes (tall and standard), cruet, syrup, toothpick holder, shakers, punch set, plates (four sizes), pickle dishes (three sizes), water bottle, and a vase. The glass is heavy and clear and the quality superior. In addition, the compote is found in a rare sapphire blue (two reported).

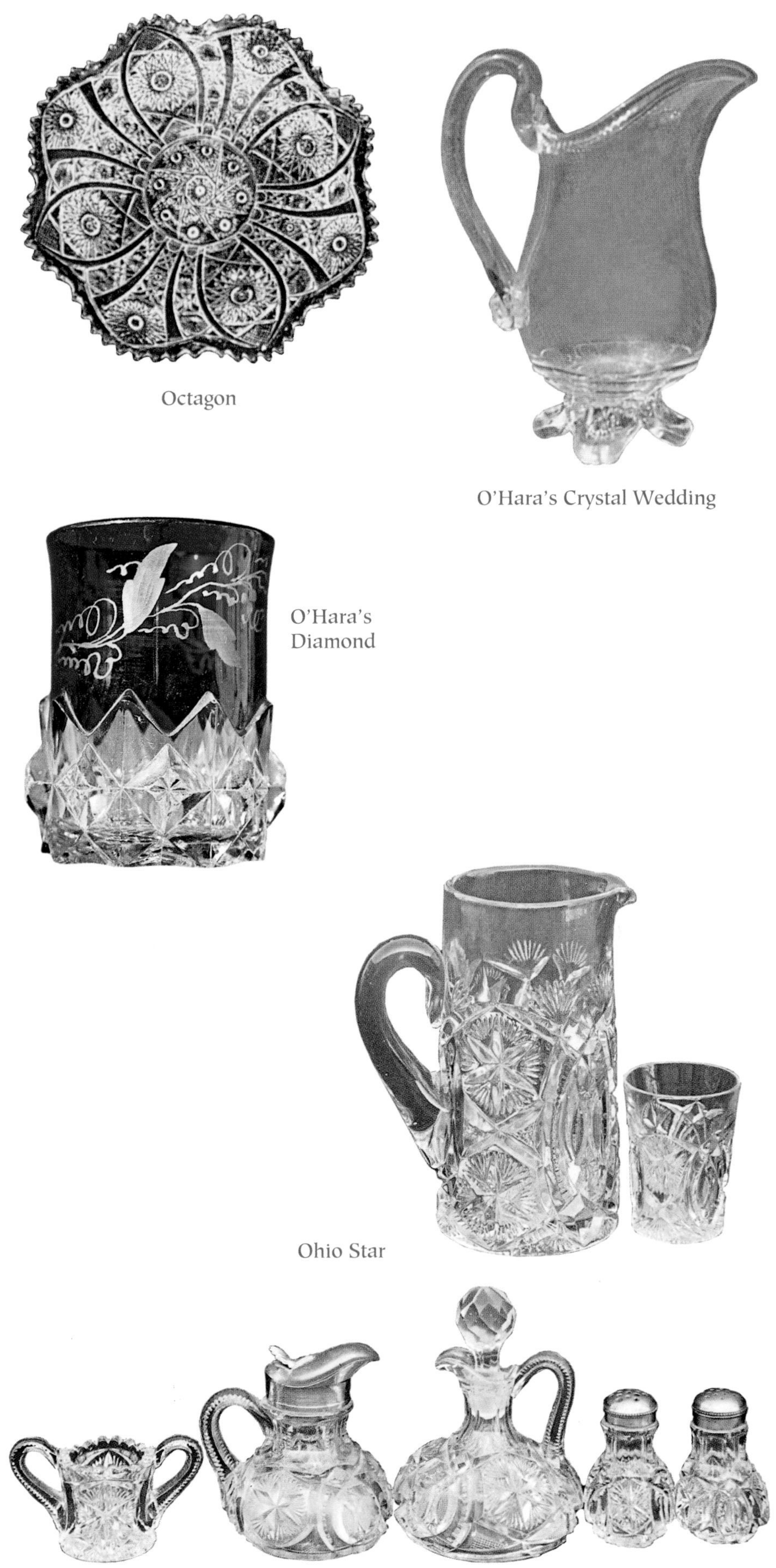

Octagon

O'Hara's Crystal Wedding

O'Hara's Diamond

Ohio Star

Old Colony

Old Glory

Omero

Omnibus

One-O-One

Open Plaid

Old Colony

Advertised as #97 under the name Old Colony, this pattern is found in clear or with gold trim as shown. Shapes include a table set, water set, and berry set. This pattern dates to the 1910 – 1912 era and is simple but very dynamic.

Old Glory

Also called Mirror Star and made by New Martinsville Glass Company in 1910, this pattern is known in a table set and water set. The original pattern number was 719, and pieces are both clear and gold trimmed.

Omero

Made by the Imperial Glass Company in the 1916 – 1922 era, this was their name for a line of nearly plain glass with wide paneling, made in iridized glass, crystal, amber, green, and rose. Some was decorated and shapes included a table set, rose bowl, nappy, bonbon, berry set, sherbet and sherbet plate, vases, pickle dish, celery tray, and handled compote.

Omnibus

Made by U. S. Glass as #15124 as part of their South American export line, Omnibus can be found in a table set, 8" deep bowl, berry set, pickle dish, celery tray, shallow 9" bowl, and possibly a water set.

One-O-One

Also called Beaded 101, this was a product of Duncan and Sons in 1885, but shards have been found at Burlington Glass in Canada. Shapes include a table set, cake stand, celery vase, covered compotes, goblet, oil lamps in standard or hand versions, pickle dish, water set, bread plate (Give Us This Day), dinner plate, relish tray, shakers, vase, and wine.

Open Plaid

Also called Open Basketweave, this is attributed to Central Glass in 1885 and U. S. Glass in 1891. Shapes include a table set, berry set, cordial, plate, salt shakers, water set, juice tumbler, champagne, wine, and syrup.

Open Rose (Imperial)

Open Rose (Imperial)

One of Imperial Glass Company's most popular patterns (their #489), it can be found in carnival glass, clear crystal, and some rare colored crystal like the large rose bowl shown (this one has the old Imperial Iron-Cross trademark). Shapes include a plate, berry sets, and the rose bowl in two sizes. A sister pattern called Lustre Rose has the same catalog number and is made in many additional shapes.

Open Rose (Moss Rose)

Open Rose (Moss Rose)

Also called Moss Rose (a better name), this is from an unknown maker despite shards found at Boston and Sandwich. Shapes include round or oval bowls, a table set, cake stand, celery vase, covered compote (6", 7", 8", 9"), open low compote (6", 7", 7½", 8", 9"), cordial, egg cup, goblet (gents' or ladies'), pickle dish, milk pitcher, relish tray, water set, salt dip, and a sauce.

Opposing Pyramids

Opposing Pyramids

Opposing Pyramids, also known as Truncated Cube or Flora, was found in clear or etched glass from Bryce, Higbee Glass in 1890. Shapes include a table set, water set, cake slaver, celery vase, compote, goblet, shakers, a vase, and a wine. The pattern seems to be a bit hard to find, and there are two pitcher sizes (a quart pitcher and one gallon tankard), but only the tankard has been found to date.

Optic

Optic

Virtually covered in gold trim, this tiny salt dip has more angles that anything else and would be a standout in a salt dip collection. It dates to the early 1900s.

Orange Peel

Orange Peel

Primarily a pattern that is known in carnival glass, this Westmoreland design is also known in decorated crystal or clear. Shapes are a punch set, custard cups (flared tops), and stemmed sherbets, all made in the 1915 – 1920 era.

Orange Tree

Oregon

Oriental

Oriental Poppy

Orinda

Orion Thumbprint

Orange Tree

Made by the Fenton Art Glass Company and best known in carnival glass, this pattern was made in a wide range of shapes in other types of glass as well. The mug shown is a pale pink glass and was made in 1929, but crystal and colored pieces date to a decade earlier, especially in the mug shape.

Oregon

This is U. S. Glass pattern #15073, made in 1901, and for many years. Shapes include a water carafe, table set, bowls (open or covered), cake stands, celery vase, covered compotes, cruet, goblet, honey dish, covered horseradish, mug, olive dish, pickle dish, water set, bread plate, relish, salt dips (master and individual), sauce, syrup, vase, toothpick holder, and wine.

Oriental

Apparently the maker of this pattern isn't known, but the date of production is believed to be around 1885. Shapes include a table set, celery vase, covered compote, pickle jar (shown), tray, water set, goblet, wine, and various bowls.

Oriental Poppy

This famous pattern was made by the Northwood Company, primarily in carnival glass where the pitcher was a tankard shape. Here in the seldom seen crystal example, the pitcher is a squat or standard shape. Just why the company decided to change styles is a mystery. Production for both treatments was in the early 1900s.

Orinda

From National Glass Company as their #1492 in 1901, shapes include a table set, toothpick holder, pickle dish, shakers, berry set, syrup, milk pitcher, water pitcher, and celery vase.

Orion Thumbprint

From the Canton Glass Company in 1894, this pattern can be found in crystal, milk glass, colored crystal, and black glass. Shapes include a water set, table set, goblet, celery vase, compote (open or covered), oval platter (Daisy and Button center), and sauce.

Ornate Star

This pattern, from Tarentum Glass in 1907, is also called Hobstar Fancy, Divided Star, or Ladders and Diamonds with Star. It was once believed to be a Millersburg pattern by some. Shapes include a berry set, water set, table set, celery vase, pickle tray, goblet, wine, cordial, and a stemmed dessert.

Our Girl/Little Bo-Peep

Made by McKee & Brothers about 1887, this mug is a companion to the Our Boy/Jester on a Pig mug by the same company. It stands 3⅜" tall and can be found in clear, amber, blue, canary, and apple green. A girl with a lamb is shown on one side while the reverse side is lettered "Our Girl."

Oval Diamond Panel

Also known as Oval Panel, this pattern is known in the goblet shown, in both crystal and vaseline. The design is simple but effective with pointed ovals that are filled with diamond crosshatching. The maker is unknown at least to us, and we'd appreciate any information about this pattern from readers.

Oval Loop

Also called Question Mark, this is a U. S. Glass pattern made in 1891. It is found in clear, frosted, and gold-trimmed glass. Shapes include oval and round bowls, table set, candlesticks, celery vase, open and covered compotes, goblet, pickle jar, water set, milk pitcher in standard or tankard sizes, shakers, sauce, sugar shaker, bread tray, and wine.

Oval Medallion

Also called Argyle or Beaded Oval Window, this is a U.S. Glass pattern from 1891. It is found in clear, canary, amber, blue, and a rare amethyst. Shapes include a table set, bowls, pickle dish, toy table set, toy water set, toy berry set, compotes, a goblet, and a wine. Footed and oval pieces have a Maltese cross in relief on the bottom, and covered pieces have a finial that is a large flat double ellipse on each side of what appears to be a raised relief of a Maltese cross.

Ornate Star

Oval Diamond Panel

Our Girl/Little Bo-Peep

Oval Loop

Oval Medallion

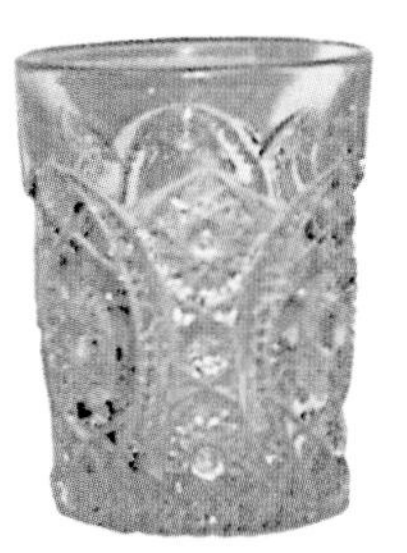

Oval Star

Overall Lattice

Overshot

Owen Coin Blank Lamp

Owl and Possum

Oval Star

The only shape we've found in this well-done pattern is the toy water set (some collectors think the tumbler shown is a toothpick holder). It was made by Indiana Glass in 1910 as their #300 pattern. If anyone knows of additional shapes in this pattern, we'd certainly like to hear from them.

Overall Lattice

From the Indiana Tumbler and Goblet Company of Greentown, Indiana, this pattern is found in crystal and vaseline glass. Shapes include a table set, wine, plate, ruffled bowl, goblet, and compote.

Overshot

While this has often been attributed to Hobbs, the Overshot pieces are apparently not from that maker and more likely came from Boston and Sandwich Glass. Some collectors call this Snakeskin, and it is found in table sets, goblets, water sets, bowls of several shapes, plates, compotes, etc. Shown are two pitchers, one in milk size and a second which has a huge glass bladder opening behind the handle. Overshot was made in the 1870s and 1880s.

Owen Coin Blank Lamp

The owner of this lamp tells us this was its name and that it was a product of U.S. Glass in 1893 and was made until 1909. Besides the vaseline shown, we feel confident this lamp was also made in crystal and possibly other colors.

Owl and Possum

We've learned practically nothing about this very imaginative goblet except it seems to be found only in this one shape and was probably made in the 1880s. On one side is the owl in the tree and on the other a possum in the same tree. The goblet's stem is a tree trunk pattern, and the whole piece has a rich, whimsical look.

Owl and Pussycat

Owl and Pussycat

We don't know the maker of this unusual covered cheese dish, but can say the mould work is exceptional with the design well done. The owl holds the cat by the tail around the top while standing on a brick wall, and the scene is again displayed on the inside of the base. We'd appreciate any information on this pattern, especially if there are other pieces.

Owl in Horseshoe

Owl in Horseshoe

Rather difficult to see, the design is one of a well-done owl suspended within a horseshoe. It is etched. We do not know the maker or date of manufacturing, and only the goblet shape seems to be available. Any information on this pattern would be appreciated.

Owl on a Branch

Owl on a Branch

Credited to Dithridge and Company partly because of the crystalography treatment, this mug has an unusual shape and a pedestal base. Only clear has been reported, and the mug is large (3¾" tall). The date of production is about 1879, and the design is a simple one, owls sitting on branches on both sides of the mug.

Paddle Wheel

Paddle Wheel

This interesting pattern dates to the 1900s and can be found in a table set, shakers, jelly compote, pickle dish, relish, celery vase and tray, and water set. The tall compote shown is a beautiful item and quite showy. It was made by Westmoreland.

Paden City #206

Paden City #206

Made about 1918 by the Paden City Glass Company as their #206 24 oz. jug, this pattern is a nice one for such a late production date. Shown in amber glass, this piece was also made in clear and despite no evidence in company ads, we feel confident other shapes were made including a table set. Anyone know more about this pattern?

Palisades

Palm Beach

Palmette

Palm Leaf Fan

Palisades

Made by the Dugan Glass Company in 1910 and then continued when the factory became Diamond Glass. The vase is called Lined Lattice by carnival glass collectors where it is most often seen, but opalescent examples are well known too. It is found in crystal, green, opalescent, or carnival glass and can be as short as 5" or pulled to 14" sizes.

Palm Beach

From U. S. Glass as their #15119 in 1909, Palm Beach is best known in carnival glass and opalescent glass but crystal and decorated crystal exist. Shapes include a table set, water set, berry set, jelly compote, wine, cruet, shakers, and celery vase.

Palmette

Also called Hearts and Spades or just Spades, this 1870s pattern can be found in a berry set, table set, cake stand, high or low compote, both open or covered, water set, goblet, master salt, wine, relish, oil lamp (two sizes), cake plate, bread plate, celery vase, champagne, cup, plate, shakers, syrup, and egg cup. The syrup is known in milk glass. It is possibly a Canadian pattern.

Palm Leaf Fan

Palm Leaf Fan was made by Bryce, Higbee in 1904. Shapes include a water set, table set, large bowl, cake stand, celery vase, compote, wine, shakers, sauce, and cruet. The design is quite good and the glass is quality. Some pieces may be gold trimmed.

Panama

Made by U. S. Glass as #15088 in 1904, this well-known pattern's shapes include a table set, water set, berry set, toothpick holder, salt shakers, celery vase, celery tray, and both round and rectangular bowls. It is sometimes found with gold trim.

Panama

Panelled 44

Often called Reverse 44 or Athenia, this U. S. Glass pattern #15140 can be found in clear, gold trimmed, platinum stained, blue stained, rose stained, or green stained. Made in 1912, shapes include a water set, table set, mug, bowls, cruet, shakers, toothpick holder, bonbon, candlestick, finger bowl, lemonade set, olive, sugar shaker, vase (loving cup shape), and a wine.

Panelled 44

Panelled Dewdrop

Panelled Dewdrop was made by Campbell, Jones Glass Company in 1879. Shapes include a table set, cordial, wine, pickle dish, pickle jar (shown), celery vase, footed sauce, jam jar, goblet, and a celery boat. The pattern is subdued but effective and quite collectible.

Panelled Dewdrop

Panelled Diamond Blocks

Made by George Duncan and Sons as their #24, this is also known as Quartered Block by some collectors. It was made in 1894, and the shapes include a berry set, carafe, table set, open or covered compote, custard cup, goblet, orange bowl, oil lamp, water set, sauce, syrup, toothpick holder, vase, wine, and the ice tub shown.

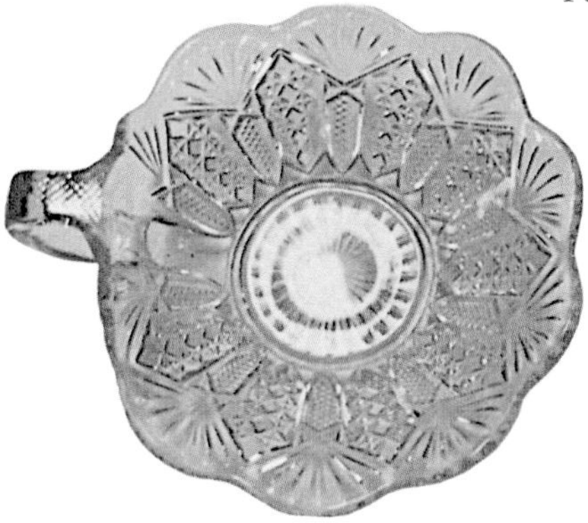

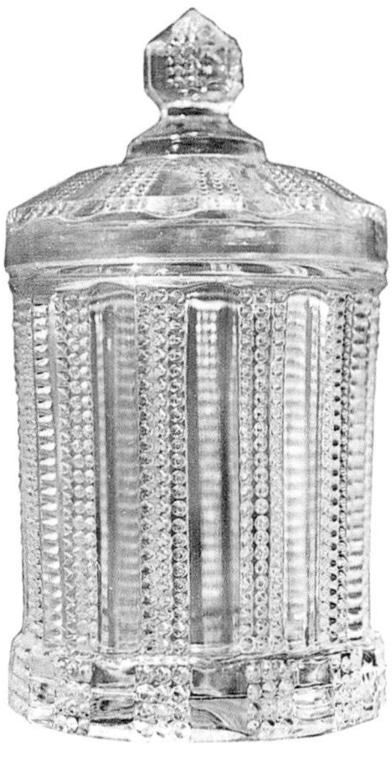

Panelled Diamond Blocks

Panelled Fishbone

Panelled Forget-Me-Not

Panelled Holly

Panelled Heather

Panelled Jewels

Panelled Fishbone

Very little information about this pattern seems to be available. We do know it was made in salt and pepper shakers as well as the oval bread tray shown, and we suspect both compotes and bowls were made also. The simple design indicates this pattern came along in the 1880s, so many other shapes are possible.

Panelled Forget-Me-Not

From U. S. Glass (Bryce) in 1891, this well-known pattern can be found in a covered bowl, bread plate, table set, covered compote, celery vase, jam jar, pickle dish, spooner, and a scarce wine. The design is uncomplicated, typical of glassware before 1900.

Panelled Heather

Often mistaken for Jefferson's #271 pattern, Panelled Heather was made by Indiana Glass in the early 1900s as their #126 design. It is found in crystal, sometimes decorated and with gilt. Shapes include a table set, berry set, water set, sauce, cake stand, covered compote, wine, pickle dish, celery tray, and a vase.

Panelled Holly

Made by the Northwood Glass Company in 1905, Panelled Holly can be found in opalescent, carnival, and decorated crystal. The design is a favorite, especially with Northwood collectors and shapes include a berry set, water set, table set, and bonbon, as well as a cruet and relish, but not all shapes are available in all treatments.

Panelled Jewels

Made by the Bellaire Goblet Company, this pattern should not be confused with the Michigan pattern from U. S. Glass that is sometimes called Panelled Jewel. It can be found in clear, amber, canary, and blue glass, but apparently only the goblet shape is known.

Panelled Oak

Panelled Oak

Credited to the Lancaster Glass Company in 1900, Panelled Oak was made in a table set, celery vase, plate, bowl, water set, and perhaps a goblet, and was also made in goofus. The design is a good one with realistic leaves and acorns, while the top of the pitcher has a notched effect above a band and crosshatching design. It is very collectible.

Panelled Octagon

Panelled Pleat

Panelled Octagon

Shown in Butler Brothers catalogs in the 1912 – 1920 period, this stemmed creamer was part of a table set, completely gilded to resemble a gold service. With so much gilding, it was good to keep the design a simple one. The maker is unknown.

Panelled Pleat

Made by Robinson Glass Company of Zanesville, Ohio, in 1894, this pattern is also known as Ladders and shapes include a table set, water set, berry set, and goblet.

Panelled Strawberry

A product of the Indiana Glass Company of Dunkirk, Indiana, in 1913, this very stately pattern is known in clear, rose colored, decorated, or gold trimmed. Shapes include a water set, table set, berry set, celery vase, goblet, and three sizes of sauces.

Panelled Strawberry

Panelled Sunflower

Panelled Thistle

Panel, Rib, and Shell

Panel with Diamond Point

Panelled Sunflower

Also called Delta, this is a Higbee pattern made in 1910, and later produced by the Dominion Glass Company in Canada in 1920. Shapes are a basket in three sizes, table set, cake stand, celery vase, salt dip, celery tray, cruet, goblet, syrup, honey dish, pickle dish, water set, covered bean pot, and plates in 7½", 8½", 9½", and 10½" sizes. It is also credited to Jenkins.

Panelled Thistle

Some call this pattern Late Thistle. It was made by Higbee in 1910, by Jefferson in 1920, and also at Dominion of Canada. Shapes are many and include a wine, baskets in three sizes, table set, berry set, cake stand, celery tray, compote, cruet, covered honey dish, goblet, pickle dish, water set, salt dip, shakers, toothpick holder, and plates in four sizes. It is widely available and has been reproduced.

Panel, Rib, and Shell

Shown is a large water pitcher that Kamm calls by this name. It rests on a stand that follows the contours of the pitcher top which is roughly a rectangle with angled corners. The handle is most unusual with curves that do not match the rest of the design. In each corner of the panel are shell designs and this panel may be plain or engraved as the example shown here. The pitcher is 10½" high and probably had companion pieces, but we have no evidence of them. This was made by Central Glass in the 1880s.

Panel with Diamond Point

Also known as Late Diamond Point or Late Diamond Point Band, this pattern was from Central Glass Company of Wheeling, West Virginia, from 1875 – 1882. Shapes reported are a berry set, table set, water set, cake stand (5 sizes, 8" – 12"), covered cheese dish, open compote, goblet, pickle jar, water set, wine, and plates in five sizes (5" – 9"). The compote is known in rare cobalt with clear stem, and the wine is known in turquoise blue.

Panther

From the Fenton Art Glass Company in 1914, this specialty pattern is best known in carnival glass but was also made in chocolate glass (rare small berry bowls) and opaque treatments as well as crystal. Bowls only are known in 10" and 5" sizes. All have three ball-and-claw type feet.

Parker & Whipple Clock Frame

This beautiful 5" pedestal clock frame is marked "Parker & Whipple Co., Meridan, Conn." It was made in 1884 and can be found in crystal as well as the vaseline shown. Only the working parts and face are missing.

Parrot

This pattern is also called Parrot and Fan or Owl and Fan. Possible makers seem to be Richards & Hartley, but this hasn't been confirmed. Made in the 1880s and only the goblet and a rare wine are reported at this time, although one writer lists this pattern in an extended table service. Please write us if you have additional information about this pattern.

Pattee Cross

From U. S. Glass, this pattern was listed in 1912, in a Sears, Roebuck catalog as Gloria. It dates to 1900 and can be found in berry sets, water sets, table sets, jelly compote, open compote, cruet, goblet, nappy, olive nappy, pickle dish, salt dip, shakers, syrup, wine, and 6" vase. Besides clear, this pattern is found in green or with rose stain.

Pavonia

Pavonia was from Ripley and Company in 1885 and then U.S. Glass after 1891 and is also known to collectors as Pineapple Stem. Made in clear, engraved, and with ruby stain. Shapes are many and include bowls, finger bowl, waste bowl, table set, cake plate, cake stand, celery vase, covered or open compotes (5", 6", 7", 8", 9", 10") hotel creamer, custard cup, goblet, mug, pickle dish (square or oblong), plate, milk pitcher, lemonade pitcher, water set, salt dips, sauce, sherbet, bread tray, water tray, and a wine.

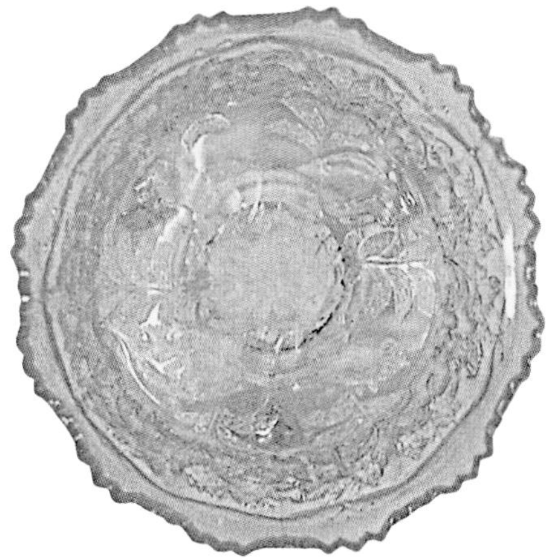

Panther

Parker & Whipple Clock Frame

Parrot

Pattee Cross

Pavonia

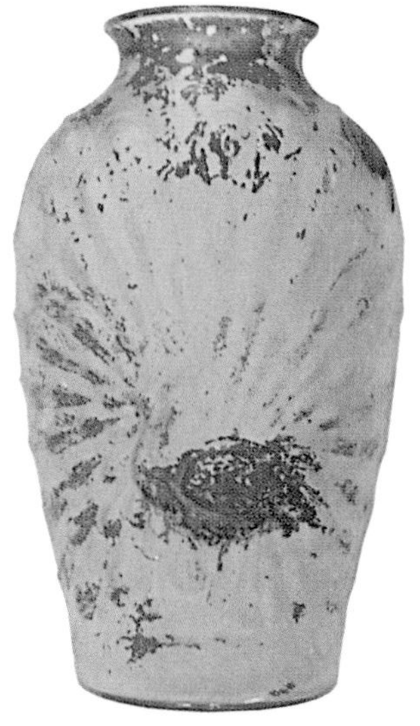

Peacock

Peacock and Urn

Peacock at the Fountain

Peacock Feather

Peanut Lamp

Peacock

This strange 10½" vase (or lamp base if a hole has been drilled in the base) can be found in clear, carnival glass (with the exterior iridized and the interior painted), or with a goofus treatment as this piece once had. The maker hasn't been verified at this time.

Peacock and Urn

Several makers had versions of this pattern but this is Northwood's. It is found in small or large bowls, primarily in carnival glass. The 6" custard sauce shown is unusual in that the bee at the end of the bird's beak and the fluting on the column and urn are not finished. This shape is called an ice cream bowl and the stain is nutmeg. Thanks to Martin C. Puyear for sharing this pattern with us.

Peacock at the Fountain

This is one of Northwood's best-known carnival glass patterns and is sometimes called Peacock and Palm. Very rare pieces in emerald green glass with gold trim are known. Shown is a water pitcher, and tumblers are reported as are pieces of the berry set (the small bowls do not have a peacock). This pattern dates to 1912 when it was patented.

Peacock Feather

Also called Georgia or Peacock Eye, this U. S. Glass pattern (#15076) was made in crystal or blue. Shapes include a table set, berry set, water set, mug, cruet, cake stand, shakers, jelly compote, syrup, large compote, 7" and 9" lamps, plate, sauce, relish, toy table set, celery tray, high or low covered compotes, pickle dish, decanter, and condiment set on a stand.

Peanut Lamp

We now understand this oil lamp, made in five sizes, was a product of U.S. Glass (their number 9939), and was produced at Gillinder, the G factory of the combine. Each of the lamps has a matching shade (two styles of chimneys were made).

Peas and Pods

This is #5602 made by U.S. Glass (Bryce Factory) in 1891. It is found in crystal and ruby stain. The only shapes documented are a wine set consisting of a decanter, stemmed wine, and tray. The decanter is known both with and without a handle.

Peek-A-Boo

Also called Cherub by some collectors, this piece is either a toothpick or a match holder, and has been reproduced. It is credited to McKee in 1900. We understand there may be a matching perfume bottle as well, but we haven't seen it.

Peerless

Peerless is sometimes called Model Peerless because it was a Model Flint Glass product in 1896. Colors are clear, amber, blue, canary, canary opalescent, and green. Shapes include an 8" berry bowl, finger bowl, handled round bowl, table set, cake stand, celery vase compote, cordial, cracker dish, cruet, punch cup, decanters, footed fruit bowl, mustard dish, covered jelly compote, plate, rose bowl, shakers, shot glass, toothpick holder, trays, vases, water bottle, wine, wine set, brandy set, and the condiment set with the clover tray shown.

Penelope

Also known as Leaf in Oval and found in clear, ruby stained, or gold trimmed, this unusual pattern's shapes include a table set, pickle dish, punch set, water set, and berry set, as well as the pickle tray shown.

Pennsylvania

Also known as Balder or Kamoni, this is a U. S. Glass pattern, #15048, made in 1898 in clear, emerald green, or ruby stained glass. Shapes include a table set, water set, berry set, toy table set, water carafe, covered cheese dish, round or square sauce, toothpick holder made from a toy spooner, oil bottle, goblet, celery tray, cruet, and several other shapes.

Peas and Pods

Peek-A-Boo

Peerless

Pennsylvania

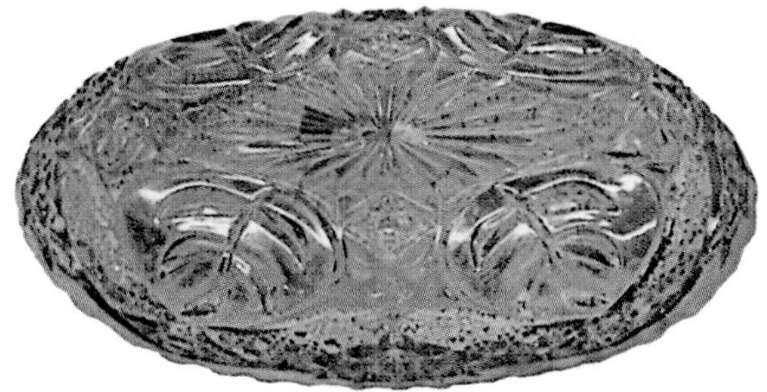

Penelope

Pentagon

Pequot

Perkins

Persian

Pert

Pentagon

This pattern, also known as Oval Five-Footed, is found in crystal and ruby stain. The maker hasn't been identified to the best of our knowledge and the shapes we've heard about are a wine decanter and stemmed wine. In addition examples with etched designs are known.

Pequot

The maker of this pattern seems to be in question, but shards have been found at the Burlington Glass Works of Canada. It is found in clear, blue, or amber and shapes include a table set, celery vase, champagne, covered or open compotes, goblet, jam jar, water set, caster set, wine, and sauce.

Perkins

First made as Fortuna by Higbee, this pattern was later released as New Martinsville's #100F and called Perkins. It can be found in a table set, celery vase, 12" handled cake plate, and cruet. Pieces may be clear or gold trimmed.

Persian

Persian, also known as Block and Pleat, was made by Bryce, Higbee and Company in 1885 and then U. S. Glass. Shapes include a table set, shakers, syrup, cruet, toothpick holder, claret, sauce, berry set, salt dip, cheese dish, water set, jelly compote, carafe, celery vase, celery dish, cup, finger bowl, and the goblet shown.

Pert

Also called Ribbed Forget-me-not, this was a Bryce Brothers pattern in the 1880s and U.S. Glass in 1891. Shapes besides the mug shown include a table set, toy table set, handled mustard with lid, bowls, cake stands (9", 10", 11"), celery vase, covered or open compotes, goblet, water set, plates, master salt, sauce, cup and saucer, toothpick holder, water tray (Herons, Aquatic, or Storks), and a wine. It can be found in clear, amber, blue, canary, or amethyst.

Petal and Loop

This is a flint glass pattern made first by Boston & Sandwich in the 1850s and then by O'Hara Glass. It is found in clear and colors. Here we show the candlesticks in canary glass. Other shapes include a table set, wine, cordial, champagne, plate, celery vase, pickle dish, and possibly others.

Petaled Medallion

From Riverside Glass Company and also known as Miami or Brilliant, this was their #436 pattern. It was made in clear, ruby, or amber stained and is sometimes found with engraving. Shapes include a berry set, table set, celery vase, covered compote, goblet, water set, shakers, sauce, syrup, toothpick holder, and wine.

Peter Rabbit

Another of the very collectible candy containers made for children, this one has outstanding detail and very good glass quality. We've seen this piece with black enameled eyes.

Petticoat

Petticoat, also known as Riverside's National, was made by the Riverside Glass Company in 1899 in clear, gilded, and vaseline (plain or gilded). Shapes include a table set, toothpick holder, water set, shakers, berry set, cruet, syrup, spoon tray, mustard jar, match holder, mug, hat toothpick, spooner, match holder, and match sugar base, compote, salver, and vase.

Pheasant (Frosted)

We believe this is a U. S. Glass pattern from 1891 but have no proof. It is found either with the bird plain or frosted. We show it on a fine low standard covered compote and would appreciate any further information about this pattern, maker, or the shapes available.

Picket Band

Also called Staves with Scalloped Band or Pen, this pattern was made by Doyle and Company in 1876 and is found in both crystal and blue glass. Shapes include a table set, toothpick holder, pickle dish, celery vase, goblet, open compote, covered compote (shown), shakers, and a wine.

Petal and Loop

Petaled Medallion

Peter Rabbit

Petticoat

Pheasant (Frosted)

Picket Band

Pickle Vine

Pigs in Corn

Pilgrim Bottle

Pillow Encircled

Pimlico

Pickle Vine

Credited to U. S. Glass, this well-done covered pickle jar with matching lid is a bit of mystery (we haven't been able to locate it in any references). The design is very realistic with a leafed vine trailing around the center of the jar with pickles suspended. Surely other shapes exist, and we'd like to hear from anyone who can shed light on this pattern.

Pigs in Corn

The maker of this goblet pattern is unknown but date of production seems to be the 1875 – 1885 period. The goblet is a very collectible item, much sought. The corn decoration can be found bent either to the left or to the right.

Pilgrim Bottle

Pilgrim Bottle was made by Central Glass (#731) in 1885, in clear, amber, blue or canary. Shapes include a table set, cruet, shakers, syrup, celery dish, and a pickle dish.

Pillow Encircled

Also called Midway, this was Model Flint's #857 pattern made in the 1890s, in crystal, frosted, etched, decorated, and ruby stained glass. Shapes include bowls (4", 7", 8"), nut bowl, table set, cake salver, celery vase, covered compote (5", 6", 7", 8"), shakers, half-gallon pitcher, quart pitcher, tumbler, and a toothpick holder. Cambridge may have continued this pattern in 1903.

Pimlico

Also called Lotus Leaf (Kamm), this pattern is reported to be from New Martinsville Glass in the 1900 – 1910 era. Shown in a handled cake plate but also known in a celery vase, pickle dish, open salt, goblet, and a table set, this pattern has a ring of leaves on a stippled background with a net of crosslines that have flower centers. The center has a six-pointed star of raised prisms with a hex-button center.

Pineapple

Also known as Pineapple and Bows, this Sowerby (England) pattern is better known to carnival glass collectors but can also be found in crystal or the azure blue shown. Shapes include a creamer, covered butter dish, open sugar that can be stemmed or flat, a rose bowl, or the bowl shape shown on a separate base. The butter dish has the pattern on the inside of the lid, and bowls range from 6" to 8".

Pineapple and Fan

This U. S. Glass pattern, made in 1895, was their #15041. It was first made by Adams & Company and is sometimes known as Holbrook or Cube with Fan. Shapes include a table set, berry set, cake stand, celery vase, custard cup, goblet, mug, relish, water set, cruet, decanter, plate, rose bowl, and punch set. It can be found in clear, emerald green, ruby stained, and rarely in carnival glass.

Pipe Match Holder

This piece may be a toothpick holder but it seems more appropriate to call it a match holder. It is milk glass and shows signs of gilding or other decoration. We have no knowledge of the maker and would welcome any information readers have about this piece.

Pistol

Here is another of the popular collectible candy containers that were made for children. Cambridge made a similar 5½" pistol container, a revolver, and this small pistol, their #2842. Sometimes these containers were enameled or gilt trimmed.

Pittsburgh Fan

Pittsburgh Fan can be found in a table set, goblet, cake stand, pickle dish, and the plate. Other shapes probably exist. The maker isn't known, at least to us, but the pattern dates to the late 1880s. Shown is a gilded pickle boat in emerald green, a rare color for this pattern.

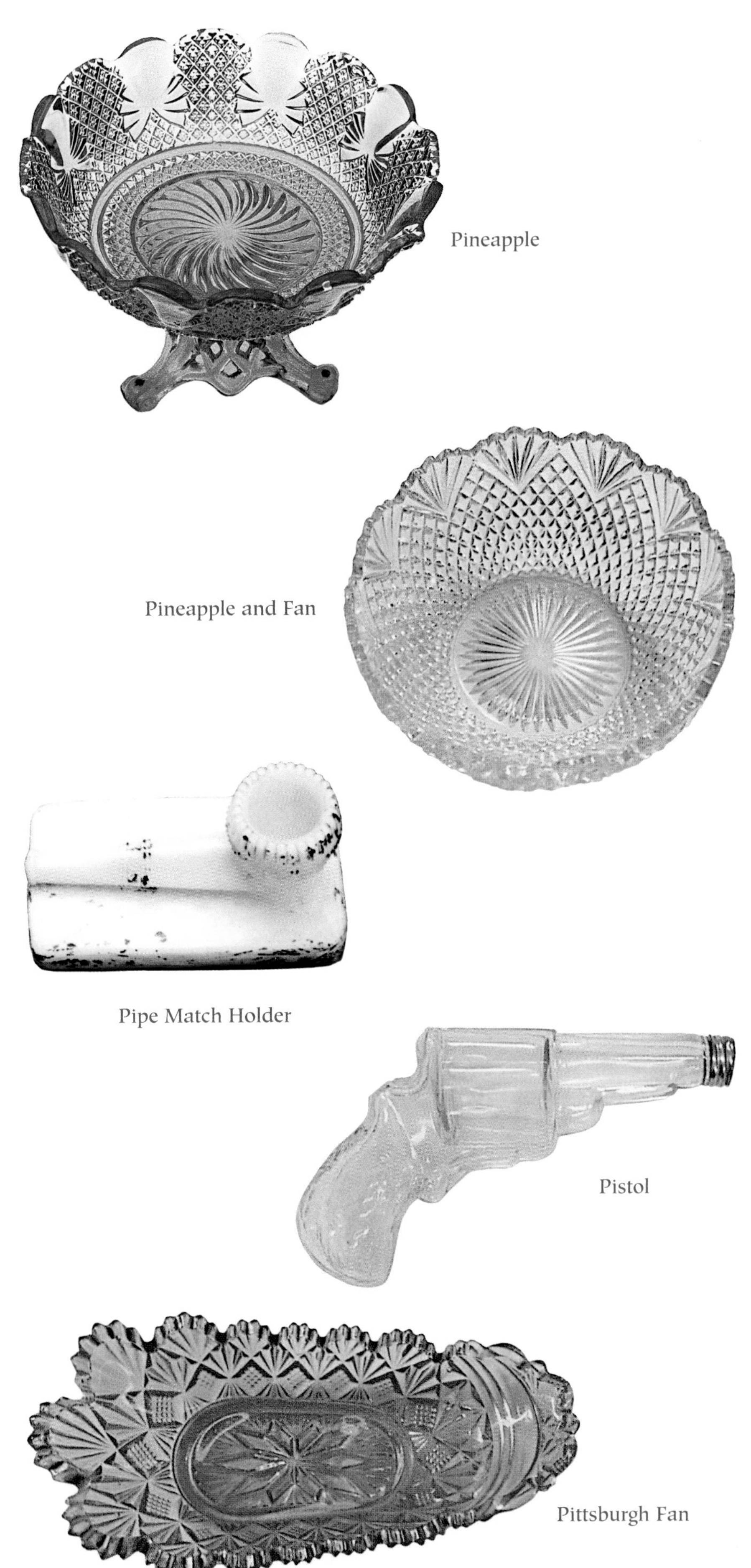

Pineapple

Pineapple and Fan

Pipe Match Holder

Pistol

Pittsburgh Fan

Plain

Pleat and Panel

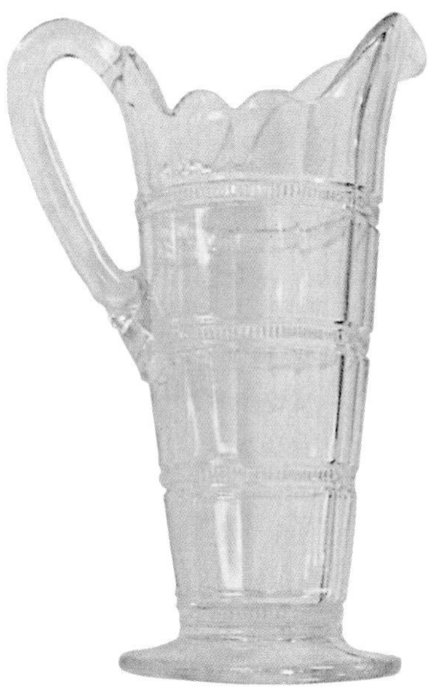

Pleated Bands

Plume (Adams)

Pleated Medallion

Plain

We do not know who made this water set, but it is very similar to one called Pleat Band from Indiana Tumbler and Goblet Company of Greentown, Indiana. The example shown has frosted flowers, fern, and a script "S," obviously decorated for someone with this initial. Surely other shapes are known to match but we haven't seen them.

Pleat and Panel

Pleat and Panel was from Bryce, Walker and Company in the late 1870s and then U. S. Glass in 1891 and can be found in clear, amethyst, canary, and blue. Shapes include a table set, compote, covered bowl, cake stand, square plate, water tray, lamp, candy jar with lid, relish dish, bread tray, shakers, and footed sauce.

Pleated Bands

While we haven't been able to come up with the maker of this interesting pattern, we have learned it was made in the tankard pitcher and matching tumblers as well as a goblet. We suspect it was also made in the usual table pieces that include a table set, pickle tray, and perhaps other stemmed pieces but can't be sure.

Pleated Medallion

Pleated Medallion was produced in 1908 as New Martinsville #713. Shapes include a table set, cruet, plate, toothpick holder, pickle dish, and cake stand. Some pieces may be gold trimmed or even ruby stained with gold trim.

Plume (Adams)

Plume was made by Adams and Company in 1874 and U.S. Glass in 1891, in bowls, cake stand, sauce, celery vase, footed bowls, lamp, goblet, table set, and various footed and non-footed pieces. Can be found in clear or ruby-stained glass. The design can be either horizontal or vertical.

Plums and Cherries

Plums and Cherries was made by the Northwood Glass Company and found in rare carnival items and decorated crystal where a water set, table set, and covered bowl are known. On the piece shown, the lid has the cherries (stained red), and the base has the plums (purple) while both pieces have gold trim. The pattern dates to 1906.

Plutec

Plutec was part of McKee Glass Company's "tec" series in 1900. Shapes include a table set, water set, berry set, celery vase, compote, decanter, goblet, pickle dish, 11" plate, syrup, water tray, cake stand, wine, and nut bowl. Pieces are marked "Pres-Cut."

Pointed Jewel

Pointed Jewel was made by Columbia Glass and then U.S. Glass as their #15006 pattern. The child's table service is called Long Diamond in this pattern. Shapes include a table set, cup, toy table set, celery vase, pickle dish, bowls, shakers, syrup, compote (shown), goblet, and a wine. It seems to be found only in crystal.

Pointing Dog

This pattern was first made by Bryce in the 1880s and then as U.S. Glass after 1891, in clear, frosted, amber, blue, and milk glass. The mug is 2⅝" tall and has a diameter of 2⅜". The design shows a dog on both sides of the mug.

Polar Bear

Also called Alaska, Ice Berg, North Pole, or Polar Bear and Seal, this pattern is now attributed to the Crystal Glass Company of Pittsburgh, Pennsylvania (some items are marked "C.G.C"). Made in clear or machine ground, shapes include an ice bowl, waste bowl, goblet, pickle dish, water pitcher, bread tray, sauce, oval or round tray. It was originally advertised as Arctic pattern in June 1880.

Plums and Cherries

Plutec

Pointed Jewel

Pointing Dog

Polar Bear

Polka Dot

Polka Dot
(Geo. Duncan and Sons)

Popcorn

Poppy

Polka Dot

Also called Inverted Coin Dot by many collectors, this pattern is found in crystal, sapphire, marine green, cranberry, rubina, rubina verde, and amber as well as opalescent colors. Examples were made by Hobbs, Brockunier as well as Fenton, Northwood, and Dugan. Shapes are many and include table sets, berry sets, water set (several shapes and sizes), bar bottles, cruets, decanters, carafes, mugs, custard cups, celery vase, footed bowls, mustard jar with lid, and both salt and sugar shakers. Hobbs pieces date to 1884 and the rest to the early 1900s.

Polka Dot (Geo. Duncan and Sons)

Polka Dot was made by Geo. Duncan and Sons (Factory D of USGC), 1891, in both pressed and earlier blown glass (1884 – 1890). It can be found in clear, canary, amber or blue. Shapes include finger bowls, cruet, shakers, tankard pitcher, toothpick holder, syrup, champagne glass, tumbler, water bottles (four shapes and sizes), footed bowls, covered compote, celery vase, covered cheese dish, sauces, wine, cordial, claret, goblet, and a pedestal-based pitcher.

Popcorn

Popcorn was made by Boston & Sandwich Glass in the late 1860s. It can be found with some variations (raised ear of corn or flat ear of corn). Shapes include a table set, cake stands (8" or 11"), cordial, goblet (with ear or with lined ear), sauce, water pitcher, or wine (shown).

Poppy

As well known as the Cabbage Rose puffed vase, the Poppy version is found in goofus, opaque glass, and decorated glass in 4", 6", 8", 10" sizes. Some are tall and stately, and some are squat. In addition, there are shakers called Poppy Blossom that nearly match.

Poppy Variant

Most often found in carnival glass on the exterior of small 7" – 8" bowls, this pattern is often overlooked in the wake of the regular Poppy pattern, also from Northwood. The only shape seen in the variant in crystal is the one shown, and it was made to be sold with a goofus treatment. The example shown still has traces of this in the seams of the design.

Portland Birch Leaf

Metz credits this leaf-shaped sauce bowl to the Portland Company. The pattern is very similar to the Hobbs Tree of Life design. Colors reported are crystal, ruby, canary, blue, or green.

Post Script

Made by Tarentum Glass Company in 1905, this pattern is quite well balanced and was made in a table set, shakers, berry set, individual creamer and sugar, cruet, goblet, handled olive, salt shakers, and wine.

Potpourri

From the Millersburg Company, in crystal or carnival glass (a rare compote is known in sapphire blue), this pattern is much like the Country Kitchen design from the same maker, except Potpourri has an added daisy wheel. It can be found on rare milk pitchers and 7" tall compotes in deep, flared, or salver shapes. Carnival glass compotes have the Poppy pattern on the interior while crystal ones do not. Potpourri is very desirable in all shapes.

Powder and Shot

Powder and Shot is attributed to Boston and Sandwich, Portland Glass, and others from the 1870s. Shapes include a table set, caster bottle, celery vase, egg cup, goblet, water pitcher, sauce, tumbler, covered compote, and master salt.

Prayer Rug

From the Fenton Art Glass Company in 1915, this pattern is primarily a custard glass one, but it has been found in rare iridized custard on the bonbon shape and plate. It is also found on decorated custard, and the shapes are a bonbon, a bowl, and a plate shape.

Poppy Variant

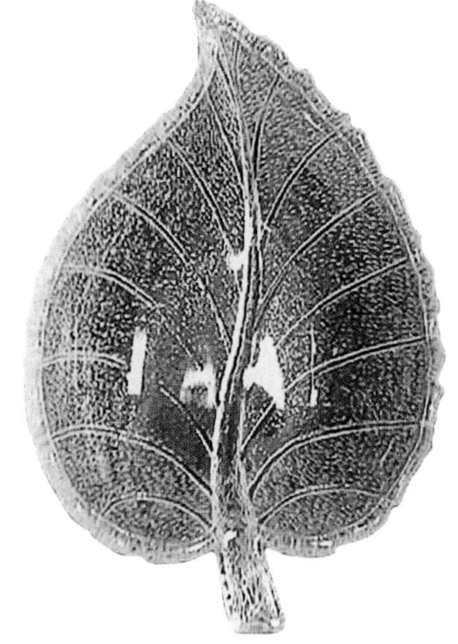

Portland Birch Leaf

Post Script

Potpourri

Powder and Shot

Prayer Rug

Pressed Diamond

Pressed Leaf

Pride

Primrose

Prince of Wales Plumes

Pressed Diamond

Pressed Diamond, also called Block and Diamond or Zephyr, was made by the Central Glass Company (#775) in 1885 and then by U.S. Glass in 1891. Colors found are clear, amber, blue, or canary, and shapes include berry sets, a table set, finger bowl, cake stand, celery vase, open or covered compotes, cruet, custard cup, goblet, water set, 11" plate, salt dip, shakers, and a wine.

Pressed Leaf

This simple pattern, also called New Pressed Leaf, was first made by McKee Brothers in 1868 and later by Central Glass in 1881. It can be found in a table set, compote, wine, cake stand, oval dish, cordial, egg cup, lamp, berry set, syrup, water set, and goblet. The compotes are found in both open and covered as well as low or high stems.

Pride

This pattern, also known as Bevelled Star, came from the Model Flint Glass Company in 1900. It was made in crystal, emerald green, cobalt blue, vaseline, and amber glass. Shapes are table sets, berry sets, water sets, celery tray (5" x 10½"), salt shakers, cruet, and a tall standard covered compote. Sold through Sears in 1900, all colors bring higher prices than crystal.

Primrose

From the Canton Glass Company as their #10 in 1885 and also known as Stippled Primrose, this pattern is found in crystal, amber, blue, canary, apple green (scarce), milk glass, slag, or black opaque glass. Shapes include a berry set, waste bowl, cake stand, high or low compotes in several sizes, cordial, creamer, egg cup, goblet, finger lamp, pickle dish, water set, milk pitcher, plates (4", 6", 7", 8", 9"), oval platter (shown), relish tray, sauce, water tray, and a wine.

Prince of Wales Plumes

From the A. H. Heisey Company, this was their #335 made in 1900. Both gilded and decorated pieces are known and shapes are a table set, water set, shakers, berry set, and toothpick holder. The design is a very strong one and very collectible.

Priscilla

Also known as Alexis or Sun and Star, this is a Dalzell, Gilmore & Leighton product from 1888. Shapes include a banana stand, biscuit jar, covered bowls, square bowl, rose bowl, table set, cake stands, celery vase, compote, covered jelly compote, condiment set, cracker jar, cruet, cup, donut stand, goblet, mug, pickle dish, water set (bulbous or tankard), plate, relish, shakers, syrup, toothpick holder, and wine.

Prism

Made by McKee and others, this common pattern was made from 1860 to the 1920s by various companies in most standard shapes that include table sets, water sets, berry sets, champagne, decanter, goblet, wine, egg cup, and shakers.

Prism Bars

Made in the 1890s (maker unknown), this prism design with the double banded top can be found in a table set, celery vase, goblet, water set, berry set, relish, and pickle tray.

Prize, The

The Prize, from the National Glass Company (McKee) in 1901 can be found in clear, emerald green, and ruby stained glass. Shapes include a table set, water set, toothpick holder, shakers, syrup, goblet, pickle dish, and cruet. Please note the ornate metal crown on the pitcher shown.

Pulled Loop

Better known in both carnival glass and opalescent glass, this Dugan/Diamond vase pattern was also made in crystal in limited amounts. Sizes range from 9" to 15" tall, depending on the amount of swinging or slinging done. The design is simple but effective.

Punty and Diamond Point

Punty and Diamond Point was made by Heisey as their #305 (1899 – 1913). Shapes include a berry set, punch set, cruet, shakers, vase, water set, water carafe, decanter, sugar shaker, platter, toothpick holder, bitters bottle, sauce, and the celery dish shown.

Priscilla

Prism

Prism Bars

Prize, The

Pulled Loop

Punty and Diamond Point

Punty Band

Pure Pack Mug

Puritan (McKee's)

Quadruped

Quartered Block

Punty Band

This was Heisey's #1220 from 1896. Shapes include a table set, water set, syrup, mug, shakers, salt dip, cake basket, candy dish, toothpick holder, goblet, wine, cake stand, banana compote, and spoon tray. Punty Band was made in clear and in ruby stained glass and often used as souvenir pieces, as shown.

Pure Pack Mug

Made from the same mould as another mug called Necco Sweets, the Pure Pack mug is an equal mystery since we have no knowledge of who made either. Both are 2⅛" tall and have a 1⅝" diameter, with banded top and twelve panels around it. Both have been seen only in clear glass.

Puritan (McKee's)

Several companies had Puritan patterns but this one was made by McKee Glass in 1910. It was made in crystal, as well as ruby stained glass. Shapes include a water set, table set, and a toothpick holder. Other shapes may exist and we'd like to hear from readers about any of them.

Quadruped

While many collectors call this pattern Chippendale and we showed it as that in the last book, we will attempt to give it its more proper name here. This pattern was made by Indiana Glass in 1908 and is found in clear as well as ruby stain. Shapes include a table set, berry set, jelly compote, vase, sundae dish, shakers, tumbler, short stemmed compote, pickle dish, relish dish, hotel creamer and sugar, and a mid-size bowl. Do not confuse this pattern with Ohio Flint's Chippendale pattern.

Quartered Block

This very sturdy oil lamp dates to the 1880s and was continued in production for two decades. It can be found in at least four sizes that include a flat handled lamp, stemmed handled lamp, and two sizes of stemmed parlor lamps. This was made by Duncan & Miller in 1905.

Quatrefoil

The maker of this distinct pattern seems to be a mystery, but we know it was made in the 1880s in clear and apple green glass. Shapes include a covered or open compote, table set, water set, rare goblet, bowls, and salt shakers.

Quebec Diamond Band

We've learned absolutely nothing about this pattern except its name, so we are showing it in hope someone out there can give us some facts. Shown is a wine goblet from the collection of John Gregory.

Queen

Also known as Pointed Panel, Panelled Daisy and Button, or Sunk, Queen was made by McKee and Brothers Company in 1894. Shapes are a table set (three styles), cake stand, claret, covered compote, open compote, oval dish, goblet, water set, wine, cruet, relish dish, celery vase, and sauce.

Queen Anne

Queen Anne was credited to LaBelle Glass Company in 1880 as their #12006 and made in clear, copper engraved, or amber. Shapes are confusing and show variations but include covered bowls, table set, 7" or 8" casserole, celery vase, high or low covered compotes, egg cup, water set, milk pitcher, plate, shakers, sauce, and syrup. Some shapes are known as Viking or Bearded Man pieces because of the faced pouring spouts.

Quatrefoil

Quebec Diamond Band

Queen

Queen Anne

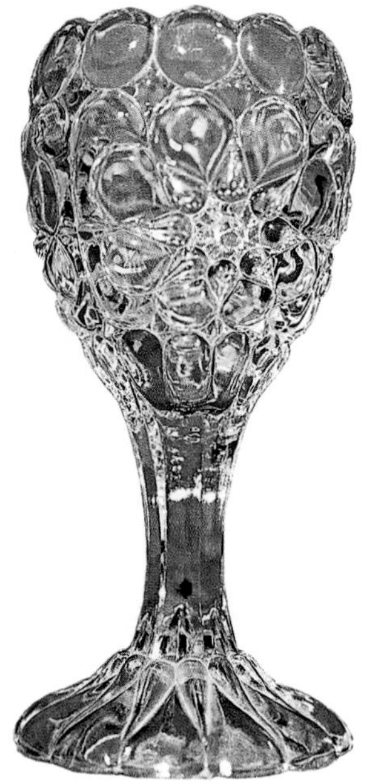

Queen's Necklace

Rabbit Sitting

Rabbit Upright

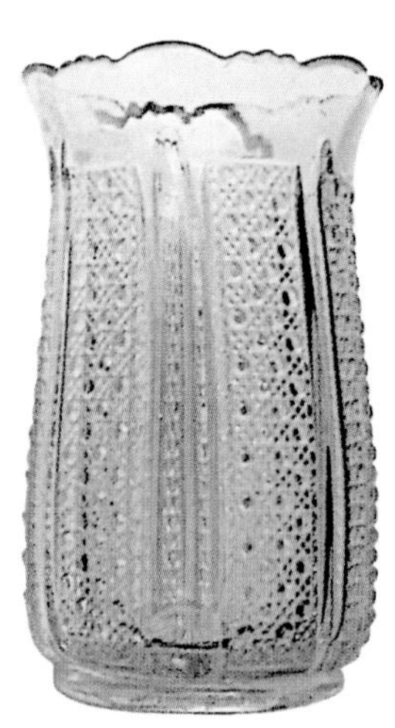
Rainbow

Racing Deer

Railroad Platter

Queen's Necklace

Also called Queen's Jewel(s), this was a Bellaire Glass pattern first (1891) and then U.S. Glass (after 1891). Shapes include a 10" bowl, table set, cake salver, celery vase, cologne bottle, open 10" compote, cruet, goblet, lamp, oil bottle, rose bowl, shakers, syrup, vases (8", 9", 10"), water set, and wine. One rare stemmed vase is known in iridized glass.

Rabbit Sitting

Rabbit Sitting was first from the Central Glass Company in the 1880s and then U.S. Glass after 1891 and is found on both clear and amber glass. This mug is $3\frac{3}{8}$" tall and has a $3\frac{1}{8}$" diameter and features rabbits sitting on one side and running on the other.

Rabbit Upright

Made in the 1880s like many other mugs, this one is found in clear, amber, blue, apple green, and probably canary glass. The mould is identical to one called Wolf and has a rabbit standing on its hind legs on both sides. Actually a closer look at the animal convinces us it is a kangaroo, not a rabbit.

Racing Deer

Sometimes called Racing Deer and Doe, Racing Deer was made by the Indiana Tumbler and Goblet Company (Greentown) in the late 1890s in both clear or chocolate glass. this pitcher can be found with either a flat top or with scallops. The Dalzell, Gilmore, and Leighton attribution of this pattern by some writers is in error.

Railroad Platter

We have conflicting reports as to the maker of this piece; one writer says it came from Bakewell, Pears Glass of Pittsburgh, but recent research points to Canton Glass as the maker in 1882. The design is very good with fine realism. The rim features four sections of fine file and splayed leaves.

Rainbow

From McKee and Brothers in 1894 in clear, rose, or gold trimmed, shapes include a table set, celery vase, shakers, carafe, cigar jar, water set, wine, and bowls.

Raindrop

Raindrop is similar to the Inverted Thumbprint pattern except the raised dots are on the outside of the pieces and not to be confused with Thousand Eye where the dots are smaller. The maker of Raindrop is unknown, but it is believed to date to the 1885 – 1895 era. Colors are clear, amber, blue, apple green, or canary. Shapes include a celery vase, table set, tumbler, miniature lamp, high standard compote (shown), a sauce, and a pickle dish.

Rampant Lion

From Gillinder & Sons of Philadelphia in 1877, this certainly may be a part of the Lion pattern. At any rate, this great covered compote has a frosted Tree Trunk stem as well as a frosted Lion finial with the lion raised to rest its front paws on a tree branch. Also present is the same cable on the lid's bottom rim. It is truly beautiful compote.

Ram's Head

The mugs shown here have a satinized ram's head similar to the Roaring Lion pattern we showed in a goblet in our second edition and in a plate in this edition. We suspect that these are English. Ram's Head mugs are known in crystal and the vaseline shown and may have been made in additional colors as well.

Ransom

Many collectors know this pattern as Gold Band because some items have gilding, but the Ransom name is a better one. Made by Riverside Glass in 1899 and found in crystal or vaseline, the shapes include a table set, bowls, a cruet, and perhaps several other shapes. We welcome additional information on this pattern from readers.

Rayed Flower

Rayed Flower was made by Indiana Glass in 1920 and is similar to their Flower with Cane pattern, shapes include a table set, water set, berry set, milk pitcher, toothpick holder, custard cup, shakers, celery vase, and pickle dish. Pieces are clear or decorated, often gold trimmed.

Raindrop

Rampant Lion

Ram's Head

Rayed Flower

Ransom

Rayed Heart

Red Block

Reaper

Reeded Star

Regal Swan

Rayed Heart

Credited to the Jefferson Glass Company in 1910 and then to Dominion of Canada in 1916 (Jefferson was the parent company of Dominion), Rayed Heart is found in opalescent glass in the goblet shape and in crystal in a berry set, table set, water set, pickle tray and relish tray, besides the goblet. Dominion called this their #275 pattern, and it would be hard to tell whether pieces came from Montreal or from Jefferson's plant.

Reaper

This oval bread platter is actually part of the Picket line (also called Picket Fence or London). It was made in the 1890s by the King Glass Company, but shards have been found at the Burlington Glass Works in Canada. The Picket line can be found in clear, amber, apple green, or blue. This platter is also called Stuart's McCormick Reaper.

Red Block

Red Block was first made by Bryce Brothers (#175), then by U. S. Glass in 1898, and by Central Glass (#881 and #893), Model Flint Glass, as well as Pioneer Glass (#250). It can be found in clear, clear with amber, and ruby stained glass. Shapes include a water set, table set, syrup, mustard jar with saucer, shakers, cruet, cup, lamp, round bowls, and rectangular bowls.

Reeded Star

Shown in an Imperial 1909 catalog as their #302½ pattern, the shapes in this fine pattern seem to be limited and include a jelly compote, a goblet, iced tea tumbler, and the 6½" cologne bottle with stopper shown. Certainly other shapes were probably made but are not shown in the 1909 catalog.

Regal Swan

The master salt dip shown couldn't be called anything other than regal. The head, neck, and wings are sterling silver and are fitted onto a moulded glass body with tail section that holds the salt. Detailing is remarkable with the glass section as intricate as the silver piece. Surely this piece had to grace a mansion's table.

Reticulated Cord

This pattern was made by U.S. Glass (O'Hara) in 1891 in crystal, blue or canary (colors are scarce). Shapes include a table set, water set, flat sauce, relish, celery vase, 11" round plate, large cake stand, and a wine.

Reverse Drapery

Reverse Drapery was made by the Fenton Art Glass Company and is known in bowls, plates, and vases all from the same mould. Mostly known in carnival glass or opalescent glass, some crystal pieces exist as shown by this pale pink bowl that came about a decade after the 1910 carnival glass production.

Reverse Fan and Diamond

We haven't been able to learn much about this pattern and must say "maker unknown" at this time. It was more than likely made in other shapes, including a table set or berry set, but to date we've seen only the water set. Any information from readers would be appreciated. The name is ours.

Reverse Twist

We believe this child's mug is from Columbia Glass Company of Finley, Ohio. It matches another they made called Prism in shape and size. We've named this Reverse Twist because it turns in the opposite direction from the Twist toy table set pieces made by the Albany Glass Company.

Rexford

Also known as Euclid or Boylan, this Higbee pattern was produced in 1910 in table sets, large cake stand, water set, compote, two handled celery vase, goblet, covered jam jar, 7" square plate, wine, and toothpick holder. Rexford is known in clear crystal only.

Rhine Star

When we first saw this very nice vase pattern, we were impressed, but turning it over, we saw it was marked "Germany," and we realized this was a piece of import glass. It stands 6½" tall. The glass is quite heavy and sparkling clear.

Reticulated Cord

Reverse Drapery

Reverse Fan and Diamond

Reverse Twist

Rexford

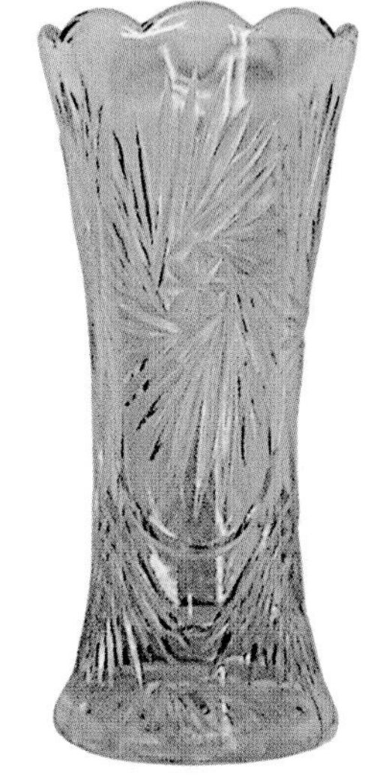

Rhine Star

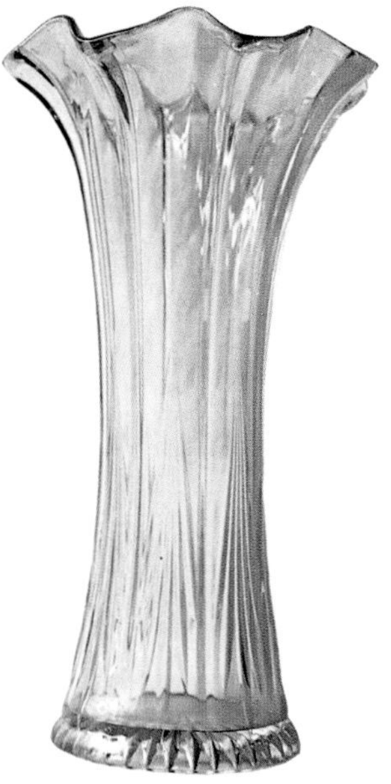

Rib and Flute

Rib Band

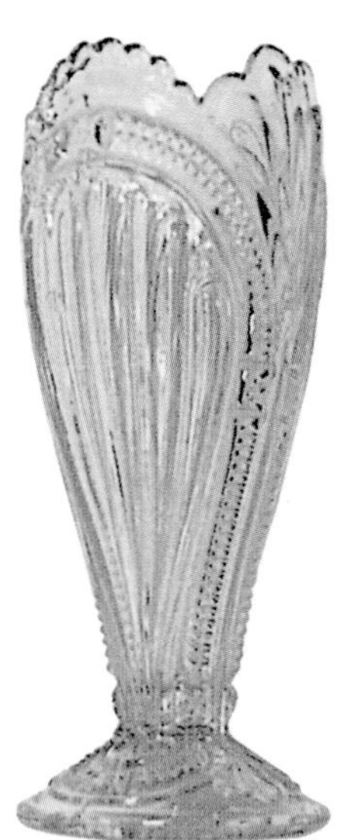

Ribbed Ellipse

Ribbed Forget-Me-Not

Ribbed Leaves Variant

Ribbed Palm

Rib and Flute

This vase pattern is primarily known in carnival glass. It has v-shaped wedges of ribbing rising from the base to join panels of flute or wide paneling. The maker has not been identified, but we strongly suspect Dugan or Diamond Glass.

Rib Band

This rather simple pattern has little going for it except quality. The handle is applied, and there is a short pedestal base. Only table sets and water sets have been reported, and the maker is unknown. Similar pieces are known in milk glass.

Ribbed Ellipse

Ribbed Ellipse, also called Admiral, was from J. B. Higbee Glass Company in 1905. Shapes include a table set, cake plate, mug, plate, compote, berry set, water set, and the vase shape shown. The design is a well done one and reminds us of the Prince of Wales Plumes pattern shown on page 206.

Ribbed Forget-Me-Not

This pattern from Bryce Brothers and then U.S. Glass in 1891 is also called Pert Set. Colors are clear, amber, blue, and canary (all colors are scarce). Shapes include a toy table set, handled mustard, cup, and an individual creamer. Shown is the 4" creamer in canary.

Ribbed Leaves Variant

Ribbed Leaves Variant was made by the Federal Glass Company and shown in the Federal Glass Company's Packer's Catalogue in 1914. Made only in clear, it is 2⅝" tall. There is another Ribbed Leaves mug that is not the variant that stands 3⅜" tall and may also be a Federal product, but we have no proof it is.

Ribbed Palm

Ribbed Palm was from McKee Brothers in the 1860s as design #1748 and reproduced by Imperial Glass (goblet only) in clear. Shapes include a table set, celery vase, champagne, covered compote, open compote, egg cup, goblet, lamp, water set, 6" plate, master salt dip, sauce, and wine.

Ribbed Window Vase

Here is the ribbed window vase like the other shown elsewhere from the New Martinsville Glass Company. It was used for stack shelving in window or glass displays. The top and the base were made wide to support the shelves and to distribute the weight.

Ribbon

From Bakewell, Pears & Company in 1870 and Geo. Duncan in 1878, this pattern may be clear or frosted. It is also known as Rebecca at the Well, or Frosted Ribbon. Shapes include a cologne bottle, berry set, waste bowl, table set, cake stand, celery vase, champagne, covered cheese dish, covered or open compotes, the famous Dolphin compote in round or oval (shown), goblet, pickle jar, water set, milk pitcher, plate, platter, shakers, sauce, water tray, or wine.

Rib Over Drape

This was made by the D.C. Jenkins Glass Company as their Drape pattern. Shapes include a pitcher, ice bucket, nappy, 8" bowl, spooner, tumbler, ice tea glass, soda glass, covered butter dish, sugar, spooner, and a vase.

Ring Neck

This pattern is actually part of a line of practical drink items from Perfection Glass Company of Washington, Pennsylvania, and advertised as their "Imperial" or style #251. These items, carafes, syrups, decanters, etc., all have the easily removed necks so they could be filled with more ease.

Ripple

Made in several sizes in carnival glass and rarely in opalescent glass, the Ripple vase from Imperial Glass was also made in crystal in three base diameters and several heights. The pattern is very much like one called Ribbed Spiral made by Model Flint Glass of Albany, Indiana, in 1902, in opalescent glass.

Ribbed Window Vase

Rib Over Drape

Ribbon

Ring Neck

Ripple

Rising Sun

Riverside Colonial Lamp

Riverside Elk

Riverside's Derby

Roaring Lion

Robin Hood

Rising Sun

This well-known pattern from U. S. Glass was their #15110 made in 1908. Shapes include a water set (two pitcher shapes), cruet, table set (three shapes known in the sugar), wine, toothpick holder, compote, and large water tray. Rising Sun is well known in carnival glass and decorated glass also.

Riverside Colonial Lamp

This lamp is part of the Lucille line from Riverside like the Wild Rose Lamp shown elsewhere. Millersburg glass bought the moulds for this line when Riverside closed and many of the shapes and sizes were made by them in carnival glass.

Riverside Elk

Also known as Elk Medallion, this pattern is from Riverside Glass in the 1880s. Shapes known are the covered pickle jar shown and a goblet, but we feel confident other shapes exist and would like to have any readers' information about this pattern.

Riverside's Derby

This is #1897, also known as Riverside's Derby. It was made in 1897 and can be found in crystal, vaseline, or gilded vaseline. Shapes include a table set, individual creamer and sugar, toothpick holder, water set, jelly compote, goblet, berry set, square berry bowls (small), 8" octagon bowl, cruet, covered compote (5", 6", 7"), open compote (7½", 8½"), breakfast set (creamer and sugar), and probably a pickle dish as well as a wine goblet.

Roaring Lion

While we have no new information about the maker of this pattern (we still feel it is English), we are able to show a beautiful plate to add to the goblet shown in our second edition. We suspect there are more shapes and welcome information about this pattern.

Robin Hood

From Fostoria Glass Company in 1898, this striking pattern can be found in a table set, salt shakers, compote, jelly compote, celery vase, water set, syrup (scarce), milk pitcher, goblet, an pickle dish.

Robin in Tree

Like so many other mugs, this one was made by Bryce Brothers and then U.S. Glass after 1891. Mosser reproduced it with their "M-inside-Ohio" trademark, so be cautious. It originally was made in clear, amber, blue, canary, and light amethyst glass. It is 3¾" tall.

Rock Crystal

Made by McKee Glass Company in 1894, this is a well-known design. Shapes include a table set, water set, salt shakers, sherbet, candlesticks, finger bowl, pickle tray, cruet, punch set, goblet, and custard cup.

Rocket

Made by Indiana Glass Company and shown in Butler Brothers catalogs from 1914 to 1926, this is a very recognizable pattern. Shapes include a water set, table set, berry set, compote, cake stand, and stemmed celery vase.

Roman Key with Ribs

This is called with Ribs by some collectors, or just Roman Key by others. It is attributed to the Union Glass Company in the 1860s. Shapes include bowls, a table set, caster set, celery vase, high or low compotes, a cordial, custard cup, decanter, egg cup, goblet, oil lamp, mustard jar, pickle dish, milk pitcher, water set, plate, relish, shakers, and wine.

Roman Rosette

Roman Rosette is a popular pattern first from Bryce, Walker in 1875 and then from U. S. Glass in 1898 as their #15030, where it was made in both clear and ruby stained glass. Shapes include a table set, water set, bowls in five sizes, bread plate (oval), two sizes of cake stands, caster set, celery vase, open compote, covered compotes in five sizes, goblet, large and small mugs, pickle dish, shakers, wine, and plate.

Robin in Tree

Rock Crystal

Rocket

Roman Key with Ribs

Roman Rosette

Romeo

Rose

Rose (and other flowers)

Roseland

Rose in Snow

Romeo

Also called Block and Fan, this was Richards and Hartley's #544 from 1888, then from U. S. Glass in 1891, in clear, ruby stained, and milk glass. Shapes include a table set, cake stand, biscuit jar, berry set, finger bowl, rose bowl, waste bowl, carafe, caster set, cake stand, celery tray and vase, open and covered compotes, condiment set, decanter, goblet, ice bucket, lamp, water set, milk pitcher, plate, sugar shaker, and wine.

Rose

Rose wade by U.S. Glass (#15318) in vaseline, blue, clear, and green with finishes in satin or opalescent treatment. Shapes include a covered trinket box, a compote, cologne bottles, console bowl, candlesticks, a handled cake plate, a trinket tray, large dresser tray. This pattern was once misnamed Roses and Ruffles, but that name is hopefully behind us.

Rose (and other flowers)

This strangely named pattern is from U.S. Glass (Factory E of Richards & Hartley). It dates to 1891 and has four panels that show a different flower on each. It is found in 5" and 9" berry dishes, and we show the smaller size in canary.

Rose in Snow

Rose in Snow was made by Bryce Brothers (square form #125) in the 1880s, Ohio Glass (round form), and then by U. S. Glass in 1891. It can be found in clear, amber, blue, or canary. Shapes include a bitters bottle, covered or open compotes, table set, cake stand, oval dish, goblet, jam jar, mug, pickle dish (double or single), water set, plates (four sizes), oval platter, relish dish, sauces (flat or footed), covered sweetmeat, and toddy jar.

Roseland

Like the Late Tomato Vine pattern shown on page 158, this one came along in the 1920s. It can be found in a water set (the tumbler is shown) and berry set, and there may well be other shapes we haven't encountered at this time. The maker is unknown to us.

Rose Point Band

Rose Point Band was from Indiana Glass Company in 1913 and is also called Waterlily or Clematis. Shapes include a table set, sauce, compote, celery vase, footed bowl, berry set, water set, and goblet.

Roses in the Snow

Well known to collectors of goofus glass, this pattern has a variant that has a netted background. Shapes include a fine 10" oil lamp, an 11" plate, and the 9" bowl. Oother shapes may exist.

Rose Sprig

This pattern from Campbell, Jones, and Company in 1886 can be found in crystal, amber, blue, and canary. Shapes include a biscuit jar, sietz shape bowl, cake stand, celery vase, covered compotes (7", 8"), open compotes (high or low in 7", 8"), goblet, mug, square nappy, pickle dish, plate (6", 6½", 8", 10"), footed punch bowl, relish tray, salt (sleigh shape), sauce (flat or footed), water tray, water set, and a wine.

Rosette

Also known as Magic, this was made by U. S. Glass in 1891. Shapes include a table set, plate, tray, shakers, water set, jelly compote, covered bowl, tall celery vase, fish relish, and handled plate.

Rosette and Palms

Made by the J. B. Higbee Glass Company in 1910, shapes include a table set, water set, goblet, wine, salt shakers, relish tray or dish, 9" plate, celery vase, banana stand, cake stand, and sauce.

Rose Point Band

Roses in the Snow

Rose Sprig

Rosette

Rosette and Palms

Rosette Band

Rosette with Pinwheels

Rotec

Royal Crystal

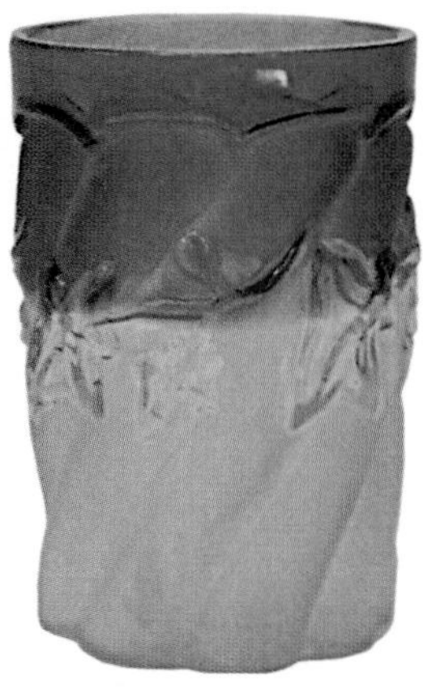

Royal Ivy

Rosette Band

Also called Chrysanthemum or Double Daisy, this pattern was made by the Riverside Glass Works in 1893 and can be found in clear, engraved, or with ruby stain. Shapes include an 8" berry bowl with slotted lid, table set, and the rare compote shown. We apologize for calling this pattern Rosette Row in the first edition of this book and hope our efforts to correct our mistakes as quickly as possible make amends.

Rosette with Pinwheels

Issued by Indiana Glass Company as their #171 design in 1905, this very active pattern can be found in a table set, celery vase, jelly compote, footed cup, water set, and honey dish (square) as well as the footed bowl shown. It is amazing how much good glass came from this small Dunkirk, Indiana, company, and this is one of the best.

Rotec

Rotec was made by McKee in 1904 in crystal or ruby stained glass. Shapes include a table set, water set, berry set, and a punch set that includes a large punch tray. Like most of the "tec" lines, this one was produced in quantity over several years, so a lot of it exists today.

Royal Crystal

Royal Crystal, also called Tarentum's Atlanta, Diamond and Teardrop, or Shining Diamonds, was made by Tarentum Glass in 1894. Colors include clear or clear with ruby stain, and shapes include flared or straight bowls (5", 6", 7", 8"), rectangular bowls, square bowls, cologne bottle, water bottle, table set, cake stands, celery vase, compotes (6", 7"), cracker jar, cruet (two sizes), goblet, candy jar, milk pitcher, water set (bulbous or tankard), plate (oval or round), shakers, sauce (flat or footed), syrup, toothpick holder, and a wine.

Royal Ivy

Found in clear or frosted glass that fades to pink as well as in amber craquelle glass, this is a Northwood product made in 1890 in berry sets, table sets, water sets, shakers, syrup, toothpick holder, pickle caster, cruet, jam jar, and even a lamp.

Royal Jubilee

Royal Jubilee, found primarily in opalescent glass in blue or canary, was made by Greener & Company of Sunderland, England. This footed novelty basket is a real find without the opal treatment. The design dates to the 1890s when James A. Jobling controlled the factory.

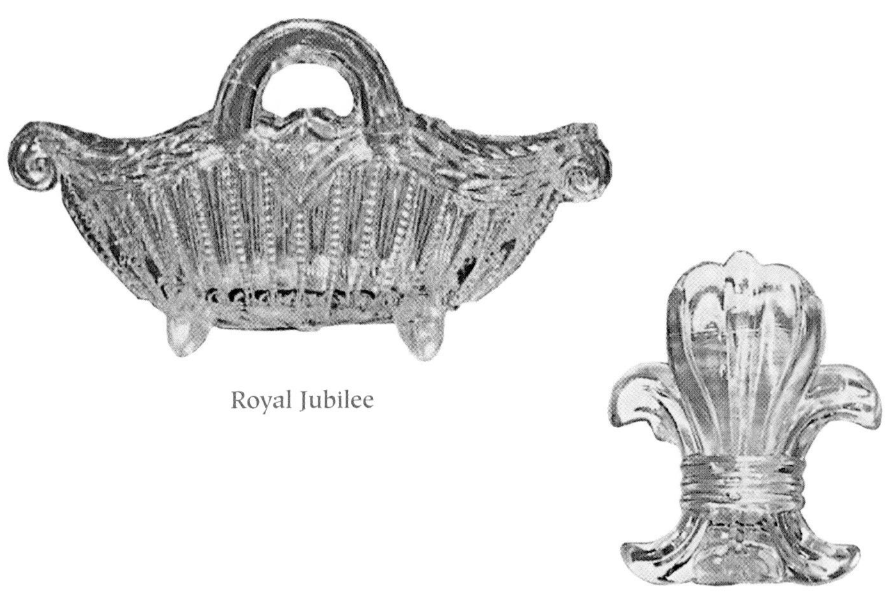

Royal Jubilee

Royal King

We were told by the owner of this piece it was made by King Glass of Pittsburgh (became Factory K of U.S. Glass Combine in 1891). Other than that, we have very little information and would certainly like to hear from anyone with additional knowledge about the pattern. The piece shown is a shot glass that is ruby stained and lettered "EUGENE, OREGON."

Royal King

Royal Lily

This beautiful toothpick holder, shaped like a fleur-de-lis, the Royal Lily of France, was shown in a 1906 ad, along with several U. S. Glass items, so we believe it may be a product of that company but have no proof. The glass is thick and clear and of fine quality, and the pattern is also known as Fleur-de-Lis.

Royal Lily

Ruby Diamond

Like many patterns chosen to be given a ruby stain treatment, the design is little more than a geometric band at the bottom of the piece. Ruby Diamond is also found in crystal and was made in 1893. Shapes include a table set, water set, goblet, wine, toothpick holder, and sauce.

Ruby Diamond

Ruby Thumbprint

Here is the familiar King's Crown pattern with ruby stain, hence the name. It was also made by U. S. Glass in 1891 and shapes include a caster set, table set, water set, pickle caster, toothpick holder, syrup, goblet, wine, and pickle dish. In addition, some pieces have gold trim and souvenir lettering.

Ruby Thumbprint

Ruffled Eye

Saddle

Sailing Ship

Saint Bernard

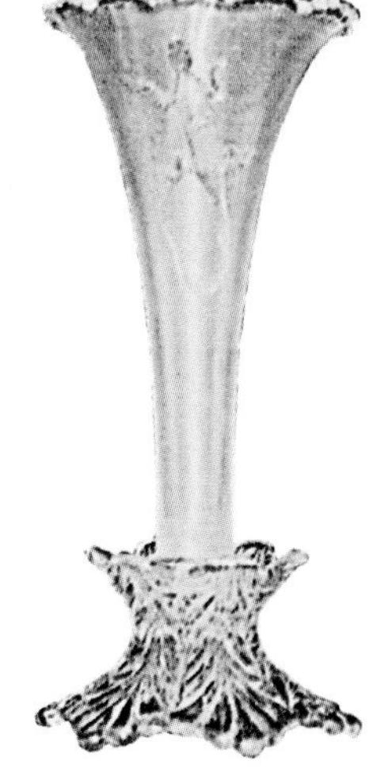
Salamander

Ruffled Eye

A product of the Indiana Tumbler and Goblet Company (Greentown), this strange pattern was advertised in a company ad in 1900 but was made earlier. Colors are crystal, canary, amber, and emerald green, as well as chocolate glass. The design is one of vining flora and strange sun-and-ray spots. The pitcher sits on three feet, making the whole design a bit awkward.

Saddle

Here is another of those scarce novelty toothpick holders or match holders made in the 1890s. The maker is unknown to us, and while we show it in amber, it was also made in crystal. It features a saddle over a barrel.

Sailing Ship

Best known as a late carnival piece, this 8" plate was also made in crystal. The pattern is intaglio on the undersurface of the base or marie. A similar plate called Columbus was made by Belmont Glass in the 1920s, but it is stippled and has a different ship, so we have to say maker unknown on the Sailing Ship plate.

Saint Bernard

Saint Bernard was made by Fostoria in 1894 as their #450 pattern in clear or copper wheel engraved glass. Shapes include a berry set, table set, cake stand, celery vase, covered high and low compotes, open low compotes, cruet, goblet, jam jar, sauce, pickle dish, water set, and salt shakers. It is also known in green or blue glass.

Salamander

Sometimes a piece of glass is found that has very special qualities, and this is one of those pieces. The vase shown is 11½" tall and has a top diameter of 5¼". The vase lily is completely threaded and on two sides has a salamander or lizard climbing up. Below the lily there is a ring of fauna that flares out to form a base. The glass seems to be all one piece. Anyone with information on this vase is urged to write us. It is also known in green or blue glass.

Sandwich Curtain Tie-Backs

From the Boston & Sandwich Company in the 1860s, these beautiful curtain tie-backs have pewter rods and were quite fashionable after the Civil War. They were made in a host of treatments and can be found in clear, amber, opaque, canary (shown), pink, blue, green, and even ebony glass, as well as in many shapes and sizes.

Sandwich Dolphin Candlestick

The Dolphin Candlestick was first made with a flat square base and then this square step base (later hexagon bases were made by Westmoreland and in Europe). It was first a product of the Boston & Sandwich Company and Mt. Washington, and later was made by Bakewell Pears. The original dates to the 1850s with this step base about ten years later. It is found in crystal, vaseline, and possibly other colors.

Sandwich Scroll Salt Dip

Typical of many items during the 1850 – 1870 period of flint glass, this beautifully designed open salt dip was high style for its day. It is found in crystal, amber, vaseline, and blue glass and had many similar "cousins."

Sandwich Star

As the name suggests, this was a pattern from Boston & Sandwich Glass, first made in the 1850s and continued into the 1860s in flint glass. It is found in clear, amethyst, and canary (all colors are rare) and shapes include a dolphin-based compote, cordial, decanter, goblet (very rare), champagne, wine, table set, and a stemmed spill holder. All shapes are considered somewhat rare.

Santa in Chimney

This novelty container is very collectible because of the subject and how well the piece is made. It shows the head and shoulders of the fictitious character sticking out of a brick chimney.

Sandwich Curtain Tie-Backs

Sandwich Dolphin Candlestick

Sandwich Scroll Salt Dip

Santa in Chimney

Sandwich Star

Sawtooth

Sawtoothed Honeycomb

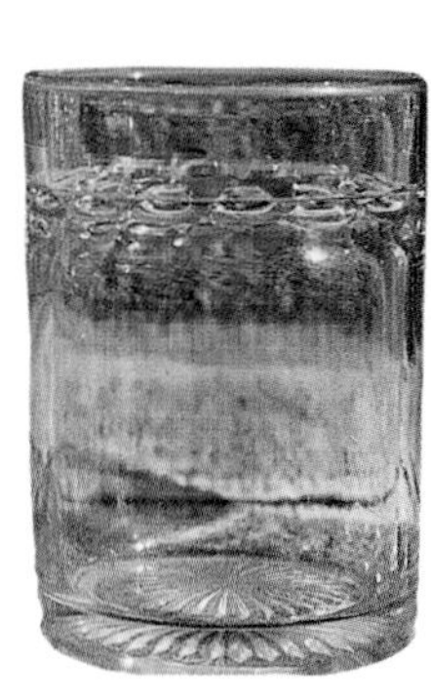

Scalloped Flange

Scalloped Skirt

Scalloped Six-Point

Sawtooth

Sawtooth was made over a long time by several companies that include Bryce, Richards, McKee, or U. S. Glass in clear, amber, amethyst, opal, sapphire blue, and milk glass. It had several other names, such as Diamond Point or Pineapple Mitre. Shapes include the usual table pieces plus a carafe, child's table set, decanter, pomade jar, oil lamps, spillholder, and cordial.

Sawtoothed Honeycomb

Also known as Serrated Block and Loop or Union's Radiant, this pattern was first made by Steiner Glass in 1906, and two years later the moulds were sold to Union Stopper Company. Shapes include a punch set, table set, bonbon, goblet, sauce (flat or footed), syrup, toothpick holder, celery vase, compote, water set, and shakers. An advertising nappy is shown in another section of this book.

Scalloped Flange

Made by the Perfection Glass Company of Washington, Pennsylvania, in 1903, this tumbler comes in five styles (we show three, #34, #50, and #40). Inside the tumbler are teeth in a row that were designed to keep ice away from the mouth, "avoiding an embarrassing sipping noise."

Scalloped Six-Point

From George Duncan and Sons as their #30 in 1900, this pattern can be found in round or square bowls, table set, butter pat, cake stand (round or square), celery vase and tray, claret, cocktail, high or low compotes, cordial, cracker jar, cruet, custard cup, sherbet cup, egg cup, goblet, mustard pot, nappy, pickle dish, water set in tankard or bulbous, ice cream plate, rose bowl, and vases.

Scalloped Skirt

This pattern was made by Jefferson Glass in 1904 and is found in table sets, berry sets, a jelly compote, toothpick holder, pickle dish, a vase, and various bowls. It was made in crystal, blue, green, amethyst, and can be often found with enameled work and gilding.

Scalloped Swirl

Scalloped Swirl was first a Ripley and Company pattern and then U.S. Glass pattern #15026 in 1892. It is found in crystal, ruby stained, and green (scarce). Shapes include a berry bowl, table set, cake plate, celery vase, goblet (shown), toothpick holder, a water set, as well as compotes.

Scheherezade

We believe the Dugan/Diamond factory made this pattern, mostly in opalescent glass. The design closely resembles another of their patterns called Reflecting Diamonds, also found on opalescent bowls. Scheherezade combines file triangles, fine cut triangles, and hobstars in a rather unique way on this rare bowl.

Scroll with Cane Band

Made by West Virginia Glass Company in 1897, this very recognizable pattern is well designed. Shapes include a table set, celery vase, toothpick holder, salt shakers, compotes, cruet, and water set. Some pieces have gold trim.

Scroll with Flowers

Made by McKee Glass in their Modern line, Scroll with Flowers is found in clear, amber, green, and blue. Shapes include a table set, cake plate with handles, cordial, egg cup, goblet, water set, covered mustard, salt dip with handle, wine, plate, and relish. The plate is double handled as is the sauce.

Sedan

Sedan is also called Panelled Star & Button. The maker is unknown and the date of production seems to be in dispute (1870s by one writer, 1900 by another). Shapes include a berry set, table set, water set, celery tray, celery vase, covered or open compotes, goblet, mug, pickle tray with double handles, relish tray, salt shaker, and the wine shown.

Sensbush Ink Well

Made by the Sensbush Inkwell Company in Milwaukee, Wisconsin, and with a patent #1-1507, this product is called a "self-closing inkwell" and has a novel insert top that springs closed when the pen is removed. The glass portion is heavy and of fine quality.

Scalloped Swirl

Scheherezade

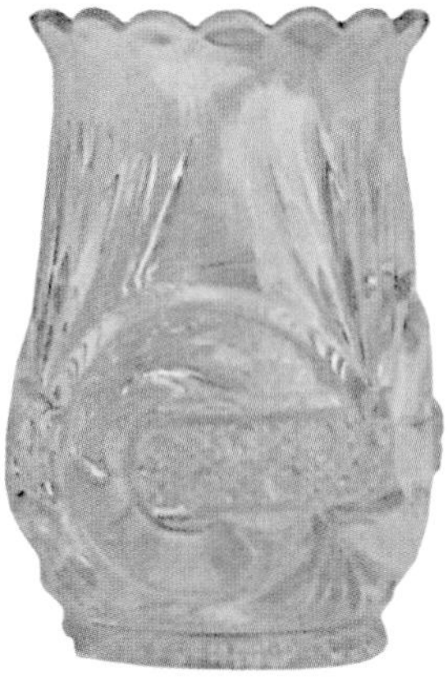

Scroll with Cane Band

Scroll with Flowers

Sedan

Sensbush Ink Well

Sequoia

Sextec

Serrated Flute

Shasta Daisy

Sheaf and Block

Sequoia

Also known as Heavy Panelled Finecut and Panelled Diamond Cross, Sequoia was made by U. S. Glass (Duncan's #800) in 1891 in clear, blue, amber, and canary. Shapes include a table set, finger bowl, tray, plate, berry set, butter pat, decanter, pickle jar, canoe-shaped bowl, relish, salt dip, covered or open compotes, celery vase or boat, wine, goblet, water set, nappy, cheese plate, shakers, cruet, and syrup.

Serrated Flute

This vase is thought to be from the Imperial Glass Company and is known in carnival glass as well as crystal. The paneling is on the interior, the base has a many-rayed star, and the typical Imperial serrated top is the most prominent feature. It is scarce in both carnival and crystal.

Sextec

Made by McKee Glass Company in 1894 as one of the "tec" series, this superior pattern's shapes include a table set, berry set, berry creamer, punch set, syrup, cruet, shakers, pickle jar, orange bowl, plate, nut bowl with handle, goblet, wine relish, and celery tray.

Shasta Daisy

Shown is Northwood's Shasta Daisy in their *Verre-D'or* line (1906). (Verre-D'or translates as glass of gold.) This line consisted of colored glass in cobalt, emerald green, amethyst, all with a liquid gold decoration. Various designs included Iceland Poppy, Grape Frieze, and Ribbons & Overlapping Squares. Shapes included large and small plates, shallow bowls, compotes, a handled nappy, and crimped bowls.

Sheaf and Block

Sometimes called Fickle Block, this design is from the Cooperative Flint Glass Company in 1893. Shapes include a table set, celery vase, pickle dish, goblet, shakers, berry set, water set, and wine.

Sheaf and Diamond

Made in 1905 by Bryce, Higbee, Sheaf and Diamond can be found in bowls, cake plate, pickle dish, table set, and celery plate. In design, it resembles several patterns of the age with diamonds of file flanked by fans that resemble standing sheaves of wheat.

Sheaf and Diamond

Sheep Mug

Sheep Mug

This tiny child's mug shows a standing sheep, and we do not believe it is the same mug that is called Scampering Sheep. So many glass pieces intended for children used animals as their theme, and all are now very collectible. Any information on this piece would be appreciated.

Shell and Jewel

Shell and Jewel was originally known as Victor from Westmoreland in 1893, then by Fostoria as their #618 line in 1898. It was also attributed to Sydenham Glass of Canada in 1895 as their Nugget pattern and finally to Jefferson Glass of Canada in 1920. Shapes include a table set, cake stand, compote, water set, shakers, bowls, banana dish, and water tray.

Shell and Jewel

Shell and Tassel

Shell and Tassel

This pattern was made by George A. Duncan & Sons (#555) in 1880, available in clear, etched, amber, blue, or canary glass. Shards have also been found at Canada's Burlington Glass Works. The pattern is found on either square or round shapes which include covered bowls, berry set, table set, cake stands in seven sizes, celery vase, covered compotes in eight sizes, rectangular dishes, goblet, pickle jar, water set, plates, platters, salt dip, shakers, ice cream tray, vase, and sauces (flat or footed).

Shelton Star

Very little information about this pattern seems to be available. We do know it was made in a water set, table set, and salt shakers, but surely other shapes have to be out there. Anyone knowing more is urged to let us know.

Shelton Star

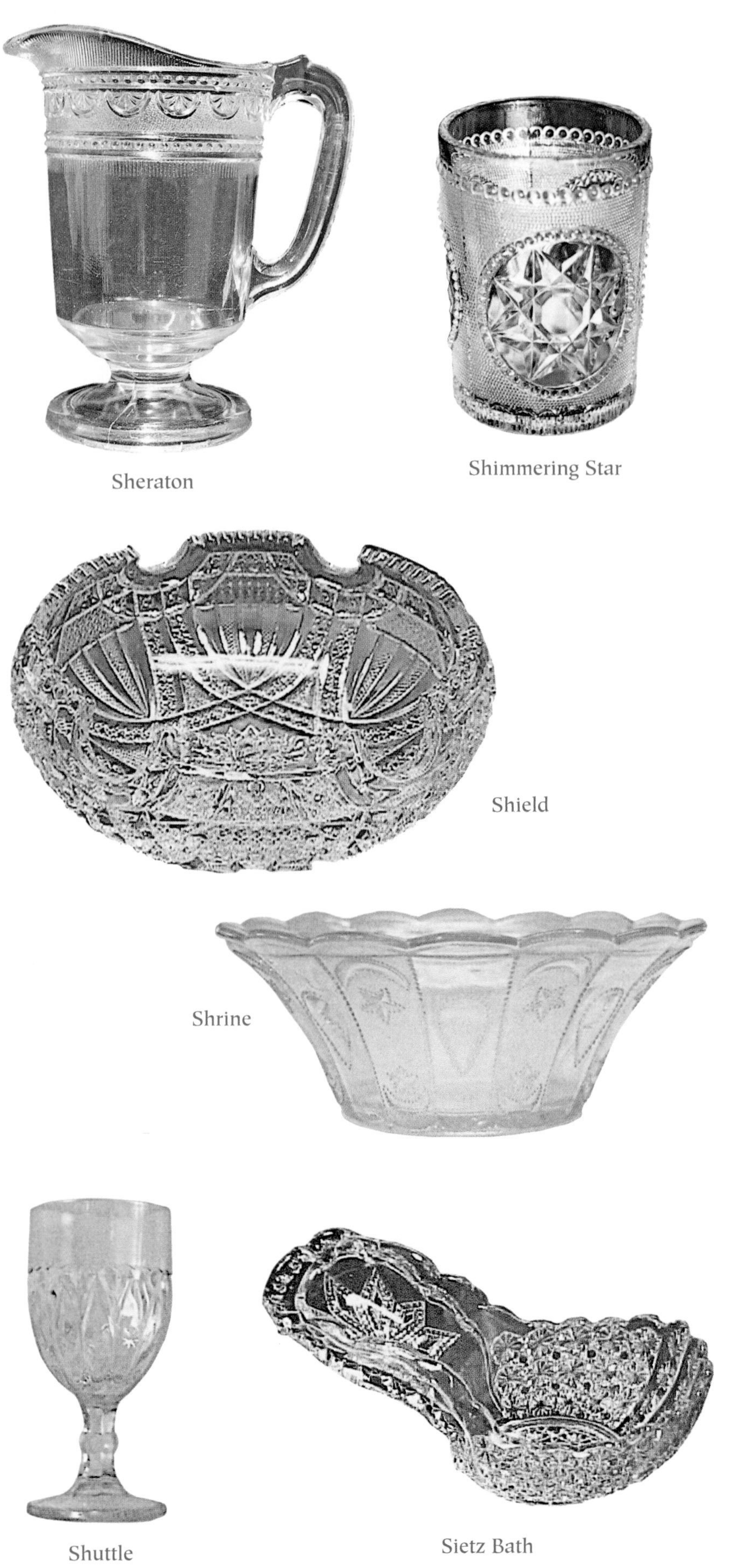

Sheraton

Shimmering Star

Shield

Shrine

Shuttle

Sietz Bath

Sheraton

Also called Ida, this is a Bryce, Higbee pattern from the 1880s. It was made in crystal, amber, blue, and green, and shapes include a berry set, table set, goblet, water set, milk pitcher, bread plate, platter, relish tray, sauce, wine, and round or eight-sided bowls.

Shield

Made by Westmoreland as their #160 line in 1899, this design is sometimes confused with a similar design by U.S. Glass. Shield shapes include a water set, 5" sauce (note the notching on the sides of the bowl), a celery vase, flower vase (14", 15", 16"), a knife rest, table set, and a goblet.

Shimmering Star

Also known as Beaded Star and credited to the Kokomo Glass Company of Kokomo, Indiana (Jenkins), this very well-done pattern was made in 1905. Shapes include a table set, berry set, water set, shakers, and a pickle dish.

Shrine

Also known as Jewelled Moon and Star, this Indiana Glass pattern (1890s), was first a 1880 design from Beatty-Brady. Shapes reported are a berry set, table set, goblet, water set, toothpick holder (scarce), pickle tray, and compote. Shrine is found in either clear or frosted crystal.

Shuttle

Also called Hearts of Loch Laven, this well-known pattern was originally from the Indiana Tumbler and Goblet factory at Greentown in 1896, and then at Indiana Glass in 1898. It was made in clear and Greentown chocolate. Shapes include a berry set, table set, celery vase, cordial, cruet, custard cup, goblet, mug, water set, shakers, sauce, and wine.

Sietz Bath

This novelty Daisy and Button piece is a very rare item that can be found in crystal, amber, blue, green, and canary. The maker isn't clear to us at this time, but we suspect it might be Hobbs, Brockunier (we could certainly be wrong). Any information on this item from readers would be appreciated.

Singing Birds

First made in 1903 by the Northwood Company, this well-known pattern is found in carnival glass, opalescent glass (mug only), custard, and clear, canary, amber, or blue glass. Shapes include a table set, water set, mug, berry set, sherbet, stemmed claret, and a goblet. Not all shapes are found in all treatments and tumblers have been reproduced in carnival and opalescent glass.

Singing Birds

Six Panel Finecut

Six Panel Finecut is credited to Dalzell, Gilmore, and Leighton in 1890, and found in clear or stained glass (amber or ruby). Shapes include a table set, water set, compote, sugar shaker, syrup, cruet, goblet, and various bowl shapes.

Six Panel Finecut

Six-Sided Candlesticks

These easily recognizable 7½" tall candlesticks are from the Imperial Glass Company and found mostly in carnival glass. The crystal examples have been reproduced in the 1960s but are marked with the "IG" mark.

Six-Sided Candlesticks

Skilton

Skilton was made by Richards and Hartley (1890), then U.S. Glass in 1891, in crystal or ruby stained glass. Shapes include bowls (4", 5", 6", 7", 8", 9"), a table set, cake stand, celery vase, covered compotes (7", 8"), open compotes (7", 8"), goblet, olive dish, pickle dish, milk pitcher, water set, shakers, water tray, and a wine. This pattern is also called Early Oregon but shouldn't be confused with the States pattern called Oregon.

Skilton

Slewed Horseshoe

Also called Radiant Daisy or U.S. Peacock, this was a pattern by U.S. Glass, their #15111, made in 1908. Shapes include a berry set, table set, punch set, punch tray, stemmed wine, syrup, ice cream tray, goblet, and a stemmed vase shape. Be advised this pattern has been reproduced in Europe in crystal and iridized glass in the 1930s.

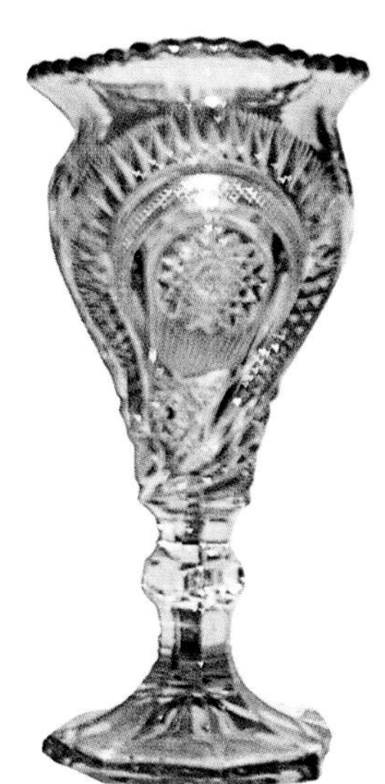

Slewed Horseshoe

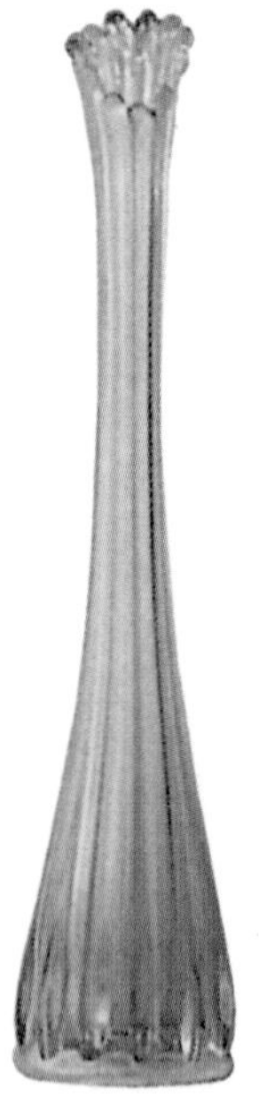

"Slick Willie"

Snail

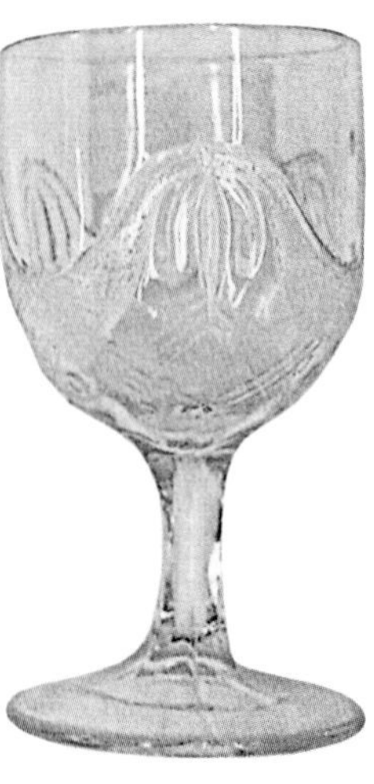

Snake Drape

Snow Flake

Snow Star

"Slick Willie"

The first of these we'd seen was in carnival glass, and we gave it this name because it was marked "Hale Baths — Hot Springs, Arkansas," so we've kept that name here. These vases are 11" – 17" usually and are shown in Butler Brothers ads over several years, but the maker seems to be unknown.

Snail

George Duncan and Sons made Snail in 1890 (some pieces were still being made by U.S. Glass in 1904), in crystal, engraved crystal, and ruby stained glass (blue reported). Shapes include a table set, open and covered compotes, berry set, covered bowls, celery vase, fruit stand, cake stand, rose bowl, syrup, cruet, goblet, shakers, tankard table set, tankard water set, squat water set, finger bowl, pickle dish, custard cup, and a sugar shaker.

Snake Drape

Apparently the goblet shown is the only reported shape in this pattern, made in the 1880s (maker unknown). The design is interesting and unusual with stippled draping above a section of criss-cross threading. Any information about this pattern would be helpful.

Snow Flake

This is Cambridge Glass Company's #2635. It was made in several shapes including a water set, table set, toothpick holder, nappy (four sizes), compote (three sizes), bread plate, pickle tray, celery tray, celery vase, oil bottle, salt shakers, condiment set on a tray, and vases in 6" and 8½" sizes. This pattern is also known as Snowflake and Sunburst, and as Fernland.

Snow Star

Snow Star was made by Bryce, Higbee in 1905, then Higbee in 1909, and was often advertised with Palm Leaf Fan and Atlanta designs. Shapes include a table set, celery vase, and assorted bowls. This pattern was well advertised in Butler Brothers from 1906 to 1909. Snow Star is our name since no one seems to have given this pattern a name before now.

Stellar

Also called Squared Sunburst, this U. S. Glass pattern was their #15103 made in 1907. It was made in a table set, berry set, water set, compote, and perhaps other table pieces.

Sterling

Made by Westmoreland Glass in 1891 and again in 1917 and also known as Pinwheels or Blazing Star, this pattern's shapes include a table set, toy table set, water set, punch set, goblet, wine, and compote. The piece shown is marked on the finial: "PAT FEB 25–1896–W.G. Co."

Stippled Bar

Stippled Bar was from U. S. Glass Company as their #15044 made in 1895. Shapes include a table set, water set, various bowls, and the plate shown. Some variations in the pattern appear from shape to shape and the design isn't always easy to recognize, but the main design shown on the plate is the wider panel with serrated edges that is stippled except for the cross bar.

Stippled Chain

Stippled Chain was made by Gillinder and Sons in 1880 with applied handles in clear only. Shapes include a berry set, table set, cake stand, celery vase, oval dish, egg cup, goblet, pickle tray, water set, relish dish, and master salt dip.

Stippled Cherry

Dating to the 1880s, this pattern's maker is unknown. Shapes include a berry set, table set, water set, 6" plate, 9" bread plate, mug, celery vase, and relish dish. The design is realistic and the mould work well done.

Stippled Daisy

Despite its name, this pattern can be found either plain or stippled. It was made in the 1880s, but the maker hasn't been determined. Shapes are a table set, open compote, oblong dish, flat sauce, goblet, wine, and relish.

Stellar

Sterling

Stippled Bar

Stippled Chain

Stippled Cherry

Stippled Daisy

Stippled Forget-Me-Not

Stippled Forget-Me-Not with Kitten

Stippled Medallion

Stippled Peppers

Stippled Sandbur

Stork and Rushes

Stippled Forget-Me-Not

Stippled Forget-Me-Not was from the Finley Flint Glass Company (1890) and Model Flint (1891) in clear, amber, blue, white, or milk glass. Shapes include a berry set, waste bowl, table set, cake stands in 9", 10", and 12", celery vase, toy table set, toy mug, large mug, covered compotes in three sizes, open compotes in three sizes, cordial, cup, goblet, water set, milk pitcher, plates (baby face, star, or kitten centers), oval relish master salt, syrup, toothpick holder, water tray, and wine.

Stippled Forget-Me-Not with Kitten

Made by the Finley Glass Company in 1891 (shards were also found at the Model Flint factory from 1891), this plate with the unusual center is not generally mentioned as part of this pattern. (A similar 7" plate called Baby Face is known with the Stippled Forget-Me-Not edging.) The piece shown has a cat in the center of pussy willow branches.

Stippled Medallion

Made by the Union Glass Company in the late 1860s, shapes include a table set, egg cup, plate, cake plate, sauce, goblet, and low compote.

Stippled Peppers

Stippled Peppers was from Boston & Sandwich Glass in the 1870s and is found only in crystal. Shapes include a table set, water pitcher, footed tumbler, egg cup, footed salt, and sauce. Shown is the footed tumbler.

Stippled Sandbur

Made by Beatty-Brady Glass Company in 1903, this nice pattern with the unusual name can be found in a berry set, table set, water set, celery vase, covered compote, goblet, toothpick holder, pickle jar, and wine.

Stork and Rushes

Made by the Dugan (Diamond) Glass Company primarily in carnival glass, the pattern can also be found in opalescent glass in the mug or tumbler shapes, and infrequently in crystal, where shapes include a water set, punch set, handled basket (made from a tumbler), and berry set pieces.

Strawberry and Cable

From the Northwood Glass Company and a companion to their Cherry and Cable pattern, this one has added cut-type trim. It dates to 1907 and is usually decorated with gold trim. Shapes include a water set, table set, berry set, sweetmeat, covered compote, goblet, wine, and salt shakers. It has been reproduced.

Strawberry and Currant

Made by Dalzell, Gillmore, and Leighton in the 1890s (pattern line #9D), shapes include a table set, celery vase, celery dish, covered or open compotes, mug, milk pitcher, water set, syrup, sauce, egg cup, covered cheese dish, and goblet.

Strawberry and Cable

Strawberry and Currant

Strawberry and Pear

This pattern is credited to Bryce Brothers in the 1880s and possibly U.S. Glass after 1891 by some writers. This mug is found in clear, amber, blue, or canary but was reproduced in the 1940s. The old examples have an eight-pointed star on the base while new ones have a 24-pointed star.

Strawberry and Pear

Strigil

Also called Nelly, this McKee Brothers pattern was made in 1892 in clear glass only. Shapes include a table set, water set, berry set, egg cup, celery vase, compote, wine glass, and goblet. As in the bowl shown, some pieces are gold trimmed.

Studio

Made by the New Martinsville Glass Company in clear or ruby stained crystal (often with gold trim), this little-known pattern can be found in a table set as well as a hair receiver (this is the only piece pictured in one company catalog). The hair receiver is called their #721 Studio pattern. Anyone knowing of additional shapes is urged to write.

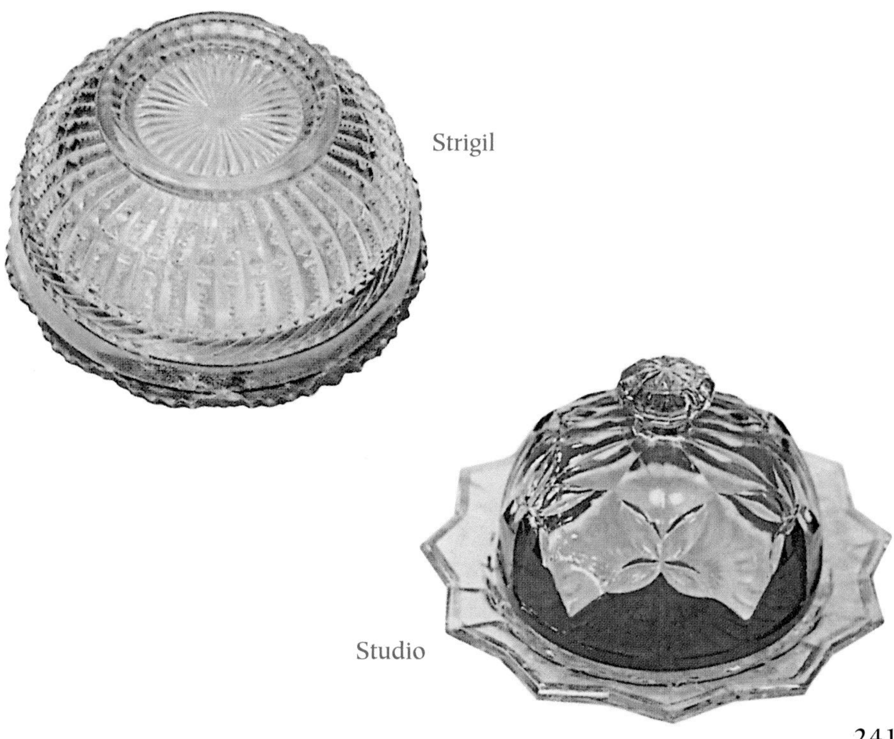

Strigil

Studio

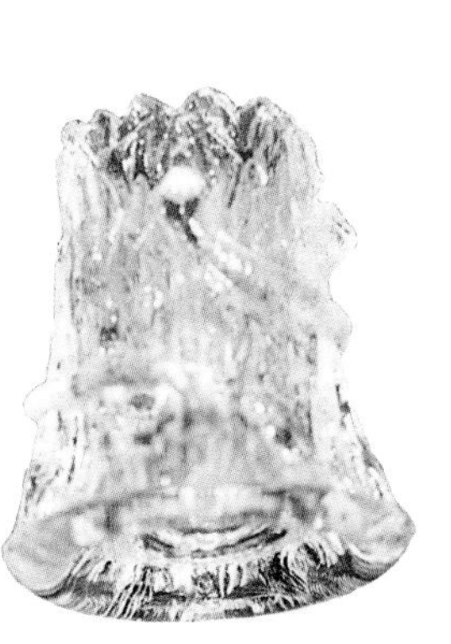
Stump

Summit

Sunbeam

Sunburst

Sunburst on Shield

Stump

Made by the Model Flint Glass Company, first in Findlay, Ohio, and then at the Albany, Indiana, plant (1880s – 1902), this naturalistic toothpick holder is found in crystal, amber, blue, or green. Researchers feel only the crystal pieces were made in Findlay while crystal and colors came from Albany. Some collectors call this the Serpent toothpick holder because it shows a snake wrapping around the stump. All pieces are rare and desirable.

Summit

Also known as X-Bull's-Eye, this pattern is from Thompson Glass Company of Uniontown, Pennsylvania, in 1895. Found in clear or ruby stained, shapes include a table set, berry set, water set, shakers, wine, and the compote shown.

Sunbeam

From McKee and Brothers in 1898 – 1902 in crystal or emerald green, shapes include a table set, berry set, water set, wine, salt shakers, compote, sauce, pickle dish, cup, toothpick holder, water carafe, and cruet.

Sunburst

Starburst is also called Squared Sunburst and was made by Jenkins Glass Company in 1910. Shapes include a table set, cake stand, shakers, water set, cordial, egg cup, wine, compotes, plates, and celery vase.

Sunburst on Shield

Sunburst on Shield was orginally called Diadem (a wonderful name) and from the Northwood Glass Company where it is best known in opalescent glass. Shapes include a table set, a breakfast set, a water set, celery tray, pickle tray, cruet, and shakers. Shown is the crystal water pitcher.

Sunflower

Sunk Daisy

Sunken Bull's-Eye

Sunken Primrose

Sunken Teardrop

Sunk Honeycomb

Sunflower

Sunflower, also called Lily, was from Atterbury and Company in 1881 and made in clear, blue, mosaic, and opalescent glass. Shapes include a table set, water set, and berry set.

Sunk Daisy

Also called Kirkland, this is a Cooperative Flint Glass pattern made in 1898 in crystal, green, or decorated glass. Shapes include a water carafe, table set, compote, cracker jar, water set, goblet, wine, toothpick holder, and salt shakers.

Sunken Bull's-Eye

Attributed to Dalzell, Gilmore & Leighton by the owner and to Boston and Sandwich (as Barrel Excelsior) by another writer, shapes include a table set, water set, and goblet. We appreciate any firm information about this pattern to help us properly classify it.

Sunken Primrose

This was from Greensburg Glass Company in 1893 and can be found in crystal, emerald green, and ruby stain with yellow flowers. Shapes are many, including a berry set, table set, high stemmed compote, high stemmed banana bowl, toothpick holder, relish dish, salt shaker, and a lamp.

Sunken Teardrop

About the only notable thing on this pattern is the creamer's spout which has a teardrop design. The maker is a mystery, at least to us. Shapes include a table set, water set, berry set, shakers, goblet, pickle dish, and wine.

Sunk Honeycomb

Sunk Honeycomb, also called Corona, was made by the Greensburg Glass Company and later McKee Brothers in 1903. Shapes include a cruet, decanter, jelly compote, toothpick holder, mug (shown), shakers, table set, berry set, individual creamer and sugar, and a wine. It can be found in crystal and ruby stained glass.

Sunk Jewel

Swag with Brackets

Swan

Swan (Bryce Brothers)

Swan and Egret

Sunk Jewel

From the Fostoria Company in 1903, this pattern is found on a water pitcher, tumblers, and the nappy shown, however other shapes probably exist. The design is interesting with inverted teardrops that contain a hobstar above prisms. We'd be interested in hearing from readers who have other shapes in this pattern.

Swag with Brackets

Swag with Brackets was from Jefferson Glass in 1903. It can be found in opalescent glass, crystal, vaseline, amethyst, and blue glass, often decorated. Shapes include a table set, water set, jelly compote, shakers, toothpick holder, cruet, celery vase, and several novelties.

Swan

Perhaps this very attractive covered compote itself should be named Swirl Based Swan since the design is etched except for the mould swirl of the stem and base, the tiered finial, and the rope edging at the top of the bowl. We haven't a clue about the maker or other pieces, but would like to hear any information on this piece.

Swan (Bryce Brothers)

Also from Bryce Brothers in the 1880s and then U.S. Glass after 1891, this mug is found in clear, frosted, amber, milk glass, and opaque blue glass. It is also called Water Fowl and Federal #3802 and was found in a Federal Glass packer's catalog in 1914, indicating they also made it for use as a container for condiments.

Swan and Egret

Most likely a product of the 1880s, this mug is only reported in clear glass and measures 2⅛" tall and has a diameter of 1⅞". It shows a swan on one side and an egret on the other. The maker is unknown to us at this time.

Swan Nappy

The owner of this fine nappy says it is similar only to the Flying Swan pattern. It measures 4½" across the top and has a fine handle designed to resemble the head and neck of a swan. The design inside the bottom has a finely structured swan with cattails on the right and flowers on the left and fern fronds around the outside rim.

Swan on Pond

Also called Swan Two by one writer, this pattern seems to be pretty much a mystery. It is known in clear, blue, amber, and possibly milk glass. Shapes may include a table set, water set, and a goblet.

Swan with Mesh

Also called Plain Swan or Swan, this pattern has been attributed to the Canton Glass Company in 1882. It was made in clear, amber, blue, or canary. Shapes include a table set, water set, covered dish, sauce, jam jar, covered or open compotes, goblet, bread tray, footed sauce, pickle jar, and wine that is rare.

Swan with Ring Handle

Attributed to Atterbury & Company in the 1880s, this mug is found in clear, amber, blue, milk glass, flint opalescent, blue alabaster, brown alabaster, pink alabaster, amber alabaster, and opaque black (ebony). The handle is quite distinctive and really sets the mug off while the large swan is very well done.

Swan with Tree

Swan with Tree is from U.S. Glass (Bryce or Indiana plants). It is known in a pitcher, goblet, and rare dome-based bowl. Production was in the 1880s but the design is much older, being part of an Atterbury line of lamps patented in 1868 and using the same design (both on the lamp's font and as a base design). The lamps were no longer made by 1881 and we believe U.S. Glass copied the design after that.

Swan Nappy

Swan with Ring Handle

Swan on Pond

Swan with Mesh

Swan with Tree

Swirl and Ball

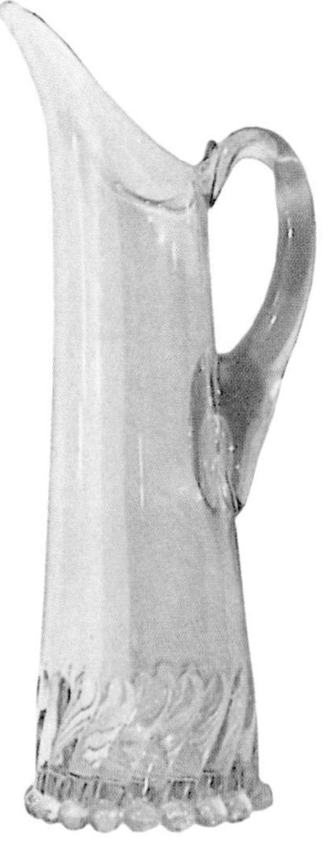
Swirl and Ball (Ray)

Swirl and Cable

Swirled Column

Swirled Star

Swirl and Ball

The child's mug shown is made by J. Beatty & Sons but other makers, including McKee Brothers, had a try at this pattern in 1894. Other shapes include a table set, shakers, celery vase, 6" plate, cordial set, syrup, footed jelly, cake stand, and candlesticks. Some makers used plain handles and no top ring.

Swirl and Ball (Ray)

From McKee Brothers Glass in 1894 and sometimes called Ray, this pattern should not be confused with a similar design called Ball and Swirl. Shapes include a table set, water set, berry set, shakers, celery vase, 6" plate, cordial set, syrup, jelly compote, candlesticks, and cake stand.

Swirl and Cable

This pattern was shown in an 1893 ad for Dazell, Gilmore, and Leighton in a pitcher and bowl shape. Listings from the factory include a honey dish, jelly compote, a mug, and a creamer. Bowls are known in 6" and 8" and the creamer and pitcher are found in two sizes.

Swirled Column

Also called Beaded Swirl which seems a better name, this is a George Duncan pattern, their #335, made in clear, emerald green, and gold trimmed and in 1891 it was produced by U. S. Glass. Shapes include a table set, water set, cup, sauce, bowl, celery vase, plate, shakers, cruet, sugar shaker, syrup, cake stand, egg cup, goblet, mug, and wine. Bowls are covered or open, flat or footed.

Swirled Star

We've now seen evidence this pattern was from Jefferson's Canadian plant in the 1888 – 1895 period. Shapes include a berry set, table set, water set, and a wine. Jefferson called it their #200 design.

Swirl Hobnail

Made by Millersburg around 1911, this pattern is usually found in carnival glass in rose bowls, spittoon whimsies, or vases, all from the same mould. Here we show one of two reported non-carnival pieces, both spittoon whimsies. One is amethyst and the other crystal and both are probably pieces that were just missed by the sprayer who did the iridizing.

Swirl Hobnail

Swirl-Stem Hobstar

The maker of this distinctive 11" pedestal vase is unknown to us, and anyone with information about this pattern is urged to write us. There are four sections of hobstars, one above the other, and these are separated by bars of broken columns. Beneath this design is a swirl above the base.

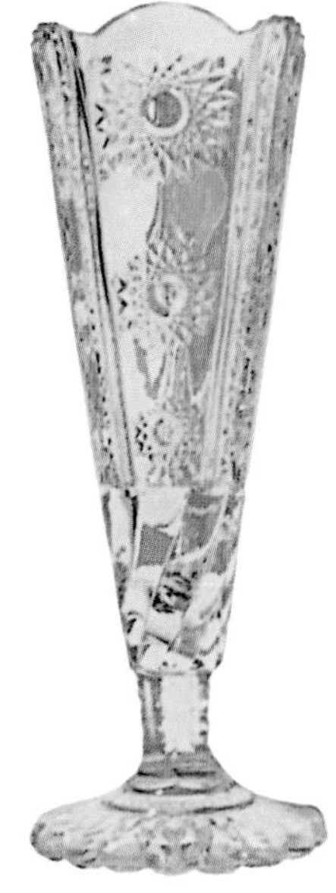

Swirl-Stem Hobstar

Sword

Made by U. S. Glass (Bryce Brothers, Factory B) and shown in a company ad with an assortment of novelty items, this very unusual pickle dish illustrates the originality of glassmakers early in this century. It is about 7" long, 4¼" wide, and ¾" deep.

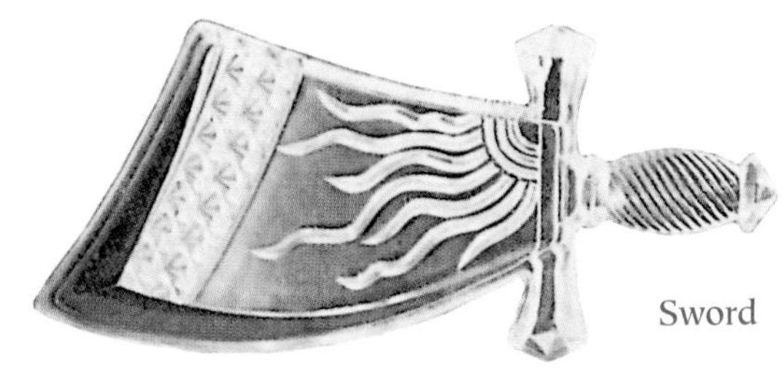

Sword

Sydney

Made by the Fostoria Glass Company in 1905, this pattern, often confused with one called Pillow and Sunburst, can be found in 6", 8", 9" bowls, table set, celery vase, covered or open compotes, pickle dish in 6", 8", 9" sizes, water set, salt shakers, and jam jar.

Sydney

Tacoma

Tacoma was made by Greensburg Glass in 1894 and National after 1900, in clear, green, amber stained, and ruby stained. The pattern is also called Triple X or Jeweled Diamond and Fan. Shapes include a finger bowl, table set, cake salver, celery vase, celery tray, footed compote (7", 8"), cracker jar, cruet, cup, decanter, fruit bowl, ice cream nappy, jelly compote, molasses jar, oblong tray, pickle jar, cruet, squat pitcher, plate, punch bowl (12", 15"), rose bowls (3½", 4½", 5½", 6½"), berry bowls, salad bowl, square compote, syrup, tobacco jar, toothpick holder, tankard water set, vases (two types and three sizes), water bottle, and a wine.

Tacoma

Tandem Diamonds and Thumbprint

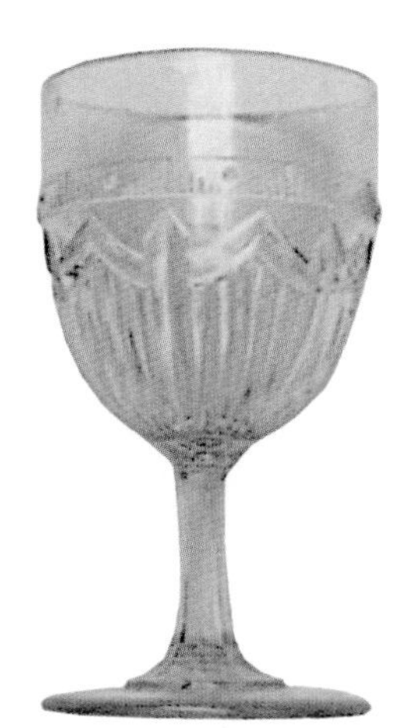
Tape Measure

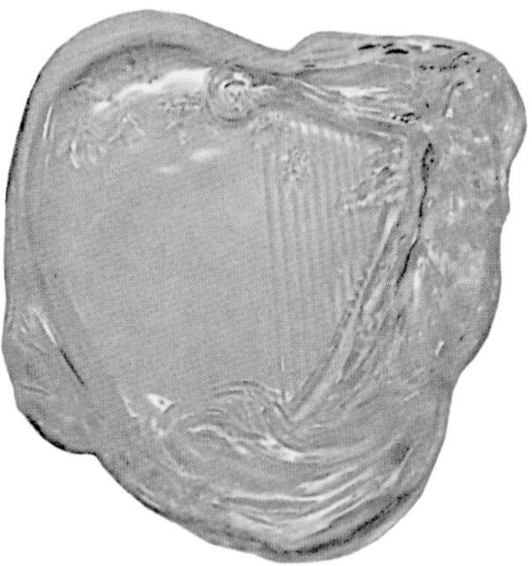
Tara's Harp

Tarentum's Manhattan

Tarentum's Virginia

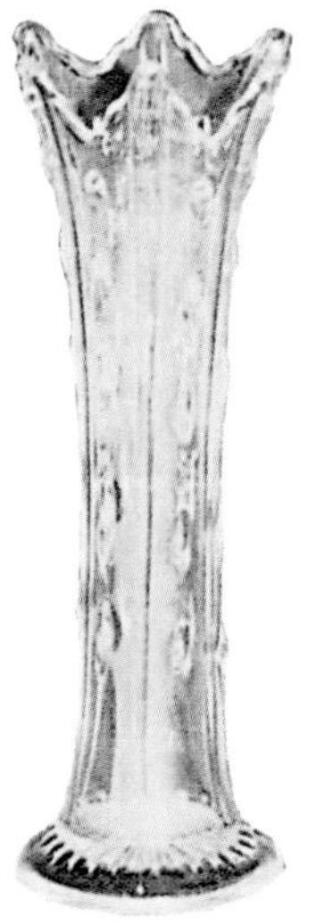
Target

Tandem Diamonds and Thumbprint

The maker of this pattern of the 1880s doesn't seem to be known to researchers, but shapes available are a table set, water set, and goblet. The pattern is a simple one of rows of diamonds linked together by banding with rows of thumbprints between.

Tape Measure

From the Portland Glass Company in 1872, shapes include a table set, water set, sauce, and goblet. This pattern is also called Shields by some collectors.

Tara's Harp

Despite the attractive look of this Art Nouveau dresser tray, the name is certainly wrong since the item behind the lady is a fluted column, not a harp. Nevertheless, the mould work is exceptional and the free-form shape very nice. The glass has a slight pinkish tinge and shows signs of having once had a goofus treatment. It measures 8¼" tall and about the same across.

Tarentum's Manhattan

Not to be confused with the U.S. Glass pattern called Manhattan, the Tarentum Glass pattern was their #15078 pattern made from 1902 to 1910. The pattern is sometimes mistaken for Millersburg's Diamond because they are similar. Shapes include a table set, berry set, cake stand, open compote, salt shaker, goblet, tumbler, syrup, cruet, oval dish, and plates in 6" and 8" sizes. It can be found in crystal or in ruby stained glass.

Tarentum's Virginia

This was made in 1895 by Tarentum Glass, in crystal and green. Forty shapes are known, including a table set, water set, berry set, shakers, cruet, compote, pickle tray, goblet, wine, celery vase, syrup, celery tray, egg cup, cordial, mustard pot, and jam jar.

Target

From Dugan/Diamond Glass, this vase pattern is better known in carnival glass or opalescent glass than in crystal, shown here, quite a scarce item. Production began in carnival glass in 1909, and the clear examples were still being shown in a 1919 Butler Brothers catalog along with Depression pink ones.

Teardrop and Tassel

From the Indiana Tumbler and Goblet Company (Greentown) around 1900, there are two variations of this pattern, the tumbler shown being the less elaborate version. Colors of amber, teal blue, cobalt blue, canary, several shades of green, Nile green, white opaque, and chocolate glass are all known besides the clear pieces. Shapes include a table set, water set, goblet, wine, and shakers.

Teasel

Teasel was made by Bryce Brothers Glass in 1870s. Do not confuse this pattern with Long Leaf Teasel from New Martinsville Glass which has no fans. Teasel is found in clear, green, amber, milk glass, Nile green, chocolate, and blue. Shapes include a table set, celery vase, compote, cruet, sauce, plate, shakers, cake stand, wine, bowl, cracker jar, toothpick holder (scarce), covered honey dish, and goblet.

Tepee

This is also known as Wigwam or Nemesis. It was first made by George Duncan and Sons (their #28) and then U. S. Glass in 1897. Shapes include a table set, wine, berry set, syrup, handled jelly, jelly compote, shakers, rare covered fish dish, water set, plate, and rare toothpick holder in green.

Ten-Pointed Star

Made by J. B. Higbee in 1907, crystal shapes include a water set, table set, berry set, milk pitcher, cruet, 12" vase, ice cream bowl, plate, square or round pickle dish, 7½" square plate, compotes in two sizes, stemmed cake salver, and something called an 8" "compotier." The design varies widely from shape to shape, and the star in the base of the bowl has only eight points.

Terrapin

The Garden of Eden pattern is also known as Turtle, so we've named this imaginative novelty pickle dish something different. It measures 10" long from head to tail and 5½" across the middle, stands on four realistic feet and has the shell design on the underside. Anyone knowing more about this piece is urged to write us.

Teardrop and Tassel

Tepee

Teasel

Ten-Pointed Star

Terrapin

Texas

Thistle

Texas Star

Thonged Star

Thousand Eye

Texas

Texas, also known as Loop with Stippled Panels, was made by U. S. Glass as their #15067 in 1900. It can be found in clear, rose stained, ruby stained, and gold trimmed. Shapes include a carafe, open and covered bowls, cake stands, bread tray, compotes, cruet, goblet, covered horseradish, olive dish, pickle tray, water set, plate, shakers, hotel salt, master salt, sauce, syrup, toothpick holder, wine, and vases.

Texas Star

Also known as Snowflake Base, this pattern was made by the Steiner Glass Company in 1891. Shapes reported are a berry set, water set, shakers, oval bowls (two sizes), and plate. The design is only on the base on most pieces, giving a very different look to some shapes, making descriptions difficult from shape to shape.

Thistle

Thistle was from Bryce, McKee & Company in 1872 and found in clear only. It is also called Early Thistle or Scotch Thistle. Shapes include a berry set, table set, cake stand, covered compote, open compotes (6", 8"), cordial, oval dish, egg cup, goblet, pickle dish, milk pitcher, water set, large plate, relish tray, master salt, syrup, and a wine.

Thonged Star

Here is Imperial Glass pattern #91/538 and 564, shown in their 1909 catalog. It can be found in an oval 7½" dish as well as the flat, two-handled olive dish shown. The pieces are marked "Nu-Cut" and some show traces of gold trim.

Thousand Eye

Thousand Eye was made by many companies including Adams & Company (1874), Richards & Hartley (1880), and U.S. Glass (1891) in crystal, amber, blue, vaseline, green, and opalescent colors. Shapes include an ABC plate, cologne bottle, bowls, table set, cake stand, celery vase (two variations), open compotes (6", 7", 8", 9", 10"), cordial, cruet (shown), square dish, honey bowl, inkwell, jelly jar, lamp (12", 15"), mug (two sizes), pickle dish, milk pitcher, water set, square plate (6", 8", 10"), platters, salt dips, sauce (flat or footed), string holder, syrup, toothpick holder (three variations), water tray (round or oval), and a wine.

Thousand Eye Variant Lamp

Although our knowledge of oil lamps is limited, we believe this is a lamp in the above pattern. It has an opaque white pressed glass base and was made in crystal, blue, amber, and vaseline in the 1890s. We welcome any further information from readers on this and any other glass (especially lamps) we show.

Thousand Eye with Fan

The owner of this stemmed compote suspects it to be from England or Europe and we'd certainly like to hear from anyone with additional information about it. In this country Thousand Eye was made by a host of glass companies so tracking each one is difficult.

Threading

Since we first wrote about this Geo. Duncan and Sons pattern, we've learned of additional shapes that include a berry set, table set, sauce, nappy, goblet, compote, celery vase (shown), wine, and a water set. This pattern is also called English Thread by some collectors.

Three Birds

From Dalzell, Gilmore & Leighton Glass Company in the 1880s, this strange pattern seems to be known only on the water pitcher shown. On one side are the three birds sitting in tree branches, and on the other a wicker basket filled with fruit sitting on what appears to be a brick wall.

Three Dolphins

Credited to Bryce Brothers, this is also called just Dolphin by some collectors. It is for matches or toothpicks and can be found in clear, amber, or possibly blue. The piece has also been seen without the dolphins.

Thousand Eye Variant Lamp

Thousand Eye with Fan

Threading

Three Dolphins

Three Birds

Three Face

Three Fruits

Three-In-One

Three Panel

Three Face

Three Face was made by Geo. Duncan and Sons in 1878 and U.S. Glass in 1891 and has been highly reproduced over the years. Shapes include a biscuit jar, bowls on high or low standards, a table set, cake stand, celery vase, champagne, covered or open compote, goblet, cordial, jam jar, water set, milk pitcher, and several sizes of oil lamps.

Three Fruits

From Northwood, this pattern is usually found in carnival glass bowls or plates (a variant stemmed bonbon is also known). The crystal pieces are quite scarce. Here is the plate shape that measures about 9" in diameter. The fruits are cherries, pears, and apples.

Three-In-One

Originally Imperial's #1 pattern known to some collectors as Fancy Diamonds, this well-known pattern was shown in a 1909 factory catalog in a 13" salver, 9" and 10" cake stands, 8" salver, handled olive, 4", 4½", 5", 7", 8", 9", 9½" bowls, punch set, 6", 8", 9" covered compotes, 10" 11" footed fruit bowls, 6", 7", 8" 9" open stemmed bowls, stemmed jelly compotes in 4½" and 5", wine, goblet, water set, whiskey decanter and tumblers, wine decanter, carafe, catsup cruet, oil cruet, syrup, candlesticks, covered mustard, 6", 8", 10" pedestal vases, table set, and covered cracker jar. It is known in some shapes in carnival.

Three Panel

Three Panel was first Richards & Hartley pattern #25 in the 1880s and then it was reissued by U. S. Glass in 1891 in clear, amber, blue, and vaseline. Shapes include bowls in three sizes, table set, celery vase, open compotes, cruet, goblet, large or small mug, water set, milk pitcher, and sauce.

Thumbprint

Also known as Argus Thumbprint, this is not the same pattern as Argus shown elsewhere. Made by Bakewell, Pears & Company in the 1860s in clear, milk glass, and rare colors, it has been widely reproduced by Fenton in a similar pattern. Shapes include an ale glass, banana boat, caster bottle, bitters bottle, cologne, water set, berry set, punch set, table set, cake stand, celery vase, champagne, claret, compotes, cordial, jelly dish, egg cup, goblet, salt dip, mug, pickle dish, plate, and relish.

Tidy

Made by McKee and Brothers in 1880, shapes include a table set, water set, compote, goblet, wine, and celery vase. In addition, there are two variations of this pattern, one with a short shield and one with a long shield. Other names for this pattern are Stayman or Drapery Variant.

Tile

Tile is also known as Optical Cube (a better name) and was from the Thompson Glass Company (their #19) in 1890 and made in a long list of shapes (75 items). These include a table set, water set, open or covered compote, goblet, cruet, shakers, pickle dish, cake stand, toothpick holder, wine, and cordial.

Togo

Made by Indiana Glass of Dunkirk, Indiana, about 1913, shapes include a table set, individual creamer and sugar, cruet, jelly compote, 5" square plate, leaf-shaped olive dish, berry set, 7" footed bowl, and water set with pedestal based pitcher. It is also called Bismarc Star.

Tokyo

Tokyo was made by the Jefferson Glass Company as their #212 pattern in 1904. It is primarily found in opalescent glass, but crystal and colors that include blue, canary, or green exist. Shapes include a table set, water set, berry set, shakers, vase, jelly compote, syrup, plate, and a toothpick holder. Non-opalescent pieces were often gilded as shown.

Thumbprint

Tidy

Tile

Tokyo

Togo

Tong

Torpedo

Touring Car

Tree

Tree Bark

Tong

Probably from the early 1870s, this unusually strong pattern is found in a table set, berry set, pickle jar (shown), pickle dish, celery vase, water set, goblet, and wine. Other shapes probably exist, but we can't confirm them at this time.

Torpedo

Also known as Pigmy or Fish Eye, this is a Thompson Glass pattern made in 1889. Shapes include a banana stand, covered or open bowls in five sizes, table set, cake stand, celery vase, covered compote, cruet, cup and saucer, decanter, finger bowl, lamps, goblet, jam jar, pickle caster, water set, milk pitcher, salt dips, syrup, trays, and wine.

Touring Car

This very collectible candy container is from the Cambridge Glass Company, listed in their ads as #2845 Automobile, but most collectors know it as Touring Car. It is a 2½ oz. container, clear with a black enameled roof and great detail.

Tree

We've still learned little about this pattern except that it was made by Paden City Glass in 1918, and there seem to be slight variations from one shape to another. Minnie Watson Kamm describes this pattern as a "stiff formal evergreen or column of graduated herringbone with long oval thumbprints around the body." Shapes include a table set, water set, toothpick holder, and celery vase. Some pieces are ruby stained, green stained, or gold trimmed. This was Paden City's #202 pattern.

Tree Bark

Tree Bark can be found in a table set, water set, berry set, and probably other shapes, and is known in crystal and amber glass. The maker is unknown, at least to us and while the design is a bit on the weak side, the quality is good and the shapes are interesting.

Tree of Life

Tree of Life was made by the Portland Glass Company (1870), Hobbs, Brockunier (1888) in limited amounts, and Sandwich Glass in the 1880s. Known in clear, amber, pastel blue, cobalt blue, canary, green, cranberry, and amethyst glass. Shapes include oval or round bowls, table set, celery vase, champagne, covered or open high or low compotes, epergne, sauce, goblet, mug, milk pitcher, water set, plates, master salt, leaf-shaped sauce, toothpick holder, water tray, wine, and vases in several sizes. The design has been copied through the years in carnival and other types of glass.

Tree of Life

Tree of Life with Hand

Dating to 1879 and made by Hobbs, Brockunier, this pattern was an extension of their Tree of Life line and consisted of compotes (4", 6", 8", and 10") as well as a "bouquet" vase (a stemmed piece with armed lilies for flowers), as well as lamps with the same Hand stems. The lamps are found in crystal, while the other pieces are also known in marine green, canary, or sapphire blue as well as crystal. Shown is a rare cake stand, and there is also a four-piece table set.

Tree of Life with Hand

Tree Stump

Tree of Love

Found mostly as an opalescent pattern and reported to have been seen marked "Sabino," this pattern was made in France in the 1920s, again in the 1930s, and even revived in the 1960s. Shapes reported are bowls, plates, cups, a compote, and the covered cheese dish shown.

Tree of Love

Tree Stump

Reported by Heacock to have been made by the Portland Glass Company in 1870, this is a very difficult pattern to locate, and little has been written about it. The shapes we can confirm are 4" footed sauces or berry dishes with handles and the covered compote shown with a tree trunk stem, handles, and a fine engraved design. In addition large bowls, both covered and open, have been reported.

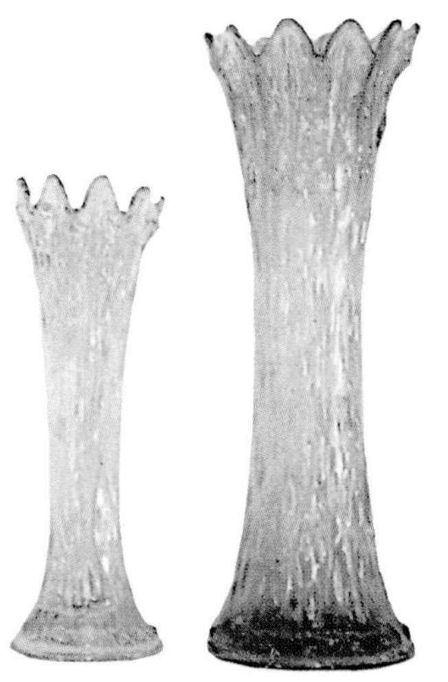

Tree Trunk

Trefoil Finecut

Triple Thumbprints

Triple Triangle (Doyle & Co.)

Triple Triangle (U.S. Glass)

Tripod Stem

Tree Trunk

The Northwood Glass Company made this vase, mostly in carnival glass or opalescent glass, but here is one in crystal, and it was also made in custard glass. The design is often confused with a Fenton vase pattern called Rustic which has a similar design. The Tree Trunk vase usually brings higher prices than the Rustic vase.

Trefoil Finecut

One of Millersburg's fine exterior bowl patterns, this one is mostly found in carnival glass with a Many Stars pattern on the interior. It is also known in a rare non-interior marigold ruffled plate, and in crystal there are bowls of several shapes that include flared, ruffled, or straight sided. All pieces in this pattern are rare and desirable.

Triple Thumbprints

Shapes of this pattern include a table set, water set, berry set, goblet, and pickle dish. The maker is unknown to us, but we believe the date of manufacture is about 1890 – 1900. Any information on this pattern would be appreciated.

Triple Triangle (Doyle & Co.)

Triple Triangle was made by Doyle and Company as their #76 pattern and then by U.S. Glass in 1891 in crystal or ruby stained crystal. Shapes include a table set, goblet, mug, water set, wine, pickle dish, celery vase, and various bowl shapes.

Triple Triangle (U.S. Glass)

This pattern was made by U. S. Glass Company in 1891 and can be found in clear or ruby stained glass. Shapes include a table set, water set, cup, mug, wine, and possibly goblet.

Tripod Stem

Also known as Arched Tripod and made in 1885 (maker unknown), shapes include a table set, water set, celery vase, goblet, and wine. A band repeats the design found on all three of the stems.

Tropical Villa

This is a fine covered compote, but we have no clue as to the maker, years of production, or other shapes. The design of palm trees, pyramids, and temples make this a fitting companion piece to the Egyptian or Parthenon pattern. We welcome any information about this pattern.

Trout and Fly

This extremely rare bowl (two crystal examples known) is mostly found in carnival glass. It was made by Millersburg and is a prized pattern to collectors. Here we show a bowl that has been whimsied into a hat shape.

Truncated Cube

Truncated Cube, from the Thompson Glass Company as their #77 pattern in 1894, can be found in clear or with ruby stain. Shapes include a berry set, table set, celery vase, cruet, decanter, goblet, milk pitcher, water set, shakers, sauce, squat or tall syrup, toothpick holder, water tray, and wine. A large open compote has been reported but not verified.

Tulip

From Bryce, Richards and Company in the 1860s, this well-known design's shapes include a table set, celery vase, decanter, wine, compote (high or low), pint jug, quart jug, water set, wine, and goblet. The decanter comes in several sizes. This pattern and the Tulip with Sawtooth are similar patterns from the same maker.

Tulip with Sawtooth

If you compare this pattern from Bryce, Richards with the Tulip above, you will see the slight differences. Tulip with Sawtooth dates to 1854 but was later made by U.S. Glass in 1891 in clear, milk glass, and opalescent glass. Shapes include a bar bottle, table set, celery vase, champagne, covered and open compotes (high or low) in four sizes, cruet, decanter, egg cup, goblet, honey dish, mug, water set, plate, pomade jar, wine, master salt dip, and whiskey tumbler.

Tropical Villa

Trout and Fly

Truncated Cube

Tulip

Tulip with Sawtooth

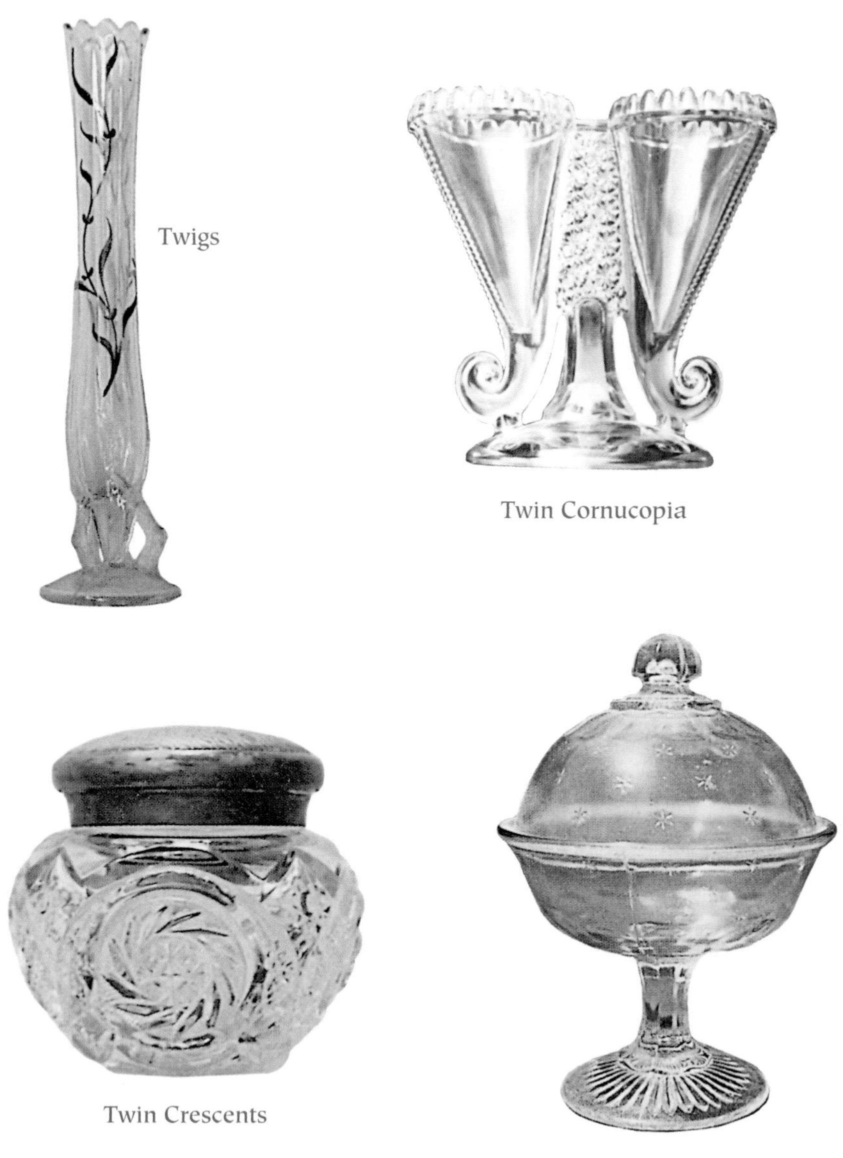

Twigs

Twin Cornucopia

Twin Crescents

Twinkle Star

Twins

Twigs

From the Dugan/Diamond Company of Indiana, Pennsylvania, this vase and its sister design called Beauty Bud Vase (doesn't have the twig feet) are found in many treatments that include carnival glass, opalescent glass, crystal, silver-decorated, and even a strange "tortoise shell" treatment that may be plain or iridized.

Twin Cornucopia

From Bryce, Higbee & Company in 1887, this novelty vase is really quite a rare item. It is 5¾" tall and 6" across the top and can be found in all crystal (often engraved), amber and clear, and blue and clear. The dual color work is unique and very interesting, and some pieces may have been made all in color, but we haven't seen them.

Twin Crescents

Similar in design to a Cambridge pattern called Near-Cut #2697, the piece shown here seems to be found in a table set and the pomade jar shown. Of course there may be other shapes, but we are unaware of them at this time. These pieces date to the late 1800s, we think, but we do not know the maker.

Twinkle Star

Also known as Utah, Frost Flower, or Starlight, this was the U. S. Glass pattern #15080 made in 1903 in clear or frosted. Shapes include covered or open bowls, table set, cake stand, cake plate, celery vase, covered and open compotes, condiment set, cruet, goblet, pickle tray, water set, shakers, sauce, syrup, and wine.

Twins

Carnival glass collectors use this name for this Imperial pattern, but others know it as Horseshoe Curve. It is shown in a 1909 factory catalog in a water set advertised as #411. Also shown is a berry set, 6" bowl, 7" grape plate, 10" bowl, 7" rose bowl, 7½" flat plate, and fruit bowl with stand. Only the last piece and the bowl shapes are known in carnival glass.

Twin Snowshoes

Twin Snowshoes was from U. S. Glass (#15139) in 1918. Shapes include a table set, water set, compotes, cake stand, cruet, cup, celery vase, relish dish, toothpick holder, toy table set, handled relish dish, and wine. Some pieces were gold trimmed.

Twin Teardrops

Made by Higbee, this 1890s pattern is found on a table set, 6" bowl, celery vase, open compote, cruet, banana plate, goblet, round 10" plate, square 8" plate, sauce, custard cup, and relish dish. The design is a good one, well balanced with even geometric planning.

Twisted Rib

Made by the Dugan/Diamond Company in 1906, this was their #1016 vase, twisted from the standard Wide Rib vase. Found primarily in carnival glass or opalescent glass, it is a bit unusual to find a crystal one. These vases will vary in size from 7" to 13".

Two Band

The maker is unknown, but this pattern dates to the 1880s. Shapes include a table set, celery vase, compote, water set, handled plate, shakers, toy table set, pickle dish, and covered low compote with handles.

Two Owls

We've learned very little about this fine covered compote with a finial of two owls and a short stem. Anyone having information about this pattern, please contact us.

Twin Snowshoes

Two Owls

Twin Teardrops

Twisted Rib

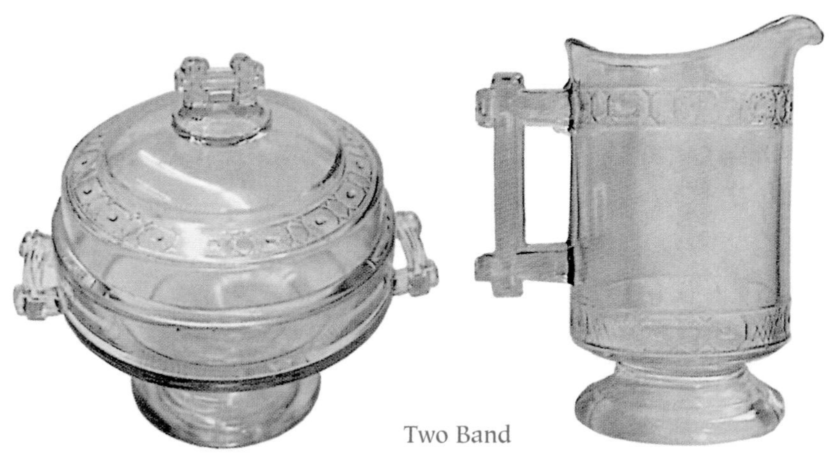

Two Band

Two Panel

Two Post Lamp

U. S. Comet

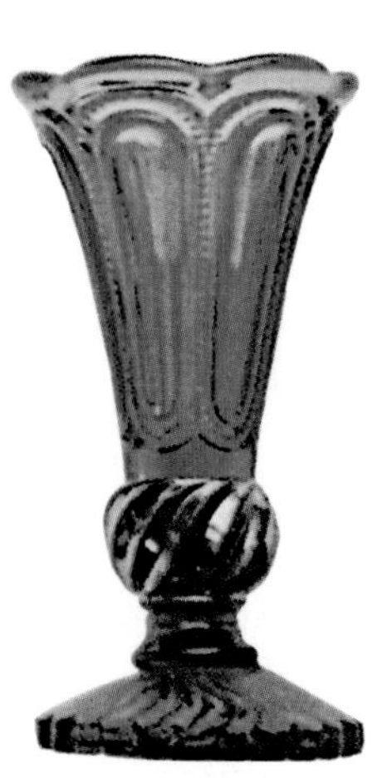
U. S. #16046

U. S. Glass #25

Two Panel

Two Panel was made by Richards and Hartley and then U. S. Glass in 1891. Other names used are Daisy in Square or Daisy in Panel. Shapes include a table set, 7", 8", 9" bowls, celery vase, covered compote, open compote, goblet, tall oil lamp, master salt, individual salt, water set, handled tray, wine, shakers, and mug. Treatments are clear, apple green, amber, blue, and canary.

Two Post Lamp

Attributed to the Dalzell, Gilmore, and Leighton Glass Company in about 1901 as part of an extensive oil lamp production, the Two Post Lamp actually has two variations in the base design. One has daisy wheels on four corners, and the one shown has an almond chain design.

U. S. Comet

U.S. Comet, also known as Doyle's Comet, was made by Doyle & Company in the 1880s and then by U.S. Glass after 1891. It is found in clear, amber, or vaseline. Some collectors call it Draped Fan as well. Shapes include a table set, water set, bowls, celery vase, goblet, wine, and a pickle dish.

U. S. #16046

Made by U. S. Glass Company and shown in an ad with a group of like vases in 1898, this vase (and the rest) apparently has no name, only numbers. They are all emerald green with gold trim, and the one shown is listed in both 6" and 7½" sizes. We are sure these were also made in clear glass.

U. S. Glass #25

Shown in a Butler Brothers catalog dated 1915, this pattern was listed with a group of export glass from U. S. Glass Company to Mexico and South America. We can't seem to locate a pattern name but know it was listed as #25, made in water sets, table sets, and berry sets. The design depends on the uneven scrolled band at the top and the decorative finials on the handles.

U. S. Glass Late Block

This is also called Waffle Block and was made by U.S. Glass in 1891 from a Duncan pattern. Shapes include a table set, water set, berry set, lamp, celery boat, square or rectangular bowls, punch set, ice tub, handled relish, jelly compote, sugar shaker, shakers, rose bowls, syrup, cruet, water bottle, horse-radish bottle, pickle dish, and mustard pot. It is found in both crystal and ruby stained crystal.

U. S. Nursery Rhyme

Credited to the U.S. Glass Company in 1908, this child's delightful pattern shows several tableau scenes from the nursery rhymes children used to learn. Shapes are a water set and table set as far as we know, but other shapes may well exist.

U. S. Rib

From the U. S. Glass Company as their #15061 in 1900, this plainish pattern is found in a table set, cruet, toothpick holder, stemmed sherbet, celery tray, bread tray, cake stand, relish, pickle dish, and shakers. It was made in clear, green, and gold-trimmed crystal, and is also known as New York.

U. S. Sheraton

Made by U.S. Glass as the name indicates, this pattern (their #15144) is also known as Greek Key and dates to 1912. It is found in crystal, gilded with gold or platinum, or in pale green. Shapes include a bonbon, bowl, table set, jelly compote (two sizes), creamers in three sizes, cruet, finger bowl, goblet, mini-lamp, jam jar, mug, mustard jar with lid, pickle dish, pin tray, water set (squat or tankard), plate in two sizes, pomade jar, puff box, punch set (covered bowl), shakers (two sizes), individual salt, sherbet, syrup, toothpick holder, ice tea tumbler, ring stand, and dresser tray.

U. S. Wicker Edge

From U. S. Glass as their #98 pattern, this is a specialty pattern found in footed fruit bowls or compotes. These came in four sizes in clear, white opaque, and turquoise.

U. S. Sheraton

U. S. Glass Late Block

U. S. Nursery Rhyme

U. S. Wicker Edge

U. S. Rib

Valencia Waffle

Venetian (Kenneth)

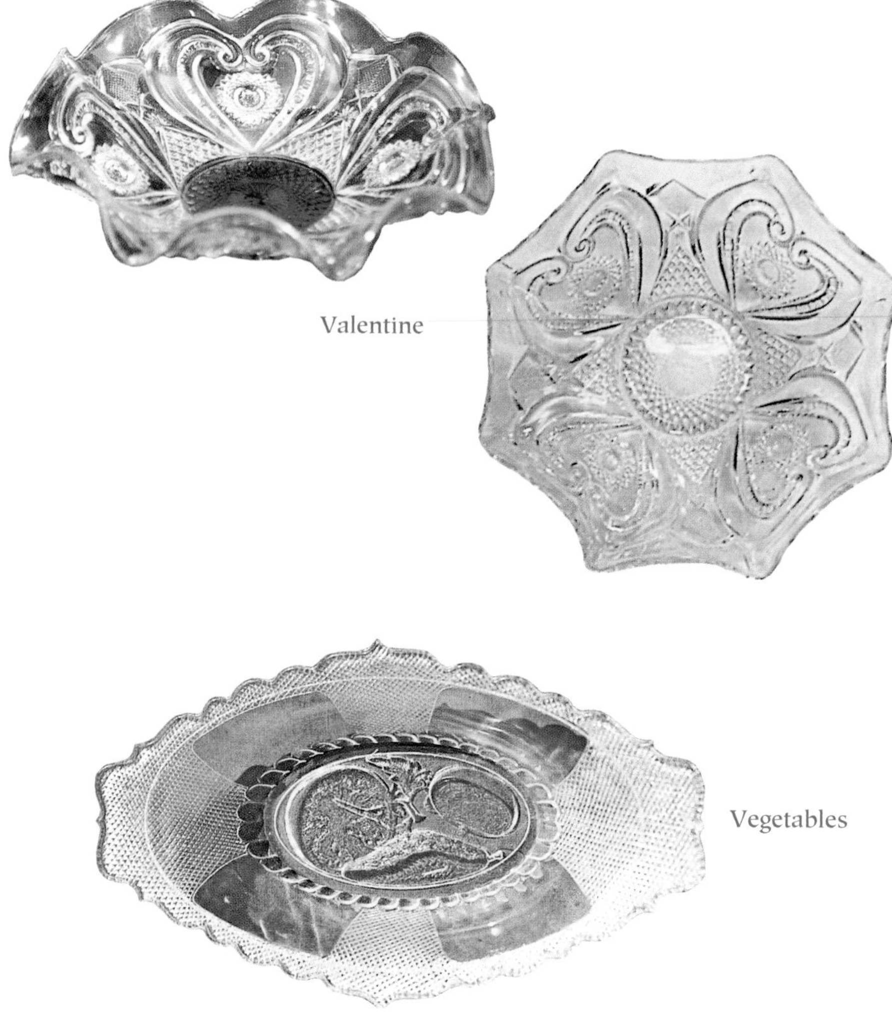

Valentine

Vegetables

Valencia Waffle

Valencia Waffle was first called Adams #85 and made by Adams & Company in 1885 and then by U. S. Glass in 1891 in clear amber, blue, apple green, and vaseline glass. Shapes include a berry set, bread plate, table set, cake stand, caster set, celery vase, high or low compotes, oblong 7", 8", 9" bowls, goblet, pickle dish, pickle jar, milk pitcher, water set, relish dish, shakers, salt dip, flat or footed sauce, syrup, and water tray.

Valentine

Northwood's #14 pattern, found in berry sets in both carnival glass and crystal, is a very good design that can also be seen with gold edging and is known (at least in crystal) in a 10" cake plate, square plate, square bowl, and flared bowl. A 1906 Northwood catalog called this pattern their "superb crystal berry assortment."

Vegetables

From the 1880s (maker is unknown to us), this very nice pickle or relish tray has a tomato, an onion, and celery stalks, a cable winding around the design, and sections of plain and fine file. Perhaps this was just a specialty item, but it seems a shame that there do not seem to be any matching pieces.

Venetian (Kenneth)

Venetian was first called Kenneth and made by Ohio Flint Glass as part of their Krys-tol line in 1905. It then moved to Jefferson Glass when Ohio Flint Glass closed in 1908. In 1909 some mould shapes then went to the Millersburg plant where the 9" vase and the table set pieces were made in carnival glass. Shapes in this pattern include a berry set, table set, water set, squat water pitcher, milk pitcher, hotel creamer and sugar, cruet, compotes in several sizes, three sizes of punch sets, stemmed sherbet, pickle dish, celery tray. In 1913, Millersburg closed and the 9" vase mould went to Cambridge as their #2340 lamp base.

Venice

Information seems to be limited about this pattern, but the owner tells us it was manufactured at the Adams factory by U.S. Glass in 1891. Colors are amber or canary, but we're sure clear was made. Shown is the rare decorated water pitcher, and it is a beauty. Thanks to Steve and Radka Sandeman for sharing this with us.

Venice

Venus (Royal)

Made by Belmont Glass of Bellaire, Ohio, there is some confusion about this pattern. It is called Royal or Royal Lady when found with ball feet (1881) and Venus when found with a collar base as shown. This latter version is said to have been made in 1883. The question remains: is this one pattern with a mould change for easier production, or really two separate patterns? Shapes include a bread plate (Crying Baby), table set, celery vase, covered 8" compote, shakers, and water set.

Venus (Royal)

Viking

Victorian (Riverside)

Made in 1894 by Riverside Glass in 35 shapes, Victorian is found in crystal and with ruby or amber stain. Shapes include a berry set, table set, water set, toothpick holder, breakfast creamer, cruet, jelly compote, tall compote, syrup, pickle jar, pickle dish, celery vase, sauce, shakers, a goblet, and a wine. The staining was done by the Mueller Glass Staining Company we are told. The breakfast creamer is really the toothpick holder with a handle added.

Victorian (Riverside)

Viking

Viking was made by Hobbs, Brockunier in 1876 and is also called Hobbs Centennial, Bearded Head, or Old Man of the Mountains. Shapes include an apothecary jar, covered bowls, table set, covered casserole, celery vase, covered high and low compotes, open compote, footed cup, egg cup, jam jar, mug, pickle dish, water pitcher, bread platter, relish tray, and master footed salt dip. Shapes have "Viking head" feet and finials.

Vinegar and Oil Cruet

V-in-Heart

Wading Heron

Waffle Block

Waffle and Finecut

Waffle and Star Band

Vinegar and Oil Cruet

Probably from Central Glass Company, this piece bears the following marking: "Pat'd 10/6/14." It has lines indicating how much vinegar and how much oil were needed for salad dressing, flared lip, and very attractive stopper.

V-in-Heart

Surely other shapes in this well-done pattern were made, but we've only been able to document the water pitcher shown, and it is now also known in a cake stand. Other references listed only the pitcher, so maybe we have to be satisfied with that. It was made by Bryce, Higbee (1895 – 1905).

Wading Heron

Wading Heron was made by U.S. Glass as #6404 in 1915 in crystal and the rare emerald green shown. The pitcher is pedestal- based and has a ring of scaling above the pedestal. The heron stands in wavy water, and there are clusters of cattails on either side.

Waffle and Finecut

From U.S. Glass in 1891, this pattern is also known as Orion or Cathedral. Shapes are a table set, bowl, wine, water set, and the unusual boat shape shown. It measures just over 12" in length. Other shapes are a cake stand, covered or open compotes, egg cup, and sauces in flat or footed variations. It was made in vaseline, amber, and blue glass also.

Waffle and Star Band

Made by Tarentum Glass in 1910 and also known as Block and Star Spear Point and Verona, this pattern is found in clear or ruby stained glass. Shapes include a table set, water set, toothpick holder, berry set, pickle dish, goblet, compote, shakers, and celery vase.

Waffle Block

Also called Monticello, this is Imperial's #698. Among the 40 known shapes are water sets, table sets, handled basket, punch set, vase, rose bowl, 6" plate, 7" – 9" bowls, stemmed parfait, shakers, fruit bowl with stand, pickle dish, compote, celery tray, and syrup.

Waffle Variant

Waffle Variant was made by George Duncan and Sons as #308 in 1890 and U.S. Glass in 1891. Shapes include a table set, 7" tray, 8" tray, celery vase (flat or footed), sugar shaker, cruet, carafe, covered cheese dish, ice cream tray, and berry set.

Waffle Variant

Waffle Window

Waffle Window

Apparently made only in these shakers with the very fancy metal top, this is Imperial's pattern #370, shown in a 1909 factory catalog that has recently surfaced. The design is a simple one, repeated on all four sides of the shaker, and I suspect these were made for commercial use in hotels and restaurants.

Washington Centennial

This was from Gillinder & Company in 1876 (shards have also turned up at Burlington Glass site in Canada). Shapes besides the well-known oval platter which may have any of three subjects (Washington, Carpenter's Hall, or Independence Hall) include 7", 8", 9" oval bowls, 7", 8", 9" round bowls, table set, cake stand in two sizes, celery vase, champagne, open or covered compotes, pickle dish, egg cup, goblet, pitcher, milk pitcher, plate, the platters, relish tray, salt dips, shakers, sauce, syrup, and wine.

Washington Centennial

Wedding Ring

Waterford

Attributed to the Portland Glass Company of Portland, Maine, the piece shown is a double relish dish, but we are sure this pattern came in several table shapes including a table set, celery vase, pickle dish, and a goblet. The date of production is estimated to be 1870s.

Wedding Ring

This pattern is also called Double Wedding Ring, and dates from the 1870s to the early 1900s. It may be found in flint as well as non-flint glass, and was reproduced in the late 1900s. Shapes include a table set, celery vase, champagne glass, cordial, decanter, goblet, oil lamp, relish tray, sauce, water set, syrup, and a wine. The maker is unknown at this time.

Waterford

Wellington

Westmoreland's #98

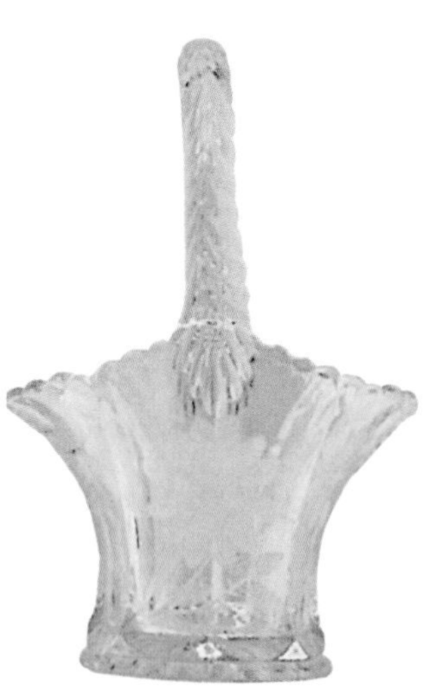

Westmoreland's #750

Westmoreland's #777

Westward Ho

Wellington

Wellington, also called Staple, was made by Westmoreland in 1903 and then by Federal in 1914. It can be found in crystal or ruby stain. Shapes include a table set, water set, berry set, pickle dish, goblet, and wine (shown).

Westmoreland's #98

Introduced by Westmoreland in 1898, this well-done pattern is found on both table sets and bowls of various sizes. It was made in both plain and gold-trimmed crystal as well as emerald glass in either plain or gold trimmed. In 1904, this pattern was expanded to 54 pieces that included a water set, celery vase, cruet, shakers, pickle tray, celery tray, and syrup.

Westmoreland's #750

This waas made in 1921 by Westmoreland as their #750 basket in 3", 4", 5", 6", 7", 8" sizes. Besides the etched example shown, it was also treated with a silvered design, and opal pieces were made for special orders.

Westmoreland's #777

First listed in the Westmoreland line in 1917, seven shapes were made including a nappy, table set, and berry set. The nappy (shown) was dropped in 1924, and the other pieces were continued until 1927. The pattern was known as #777 and remains without another name (as far as we know) to this day.

Westward Ho

Also known as Pioneer or Tippecanoe and first made by Gillinder and Sons in 1879, Westward Ho has been widely reproduced through the years, even up to the present. Old shapes include a table set, celery vase (three sizes), covered and open compotes (high or low), jam jar, mugs in two sizes, pickle dish, milk pitcher, water set, bread plate, oval platter, sauces, wine, and goblet.

Wheat and Barley
First made by Bryce Brothers in the 1870s and then as a part of U.S. Glass in the 1890s, this pattern is also known as Duquesne, Hops and Barley, or Oats and Barley. Shapes are a table set, cake stand, open or covered compotes, goblet, mug, water set, syrup, shakers, berry set, and handled plates in 7" and 9" sizes.

Wheat Sheaf
Wheat Sheaf was made in 1908 by the Cambridge Glass Company as their #2660 pattern. Shapes include celery vase, compotes (5½", 8"), fruit compotes (8", 9"), sweetmeat with lid, cruet, milk pitcher, decanter, wine, punch set, stemmed 9" vase, tankard pitcher, half gallon pitcher, tumbler, a tray, rose bowl, and a handled basket.

Wheels
Wheels was made by Imperial Glass in 1909 as their #3888 and can be found in both crystal and carnival glass. Shapes include a berry set, 7½" rose bowl, and 10" fruit bowl. A tumbler is also known with gold trim so surely there is a pitcher out there somewhere.

Whirled Sunburst in Circle
From Beatty-Brady Glass Company in 1908, this well-known pattern can be found in a table set, water set, and berry set. The design is a good one with interesting oval shapes, plain ovals, fans, and diamond sections around a whirling star.

Whirlwind
We've learned little about this pattern except that it is found in several shapes that include bowls, a water set, shakers, and the large open compote shown. The primary pattern is a whirling star inside a beaded circle but there are alternate sections of diamond file, triangular hobstars, and triangular sunbursts. We'd appreciate any further information about this pattern.

Wheat and Barley

Wheat Sheaf

Wheels

Whirled Sunburst in Circle

Whirlwind

Whisk Broom

Wide Rib

Wildflower

Wild Rose Lady's Medallion Lamp

Wild Rose Lamp

Whisk Broom

This novelty pickle dish, made by Campbell & Jones as well as Geo. Duncan & Sons (1886), comes in two sizes and can be found in crystal, canary, blue, or amber. It is marked "Pat appd for" and we can't explain why Campbell & Jones received the patent and then let Duncan make it.

Wide Rib

Wide Rib was made by the Northwood Glass Company in 1907 in carnival glass, opalescent glass, clear, and colored crystal. There are several variations of this simple pattern, and almost all are covered in our writings in carnival glass. Wide Rib vases measure 7" to 13" tall usually but taller examples are sometimes found.

Wildflower

First Adams in 1874, then U.S. Glass in 1891 made this well-known pattern. Found in amber, apple green, blue, vaseline, etched, and clear. Shapes include oval cake basket, round and square bowls, table set, cake stand, celery vase, champagne, covered compotes, goblet, water set, cake plate, oval bread plate, platter, relish, shakers, salt dip, syrup, water tray, and wine. It has been reproduced.

Wild Rose Lady's Medallion Lamp

This is shown in the goofus treatment and was first made by the Riverside Glass Company before 1907 and then retooled after 1909 by the Millersburg Glass Company and made in a rare carnival glass version. All treatments are considered very collectible, and the Millersburg versions of this lamp are all rare. It is also called Riverside Lady or Lucille.

Wild Rose Lamp

This pattern was first made by Riverside Glass as part of their Lucille line of oil lamps, and later by the Millersburg Glass Company (1910) in carnival glass. Found in fours sizes (here we show the first reported handled hand lamp), these lamps are companions to the Riverside Ladies (Ladies Medallion) lamp as well as the Riverside Colonial lamp.

Wild Rose with Bow Knot

This was made by McKee and Sons (National Glass 1901) and can be found in crystal, frosted crystal, colors, and goofus decorated. Shapes include a table set, water set, toothpick holder, shakers, sauce, berry set, smoke set on a tray, and rectangular tray (shown).

Wild Rose with Bow Knot

Wild Rose Wreath

Also known as Miniature Intaglio to some carnival glass collectors, this U.S. Glass pattern was advertised as a "stemmed almond" so we know it was a nut cup. In carnival glass, it can be found in marigold or white and in crystal most examples have a gold or goofus treatment. The nut bowl stands 2½" tall and is about 3" across the bowl.

Wild Rose Wreath

Willow Oak

Willow Oak was a Bryce pattern in 1890 and a U.S. Glass member in 1891. This pattern is also known as Oak Leaf, Stippled Star, Acorn, Thistle, or Wreath. Shapes are a tray, plate, mug, shakers, water set, sauce, celery vase, waste bowl, cake stand, and berry set.

Willow Oak

Wiltec

Wiltec, made by McKee Glass about 1905, was one of the well-advertised "tec" patterns. Pieces are usually marked with McKee's "Prescut" mark. Shapes include a berry set, table set, water set, bonbon, cigar jar, custard cup, a scarce flower pot, punch sets, and plates in 6", 8", 10", and 12" sizes. The water pitchers can be squat or tankard and are very massive.

Wiltec

Wilted Flowers

Also known as Single Flower by carnival glass collectors, this Dugan/Diamond pattern was part of the Intaglio line from 1906 to 1911. It was made in clear, goofus, opalescent, and carnival glass. Shapes are mostly bowls or rare plates, but handles have also been applied to some pieces to form baskets.

Wilted Flowers

Windflower

Found primarily in carnival glass, this Dugan/Diamond pattern was also made in crystal and in opalescent glass. Shapes are mostly bowls, but plates and the handled nappy are known in all treatments. The design is a nice one with a lot of flow.

Windflower

Windmill Server

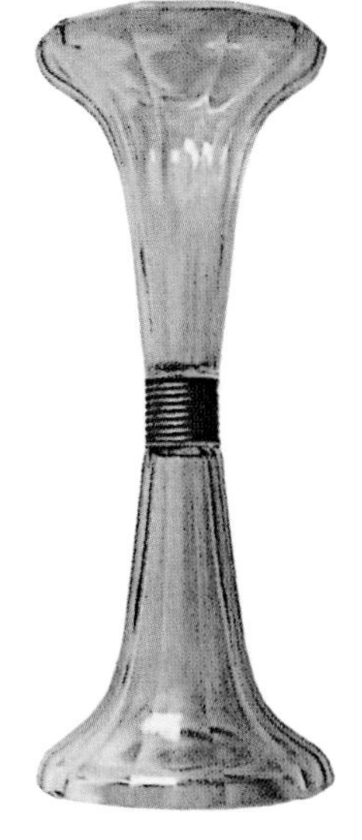
Window Trim Vase

Windmill Server

We suspect this interesting item is European. It came along in the early 1900s according to *Yellow-Green Vaseline* by Jay Glickman and Terry Fedosky, who say it is nickel plated and that the windmill actually turns. We welcome any more information about this item.

Window Trim Vase

Here is the second variety of window trim vases from New Martinsville. This one has the metal connecting spacer in the center and was a stronger vase than the other we show.

Windsor Anvil

Windsor Anvil

Attributed to the Windsor Glass Company of Pittsburgh in 1887 – 1889, this novelty paperweight is in the shape of a blacksmith's anvil. It is found in clear, amber, or blue glass.

Winged Scroll

Winged Scroll

Winged Scroll was made by the A.H. Heisey Company in about 1888 and can be found in clear, milk glass, custard, and this emerald green. The pattern is called Ivorina Verde in opaque glass. Shapes include a syrup, table set, smoker's set, cruet, berry set, bonbon (no handles), pickle dish, cup and saucer, cake stand, cologne, trinket box, humidor, celery vase, olive dish, toothpick holder, and a high standard compote.

Wisconsin

Wisconsin

Sometimes called Beaded Dewdrop, this is U.S. Glass's State Series pattern #15079, made in 1903 in shapes that include a banana stand, bonbon, oil bottle, covered and open bowls, celery tray, table set, cake stand, covered and open compotes, saucer in a stem, custard cup, five-piece condiment set, cruet, cup and saucer, goblet, jelly dish, jam jar, mug, mustard jar, pickle dish and jar, water set, milk pitcher, plates, preserve dish, relish, shakers in two shapes, sherbet cup, syrup, sugar shaker, toothpick holder, wine, and 6" round vase.

Wolf

Also a product of the 1880s, this mug is 3¾" tall and has a diameter of 3¾". It is found in clear, amber, blue, apple green, and probably canary. The handle is like that on Rabbit Upright and Diamond with Circle mugs so probably came from the same glasshouse.

Wooden Pail

Wooden Pail was first made by Bryce, Higbee in the 1880s and then by U.S. Glass in 1891. Colors include amber, amethyst, blue, canary, and clear. Shapes include a table set, toy table set, toothpick holder in three sizes, water set, jelly bucket, ice bucket, and open sugar pail.

Wyoming

Made by U.S. Glass in 1903, this pattern is also called Enigma by some collectors. It can be found in a water set, covered compote, open compote, table set (both covered and open sugars known), cake plate, shakers, berry sets, and wine. The main pattern recognition is the owl-like figure.

X-Log

Also known as Prism Arc, this 1880s pattern is found in crystal or opaque white glass. The maker is unknown, but shapes include table sets, oval bowl, cake stand, goblet, mug, wine, shakers, pickle dish, and sauce.

X-Ray

X-Ray was a product of Riverside Glass Company in 1899 in crystal, emerald green, amethyst (scarce), and gold trimmed. Shapes include a table set, rare syrup, shakers, cruet, jelly compote, toothpick holder, berry set, cloverleaf tray, compote, and celery vase.

Wolf

Wooden Pail

Wyoming

X-Log

X-Ray

Yale

Yoke and Circle

Yutec

Zenith

Zig-Zag Band

Yale

Sometimes called Crow-Feet, this McKee Glass Company pattern was made in 1894 in a berry set, table set, cake stand, celery vase, covered compote (high), open compote (high or low), goblet, water set, oval relish, shakers, flat or footed sauce, and syrup.

Yoke and Circle

Yoke and Circle is also called New Era and was made by J.B. Higbee Company. Shapes include a table set, water set, berry set, goblet, shakers, milk pitcher, rose bowl, pickle dish, celery vase, and mustard jar. The design is a very good one with interesting patterns.

Yutec

From McKee Brothers in 1909 as part of their "tec" line, Yutec is found in berry sets, water sets, table sets, a wine, cordial or champagne goblet, pickle dish, relish tray, and a punch set (bowl and base shown). The pattern features two strong components consisting of sections of cane and a section of a radiating star. Yutec was reproduced by Kemple Glass in colors.

Zenith

Besides the candlestick shown, this pattern is found in a cruet and salt shaker. It is made in crystal and a scarce pale blue glass, but the date of production and the maker are not known, at least to us.

Zig-Zag Band

Zig-Zag Band was made in the 1880s (maker unknown) and can be found on a creamer, a sugar, and the covered bowl shown. (There were probably other table pieces but we haven't verified them.) All the covered pieces have the squirrel final and the name is derived from the banding of zig-zagging around each piece.

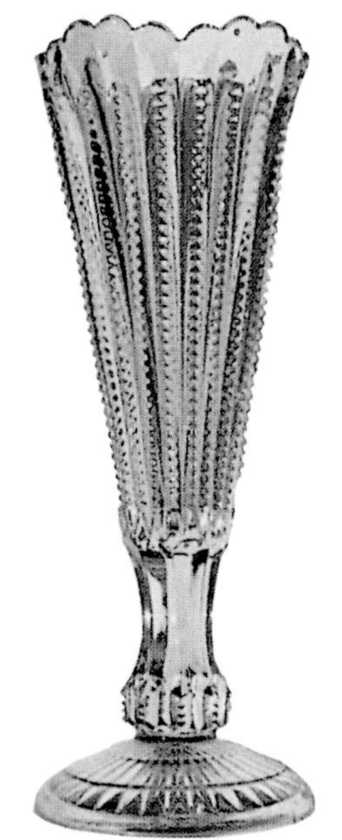

Zipper

Zipper Cross

Zipper

Originally called Cobb, it is also known as Late Sawtooth and is found in crystal or blue. Shapes include a bowl, table set, celery vase, cheese dish, covered high or low compote, open high compote, cruet, goblet, jam jar, water set, milk pitcher, relish tray, salt dip, sauce, and stemmed vase.

Zipper Cross

Zipper Cross was first made by Bryce, Higbee until 1907 and then J.B. Higbee and finally New Martinsville Glass after 1918, and shown in Montgomery Ward ads in 1900 as Paris. Shapes are many and include a berry set, table set, compotes, a mug, pickle dish, celery dish, and vase.

Zippered Corner

Zippered Corner

We believe this is also known as Zippered Block. Date of production was in the 1890 – 1905 era, and the maker seems to be unknown (some collectors think it was by Cambridge from Northwood moulds). Shapes we can verify are a full table set, a syrup, a bowl, and a pickle dish, but certainly others may exist.

Zippered Heart

Made by Imperial Glass in 1909 as their #292 pattern, it is found in crystal and scarce carnival glass. Shapes include a table set, celery vase, breakfast set, pedestal rose bowl, vase, small pitcher, water set, sherbet, finger bowl, plate, custard cup, jelly compote, punch set, orange and fruit bowls, nut bowls, berry set, nappy, spoon tray, mayonnaise set, and various bowls.

Zippered Heart

Zippered Windows

Zipper Loop

Zipper Slash

Zippered Windows

We suspect this wine is from Iowa City Glass (it is shown in Miriam Righter's *Iowa City Glass*) and is listed as simply the Iowa City wine. We believe it dates to the 1890s and can't speculate on other shapes but they may well exist.

Zipper Loop

Zipper Loop was made by the Imperial Glass Company as their #201½ and shown in their 1909 company catalog in three sizes of hand lamp, four sizes of medium stand lamps, and four sizes of large stand lamps. At least three sizes of these lamps (one hand, one medium stand, and one large) are known in carnival glass and have been reproduced in this treatment.

Zipper Slash

This was George Duncan & Sons' #2005 from the 1890s and can be found in crystal, frosted, ruby stained, and amber stained glass. Shapes include a table set, water set, toothpick holder, wine, berry set, celery vase, sherbet, cup, open and covered compotes, banana dish, and footed sauce.

Commemorative and Advertising Patterns

ABC Clock Plate

Admiral Dewey Plate

Admiral Dewey Tumbler

Alphabet & Children Mug

ABC Clock Plate

Credited to Ripley and Company Glass of Pittsburgh (they became part of U.S. Glass in 1891 as Factory F), this well-designed ABC plate with the clock face and the notched edges was advertised as U.S. Glass. Its purpose was threefold, teaching children their ABCs, their numbers, and how to tell time.

Admiral Dewey Plate

While the Beatty-Brady Glass Company made the water sets in Spanish American and Dewey patterns, we can't say with certainty who made this nice pierced border plate that has a photo transfer design showing the Admiral and a flag and says "Admiral George Dewey," edged by a circle to roping.

Admiral Dewey Tumbler

One of several similar tumblers honoring Admiral Dewey in the Spanish-American War, this one has a photo picture, a wreath, and lettering that says, "Admiral Dewey...The Nelson of America...Battle of Manila Bay...May 1st, 1898."

Alphabet & Children Mug

This mug was made by Adams & Company in the 1880s and then U.S. Glass after 1891, in clear, amber, blue, green, or opaque blue glass. One side shows a girl decorating a tree (Christmas), and the other features a boy seated at a desk.

Alphabet Plate

Aztec Sunburst

Ball Brothers Glass Mfg. Company

Bates Plate

Beaver Band

Alphabet Plate

Alphabet plates of one type or another were very popular when they were made. Here is one with a nice ruffled edge that is beaded but with no center design (the many rayed star you see is on the exterior of the marie). We know the maker of this plate is Bryce, Higbee since it was featured in one of their ads of 1893, but it was later made by New Martinsville in 1919 and by Viking Glass after 1944. Old pieces are known in clear, blue, and amber. Later production by Viking added a tinted amethyst.

Aztec Sunburst

Shown is a 5" compote with advertising in McKee's Sunburst (McKee called this pattern simply Sunburst and this is their jelly compote). It reads "GREATER HAROLD FURNITURE CO., 812 PENN ST."

Ball Brothers Glass Mfg. Company

The Ball Brothers Glass Company is in Muncie, Indiana, and has long been known for production of glass canning jars. Here is a plate that honors that company, showing a typical glass canning jar, with the lettering "Ball Bros Glass Mfg. Co...Muncie, Ind." The maker of this fine plate is unknown to us, so if readers have any more information, we urge them to contact us.

Bates Plate

Some question exists as to the man in the portrait and while we listed him as John Coulter Bates, other sources say it is John Adams (founder of Adams and Company). The plate has a scalloped edge bordered with dewdrops and a vine. It measures 8". We certainly welcome any information on this piece.

Beaver Band

From Excelsior Glass Company of Canada, this fine goblet has the maple leaf, the band of beavers, and on the underside of the base lettering that reads: "St. Jean Baptiste – Quebec – 24 June 1880." The date of production is believed to have been just prior to the date on the base.

Be Industrious

This very interesting platter is a bit of mystery. It is attributed to Crystal Glass Works by one researcher and to Iowa City Flint Glass by another. We know it was around 1879 when the patent for "crystalography" (the design feature around the tray's rim) was received by the lithographer Henry Feurhake. The process was then assigned to mould maker Washington Beck for Dithridge & Company, so only time will tell who made this piece and the exact date.

Be Industrious — The Lion Shall Lie Down with the Lamb

This product was like the regular Be Industrious platter or Beehive Platter, with added lettering around the outer rim. We feel this platter is probably a product of Iowa City Flint Glass but some researchers attribute it to the Crystal Glass Works.

Be True

Part of a series of plates (Be Thankful, Be Gentle, Be Affectionate, and Be True), this plate was made by the Iowa City Flint Glass Works of Iowa City. As you can see, the Be True plate features a dog center, but the others had a kitten (Be Playful), lamb (Be Gentle), a calf and mother cow (Be Affectionate). These plates all seem to have been tied in with other products with figures and sayings like the beehive plate above (Be Industrious).

Boat Relish

From Atterbury Glass in 1874, this rarely found boat-shaped relish is very interesting. It has "Patented 1874" in the boat's bottom and says "Pickles" on both sides of the bow. There is even a rudder, realistic beams, and boarding in the moulding.

British Lion

This well-done paperweight was issued to commemorate the laying of the second Atlantic cable in 1876. It is inscribed on the base: "Gillinder and Sons Centennial Exhibition." It is frosted crystal, 5⅝" long and 2¾" tall.

Be Industrious

Be Industrious — The Lion Shall Lie Down with the Lamb

Be True

Boat Relish

British Lion

Buckingham Advertising Whimsey

Button Center ABC Plate

By Jingo Mug

Centennial Drape

Carson Furniture

Buckingham Advertising Whimsey

Made by U.S. Glass, Buckingham, also known as Crosby, dates to 1906 and can be found in many shapes. Here we show a 6½" tricornered whimsey bowl with advertising. It reads "Cohn – – Penn & Collins." All advertising items in crystal have become collectible, and this one seems a bit special.

Button Center ABC Plate

Much like the Cane pattern shown on page 51, this center design is called Button Center by collectors and Hobnail by others. The plate shown has this center and the alphabet letters around the outer rim on a stippled background. We do not know the maker of this plate at this time.

By Jingo Mug

Made around 1880 (maker unknown), this interesting mug is found in two sizes (2½" tall or 3⅜" tall). Colors are clear (shown), amber, or blue. The design features a man wearing a hat sitting on a bench.

Carson Furniture

This advertising pickle dish has the U.S. Glass's Oregon pattern around the rim and the wording says "Complete Home Furnishings–Carson Furniture Co.–1825 Carson's SS Pittsburgh." The Oregon pattern was made in many shapes that included a water bottle, covered or open bowls, table set, cake stands, celery vase, compote, saucer bowls, cruet, goblet, honey dish, mug, milk pitcher, water set, plate, relish dish, syrup, toothpick holder, vase, and wine.

Centennial Drape

Also called Centennial 1876, this pattern is found in a table set, bread plate, pickle dish, celery vase, goblet, and various bowls. The lettering says "Centennial 1876," and the pieces were made to celebrate the Philadelphia Exposition.

Centennial Exhibition Shoe

Made by Gillinder and Sons in 1876, this shoe or slipper is a Centennial Exhibition article and, as you can see, came in clear or satin crystal. They have a very stylish look about them and are very collectible.

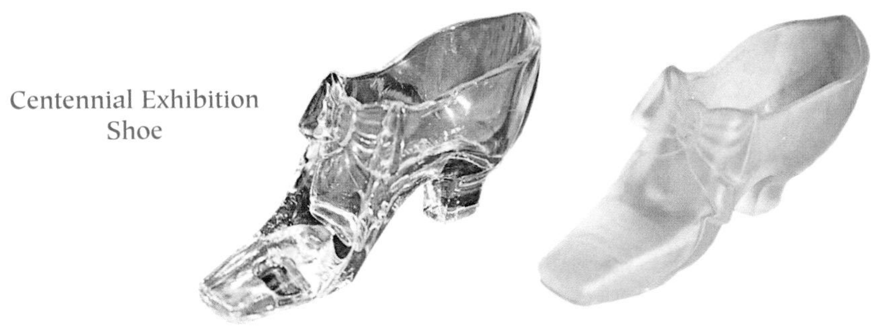

Centennial Exhibition Shoe

Clark's Teaberry

This pedestal advertising change tray has become a popular collectible. It is most often seen in vaseline glass but was made in emerald green and the scarce crystal clear version shown.

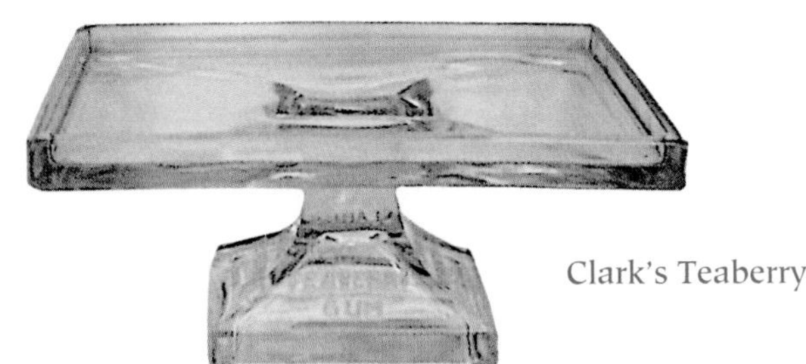

Clark's Teaberry

Cleopatra

This is actually part of the Egyptian or Parthenon pattern, made by Adams and Company in 1884. This tray is known as the Cleopatra platter and measures 8½" x 12". It shows a seated queen with palm trees and a portion of temple column and rail in the background. It is lettered "Give Us This Day Our Daily Bread."

Cleopatra

Columbus Landing

This is a well-designed mug with the image of the Santa Maria, the Columbus flagship on one side and Columbus and his men raising the flag of Spain on the other. On the base is "World's Fair...1893." We've heard of this mug only in clear crystal.

Columbus Landing

"Compliments — Louis Mankowitz"

This can be found on the Millersburg Country Kitchen pattern in both plates and bowls are several advertising items. The one shown is a shallow bowl shape known as an ice cream bowl. It says "Compliments – Louis Mankowitz – Cloaks & Suits – #2 Milwaukee Ave. – Chicago." All Millersburg advertising items are rare whether in crystal or carnival glass.

"Compliments — Louis Mankowitz"

Compliments S.I. Frank

Constitution Platter

Compliments of St. Louis Coffin Company

Continental Platter

Compliments S.I. Frank

This very rare rose bowl in Millersburg's Country Kitchen pattern is lettered "Compliments of S.I. Frank Furniture & Stoves – Credit To All – 709-711 W. North Ave." This is the first advertising rose bowl to surface in this pattern and the only known example with S.I. Frank advertising, indicating it may have been a sample that was never produced.

Compliments of St. Louis Coffin Company

The punch bowl shown is seldom discussed, even without the unusual advertising that says "Compliments of St. Louis Coffin Co.—F.D. Gardner." The advertising is on the exterior of the bowl's marie or collar base while inside is the Cambridge trade mark "Near Cut." Cambridge seems to have few advertising pieces, and this punch bowl is a real find.

Constitution Platter

This well-known bread platter has the following lettering: "Give Us This Day...Our Daily Bread...Liberty and Freedom...1776." In the center is the American eagle with a copy of the Constitution clutched in its talons. It is crystal, measures 12½" x 9", and is fairly plentiful.

Continental Platter

Not to be confused with the Continental pattern by Heisey, this beautiful platter shows a large public building and the dates 1776 – 1876 as well as "Give Us This Day Our Daily Bread." The handles are hands clasping barbells, with an inner ring of round file and divided diamonds. This piece was made by Atterbury Glass in 1876 and is much sought by collectors.

Daisy & Button Advertising Slipper

Patented by the Geo. Duncan & Sons Company in 1886, this Daisy & Button patterned slipper is very similar to one by Bryce (the patents for both were issued the same day). At any rate, Duncan called this their "Hob Nail Slipper," made in crystal, amber, blue, canary, and ruby glass. The Duncan slipper says, "Patd...Oct...19/86," and the heel is higher than that on the Bryce version.

Dewey

Credited to Beatty-Brady in the late 1890s and similar to the Spanish-American set shown elsewhere, this one is much more detailed, has a better glass quality, and is scarcer. The pitcher shows shells standing on end, a laurel-wreathed portrait of Admiral Dewey, as well as a scroll, flags, sunbursts, and a column with a globe on top. Both tumblers (rare) and the pitcher (very scarce) are known, and both are very desirable. It is also known as Gridley.

Dewey Bust

Among the many items honoring Admiral George Dewey is this 5½" tall satinized bust or statuette. It is on clear glass with an acid finish. It says: "Dewey...Manila...1898." As we said earlier, Dewey was a hero of the Spanish-American War, defeating the Spanish fleet at Manila Bay on May 1, 1898.

Dice

We haven't a clue as to who made this novelty advertising piece but have to admit it is a winner. It is a paperweight, shaped and marked like real dice, and it bears the advertising Bristol Diced Mints. We'd certainly like to have any additional information on this item or the candy company it represents.

Dog Plate

Made by Bryce, Higbee in 1893 and shown in one of their catalogs, this ABC plate with a dog is the center was later made by New Martinsville Glass in 1919. Original colors include clear, blue, or amber. It was originally called Rovers in the company ads and measures 6½" in diameter. New Martinsville examples may be marked with "S.I." between the letters of T and U, indicating reproductions were issued for the Smithsonian Institute.

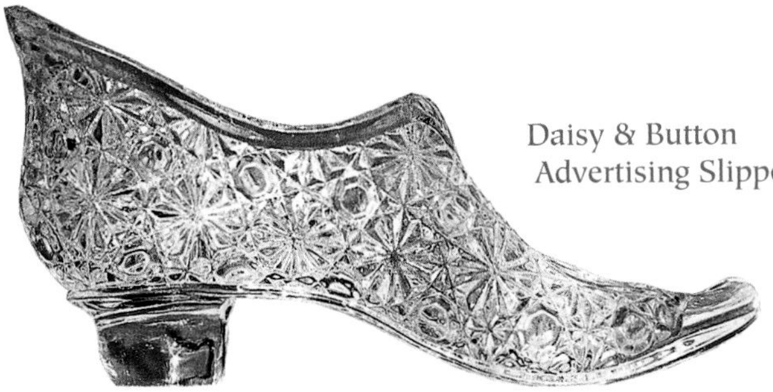

Daisy & Button Advertising Slipper

Dewey

Dewey Bust

Dog Plate

Dice

Donald & Company

Donald & Company

Just like The Globe advertising piece, this one has the Brazilian (or Cane Shield) pattern but has the following advertising: "Donald & Co. – 69 – 71 Market St. – Newark – Furniture – Carpenters & Stoves." The shape is like a wedge of pie and is, of course, a pickle dish. This was a product of Fostoria in 1898 as their #600 pattern.

Easter Greetings Chick

Easter Greetings Chick

Made by several companies over a long span of time, these little plates are found with various edge treatments, several seasonal themes, and in many types of glass. The example shown is on crystal with goofus treatment, dating it to about 1905.

Flower Bouquet ABC Plate

Flower Bouquet ABC Plate

Credited to Gillinder & Sons of Philadelphia, in 1891 a member of U.S. Glass (Factory G), this is one of the better ABC plates. It has a very well done center design of floral spray with the alphabet around the outer rim on a stippled background. We believe this piece dates to the 1880s.

For Auld Lang Syne

For Auld Lang Syne

We've been able to learn little about this very well done plate except it has the same border treatment as another called the Rule Brittania Plate, so both are probably British in origin. Since the one plate is dated 1900, we believe this plate was from around that time also.

Franklin Caro

Franklin Caro

Made in 1915 by the Franklin Caro Company of Richmond, Virginia, this container held chewing gum! The containers were made from 1915 to 1918 only, and the advertisement is on the lid. Today, these pieces are scarce and very collectible, especially to Virginians. A similar piece was made to advertise Coca-Cola gum, and it is very rare.

Frosted Stork ABC Plate

Very different from the iridized Stork ABC plate made by Belmont in Depression glass years, the one shown here is part of a set of known flat glass items (see the oval platter shown on page 116). The design shows the stork, fern branches, a palm tree, and tropical plants. It was made by Iowa City Flint Glass Company.

Garden of Eden "Our Daily Bread"

We are happy to show the oval bread plate or tray with the "Give Us This Day Our Daily Bread" slogan that was part of the Garden of Eden pattern, made in the 1870s or early 1880s (maker unknown). The rest of the piece duplicates the design in this unusual pattern. Pieces are found with or without a serpent in many shapes that are discussed elsewhere.

GAR Encampment Goblet (Milwaukee)

Aside from the goblet shown, there were others (GAR St. Louis Encampment). This says "23rd National Encampment...Milwaukee...Aug. 27th to 30th...1889" (the St. Louis Encampment was in 1887). These items were issued to honor the Grand Army of the Republic, organized in 1866, and composed of men who enlisted in the army of the Union 1861 – 1865. The goblet is 6¾" tall.

Garfield Alphabet Plate

Not part of the Garfield Drape pattern, this memorial plate is by Campbell, Jones and Company in 1881. It measures about 7" in diameter, with a portrait and the letters of the alphabet. Garfield's death brought on a wave of these commemorative items.

Garfield and Lincoln Mug

This mug was made by Adams & Company in 1881 to commemorate the deaths of the two assassinated presidents with a bust of Garfield on one side and Lincoln on the other. The bottom of the mug says, "Our Country's Martyrs," and there are the names, birthdates, and dates of the deaths of the two presidents.

Frosted Stork ABC Plate

GAR Encampment Goblet (Milwaukee)

Garden of Eden "Our Daily Bread"

Garfield Alphabet Plate

Garfield and Lincoln Mug

Garfield Drape Mourning Plate

Garfield Memorial

Garfield Plate with One-O-One Border

Garfield Star Plate

Give Us Our Daily Bread

Glassport Brave

Garfield Drape Mourning Plate

As a part of the Lee & Adams Garfield Drape line produced after President Garfield's death in 1881, this mourning plate bears a picture of the President, the familiar drape pattern, and the wording "We Mourn Our Nation's Loss." A second plate with a star center was also made in this pattern.

Garfield Memorial

Like the Garfield Alphabet plate shown on page 283, this one is from Campbell, Jones and Company in 1881. It simply says, "Memorial" and has a portrait and a wreath of laurel leaves. Perhaps the popularity of these items accounts for so many offerings by the same company.

Garfield Plate with One-O-One Border

Evidence seems to indicate that this plate, like others with this One-O-One border, are products of Iowa City Glass despite being previously attributed to Crystal. At any rate, this very nice piece dates to 1881 and has a frosted bust of Garfield.

Garfield Star Plate

Credited to the Crystal Glass Company in 1880 – 1881, this 6" plate has a bust of Garfield, a starred border with thirteen stars, and a flag shield. Garfield's name is inscribed below his portrait which may be clear or frosted as shown.

Give Us Our Daily Bread

This plate has a well-known theme and the example shown is part of the Dewdrop line (or Dewdrop with Star) made by Campbell, Jones & Company in 1877. Some collectors refer to this bread plate as the Sheaf of Wheat plate.

Glassport Brave

What an exciting piece of advertising crystal! It is 5½" tall and 4¼" wide and reads "1903–Buy Glassport Lots." Obviously made by U. S. Glass at their Glassport factory, this piece has also been seen in cobalt and amber glass, and both are rare finds today.

"The Globe"

Found on a pickle tray that bears the Brazilian pattern (minus the exterior rays), this neat advertising piece is 8" long and 4¼" wide at the back. The advertising says, "The Globe–5th and Central Ave.–Furniture & Carpet Co." Brazilian is a pattern from Fostoria Glass (their #600, made in 1898) and is also known as Cane Shield.

A Good Boy

The maker of this mug and its companion, A Good Girl, is unknown. It is 3½" tall, has a 3" diameter, and dates to the 1880s we believe. It can be found in crystal, amber, and blue.

Good Luck

This interesting relish dish is not part of the Good Luc or Prayer Rug design but has a strong interlocking six-pointed star and band design of its own. It does have a horseshoe in the center and the words "good luck." We do not know the maker at this time.

Hatchet

Found in several early 1900s ads in the Butler Brothers catalogs, this small hatchet (7¾" long) has a ruby stained handle and a gilded blade. Various advertising mottos are found on these, and the one shown has "Souvenir of Fredricksburg, VA" on it. These were listed as 97 cent items at the time.

Heroes of Bunker Hill

Made by Gillinder and Company for the Philadelphia Exposition in 1876, this oval bread plate has it all. Handles are flag shields and lettering that says, "Prescott – Stark – Warren – Putnam – 1776 – 1876 The Heroes of Bunker Hill – The Spirit of Seventy-Six." In the center is the monument, the town, and wording "Birthplace of Liberty."

"The Globe"

Hatchet

A Good Boy

Good Luck

Heroes of Bunker Hill

Hey Diddle Diddle

Higbee Advertising Mug

Hobstar Band

The Hub

Humpty Dumpty Mug

Hey Diddle Diddle

This is another in the series of nursery rhyme plates for children. The series consists of this plate, a Little Bo Peep plate, and a This Little Pig Went to Market plate. The maker is unknown, at least to us.

Higbee Advertising Mug

What a treat to read this mug. It says "Higbee hot or cold sanitary vacuum bottle...for home & domestic use...keeps hot 48 hours...keeps cold 48 hours. Compliments John B. Higbee Glass Co...Bridgevill, PA...Higbee Sanitary Bottle" (photo of a bottle). The lettering says it all on this clear mug, and the bottle it advertises is quite rare.

Hobstar Band

This is primarily a carnival glass pattern where it is found on two types of pitchers (flat or pedestal based), tumblers, bowl, and handled celery vase. The pieces of crystal known aren't so numerous. So far the pedestal pitcher shown, inscribed "Bernheimer Bros. Anniversary 1913," and the large berry bowl are all that we've found. The maker of this pattern is in question, but many think it is U.S. Glass.

The Hub

Here is the second advertising piece found on pieces of Northwood's Memphis pattern, this time on a 10" fruit bowl and stand. The lettering says "The Hub...Furniture...Carpets...7th & D Sts...NW...Washington, D.C." Only crystal is reported, and this set is considered very rare by collectors of Northwood glass.

Humpty Dumpty Mug

Dating to the 1880s and found in clear and amber and believed to exist in pink, blue, or green as well, this mug says Humpty Dumpty on one side and Tom, Tom, the Piper's Son on the other, with illustrations of both characters.

I.H.S.

We have very little information about the unusual oval plate or tray shown. The maker is unknown, and the only clues are the beaded cross in the center and the IHS banner, which is a miscopy of the IHE OTE monogram for Jesus, Savior of Men. Anyone having more information about this piece is urged to write us.

I.H.S.

It Is God's Way — His Will Be Done

Independence Hall Mug

Made by Boston & Sandwich Glass and with the same moulding as the Plain Dodecagon mug by the same company, this one says, "Independence Hall," with a picture of the building. In addition, the example shown is engraved "Alice...1876," indicating it was indeed produced for the Philadelphia Centennial Exhibition.

Independence Hall Mug

"In Remembrance"

This well-known memorial platter was issued following the Garfield assassination in 1881. The platter shows Garfield, Washington, and Lincoln and can be found totally clear or with frosted portraits. Some examples have been reported with gilding also.

"In Remembrance"

It Is God's Way — His Will Be Done

This small plate or oval platter is another of those memorial items created to honor the fallen McKinley in 1901. It has a full-length portrait of him in the center with a laurel wreath edge. It says, "It Is God's Way — His Will Be Done." It also lists McKinley's date of birth and death. It is another fine memorial piece.

Jenny Lind Match Safe

Also known as The Goddess of Liberty match safe, this one is made on frosted glass and is marked Pat'd. June 13, 1876. It is 4½" tall and is pierced on the back for hanging. The design actually looks more like the liberty lady and is so draped. Note there is a glass plate at the bottom for striking matches.

Jenny Lind Match Safe

John Bull Eye Cup

Katzenjammer

Knights of Labor Goblet

Knights of Labor Mug

John Bull Eye Cup

The title pretty much says it all, but this nice example of an eye cup says on the base "Pat. Aug 14, 1917 – 23659 – Trade Mark – USA – John Bull – Reg. U.S. Pat. Off. " Eye cups were used in the early part of the century by both doctors and people at home, and the old ones are quite collectible (many reproductions exist however).

Katzenjammer

This strange mug is a mystery in several ways. It has three panels of cats (licking a paw, paw on a jug, and paws on a banner). One panel reads "Dercemeinehauskater," another reads "Dercefleck-tewalokater," and the third "Dascraueeleno and Katzenjammer." The mug is 5" tall. Anyone with additional information is asked to contact us.

Knights of Labor Goblet

Just like the stein or mug shown below, this goblet was made by the Central Glass Company as an honor to the Knights of Labor organization and again, shows a worker and a union knight shaking hands. It says "Knights of Labor." There is also a matching crystal platter that measures 11¾" in length with the same center design and a border that shows railroads, ship, a horse, a farm worker, and the lettering "United We Stand...Divided We Fall."

Knights of Labor Mug

Credited to the Central Glass Company by many collectors (they made the Knights of Labor goblet above), this mug can be found in two sizes (4¾" tall or 6½" tall). Made only in clear, the mug or stein reads "Knights of Labor" and shows figures of a laborer shaking hands with the union's knight. This union was established in 1869.

Lady Bust

This interesting paperweight is marked "U.S. Glass Co...Pittsburgh, PA." The bust of a lady is in the center and is satinized, while around her is a beaded oval. Often glass companies made advertising items to promote their own business and this one, like the Glassport Brave, is an example of this practice.

Lady Bust

Lansburgh & Bros. Advertising Nappy

From U.S. Glass, this advertising piece has the #15110 Rising Sun pattern produced in 1908 as its background. The advertising says "Lansburgh & Bros — Dry Goods Only — Washington, DC." The piece has three handles and is called a sweetmeat in the company ads; one book calls it a "three handled jelly."

Lansburgh & Bros. Advertising Nappy

Let Us Have Peace Plate

Actually part of the Maple Leaf pattern made by Gillinder and Sons in 1885, this 10½" plate notes the passing of U.S. Grant. It can be found in clear, amber, blue, canary, and frosted glass, and has never been reproduced, making it quite collectible.

Let Us Have Peace Plate

Liberty Bell

Also called Centennial, this pattern was made by Adams and Company in 1876 (a reproduction that shows dates from 1776 – 1976 exists in some shapes). Old pieces are found in crystal and rarely in milk glass, and shapes include a berry set, table set, celery vase, compotes, goblet, toy table set, mugs, pickle dish, water set, plates, platters, salt dip, shakers, and sauce in flat or footed styles.

Liberty Bell

Liberty Bell Bank

Made for small coins, this is 4⅛" tall and can be found in clear and amber glass. The bottom is a threaded metal base that is lettered "Robinson & Loeble...723 Wharton St...Phila. PA." The bell itself says "Liberty 1776" and "Patented Sept., 22, 1885."

Liberty Bell Bank

Lion and Cable
Bread Plate

Lion and Cable Bread Plate

As part of the regular Lion and Cable line from Richards & Hartley Glass Company, this lettered bread plate is a very attractive piece of glass. In the center is the "proud lion" design while the lettering around the outer rim says "Give Us This Day...Our Daily Bread." The outer rim is bound with a cable effect, and there are two handles that match those on the covered butter dish.

Little Bo Peep

Little Bo Peep

One of several designs that feature this child's subject, this one is part of a nursery rhyme set that features Hey Diddle Diddle and This Little Pig Went To Market subjects, all the same size and with the same figural borders.

Little Bo-Peep (Dithridge)

Little Bo-Peep (Dithridge)

Made by Dithridge & Company in 1879, this mug was an advertisement for the crystalography surface treatment used. It says Little Bo-Peep on one side and Has Lost Her Sheep on the other. Several sheep with a fence in the background are shown, while the Bo-Peep side shows the girl and a dog.

Little Buttercup

Little Buttercup

Also from Dithridge & Company in 1879, this mug says "Little Buttercup" on one side with a picture of girls and a ship's crew standing on the deck of a ship and "H.M.S. Pinafore" on the other, with a ship. The surface is the crystalography treatment, and the mug is the same mould shape as the Little Bo-Peep mug.

Louisiana Purchase Exposition

Louisiana Purchase Exposition

This was made in clear, frosted, and milk glass for the World's Fair Exposition in St. Louis in 1904 to commemorate the centennial of the Louisiana Purchase. Shapes of these souvenirs include a 7¼" Festival Hall plate and the iced tea tumbler shown. Other shapes probably exist also.

"Loves Request Is Pickles"

Some question as to the maker now exists and while we credited this pattern to Crystal, Riverside, and LaBelle glassworks, we are told the maker was Adams and Company. The center design is a figure of a girl that was thought to be one of the Actress line. We welcome any information that will clear up this puzzle.

Millner's Ashtray

J.R. Millner Company is a Lynchburg, Virginia, concern that must have believed in advertising because the famous Millner tumbler in carnival glass is well known. It has the Cosmos and Cane design by U.S. Glass. Here we have a very plain, modern ashtray in crystal that measures 4" long and has cigarette dips on opposing corners. The lettering is on the bottom.

Moerleins

This beer pilsner or ale goblet is 6" tall and bears the inscription "Moerleins – National Lager Beer — Good Luck — Cincinnati." It was obviously an advertising give-away item from a Cincinnati company. It was made by the Bellaire Goblet Company that moved to Findlay, Ohio, in 1888 from Bellaire, Ohio.

Northwood's #12 Advertising (Near-Cut)

This very nice advertising nappy, found on Northwood's #12 or Near-Cut pattern, had the pattern and advertising on the exterior. The pattern was introduced in 1906 in a water set, table set, berry set, nappy, two-handled mayonnaise dish, cake plate, oval pickle dish, and shakers. The advertising piece is rare and says, "Your Credit Is Good — Nuf Ced." along with an anchor.

Northwood's Good Luck

This pattern, found in bowls or plates from the same mould, usually in carnival glass, was made in 1909. Rare examples are known in crystal and scarce bowls are found in custard glass (shown here with a nutmeg stain). The mould was advanced from an advertising pattern called Jockey Club and may have either a basketweave or a fine rib exterior.

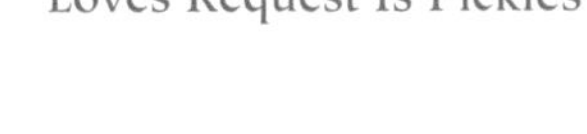

"Loves Request Is Pickles"

Millner's Ashtray

Northwood's #12 Advertising (Near-Cut)

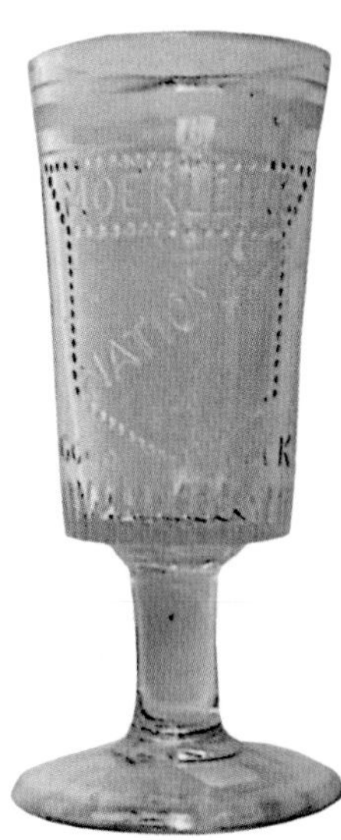

Moerleins

Northwood's Good Luck

Oklahoma Vinegar Company

Old State House

Pickering Furniture and Carpets

Pope Leo XIII Plate

Peabody

President McKinley Assassination Water Set

Oklahoma Vinegar Company

This very nice advertising piece is 5½" tall and has a 2¼" top diameter. The base is hollow for more than 1½" and the advertising reads "Oklahoma Vinegar Co. — Fort Smith, Ark." All vinegar advertising items are highly collectible.

Old State House

Made by Cooperative Flint Glass in 1876, this fine round plate or platter bears a picture of the building and says, "Old State House — Philadelphia." The border design contains Daisy and Button with ovals of fine file, and the platter is edged with roping.

Peabody

From the Wear Flint Glass Company (also known as H. Greener & Company) with a registry mark on July 31, 1869, this fine mug and saucer (a creamer and bowl are also known) honor George Peabody (1795 – 1869), a philanthropist well known in both England and America. Pieces are found in clear, blue, and amethyst glass.

Pickering Furniture and Carpets

This very collectible nappy, made by the Northwood Glass Company in their famous Memphis pattern, is a real find. It says, "Pickering Furniture and Carpets — 10 & Penn — NufCed." Originally the lettering was gilded, but most pieces have lost this long ago.

Pope Leo XIII Plate

This rare plate was made by Bryce, Higbee in 1903 to commemorate the death of the Pope in that year. It shows a side-view bust of the Pope and various Roman Catholic religious symbols around the rim between sections of raised beading. It seems to have been made only in crystal.

President McKinley Assassination Water Set

William McKinley was the twenty-fifth president of the United States and was assassinated by an anarchist in 1901. This scarce water set was made in commemoration of his death and says "Our Martyr'd President." It bears a portrait of McKinley, his signature, and the dates of his birth and death.

Protection and Plenty

Made by McKee Brothers and Company for the election of 1896, this mid-size plate shows presidential candidate McKinley's bust on a shield with the lettering, "Protection and Plenty." There is also a mug in this pattern shown on the facing page.

Protection and Plenty

Protection and Plenty Mug

Just like the plate shown before, this mug (the cover is missing) was made by McKee Brothers and Company for the 1896 presidential campaign of McKinley. The front of the mug has a McKinley bust with his name, "Maj. Wm. McKinley" beneath it, and above it says "Protection and Plenty." The opponent, William Jennings Bryan, had a similar covered mug.

Protection and Plenty Mug

"Remember Me" Mug

Mugs for children have a charm all their own, and this one has to be near the top of the heap. It is faced with an irregular shield that says "Remember Me." Below the shield are crossed leaves with leaves and scroll above it. I have a strong feeling this may be U.S. Glass since it is shaped like so may mugs from that company. Found mostly on amber, here is a scarce clear example.

"Remember Me" Mug

Richard Wallace Compote

Richard Wallace was the natural son of the Marquis of Hertford; he inherited much of the Marquis's estate. He served as Commissioner of the Paris Exhibition in 1878, was made a Knight Commander of the Bath, and a trustee of the National Gallery. When he died, he left the estate as a house museum to the English nation. This compote was made by the Greener Glass Company and bears their 1877 Lion and Star trademark. It is a superb piece of glass with outstanding design.

Rooster ABC Plate

Credited to the King Glass Company of Pittsburgh (became U.S. Glass Factory K in 1891), this alphabet plate shows a large rooster and smaller chickens with a brick wall in the background. The design is good but not outstanding. No collection of alphabet pieces would be complete without it.

Rooster ABC Plate

Richard Wallace Compote

Salt Lake Temple Platter

Salt Lake Temple Platter

As part of the Egyptian (Parthenon) line by Boston & Sandwich Glass in 1870, the Salt Lake Temple platter is one of the most sought and desirable pieces. It shows the great temple of Salt Lake City in a satinized portrait, is lettered "Salt Lake Temple," and measures 8½" x 13".

Sawtoothed Honeycomb

Sawtoothed Honeycomb

Originally called either Radiant or Serrated Block and Loop, this pattern has a puzzling background. It was first made by Steiner Glass of West Virginia and then Union Stopper in 1908. Shapes known are a table set, punch set, berry set, goblet, syrup, toothpick holder (clear or ruby stained), and the nappies shown which advertise Bernheimer Brothers. A sauce is also known either flat or footed, and there are two variations of the advertising nappy.

Schrafft's Chocolates

Star-in-Bullseye Advertising

Schrafft's Chocolates

Advertising items have an appeal all their own, and this one certainly fills that bill. It is a square plate with a nice geometric design and a small centered rectangle that says "Schrafft's Chocolates." The maker is unknown to us.

Spanish-American

Spanish-American

Made in Dunkirk, Indiana, by Beatty-Brady Glass as a commemoration of Admiral Dewey's part in the Spanish-American War, this pitcher and matching tumbler and a second water set called Dewey came into being in the 1890s. The Dewey pitcher and tumblers are very hard to find, and they have bullets rather than the cannon balls in the design, as well as other pattern changes.

Star-in-Bullseye Advertising

Like the example shown on page 289 this one is advertising "Lansburg & Bros. – Dry Goods Only – Washington, D.C." It was made in 1905 by U.S. Glass with an exterior pattern called Star-in-Bullseye (U.S. Glass pattern #15092). The pattern was later made by New Martinsville Glass (1918) but without the advertising. Thanks to Bill Holmeide for sharing this piece with us.

St. Louis Encampment

This unusual goblet is lettered "21 Encampment — September 27, '87 — St. Louis, Mo." On the reverse side there is an American flag and shield, topped by an eagle, with a military emblem below them all. We haven't been able to learn the maker but feel this is a scarce and very collectible item.

St. Louis World's Fair Hatchet

There are really two versions of this hatchet. The one shown here has a portrait of George Washington and the lettering "The Father of His Country" on one side and the other has on the handle "St. Louis World's Fair 1904." The hatchet measures 8" long. The second version is shown under Washington Hatchet.

Theodore Roosevelt Platter

Honoring the nation's twenty-sixth president, this platter is a beauty. It has a portrait of Roosevelt in the center (can be either frosted or clear) and a rim of symbols that include teddy bears, golf, tennis, hunting, music, dancing (all things associated with Roosevelt), an eagle, shield, and crossed clubs. Border lettering reads "A Square Deal," Roosevelt's slogan. The platter measures 7¾" x 10¼".

This Little Pig Went to Market

Here is the third in the series of nursery rhyme plates that have the same border. The other pieces, Little Bo Peep and Hey Diddle Diddle, complete the set.

St. Louis Encampment

St. Louis World's Fair Hatchet

Theodore Roosevelt Platter

This Little Pig Went to Market

U.S. Grant — Patriot and Soldier

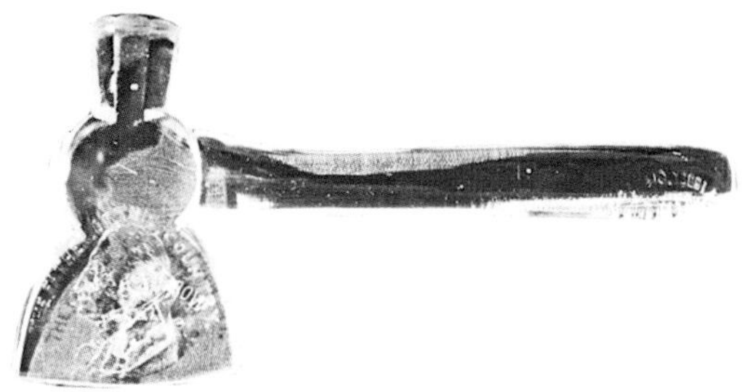
Washington Hatchet

Wm. J. Bryan Tumbler

U.S. Grant — Patriot and Soldier

This beautiful 11" square plate can be found in crystal and rarely in amber. It shows a portrait of Grant in military uniform and the lettering says "The Patriot and Soldier. . . Gen. Ulysses S. Grant." Corners of the plate are mitered and the edge has a bead moulding, while the interior has a stylized daisy design. It was made in 1885 by Bryce, Higbee.

Washington Hatchet

Here is the second version of this hatchet and like the first, it has a portrait of George Washington on the blade and the lettering "The Father of His Country." On the handle are the words "Libbey Glass Co. Toledo, Ohio." On the reverse side of the blade is the lettering "World's Fair...1893." Both of these hatchets were made by Libbey Glass, we believe, for they are identical in form and measure 8" long.

Wm. J. Bryan Tumbler

William Jennings Bryan was Democratic presidential candidate in 1896 and again in 1900 (losing both times to McKinley) and a third time in 1908 (losing to Theodore Roosevelt) and later Wilson's Secretary of State. The tumbler says, "The people's choice...1896 – 1900...Wm. J. Bryan." The decoration is like that of the Dewey tumbler shown on page 275.

Bibliography

Bredehoft, Neila and Tom. *Hobbs, Brockunier & Company Glass*. Paducah, Kentucky: Collector Books, 1997.

Bredehoft, Neila M., Geo. A. Fogg, and Francis C. Maloney. *Early Duncan Glassware*. Self Published, 1987.

Davis, Sue C. *Picture Book of Vaseline Glass*. Atglen, Pennsylvania; Schiffer Books.

Edwards, Bill. *Millersburg Crystal Glassware*. Paducah, Kentucky: Collector Books, 1982.

________. *Standard Encyclopedia of Opalescent Glass*. Paducah, Kentucky: Collector Books, 1997.

Edwards, Bill and Mike Carwile. *The Standard Encyclopedia of Carnival Glass, 6th Edition*. Paducah, Kentucky: Collector Books, 1998.

Glickman, Jay L., and Terry Fedosky. *Yellow-Green Vaseline*. Marietta, Ohio: Glass Press, 1998.

Heacock, William. *Fenton Glass – The First Twenty-Five Years*. Marietta, Ohio: O-Val Advertising Corp, 1978.

________. *Old Pattern Glass*. Marietta, Ohio: Antiques Publications, 1981.

Heacock, William and Fred Bickenheuser. *Encyclopedia of Victorian and Colored Glass – Book 5*. Marietta, Ohio: Antiques Publications, 1978.

Heacock, William, James Measell, and Berry Wiggins. *Harry Northwood – The Early Years*. Marietta, Ohio: Antiques Publications, 1991.

________. *Harry Northwood – The Wheeling Years 1901 – 1925*. Marietta, Ohio: Antiques Publications, 1993.

________. *Dugan/Diamond*. Marietta, Ohio: Antiques Publications, 1993.

Jenks, William and Jerry Luna. *Early American Pattern Glass, 1850 – 1910*. Radnor, Pennsylvania: Wallace-Homestead Book Company, 1990.

Lecher, Doris Anderson. *Toy Glass*. Marietta, Ohio: Antiques Publications, 1989.

Loomis, Jean Chapman. *Krys-tol! Kryst-tol! Krys-tol!* Self published, 2001.

McCain, Mollie Helen. *Collector's Encyclopedia of Pattern Glass*. Paducah, Kentucky: Collector Books, 1994.

McGee, Marie. *Millersburg Glass*. Marietta, Ohio: The Glass Press, 1995.

Measell, James. *Greentown Glass*. Grand Rapids, Michigan: Grand Rapids Museum Association, 1979.

Metz, Alice Hulett. *Early American Pattern Glass*. Paducah, Kentucky: Collector Books, 1977 – 1978.

Mordock, John B. and Walter L. Adams. *Pattern Glass Mugs*. Marietta, Ohio: Antiques Publications, 1995.

Righter, Miriam. *Iowa City Glass*. Self published, 1981, J.W. Carlberry.

Schroy, Ellen Tischbein. *Warman's Pattern Glass*. Radnor, Pennsylvania: Wallace-Homestead Book Company, 1993.

Spillman, Jane Shadel. *Knopf Collector's Guide to American Antiques – Glass, Tableware, Bowls, and Vases,* Alfred A. Knopf. New York, New York: Chanticleer Press, Inc.

Stevens, Gerald. *Canadian Glass, 1825 – 1925*. Toronto, Canada: Coles Publishing Company Limited, 1979.

Teal, Ron Sr. *Albany Glass*. Marietta, Ohio: Antiques Publications, 1997.

Vogel, Clarence W. *Heisey's Art and Colored Glass, 1922 – 1942, Heisey's Colonial Years, 1906 – 1922, Heisey's First Ten Years, 1896 – 1905, Heisey's Early and Late Years, 1896 – 1958* Books I, II, III, and IV.

Weatherman, Hazel Marie. *Colored Glass of the Depression Era II*. Ozark, Missouri: Weatherman Glass Books, 1974.

Welker, John and Elizabeth. *Pressed Glass in America*. Antique Acres Press, 1985.

Welker, Mary, Lyle and Lynn. *The Cambridge Glass Company, A Reprint of Old Company Catalogs*, Books I, II. Self Published, 1970 and 1974.

Whitmyer, Margaret and Kenn. *Fenton Art Glass*. Paducah, Kentucky: Collector Books, 1996.

Wilson, Charles West. *Westmoreland Glass*. Paducah, Kentucky: Collector Books, 1996.

Price Guide

All values are for crystal, unless indicated otherwise. For Special treatment items, the following should be applied:

Acid Etched – add 15% | Decorated (enameling) – add 15% | Engraved – add 15%
Frosted – add 10% | Gilding – add 10% | Silver or platinum overlay – add 10%

ABC CLOCK
Plate . . . 55.00

ACORN
Butter . . . 90.00
Celery Vase . . . 25.00
Compote, Covered . . . 65.00
Compote, Open . . . 40.00
Creamer or Spooner . . . 30.00
Egg Cup . . . 20.00
Goblet . . . 50.00
Pitcher . . . 110.00
Sugar . . . 40.00

ACORN BAND
Bowl . . . 30.00
Bowl, Covered . . . 50.00
Celery Vase . . . 20.00
Compote, Open . . . 25.00
Compote, Covered . . . 55.00
Creamer or Spooner . . . 25.00
Dessert, Stemmed . . . 15.00
Egg Cup . . . 15.00
Goblet . . . 40.00
Pitcher . . . 85.00
Tumbler . . . 25.00
Sauce, Flat or Ftd. . . . 10.00
Sugar . . . 30.00
Wine . . . 15.00

ACTRESS
Bowl, 6" – 9½" . . . 50.00 – 90.00
Butter . . . 135.00
Cake Stand, 9" – 10" . . . 165.00
Candlesticks, ea. . . . 120.00
Celery Vase, Actress Head . . . 145.00
Celery Vase, HMS Pinafore . . . 170.00
Cheese Dish . . . 250.00
Compote, Covered, 8" – 12" . . . 300.00
Compote, Open, High, 10" – 12" . . . 110.00
Compote, Open, Low, 5" – 7" . . . 60.00
Creamer or Spooner . . . 75.00
Dresser Tray . . . 70.00
Goblet . . . 95.00
Jam Jar . . . 140.00
Milk Pitcher . . . 300.00
Mug . . . 50.00
Pickle Dish . . . 40.00
Platter, HMS Pinafore . . . 100.00
Platter, Miss Neilson . . . 80.00
Pitcher . . . 275.00
Tumbler . . . 75.00
Relish, 3 Sizes . . . 40.00
Salt, Master . . . 75.00
Sauce, 4" – 5", Flat or Ftd. . . . 25.00
Sugar . . . 125.00

ADA (Condensed List)
Berry Bowl, Sm. . . . 15.00
Berry Bowl, Lg. . . . 45.00
Butter . . . 75.00
Celery Dish . . . 20.00
Compotes, Various . . . 25.00 – 55.00
Creamer or Spooner . . . 25.00
Cruet . . . 45.00
Pickle Dish . . . 15.00
Pitcher . . . 95.00
Tumbler . . . 25.00
Shakers, ea. . . . 20.00
Sugar . . . 30.00

ADAM'S APOLLO
Lamp . . . 75.00
Amber . . . 110.00
Vaseline . . . 175.00
Green/Blue . . . 150.00

ADAM'S PLUME
Bowls, Flat . . . 10.00 – 30.00
Ruby Stain . . . 15.00 – 40.00
Bowls, Ftd. . . . 15.00 – 35.00
Ruby Stain . . . 20.00 – 50.00
Butter . . . 50.00
Ruby Stain . . . 75.00
Cake Stand . . . 45.00
Ruby Stain . . . 50.00
Celery Vase . . . 25.00
Ruby Stain . . . 30.00
Creamer or Spooner . . . 25.00
Ruby Stain . . . 30.00
Goblet . . . 30.00
Ruby Stain . . . 55.00
Lamp . . . 65.00
Ruby Stain . . . 100.00
Sauce . . . 10.00
Ruby Stain . . . 20.00
Sugar . . . 30.00
Ruby Stain . . . 50.00

ADMIRAL DEWEY
Tumbler . . . 65.00

ADIMRAL DEWEY PLATE
Plate, 7" . . . 90.00

ADONIS
Berry Bowl, Sm. . . . 10.00
Vaseline . . . 20.00
Green/Blue . . . 25.00
Berry Bowl, Lg. . . . 30.00
Vaseline . . . 65.00
Green/Blue . . . 55.00
Butter . . . 50.00
Vaseline . . . 150.00
Green/Blue . . . 100.00
Cake Plate . . . 25.00
Vaseline . . . 60.00
Green Blue . . . 65.00
Cake Stand . . . 35.00
Vaseline . . . 70.00
Green/Blue . . . 80.00
Celery Vase . . . 20.00
Vaseline . . . 35.00
Green/Blue . . . 40.00
Compote, Covered . . . 45.00
Vaseline . . . 150.00
Green/Blue . . . 110.00
Compote, Open . . . 30.00
Vaseline . . . 55.00
Green/Blue . . . 65.00
Creamer or Spooner . . . 20.00
Vaseline . . . 30.00
Green/Blue . . . 35.00
Jelly Compote . . . 25.00
Vaseline . . . 30.00
Green/Blue . . . 35.00
Plate, 10" – 11" . . . 25.00
Vaseline . . . 30.00
Green/Blue . . . 35.00
Pitcher . . . 60.00
Vaseline . . . 185.00
Green/Blue . . . 150.00
Tumbler . . . 15.00
Vaseline . . . 25.00
Green/Blue . . . 25.00
Relish Tray . . . 10.00
Vaseline . . . 20.00
Green/Blue . . . 25.00
Shakers, ea. . . . 20.00
Vaseline . . . 45.00
Green/Blue . . . 50.00
Sugar . . . 30.00
Vaseline . . . 50.00
Green/Blue . . . 55.00
Syrup . . . 60.00
Vaseline . . . 155.00
Green/Blue . . . 170.00

AFRICAN SHIELD
Vase, 2⅞" . . . 20.00

ALABAMA
Bowl, 8" . . . 50.00
Butter . . . 60.00
Ruby Stain . . . 165.00
Cake Stand . . . 40.00
Celery Vase . . . 25.00
Ruby Stain . . . 100.00
Compote, Covered . . . 55.00
Compote, Open . . . 45.00
Creamer or Spooner . . . 25.00
Ruby Stain . . . 65.00
Honey Dish w/Lid, Rare . . . 75.00
Nappy . . . 30.00
Pitcher . . . 80.00
Tumbler . . . 20.00
Relish Dish, 3 Sizes . . . 15.00 – 35.00
Ruby Stain . . . 40.00
Sugar . . . 30.00
Syrup . . . 70.00
Ruby Stain . . . 225.00
Toothpick . . . 65.00
Ruby Stain . . . 150.00

ALASKA (NORTHWOOD)
Berry Bowl, Lg. . . . 40.00
Green/Blue . . . 65.00
Berry Bowl, Sm. . . . 25.00
Green/Blue . . . 35.00
Butter Dish . . . 75.00
Green/Blue . . . 150.00
Creamer, Spooner, or Sugar . . . 35.00
Green/Blue . . . 55.00
Cruet . . . 185.00
Green/Blue . . . 265.00
Jewel Tray . . . 40.00
Green/Blue . . . 50.00
Pitcher . . . 125.00
Green/Blue . . . 225.00
Tumbler . . . 30.00
Green/Blue . . . 50.00
Rose Bowl . . . 45.00
Green/Blue . . . 70.00

ALDINE (BEADED ELLIPSE)
Bowl, Covered . . . 45.00
Butter . . . 60.00
Chocolate . . . 235.00
Celery Dish . . . 25.00
Creamer or Spooner . . . 30.00
Chocolate . . . 90.00
Pickle Dish . . . 25.00
Pitcher . . . 95.00
Tumbler . . . 20.00
Sugar . . . 40.00
Chocolate . . . 125.00
Wine . . . 30.00

ALEXIS (FOSTORIA)
Bowls, Various . . . 10.00 – 45.00
Butter . . . 60.00

Catsup . . . 45.00
Celery Tray . . . 25.00
Celery Vase . . . 30.00
Champagne . . . 20.00
Claret . . . 25.00
Cocktail . . . 20.00
Cordial . . . 25.00
Creamer or Spooner . . . 30.00
Cruet, 3 Sizes . . . 35.00 – 70.00
Custard . . . 15.00
Decanter . . . 65.00
Egg Cup . . . 20.00
Finger Bowl . . . 20.00
Goblet . . . 35.00
Ice Bowl w/Underplate . . . 65.00
Ice Tea Set w/Plates . . . 80.00
Mayonnaise Plate/Bowl . . . 40.00
Nasturtium Vase . . . 40.00
Nut Bowl . . . 25.00
Olive Tray . . . 20.00
Pickle Tray . . . 15.00
Pitcher, 3 Sizes . . . 75.00 – 145.00
Tumbler, 3 Sizes . . . 20.00 – 35.00
Tumbler, Whiskey . . . 30.00
Relish Jar . . . 20.00
Salt, 2 Sizes . . . 15.00 – 25.00
Shakers, ea . . . 25.00
Sherbet . . . 15.00
Sugar . . . 45.00
Sugar Sifter . . . 55.00
Sweet Pea Vase . . . 25.00
Syrup . . . 65.00
Toothpick . . . 50.00
Water Bottle . . . 45.00
Wine . . . 15.00

ALMOND (U.S. GLASS)
Stemmed Wine . . . 25.00
Wine Decanter . . . 65.00
Wine Tray . . . 30.00

ALMOND THUMBPRINT
Butter . . . 65.00
Celery Vase . . . 25.00
Champagne . . . 30.00
Creamer or Spooner . . . 35.00
Compote, High Covered, 5", 7", and 10" . . . 40.00 – 85.00
Compote, Low Covered, 5", 7", and 10" . . . 35.00 – 80.00
Cordial . . . 20.00
Cruet . . . 60.00
Decanter . . . 45.00
Goblet . . . 35.00
Pitcher . . . 95.00
Punch Bowl . . . 120.00
Punch Cup . . . 15.00
Salt Dips, 2 Sizes . . . 10.00 – 20.00
Sugar . . . 35.00
Sweetmeat, Covered . . . 65.00
Tumbler . . . 20.00
Wine . . . 15.00

ALPHABET AND CHILDREN
Mug . . . 40.00

ALPHABET PLATE
Plate . . . 80.00

AMARYLLIS
Bowl, 8" . . . 45.00

AMAZON
Banana Stand . . . 50.00
  Engraved . . . 95.00
Bowl, Oval, Covered . . . 40.00
  Engraved . . . 50.00
Bowl, Rnd., w/Lid, 5" – 7" . . . 35.00
Bowl, Rnd., w/Lid, 8" – 9" . . . 45.00
Butter . . . 55.00
  Engraved . . . 80.00
Celery Vase, Ftd. or Flat . . . 25.00
  Engraved . . . 40.00
Champagne . . . 30.00
Child's Table Set . . . 95.00
Claret . . . 25.00
  Engraved . . . 45.00
Compote, Covered, 4" – 6" . . . 30.00
Compote, Covered, 7" – 8" . . . 45.00
Compote, Open, 4" – 6" . . . 25.00
  Engraved . . . 50.00
Compote, Open, 7" – 8" . . . 35.00
Cordial . . . 25.00
  Engraved . . . 45.00
Creamer or Spooner . . . 20.00
  Engraved . . . 35.00
Cruet . . . 45.00
  Engraved . . . 55.00
Egg Cup . . . 20.00
Goblet, 3 Sizes . . . 30.00
  Engraved . . . 40.00
Pitcher . . . 65.00
  Engraved . . . 80.00
Tumbler . . . 15.00
  Engraved . . . 35.00
Sauce . . . 10.00
  Engraved . . . 15.00
Salt Dip, Ind . . . 15.00
Salt Dip, Master . . . 20.00
Sugar . . . 25.00
  Engraved . . . 60.00
Syrup . . . 45.00
  Engraved . . . 75.00
Vase . . . 25.00
  Engraved . . . 35.00
Wine . . . 20.00
  Engraved . . . 30.00

AMBERETTE
(All crystal pieces have amber stain.)
Bowl, Covered, 7" – 8" . . . 75.00
  Vaseline . . . 100.00
  Green/Blue . . . 85.00
Bowl, Open, 7" – 8" . . . 40.00 – 65.00
  Vaseline . . . 90.00
  Green/Blue . . . 80.00
Bowl, Oval, 5" – 8" . . . 45.00 – 70.00
  Vaseline . . . 80.00
  Green/Blue . . . 75.00
Bowl, Sq., 5" – 8" . . . 45.00 – 75.00
  Vaseline . . . 80.00
  Green/Blue . . . 75.00
Butter . . . 135.00
  Vaseline . . . 165.00
  Green/Blue . . . 150.00
Butter Pat . . . 30.00
  Vaseline . . . 40.00
  Green/Blue . . . 35.00
Cake Stand . . . 130.00
  Vaseline . . . 165.00
  Green/Blue . . . 145.00
Celery Tray . . . 50.00
  Vaseline . . . 65.00
  Green/Blue . . . 60.00
Celery Vase . . . 80.00
  Vaseline . . . 95.00
  Green/Blue . . . 85.00
Compote, 8" – 9" . . . 100.00
  Vaseline . . . 135.00
  Green/Blue . . . 125.00
Creamer or Spooner . . . 75.00
  Vaseline . . . 95.00
  Green/Blue . . . 85.00
Cruet . . . 90.00
  Vaseline . . . 150.00
  Green/Blue . . . 135.00
Finger Bowl . . . 45.00
  Vaseline . . . 55.00
  Green/Blue . . . 50.00
Gas Shade . . . 90.00
  Vaseline . . . 120.00
  Green/Blue . . . 100.00
Milk Pitcher . . . 130.00
  Vaseline . . . 150.00
  Green/Blue . . . 140.00
Olive Dish . . . 30.00
  Vaseline . . . 45.00
  Green/Blue . . . 40.00
Pickle Dish . . . 30.00
  Vaseline . . . 45.00
  Green/Blue . . . 40.00
Plate, 7" – 11" . . . 45.00
  Vaseline . . . 65.00
  Green/Blue . . . 55.00
Pitcher . . . 200.00
  Vaseline . . . 250.00
  Green/Blue . . . 225.00
Tumbler . . . 45.00
  Vaseline . . . 65.00
  Green/Blue . . . 60.00
Sauce, Flat, 4" – 4½" . . . 20.00
  Vaseline . . . 35.00
  Green/Blue . . . 30.00
Sauce, Collared, 4" – 4½" . . . 25.00
  Vaseline . . . 40.00
  Green/Blue . . . 35.00
Shakers, ea . . . 40.00
  Vaseline . . . 65.00
  Green/Blue . . . 50.00
Sugar . . . 110.00
  Vaseline . . . 150.00
  Green/Blue . . . 120.00

AMBOY
Berry Bowl, Sm . . . 15.00
Berry Bowl, Lg . . . 40.00
Butter . . . 65.00
Celery Dish . . . 15.00
Creamer or Spooner . . . 20.00
Goblet . . . 35.00
Pickle Dish . . . 15.00
Spoon Dish . . . 15.00
Sugar . . . 25.00

AMERICAN BEAUTY
Berry Bowl, Sm . . . 10.00
Berry Bowl, Lg . . . 35.00
Butter . . . 55.00
Creamer or Spooner . . . 20.00
Jelly Compote . . . 30.00
Pitcher . . . 75.00
Tumbler . . . 20.00
Sugar . . . 25.00

ANGEL'S CROWN
Jelly Tumbler . . . 60.00

ANGELUS
Butter . . . 60.00
Celery Vase . . . 20.00
Creamer or Spooner . . . 25.00
Pickle Dish . . . 20.00
Pitcher . . . 80.00
Sugar . . . 30.00
Tumbler . . . 20.00
Waste Bowl . . . 25.00
Wine . . . 30.00

ANGULAR
Butter . . . 65.00
Compote, Covered . . . 45.00
Creamer or Spooner . . . 20.00
Pitcher . . . 85.00
Tumbler . . . 25.00
Sugar . . . 30.00

APPLE TREE
Giant Spittoon, from Pitcher, Rare . . . 325.00
  Black . . . 400.00

APPLIED FILIGREE
Footed Pitcher, Amber . . . 350.00

APPOMATTOX
Hand Mirror, Glass Hndl . . . 75.00

AQUARIUM
Pitcher, Very Scarce . . . 310.00

AQUARIUS
Lamp . . . 95.00
  Amber . . . 125.00
  Vaseline . . . 195.00
  Green/Blue . . . 165.00

ARCADIA LACE
Berry Bowl, Sm . . . 15.00
Berry Bowl, Lg . . . 40.00
Butter . . . 55.00
Candy Dish, Covered . . . 35.00
Celery Vase . . . 25.00
Compote, Covered . . . 45.00
Creamer or Spooner . . . 25.00
Jelly Compote . . . 25.00

Nappy 30.00
Plate, 6" 25.00
Plate, 11" 30.00
Pickle Dish 20.00
Pitcher 70.00
Tumbler 20.00
Rose Bowl 30.00
Sugar 25.00
Vase, 6" and 10", 2 Styles . . . . 30.00 – 35.00
Wine 20.00

ARCH AND FORGET-ME-NOT BANDS

Berry Bowl, Sm. 15.00
Berry Bowl, Lg. 35.00
Butter 45.00
Creamer or Spooner 25.00
Jam Jar 30.00
Sauce 10.00
Sugar 30.00

ARCHED FLEUR-DE-LIS

Banana Stand 35.00
Ruby Stain 125.00
Butter 65.00
Ruby Stain 100.00
Cake Stand 40.00
Creamer or Spooner 25.00
Ruby Stain 65.00
Dish, 7" 15.00
Jelly Compote 30.00
Mug 40.00
Ruby Stain 50.00
Olive, Hndl. 20.00
Plate, 7", Sq. 20.00
Ruby Stain 50.00
Pitcher 100.00
Ruby Stain 300.00
Tumbler 30.00
Ruby Stain 55.00
Relish 15.00
Sauce 10.00
Ruby Stain 25.00
Shakers, ea. 20.00
Ruby Stain 65.00
Sugar . . . . 20.00 – 35.00
Ruby Stain . . . . 70.00 – 100.00
Toothpick Hldr. 65.00
Ruby Stain 100.00
Vase 30.00
Ruby Stain 75.00
Wine 20.00
Ruby Stain 55.00

ARCHED GRAPE

Butter 55.00
Celery Vase 20.00
Champagne 25.00
Compote, Covered 60.00
Creamer or Spooner 30.00
Goblet 55.00
Pitcher 85.00
Tumbler 20.00
Sauce, Flat or Ftd. 10.00
Sugar 45.00
Wine 20.00

ARCHED OVALS

Berry Bowl, Sm. 20.00
Green/Blue 30.00
Berry Bowl, Lg. 45.00
Green/Blue 55.00
Butter 60.00
Green/Blue 85.00
Ruby Stain 100.00
Cake Stand 40.00
Celery Vase 25.00
Green/Blue 35.00
Compote, Covered 45.00
Compote, Open 35.00
Creamer or Spooner 25.00
Green/Blue 35.00
Ruby Stain 40.00
Cruet 45.00
Green/Blue 75.00
Goblet 30.00
Green/Blue 40.00
Ruby Stain 50.00
Mug 25.00
Green/Blue 30.00
Ruby Stain 35.00
Plate 30.00
Green/Blue 35.00
Pitcher 65.00
Green/Blue 100.00
Tumbler 20.00
Relish 25.00
Sauce 15.00
Shakers, ea. 25.00
Green/Blue 60.00
Sugar 25.00
Green/Blue 65.00
Syrup 55.00
Toothpick, Hldr. 30.00
Green/Blue 35.00
Ruby Stain 40.00
Wine 15.00
Green/Blue 25.00
Ruby Stain 35.00

ARGENT

Bread Plate, 9"x13" 45.00
Butter 65.00
Cake Stand 45.00
Celery Vase 30.00
Compote, Covered 60.00
Creamer or Spooner 25.00
Goblet 35.00
Plate, 7" 25.00
Platter 35.00
Sugar, Open 25.00
Tumbler 20.00
Wine 15.00

ARGUS (THUMBPRINT)

Ale Glass 50.00
Berry Bowl, Sm. 15.00
Berry Bowl, Lg. 35.00
Bitters Bottle 65.00
Bowls, Various . . . . 15.00 – 45.00
Butter 55.00
Celery Vase 30.00
Champagne 25.00
Creamer, Spooner or Sugar 25.00
Compote, Covered, Various . . . . 35.00 – 75.00
Compote, Open 35.00
Cordial 25.00
Decanter 60.00
Egg Cup 30.00
Honey Dish 25.00
Jelly Glass 20.00
Mug 55.00
Oil Lamp 75.00
Paper Weight 25.00
Pickle Jar 35.00
Punch Bowl 75.00
Pitcher 110.00
Tumbler 25.00
Salt Dip, Master 25.00
Salt Dip, Ind. 10.00
Sauce Bowl 15.00
Whiskey, Hndl., Scarce 75.00
Wine 20.00

ARMY HAT

Novelty, 3½"x1" 100.00

ARROWHEAD

Butter 55.00
Vaseline 110.00
Celery Dish 20.00
Vaseline 35.00
Compote 35.00
Vaseline 125.00
Creamer or Spooner 25.00
Vaseline 45.00
Pickle Dish 20.00
Vaseline 35.00
Sugar 30.00
Vaseline 65.00

ARROWHEAD-IN-OVAL

Basket 50.00
Berry Bowl, Sm. 20.00
Berry Bowl, Lg. 45.00
Butter 80.00
Cake Stand 35.00
Celery 20.00
Creamer or Spooner 25.00
Plate, 7" 20.00
Pitcher 90.00
Tumbler 20.00
Punch Bowl 125.00
Punch Cup 10.00
Rose Bowl, Stemmed 35.00
Sherbet 15.00
Sugar 30.00
Toy Table Set 100.00

ART

Banana Stand 70.00
Ruby Stain 150.00
Berry Bowl, Sm. 15.00
Berry Bowl Lg. 40.00
Ruby Stain 80.00
Biscuit Jar 120.00
Ruby Stain 175.00
Butter 70.00
Ruby Stain 145.00
Cake Stand 40.00
Celery Vase 45.00
Ruby Stain 95.00
Compote, Open 40.00
Compote, Covered, 7" – 10" 55.00
Ruby Stain 175.00
Creamer or Spooner 20.00
Ruby Stain 85.00
Cracker Jar 50.00
Cruet 100.00
Ruby Stain 225.00
Fruit Basket, 10" 65.00
Goblet 40.00
Milk Pitcher 100.00
Ruby Stain 165.00
Mug 30.00
Pitcher, Various 85.00
Tumbler 20.00
Relish 20.00
Ruby Stain 60.00
Sauce, Flat 15.00
Sugar 30.00
Ruby Stain 125.00
Wine 20.00

ARTICHOKE

Bobeche 40.00
Bowl, 7" – 8" 35.00
Butter 75.00
Cake Stand 50.00
Celery Vase 35.00
Compote, Covered, 6" – 7" . . . . 80.00 – 95.00
Compote, Open, 8" – 10" . . . . 55.00 – 70.00
Creamer or Spooner 40.00
Cruet 65.00
Finger Bowl 45.00
Oil Lamp 275.00
Pitcher, Bulbous 100.00
Pitcher, Tankard 150.00
Tumbler 40.00
Sauce, Flat or Ftd. 15.00
Shakers, ea. 20.00
Sugar 60.00
Syrup 75.00
Water Tray 50.00
Vase 35.00

ASHBURTON

Ale Glass 35.00
Amber 45.00
Vaseline 65.00
Green/Blue 55.00
Amethyst 60.00
Bitters Bottle 55.00
Amber 65.00
Vaseline 90.00
Green/Blue 70.00
Amethyst 75.00
Bowl 25.00
Amber 40.00

Vaseline........................65.00
Green/Blue......................50.00
Amethyst........................55.00
Butter..........................65.00
Amber...........................80.00
Vaseline.......................115.00
Green/Blue......................90.00
Amethyst........................85.00
Cake Stand......................35.00
Amber...........................55.00
Vaseline........................75.00
Green/Blue......................65.00
Amethyst........................75.00
Candlesticks, ea................20.00
Amber...........................35.00
Vaseline........................50.00
Green/Blue......................40.00
Amethyst........................60.00
Celery Vase.....................20.00
Amber...........................30.00
Vaseline........................55.00
Green/Blue......................40.00
Amethyst........................55.00
Champagne.......................15.00
Amber...........................25.00
Vaseline........................35.00
Green/Blue......................30.00
Amethyst........................45.00
Claret..........................15.00
Amber...........................25.00
Vaseline........................45.00
Green/Blue......................40.00
Amethyst........................40.00
Compote, Open...................30.00
Amber...........................40.00
Vaseline........................70.00
Green/Blue......................60.00
Amethyst........................70.00
Cordial.........................15.00
Amber...........................25.00
Vaseline........................40.00
Green/Blue......................35.00
Amethyst........................45.00
Creamer or Spooner..............20.00
Amber...........................30.00
Vaseline........................50.00
Green/Blue......................40.00
Amethyst........................45.00
Decanter........................35.00
Amber...........................50.00
Vaseline........................90.00
Green/Blue......................75.00
Amethyst........................80.00
Egg Cup.........................25.00
Amber...........................35.00
Vaseline........................55.00
Green/Blue......................40.00
Amethyst........................40.00
Goblet..........................30.00
Amber...........................40.00
Vaseline........................65.00
Green/Blue......................50.00
Amethyst........................55.00
Lamp............................70.00
Amber...........................90.00
Vaseline.......................175.00
Green/Blue.....................145.00
Amethyst.......................155.00
Mug.............................15.00
Amber...........................30.00
Vaseline........................65.00
Green/Blue......................45.00
Amethyst........................50.00
Pitcher.........................70.00
Amber...........................85.00
Vaseline.......................140.00
Green/Blue.....................115.00
Amethyst.......................130.00
Sauce...........................10.00
Amber...........................20.00
Vaseline........................35.00
Green/Blue......................30.00

Amethyst........................35.00
Sugar...........................25.00
Amber...........................35.00
Vaseline........................60.00
Green/Blue......................45.00
Amethyst........................50.00
Tumbler.........................15.00
Amber...........................25.00
Vaseline........................45.00
Green/Blue......................35.00
Amethyst........................40.00
Vase............................20.00
Amber...........................35.00
Vaseline........................65.00
Green/Blue......................50.00
Amethyst........................45.00
Wine............................10.00
Amber...........................20.00
Vaseline........................40.00
Green/Blue......................35.00
Amethyst........................35.00

ASHMAN

Bowl............................25.00
Bread Tray......................30.00
Butter..........................60.00
Cake Stand......................35.00
Compote Covered.................45.00
Compote, Open...................30.00
Creamer or Spooner..............20.00
Goblet..........................40.00
Pickle Jar......................35.00
Pitcher.........................75.00
Tumbler.........................20.00
Relish..........................15.00
Sugar...........................25.00
Water Tray......................25.00
Wine............................15.00

ATLANTA

Berry Bowl, Lg..................35.00
Berry Bowl, Sm..................15.00
Butter..........................45.00
Celery Vase.....................30.00
Compote, Jelly..................35.00
Creamer, Spooner, or Sugar......25.00
Goblet..........................30.00
Lamp Shade, Gas or Ele..........50.00
Shakers, ea.....................20.00
Syrup...........................45.00
Toothpick Hldr..................30.00
Wine............................25.00

ATLANTIS

Tray (Master Salt)..............55.00

ATLAS (ATTERBURY)

Compote, Milk Glass............250.00

ATLAS (BRYCE, U.S. GLASS)

Bowl, Covered, 4 Sizes........50.00 – 90.00
Ruby Stain...................65.00 – 120.00
Bowl, Open, 4 Sizes...........30.00 – 65.00
Ruby Stain....................50.00 – 90.00
Butter..........................70.00
Ruby Stain.....................145.00
Cake Stand, 3 Sizes...........35.00 – 70.00
Ruby Stain...................60.00 – 100.00
Celery Vase.....................25.00
Ruby Stain......................40.00
Compote, Covered, 3 Sizes.....65.00 – 95.00
Ruby Stain...................70.00 – 140.00
Compote, Open, 3 Sizes........35.00 – 70.00
Ruby Stain...................50.00 – 110.00
Cordial.........................20.00
Ruby Stain......................35.00
Creamer or Spooner..............25.00
Ruby Stain......................45.00
Finger Bowl.....................20.00
Ruby Stain......................35.00
Goblet..........................35.00
Ruby Stain......................50.00
Hotel Butter....................55.00
Ruby Stain......................75.00
Hotel Creamer or Spooner........20.00
Ruby Stain......................40.00
Hotel Sugar.....................35.00

Ruby Stain......................50.00
Jam Jar.........................35.00
Ruby Stain......................65.00
Mug.............................30.00
Ruby Stain......................45.00
Milk Pitcher....................60.00
Ruby Stain......................95.00
Pitcher.........................85.00
Ruby Stain.....................130.00
Salt, Lg. or Sm.................20.00
Ruby Stain......................30.00
Salt, Flat or Ftd...............25.00
Ruby Stain......................35.00
Shakers, ea.....................20.00
Ruby Stain......................65.00
Sugar...........................35.00
Ruby Stain......................50.00
Syrup...........................65.00
Ruby Stain......................80.00
Toothpick Hldr..................40.00
Ruby Stain......................50.00
Tumbler.........................25.00
Ruby Stain......................30.00
Whiskey Tumbler.................20.00
Ruby Stain......................35.00
Wine............................25.00
Ruby Stain......................30.00

AURORA

Bread Plate, 10"................35.00
Ruby Stain......................65.00
Butter..........................75.00
Ruby Stain......................95.00
Compote, Covered................65.00
Ruby Stain.....................125.00
Compote, Open...................40.00
Ruby Stain......................80.00
Creamer or Spooner..............30.00
Ruby Stain......................55.00
Decanter........................75.00
Ruby Stain.....................135.00
Goblet..........................60.00
Ruby Stain......................70.00
Pickle Dish.....................20.00
Ruby Stain......................35.00
Pitcher.........................85.00
Ruby Stain.....................145.00
Tumbler.........................25.00
Ruby Stain......................40.00
Shakers, ea.....................40.00
Ruby Stain......................85.00
Sugar...........................40.00
Ruby Stain......................65.00
Tray............................30.00
Ruby Stain......................55.00
Wine............................20.00
Ruby Stain......................55.00

AUSTRIAN

Banana Stand....................55.00
Amber..........................100.00
Vaseline.......................350.00
Berry Bowl, Sm..................15.00
Vaseline........................60.00
Berry Bowl, Lg..................40.00
Vaseline.......................100.00
Bowl, Rectangular...............70.00
Vaseline.......................200.00
Butter..........................85.00
Amber..........................200.00
Vaseline.......................425.00
Cake Stand.....................125.00
Vaseline.......................350.00
Child's Table Set..............175.00
Vaseline......................1100.00
Child's Butter..................75.00
Vaseline.......................525.00
Child's Creamer.................25.00
Vaseline.......................150.00
Child's Spooner.................25.00
Vaseline.......................150.00
Child's Sugar...................50.00
Vaseline.......................275.00
Compotes, Open, High & Low...30.00 – 45.00

Vaseline . . . 225.00 – 325.00
Cordial . . . 50.00
Amber . . . 125.00
Vaseline . . . 150.00
Creamer or Spooner . . . 30.00
Amber . . . 100.00
Vaseline . . . 145.00
Goblet . . . 45.00
Vaseline . . . 200.00
Mug, Child's . . . 30.00
Vaseline . . . 75.00
Nappy, Covered . . . 35.00
Vaseline . . . 265.00
Pitcher . . . 80.00
Vaseline . . . 425.00
Tumbler . . . 20.00
Amber . . . 140.00
Vaseline . . . 125.00
Plate, Sq. . . . 70.00
Vaseline . . . 225.00
Punch Bowl . . . 165.00
Punch Cup . . . 15.00
Amber . . . 100.00
Vaseline . . . 125.00
Rose Bowl, 3 Sizes . . . 25.00 – 50.00
Amber . . . 100.00 – 150.00
Vaseline . . . 200.00 – 225.00
Shakers, ea. . . . 45.00
Vaseline . . . 150.00
Sugar . . . 30.00
Vaseline . . . 250.00
Vase, 6" – 10" . . . 20.00 – 40.00
Vaseline . . . 200.00 – 350.00
Wine . . . 20.00
Amber . . . 165.00
Vaseline . . . 150.00

AZMOOR
Butter . . . 60.00
Bowl, Deep . . . 25.00
Creamer or Spooner . . . 25.00
Cruet . . . 45.00
Nappy . . . 20.00
Pitcher . . . 85.00
Punch Bowl . . . 130.00
Punch Cup . . . 15.00
Relish, Oval . . . 25.00
Sugar . . . 35.00
Tumbler . . . 20.00

AZTEC
Berry Bowl, Lg. . . . 40.00
Ruby Stain . . . 60.00
Berry Bowl, Sm. . . . 20.00
Ruby Stain . . . 25.00
Butter . . . 60.00
Ruby Stain . . . 90.00
Celery Bowl . . . 25.00
Ruby Stain . . . 35.00
Champagne Glass . . . 25.00
Ruby Stain . . . 40.00
Claret . . . 20.00
Ruby Stain . . . 30.00
Cordial . . . 30.00
Ruby Stain . . . 45.00
Creamer or Spooner . . . 30.00
Ruby Stain . . . 55.00
Goblet . . . 40.00
Ruby Stain . . . 60.00
Pickle Dish . . . 15.00
Ruby Stain . . . 25.00
Pitcher . . . 75.00
Ruby Stain . . . 150.00
Punch Bowl . . . 115.00
Ruby Stain . . . 195.00
Punch Cup . . . 10.00
Ruby Stain . . . 20.00
Rose Bowl . . . 25.00
Ruby Stain . . . 50.00
Sugar . . . 35.00
Ruby Stain . . . 65.00
Water Bottle . . . 45.00
Ruby Stain . . . 80.00
Wine . . . 20.00
Ruby Stain . . . 30.00

AZTEC SUNBURST
Berry Bowl, Sm. . . . 15.00
Berry Bowl, Lg. . . . 40.00
Berry Creamer & Open Sugar . . . 30.00
Butter . . . 65.00
Cake Plate, Tall . . . 55.00
Celery Vase . . . 30.00
Celery Tray . . . 30.00
Compote, 7", 8" & 9" . . . 45.00 – 75.00
Compote, Tall . . . 55.00
Cracker Bowl . . . 35.00
Creamer or Spooner . . . 25.00
Handled Nappy . . . 25.00
Pickle Dish . . . 20.00
Rose Bowl . . . 50.00
Rose Bowl, Tall Ftd. . . . 60.00
Salver . . . 60.00
Saucer, 8" . . . 35.00
Shakers, ea. . . . 30.00
Sugar . . . 25.00
Vase . . . 25.00
Vase, Sweet Pea . . . 30.00

BABY ANIMALS
Mug . . . 175.00

BABY FACE
Butter . . . 275.00
Celery Dip . . . 65.00
Celery Vase . . . 90.00
Champagne . . . 115.00
Compote, Covered, 5" – 8" . . . 175.00 – 250.00
Compote, Open, 7" – 8" . . . 85.00 – 135.00
Cordial . . . 80.00
Creamer of Spooner . . . 110.00
Goblet . . . 125.00
Pitcher . . . 350.00
Salt Dip . . . 60.00
Sugar . . . 215.00
Wine . . . 175.00

BALKY MULE
Water Tray, 9½" – 12½" . . . 75.00 – 130.00

BALL AND SWIRL
Butter . . . 55.00
Ruby Stain . . . 85.00
Opaque White . . . 75.00
Cake Stand . . . 30.00
Ruby Stain . . . 45.00
Opaque White . . . 40.00
Candlesticks, ea. . . . 25.00
Ruby Stain . . . 30.00
Opaque White . . . 25.00
Celery Vase . . . 15.00
Ruby Stain . . . 25.00
Opaque White . . . 20.00
Cordial . . . 10.00
Ruby Stain . . . 25.00
Opaque White . . . 20.00
Creamer or Spooner . . . 20.00
Ruby Stain . . . 30.00
Opaque White . . . 25.00
Decanter & Cordials . . . 95.00
Ruby Stain . . . 145.00
Opaque White . . . 120.00
Jelly . . . 25.00
Ruby Stain . . . 35.00
Opaque White . . . 30.00
Mug . . . 20.00
Ruby Stain . . . 35.00
Opaque White . . . 30.00
Plate, 6" . . . 25.00
Ruby Stain . . . 25.00
Opaque White . . . 25.00
Pitcher . . . 70.00
Ruby Stain . . . 120.00
Opaque White . . . 100.00
Shakers, ea. . . . 20.00
Ruby Stain . . . 30.00
Opaque White . . . 25.00
Sugar . . . 30.00
Ruby Stain . . . 45.00
Opaque White . . . 40.00
Syrup . . . 65.00
Ruby Stain . . . 85.00
Opaque White . . . 75.00
Tumbler . . . 15.00
Ruby Stain . . . 25.00
Opaque White . . . 25.00

BALL BROTHERS
Plate . . . 100.00

BALTIMORE PEAR
Bowl, Covered, 5" – 9" . . . 25.00 – 60.00
Bowl, Open, 5" – 9" . . . 15.00 – 40.00
Bread Plate . . . 35.00
Butter . . . 75.00
Cake Plate . . . 30.00
Cake Stand . . . 45.00
Celery Vase . . . 25.00
Compote, Covered, 5" – 8" . . . 30.00 – 60.00
Compote, Open, 5" – 8" . . . 20.00 – 45.00
Creamer or Spooner . . . 15.00
Goblet . . . 60.00
Honey Dish . . . 30.00
Milk Pitcher . . . 65.00
Pickle Tray . . . 20.00
Plate, 8" – 10" . . . 40.00
Pitcher . . . 110.00
Tumbler . . . 30.00
Relish Tray . . . 20.00
Sauce . . . 10.00
Sugar . . . 20.00
Water Tray . . . 30.00

BAMBOO BEAUTY
Berry Bowl, Sm. . . . 25.00
Berry Bowl, Lg. . . . 55.00
Butter . . . 90.00
Creamer or Spooner . . . 35.00
Pitcher . . . 110.00
Tumbler . . . 25.00
Sugar . . . 40.00

BAND
Violet Basket in Holder . . . 45.00

BAND AND DIAMOND SWIRL
Vase, 6" . . . 65.00

BANDED BUCKLE
Bowl . . . 30.00
Butter . . . 65.00
Compote, Open . . . 35.00
Compote, Covered . . . 50.00
Cordial . . . 20.00
Creamer or Spooner . . . 25.00
Egg Cup . . . 30.00
Goblet . . . 40.00
Pitcher . . . 85.00
Tumbler . . . 20.00
Salt Dip, Ftd. . . . 20.00
Sugar . . . 25.00

BANDED DIAMOND POINT
Berry Bowl, Sm. . . . 10.00
Berry Bowl, Lg. . . . 35.00
Butter . . . 50.00
Creamer or Spooner . . . 20.00
Goblet . . . 35.00
Sugar . . . 25.00

BANDED DIAMOND W/PEG
Butter . . . 45.00
Creamer, Spooner, or Sugar . . . 25.00
Pitcher . . . 65.00
Tumbler . . . 20.00
Shakers, Ea. . . . 25.00
Toothpick Hldr. . . . 35.00

BANDED FINECUT
Goblet . . . 55.00
Nappy . . . 25.00
Wine . . . 20.00

BANDED FLEUR-DE-LIS
Butter . . . 65.00
Celery Vase . . . 20.00
Creamer or Spooner . . . 20.00
Egg Cup . . . 30.00
Jelly Compote . . . 25.00
Milk Pitcher . . . 60.00
Pitcher . . . 85.00
Tumbler . . . 20.00
Shakers, ea. . . . 15.00

Sugar 30.00
Syrup 45.00

BANDED RAINDROPS

Bowls, Various . . . . . 15.00 – 40.00
Amber . . . . . 20.00 – 50.00
Milk Glass . . . . . 15.00 – 45.00
Butter 60.00
Amber 85.00
Milk Glass 75.00
Compote, Covered, 7" 45.00
Amber 65.00
Milk Glass 60.00
Creamer or Spooner 20.00
Amber 30.00
Milk Glass 25.00
Cup & Saucer 45.00
Amber 55.00
Milk Glass 50.00
Goblet 60.00
Amber 80.00
Milk Glass 75.00
Plate, 7½" – 9" . . . . . 15.00 – 30.00
Amber . . . . . 20.00 – 55.00
Milk Glass . . . . . 15.00 – 50.00
Pitcher 85.00
Amber 135.00
Milk Glass 125.00
Tumbler 15.00
Amber 25.00
Milk Glass 20.00
Relish, Sq. 15.00
Amber 20.00
Milk Glass 15.00
Sauce 10.00
Amber 15.00
Milk Glass 10.00
Shakers, ea. 20.00
Amber 45.00
Milk Glass 40.00
Sugar 30.00
Amber 45.00
Milk Glass 40.00
Wine 10.00
Amber 25.00
Milk Glass 20.00

BANDED STAR

Butter 50.00
Celery Vase 15.00
Compote, Covered, High 65.00
Compote, Covered, Low 55.00
Creamer or Spooner 25.00
Creamer, Ind. 20.00
Pickle Dish 15.00
Pitcher 90.00
Tumbler 20.00
Sauces 10.00
Sugar 30.00
Sugar, Ind. 25.00

BANNER

Butter, Scarce 70.00

BAR AND BLOCK (NICKEL PLATE'S RICHMOND)

Butter 80.00
Celery Vase 20.00
Creamer or Spooner 25.00
Finger Bowl 15.00
Mustard Jar 50.00
Pitcher 95.00
Tumbler 25.00
Shakers, ea. 15.00
Sugar 35.00
Wine 15.00

BAR AND DIAMOND

Butter 50.00
Ruby Stain 90.00
Celery Vase 20.00
Ruby Stain 30.00
Compotes, Various . . . . . 15.00 – 40.00
Ruby Stain . . . . . 25.00 – 55.00
Creamer or Spooner 30.00
Ruby Stain 40.00
Cruet 55.00
Ruby Stain 85.00
Decanter 45.00
Ruby Stain 65.00
Lamp, Hand Size 65.00
Ruby Stain 120.00
Shakers, Ea. 25.00
Ruby Stain 35.00
Sugar 40.00
Ruby Stain 55.00
Sugar Shaker 50.00
Ruby Stain 70.00
Toy Table Set, Complete 85.00
Ruby Stain 145.00
Wine 15.00
Ruby Stain 25.00

BARBERRY

Bowls, Various, 5" – 9" . . . . . 20.00 – 35.00
Bowls, Covered, 6" – 8" . . . . . 25.00 – 50.00
Butter, 2 Styles 85.00
Cake Stand 135.00
Celery Vase 35.00
Compote, Covered, 6" – 8" . . . . . 50.00 – 70.00
Compote, Open, 7" – 8" . . . . . 40.00 – 55.00
Cordial 35.00
Creamer or Spooner 35.00
Cup Plate 15.00
Dish, 2 Styles 15.00
Egg Cup 35.00
Goblet 30.00
Honey Dish 20.00
Pickle Tray 15.00
Pitcher 145.00
Tumbler 30.00
Plate 25.00
Salt, 2 Styles 30.00
Sauce 15.00
Sugar 60.00
Syrup 135.00
Wine 25.00

BARLEY

Butter 50.00
Cake Stand, 4 Sizes . . . . . 35.00 – 60.00
Celery Vase 30.00
Compote w/Lid 40.00
Cordial 25.00
Creamer, Spooner, or Sugar 25.00
Goblet 30.00
Jam Jar 35.00
Pickle Dish 25.00
Pitcher 70.00
Tumbler 20.00
Oval Dish 25.00
Plate, 6", Scarce 50.00
Platter, Oval, Scarce 70.00
Relish 25.00
Sauce, Ftd. 20.00
Wine 25.00

BARRELLED THUMBPRINT

Bowl, 7" – 9" 30.00
Butter 55.00
Celery Vase 25.00
Creamer, Spooner, or Sugar 25.00
Goblet 30.00
Nappy, 4 Sizes . . . . . 25.00 – 40.00
Pickle Dish 30.00
Pitcher 80.00
Tumbler 15.00
Shakers, ea. 25.00
Water Bottle 60.00
Wine 25.00

BARRY

Plate 35.00

BASKET EPERGNE

6 Basket Centerpiece 250.00

BASKETWEAVE

Berry Bowl, Sm. 10.00
Amber 15.00
Vaseline 20.00
Green/Blue 20.00
Berry Bowl, Lg. 30.00
Amber 35.00
Vaseline 50.00
Green/Blue 45.00
Butter 65.00
Amber 85.00
Vaseline 145.00
Green/Blue 130.00
Cake Plate 40.00
Amber 50.00
Vaseline 70.00
Green/Blue 65.00
Compote, Open, High or Low . . . 25.00 – 40.00
Amber . . . . . 30.00 – 50.00
Vaseline . . . . . 40.00 – 60.00
Green/Blue . . . . . 35.00 – 55.00
Compote, Covered, High or Low . 40.00 – 65.00
Amber . . . . . 45.00 – 70.00
Vaseline . . . . . 55.00 – 80.00
Green/Blue . . . . . 50.00 – 75.00
Cordial 20.00
Amber 25.00
Vaseline 35.00
Green/Blue 30.00
Creamer or Spooner 25.00
Amber 30.00
Vaseline 40.00
Green/Blue 35.00
Egg Cup, Single & Double . . . . . 15.00 – 25.00
Amber . . . . . 20.00 – 35.00
Vaseline . . . . . 30.00 – 45.00
Green/Blue . . . . . 25.00 – 40.00
Finger Bowl 25.00
Amber 30.00
Vaseline 35.00
Green/Blue 30.00
Goblet 45.00
Amber 55.00
Vaseline 60.00
Green/Blue 55.00
Milk Pitcher 60.00
Amber 75.00
Vaseline 95.00
Green/Blue 90.00
Mug 35.00
Amber 40.00
Vaseline 50.00
Green/Blue 45.00
Pickle Dish 20.00
Amber 25.00
Vaseline 30.00
Green/Blue 30.00
Pitcher 90.00
Amber 115.00
Vaseline 165.00
Green/Blue 125.00
Tumbler 15.00
Amber 20.00
Vaseline 30.00
Green/Blue 25.00
Salt Dip, Flat or Ftd. 20.00
Amber 30.00
Vaseline 40.00
Green/Blue 35.00
Sauce 10.00
Amber 15.00
Vaseline 20.00
Green/Blue 20.00
Saucer 15.00
Amber 20.00
Vaseline 25.00
Green/Blue 25.00
Sugar 40.00
Amber 50.00
Vaseline 65.00
Green/Blue 60.00
Syrup 70.00
Amber 90.00
Vaseline 125.00
Green/Blue 100.00
Waste Bowl 20.00
Amber 25.00
Vaseline 30.00
Green/Blue 25.00
Water Tray 40.00
Amber 45.00

Vaseline 65.00
Green/Blue 50.00
Wine 20.00
Amber 25.00
Vaseline 30.00
Green/Blue 25.00

BEACON #410 INNOVATION
Basket, Hndl 65.00
Bowl, Ftd., Round 30.00
Bowl, Ftd., Oval 40.00
Cylinder Vase, Etched, 12" 55.00
Sq. Vase, 10" – 12" 45.00

BEAD AND SCROLL
Butter 55.00
Creamer or Spooner 25.00
Goblet 50.00
Jelly Compote 35.00
Pitcher 80.00
Tumbler 25.00
Shakers, ea. 30.00
Sugar 35.00
Toothpick Hldr. 30.00
Toy Table Set, Rare 125.00

BEAD COLUMN
Berry Bowl, Sm. 10.00
Berry Bowl, Lg. 35.00
Butter 55.00
Creamer or Spooner 20.00
Pitcher 70.00
Tumbler 15.00
Sugar 20.00

BEADED ARCH PANELS
Butter 60.00
Creamer or Spooner 25.00
Goblet 45.00
Mug 30.00
Sugar 35.00

BEADED BAND
Butter 50.00
Compote 45.00
Cordial 25.00
Creamer, Spooner, or Sugar 20.00
Salt Shaker, ea. 20.00
Syrup 50.00
Wine 30.00

BEADED BEAUTY
Compote, Covered 90.00
Compote, Open 65.00

BEADED CHAIN
Butter 70.00
Celery Vase 25.00
Creamer or Spooner 25.00
Goblet 35.00
Plate 30.00
Sauce 15.00
Sugar 30.00

BEADED COARSE BARS
Butter 50.00
Creamer or Spooner 20.00
Goblet 40.00
Mug 25.00
Pickle Dish 25.00
Shakers, ea. 20.00
Sugar 30.00
Water Carafe 35.00

BEADED COMET BAND
Berry Bowl, Lg. 35.00
Berry Bowl, Sm. 15.00
Butter 50.00
Creamer, Spooner, or Sugar 25.00
Cruet 45.00
Pickle Dish 30.00
Plate, 10" 40.00

BEADED DIAMOND
Berry Bowl, Sm. 20.00
Berry Bowl, Lg. 40.00
Butter 55.00
Creamer or Spooner 20.00
Pitcher 75.00
Tumbler 20.00
Sugar 25.00

BEADED GRAPE (CALIFORNIA)
Berry Bowl, Sm. 15.00
Green/Blue 45.00
Berry Bowl, Lg. 35.00
Green/Blue 65.00
Bowl, Rnd. or Sq., Various . . . . . 10.00 – 40.00
Green/Blue . . . . . 20.00 – 70.00
Bread Plate 25.00
Green/Blue 55.00
Butter 70.00
Green/Blue 75.00
Cake Stand 90.00
Green/Blue 125.00
Compote, Covered . . . . . 50.00 – 100.00
Green/Blue . . . . . 60.00 – 125.00
Compote, Open . . . . . 25.00 – 75.00
Green/Blue . . . . . 30.00 – 90.00
Cordial 85.00
Green/Blue 110.00
Creamer or Spooner 25.00
Green/Blue 50.00
Milk Pitcher 75.00
Green/Blue 100.00
Pickle Dish 20.00
Green/Blue 35.00
Pitcher, Rnd. or Sq. 100.00
Green/Blue 125.00
Tumbler, Rnd. or Sq. 25.00
Green/Blue 50.00
Sauce, Various 15.00
Green/Blue 25.00
Shakers, ea. 30.00
Green/Blue 55.00
Sugar 35.00
Green/Blue 75.00
Toothpick Hldr. 40.00
Green/Blue 90.00
Vase, 3 Sizes . . . . . 50.00 – 100.00
Green/Blue . . . . . 75.00 – 125.00
Wine 50.00
Green/Blue 75.00

BEADED GRAPE MEDALLION
Bowl, Rnd. or Sq., Various . . . . . 20.00 – 30.00
Butter 65.00
Cake Stand 135.00
Caster Set, Complete 165.00
Celery Vase 45.00
Champagne 50.00
Compote, Covered . . . . . 45.00 – 70.00
Compote, Open . . . . . 30.00 – 50.00
Cordial 55.00
Creamer or Spooner 45.00
Dish, Covered, Various . . . . . 55.00 – 75.00
Egg Cup 30.00
Goblet, Various 40.00
Pickle Dish 20.00
Plate 25.00
Pitcher 145.00
Tumbler 25.00
Relish 20.00
Salt, Ind. 25.00
Salt, Master 30.00
Sugar 55.00
Wine 25.00

BEADED MEDALLION
Butter 45.00
Celery Vase 25.00
Creamer or Spooner 25.00
Egg Cup 20.00
Jelly Compote 30.00
Open Salt 20.00
Pitcher 65.00
Tumbler 15.00
Sugar 25.00

BEADED PANEL AND SUNBURST
Butter 50.00
Creamer or Spooner 20.00
Sugar 25.00
Toothpick Hldr. 25.00

BEADED SHELL
Berry Bowl, Lg. 30.00
Green/Blue 35.00
Berry Bowl, Sm. 10.00
Green/Blue 15.00
Butter 45.00
Green/Blue 55.00
Compote 35.00
Green/Blue 40.00
Creamer or Spooner 30.00
Green/Blue 35.00
Cruet 55.00
Green/Blue 75.00
Cruet Set 95.00
Green/Blue 115.00
Mug 35.00
Green/Blue 40.00
Pitcher 80.00
Green/Blue 135.00
Tumbler 15.00
Green/Blue 25.00
Shakers, ea. 25.00
Green/Blue 35.00
Sugar 45.00
Green/Blue 50.00
Toothpick Hldr. 40.00
Green/Blue 45.00

BEADED STARS AND SWAG
Banana Bowl 65.00
Bowls, Various . . . . . 15.00 – 35.00
Plates, Various . . . . . 20.00 – 50.00
Rose Bowl, Advertising, "Lion Store, Hammond, Louisiana," Rare 100.00
Rose Bowls, Various . . . . . 25.00 – 60.00

BEADED SWAG
Cup & Saucer 45.00
Green/Blue 55.00
Ruby Stain 75.00
Custard 60.00
Mug 35.00
Green/Blue 45.00
Ruby Stain 55.00
Custard 50.00

BEADED SWIRL AND BALL
Child's Mug 30.00

BEADED SWIRL AND LENS
Butter 75.00
Cake Stand 35.00
Celery Vase 20.00
Compote, Covered 50.00
Compote, Open 40.00
Creamer or Spooner 20.00
Egg Cup 20.00
Goblet 60.00
Mug 30.00
Pitcher 95.00
Tumbler 20.00
Sauce, Flat or Ftd. 15.00
Sugar 30.00
Syrup 45.00
Wine 15.00

BEADED TULIP
Bowls, Various . . . . . 10.00 – 40.00
Bread Plate 25.00
Butter 85.00
Green/Blue 135.00
Cake Stand 35.00
Champagne 25.00
Compote, Covered 45.00
Compote, Open 25.00
Creamer or Spooner 35.00
Green/Blue 85.00
Goblet 35.00
Ice Cream Dish 20.00
Jam Jar 40.00
Milk Pitcher 45.00
Green/Blue 80.00
Pickle Dish, Oval 20.00
Plate 20.00
Pitcher 75.00
Tumbler 15.00
Sauce 10.00
Sugar 30.00
Green/Blue 80.00
Water Tray 25.00

Wine 10.00
Wine Tray 25.00

BEAUMONT'S COLUMBIA

Berry Bowl, Sm. 10.00
Vaseline. 15.00
Ruby Stain. 15.00
Amber Stain. 15.00
Berry Bowl, Lg. 25.00
Vaseline. 35.00
Ruby Stain. 45.00
Amber Stain. 45.00
Butter 60.00
Vaseline. 115.00
Ruby Stain. 90.00
Amber Stain. 85.00
Celery Tray. 20.00
Vaseline. 25.00
Ruby Stain. 30.00
Amber Stain. 35.00
Celery Vase 25.00
Vaseline. 30.00
Ruby Stain. 30.00
Amber Stain. 35.00
Compote. 30.00
Vaseline. 40.00
Ruby Stain. 45.00
Amber Stain. 45.00
Creamer or Spooner. 30.00
Vaseline. 35.00
Ruby Stain. 40.00
Amber Stain. 40.00
Cruet 60.00
Vaseline. 85.00
Ruby Stain. 85.00
Amber Stain. 80.00
Jelly Compote. 25.00
Vaseline. 35.00
Ruby Stain. 45.00
Amber Stain. 45.00
Pitcher 80.00
Vaseline. 130.00
Ruby Stain. 145.00
Amber Stain. 135.00
Tumbler 15.00
Vaseline. 40.00
Ruby Stain. 35.00
Amber Stain. 35.00
Plates, Various . . . . 15.00 – 25.00
Vaseline . . . . 20.00 – 40.00
Ruby Stain . . . . 25.00 – 50.00
Amber Stain . . . . 25.00 – 50.00
Salt Dip 20.00
Vaseline. 25.00
Ruby Stain. 30.00
Amber Stain. 30.00
Sugar 35.00
Vaseline. 45.00
Ruby Stain. 50.00
Amber Stain. 45.00
Syrup 70.00
Vaseline. 95.00
Ruby Stain. 100.00
Amber Stain. 95.00
Toothpick Hldr. 35.00
Vaseline. 65.00
Ruby Stain. 55.00
Amber Stain. 50.00
Vase. 30.00
Vaseline. 50.00
Ruby Stain. 45.00
Amber Stain. 45.00

BEAVER BAND

Goblet, Very Rare 1000.00

BEE

Butter w/Cover 125.00*
Amber 150.00*
Vaseline. 350.00*
Green/Blue. 175.00*

BEGGING DOG

Mug 50.00
Amethyst 85.00

"BE INDUSTRIOUS" (Either lettering)

Platter, Oval. 80.00

BELLADONNA

Berry Bowl, Lg.. . . . . 45.00
Green/Blue. 55.00
Ruby Stain. 65.00
Berry Bowl, Sm. 20.00
Green/Blue. 25.00
Ruby Stain. 30.00
Butter. 60.00
Green/Blue. 70.00
Ruby Stain. 90.00
Creamer or Spooner. 35.00
Green/Blue. 40.00
Ruby Stain. 45.00
Pitcher 85.00
Green/Blue. 100.00
Ruby Stain. 135.00
Tumbler 25.00
Green/Blue. 30.00
Ruby Stain. 40.00
Sugar 45.00
Green/Blue. 50.00
Ruby Stain. 65.00
Toothpick Hldr. 40.00
Green/Blue. 45.00
Ruby Stain. 55.00

BELLFLOWER

Bowls, Various . . . . 15.00 – 35.00
Amber. . . . . 20.00 – 40.00
Vaseline . . . . 25.00 – 65.00
Green/Blue . . . . 25.00 – 45.00
Milk Glass . . . . 20.00 – 35.00
Butter. 55.00
Amber 70.00
Vaseline. 110.00
Green/Blue. 85.00
Milk Glass. 70.00
Cake Stand, 2 Sizes. . . . . 20.00 – 35.00
Amber. . . . . 25.00 – 50.00
Vaseline . . . . 40.00 – 65.00
Green/Blue . . . . 35.00 – 50.00
Milk Glass . . . . 30.00 – 45.00
Caster Set. 70.00
Amber 85.00
Vaseline. 145.00
Green/Blue. 120.00
Milk Glass. 100.00
Celery Vase 20.00
Amber 30.00
Vaseline. 50.00
Green/Blue. 40.00
Milk Glass. 35.00
Champagne 15.00
Amber 20.00
Vaseline. 35.00
Green/Blue. 25.00
Milk Glass. 25.00
Compote, Covered or Open . . . . . 25.00 – 35.00
Amber. . . . . 30.00 – 45.00
Vaseline . . . . 45.00 – 70.00
Green/Blue . . . . 35.00 – 60.00
Milk Glass . . . . 30.00 – 55.00
Cordial. 10.00
Amber 20.00
Vaseline. 35.00
Green/Blue. 30.00
Milk Glass. 25.00
Creamer or Spooner. 20.00
Amber 30.00
Vaseline. 45.00
Green/Blue. 40.00
Milk Glass. 30.00
Decanter, 2 Sizes . . . . 25.00 – 35.00
Amber. . . . . 30.00 – 45.00
Vaseline . . . . 65.00 – 90.00
Green/Blue . . . . 50.00 – 75.00
Milk Glass . . . . 40.00 – 55.00
Egg Cup 15.00
Amber 20.00
Vaseline. 35.00
Green/Blue. 30.00
Milk Glass. 25.00
Goblet . . . . 15.00 – 35.00
Amber. . . . . 20.00 – 40.00
Vaseline . . . . 25.00 – 55.00
Green/Blue . . . . 25.00 – 40.00
Milk Glass . . . . 20.00 – 35.00
Hat Shape 15.00
Amber 20.00
Vaseline. 35.00
Green/Blue. 30.00
Milk Glass. 25.00
Honey Dish 15.00
Amber 20.00
Vaseline. 40.00
Green/Blue. 30.00
Milk Glass. 30.00
Lamp 65.00
Amber 80.00
Vaseline. 125.00
Green/Blue. 100.00
Milk Glass. 85.00
Milk Pitcher. 45.00
Amber 60.00
Vaseline. 85.00
Green/Blue. 70.00
Milk Glass. 65.00
Mug 20.00
Amber 30.00
Vaseline. 60.00
Green/Blue. 45.00
Milk Glass. 40.00
Pickle Dish 10.00
Amber 20.00
Vaseline. 35.00
Green/Blue. 30.00
Milk Glass. 25.00
Pitcher 60.00
Amber 75.00
Vaseline. 120.00
Green/Blue. 100.00
Milk Glass. 85.00
Plate. 15.00
Amber 30.00
Vaseline. 55.00
Green/Blue. 40.00
Milk Glass. 35.00
Relish Dish 10.00
Amber 20.00
Vaseline. 35.00
Green/Blue. 30.00
Milk Glass. 25.00
Salts. 20.00
Amber 25.00
Vaseline. 35.00
Green/Blue. 30.00
Milk Glass. 25.00
Sauce 10.00
Amber 15.00
Vaseline. 25.00
Green/Blue. 20.00
Milk Glass. 20.00
Sugar 30.00
Amber 40.00
Vaseline. 65.00
Green/Blue. 45.00
Milk Glass. 35.00
Syrup 50.00
Amber 65.00
Vaseline. 85.00
Green/Blue. 70.00
Milk Glass. 55.00
Sweetmeat 60.00
Amber 70.00
Vaseline. 95.00
Green/Blue. 80.00
Milk Glass. 65.00
Tumbler 15.00
Amber 20.00
Vaseline. 45.00
Green/Blue. 30.00
Milk Glass. 25.00
Whiskey Tumbler. 10.00

Amber 20.00
Vaseline 30.00
Green/Blue 25.00
Milk Glass 20.00

BELMONT #100 (DAISY AND BUTTON)
Butter 85.00
Vaseline 250.00
Green/Blue 300.00
Bowl w/Underplate 45.00
Vaseline . . . . 250.00 – 350.00
Compote, Covered 95.00
Vaseline 250.00
Celery Vase, Scarce 80.00
Vaseline 300.00
Creamer or Spooner 35.00
Vaseline 125.00
Sauce, Flat or Ftd . . . . 15.00 – 20.00
Vaseline . . . . 45.00 – 65.00
Sugar 50.00
Vaseline 175.00

BELMONT DIAMOND
Bowl, Oval 35.00
Bowl, Rnd 30.00
Cruet 50.00

BERLIN
Bowl, 7" 30.00
Butter 90.00
Compote, Covered 85.00
Compote, Open 60.00
Creamer or Spooner 40.00
Dish, Oval 25.00
Egg Cup 25.00
Honey Dish 30.00
Milk Pitcher 100.00
Pickle Dish 30.00
Pitcher 150.00
Tumbler 30.00
Plate, 7" 30.00
Shakers, ea 45.00
Sauce 15.00
Sugar 50.00

BERRY
Butter 65.00
Creamer or Spooner 30.00
Sugar 45.00

BERRY CLUSTER
Butter 55.00
Celery Vase 20.00
Creamer or Spooner 20.00
Goblet 30.00
Pitcher 75.00
Sugar 30.00
Tumbler 20.00

BERRY SPRAY
Egg Cup 25.00

BETHLEHEM STAR
Butter 45.00
Celery Vase 20.00
Compote, Covered, 4½" – 8" . . . . 30.00 – 45.00
Creamer or Spooner 20.00
Cruet 50.00
Goblet 25.00
Pitcher 55.00
Tumbler 10.00
Relish 15.00
Sauce 10.00
Sugar 25.00
Wine 15.00

BE TRUE
Plate 125.00

BEVELLED BUTTONS
Bowls . . . . 15.00 – 30.00
Butter 45.00
Celery Vase 20.00
Compote 30.00
Creamer or Spooner 20.00
Pickle Jar 30.00
Sauce 10.00
Sugar 25.00

BEVELLED DIAGONAL BLOCK
Butter 65.00
Cake Stand 35.00
Celery Vase 20.00
Cordial 20.00
Creamer or Spooner 20.00
Goblet 45.00
Jam Jar 40.00
Plate 20.00
Pitcher 85.00
Tumbler 20.00
Shakers, ea 20.00
Sugar 30.00
Wine 15.00

BEVELLED DIAMOND AND STAR
Bowl, 7" – 8" 20.00
Ruby Stain 35.00
Bread Plate 30.00
Ruby Stain 45.00
Butter 75.00
Ruby Stain 100.00
Cake Stand 40.00
Ruby Stain 100.00
Celery Vase 30.00
Ruby Stain 70.00
Compote, 5" – 7", Covered . . . . 45.00 – 70.00
Ruby Stain 200.00
Compote, 5" – 8", Open . . . . 30.00 – 50.00
Ruby Stain 135.00
Cracker Jar w/Lid 50.00
Ruby Stain 165.00
Creamer or Spooner 25.00
Ruby Stain 65.00
Cruet 65.00
Ruby Stain 125.00
Decanter w/Stopper 75.00
Ruby Stain 165.00
Goblet 40.00
Ruby Stain 80.00
Milk Pitcher 45.00
Ruby Stain 125.00
Pickle Dish 15.00
Ruby Stain 25.00
Plate 15.00
Ruby Stain 25.00
Pitcher 95.00
Ruby Stain 200.00
Tumbler 20.00
Ruby Stain 45.00
Shakers, ea 15.00
Ruby Stain 50.00
Sugar 35.00
Ruby Stain 90.00
Syrup 45.00
Ruby Stain 125.00
Toothpick 35.00
Ruby Stain 80.00
Tray 40.00
Ruby Stain 80.00
Wine 15.00
Ruby Stain 50.00

BEVELED STAR
Bowl, 9" 35.00
Berry Bowl, Lg 40.00
Berry Bowl, Sm 15.00
Butter 55.00
Celery Tray 35.00
Compote, Covered 50.00
Creamer, Spooner, or Sugar 25.00
Cruet 45.00
Pitcher 70.00
Tumbler 20.00
Syrup 65.00

BICYCLE GIRL
Pitcher, Rare 475.00

BIG BASKETWEAVE
Vase 30.00
Celeste Blue 75.00

BIG FISH
Bowl, Very Rare 1500*

BILIKEN FLUTE
Butter 55.00
Creamer or Spooner 20.00
Goblet 30.00
Pickle Dish 20.00
Sugar 30.00
Wine 15.00

BIRCH LEAF
Butter 80.00
Celery Vase 20.00
Compote, Covered 65.00
Compote, Open 45.00
Creamer or Spooner 30.00
Egg Cup 25.00
Goblet 50.00
Pickle Dish 20.00
Salt Dip, Master 20.00
Sugar 40.00
Wine 15.00

BIRD AND CHERRY
Mustard Jar Holder 25.00
Vaseline 75.00

BIRD AND HARP
Mug 55.00
Purple Slag 80.00

BIRD AND STRAWBERRY
Berry Bowl, Sm 15.00
Berry Bowl, Lg 35.00
Bowls, 5" – 10½" . . . . 10.00 – 40.00
Butter 100.00
Cake Stand 75.00
Celery Tray 50.00
Celery Vase 45.00
Chop Plate 150.00
Compote, 4" – 6" 110.00
Creamer or Spooner 55.00
Cup 25.00
Goblet, Rare 400.00
Hat, from Tumbler, Rare 200.00
Pitcher 250.00
Tumbler 50.00
Relish 25.00
Rose Bowl, Ftd., Lg 175.00
Sandwich Plate 100.00
Sugar 65.00
Wine 75.00

BIRD BASKET
Match Hldr 85.00

BIRD IN NEST WITH FLOWERS
Mug 65.00
Purple Slag 100.00

BIRD ON A BRANCH
Child's Mug 160.00

BIRDS AT FOUNTAIN
Bowl, Sm 25.00
Butter 175.00
Compote, Covered 135.00
Creamer or Spooner 70.00
Goblet 85.00
Mug, Miniature 65.00
Sauce 25.00
Sugar 90.00

BIRDS IN SWAMP
Goblet 75.00

BLACKBERRY (HOBB'S)
Butter 60.00
Milk Glass 75.00
Celery Vase, 2 Sizes . . . . 50.00 – 60.00
Milk Glass . . . . 90.00 – 110.00
Champagne 30.00
Milk Glass 55.00
Compote, Covered, 2 Sizes . . . . 40.00 – 65.00
Milk Glass . . . . 60.00 – 85.00
Creamer or Spooner 50.00
Milk Glass 75.00
Dish, Oval 15.00
Milk Glass 35.00
Egg Cup, Single 35.00
Milk Glass 40.00
Egg Cup, Double 45.00
Milk Glass 55.00
Goblet 60.00
Milk Glass 75.00
Honey Dish 15.00
Milk Glass 25.00
Lamp, 3 Sizes . . . . 95.00 – 165.00
Pitcher 125.00

Milk Glass 175.00
Tumbler 30.00
Milk Glass 50.00
Relish 20.00
Milk Glass 35.00
Salt Dip, Master 30.00
Milk Glass 40.00
Sauce 15.00
Milk Glass 20.00
Sugar 75.00
Milk Glass 95.00
Syrup 165.00
Milk Glass 250.00
Wine 30.00
Milk Glass 45.00

BLAZING CORNUCOPIA
Berry Bowl, Sm. 20.00
Berry Bowl, Lg. 45.00
Butter 100.00
Celery Tray 25.00
Creamer or Spooner 30.00
Cruet 65.00
Cup 20.00
Goblet 65.00
Jelly Compote 35.00
Nappy 30.00
Olive Dish 20.00
Pickle Dish 25.00
Pitcher 165.00
Tumbler 25.00
Sugar 40.00
Toothpick Hldr. 35.00
Wine 15.00

BLEEDING HEART
Bowl w/Lid, 3 Styles, 4 Sizes . . . . 25.00 – 60.00
Butter 70.00
Cake Stand, 9" – 11" 45.00
Compote, Oval or Rnd. 40.00
Compote w/Lid, 7" – 9" 60.00
Creamer or Spooner 25.00
Egg Cup 30.00
Goblet 40.00
Honey Dish 25.00
Jelly 30.00
Mug 35.00
Pitcher 90.00
Tumbler 20.00
Pickle Tray 25.00
Plate 30.00
Platter, Oval 40.00
Relish Tray 25.00
Salt, Ind. 10.00
Salt, Master 30.00
Sauce 15.00
Sugar 30.00
Waste Bowl 20.00

BLOCKADE
Butter 65.00
Celery Vase 20.00
Compote, Covered, 6" – 8" . . . . . 35.00 – 65.00
Compote, Open, 4" – 8" . . . . . 20.00 – 45.00
Creamer or Spooner 20.00
Dish, Sq., 7" – 9" . . . . . 15.00 – 30.00
Finger Bowl 20.00
Goblet 45.00
Nappy, 4½" – 6" 30.00
Pitcher 85.00
Tumbler 20.00
Sugar 25.00

BLOCK AND BAR
Creamer 40.00
Vaseline 60.00
Goblet 65.00
Vaseline 80.00
Pitcher 120.00
Vaseline 185.00
Sugar 50.00
Vaseline 70.00

BLOCK AND CIRCLE
Berry Bowl, Sm. 10.00
Berry Bowl, Lg. 35.00
Butter 55.00
Celery Vase 20.00
Compote, Covered 45.00
Compote, Open, 7" – 9" 30.00
Creamer or Spooner 20.00
Dish, Oval, 7" – 9" . . . . . 15.00 – 30.00
Goblet 40.00
Lamp, Mini 85.00
Mug 35.00
Pitcher 85.00
Tumbler 20.00
Sugar 30.00

BLOCK AND JEWEL
Wine 30.00

BLOCK AND PANEL
Butter 45.00
Celery Vase 25.00
Creamer or Spooner 25.00
Shakers, ea. 20.00
Sugar 30.00

BLOCK AND PILLAR
Shakers, ea. 20.00
Vase 30.00

BLOCK AND TRIPLE BARS
Butter 45.00
Creamer or Spooner 20.00
Goblet 35.00
Sugar 25.00

BLOCKED THUMBPRINT BAND
Cruet 50.00
Ruby Stain 75.00
Mug 35.00
Ruby Stain 45.00
Shot Glass 30.00
Ruby Stain 40.00
Toothpick Hldr. 45.00
Ruby Stain 60.00
Wine 15.00
Ruby Stain 25.00

BLOOMS AND BLOSSOMS (MIKADO)
(All prices in crystal column are for decorated pieces.)
Bowls, Various . . . . . 15.00 – 60.00
Vaseline . . . . . 20.00 – 75.00
Green/Blue . . . . . 20.00 – 50.00
Butter 150.00
Vaseline 185.00
Green/Blue 130.00
Compote 65.00
Vaseline 80.00
Green/Blue 60.00
Creamer or Spooner 45.00
Vaseline 65.00
Green/Blue 40.00
Cruet 165.00
Vaseline 195.00
Green/Blue 130.00
Nappy 35.00
Vaseline 65.00
Green/Blue 35.00
Plate 40.00
Vaseline 75.00
Green/Blue 40.00
Pitcher 225.00
Vaseline 265.00
Green/Blue 175.00
Tumbler 35.00
Vaseline 75.00
Green/Blue 35.00
Sugar 55.00
Vaseline 75.00
Green/Blue 55.00

BOAT RELISH
One Shape 75.00

BOHEMIAN DRAPE
Bowl, 10", Vaseline 70.00
Jar, Covered, Vaseline 95.00

BOSC PEAR
Berry Bowl, Lg. 30.00
Purple Flash 50.00
Berry Bowl, Sm. 10.00
Purple Flash 20.00
Butter 50.00
Purple Flash 90.00
Celery Vase 25.00
Purple Flash 30.00
Creamer or Spooner 30.00
Purple Flash 35.00
Pitcher 75.00
Purple Flash 110.00
Tumbler 20.00
Purple Flash 30.00
Sugar 35.00
Purple Flash 50.00

BOW TIE
Bowls, 7" – 11" . . . . . 15.00 – 55.00
Butter 75.00
Butter Pat 20.00
Cake Stand 55.00
Celery Vase 20.00
Compote, High, 7" – 11" . . . . . 35.00 – 85.00
Compote, Low, 7" – 11" . . . . . 25.00 – 75.00
Creamer or Spooner 25.00
Goblet 55.00
Jam Jar 35.00
Milk Pitcher, 2 Sizes . . . . . 45.00 – 70.00
Orange Bowl 45.00
Pitcher, 3 Sizes . . . . . 65.00 – 110.00
Tumbler 25.00
Punch Bowl 150.00
Relish 20.00
Salt, Master 20.00
Salt, Ind. 10.00
Sauce, Flat or Ftd. 10.00
Sugar 30.00

BOXED STAR
Butter 55.00
Carafe, Water 40.00
Creamer or Spooner 20.00
Goblet 50.00
Pitcher 65.00
Tumbler 20.00
Sugar 25.00
Wine 20.00

BOX PLEAT
Butter 45.00
Cake Stand 40.00
Celery Vase 20.00
Compote 30.00
Creamer or Spooner 20.00
Pitcher 65.00
Tumbler 10.00
Sugar 25.00

BOY AND GIRL FACE
Cup w/Saucer 65.00
Amber 110.00
Green/Blue 85.00

BOY WITH BEGGING DOG
Mug 55.00
Green/Blue 85.00
Milk Glass 95.00

BRANCHED TREE
Butter 145.00
Celery Vase 35.00
Compote, Covered 90.00
Creamer or Spooner 40.00
Goblet 65.00
Pitcher 170.00
Tumbler 35.00
Sugar 60.00

BRASS NAILHEAD (FRANCE)
Mug 50.00
Opal 70.00

BRAZEN SHIELD
Berry Bowl, Sm. 15.00
Berry Bowl, Lg. 45.00
Butter 75.00
Creamer or Spooner 25.00
Goblet 50.00
Jelly Compote 35.00
Pickle Dish 20.00
Pitcher 95.00
Tumbler 20.00
Shakers, ea. 20.00
Sugar 30.00
Wine 20.00

BRAZILIAN
- Berry Bowl, Sm. 20.00
- Berry Bowl, Lg. 45.00
- Butter 65.00
- Carafe 40.00
- Celery Tray (shown) 25.00
- Celery Vase 30.00
- Compote 35.00
- Cracker Jar, 7" – 9" . . . . . 25.00 – 40.00
- Creamer or Spooner 25.00
- Cruet 60.00
- Finger Bowl 20.00
- Pitcher 80.00
- Tumbler 25.00
- Olive, Hndl. 25.00
- Pickle Jar 30.00
- Rose Bowl 35.00
- Salt Shaker 20.00
- Sauce 15.00
- Sherbet 20.00
- Sugar 30.00
- Toothpick Hldr. 30.00
- Vase 35.00

BRINGING HOME THE COWS
- Butter 300.00
- Creamer or Spooner 200.00
- Pitcher, Tankard 650.00
- Sugar 250.00

BRINKERHOFF INKWELL
- One Shape 25.00

BRITISH LION
- Paperweight 250.00

BRITANNIC
- Banana Stand 85.00
  - Ruby Stain 110.00
- Bowl, Oval, 7" – 9" 30.00
  - Ruby Stain 45.00
- Bowl, Rnd., 8" 25.00
  - Ruby Stain 40.00
- Bowl, Sq. 30.00
  - Ruby Stain 55.00
- Butter 55.00
  - Ruby Stain 125.00
- Cake Stand, Lg. or Sm. . . . . . 35.00 – 45.00
- Carafe 50.00
- Castor Set 80.00
  - Ruby Stain 200.00
- Celery Tray 30.00
- Celery Vase 25.00
- Cologne 35.00
- Compote, Covered 45.00
  - Ruby Stain 85.00
- Compote, Open, 5" – 7" . . . . . 25.00 – 35.00
  - Ruby Stain 65.00
- Compote, Open, 8½" – 10" . . . . . 40.00 – 50.00
  - Ruby Stain 70.00
- Cracker Jar 35.00
- Creamer or Spooner 20.00
- Cruet 55.00
  - Ruby Stain 165.00
- Custard Cup 10.00
- Fruit Basket 30.00
- Goblet 30.00
  - Ruby Stain 65.00
- Honey Jar 35.00
- Ice Cream Tray 25.00
- Lamp, 2 Types, 2 Sizes . . . . . 50.00 – 65.00
- Mug 20.00
  - Ruby Stain 45.00
- Olive Dish 20.00
- Pickle Dish 20.00
- Pitcher 75.00
  - Ruby Stain 135.00
- Tumbler 20.00
  - Ruby Stain 45.00
- Rose Bowl 30.00
  - Ruby Stain 80.00
- Sauce, Rnd. or Sq. 15.00
  - Ruby Stain 35.00
- Shakers, ea. 20.00
  - Ruby Stain 90.00
- Sugar 30.00
  - Ruby Stain 85.00
- Syrup 45.00
  - Ruby Stain 100.00
- Toothpick Hldr. 20.00
  - Ruby Stain 175.00
- Vase 25.00
  - Ruby Stain 60.00
- Wine 15.00
  - Ruby Stain 55.00

BRITANNIC FLORAL
- Creamer 30.00
  - Vaseline 70.00

BROKEN ARCHES
- Bowl, 8½" 25.00
- Punch Bowl 75.00
  - Vaseline 400.00
- Punch Cup 10.00
  - Vaseline 30.00

BROKEN COLUMN
- Banana Dish 30.00
- Basket, Hndl. 40.00
- Berry Bowl, Sm. 15.00
  - Ruby Stain 25.00
- Berry Bowl, Lg. 35.00
  - Ruby Stain 55.00
- Biscuit Jar 75.00
  - Ruby Stain 175.00
- Bowl, Covered, 5" – 8" . . . . . 40.00 – 70.00
  - Ruby Stain . . . . . 125.00 – 225.00
- Bread Plate 50.00
  - Ruby Stain 125.00
- Butter 55.00
  - Ruby Stain 200.00
- Cake Stand 40.00
  - Ruby Stain 225.00
- Celery Tray 25.00
  - Ruby Stain 85.00
- Celery Vase 30.00
  - Ruby Stain 125.00
- Compote, Covered, 5" – 8" . . . . . 60.00 – 80.00
  - Ruby Stain . . . . . 175.00 – 325.00
- Compote, Open, 5" – 8" . . . . . 35.00 – 60.00
  - Ruby Stain . . . . . 75.00 – 165.00
- Creamer or Spooner 25.00
  - Ruby Stain 100.00
- Cruet 60.00
  - Ruby Stain 165.00
- Custard Cup 15.00
  - Ruby Stain 35.00
- Finger Bowl 20.00
- Goblet 60.00
  - Ruby Stain 125.00
- Pickle Castor 125.00
  - Ruby Stain 400.00
- Plate, 7½" 25.00
  - Ruby Stain 45.00
- Pitcher 100.00
  - Ruby Stain 225.00
- Tumbler 35.00
  - Ruby Stain 65.00
- Sauce 15.00
  - Ruby Stain 25.00
- Shakers, ea. 25.00
  - Ruby Stain 75.00
- Sugar 65.00
  - Ruby Stain 125.00
- Syrup 125.00
  - Ruby Stain 385.00
- Wine Carafe 80.00
  - Ruby Stain 165.00

BROKEN PILLAR AND REED
- Bonbon 15.00
  - Amber 20.00
  - Green/Blue 30.00
  - Maiden's Blush 35.00
- Bowl, 8" 20.00
  - Amber 25.00
  - Green/Blue 40.00
  - Maiden's Blush 45.00
- Butter 45.00
  - Amber 55.00
  - Green/Blue 75.00
  - Maiden's Blush 70.00
- Cake Stand 35.00
  - Amber 40.00
  - Green/Blue 50.00
  - Maiden's Blush 55.00
- Celery Tray 20.00
  - Amber 25.00
  - Green/Blue 35.00
  - Maiden's Blush 40.00
- Celery Vase 25.00
  - Amber 30.00
  - Green/Blue 40.00
  - Maiden's Blush 40.00
- Cologne 40.00
  - Amber 45.00
  - Green/Blue 55.00
  - Maiden's Blush 60.00
- Compote 35.00
  - Amber 40.00
  - Green/Blue 45.00
  - Maiden's Blush 45.00
- Creamer or Spooner 30.00
  - Amber 35.00
  - Green/Blue 40.00
  - Maiden's Blush 45.00
- Custard Cup 15.00
  - Amber 20.00
  - Green/Blue 25.00
  - Maiden's Blush 25.00
- Jelly Compote 25.00
  - Amber 30.00
  - Green/Blue 35.00
  - Maiden's Blush 35.00
- Pickle Tray 20.00
  - Amber 25.00
  - Green/Blue 30.00
  - Maiden's Blush 30.00
- Plate 20.00
  - Amber 25.00
  - Green/Blue 30.00
  - Maiden's Blush 35.00
- Pitcher, 2 Sizes . . . . . 55.00 – 70.00
  - Amber . . . . . 65.00 – 80.00
  - Green/Blue . . . . . 75.00 – 100.00
  - Maiden's Blush . . . . . 80.00 – 125.00
- Tumbler, 2 Sizes . . . . . 15.00 – 25.00
  - Amber . . . . . 20.00 – 30.00
  - Green/Blue . . . . . 25.00 – 35.00
  - Maiden's Blush . . . . . 30.00 – 40.00
- Shakers, ea. 20.00
  - Amber 25.00
  - Green/Blue 30.00
  - Maiden's Blush 40.00
- Sugar 35.00
  - Amber 40.00
  - Green/Blue 50.00
  - Maiden's Blush 55.00
- Syrup 60.00
  - Amber 75.00
  - Green/Blue 90.00
  - Maiden's Blush 110.00
- Soap Dish 20.00
  - Amber 25.00
  - Green/Blue 30.00
  - Maiden's Blush 35.00
- Toothpick Hldr. 40.00
  - Amber 50.00
  - Green/Blue 55.00
  - Maiden's Blush 65.00
- Tray 30.00
  - Amber 35.00
  - Green/Blue 40.00
  - Maiden's Blush 45.00

BRYAN, WM. J.
- Tumbler 95.00

BRYCE FASHION
- Butter Dish, Amber 135.00
  - Vaseline 235.00
  - Green/Blue 150.00
  - Ruby Stain 135.00
  - Amethyst 140.00
- Creamer, from Cup 30.00

- Amber ... 35.00
- Vaseline ... 50.00
- Green/Blue ... 45.00
- Ruby Stain ... 40.00
- Amethyst ... 45.00

Creamer, from Toothpick ... 35.00
- Amber ... 45.00
- Vaseline ... 60.00
- Green/Blue ... 55.00
- Ruby Stain ... 45.00
- Amethyst ... 50.00

Cup ... 20.00
- Amber ... 25.00
- Vaseline ... 35.00
- Green/Blue ... 30.00
- Ruby Stain ... 25.00
- Amethyst ... 35.00

Toothpick Hldr. ... 25.00
- Amber ... 30.00
- Vaseline ... 45.00
- Green/Blue ... 45.00
- Ruby Stain ... 30.00
- Amethyst ... 40.00

BRYCE HOBNAIL

- Bowls, Various ... 15.00 – 30.00
  - Ruby Stain ... 25.00 – 60.00
- Butter ... 45.00
  - Ruby Stain ... 75.00
- Celery Vase ... 25.00
  - Ruby Stain ... 35.00
- Compote, Covered ... 45.00
  - Ruby Stain ... 60.00
- Compote, Open ... 35.00
  - Ruby Stain ... 40.00
- Creamer or Spooner ... 30.00
  - Ruby Stain ... 40.00
- Goblet ... 40.00
  - Ruby Stain ... 55.00
- Mug ... 35.00
  - Ruby Stain ... 50.00
- Pickle Dish ... 20.00
  - Ruby Stain ... 25.00
- Sugar ... 40.00
  - Ruby Stain ... 60.00
- Wine ... 20.00
  - Ruby Stain ... 30.00

BRYCE PANEL

- Butter ... 50.00
- Celery Vase ... 20.00
- Creamer or Spooner ... 20.00
- Sugar ... 25.00
- Syrup ... 45.00

BRYCE RIBBON CANDY

- Bowl, Oval, w/Lid, 4" and 5" ... 45.00
- Bowl, Oval, w/Lid, 6" and 8" ... 65.00
- Bowl, Oval, Open, 4" and 5" ... 35.00
- Bowl, Oval, Open, 6" and 8" ... 50.00
- Bread Plate ... 25.00
- Butter ... 60.00
- Cake Plate ... 35.00
- Cake Stand ... 50.00
- Celery Vase ... 25.00
- Child's Table Set ... 100.00
- Claret ... 20.00
- Compote w/Lid, High or Low,
  - 5" and 6" ... 30.00 – 50.00
  - 7" and 8" ... 35.00 – 60.00
- Compote, Open, High or Low,
  - 5", 6", and 7" ... 20.00 – 40.00
  - 8" and 10" ... 30.00 – 50.00
- Cordial ... 20.00
- Creamer or Spooner ... 20.00
- Cruet ... 50.00
- Cup & Saucer ... 30.00
- Goblet ... 35.00
- Honey Dish ... 25.00
- Lamp ... 70.00
- Milk Pitcher ... 55.00
- Pickle Dish ... 20.00
- Plate, 6" and 7" ... 20.00
- Plate, 8" – 10" ... 30.00
- Pitcher ... 75.00
- Tumbler ... 20.00
- Relish ... 20.00
- Sauce, Flat or Ftd. ... 15.00
- Shakers, ea. ... 25.00
- Sugar ... 25.00
- Syrup ... 60.00
- Wine ... 15.00

BUCKINGHAM

- Basket ... 45.00
- Bowl, Adv., Tri-corner ... 60.00
- Butter ... 60.00
- Celery Vase ... 25.00
- Compote, Covered ... 45.00
- Compote, Open ... 35.00
- Creamer or Spooner ... 25.00
- Goblet ... 40.00
- Pitcher ... 85.00
- Tumbler ... 20.00
- Toothpick Hldr., 3 Hndls. ... 30.00
- Sugar ... 30.00

BUCKLE AND DIAMOND

- Bowls ... 10.00 – 35.00
- Butter ... 65.00
- Creamer or Spooner ... 20.00
- Goblet ... 45.00
- Pitcher ... 80.00
- Tumbler ... 20.00
- Sugar ... 30.00

BUCKLE WITH ENGLISH HOBNAIL

- Berry Bowl, Sm. ... 15.00
- Berry Bowl, Lg. ... 40.00
- Butter ... 70.00
- Celery Vase ... 30.00
- Creamer or Spooner ... 25.00
- Pickle Dish ... 25.00
- Shakers, ea. ... 25.00
- Sugar ... 25.00

BUCKLE WITH STAR

- Bowls, Covered, 7" – 10" ... 35.00 – 75.00
- Butter ... 75.00
- Cake Stand ... 35.00
- Celery Vase ... 25.00
- Cologne Bottle ... 50.00
- Compote, Covered, 7" ... 55.00
- Compote, Open, 9½" ... 40.00
- Creamer or Spooner ... 25.00
- Goblet ... 55.00
- Honey Dish ... 20.00
- Mug ... 35.00
- Mustard Jar ... 40.00
- Pitcher ... 110.00
- Tumbler ... 20.00
- Tumbler, Hndl. ... 30.00
- Relish Tray ... 20.00
- Salt, Master ... 20.00
- Sauce, Flat or Ftd. ... 15.00
- Sugar ... 35.00
- Syrup ... 70.00
- Wine ... 15.00

BULLET EMBLEM

- Butter ... 475.00
- Creamer or Spooner ... 225.00
- Sugar ... 350.00

BULLS-EYE AND DAISY

- Butter ... 50.00
  - Ruby Stain ... 100.00
  - Green Stain ... 65.00
- Creamer or Spooner ... 25.00
  - Ruby Stain ... 45.00
  - Green Stain ... 30.00
- Goblet ... 25.00
  - Ruby Stain ... 50.00
  - Green Stain ... 30.00
- Pitcher ... 65.00
  - Ruby Stain ... 145.00
  - Green Stain ... 75.00
- Tumbler ... 20.00
  - Ruby Stain ... 30.00
  - Green Stain ... 25.00
- Shakers, ea. ... 30.00
  - Ruby Stain ... 50.00
  - Green Stain ... 35.00
- Sugar ... 25.00
  - Ruby Stain ... 70.00
  - Green Stain ... 40.00
- Syrup ... 45.00
  - Ruby Stain ... 135.00
  - Green Stain ... 65.00
- Toothpick Hldr. ... 35.00
  - Ruby Stain ... 65.00
  - Green Stain ... 45.00
- Wine ... 20.00
  - Ruby Stain ... 40.00
  - Green Stain ... 30.00

BULLS-EYE AND FAN

- Berry Bowl, Lg. ... 25.00
  - Green/Blue ... 35.00
  - Sapphire Stain ... 35.00
- Berry Bowl, Sm. ... 10.00
  - Green/Blue ... 15.00
- Butter ... 70.00
  - Green/Blue ... 95.00
- Cake Stand ... 55.00
- Creamer or Spooner ... 30.00
  - Green/Blue ... 45.00
  - Sapphire Stain ... 45.00
- Goblet ... 35.00
  - Green/Blue ... 50.00
  - Amethyst Stain ... 60.00
- Mug ... 30.00
- Pitcher, 2 Sizes ... 50.00 – 75.00
  - Green/Blue ... 100.00
  - Sapphire Stain ... 120.00
- Tumbler ... 20.00
  - Green/Blue ... 50.00
  - Sapphire Stain ... 55.00
- Sugar ... 40.00
  - Green/Blue ... 60.00
  - Amethyst Stain ... 65.00
- Toothpick Hldr. ... 30.00
  - Green/Blue ... 45.00
- Wine ... 20.00
  - Green/Blue ... 40.00
  - Sapphire Stain ... 45.00

BUTTERFLY

- Bowls, Various ... 20.00 – 50.00
- Butter ... 95.00
- Celery Vase ... 40.00
- Compote, Covered ... 65.00
- Creamer or Spooner ... 35.00
- Mustard Jar ... 60.00
- Pickle Dish ... 30.00
- Pitcher ... 250.00
- Tumbler ... 35.00
- Relish Dish ... 25.00
- Shakers, ea. ... 35.00
- Sugar ... 50.00

BUTTERFLY AND BERRY (FENTON)

- Vase, Scarce ... 40.00
  - Red ... 125.00

BUTTERFLY AND THISTLE

- Bowl, 9", Scarce ... 50.00

BUTTERFLY (PLAIN) (U.S. GLASS)

- Butter ... 115.00
- Celery Vase ... 65.00
- Compote, Covered ... 145.00
- Creamer or Spooner ... 45.00
- Shakres, ea. ... 40.00
- Sugar ... 60.00

BUTTERFLY (FROSTED) (AETNA)

- Butter ... 135.00
- Celery Vase ... 75.00
- Compote, Covered ... 165.00
- Creamer or Spooner ... 60.00
- Shakers, ea. ... 55.00
- Suger ... 70.00

BUTTERFLY WITH SPRAY

- Butter ... 75.00
- Celery ... 20.00
- Compote, Covered, High or Low ... 50.00
- Creamer or Spooner ... 20.00
- Mug ... 25.00
- Mug, Child's ... 40.00
- Pitcher ... 90.00

Tumbler 20.00

BUTTON ARCHES

Bowl 20.00
Ruby Stain 45.00
Butter 55.00
Ruby Stain 125.00
Cake Stand 45.00
Ruby Stain 175.00
Celery Vase 25.00
Ruby Stain 75.00
Compote, Jelly 30.00
Ruby Stain 45.00
Creamer or Spooner 20.00
Ruby Stain 45.00
Cruet 40.00
Ruby Stain 165.00
Milk Pitcher 35.00
Ruby Stain 100.00
Mustard Jar 25.00
Ruby Stain 125.00
Pitcher 75.00
Ruby Stain 145.00
Tumbler 20.00
Ruby Stain 40.00
Toothpick Hldr 25.00
Ruby Stain 50.00
Salt Shaker, Ea 20.00
Ruby Stain 40.00
Sauce 15.00
Ruby Stain 25.00
Syrup 60.00
Ruby Stain 185.00
Toy Mug 30.00
Ruby Stain 60.00
Amethyst 100.00
Wine 20.00
Ruby Stain 35.00

BUTTON CENTER ABC

Plate 75.00

BUTTON PANEL

Berry Bowl, Sm 15.00
Berry Bowl, Lg 35.00
Butter 60.00
Creamer or Spooner 25.00
Cruet 55.00
Pickle Dish 20.00
Sauce 15.00
Sugar 20.00
Toothpick Hldr 35.00
Toy Table Set, Complete 85.00

BUTTRESSED LOOP

Bowl, Covered 50.00
Butter 55.00
Compote 30.00
Creamer or Spooner 20.00
Sugar 25.00

BUZZ-STAR

Berry Bowl, Sm 20.00
Berry Bowl, Lg 45.00
Butter 65.00
Creamer or Spooner 25.00
Goblet 45.00
Pickle Dish 20.00
Pitcher 85.00
Tumbler 20.00
Salt Dip 15.00
Sugar 30.00
Toy Punch Set 145.00
Toy Table Set (Whirligig) 125.00
Wine 15.00

BY JINGO

Mug 60.00

CABBAGE ROSE

Basket, Hndl 75.00
Bitters Bottle 65.00
Bowl, Oval or Rnd., 6" – 8" . . . . . 20.00 – 40.00
Butter 65.00
Cake Plate 30.00
Cake Stand, 9" – 12½" . . . . . 30.00 – 55.00
Celery Vase 20.00
Champagne 15.00
Compote, Covered, 6" – 11" . . . . . 45.00 – 90.00
Cordial 25.00
Creamer or Spooner 20.00
Egg Cup 25.00
Goblet 45.00
Milk Pitcher 70.00
Mug 30.00
Pickle Dish 15.00
Pitcher 90.00
Tumbler 20.00
Relish Dish 15.00
Salt Dip, Master 20.00
Sugar 30.00
Wine 25.00

CABLE AND THUMBPRINT

Match Holder 30.00
Vaseline 80.00

CACTUS

Bowl, 8" – 9½", Rare 400.00

CAMBRIDGE #2351

Berry Bowl, Sm 10.00
Berry Bowl, Lg 35.00
Butter 75.00
Celery, Tall 25.00
Cologne Bottle 45.00
Compote, Lg 60.00
Creamer or Spooner 25.00
Custard Cup 10.00
Jelly Compote 30.00
Jug, Squat 55.00
Oil Bottle 40.00
Olive, Hndl 25.00
Orange Bowl Ftd 55.00
Pitcher 90.00
Tumbler 20.00
Punch Bowl 125.00
Punch Cup 10.00
Shakers, ea 25.00
Sherbet 15.00
Spoon Tray 20.00
Sugar 30.00
Vase, 7" 25.00
Vase, Pedestal 30.00
Whiskey Set w/tray 100.00

CAMBRIDGE #2467

Punch Bowl & Base 145.00
Adv. Punch Bowl, & Base, Rare 250.00

CAMBRIDGE #2658

Creamer 30.00
Ruby Stain 45.00
Mug 50.00
Ruby Stain 60.00

CAMBRIDGE #2660

Basket 45.00
Bowl, Sq., 6" 25.00
Butter 65.00
Cake Stand 45.00
Celery Tray 30.00
Celery Vase 25.00
Cologne Bottle 35.00
Compote 40.00
Creamer or Spooner 25.00
Cruet 65.00
Custard Cup 15.00
Decanter 55.00
Jelly Compote 25.00
Oil Lamp, 18" w/10" Shade 225.00
Plate, Sq., 7" 45.00
Punch Bowl 175.00
Punch Cup 20.00
Pitcher 90.00
Tumbler 25.00
Rose Bowl 30.00
Sauce 15.00
Sherbet, Hnld., on Stem 40.00
Toy Punch Set, Complete 75.00
Wine 15.00

CAMBRIDGE BUZZ SAW

Basket, Squat Hndl 50.00
Berry Bowl, Sm 15.00
Berry Bowl, Lg 40.00
Bowl, 5" – 7" 20.00
Bowl, 8" – 9" 45.00
Butter 65.00
Celery Tray 30.00
Celery Vase 25.00
Cologne 70.00
Creamer or Spooner 25.00
Cruet 75.00
Milk Pitcher, 2 Sizes . . . . . 45.00 – 60.00
Nut Bowl, 5" – 7" 25.00
Olive Nappy 20.00
Pitcher 95.00
Tumbler 25.00
Rose Bowl 35.00
Shakers, ea 25.00
Sherbet 25.00
Sugar 30.00
Syrup 65.00

CAMBRIDGE HERON

Figure Flower Holder, 9" – 20" . . . . . 65.00 – 165.00

CAMBRIDGE NEAR-CUT #2653

Celery Vase 35.00
Cracker Jar w/Lid 80.00
Goblet 45.00
Ice Cream Bowl, Sm., Rect 20.00
Ice Cream Bowl, Lg., Rect 45.00
Jelly Compote 35.00
Pickle Tray 20.00
Pitcher, 1 Qt., Squat 80.00
Pitcher 125.00
Tumbler 25.00
Punch Bowl w/Base 175.00
Punch Cup 15.00
Sherbet 20.00

CAMBRIDGE SEMITAR #2647

Bonbon, Ftd 25.00
Bowls, 4½" – 9" . . . . . 15.00 – 45.00
Bowl, Special Deep, 9" 50.00
Butter 70.00
Celery Tray 30.00
Creamer or Spooner 30.00
Cruet 70.00
Custard Cup 15.00
Jelly Compote 25.00
Nappy 20.00
Pickle Tray 25.00
Plate, 6" – 8" 35.00
Pitcher, 2 Sizes . . . . . 70.00 – 95.00
Punch Bowl, 2 Sizes . . . . . 125.00 – 160.00
Punch Bowl, Advertising 300.00
Tumbler 25.00
Whiskey Tumbler 30.00
Shakers, ea 25.00
Spoon Tray 30.00
Sugar 50.00
Water Bottle 60.00

CANADIAN

Bowls, Covered . . . . . 35.00 – 75.00
Bowls, Open . . . . . 20.00 – 55.00
Bread Plate 35.00
Butter 90.00
Cake Stand 50.00
Compote w/Lid, High, 6" – 10" . . . . . 50.00 – 110.00
Compote w/Lid, Low, 6" – 8" . . . . . 35.00 – 85.00
Compote, Open, High or Low . . . . . 25.00 – 65.00
Creamer or Spooner 85.00
Goblet 70.00
Jam Jar 65.00
Milk Pitcher 75.00
Mug 45.00
Plate, 6" – 12" . . . . . 20.00 – 50.00
Pitcher 110.00
Tumbler 25.00
Sauce 20.00
Sugar 90.00
Wine 35.00

CANE

Berry Bowl, Sm 10.00
Amber 15.00
Vaseline 25.00
Green/Blue 20.00
Berry Bowl, Lg 25.00
Amber 30.00
Vaseline 35.00

Green/Blue. 35.00
Bowl, Oval 30.00
Amber 50.00
Vaseline. 65.00
Green/Blue. 70.00
Butter. 45.00
Amber 60.00
Vaseline. 95.00
Green/Blue. 75.00
Celery Vase 20.00
Amber 25.00
Vaseline. 30.00
Green/Blue. 25.00
Compote. 25.00
Amber 40.00
Vaseline. 55.00
Green/Blue. 45.00
Cordial 15.00
Amber 20.00
Vaseline. 30.00
Green/Blue. 40.00
Creamer or Spooner. 20.00
Amber 30.00
Vaseline. 45.00
Green/Blue. 45.00
Finger Bowl 15.00
Amber 20.00
Vaseline. 30.00
Green/Blue. 25.00
Goblet 20.00
Amber 30.00
Vaseline. 45.00
Green/Blue. 40.00
Honey Dish 15.00
Amber 20.00
Vaseline. 30.00
Green/Blue. 25.00
Match Hldr, Kettle Shape. 35.00
Amber 50.00
Vaseline. 75.00
Green/Blue. 90.00
Milk Pitcher. 40.00
Amber 65.00
Vaseline. 100.00
Green/Blue. 100.00
Pickle Dish. 15.00
Amber 20.00
Vaseline. 30.00
Green/Blue. 25.00
Plate, 4½". 15.00
Amber 20.00
Vaseline. 35.00
Green/Blue. 25.00
Pitcher 70.00
Amber 95.00
Vaseline. 145.00
Green/Blue. 165.00
Tumbler 20.00
Amber 25.00
Vaseline. 40.00
Green/Blue. 30.00
Relish. 15.00
Amber 20.00
Vaseline. 35.00
Green/Blue. 45.00
Sauce, Flat or Ftd. 15.00
Amber 20.00
Vaseline. 25.00
Green/Blue. 25.00
Amber 25.00
Shakers, ea. 25.00
Vaseline. 65.00
Green/Blue. 60.00
Slipper 25.00
Amber 30.00
Vaseline. 60.00
Green/Blue. 45.00
Sugar 25.00
Amber 40.00
Vaseline. 65.00
Green/Blue. 70.00
Tray 25.00
Amber 30.00
Vaseline. 70.00
Green/Blue. 45.00
Wine 20.00
Amber 25.00
Vaseline. 40.00
Green/Blue. 40.00
Waste Bowl 15.00
Amber 20.00
Vaseline. 30.00
Green/Blue. 30.00

CANE COLUMN
Butter. 45.00
Celery Vase 20.00
Creamer or Spooner. 20.00
Cruet 45.00
Pitcher 60.00
Tumbler 15.00
Sauce 10.00
Sugar 30.00
Wine 15.00

CANE HORSESHOE
Berry Bowl, Sm. 20.00
Berry Bowl, Lg. 45.00
Butter. 60.00
Cake Stand. 40.00
Celery Tray. 25.00
Compote. 35.00
Creamer or Spooner. 25.00
Cruet 50.00
Pitcher 60.00
Tumbler 15.00
Shaker 35.00
Sugar 25.00

CANE INSERT
Berry Bowl, Sm. 15.00
Berry Bowl, Lg. 35.00
Butter. 45.00
Cake Stand. 30.00
Carafe 40.00
Celery Vase, Rare. 75.00
Compote. 35.00
Creamer or Spooner. 20.00
Goblet 35.00
Hair Receiver. 40.00
Mug 30.00
Pitcher 70.00
Tumbler 20.00
Sugar 30.00

CANE PINWHEEL
Berry Bowl, Sm. 20.00
Berry Bowl, Lg. 50.00
Bowls, Various . . . . . 10.00 – 35.00
Butter. 75.00
Celery Tray. 20.00
Cologne Bottle 45.00
Creamer or Spooner. 25.00
Cruet 50.00
Pitcher, Qt., 2 Shapes . . . . . 100.00 – 135.00
Sugar 35.00
Syrup 60.00

CANNONBALL PINWHEEL
Berry Bowl, Sm. 15.00
Berry Bowl, Lg. 35.00
Butter. 70.00
Celery Vase 25.00
Cherry Tray, 10". 30.00
Creamer or Spooner. 20.00
Cup 15.00
Fruit Plate, 9". 25.00
Goblet 35.00
Jelly Compote. 25.00
Milk Pitcher. 55.00
Nappy 25.00
Olive Dish, Sq. 25.00
Pickle Dish. 20.00
Plate, 6", Sq. 20.00
Pitcher 75.00
Tumbler 15.00
Shakers, ea. 20.00
Sherbet. 15.00
Sugar 25.00
Tall Sugar, Hndl. 30.00
Wine 20.00

CAPITOL
Creamer 25.00
Mug 40.00
Perfume 45.00
Puff Box 50.00
Sugar 30.00
Toothpick Hldr. 35.00

CAPRICE (Condensed List)
Bowls, Various . . . . . 10.00 – 45.00
Bitters Bottle 65.00
Cigarette Ashtray 25.00
Cigarette Box 45.00
Cigarette Hldr. 35.00
Compote, Various . . . . . 25.00 – 65.00
Condiment Set 100.00
Decanter 70.00
Goblet 30.00
Ice Bucket 65.00
Pitcher 125.00
Tumbler 30.00
Shakers, ea. 25.00

CARDINAL
Berry Bowl, Sm. 25.00
Berry Bowl, Lg. 55.00
Butter. 80.00
Cake Stand. 40.00
Creamer or Spooner. 30.00
Goblet 60.00
Honey Dish, Covered or Open . . 35.00 – 60.00
Pitcher 125.00
Tumbler 25.00
Sauce, Flat or Ftd. 20.00
Sugar 35.00

CARLTEC
Basket 45.00
Berry Bowl, Lg. 40.00
Berry Bowl, Sm. 15.00
Bonbon 20.00
Bowls, Various . . . . . 20.00 – 35.00
Butter. 65.00
Celery Bowl 20.00
Compote, Hndl. 45.00
Creamer or Spooner. 30.00
Olive Tray 25.00
Pickle Dish. 20.00
Plate 30.00
Pitcher 85.00
Preserve Dishes, Various . . . . . 20.00 – 30.00
Rose Bowl 30.00
Spoon Tray 35.00
Sugar 40.00
Tumbler 20.00

CARNATION (LANCASTER)
Berry Bowl, Sm. 15.00
Berry Bowl, Lg. 40.00
Butter. 60.00
Creamer or Spooner. 20.00
Goblet 40.00
Milk Pitcher. 65.00
Pickle Dish. 15.00
Pitcher 80.00
Tumbler 20.00
Sugar 25.00

CARNATION (NEW MARTINSVILLE)
Goblet 35.00
Ruby Stain. 45.00
Pickle Dish. 20.00
Ruby Stain. 25.00
Pitcher 60.00
Ruby Stain. 80.00
Tumbler 15.00
Ruby Stain. 25.00
Toothpick Hldr. 35.00
Ruby Stain. 45.00
Wine 20.00
Ruby Stain. 25.00

CARNATION WITH ELK
Plate, 9" – 13" . . . . . 35.00 – 60.00

CARSON FURNITURE
Advertising Pickle Tray 45.00

CATHEDRAL
Bowl, 5" – 6" . . . 20.00
Amber . . . 30.00
Vaseline . . . 30.00
Green/Blue . . . 40.00
Amethyst . . . 65.00
Bowl, 7" – 8" . . . 45.00
Amber . . . 35.00
Vaseline . . . 50.00
Green/Blue . . . 45.00
Amethyst . . . 85.00
Butter . . . 45.00
Amber . . . 65.00
Vaseline . . . 125.00
Green/Blue . . . 75.00
Amethyst . . . 125.00
Cake Stand . . . 35.00
Amber . . . 45.00
Vaseline . . . 125.00
Green/Blue . . . 55.00
Amethyst . . . 85.00
Celery Vase . . . 25.00
Amber . . . 30.00
Vaseline . . . 55.00
Green/Blue . . . 40.00
Amethyst . . . 55.00
Compote, Covered . . . 55.00
Amber . . . 65.00
Vaseline . . . 150.00
Green/Blue . . . 75.00
Amethyst . . . 100.00
Compote, Open . . . 40.00
Amber . . . 45.00
Vaseline . . . 95.00
Green/Blue . . . 50.00
Amethyst . . . 80.00
Creamer or Spooner . . . 20.00
Amber . . . 25.00
Vaseline . . . 55.00
Green/Blue . . . 35.00
Amethyst . . . 50.00
Cruet . . . 60.00
Amber . . . 85.00
Vaseline . . . 150.00
Green/Blue . . . 90.00
Amethyst . . . 125.00
Goblet . . . 45.00
Amber . . . 60.00
Vaseline . . . 70.00
Green/Blue . . . 75.00
Amethyst . . . 100.00
Lamp . . . 75.00
Green/Blue . . . 200.00
Mug . . . 30.00
Amber . . . 40.00
Vaseline . . . 55.00
Green/Blue . . . 45.00
Amethyst . . . 65.00
Pitcher . . . 70.00
Amber . . . 95.00
Vaseline . . . 145.00
Green/Blue . . . 115.00
Amethyst . . . 165.00
Tumbler . . . 20.00
Amber . . . 30.00
Vaseline . . . 50.00
Green/Blue . . . 40.00
Amethyst . . . 55.00
Relish Tray . . . 15.00
Amber . . . 25.00
Vaseline . . . 55.00
Green/Blue . . . 30.00
Amethyst . . . 40.00
Salt Boat . . . 20.00
Amber . . . 30.00
Vaseline . . . 40.00
Green/Blue . . . 40.00
Amethyst . . . 50.00
Sauce . . . 15.00
Amber . . . 20.00
Vaseline . . . 20.00
Green/Blue . . . 30.00
Amethyst . . . 40.00
Sugar . . . 30.00
Amber . . . 40.00
Vaseline . . . 65.00
Green/Blue . . . 50.00
Amethyst . . . 70.00

CAT IN A TANGLE
Mug . . . 70.00
Amber . . . 90.00

CAT'S EYE (BRETON)
Bowls, Various . . . 20.00 – 50.00
Butter . . . 70.00
Creamer or Spooner . . . 25.00
Pickle Dish . . . 20.00
Sugar . . . 30.00
Wine . . . 40.00

CAT'S EYE AND FAN
Berry Bowl, Sm. . . . 20.00
Berry Bowl, Lg. . . . 45.00
Bowl, Lg., Ftd. . . . 40.00
Butter . . . 55.00
Compote . . . 35.00
Creamer or Spooner . . . 25.00
Sauce . . . 15.00
Sugar . . . 30.00

CAT UP A TREE WITH DOG
Pitcher, Tall, Rare . . . 450.00

CENTENNIAL DRAPE
Bread Plate . . . 35.00
Butter . . . 65.00
Creamer or Spooner . . . 30.00
Goblet . . . 50.00
Pickle Dish . . . 25.00
Sugar . . . 45.00

CENTENNIAL EXHIBITION SHOE
Slipper . . . 200.00

CENTER MEDALLION
Butter . . . 65.00
Compote, Covered . . . 45.00
Creamer or Spooner . . . 20.00
Sugar . . . 30.00

CENTIPEDE
Butter . . . 45.00
Creamer or Spooner . . . 20.00
Pickle Dish . . . 15.00
Relish . . . 20.00
Shakers, ea. . . . 25.00
Sugar . . . 25.00

CENTRAL'S CABBAGE ROSE
Basket . . . 55.00
Bitters Bottle . . . 80.00
Bottle . . . 65.00
Bowl, Oval . . . 30.00
Bowl, Round . . . 25.00
Butter . . . 75.00
Cake Plate, 6 Sizes . . . 30.00 – 75.00
Celery Vase . . . 25.00
Champagne . . . 25.00
Compote, Covered, 8 Sizes . . . 60.00 – 110.00
Compote, Open, 4 Sizes . . . 45.00 – 90.00
Cordial . . . 20.00
Creamer or Spooner . . . 25.00
Egg Cup . . . 25.00
Goblet . . . 30.00
Mug . . . 35.00
Pickle Dish . . . 20.00
Pitcher . . . 100.00
Relish Dish . . . 20.00
Salt, Master . . . 25.00
Sauce . . . 15.00
Sugar . . . 40.00
Tumbler . . . 25.00
Wine . . . 20.00

CHAIN
Berry Bowl, Sm. . . . 10.00
Berry Bowl, Lg. . . . 30.00
Butter . . . 45.00
Compote, Covered . . . 35.00
Cordial . . . 15.00
Creamer or Spooner . . . 20.00
Sugar . . . 25.00
Wine . . . 15.00

CHAIN AND SHIELD
Butter . . . 65.00
Celery Vase . . . 20.00
Creamer or Spooner . . . 20.00
Goblet . . . 55.00
Plate, 7" – 11" . . . 20.00 – 40.00
Platter, Oval . . . 35.00
Pitcher . . . 90.00
Tumbler . . . 20.00
Sauce . . . 10.00
Sugar . . . 30.00
Wine . . . 15.00

CHAIN WITH STAR
Berry Bowl, Sm. . . . 20.00
Berry Bowl, Lg. . . . 40.00
Butter . . . 55.00
Cake Stand . . . 30.00
Creamer or Spooner . . . 25.00
Pickle Dish . . . 20.00
Plate . . . 25.00
Relish . . . 20.00
Sauce . . . 15.00
Shakers, ea. . . . 20.00
Sugar . . . 25.00
Wine . . . 20.00

CHANDELIER
Banana Stand . . . 125.00
Engraved . . . 145.00
Bowl . . . 40.00
Engraved . . . 50.00
Butter . . . 70.00
Engraved . . . 80.00
Cake Stand . . . 80.00
Engraved . . . 95.00
Caster Set, Complete . . . 125.00
Engraved . . . 150.00
Celery Vase . . . 35.00
Engraved . . . 40.00
Compote, Covered . . . 85.00
Engraved . . . 100.00
Compote, Open, 8" – 9½" . . . 55.00
Engraved . . . 60.00
Creamer or Spooner . . . 55.00
Engraved . . . 60.00
Finger Bowl . . . 35.00
Engraved . . . 40.00
Goblet . . . 75.00
Engraved . . . 85.00
Inkwell, Lettered & Dated . . . 110.00
Engraved . . . 125.00
Pitcher . . . 165.00
Engraved . . . 200.00
Tumbler . . . 50.00
Engraved . . . 60.00
Salt, Master . . . 25.00
Engraved . . . 30.00
Sauce . . . 20.00
Engraved . . . 25.00
Shakers, ea. . . . 100.00
Engraved . . . 125.00
Sugar . . . 90.00
Engraved . . . 100.00
Sugar Shaker . . . 130.00
Engraved . . . 155.00
Violet Bowl . . . 35.00
Engraved . . . 40.00
Water Tray . . . 40.00
Engraved . . . 45.00

CHATELAINE
Pitcher . . . 175.00
Tumbler . . . 40.00

CHERRY
Berry Bowl, Lg. . . . 55.00
Berry Bowl, Sm. . . . 20.00
Bowls, Novelty . . . 20.00 – 45.00
Butter . . . 70.00
Champagne . . . 25.00
Compote, Covered . . . 60.00
Compote, Open . . . 35.00
Creamer or Spooner . . . 25.00
Goblet . . . 30.00
Plate . . . 35.00

Sugar 40.00
Wine 25.00

CHERRY

Child's Mug 30.00

CHERRY AND CABLE

Berry Bowl, Sm. 25.00
Berry Bowl, Lg. 55.00
Butter 80.00
Compote 55.00
Creamer or Spooner 30.00
Pitcher 125.00
Tumbler 25.00
Punch Bowl, Rare 300.00
Punch Cup, Scarce 25.00
Sugar 35.00
Syrup 80.00

CHERRY AND FIG

Berry Bowl, Sm. 15.00
Berry Bowl, Lg. 55.00
Butter 85.00
Celery Vase 20.00
Compote, Covered 55.00
Compote, Open 30.00
Creamer or Spooner 25.00
Goblet 60.00
Pickle Dish 20.00
Pitcher 110.00
Tumbler 25.00
Sugar 35.00
Wine 20.00

CHERRY LATTICE

Berry Bowl, Sm. 25.00
Berry Bowl, Lg. 55.00
Butter 70.00
Compote 50.00
Creamer or Spooner 25.00
Pitcher 90.00
Tumbler 20.00
Sugar 30.00

CHERRY WITH THUMBPRINTS

Bean Pot, Covered 45.00
Berry Bowl, Sm. 15.00
Berry Bowl, Lg. 35.00
Covered Bowls, Several Sizes . . . 20.00 – 50.00
Lemonade Tumbler 25.00
Mug 20.00
Pitcher 65.00
Tumbler 15.00
Sauce 15.00
Syrup 50.00
Toothpick Hldr. 30.00
Wine 20.00

CHESTNUT OAK

Butter 65.00
Celery Dish 20.00
Compote, Covered 55.00
Compote, Open 35.00
Creamer, 2 Styles . . . . 15.00 – 25.00
Egg Cup 20.00
Goblet 35.00
Pitcher 95.00
Tumbler 20.00
Sauce, Flat 15.00
Spooner 30.00
Sugar, Open or Covered . . . . 20.00 – 35.00

CHICK AND PUGS

Mug 55.00
Amber 65.00
Vaseline 75.00
Green/Blue 85.00

CHICKEN FOOT STEM

Goblet, Rare 300.00

CHIPPENDALE

Butter 75.00
Creamer or Spooner 25.00
Goblet 50.00
Pickle Tray 25.00
Pitcher 95.00
Tumbler 20.00
Relish Dish 20.00
Shakers, ea. 30.00
Sugar 35.00

Toothpick Hldr. 40.00

CHRYSANTHEMUM LEAF

Berry Bowl, Sm. 20.00
Berry Bowl, Lg. 45.00
Butter 55.00
Carafe 35.00
Compote 35.00
Cracker Jar 30.00
Creamer or Spooner 20.00
Cruet 60.00
Pitcher 75.00
Tumbler 20.00
Sauce 15.00
Shakers, ea. 20.00
Sugar 30.00
Syrup 65.00
Toothpick Hldr. 30.00

CHRYSANTHEMUM SPRIG (PAGODA)

Berry Bowl, Lg., Custard 195.00
Berry Bowl, Sm., Custard 75.00
Butter, Custard 250.00
Celery Vase, Custard 165.00
Compote, Custard 100.00
Condiment Set, Custard 325.00
Creamer or Spooner, Custard 125.00
Cruet, Custard 225.00
Pitcher, Custard 450.00
Tumbler, Custard 95.00
Sugar, Custard 165.00
Toothpick Hldr., Custard 125.00

CHURCH WINDOWS

Bowl 20.00
Butter 65.00
Cake Stand 40.00
Celery Vase 25.00
Creamer or Spooner 20.00
Goblet 35.00
Jelly Compote, Covered 45.00
Pitcher 70.00
Sardine Dish 25.00
Sugar 25.00

CIRCULAR SAW

Berry Bowl, Sm. 15.00
Berry Bowl, Lg. 40.00
Breakfast Set 45.00
Butter 55.00
Creamer or Spooner 25.00
Cracker Jar 30.00
Pitcher 65.00
Tumbler 20.00
Punch Bowl 85.00
Punch Cup 15.00
Sauce 15.00
Shakers, ea. 20.00
Sugar 30.00

CLARK'S TEABERRY GUM

Advertising Tray 65.00
Vaseline 115.00
W/Cover, very scarce, vaseline 240.00

CLASSIC

Bowl, Covered, 7" 150.00
Butter 200.00
Celery Vase, 2 Styles 125.00
Compote w/Lid, 6½" – 12½" . . . 150.00 – 250.00
Compote, Open, 7¾" 125.00
Creamer or Spooner, 2 Styles . 125.00 – 150.00
Goblet 275.00
Marmalade Jar w/Lid 375.00
Milk Pitcher, Ftd. 475.00
Pitcher, 2 Styles 300.00
Tumbler 100.00
Plate, "Blaine" 200.00
Plate, "Cleveland" 200.00
Plate, "Hendricks" 175.00
Plate, "Logan" 250.00
Plate, "Warrior" 195.00
Sauce, Flat or Ftd. 35.00
Sugar, 2 Styles 200.00
Sweetmeat 200.00

CLASSIC INTAGLIO

Salt Hldrs. (Either), Green/Blue 150.00

CLASSIC MEDALLION

Bowls, Flat or Ftd., 6½" 25.00
Celery Vase 15.00
Compote, Covered 45.00
Compote, Open 25.00
Creamer or Spooner 15.00
Goblet 35.00
Pitcher 65.00
Sauce 10.00
Sugar 20.00

CLEAR DIAGONAL BAND

Berry Bowl, Lg. 35.00
Berry Bowl, Sm. 15.00
Butter 40.00
Celery Vase 30.00
Compote, High Standard 60.00
Compote, Low 50.00
Creamer, Spooner or Sugar 30.00
Goblet 30.00
Marmalade Jar 35.00
Pitcher 70.00
Tumbler 15.00
Platter 35.00
Shakers, Ea. 20.00

CLEAR LION HEAD

Berry Bowl, Sm. 30.00
Berry Bowl, Lg. 55.00
Butter 75.00
Cake Stand 45.00
Creamer or Spooner 35.00
Jam Jar 45.00
Pickle Dish 35.00
Sauce 25.00
Shakers, ea. 35.00
Sugar 35.00
Toothpick Hldr. 50.00
Toy Table Set 150.00

CLEAR RIBBON

Bread Tray 45.00
Butter 90.00
Celery Vase 30.00
Compote 50.00
Creamer or Spooner 25.00
Goblet 50.00
Pickle Dish 20.00
Pitcher 135.00
Tumbler 25.00
Sauce 15.00
Sugar 45.00

CLEOPATRA (EGYPTIAN)

Tray, Rectangular 95.00

CLIO

Bowl, Sauce, 2 Sizes 20.00
Bowl, Lg. (Fan Corners) 40.00
Bowl, Sm. (Fan Corners) 25.00
Bowl, 7" and 8" Ftd. w/Cover . . . . 65.00 – 75.00
Butter, 2 Sizes . . . . 50.00 – 70.00
Vaseline . . . . 115.00 – 145.00
Celery 35.00
Compote, 4½", Open 30.00
Compote, 7" and 8", Flat 50.00
Creamer, Spooner or Sugar 25.00
Plate, 7" and 10" 35.00
Vaseline . . . . 65.00 – 95.00
Pitcher 90.00
Vaseline 170.00

CLOVER (R AND H)

Berry Bowl, Sm. 15.00
Berry Bowl, Lg. 35.00
Butter 45.00
Creamer or Spooner 20.00
Pitcher 65.00
Tumbler 10.00
Sauce 10.00
Shakers, ea. 20.00
Sugar 25.00

COACHMAN'S CAPE

Goblet 40.00
Wine 25.00

COARSE ZIG ZAG

Berry Bowl, Sm. 20.00
Berry Bowl, Lg. 45.00

Butter 65.00
Creamer or Spooner 25.00
Plate 30.00
Pitcher 70.00
Tumbler 20.00
Shakers, ea. 25.00
Sugar 30.00
Wine 20.00

COIN AND DEW DROP
Goblet 50.00

COLONIAL LADY-#1700
Creamer or Sugar 35.00
Vase, 6" and 9" 45.00

COLONIAL STAIRSTEPS
Butter 55.00
Creamer or Spooner 20.00
Sugar 30.00
Toothpick Hldr. 25.00

COLONIS
Berry Bowl, Sm. 15.00
Berry Bowl, Lg. 35.00
Butter 65.00
Cake Stand 40.00
Celery Vase 30.00
Cordial 25.00
Creamer or Spooner 25.00
Egg Cup 20.00
Milk Pitcher 50.00
Oval Dish 20.00
Pickle Dish, 7" 20.00
Pitcher 80.00
Tumbler 20.00
Sugar 25.00
Syrup 70.00
Tray 30.00

COLORADO
Banana Dish 20.00
Green/Blue 50.00
Bowl, Tri-Corner 20.00
Green/Blue 50.00
Bowl, Lg. 25.00
Green/Blue 45.00
Bowl, Sm. 15.00
Green/Blue 20.00
Cheese Dish, Ftd. 20.00
Green/Blue 60.00
Compote 35.00
Green/Blue 100.00
Creamer, Spooner, or Sugar 20.00
Green/Blue 75.00
Cup, Engraved 20.00
Green/Blue 35.00
Milk Pitcher 100.00
Green/Blue 250.00
Perfume, Rare 65.00
Green/Blue 125.00
Pitcher 85.00
Green/Blue . . . . . 225.00 – 500.00
Tumbler, Flat 35.00
Green/Blue . . . . . 60.00 – 100.00
Shakers, Pr. Ftd. 50.00
Green/Blue 145.00
Toothpick Hldr. 40.00
Green/Blue 55.00
Toy Table Set, Complete 85.00
Green/Blue 175.00
Vase 35.00
Green/Blue 95.00
Violet Bowl 35.00
Green/Blue 55.00
Wine 20.00
Green/Blue 65.00

COLUMBIA
Compote 30.00
Plate, Ftd. 50.00
Vases, Various Shapes 25.00

COLUMBIA #100
Butter 70.00
Vaseline 140.00
Celery Vase 20.00
Vaseline 40.00
Creamer or Spooner 25.00
Vaseline 45.00
Pitcher 90.00
Vaseline 125.00
Sugar 35.00
Vaseline 50.00
Toothpick Hldr. 40.00
Vaseline 60.00
Tumbler 20.00
Vaseline 30.00

COLUMBIAN COIN (U.S. COIN)
Ale Glass 80.00
Berry Bowl, Sm. 25.00
Berry Bowl, Lg. 60.00
Bowl, Covered, 6" – 8" . . . . . 50.00 – 85.00
Bowl, Open, 6" – 8" . . . . . 30.00 – 55.00
Butter 175.00
Cake Stand 450.00
Celery Tray 65.00
Celery Vase 80.00
Champagne 70.00
Compote, Covered, 6" – 8" . . . . . 75.00 – 110.00
Compote, Open, 7" – 8" . . . . . 55.00 – 65.00
Claret 80.00
Creamer or Spooner 80.00
Cruet 70.00
Epergne 250.00
Goblet, 2 Styles 65.00
Milk Pitcher 225.00
Mug, Beer Size 125.00
Pickle Dish 45.00
Pickle Jar w/Lid 70.00
Pitcher 155.00
Tumbler 45.00
Shakers, ea. 110.00
Sugar 75.00
Syrup 275.00
Toothpick Hldr. 45.00
Water Tray 150.00
Waste Bowl 45.00
Wine 85.00

COLUMBUS LANDING
Mug 65.00

COLUMN BLOCK (#500)
Butter 65.00
Vaseline 110.00
Celery Vase 30.00
Vaseline 60.00
Creamer or Spooner 35.00
Vaseline 55.00
Jelly Compote 40.00
Vaseline 60.00
Pickle Dish 30.00
Vaseline 45.00
Pitcher 100.00
Vaseline 165.00
Salt Shaker 45.00
Vaseline 60.00
Sugar 45.00
Vaseline 60.00
Toothpick Hldr. 50.00
Vaseline 65.00

COLUMNED THUMBPRINTS
Berry Bowl, Sm. 10.00
Berry Bowl, Lg. 35.00
Butter 50.00
Celery Vase 20.00
Creamer or Spooner 20.00
Cruet 45.00
Cup 10.00
Pitcher 65.00
Tumbler 10.00
Shakers, ea. 15.00
Sugar 25.00
Syrup 60.00
Toothpick Hldr. 20.00

COMET
Butter 55.00
Compote 30.00
Creamer or Spooner 20.00
Goblet 40.00
Mug 25.00
Pitcher 70.00
Tumbler, 2 Sizes . . . . . 15.00 – 25.00
Sugar 25.00

COMET IN THE STARS
Berry Bowl, Lg. 35.00
Berry Bowl, Sm. 15.00
Bowl, Oval 20.00
Bowl, Sauce 15.00
Butter 45.00
Creamer, Spooner, or Sugar 25.00
Pickle Dish 30.00
Pitcher 65.00
Tumbler 15.00
Relish, Hndl. 25.00

COMPLIMENTS-LOUIS MANKOWITZ
"Country Kitchen" Advertising
Bowl, Very Scarce 350.00
Plate, Rare 425.00

COMPLIMENTS OF ST. LOUIS COFFIN CO.
Punch Bowl & Base 150.00

COMPLIMENTS S.I. FRANK
See Country Kitchen

CONNECTICUT
Basket, Hndl. 35.00
Biscuit Jar 30.00
Bowls, 5" – 8" . . . . . 10.00 – 35.00
Butter 55.00
Celery Tray 15.00
Celery Vase 20.00
Compotes, Covered . . . . . 25.00 – 45.00
Compotes, Open . . . . . 20.00 – 35.00
Creamer or Spooner 15.00
Cruet 60.00
Dish, Oblong or Rnd. 20.00
Goblet 30.00
Jam Jar 25.00
Lemonade Mug 20.00
Oil Lamp 75.00
Plate 20.00
Pitcher, 2 Styles & Sizes . . . . . 65.00 – 85.00
Tumbler 20.00
Relish Tray 15.00
Sauce, Flat or Belled Base 15.00
Shakers, 3 Shapes, ea. 20.00
Sherbet Cup 10.00
Sugar 25.00
Sugar Shaker 35.00
Toothpick Hldr. 20.00
Vase 20.00
Water Bottle 35.00
Wine 10.00

CONSOLIDATED SHELL
Rose Bowl, Rubina 85.00

CONSTITUTION PLATTER
Platter or Bread Plate 65.00

CONTINENTAL PLATTER ("GIVE US THIS DAY")
Platter, Oval, 1776 – 1876 . . . . . 90.00

CO-OP COLUMBIA
Bowl, Various . . . . . 15.00 – 35.00
Butter 50.00
Creamer or Spooner 20.00
Goblet 40.00
Pickle Dish 15.00
Relish Tray 20.00
Shakers, ea. 20.00
Sugar 25.00
Wine 15.00

CO-OP REX
Berry Bowl, Sm. 10.00
Berry Bowl, Lg. 35.00
Butter 55.00
Creamer or Spooner 15.00
Goblet 30.00
Pickle Dish 10.00
Pitcher 65.00
Tumbler 10.00
Sugar 20.00

CO-OP'S ROYAL
Bowls, Various . . . . . 15.00 – 35.00
Ruby Stain . . . . . 25.00 – 55.00
Butter 55.00
Ruby Stain 70.00
Celery Vase 25.00

Ruby Stain . . . 30.00
Creamer or Spooner . . . 30.00
Ruby Stain . . . 35.00
Goblet . . . 40.00
Ruby Stain . . . 50.00
Pickle Dish . . . 20.00
Ruby Stain . . . 30.00
Pitcher . . . 80.00
Ruby Stain . . . 115.00
Tumbler . . . 20.00
Ruby Stain . . . 25.00
Shakers, ea . . . 25.00
Ruby Stain . . . 30.00
Sugar . . . 40.00
Ruby Stain . . . 55.00
Toothpick Hldr . . . 45.00
Ruby Stain . . . 60.00
Wine . . . 20.00
Ruby Stain . . . 30.00

CORAL GABLES
Cruet . . . 55.00
Goblet . . . 40.00
Wine . . . 25.00

CORD DRAPERY
Bowls, Oval or Rnd. . . . 10.00 – 40.00
Amber . . . 15.00 – 60.00
Butter . . . 70.00
Amber . . . 90.00
Green/Blue . . . 145.00
Cake Stand . . . 30.00
Amber . . . 55.00
Green/Blue . . . 85.00
Compote, Covered, 3 Sizes . . . 25.00 – 55.00
Amber . . . 35.00 – 90.00
Green/Blue . . . 50.00 – 100.00
Compote, Open, 8½" . . . 35.00
Amber . . . 50.00
Green/Blue . . . 65.00
Compote, 10" . . . 100.00
Vaseline . . . 550.00
Creamer or Spooner . . . 20.00
Amber . . . 65.00
Green/Blue . . . 90.00
Cruet . . . 85.00
Amber . . . 275.00
Green/Blue . . . 125.00
Goblet . . . 50.00
Amber . . . 60.00
Green/Blue . . . 75.00
Mug . . . 45.00
Amber . . . 65.00
Green/Blue . . . 85.00
Pickle Dish . . . 20.00
Amber . . . 50.00
Sauce, Flat or Ftd. . . . 10.00
Amber . . . 20.00
Vaseline . . . 145.00
Green/Blue . . . 20.00
Shakers, ea . . . 25.00
Amber . . . 45.00
Green/Blue . . . 65.00
Sugar . . . 30.00
Amber . . . 135.00
Green/Blue . . . 110.00
Syrup . . . 100.00
Amber . . . 300.00
Toothpick Hldr . . . 75.00
Amber . . . 450.00
Green/Blue . . . 500.00
Water Tray . . . 25.00
Amber . . . 30.00
Green/Blue . . . 45.00
Wine . . . 95.00
Amber . . . 100.00
Vaseline . . . 400.00
Green/Blue . . . 125.00

CORNFLOWER
Decanter . . . 50.00
Green/Blue . . . 80.00
Ruby Glass . . . 85.00
Tankard Pitcher . . . 95.00
Green/Blue . . . 130.00
Ruby Glass . . . 140.00
Tumbler . . . 20.00
Green/Blue . . . 30.00
Ruby Glass . . . 50.00
Wine . . . 15.00
Green/Blue . . . 25.00
Ruby Glass . . . 40.00

CORNUCOPIA
Berry Bowl, Sm . . . 20.00
Berry Bowl, Lg . . . 50.00
Butter . . . 75.00
Cake Stand . . . 35.00
Celery Vase . . . 20.00
Compote, Covered . . . 45.00
Cordial . . . 20.00
Creamer or Spooner . . . 25.00
Goblet . . . 60.00
Lamps, Various . . . 55.00 – 90.00
Mug . . . 30.00
Pitcher . . . 85.00
Tumbler . . . 20.00
Sugar . . . 30.00
Wine . . . 15.00

CORNUCOPIA (FENTON)
One Shape . . . 20.00

CORNUCOPIA (JEANNETTE)
One Shape . . . 35.00

COSMOS
Butter . . . 70.00
Condiment Set . . . 95.00
Creamer or Spooner . . . 20.00
Lamps, Lg. or Mini . . . 65.00 – 100.00
Lemonade Set . . . 125.00
Perfume . . . 45.00
Pickle Caster . . . 35.00
Pitcher . . . 90.00
Tumbler . . . 15.00
Shakers, ea . . . 20.00
Sugar . . . 30.00
Syrup . . . 65.00
Trays . . . 20.00 – 45.00

COSMOS AND CANE
Basket, 2 Hndl., Rare . . . 100.00
Berry Bowl, 4" . . . 15.00
Spooner . . . 35.00

COSMOS DRAPE
Oil Lamp . . . 95.00

COSMOS VARIANT
Bowl . . . 40.00
Plate, Scarce . . . 65.00

COTTAGE
Banana Stand . . . 35.00
Berry Bowl, Sm . . . 10.00
Berry Bowl, Lg . . . 30.00
Bowl, Oval, 2 Styles . . . 25.00
Butter . . . 50.00
Cake Stand, 9" and 10" . . . 40.00
Celery Vase . . . 20.00
Champagne . . . 15.00
Ruby Stain . . . 85.00
Claret . . . 15.00
Compote, w/Lid, 6" – 8" . . . 45.00
Compote, Open, 4" – 7" . . . 30.00
Compote, Open, 8" – 10" . . . 40.00
Creamer or Spooner . . . 20.00
Ruby Stain . . . 55.00
Cruet . . . 60.00
Cup . . . 10.00
Finger Bowl . . . 20.00
Fruit Bowl . . . 30.00
Goblet . . . 35.00
Milk Pitcher . . . 45.00
Mug . . . 25.00
Pickle Dish . . . 15.00
Plate, 6" – 8" . . . 20.00
Ruby Stain . . . 40.00
Plate, 9" – 10" . . . 30.00
Pitcher . . . 65.00
Tumbler . . . 15.00
Relish Tray . . . 15.00
Sauce, Flat or Ftd . . . 10.00
Shakers, ea . . . 15.00
Sugar . . . 25.00
Syrup . . . 80.00
Waste Bowl . . . 20.00
Water Tray . . . 30.00
Wine . . . 15.00

COUNTRY KITCHEN (All pieces scarce)
Bowl, 5½" . . . 35.00
Bowl, 6", Flared . . . 60.00
Bowl, 7", Ice Cream Shape . . . 125.00
Bowl, 8" – 9" . . . 90.00
Bowl, 9" – 10", Ftd., Rare . . . 300.00
Bowl, Sq., Rare . . . 225.00
Bowl, Pinched in Whimsey, Rare . . . 325.00
Bowl, w/Advertising . . . 350.00
Butter . . . 200.00
Creamer or Spooner . . . 75.00
Plate, 5" . . . 75.00
Plate, 7" . . . 95.00
Plate, 10" . . . 90.00
Plate, 12" . . . 100.00
Plate, w/Advertising . . . 425.00
Rose Bowl, Sm . . . 150.00
Rose Bowl, Med . . . 200.00
Rose Bowl, Lg . . . 275.00
Rose Bowl, "S.I. Frank" Advertising . . . 900.00
Sugar . . . 150.00

COUNTRY KITCHEN VARIANT
Bowl, Rare . . . 250.00

COVERED FISH DISH
One Shape, 8" . . . 155.00
Vaseline . . . 250.00
Green/Blue . . . 200.00

CRAB CLAW
Basket, Hndl . . . 50.00
Bowl, Lg . . . 35.00
Bowl, Sm . . . 15.00
Plate, 11½" . . . 45.00
Nut Bowl . . . 30.00

CRAB CLAW VARIANT
Pitcher . . . 80.00
Tumbler . . . 15.00

CRADLED PRISMS
Butter . . . 55.00
Creamer or Spooner . . . 20.00
Goblet . . . 35.00
Sugar . . . 30.00

CRANESBILL
Berry Bowl, Sm . . . 20.00
Berry Bowl, Lg . . . 45.00
Butter . . . 60.00
Creamer or Spooner . . . 20.00
Pitcher . . . 80.00
Tumbler . . . 20.00
Sugar . . . 30.00

CRATE
Paperweight . . . 175.00

CRESTED HOBNAIL (WITH TWISTED HANDLE)
Mug . . . 65.00

CROESUS
Bowl, Covered, 8" – 10" . . . 10.00 – 75.00
Green/Blue . . . 50.00 – 165.00
Amethyst . . . 100.00 – 175.00
Bowl, Open, 4" – 8" . . . 10.00 – 35.00
Green/Blue . . . 40.00 – 100.00
Amethyst . . . 60.00 – 100.00
Butter . . . 110.00
Green/Blue . . . 200.00
Amethyst . . . 185.00
Cake Stand . . . 60.00
Green/Blue . . . 145.00
Amethyst . . . 175.00
Celery Vase . . . 85.00
Green/Blue . . . 110.00
Amethyst . . . 275.00
Compote, Covered, 5" – 7" . . . 30.00 – 45.00
Green/Blue . . . 85.00 – 130.00
Amethyst . . . 90.00 – 120.00
Compote, Open, 5" – 7" . . . 25.00 – 30.00
Green/Blue . . . 55.00 – 95.00
Amethyst . . . 65.00 – 100.00
Condiment Set, Complete . . . 200.00
Green/Blue . . . 200.00

Amethyst . . . 225.00
Creamer or Spooner . . . 40.00
Green/Blue . . . 125.00
Amethyst . . . 150.00
Creamer, Ind. . . . 55.00
Green/Blue . . . 100.00
Amethyst . . . 175.00
Cruet . . . 125.00
Green/Blue . . . 155.00
Amethyst . . . 325.00
Jelly Compote . . . 50.00
Green/Blue . . . 150.00
Amethyst . . . 165.00
Pitcher . . . 125.00
Green/Blue . . . 200.00
Amethyst . . . 300.00
Tumbler . . . 20.00
Green/Blue . . . 50.00
Amethyst . . . 70.00
Plate, Ftd., 8" . . . 25.00
Green/Blue . . . 65.00
Amethyst . . . 80.00
Relish, Boat Shape . . . 35.00
Green/Blue . . . 60.00
Amethyst . . . 70.00
Sauce, Flat or Ftd. . . . 15.00
Green/Blue . . . 35.00
Amethyst . . . 40.00
Shakers, ea. . . . 50.00
Green/Blue . . . 135.00
Amethyst . . . 110.00
Sugar . . . 100.00
Green/Blue . . . 145.00
Amethyst . . . 175.00
Sugar, Ind. . . . 85.00
Green/Blue . . . 110.00
Amethyst . . . 125.00
Toothpick Hldr. . . . 35.00
Green/Blue . . . 95.00
Amethyst . . . 130.00
Tray . . . 25.00
Green/Blue . . . 40.00
Amethyst . . . 55.00

CROSS BANDS
Butter . . . 55.00
Creamer or Spooner . . . 20.00
Sugar . . . 25.00

CROSS BAR AND CANE
Butter . . . 45.00
Creamer or Spooner . . . 20.00
Shakers, ea. . . . 15.00
Sugar . . . 25.00

CROSSED BLOCK
Bowl, Oval . . . 30.00
Butter . . . 55.00
Creamer or Spooner . . . 20.00
Goblet . . . 35.00
Pickle Dish . . . 20.00
Sugar . . . 30.00

CROSSED SHIELD
Berry Bowl, Sm. . . . 10.00
Berry Bowl, Lg. . . . 35.00
Butter . . . 65.00
Compotes, 4 Sizes . . . 20.00 – 55.00
Cordial . . . 15.00
Creamer or Spooner . . . 20.00
Goblet . . . 45.00
Pickle Dish . . . 20.00
Pitcher . . . 85.00
Tumbler . . . 15.00
Sugar . . . 25.00
Wine . . . 10.00

CROSS IN DIAMONDS
Bowls, Various . . . 10.00 – 35.00
Butter . . . 55.00
Compote . . . 30.00
Creamer or Spooner . . . 20.00
Pitcher . . . 75.00
Tumbler . . . 15.00
Sugar . . . 30.00
Tray . . . 25.00

CROWN SALT
Ind. Salt Dip . . . 20.00

CRUCIFIX
Candlesticks, ea. . . . 60.00

CRYSTAL QUEEN (Condensed List)
Basket, Hndl. . . . 55.00
Berry Bowl, Sm. . . . 20.00
Berry Bowl, Lg. . . . 55.00
Butter . . . 100.00
Celery Vase . . . 40.00
Compotes, 2 Sizes . . . 45.00 – 70.00
Creamer or Spooner . . . 30.00
Milk Pitcher . . . 80.00
Pickle Dish . . . 30.00
Pitcher . . . 150.00
Tumbler . . . 35.00
Sugar . . . 40.00
Vase . . . 30.00

CRYSTAL ROCK
Berry Bowl, Sm. . . . 20.00
Berry Bowl, Lg. . . . 45.00
Butter . . . 55.00
Creamer or Spooner . . . 20.00
Pitcher . . . 65.00
Tumbler . . . 10.00
Sugar . . . 25.00

CRYSTAL STAR
Auto Vase, Vaseline, ea. . . . 50.00

CRYSTAL WEDDING
Banana Bowl, Scarce . . . 110.00
Berry Bowl, 8" Sq. . . . 40.00
Ruby Stain . . . 85.00
Berry Bowl, 4½" Sq. . . . 20.00
Berry Bowl, Covered, 6" – 7" . . . 70.00
Ruby Stain . . . 80.00
Bowl, Sauce 4" . . . 15.00
Butter . . . 70.00
Ruby Stain . . . 125.00
Cake Plate, Flat or Ftd. . . . 45.00 – 70.00
Ruby Stain . . . 85.00
Celery . . . 35.00
Ruby Stain . . . 70.00
Claret . . . 25.00
Compote, Ftd., 3 Sizes, Covered . 45.00 – 95.00
Ruby Stain . . . 100.00 – 125.00
Compote, Flat, 3 Sizes, Open . . . 35.00 – 65.00
Ruby Stain . . . 50.00 – 70.00
Creamer or Spooner . . . 30.00 – 50.00
Ruby Stain . . . 60.00 – 80.00
Cruet, Rare . . . 145.00
Ruby Stain . . . 225.00
Goblet . . . 25.00
Ruby Stain . . . 80.00
Milk Pitcher, 2 Styles . . . 75.00 – 95.00
Ruby Stain . . . 100.00 – 185.00
Pitcher, 2 Styles . . . 90.00 – 170.00
Ruby Stain . . . 175.00 – 225.00
Pickle Dish . . . 35.00
Ruby Stain . . . 40.00
Salt Dip, 2 Sizes . . . 20.00 – 35.00
Ruby Stain . . . 40.00 – 70.00
Shaker, Sq., ea. . . . 30.00
Ruby Stain . . . 80.00
Sugar w/Lid . . . 65.00
Ruby Stain . . . 90.00
Syrup . . . 125.00
Ruby Stain . . . 225.00
Tumbler . . . 30.00
Ruby Stain . . . 50.00
Vase . . . 40.00

CUPID AND VENUS
Berry Bowl, Sm. . . . 25.00
Berry Bowl, Lg. . . . 45.00
Bowl, Flat or Ftd. . . . 35.00
Bread Plate . . . 45.00
Amber . . . 80.00
Vaseline . . . 150.00
Butter . . . 65.00
Cake Stand . . . 65.00
Celery Vase . . . 45.00
Compote, Covered, Low or High . . . 125.00
Compote, Open, Low or High . . . 55.00
Amber . . . 150.00
Cordial . . . 100.00
Creamer or Spooner . . . 40.00
Cruet . . . 150.00
Goblet . . . 90.00
Jam Jar . . . 60.00
Milk Pitcher . . . 65.00
Amber . . . 190.00
Mug, 3 Sizes . . . 45.00 – 60.00
Pickle Caster . . . 60.00
Plate, 10" . . . 35.00
Amber . . . 85.00
Pitcher . . . 75.00
Amber . . . 225.00
Tumbler . . . 30.00
Relish . . . 35.00
Sauce, Flat or Ftd. . . . 20.00
Sugar . . . 75.00
Wine . . . 100.00

CUPIDS
Bowls, Dome Base . . . 20.00 – 50.00

CURLED LEAF
Mug . . . 40.00
Vaseline . . . 65.00
Amethyst . . . 65.00
Pitcher . . . 80.00
Vaseline . . . 140.00
Amethyst . . . 145.00

CURRANT
Bowl, 7" . . . 25.00
Butter . . . 90.00
Cake Stand, 2 Sizes . . . 50.00 – 90.00
Celery Vase . . . 50.00
Compote, High, 8" – 12" . . . 100.00 – 200.00
Compote, Low 8" . . . 65.00
Cordial . . . 50.00
Creamer or Spooner . . . 45.00
Egg Cup . . . 30.00
Goblet . . . 40.00
Jam Jar w/Lid . . . 60.00
Milk Pitcher . . . 150.00
Pitcher . . . 100.00
Tumbler, Ftd. . . . 40.00
Plate, Oval, 2 Sizes . . . 25.00 – 35.00
Relish Dish . . . 20.00
Salt, Ftd. . . . 35.00
Sauce, Ftd. . . . 15.00
Sugar . . . 60.00
Wine . . . 30.00

CURRIER & IVES
Bowl, Oval, 10" . . . 40.00
Butter . . . 80.00
Cake Stand . . . 70.00
Compote, Covered, 7½" . . . 100.00
Compote, Open, 7½" . . . 60.00
Creamer or Spooner . . . 35.00
Cup & Saucer . . . 40.00
Decanter . . . 40.00
Dish, Oval, 8" . . . 30.00
Goblet . . . 40.00
Lamp, 9½" . . . 100.00
Milk Pitcher . . . 70.00
Pitcher . . . 125.00
Vaseline . . . 275.00
Tumbler . . . 50.00
Plate, 10" . . . 25.00
Relish . . . 20.00
Salt Shaker . . . 30.00
Sauce . . . 15.00
Sugar . . . 50.00
Syrup . . . 85.00
Tray, Balky Mule . . . 75.00
Vaseline . . . 140.00
Water Bottle . . . 60.00
Wine . . . 20.00

CURTAIN TIE BACK
Bowls, Sq. . . . 5.00 – 30.00
Butter . . . 45.00
Celery Tray . . . 15.00
Celery Vase . . . 20.00
Compote, Covered . . . 35.00
Creamer or Spooner . . . 15.00

Goblet, 2 Styles 35.00
Pickle Dish. 10.00
Plate. 20.00
Pitcher 65.00
Tumbler 10.00
Relish. 10.00
Sauce, Flat or Ftd. 10.00
Shakers, ea. 15.00
Sugar 20.00
Water Tray. 30.00
Wine 10.00

CURVED STAR
Bowls, Various . . . . . 10.00 – 35.00
Butter. 50.00
Cake Stand. 35.00
Celery Vase 25.00
Compote, Sm.. . . . . 30.00
Epergne, 3 Part 100.00
Rose Bowl 30.00
Vase 25.00

CUT BLOCK (HEISEY)
Breakfast Set, 2 Pcs. 85.00
Ruby Stain. 115.00
Butter. 70.00
Ruby Stain. 95.00
Celery Vase 30.00
Ruby Stain. 40.00
Creamer or Spooner. 35.00
Ruby Stain. 50.00
Cruet 90.00
Ruby Stain. 125.00
Pickle Dish. 30.00
Ruby Stain. 40.00
Sugar 45.00
Ruby Stain. 60.00
Syrup 75.00
Ruby Stain. 90.00

CUT LOG
Banana Stand 40.00
Biscuit Jar 45.00
Bowl, 7" – 10" . . . . . 25.00 – 45.00
Butter. 60.00
Creamer, Spooner or Sugar 30.00
Cake Stand, 2 Sizes 55.00
Celery Tray. 30.00
Celery Vase 25.00
Compote, 7", 8" &10", Open . . . . 30.00 – 50.00
Compote, 5½" and 7½",w/Lid 65.00
Goblet 35.00
Honey Dish 35.00
Jam Jar 25.00
Mustard Jar 30.00
Mug 40.00
Nappy 30.00
Olive Dish 20.00
Pitcher 80.00
Tumbler 20.00
Relish Dish 20.00
Sauce, Flat or Ftd. 10.00
Salt, Ind. & Master . . . . . 15.00 – 30.00
Shakers, ea. 25.00
Vase. 16" 65.00
Wine 25.00

DAHLIA (PORTLAND)
Bowl, Oval 25.00
Amber 40.00
Vaseline. 40.00
Green/Blue. 35.00
Bread Plate 20.00
Amber 60.00
Vaseline. 60.00
Green/Blue. 50.00
Butter. 50.00
Amber 100.00
Vaseline. 165.00
Green/Blue. 110.00
Cake Stands . . . . . 25.00 – 40.00
Amber 75.00
Vaseline. 125.00
Green/Blue. 60.00
Compote, Covered 60.00
Amber 100.00
Vaseline. 95.00
Green/Blue. 85.00
Compote, Open 30.00
Amber 55.00
Vaseline. 55.00
Green/Blue. 50.00
Cordial 10.00
Amber 60.00
Vaseline. 60.00
Green/Blue. 50.00
Creamer or Spooner. 40.00
Amber 45.00
Vaseline. 45.00
Green/Blue. 40.00
Egg Cup, Single 15.00
Amber 60.00
Vaseline. 70.00
Green/Blue. 55.00
Egg Cup, Double 25.00
Amber 85.00
Vaseline. 110.00
Green/Blue. 70.00
Goblet 45.00
Amber 60.00
Vaseline. 60.00
Green/Blue. 55.00
Jam Jar 55.00
Amber 70.00
Vaseline. 150.00
Green/Blue. 85.00
Milk Pitcher 50.00
Amber 80.00
Vaseline. 115.00
Green/Blue. 70.00
Mug, 2 Sizes . . . . . 30.00 – 40.00
Amber. . . . . 60.00 – 70.00
Vaseline . . . . . 55.00 – 65.00
Green/Blue . . . . . 50.00 – 60.00
Pickle Dish. 10.00
Amber 30.00
Vaseline. 30.00
Green/Blue. 25.00
Plate, Dinner 20.00
Amber 35.00
Vaseline. 35.00
Green/Blue. 30.00
Platter, 2 Styles Hndls. 30.00
Amber 60.00
Vaseline. 55.00
Green/Blue. 50.00
Pitcher 75.00
Amber 115.00
Vaseline. 175.00
Green/Blue. 100.00
Tumbler 20.00
Amber 40.00
Vaseline. 55.00
Green/Blue. 35.00
Relish. 10.00
Amber 25.00
Vaseline. 30.00
Green/Blue. 25.00
Salt Dip, Ind. 15.00
Amber 35.00
Vaseline. 35.00
Green/Blue. 30.00
Sauce, Flat or Ftd. 10.00
Amber 20.00
Vaseline. 25.00
Green/Blue. 20.00
Sugar 50.00
Amber 65.00
Vaseline. 80.00
Green/Blue. 50.00
Syrup 60.00
Amber 75.00
Vaseline. 95.00
Green/Blue. 75.00
Wine 10.00
Amber 45.00
Vaseline. 65.00
Green/Blue. 55.00

DAHLIA, GOOFUS PATTERN
Bowl, 4" 20.00
Bowl, 9" 35.00
Bowl, 10" 40.00
Plate, 11" 50.00

DAHLIA AND FAN
Bowl, 4" 15.00
Bowl, 9" – 10". 50.00
Plate, 11" 35.00

DAISY AND BUTTON (HOBBS)
Bowl. 30.00
Amber 40.00
Vaseline. 45.00
Green/Blue. 45.00
Bread Plate 25.00
Amber 40.00
Vaseline. 50.00
Green/Blue. 50.00
Butter, 2 Styles . . . . . 55.00 – 110.00
Amber. . . . . 75.00 – 130.00
Vaseline . . . . . 95.00 – 165.00
Green/Blue . . . . . 80.00 – 135.00
Butter Pat. 30.00
Amber 40.00
Vaseline. 45.00
Green/Blue. 45.00
Canoe, 4" – 14" . . . . . 10.00 – 35.00
Amber. . . . . 25.00 – 75.00
Vaseline . . . . . 45.00 – 110.00
Green/Blue . . . . . 35.00 – 95.00
Caster Set, 4 Bottle. 75.00
Amber 90.00
Vaseline. 135.00
Green/Blue. 95.00
Caster Set, 5 Bottle. 110.00
Amber 125.00
Vaseline. 180.00
Green/Blue. 125.00
Celery, Shoe Shape 30.00
Amber 50.00
Vaseline. 80.00
Green/Blue. 65.00
Compote, Covered 35.00
Amber 50.00
Vaseline. 145.00
Green/Blue. 110.00
Compote, Open 55.00
Amber 80.00
Vaseline. 100.00
Green/Blue. 90.00
Creamer or Spooner. 30.00
Amber 40.00
Vaseline. 45.00
Green/Blue. 40.00
Cruet 55.00
Amber 125.00
Vaseline. 135.00
Green/Blue. 125.00
Egg Cup 20.00
Amber 25.00
Vaseline. 30.00
Green/Blue. 25.00
Finger Bowl 25.00
Amber 30.00
Vaseline. 35.00
Green/Blue. 30.00
Goblet 35.00
Amber 45.00
Vaseline. 60.00
Green/Blue. 45.00
Hat. 20.00
Amber 30.00
Vaseline. 35.00
Green/Blue. 30.00
Ice Cream Tray. 40.00
Amber 80.00
Vaseline. 90.00
Green/Blue. 85.00
Ice Tub. 40.00
Vaseline. 85.00
Green/Blue. 80.00
Inkwell. 30.00

Amber 40.00
Vaseline 45.00
Green/Blue 40.00
Parfait 20.00
Amber 25.00
Vaseline 30.00
Green/Blue 25.00
Pickle Caster 65.00
Amber 130.00
Vaseline 165.00
Green/Blue 150.00
Pitcher, 2 Styles . . . . 60.00 – 85.00
Amber . . . . 70.00 – 130.00
Vaseline . . . . 100.00 – 195.00
Green/Blue . . . . 85.00 – 145.00
Tumbler 20.00
Amber 25.00
Vaseline 45.00
Green/Blue 30.00
Plate, Leaf Shape 20.00
Amber 35.00
Vaseline 75.00
Green/Blue 55.00
Plate, Rnd. or Sq. 15.00
Amber 20.00
Vaseline 25.00
Green/Blue 20.00
Punch Bowl w/Base 115.00
Amber 175.00
Vaseline 325.00
Green/Blue 225.00
Shakers, ea. 25.00
Amber 30.00
Vaseline 50.00
Green/Blue 35.00
Sauce 10.00
Amber 15.00
Vaseline 20.00
Green/Blue 15.00
Slipper, 2 Sizes . . . . 35.00 – 50.00
Amber . . . . 40.00 – 55.00
Vaseline . . . . 45.00 – 60.00
Green/Blue . . . . 40.00 – 50.00
Sugar 45.00
Amber 55.00
Vaseline 60.00
Green/Blue 55.00
Syrup 40.00
Amber 70.00
Vaseline 110.00
Green/Blue 60.00
Toothpick, 2 Styles . . . . 20.00 – 50.00
Amber . . . . 25.00 – 60.00
Vaseline . . . . 45.00 – 80.00
Green/Blue . . . . 30.00 – 65.00
Tray 30.00
Amber 75.00
Vaseline 95.00
Green/Blue 80.00
Vase (Wall Pocket) 125.00
Amber 145.00
Wine 15.00
Amber 25.00
Vaseline 40.00
Green/Blue 30.00

DAISY AND BUTTON ADVERTISING SHOE
Slipper 90.00

DAISY AND BUTTON BASKET
Bride's Basket 50.00
Vaseline 115.00

DAISY AND BUTTON TRIANGLE
Butter 45.00
Creamer or Spooner 20.00
Goblet 35.00
Salt Dip 25.00
Sauce 15.00
Sugar 25.00

DAISY AND BUTTON VARIANT
Butter 200.00

DAISY AND BUTTON WHEELBARROW
Novelty 185.00
Vaseline 265.00

DAISY AND BUTTON WITH CROSSBARS
Bowl, 7" – 9" 25.00
Amber 30.00
Vaseline 35.00
Green/Blue 35.00
Bowl, Oval, 6" – 9" 30.00
Amber 35.00
Vaseline 40.00
Green/Blue 40.00
Butter, Pedestal Ftd. 55.00
Amber 65.00
Vaseline 150.00
Green/Blue 90.00
Catsup Bottle 40.00
Amber 45.00
Vaseline 125.00
Green/Blue 50.00
Celery Vase 25.00
Amber 30.00
Vaseline 65.00
Green/Blue 35.00
Compote, Covered, High or Low 45.00
Amber 65.00
Vaseline . . . . 90.00 – 125.00
Green/Blue 70.00
Compote, Open, High or Low 35.00
Amber 45.00
Vaseline . . . . 65.00 – 75.00
Green/Blue 50.00
Cordial 15.00
Amber 20.00
Vaseline 40.00
Green/Blue 25.00
Creamer or Spooner 20.00
Amber 30.00
Vaseline 45.00
Green/Blue 35.00
Cruet 45.00
Amber 60.00
Vaseline 150.00
Green/Blue 100.00
Finger Bowl 20.00
Amber 25.00
Vaseline 30.00
Green/Blue 30.00
Goblet 35.00
Amber 40.00
Vaseline 65.00
Green/Blue 55.00
Milk Pitcher 45.00
Amber 70.00
Vaseline 95.00
Green/Blue 85.00
Mug, 2 Sizes 25.00
Amber 40.00
Vaseline 50.00
Green/Blue 65.00
Oil Lamp 80.00
Amber 120.00
Vaseline 250.00
Green/Blue 135.00
Pickle Dish 15.00
Amber 20.00
Vaseline 25.00
Green/Blue 30.00
Pickle Jar 25.00
Amber 30.00
Vaseline 50.00
Green/Blue 30.00
Pitcher 70.00
Amber 125.00
Vaseline 145.00
Green/Blue 125.00
Tumbler 20.00
Amber 30.00
Vaseline 35.00
Green/Blue 35.00
Plate 20.00
Amber 25.00
Vaseline 30.00
Green/Blue 30.00
Sauce, Flat or Ftd. 15.00
Amber 20.00
Vaseline 20.00
Green/Blue 25.00
Shakers, ea. 20.00
Amber 45.00
Vaseline 45.00
Green/Blue 50.00
Sugar 25.00
Amber 60.00
Vaseline 80.00
Green/Blue 65.00
Syrup 75.00
Amber 135.00
Vaseline 250.00
Green/Blue 195.00
Toothpick Hldr. 25.00
Amber 50.00
Vaseline 65.00
Green/Blue 70.00
Waste Bowl 20.00
Amber 30.00
Vaseline 30.00
Green/Blue 35.00
Water Tray 30.00
Amber 35.00
Vaseline 35.00
Green/Blue 35.00
Wine 20.00
Amber 25.00
Vaseline 30.00
Green/Blue 35.00

DAISY AND BUTTON WITH NARCISSUS
Bowl Oval 20.00
Butter 60.00
Celery Vase 35.00
Compote 45.00
Creamer or Spooner 25.00
Decanter 55.00
Ruby Stain 75.00
Fruit Bowl, Ftd. 45.00
Goblet 25.00
Pitcher 75.00
Ruby Stain 110.00
Tumbler 20.00
Shaker, ea. 25.00
Sugar 40.00
Ruby Stain 50.00
Tray 30.00
Ruby Stain 45.00
Wine 15.00
Ruby Stain 25.00

DAISY AND BUTTON WITH THUMBPRINT
Bowl, 6" 15.00
Amber 20.00
Vaseline 40.00
Green/Blue 25.00
Ruby Stain 30.00
Butter 50.00
Amber 75.00
Vaseline 115.00
Green/Blue 90.00
Ruby Stain 85.00
Cake Stand 45.00
Amber 65.00
Vaseline 95.00
Green/Blue 70.00
Ruby Stain 75.00
Celery Vase 25.00
Amber 30.00
Vaseline 65.00
Green/Blue 35.00
Ruby Stain 40.00
Compote, Open 35.00
Amber 55.00
Vaseline 60.00
Green/Blue 60.00
Ruby Stain 65.00
Creamer or Spooner 35.00
Amber 40.00
Vaseline 50.00
Green/Blue 45.00
Ruby Stain 50.00

Goblet 30.00
Amber 35.00
Vaseline. 40.00
Green/Blue. 40.00
Ruby Stain. 45.00
Pitcher 85.00
Amber 120.00
Vaseline. 150.00
Green/Blue. 125.00
Ruby Stain. 130.00
Tumbler 15.00
Amber 20.00
Vaseline. 40.00
Green/Blue. 25.00
Ruby Stain. 30.00
Sauce, Ftd. 10.00
Amber 15.00
Vaseline. 20.00
Green/Blue. 20.00
Ruby Stain. 25.00
Sugar 40.00
Amber 55.00
Vaseline. 70.00
Green/Blue. 60.00
Ruby Stain. 65.00
Wine 15.00
Amber 20.00
Vaseline. 35.00
Green/Blue. 25.00
Ruby Stain. 30.00

DAISY AND BUTTON WITH V ORNAMENT
Berry Bowl, Sm. 15.00
Amber 25.00
Vaseline. 25.00
Green/Blue. 30.00
Berry Bowl, Lg. 30.00
Amber 45.00
Vaseline. 70.00
Green/Blue. 45.00
Bowl, Octagonal 35.00
Amber 40.00
Vaseline. 40.00
Green/Blue. 45.00
Butter. 50.00
Amber 70.00
Vaseline. 125.00
Green/Blue. 100.00
Celery Vase 25.00
Amber 40.00
Vaseline. 75.00
Green/Blue. 60.00
Creamer or Spooner 20.00
Amber 30.00
Vaseline. 50.00
Green/Blue. 40.00
Finger Bowl 20.00
Amber 35.00
Vaseline. 60.00
Green/Blue. 45.00
Goblet 30.00
Amber 40.00
Vaseline. 65.00
Green/Blue. 50.00
Match Hldr. 25.00
Amber 45.00
Vaseline. 65.00
Green/Blue. 50.00
Milk Pitcher. 50.00
Amber 75.00
Vaseline. 100.00
Green/Blue. 80.00
Mug, 4 Sizes . . . . . 20.00 – 45.00
Amber. . . . . 25.00 – 60.00
Vaseline . . . . . 25.00 – 55.00
Green/Blue . . . . . 30.00 – 65.00
Pickle Caster 75.00
Amber 195.00
Vaseline. 300.00
Green/Blue. 225.00
Pickle Jar 25.00
Amber 35.00
Vaseline. 60.00
Green/Blue. 40.00
Plate, 4 Sizes. . . . . 10.00 – 35.00
Amber. . . . . 15.00 – 45.00
Vaseline . . . . . 25.00 – 50.00
Green/Blue . . . . . 20.00 – 50.00
Pitcher 65.00
Amber 85.00
Vaseline. 150.00
Green/Blue. 110.00
Tumbler 20.00
Amber 30.00
Vaseline. 40.00
Green/Blue. 35.00
Sauce 15.00
Amber 25.00
Vaseline. 25.00
Green/Blue. 30.00
Shade, Gas. 30.00
Amber 50.00
Vaseline. 50.00
Green/Blue. 55.00
Sherbet. 20.00
Amber 35.00
Vaseline. 35.00
Green/Blue. 40.00
Sugar 25.00
Amber 50.00
Vaseline. 80.00
Green/Blue. 55.00
Toothpick Hldr. 25.00
Amber 70.00
Vaseline. 70.00
Green/Blue. 75.00
Water Tray. 35.00
Amber 50.00
Vaseline. 50.00
Green/Blue. 55.00
Wine 20.00
Amber 40.00
Vaseline. 40.00
Green/Blue. 45.00

DAISY AND PLUME
Bowl, Ftd., Scarce 55.00
Compote, Stemmed, Rare. 65.00
Rose Bowl, Stemmed, Rare 75.00
Rose Bowl, Ftd., Scarce 60.00

DAISY AND SCROLL
Berry Bowl, Sm. 15.00
Berry Bowl, Lg.. . . . . 35.00
Butter. 60.00
Creamer or Spooner. 25.00
Pitcher 65.00
Tumbler 20.00
Shakers, ea. 25.00
Sugar 30.00
Syrup 55.00

DAISY AND TREE LIMB
Tray, 14" – 9½", Amber 85.00
Milk Glass. 70.00

DAISY AND X-BAND
Berry Bowl, Lg.. . . . . 40.00
Berry Bowl, Sm. 20.00
Butter. 50.00
Celery, Hndl. 35.00
Compote, Low w/Lid. 55.00
Creamer, Spooner or Sugar 30.00
Goblet 30.00
Jelly, Hndl. 30.00
Pitcher 75.00
Tumbler 20.00
Rose Bowl, 8". 40.00
Sherbet. 20.00
Sweetmeat 45.00
Vase, 10", 12" & 14" . . . . . 25.00 – 50.00

DAISY BAND
Sauce 10.00
Sherbet. 15.00

DAISY BAND (COLUMBIA AND U.S. GLASS)
Cup & Saucer. 60.00
Amber 75.00
Green/Blue. 85.00

DAISY BANDED CRYSTAL WEDDING
Compote, Covered, Scarce 150.00
Compote, Open, Scarce 65.00

DAISY BAND VARIANT
Mug 20.00

DAISY BASKET
One Shape, Hndl. 35.00

DAISY-IN-SQUARE
Berry Bowl, Sm. 10.00
Berry Bowl, Lg. 35.00
Butter. 45.00
Celery Vase 15.00
Creamer or Spooner. 15.00
Milk Pitcher. 45.00
Pickle Tray. 15.00
Pitcher 65.00
Tumbler 10.00
Sauce 10.00
Shakers, ea. 15.00
Sugar 20.00
Syrup 40.00
Vase. 20.00

DAISY MEDALLION
Berry Bowl, Sm. 20.00
Berry Bowl, Lg. 45.00
Butter. 60.00
Cake Stand. 40.00
Compote. 35.00
Creamer or Spooner. 25.00
Goblet 40.00
Pitcher 80.00
Tumbler 20.00
Sugar 30.00

DAISY PLEAT
Mug 45.00

DAISY SWAG
Creamer 30.00
Vaseline. 70.00
Open Sugar 30.00
Vaseline. 65.00

DAKOTA
Berry Bowl, Sm. 20.00
Engraved. . . . . 30.00 – 65.00
Berry Bowl, Lg. 45.00
Engraved. . . . . 40.00 – 80.00
Bottle, Cologne, Rare 85.00
Ruby Stain. 325.00
Engraved 200.00
Bottle, Pepper Sauce, Rare. 125.00
Engraved 245.00
Butter, 2 Sizes 70.00
Ruby Stain. 120.00
Engraved 80.00
Cake Basket, w/metal Hndl., Rare 225.00
Engraved 425.00
Cake Stand, Dome, 8" – 14", Rare. 200.00 – 300.00
Engraved. . . . . 300.00 – 600.00
Cake Stand, Dome,15", Extremely Rare. 425.00
Engraved 800.00
Cake Stand, Reg., 8" – 10½" . . . . 55.00 – 70.00
Ruby Stain. 250.00
Engraved 100.00
Celery Tray. 35.00
Ruby Stain. 80.00
Engraved 45.00
Celery Vase 45.00
Engraved 45.00
Compote, Covered, 5" – 12". . . . 65.00 – 140.00
Ruby Stain. 200.00
Engraved. . . . . 75.00 – 300.00
Compote, Open, 5" – 12" . . . . . 35.00 – 75.00
Ruby Stain. 100.00
Engraved. . . . . 35.00 – 75.00
Creamer or Spooner, 2 Sizes 50.00
Ruby Stain. 200.00
Engraved. . . . . 40.00 – 145.00
Cruet 100.00
Ruby Stain. 325.00
Engraved 250.00
Cruet Set 500.00
Ruby Stain. 1000.00
Engraved 850.00

Cruet Undertray . . . 35.00
Engraved . . . 325.00
Dish, 8" – 10" . . . 40.00 – 65.00
Ruby Stain . . . 60.00 – 85.00
Engraved . . . 70.00 – 100.00
Goblet . . . 40.00
Ruby Stain . . . 60.00
Engraved . . . 30.00
Honey Dish . . . 20.00
Ruby Stain . . . 40.00
Engraved . . . 30.00
Milk Pitcher, 2 Styles . . . 100.00
Ruby Stain . . . 325.00
Engraved . . . 250.00
Mug . . . 125.00
Engraved . . . 425.00
Plate . . . 65.00
Ruby Stain . . . 90.00
Engraved . . . 125.00
Pitcher, 2 Styles . . . 100.00 – 135.00
Ruby Stain . . . 200.00
Engraved . . . 175.00
Tumbler . . . 30.00
Ruby Stain . . . 60.00
Engraved . . . 45.00
Sauce, Flat or Ftd. . . . 30.00
Ruby Stain . . . 45.00
Engraved . . . 30.00
Sugar . . . 75.00
Ruby Stain . . . 130.00
Engraved . . . 100.00
Tray, 3 Sizes . . . 100.00 – 225.00
Engraved . . . 250.00 – 450.00
Waste Bowl . . . 40.00
Ruby Stain . . . 100.00
Engraved . . . 75.00
Wine . . . 40.00
Ruby Stain . . . 45.00
Engraved . . . 50.00

DALTON

Breakfast Set, 2 Pcs. . . . 65.00
Butter . . . 70.00
Creamer or Spooner . . . 30.00
Cup . . . 10.00
Goblet . . . 35.00
Plate, 10½" . . . 25.00
Pitcher . . . 70.00
Tumbler . . . 15.00
Rose Bowl, Miniature . . . 30.00
Sugar . . . 35.00
Toothpick Hldr. . . . 30.00

DALZELL SWAN

Pitcher, Very Rare . . . 1300.00

DART

Bowl . . . 25.00
Butter . . . 55.00
Creamer or Spooner . . . 25.00
Goblet . . . 50.00
Jelly Compote . . . 35.00
Pitcher . . . 70.00
Tumbler . . . 20.00
Sauce . . . 15.00
Sugar . . . 30.00

DART AND BALL

Bowl . . . 30.00

DARWIN

Match Hldr. . . . 145.00
Amber . . . 200.00

DAVIDSON TULIP VASE

Stemmed Vase . . . 50.00
Vaseline . . . 85.00

DECORATED THREE FACE

Compote . . . 95.00

DEER ALERT

Pitcher . . . 375.00
Tumbler . . . 100.00

DEER AND CASTLE (EUROPEAN)

Bowls, Various, Ruby Stain . . . 30.00 – 75.00
Compotes, Various, Ruby Stain . . . 40.00 – 95.00
Ewers, Various, Ruby Stain . . . 65.00 – 115.00
Lighting Lustres, Ruby Stain . . . 50.00 – 80.00
Pitcher, Various, Ruby Stain . . . 95.00 – 175.00
Tumbler, Various, Ruby Stain . . . 35.00 – 65.00
Vases, Various, Ruby Stain . . . 40.00 – 75.00

DEER AND COW

Mug . . . 65.00
Green/Blue . . . 65.00
Milk Glass . . . 55.00

DEER AND DOG

Butter . . . 125.00
Engraved . . . 150.00
Celery Vase . . . 80.00
Engraved . . . 110.00
Champagne . . . 135.00
Engraved . . . 150.00
Cheese Dish . . . 160.00
Engraved . . . 175.00
Compote, Covered, High, 7" – 8" . . . 160.00
Engraved . . . 175.00
Compote, Covered, Low, 7" – 8" . . . 135.00
Engraved . . . 150.00
Cordial . . . 65.00
Engraved . . . 75.00
Creamer or Spooner . . . 70.00
Engraved . . . 80.00
Goblet . . . 70.00
Engraved . . . 80.00
Marmalade Jar . . . 125.00
Engraved . . . 150.00
Mug . . . 45.00
Engraved . . . 65.00
Pitcher . . . 165.00
Engraved . . . 180.00
Sauce, Flat or Ftd. . . . 25.00
Engraved . . . 30.00
Sugar . . . 110.00
Engraved . . . 125.00
Wine . . . 70.00
Engraved . . . 85.00

DEER AND OAK TREE

Butter . . . 145.00
Vaseline . . . 175.00
Creamer or Spooner . . . 90.00
Vaseline . . . 100.00 – 125.00
Pickle Dish . . . 25.00
Vaseline . . . 40.00
Plate, Bread . . . 60.00
Vaseline . . . 95.00
Platter, Oblong . . . 85.00
Vaseline . . . 150.00
Mug . . . 70.00
Vaseline . . . 100.00
Pitcher . . . 425.00
Chocolate . . . 700.00
Sugar . . . 85.00
Vaseline . . . 125.00

DEER AND PINE TREE

Bowl, Waste . . . 50.00
Butter . . . 110.00
Amber . . . 140.00
Green/Blue . . . 150.00
Cake Stand . . . 80.00
Celery Vase . . . 80.00
Compote, Covered, 7" – 9" . . . 75.00 – 110.00
Compote, Open, 7" – 9" . . . 35.00 – 50.00
Creamer or Spooner . . . 70.00
Amber . . . 100.00
Green/Blue . . . 90.00
Dish, Oblong, 3 Sizes . . . 30.00 – 50.00
Goblet . . . 55.00
Marmalade Jar . . . 135.00
Milk Pitcher . . . 140.00
Mug, 2 Sizes . . . 45.00 – 60.00
Amber . . . 50.00 – 70.00
Green/Blue . . . 50.00 – 70.00
Pickle Dish, Green/Blue . . . 45.00
Plate . . . 60.00
Green/Blue . . . 75.00 – 85.00
Platter . . . 80.00
Amber . . . 110.00
Green/Blue . . . 125.00
Pitcher . . . 150.00
Tumbler . . . 45.00
Amber . . . 65.00
Green/Blue . . . 65.00
Sauce . . . 25.00
Sugar . . . 95.00
Tray . . . 110.00
Amber . . . 135.00
Green/Blue . . . 140.00

DELAWARE

Banana Bowl . . . 35.00
Green/Blue . . . 70.00
Ruby Stain . . . 90.00
Basket, Silver Hldr. . . . 40.00
Green/Blue . . . 100.00
Ruby Stain . . . 165.00
Berry Bowl, Sm. . . . 15.00
Green/Blue . . . 30.00
Ruby Stain . . . 40.00
Berry Bowl, Lg. . . . 30.00
Green/Blue . . . 60.00
Ruby Stain . . . 70.00
Butter . . . 50.00
Green/Blue . . . 80.00
Ruby Stain . . . 125.00
Celery Vase . . . 25.00
Green/Blue . . . 75.00
Ruby Stain . . . 90.00
Claret Jug . . . 40.00
Green/Blue . . . 125.00
Ruby Stain . . . 185.00
Compote . . . 40.00
Green/Blue . . . 85.00
Ruby Stain . . . 100.00
Creamer or Spooner . . . 25.00
Green/Blue . . . 50.00
Ruby Stain . . . 70.00
Cruet . . . 60.00
Green/Blue . . . 225.00
Ruby Stain . . . 350.00
Cup . . . 15.00
Green/Blue . . . 30.00
Ruby Stain . . . 50.00
Finger Bowl . . . 20.00
Green/Blue . . . 40.00
Ruby Stain . . . 50.00
Fruit Bowl . . . 25.00
Green/Blue . . . 35.00
Ruby Stain . . . 55.00
Pin Tray . . . 20.00
Green/Blue . . . 50.00
Ruby Stain . . . 80.00
Pitcher, Squat . . . 65.00
Green/Blue . . . 100.00
Ruby Stain . . . 125.00
Pitcher, Tankard . . . 110.00
Green/Blue . . . 175.00
Ruby Stain . . . 200.00
Tumbler . . . 40.00
Green/Blue . . . 50.00
Ruby Stain . . . 60.00
Pomade Box . . . 135.00
Green/Blue . . . 250.00
Ruby Stain . . . 400.00
Puff Box . . . 150.00
Green/Blue . . . 250.00
Ruby Stain . . . 400.00
Sauce, Oval or Rnd. . . . 20.00
Green/Blue . . . 30.00
Ruby Stain . . . 40.00
Shade, Electric . . . 100.00
Green/Blue . . . 150.00
Ruby Stain . . . 225.00
Shade, Gas . . . 100.00
Green/Blue . . . 150.00
Ruby Stain . . . 225.00
Shakers, ea. . . . 125.00
Green/Blue . . . 225.00
Ruby Stain . . . 325.00
Toothpick Hldr. . . . 40.00
Green/Blue . . . 100.00
Ruby Stain . . . 150.00
Vase, 6" – 9½" . . . 35.00
Green/Blue . . . 65.00
Ruby Stain . . . 95.00

DELTA
Pitcher ... 90.00
Tumbler ... 20.00
Syrup ... 70.00

DESPOT
Goblet ... 35.00

DEW AND RAINDROP
Berry Bowl, Sm. ... 10.00
Berry Bowl, Lg. ... 30.00
Butter ... 45.00
Creamer or Spooner ... 20.00
Goblet ... 35.00
Mug ... 20.00
Pitcher ... 65.00
Tumbler ... 15.00
Sauce ... 10.00
Shakers, ea. ... 15.00
Sherbet ... 15.00
Sugar ... 25.00
Wine ... 15.00

DEWDROP
Butter ... 50.00
Cake Tray, Hndl. ... 35.00
Caster Set ... 75.00
Creamer or Spooner ... 20.00
Goblet ... 20.00
Vaseline ... 45.00
Shakers, ea. ... 20.00
Sherbet ... 15.00
Sugar ... 25.00
Sugar Shaker ... 35.00
Tumbler ... 20.00
Vaseline ... 40.00
Wine ... 15.00

DEWDROP IN POINTS
Bread Plate ... 25.00
Butter ... 65.00
Compote, Covered ... 45.00
Compote, Open ... 30.00
Creamer or Spooner ... 20.00
Goblet ... 35.00
Pickle Dish ... 15.00
Pitcher ... 75.00
Tumbler ... 20.00
Plate ... 20.00
Sauce ... 10.00
Sugar ... 25.00

DEWDROP WITH STAR
Butter ... 50.00
Cake Stand ... 60.00
Cheese Dish ... 35.00
Compote w/Lid, High, 2 Sizes ... 65.00
Compote w/Lid, Low, 2 Sizes ... 55.00
Creamer, Spooner, or Sugar ... 30.00
Pickle Dish ... 30.00
Pitcher ... 85.00
Tumbler ... 20.00
Plates, from 4½" – 11" ... 20.00 – 40.00
Sauce ... 15.00

DEWEY
Berry Bowl, Sm. ... 20.00
Amber ... 30.00
Vaseline ... 35.00
Green/Blue ... 30.00
Chocolate ... 100.00
Berry Bowl, Lg. ... 50.00
Amber ... 60.00
Vaseline ... 135.00
Green/Blue ... 65.00
Chocolate ... 225.00
Breakfast Set, 2 Pcs. ... 65.00
Amber ... 80.00
Vaseline ... 150.00
Green/Blue ... 125.00
Butter ... 85.00
Amber ... 110.00
Vaseline ... 195.00
Green/Blue ... 135.00
Chocolate ... 250.00
Creamer or Spooner ... 70.00
Amber ... 75.00
Vaseline ... 85.00
Green/Blue ... 80.00
Chocolate ... 100.00
Cruet ... 65.00
Amber ... 100.00
Vaseline ... 175.00
Green/Blue ... 135.00
Chocolate ... 450.00
Mug ... 40.00
Amber ... 60.00
Vaseline ... 95.00
Green/Blue ... 75.00
Chocolate ... 325.00
Parfait Glass ... 30.00
Amber ... 40.00
Vaseline ... 80.00
Green/Blue ... 60.00
Chocolate ... 165.00
Plate ... 30.00
Amber ... 45.00
Vaseline ... 85.00
Green/Blue ... 60.00
Pitcher, Rare ... 75.00
Amber ... 150.00
Vaseline ... 300.00
Green/Blue ... 200.00
Tumbler, Rare ... 45.00
Amber ... 75.00
Vaseline ... 125.00
Green/Blue ... 90.00
Sauce ... 20.00
Amber ... 25.00
Vaseline ... 30.00
Green/Blue ... 25.00
Chocolate ... 75.00
Shakers, ea. ... 35.00
Amber ... 50.00
Vaseline ... 80.00
Green/Blue ... 65.00
Chocolate ... 400.00
Sugar ... 45.00
Amber ... 70.00
Vaseline ... 140.00
Green/Blue ... 90.00
Chocolate ... 125.00
Tray, 2 Sizes ... 30.00 – 55.00
Amber ... 35.00 – 60.00
Vaseline ... 70.00 – 95.00
Green/Blue ... 60.00 – 80.00
Chocolate ... 350.00

DEWEY BUST
Paperweight ... 250.00

DIAGONAL BAND
Bowl ... 35.00
Amber ... 40.00
Green/Blue ... 50.00
Bread Plate ... 30.00
Amber ... 35.00
Green/Blue ... 40.00
Butter ... 55.00
Amber ... 65.00
Green/Blue ... 75.00
Cake Stand ... 45.00
Amber ... 50.00
Green/Blue ... 60.00
Compote ... 40.00
Amber ... 45.00
Green/Blue ... 55.00
Creamer or Spooner ... 30.00
Amber ... 35.00
Green/Blue ... 45.00
Goblet ... 30.00
Amber ... 40.00
Green/Blue ... 45.00
Pitcher ... 75.00
Amber ... 80.00
Green/Blue ... 95.00
Tumbler ... 15.00
Amber ... 20.00
Green/Blue ... 30.00
Plate ... 15.00
Relish ... 30.00
Amber ... 35.00
Green/Blue ... 45.00
Sauce ... 20.00
Sugar ... 30.00
Amber ... 40.00
Green/Blue ... 50.00

DIAMOND
Berry Bowl, Sm. ... 10.00
Berry Bowl, Lg. ... 35.00
Butter ... 70.00
Compote ... 35.00
Creamer or Spooner ... 20.00
Goblet ... 45.00
Pickle Dish ... 15.00
Pitcher ... 80.00
Tumbler ... 15.00
Sugar ... 30.00
Wine ... 15.00
Vase ... 25.00

DIAMOND (MILLERSBURG)
Hat, from Tumbler, Very Rare,
Green/Blue ... 500.00
Punch Bowl, Rare ... 600.00
Punch Base, Rare ... 225.00
Tumbler ... 100.00
Amethyst ... 425.00

DIAMOND AND FAN (MILLERSBURG)
Bowl, Rare ... 500.00

DIAMOND AND SUNBURST (PORTLAND)
Butter ... 50.00
Celery Vase ... 25.00
Creamer or Spooner ... 25.00
Pickle Dish ... 15.00
Sugar ... 40.00
Wine ... 20.00

DIAMOND AND SUNBURST (U.S. GLASS)
Bowl, Sq. ... 25.00
Butter ... 55.00
Celery Vase ... 25.00
Creamer or Spooner ... 30.00
Goblet ... 35.00
Pickle Dish ... 20.00
Pitcher ... 80.00
Tumbler ... 15.00
Shakers, ea. ... 25.00
Sugar ... 45.00
Wine ... 15.00

DIAMOND BAND
Bowl, Shallow ... 20.00
Butter ... 50.00
Celery Vase ... 35.00
Compote, Ftd., Sm. ... 40.00
Creamer, Spooner, or Sugar ... 25.00
Goblet ... 30.00
Pitcher ... 70.00
Tumbler ... 20.00
Wine ... 30.00

DIAMOND BLOCK
Candlestick, ea. ... 35.00
Compote ... 45.00
Cylinder Vase ... 35.00
Juice Tumbler ... 20.00
Milk Pitcher ... 60.00
Pedestal Vase ... 40.00
Rose Bowl ... 35.00

DIAMOND BRIDGES
Berry Bowl, Sm. ... 20.00
Berry Bowl, Lg. ... 50.00
Butter ... 80.00
Compotes ... 30.00 – 55.00
Goblet ... 40.00
Pickle Dish ... 15.00
Pickle Jar ... 35.00
Pitcher ... 90.00
Tumbler ... 20.00
Sugar ... 30.00
Wine ... 15.00

DIAMOND CUT WITH LEAF
Butter ... 45.00
Amber ... 50.00
Vaseline ... 75.00
Green/Blue ... 65.00
Cordial ... 20.00

Amber 25.00
Vaseline 35.00
Green/Blue 30.00
Creamer or Spooner 25.00
Amber 30.00
Vaseline 40.00
Green/Blue 35.00
Goblet 30.00
Amber 35.00
Vaseline 45.00
Green/Blue 40.00
Mug 35.00
Amber 40.00
Vaseline 50.00
Green/Blue 40.00
Plate 25.00
Amber 30.00
Vaseline 40.00
Green/Blue 35.00
Shakers, ea 25.00
Amber 30.00
Vaseline 35.00
Green/Blue 30.00
Sugar 35.00
Amber 40.00
Vaseline 50.00
Green/Blue 40.00
Wine 20.00
Amber 25.00
Vaseline 35.00
Green/Blue 30.00

DIAMOND IN DIAMOND
Bowls . . . . . 10.00 – 40.00
Butter 65.00
Compotes . . . . . 20.00 – 55.00
Creamer or Spooner 20.00
Goblet 35.00
Pickle Dish 15.00
Pitcher 75.00
Tumbler 15.00
Sugar 25.00
Toothpick Hldr 20.00
Wine 10.00

DIAMOND LATTICE
Berry Bowl, Sm 15.00
Berry Bowl, Lg 40.00
Butter 65.00
Creamer or Spooner 20.00
Pickle Dish 20.00
Plate 25.00
Relish Dish (Club Shaped) 35.00
Sauce 10.00
Sugar 30.00

DIAMOND POINT
Vase 35.00

DIAMOND POINT BAND
Goblet 30.00
Vaseline 55.00
Green/Blue 50.00
Ruby Stain 65.00
Mug 25.00
Vaseline 35.00
Green/Blue 30.00
Ruby Stain 40.00
Wine 20.00
Vaseline 25.00
Green/Blue 25.00
Ruby Stain 30.00

DIAMOND POINT COLUMNS
Bowl 20.00
Vase 35.00

DIAMOND POINT DISC
Berry Bowl, Sm 15.00
Berry Bowl, Lg 45.00
Butter 80.00
Cake Stand 45.00
Compote 35.00
Creamer or Spooner 25.00
Salt, Ind 20.00
Shakers, ea 30.00
Sugar 40.00

DIAMOND POINT LOOP
Berry Bowl 25.00
Amber 30.00
Vaseline 40.00
Green/Blue 35.00
Butter 55.00
Amber 60.00
Vaseline 85.00
Green/Blue 80.00
Celery Dish 20.00
Amber 25.00
Vaseline 30.00
Green/Blue 30.00
Celery Vase 25.00
Amber 30.00
Vaseline 35.00
Green/Blue 35.00
Creamer or Spooner 25.00
Amber 30.00
Vaseline 40.00
Green/Blue 40.00
Goblet 30.00
Amber 35.00
Vaseline 50.00
Green/Blue 45.00
Pickle Dish 20.00
Amber 25.00
Vaseline 30.00
Green/Blue 30.00
Plate, Sq 25.00
Amber 30.00
Vaseline 35.00
Green/Blue 35.00
Sugar 35.00
Amber 40.00
Vaseline 60.00
Green/Blue 55.00

DIAMOND POINTS
Basket, 2 Hndl., Scarce 250.00
Rose Bowl, Very Scarce 375.00

DIAMOND POINTS VARIANT (YORK)
Rose Bowl, Scarce 85.00

DIAMOND POINT WITH CANNONBALLS
Butter 85.00
Creamer or Spooner 30.00
Pitcher 95.00
Tumbler 20.00
Sugar 35.00

DIAMOND QUILTED
Bowls, Oval or Rnd . . . . . 10.00 – 40.00
Amber . . . . . 15.00 – 45.00
Vaseline . . . . . 20.00 – 55.00
Green/Blue . . . . . 25.00 – 60.00
Amethyst . . . . . 20.00 – 50.00
Butter 50.00
Amber 95.00
Vaseline 165.00
Green/Blue 115.00
Amethyst 75.00
Celery Vase 20.00
Amber 30.00
Vaseline 40.00
Green/Blue 45.00
Amethyst 40.00
Champagne 15.00
Amber 20.00
Vaseline 30.00
Green/Blue 35.00
Amethyst 30.00
Compote, Open, High or Low . . . 20.00 – 35.00
Amber . . . . . 25.00 – 40.00
Vaseline . . . . . 35.00 – 60.00
Green/Blue . . . . . 40.00 – 65.00
Amethyst . . . . . 35.00 – 60.00
Compote, Covered, High or Low . 30.00 – 45.00
Amber . . . . . 35.00 – 50.00
Vaseline . . . . . 45.00 – 75.00
Green/Blue . . . . . 50.00 – 80.00
Amethyst . . . . . 45.00 – 75.00
Cordial 15.00
Amber 20.00
Vaseline 30.00
Green/Blue 35.00
Amethyst 30.00
Creamer or Spooner 35.00
Amber 40.00
Vaseline 50.00
Green/Blue 55.00
Amethyst 50.00
Goblet 30.00
Amber 35.00
Vaseline 40.00
Green/Blue 45.00
Amethyst 40.00
Mug 25.00
Amber 30.00
Vaseline 35.00
Green/Blue 40.00
Amethyst 40.00
Pitcher 80.00
Amber 90.00
Vaseline 165.00
Green/Blue 145.00
Amethyst 145.00
Tumbler 15.00
Amber 20.00
Vaseline 30.00
Green/Blue 35.00
Amethyst 35.00
Salt Dip, Ind. & Master . . . . . 20.00 – 25.00
Amber . . . . . 25.00 – 30.00
Vaseline . . . . . 30.00 – 35.00
Green/Blue . . . . . 35.00 – 40.00
Amethyst . . . . . 30.00 – 40.00
Sauce, Flat or Ftd 15.00
Amber 20.00
Vaseline 25.00
Green/Blue 30.00
Amethyst 30.00
Strawberry Plate, 10½" 65.00
Amber 70.00
Vaseline 100.00
Green/Blue 110.00
Amethyst 100.00
Sugar 45.00
Amber 50.00
Vaseline 65.00
Green/Blue 75.00
Amethyst 70.00
Vase, 9" 30.00
Amber 35.00
Vaseline 45.00
Green/Blue 50.00
Amethyst 45.00
Water Tray, 2 Shapes . . . . . 25.00 – 35.00
Amber . . . . . 30.00 – 40.00
Vaseline . . . . . 35.00 – 50.00
Green/Blue . . . . . 40.00 – 55.00
Amethyst . . . . . 35.00 – 50.00
Wine 20.00
Amber 25.00
Vaseline 30.00
Green/Blue 35.00
Amethyst 30.00

DIAMONDS AND CLUBS
Pitcher 150.00
Tumbler 25.00
Wine 15.00
Wine Decanter 85.00

DIAMOND SPEARHEAD
Berry Bowl, Sm 10.00
Berry Bowl, Lg 35.00
Butter 65.00
Celery Vase 20.00
Compote, Tall 45.00
Creamer, 2 Sizes . . . . . 15.00 – 25.00
Goblet 40.00
Jelly Compote 30.00
Mug 25.00
Pitcher 85.00
Tumbler 20.00
Rose Bowl 25.00
Shakers, ea 15.00
Spooner 25.00

Sugar . . . 40.00
Sugar Shaker . . . 50.00
Syrup . . . 55.00
Toothpick Hldr. . . . 35.00
Water Bottle. . . . 45.00

DIAMOND STRAWBERRY (FOSTORIA #402)
Pitcher . . . 95.00
Tumbler . . . 25.00

DIAMOND SUNBURST
Bowl. . . . 40.00
Cake Stand. . . . 50.00
Celery Vase . . . 35.00
Compote w/Lid . . . 60.00
Decanter . . . 65.00
Egg Cup . . . 25.00
Lamp . . . 75.00
Oval Platter . . . 40.00
Pickle Dish. . . . 30.00
Pitcher . . . 65.00
Tumbler . . . 20.00
Sauce . . . 15.00
Wine . . . 15.00

DIAMOND SWAG
Banana Compote . . . 45.00
Cracker Jar . . . 40.00
Creamer or Spooner . . . 20.00
Cruet . . . 65.00
Jelly Compote . . . 30.00
Jelly, Tri-cornered . . . 35.00
Pitcher . . . 80.00
Tumbler . . . 20.00
Relish. . . . 20.00
Spoon Tray . . . 25.00
Sugar . . . 25.00
Sugar Shaker . . . 45.00
Syrup . . . 75.00
Wine . . . 20.00
Vase. . . . 30.00

DIAMOND SWIRL
Butter. . . . 45.00
Creamer or Spooner . . . 20.00
Pitcher . . . 75.00
Tumbler . . . 15.00
Shakers, ea. . . . 20.00
Sugar . . . 25.00
Syrup . . . 50.00
Toothpick Hldr. . . . 20.00

DIAMOND THUMBPRINT
Ale Glass . . . 90.00
Bitters Bottle . . . 450.00
Butter. . . . 200.00
Celery Vase . . . 185.00
Champagne . . . 250.00
Compote, Covered . . . 250.00
Cordial . . . 300.00
Decanter . . . 175.00
Egg Cup . . . 85.00
Finger Bowl . . . 120.00
Goblet . . . 300.00
Honey Dish . . . 35.00
Milk Pitcher . . . 450.00
Mug . . . 200.00
Pitcher . . . 500.00
Tumbler . . . 125.00
Sauce . . . 10.00
Sugar . . . 25.00
Sweetmeat Jar (Covered) . . . 95.00
Tray, 7"x11" . . . 30.00
Whiskey Tumbler. . . . 125.00
Wine . . . 250.00

DIAMOND WITH CIRCLE
Mug . . . 30.00
Amber . . . 45.00
Green/Blue. . . . 55.00

DIAMOND WITH DIAMOND POINT
Butter. . . . 55.00
Celery Vase . . . 20.00
Compote. . . . 35.00
Creamer or Spooner . . . 20.00
Cup . . . 15.00
Nappy . . . 20.00
Pitcher . . . 70.00
Tumbler . . . 20.00
Shakers, ea. . . . 20.00
Sugar . . . 25.00

DIAMOND WITH DUAL FAN
Berry Bowl, Sm. . . . 10.00
Berry Bowl, Lg.. . . . 35.00
Butter. . . . 65.00
Creamer or Spooner . . . 20.00
Goblet . . . 55.00
Pickle Dish. . . . 15.00
Plate, 10" . . . 20.00
Pitcher . . . 95.00
Tumbler . . . 20.00
Shakers, ea. . . . 15.00
Sugar . . . 30.00
Toothpick Hldr. . . . 25.00
Wine . . . 10.00

DIAMOND WITH FAN
Berry Bowl, Lg.. . . . 40.00
Berry Bowl, Sm. . . . 15.00
Pitcher . . . 65.00
Tumbler . . . 20.00

DIAMOND WITH PEG
Berry Bowl, Sm. . . . 15.00
Berry Bowl, Lg.. . . . 40.00
Butter. . . . 65.00
Celery Vase . . . 20.00
Creamer or Spooner . . . 20.00
Pickle Dish. . . . 15.00
Pitcher . . . 90.00
Tumbler . . . 20.00
Shakers, ea. . . . 15.00
Sugar . . . 30.00
Toothpick Hldr. . . . 25.00

DICE
Paperweight . . . 150.00

DIVIDED HEARTS
Butter. . . . 65.00
Compote. . . . 40.00
Creamer or Spooner . . . 25.00
Egg Cup . . . 25.00
Goblet . . . 30.00
Lamp . . . 95.00
Pitcher . . . 80.00
Salt. . . . 20.00
Sugar . . . 30.00
Tumbler . . . 15.00

DOG (COLUMBIA)
Plate, 6" . . . 50.00
Amber . . . 60.00
Green/Blue. . . . 70.00

DOG CART
Plate, Scarce . . . 85.00

DOG CHASING CAT (DAVIDSON)
Creamer . . . 40.00
Opaque White . . . 65.00
Sugar . . . 60.00
Opaque White . . . 85.00

DOG CHASING DEER
Mug . . . 50.00
Amber . . . 70.00
Green/Blue. . . . 90.00
Milk Glass . . . 60.00

DOG HUNTING
Pitcher, Very Scarce . . . 325.00

DOG PLATE
Plate, Rare . . . 125.00

DOG'S HEAD ABC
Plate. . . . 150.00

DOG VASE (DAISY AND BUTTON)
One Shape, Rare . . . 150.00

DOG WITH COLLAR
Mug . . . 45.00
Amethyst . . . 65.00

DOG WITHOUT COLLAR
Mug . . . 60.00
Amethyst . . . 75.00

DOG WITH PAIL
Match Hldr. . . . 70.00

DOLPHIN (HOBBS BROCKUNIER)
Bowls, Covered, 7" and 8" . . . 350.00 – 400.00
Butter. . . . 395.00
Celery Vase . . . 125.00
Compote, Open, 8" and 9" . . . 175.00 – 200.00
Compote, Covered, 8" and 9". . 245.00 – 260.00
Creamer or Spooner . . . 150.00
Pickle Jar w/Lid . . . 350.00
Pitcher . . . 550.00
Salt, Master . . . 65.00
Sugar . . . 375.00

DOLPHIN AND HERONS
Vase, Very Rare . . . 550.00

DOLPHIN COMPOTE
Compote, 2 piece . . . 75.00
Amber . . . 85.00
Vaseline. . . . 145.00
Green/Blue. . . . 100.00

DOLPHIN MATCH HOLDER
Match Hldr. . . . 30.00
Amber . . . 45.00
Vaseline. . . . 75.00
Green/Blue. . . . 50.00

DONALD & COMPANY
Advertising Piece . . . 45.00

DOT
Berry Bowl, Sq., Sm. . . . 10.00
Berry Bowl, Sq., Lg. . . . 30.00
Butter. . . . 40.00
Creamer or Spooner . . . 20.00
Relish. . . . 20.00
Sugar . . . 25.00

DOUBLE BEETLE BAND
Butter. . . . 90.00
Celery Vase . . . 20.00
Creamer or Spooner . . . 25.00
Goblet . . . 60.00
Pickle Dish. . . . 20.00
Pitcher . . . 125.00
Tumbler . . . 20.00
Sauce, Flat or Ftd. . . . 10.00
Sugar . . . 35.00
Wine . . . 15.00

DOUBLE DRAPE
Vase, 13" . . . 55.00

DOUBLE PINWHEEL
Berry Bowl, Sm. . . . 15.00
Berry Bowl, Lg.. . . . 40.00
Bowl, 7" . . . 25.00
Butter. . . . 60.00
Compote. . . . 35.00
Compote, Covered . . . 95.00
Creamer or Spooner . . . 25.00
Pickle Dish. . . . 20.00
Pitcher . . . 75.00
Tumbler . . . 20.00
Shakers, ea. . . . 20.00
Sugar . . . 25.00

DOUBLE RELISH (CAMPBELL, JONES)
Double Relish . . . 70.00

DOUBLE RIBBON
Bread Plate . . . 20.00
Butter. . . . 65.00
Compote, Covered . . . 50.00
Compote, Open . . . 40.00
Creamer or Spooner . . . 25.00
Egg Cup . . . 20.00
Pickle Dish. . . . 25.00
Pitcher . . . 80.00
Tumbler . . . 25.00
Sauce, Ftd. . . . 25.00
Shakers, ea. . . . 25.00
Sugar . . . 30.00

DOUBLE SPEAR
Butter. . . . 45.00
Celery Vase . . . 20.00
Compote. . . . 35.00
Creamer or Spooner . . . 20.00
Goblet . . . 40.00
Pickle Dish. . . . 20.00
Relish. . . . 20.00
Sauce . . . 10.00
Sugar . . . 30.00

DOUBLE VINE
Plate. . . . 45.00

DOUGLASS
- Berry Bowl, Sm. . . . 20.00
  - Ruby Stain. . . . 30.00
- Berry Bowl, Lg. . . . 45.00
  - Ruby Stain. . . . 55.00
- Butter, 2 Styles . . . 60.00 – 75.00
  - Ruby Stain . . . 75.00 – 100.00
- Creamer or Spooner . . . 25.00
  - Ruby Stain. . . . 35.00
- Finger Bowl, Sq. . . . 30.00
  - Ruby Stain. . . . 45.00
- Pitcher . . . 85.00
  - Ruby Stain. . . . 145.00
- Tumbler . . . 25.00
  - Ruby Stain. . . . 35.00
- Punch Bowl . . . 110.00
  - Ruby Stain. . . . 225.00
- Punch Cup . . . 15.00
  - Ruby Stain. . . . 25.00
- Shakers, ea. . . . 25.00
  - Ruby Stain. . . . 40.00
- Sugar . . . 30.00
  - Ruby Stain. . . . 70.00
- Toothpick Hldr. . . . 35.00
  - Ruby Stain. . . . 45.00

DOVE VASE (CANTON)
- Cake Stand. . . . 80.00
  - Amber . . . 95.00
  - Green/Blue. . . . 135.00
- Vase . . . 65.00
  - Amber . . . 75.00
  - Green/Blue. . . . 125.00

DOYLE'S SHELL
- Butter. . . . 45.00
  - Amber . . . 55.00
  - Green/Blue. . . . 65.00
  - Ruby Stain. . . . 60.00
- Celery Vase . . . 20.00
  - Amber . . . 35.00
  - Green/Blue. . . . 45.00
  - Ruby Stain. . . . 40.00
- Creamer or Spooner . . . 25.00
  - Amber . . . 35.00
  - Green/Blue. . . . 45.00
  - Ruby Stain. . . . 40.00
- Mug . . . 30.00
  - Amber . . . 40.00
  - Green/Blue. . . . 55.00
  - Ruby Stain. . . . 50.00
- Pickle Dish. . . . 20.00
  - Amber . . . 25.00
  - Green/Blue. . . . 35.00
  - Ruby Stain. . . . 30.00
- Sugar . . . 30.00
  - Amber . . . 35.00
  - Green/Blue. . . . 45.00
  - Ruby Stain. . . . 40.00
- Water Tray. . . . 40.00
  - Amber . . . 45.00
  - Green/Blue. . . . 55.00
  - Ruby Stain. . . . 50.00
- Waste Bowl . . . 30.00
  - Amber . . . 35.00
  - Green/Blue. . . . 40.00
  - Ruby Stain. . . . 35.00
- Wine . . . 25.00
  - Amber . . . 30.00
  - Green/Blue. . . . 35.00
  - Ruby Stain. . . . 30.00

DRAGON (All pieces rare)
- Butter. . . . 300.00
- Compote, Sm. . . . 85.00
- Creamer or Spooner . . . 65.00
- Goblet . . . 100.00
- Plate. . . . 60.00
- Sugar, Open . . . 55.00

DRAPE
- Mug . . . 40.00

DRUM
- Child's Table Set . . . 85.00
  - Green/Blue. . . . 145.00
- Mug, 3 Sizes . . . 20.00 – 40.00
  - Green/Blue . . . 30.00 – 60.00

DRUM AND EAGLE
- Child's Mug . . . 35.00

DUCHESS
- Pitcher . . . 125.00
- Tumbler . . . 35.00

DUGAN'S HONEYCOMB
- Bowl, Green/Blue . . . 40.00
  - Amethyst . . . 55.00
- Nut Bowl, Green/Blue . . . 50.00
  - Amethyst . . . 65.00
- Rose Bowl, Green/Blue. . . . 65.00
  - Amethyst . . . 75.00

DUNCAN #13
- Mug . . . 40.00
- Tumbler's . . . 10.00 – 30.00

DUNCAN #40
- Bowls, Rnd. or Sq. . . . 15.00 – 40.00
- Butter. . . . 70.00
- Celery Tray. . . . 25.00
- Compote, Open, 10 Sizes . . . 20.00 – 75.00
- Creamer or Spooner . . . 25.00
- Creamer, Ind. . . . 15.00
- Finger Bowl . . . 20.00
- Nappy . . . 20.00
- Plate, 8" . . . 25.00
- Pitcher . . . 75.00
- Tumbler . . . 30.00
- Pitcher, Tankard . . . 90.00
- Pitcher w/Metal Top. . . . 135.00
- Punch Bowl . . . 200.00
- Punch Cup . . . 15.00
- Punch Tray . . . 45.00
- Shade, Gas. . . . 35.00
- Shakers, ea. . . . 15.00
- Sugar . . . 40.00
- Sugar, Ind. . . . 25.00
- Vase, 6 Sizes . . . 15.00 – 45.00

DUNCAN #98
- Berry Bowl, Lg. . . . 30.00
  - Amber . . . 35.00
  - Vaseline. . . . 55.00
  - Green/Blue. . . . 40.00
- Berry Bowl, Sm. . . . 15.00
  - Amber . . . 20.00
  - Vaseline. . . . 25.00
  - Green/Blue. . . . 20.00
- Bowl w/Underplate. . . . 55.00
  - Amber . . . 65.00
  - Vaseline. . . . 75.00
  - Green/Blue. . . . 60.00
- Jelly Set . . . 40.00
  - Amber . . . 50.00
  - Vaseline. . . . 70.00
  - Green/Blue. . . . 60.00
- Creamer . . . 20.00
  - Amber . . . 25.00
  - Vaseline. . . . 40.00
  - Green/Blue. . . . 35.00
- Sugar . . . 30.00
  - Amber . . . 40.00
  - Vaseline. . . . 55.00
  - Green/Blue. . . . 40.00

DUNCAN #904
- Bowls, Various . . . 10.00 – 35.00
- Butter. . . . 70.00
- Creamer or Spooner . . . 20.00
- Cup . . . 10.00
- Goblet . . . 45.00
- Pitcher . . . 85.00
- Tumbler . . . 20.00
- Sugar . . . 30.00

DUNCAN AND MILLER BASKET
- Novelty, One Shape . . . 45.00

DUNCAN HOMESTEAD (#63)
- Berry Bowl, Sm. . . . 10.00
- Berry Bowl, Lg. . . . 35.00
- Bowls, Various . . . 10.00 – 50.00
- Butter. . . . 65.00
- Celery Vase . . . 20.00
- Compotes . . . 25.00 – 50.00
- Creamer or Spooner . . . 20.00
- Creamer, Ind. . . . 15.00
- Cruet . . . 50.00
- Finger Bowl . . . 20.00
- Punch Bowl . . . 125.00
- Punch Cup . . . 10.00
- Salt, Ind. . . . 15.00
- Shakers, ea., 2 Styles . . . 35.00 – 45.00
- Sugar . . . 35.00
- Sugar, Ind. . . . 20.00
- Syrup . . . 55.00
- Toothpick Hldr. . . . 30.00
- Vases, Various Sizes . . . 15.00 – 40.00

DUNCAN'S CLOVER (#58)
- Butter. . . . 40.00
- Creamer, Spooner, or Sugar. . . . 20.00
- Finger Bowl . . . 25.00
- Pitcher . . . 70.00
- Tumbler . . . 20.00
- Toothpick Hldr. . . . 35.00
- Wine . . . 20.00

DUNCAN'S LATE BLOCK
- Bowl, Sq. . . . 40.00
- Bowl, Tri-Cornered. . . . 45.00
- Butter. . . . 75.00
- Celery Boat . . . 35.00
- Creamer or Spooner. . . . 30.00
- Cruet . . . 60.00
- Ice Tub. . . . 50.00
- Jelly Compote. . . . 35.00
- Mustard Jar . . . 45.00
- Parlor Lamp . . . 90.00
- Punch Bowl . . . 115.00
- Punch Cup . . . 20.00
- Relish, Hndl. . . . 30.00
- Rose Bowl . . . 45.00
- Sauce, Sq. . . . 25.00
- Salt Shaker. . . . 30.00
- Sugar . . . 35.00
- Sugar Shaker . . . 45.00
- Syrup . . . 70.00

DUTCH MILL
- Mug . . . 35.00
  - Green/Blue. . . . 55.00
  - Amethyst . . . 65.00

EARLY AMERICAN (WESTMORELAND)
- Bowl. . . . 25.00
- Cup & Saucer. . . . 35.00
- Goblet . . . 40.00
- Nut Dish . . . 20.00
- Plate, 8" . . . 20.00
- Relish Tray, 5 Part with Jar & Lid . . . 75.00
- Shakers, ea. . . . 20.00
- Sherbet. . . . 15.00

EARLY EXCELSIOR
- Ale Glass . . . 55.00
- Bar Bottle. . . . 45.00
- Bitters Bottle . . . 60.00
- Bowl, Covered . . . 135.00
- Bowl, Open . . . 50.00
- Butter. . . . 125.00
- Candlesticks, Ea. . . . 130.00
- Celery Vase . . . 65.00
- Champagne . . . 55.00
- Claret . . . 50.00
- Compote, Covered . . . 80.00
- Compote, Open . . . 110.00
- Cordial . . . 80.00
- Creamer or Spooner. . . . 65.00
- Decanter, 2 Sizes . . . 80.00 – 100.00
- Egg Cup, Single . . . 65.00
- Egg Cup, Double . . . 85.00
- Goblet, 2 Styles . . . 65.00
- Jelly Glass . . . 60.00
- Lamp . . . 110.00
- Milk Pitcher. . . . 225.00
- Mug . . . 50.00
- Pickle Jar w/Lid . . . 50.00
- Pitcher . . . 325.00
- Tumbler, Various . . . 50.00 – 70.00
- Salt. . . . 40.00
- Spillholder . . . 80.00
- Sugar . . . 95.00

Syrup . . . 150.00
Water Bottle . . . 100.00
Wine . . . 60.00
Vase . . . 75.00

EARLY PANELLED GRAPE BAND
Butter . . . 70.00
Celery Vase . . . 20.00
Creamer or Spooner . . . 25.00
Egg Cup . . . 20.00
Goblet . . . 50.00
Pickle Dish . . . 20.00
Relish . . . 20.00
Salt, Open . . . 15.00
Sugar . . . 30.00

EASTER GREETINGS CHICK
Child's Plate . . . 40.00

EDGEWOOD
Butter . . . 50.00
Carafe . . . 65.00
Creamer, Spooner, or Sugar . . . 30.00
Cup . . . 20.00
Shakers, ea . . . 25.00
Sherbet . . . 25.00
Syrup . . . 60.00
Toothpick Hldr . . . 35.00

EGG IN SAND
Bread Tray . . . 30.00
Butter . . . 65.00
Cake Stand . . . 35.00
Creamer or Spooner . . . 20.00
Dish, Swan Center . . . 35.00
Goblet . . . 35.00
Jam Jar . . . 25.00
Jelly Compote, Covered . . . 40.00
Milk Pitcher . . . 50.00
Platter, Rectangular . . . 30.00
Pitcher . . . 70.00
Tumbler . . . 20.00
Relish . . . 15.00
Sauce . . . 10.00
Shakers, ea . . . 25.00
Sugar . . . 25.00
Water Tray . . . 35.00
Wine . . . 15.00

EGYPTIAN
Bowl . . . 60.00
Bread Plate, Cleopatra . . . 95.00
Bread Plate, Temple . . . 325.00
Butter . . . 55.00
Celery Vase . . . 85.00
Compote, Covered, 2 Sizes . . . 300.00
Compote, Open, 7½" . . . 95.00
Creamer or Spooner . . . 60.00
Goblet . . . 60.00
Honey Dish . . . 20.00
Pickle Dish . . . 25.00
Pitcher . . . 245.00
Plate, Pyramids . . . 125.00
Relish Dish . . . 30.00
Sauce . . . 20.00
Sugar . . . 95.00

ELECTRIC
Bread Plate . . . 25.00
Butter . . . 50.00
Creamer or Spooner . . . 20.00
Cracker Jar . . . 35.00
Pickle Dish . . . 20.00
Relish . . . 15.00
Sauce . . . 10.00
Shakers, Ea . . . 20.00
Sugar . . . 25.00
Toothpick Hldr . . . 25.00

ELEPHANT (KING)
Wall Pocket Vase, Rare . . . 350.00

ELEPHANT HEAD
Toothpick Novelty . . . 150.00
Amber . . . 185.00
Green/Blue . . . 225.00
Milk Glass . . . 200.00

ELSON DEW DROP
Berry Bowl, Sm . . . 15.00
Berry Bowl, Lg . . . 35.00
Breakfast Set, 2 Pcs . . . 45.00
Butter . . . 65.00
Celery Vase . . . 30.00
Creamer or Spooner . . . 20.00
Pitcher . . . 80.00
Tumbler . . . 20.00
Sugar . . . 25.00

EMPRESS
Berry Bowl, Lg . . . 45.00
Green/Blue . . . 60.00
Ruby Stain . . . 50.00
Berry Bowl, Sm . . . 25.00
Green/Blue . . . 40.00
Ruby Stain . . . 30.00
Breakfast Set, 2 Pcs . . . 60.00
Green/Blue . . . 75.00
Ruby Stain . . . 65.00
Butter . . . 115.00
Green/Blue . . . 165.00
Ruby Stain . . . 145.00
Cake Stand . . . 65.00
Green/Blue . . . 85.00
Ruby Stain . . . 70.00
Celery Vase . . . 35.00
Green/Blue . . . 50.00
Ruby Stain . . . 40.00
Compote, 4 Sizes . . . 55.00 – 110.00
Green/Blue . . . 70.00 – 145.00
Ruby Stain . . . 55.00 – 125.00
Creamer or Spooner . . . 35.00
Green/Blue . . . 50.00
Ruby Stain . . . 40.00
Cruet . . . 85.00
Green/Blue . . . 110.00
Ruby Stain . . . 95.00
Jelly Compote . . . 45.00
Green/Blue . . . 60.00
Ruby Stain . . . 50.00
Ice Cream Bowls, Lg. & Sm . . . 25.00 – 50.00
Green/Blue . . . 35.00 – 70.00
Ruby Stain . . . 30.00 – 60.00
Lamps, 5 Sizes . . . 95.00 – 185.00
Green/Blue . . . 115.00 – 210.00
Ruby Stain . . . 100.00 – 195.00
Mustard Pot . . . 45.00
Green/Blue . . . 65.00
Ruby Stain . . . 55.00
Pickle Tray . . . 40.00
Green/Blue . . . 55.00
Ruby Stain . . . 45.00
Pitcher . . . 200.00
Green/Blue . . . 265.00
Ruby Stain . . . 250.00
Pitcher, Ftd . . . 225.00
Green/Blue . . . 285.00
Ruby Stain . . . 265.00
Plate, 2 Sizes . . . 35.00 – 55.00
Green/Blue . . . 50.00 – 80.00
Ruby Stain . . . 40.00 – 65.00
Salts, Master & Ind . . . 25.00 – 40.00
Green/Blue . . . 35.00 – 55.00
Ruby Stain . . . 30.00 – 45.00
Shakers, ea . . . 45.00
Green/Blue . . . 60.00
Ruby Stain . . . 45.00
Sugar . . . 60.00
Green/Blue . . . 75.00
Ruby Stain . . . 65.00
Toothpick Hldr . . . 60.00
Green/Blue . . . 70.00
Ruby Stain . . . 60.00
Tray . . . 70.00
Green/Blue . . . 85.00
Ruby Stain . . . 65.00

ENGLISH COLONIAL (Condensed List)
Berry Bowl, Sm . . . 10.00
Berry Bowl, Lg . . . 35.00
Butter . . . 50.00
Claret . . . 10.00
Compote . . . 30.00
Cordial . . . 20.00
Creamer or Spooner . . . 20.00
Cruet . . . 45.00
Decanter . . . 50.00
Jelly Compote . . . 25.00
Plate . . . 20.00
Punch Bowl . . . 75.00
Punch Cup . . . 10.00
Pitcher . . . 65.00
Tumbler . . . 15.00
Relish . . . 15.00
Sauce . . . 10.00
Shakers, ea . . . 20.00
Sugar . . . 25.00
Syrup . . . 60.00
Toothpick Hldr . . . 25.00

ENGLISH DAISY AND BUTTON
Bowl, Dome-based . . . 35.00

ENGLISH OVAL
Candlesticks, ea . . . 95.00
Vaseline . . . 225.00

ENGLISH ZIPPER FLOWER
Oval Bowl . . . 55.00
Vaseline . . . 90.00

ESSEX
Bowls, Various . . . 10.00 – 35.00
Butter . . . 55.00
Celery Vase . . . 25.00
Champagne . . . 15.00
Claret . . . 15.00
Creamer or Spooner . . . 20.00
Cup . . . 10.00
Sauce . . . 15.00
Sugar . . . 25.00
Sugar Shaker . . . 35.00
Sundae Dish . . . 20.00
Syrup . . . 65.00
Toothpick Hldr . . . 25.00
Wine . . . 15.00

ESTHER
Berry Bowl, Sm . . . 15.00
Green/Blue . . . 20.00
Berry Bowl, Lg . . . 35.00
Green/Blue . . . 50.00
Butter . . . 70.00
Green/Blue . . . 100.00
Cake Stand . . . 65.00
Green/Blue . . . 75.00
Caster Set . . . 115.00
Ruby Stain . . . 165.00
Celery Vase . . . 35.00
Green/Blue . . . 85.00
Ruby Stain . . . 75.00
Cheese Dish . . . 85.00
Green/Blue . . . 140.00
Ruby Stain . . . 115.00
Compote, Tall, Covered . . . 80.00
Green/Blue . . . 100.00
Ruby Stain . . . 125.00
Cracker Jar . . . 80.00
Green/Blue . . . 200.00
Ruby Stain . . . 185.00
Creamer or Spooner . . . 25.00
Green/Blue . . . 70.00
Ruby Stain . . . 80.00
Cruet . . . 65.00
Green/Blue . . . 250.00
Ruby Stain . . . 275.00
Goblet . . . 45.00
Green/Blue . . . 100.00
Ruby Stain . . . 80.00
Jam Jar . . . 35.00
Green/Blue . . . 125.00
Ruby Stain . . . 85.00
Jelly Compote . . . 30.00
Green/Blue . . . 80.00
Ruby Stain . . . 60.00
Lamp . . . 90.00
Green/Blue . . . 265.00
Ruby Stain . . . 300.00
Pitcher . . . 90.00
Green/Blue . . . 175.00
Ruby Stain . . . 265.00
Tumbler . . . 20.00

Green/Blue. 50.00
Ruby Stain. 60.00
Relish. 25.00
Green/Blue. 25.00
Ruby Stain. 35.00
Shakers, ea. 25.00
Green/Blue. 40.00
Ruby Stain. 35.00
Sugar 30.00
Green/Blue. 75.00
Ruby Stain. 110.00
Syrup, Rare 125.00
Green/Blue. 225.00
Ruby Stain. 200.00
Toothpick Hldr. 40.00
Green/Blue. 100.00
Ruby Stain. 115.00

ETCHED MUSTARD POT
Mustard Pot 50.00
Vaseline. 80.00

ETCHED VENICE
Pitcher, Vaseline 150.00
Green/Blue. 115.00
Tumbler, Vaseline 40.00
Green/Blue. 30.00
Tray, Vaseline 70.00
Green/Blue. 55.00

ETRUSCAN
Berry Bowl, Sm. 15.00
Berry Bowl, Lg.. . . . . . 40.00
Butter. 70.00
Cake Stand. 40.00
Compote. 35.00
Creamer or Spooner 25.00
Egg Cup 20.00
Jelly Compote 30.00
Pitcher 85.00
Tumbler 20.00
Sauce 15.00
Sugar 30.00

EVANGELINE
Bowl, Lg. 35.00
Bowl, Sm.. . . . . 15.00
Bowl, High Ftd. 60.00
Butter. 50.00
Cake Plate, Ftd. 45.00
Celery Tray. 30.00
Compote, Various Shapes 55.00
Creamer or Sugar 30.00
Goblet 25.00
Pickle Dish. 30.00
Pitcher 70.00
Tumbler 20.00
Wine 20.00

EVELYN (THUMBALLA)
Bowl, 7" – 8", Green/Blue 75.00
Plate, 8½" – 9", Green/Blue 100.00
Punch Bowl, Large 250.00
Punch Cup 20.00
Water Tray, Rect. Shape, Green/Blue. . . 125.00

EYEWINKER
Banana Dish 30.00
Berry Bowl, Sm. 15.00
Berry Bowl, Lg.. . . . . . 40.00
Bowl, Covered 55.00
Bowl, Vegetable 35.00
Butter. 75.00
Cake Stand, 8" – 10". 45.00
Celery Vase 30.00
Compote, Covered, 4" – 6" 30.00
Compote, Covered, 7" – 9" 45.00
Compote, Covered, 10" – 12½". 60.00
Compote, Open, 4" – 6" 25.00
Compote, Open, 7" – 9" 35.00
Compote, Open, 10" – 12½" 55.00
Creamer or Spooner 30.00
Cruet 75.00
Honey Dish 25.00
Milk Pitcher 70.00
Oil Lamp 125.00
Plate, Sq., 5" – 7" 25.00
Plate, Sq., 8" – 10" 35.00

Pitcher 150.00
Tumbler 25.00
Sauce, Round or Sq. 20.00
Shakers, ea. 30.00
Sugar 35.00
Syrup 70.00

FACETED FLOWER SWIRL
Butter. 45.00
Celery Vase 25.00
Creamer or Spooner 25.00
Cruet 65.00
Pitcher 90.00
Tumbler 20.00
Pickle Tray. 20.00
Sugar 30.00
Toothpick Hldr. 25.00
Water Tray. 30.00

FAIRFAX STRAWBERRY
Bowl, Oval 35.00
Butter. 55.00
Milk Glass 75.00
Celery Vase 25.00
Compote, Covered, High or Low 45.00
Creamer or Spooner 20.00
Milk Glass 90.00
Egg Cup 15.00
Milk Glass 45.00
Goblet 35.00
Milk Glass 85.00
Honey Dish 15.00
Pickle Tray. 20.00
Pitcher 75.00
Milk Glass 150.00
Tumbler 20.00
Milk Glass 45.00
Relish. 15.00
Salt, Master 15.00
Sauce 10.00
Sugar 30.00
Milk Glass 80.00
Syrup 60.00
Wine 15.00

FALLING LEAVES
Berry Bowl, Sm. 15.00
Berry Bowl, Lg.. . . . . . 35.00
Bowl, Covered, 5" – 8" 45.00
Butter. 65.00
Celery Tray. 25.00
Creamer or Spooner 20.00
Dish, Oval 15.00
Milk Pitcher 45.00
Pitcher, Pedestal, 1 Qt. 55.00
Pitcher 70.00
Tumbler 20.00
Pickle Dish. 15.00
Sugar 25.00

FAMOUS (AKA: Panelled Thumbprint)
Berry Bowl, Lg.. . . . . . 35.00
Berry Bowl, Sm. 15.00
Butter. 60.00
Celery Vase 25.00
Creamer, Spooner, or Sugar 25.00
Oil Lamp 75.00
Pickle Dish. 20.00
Pitcher 65.00
Tumbler 15.00
Shakers, Ea. 20.00
Syrup 45.00
Toothpick Hldr. 30.00

FAN BAND
Butter. 30.00
Compote. 20.00
Creamer or Spooner 15.00
Finger Bowl 15.00
Pitcher 65.00
Tumbler 15.00
Sugar 25.00
Tray 30.00
Wine 20.00

FANCY CUT (REX)
Pitcher 95.00
Tumbler 20.00

Punch Bowl 125.00
Punch Cup 15.00
Toy Table Set 85.00
Vase Whimsey 40.00

FANCY LOOP
Bonbon 35.00
Butter. 80.00
Celery Vase 20.00
Champagne 15.00
Claret 10.00
Cracker Jars . . . . . 25.00 – 45.00
Creamer or Spooner 25.00
Cruet 60.00
Goblet 50.00
Jelly Compote 20.00
Jelly Dish 15.00
Pitcher 95.00
Tumbler 25.00
Tumbler, Bar Size 35.00
Punch Bowl 125.00
Punch Cup 15.00
Salt Dip, Ind. 10.00
Salt, Master 20.00
Shakers, ea. 15.00
Sherry 15.00
Spoon Tray 20.00
Sugar 30.00
Toothpick Hldr. 35.00
Wine 10.00

FANDANGO
Banana Stand 45.00
Bar Bottle 35.00
Berry Bowl, Sm. 15.00
Berry Bowl, Lg.. . . . . . 40.00
Bowls, Various . . . . . 10.00 – 50.00
Butter. 65.00
Butter Pat. 10.00
Carafe 45.00
Celery Tray, 7" – 9" . . . . . 15.00 – 25.00
Celery Vase 20.00
Cheese Plate 30.00
Compote, 6" – 10" . . . . . 25.00 – 60.00
Cookie Jar, Tall 50.00
Cracker Jar 35.00
Creamer, 5 Sizes . . . . . 10.00 – 50.00
Cruet, 2 Sizes . . . . . 45.00 – 60.00
Custard Cup 10.00
Finger Bowl 20.00
Horseradish 35.00
Ice Bowl w/plate. 50.00
Jelly Compote. 30.00
Nappy 20.00
Pickle Tray. 15.00
Plate, Sq. 20.00
Pitcher, 2 Sizes . . . . . 85.00 – 125.00
Tumbler 25.00
Rose Bowl, 2 Sizes . . . . . 20.00 – 30.00
Salt Dip 15.00
Salt Shaker, 3 Types . . . . . 30.00 – 55.00
Salver. 40.00
Sugar, 3 Sizes . . . . . 25.00 – 50.00
Sugar Shaker 40.00
Syrup, 3 Sizes . . . . . 40.00 – 70.00
Toothpick Hldr. 30.00
Tray, 14" 25.00
Wine 10.00

FAN WITH DIAMOND
Butter. 50.00
Celery Vase 25.00
Compote, Any 40.00
Cordial 20.00
Creamer, Spooner, or Sugar 25.00
Egg Cup 25.00
Pickle Dish. 20.00
Relish. 20.00
Pitcher 65.00
Tumbler 15.00
Sauce 15.00
Wine 20.00

FAN WITH SPLIT DIAMOND
Berry Bowl, Sm. 15.00
Berry Bowl, Lg.. . . . . . 40.00

Butter . . . 60.00
Creamer or Spooner . . . 20.00
Mustard Pot . . . 35.00
Pitcher . . . 80.00
Tumbler . . . 20.00
Sugar . . . 35.00

FAN WITH STAR
Berry Bowl, Lg. . . . 35.00
Berry Bowl, Sm. . . . 15.00
Butter . . . 45.00
Celery Vase . . . 25.00
Compote . . . 40.00
Creamer, Spooner, or Sugar . . . 25.00
Goblet . . . 30.00
Plate, 7" . . . 25.00
Pitcher . . . 65.00
Tumbler . . . 15.00

FARMYARD COMPOSITE LAMP
Oil Lamp . . . 80.00
Vaseline . . . 200.00
Green/Blue . . . 160.00

FASHION
Berry Bowl, Lg. . . . 30.00
Berry Bowl, Sm. . . . 10.00
Bowl, 9", 10" & 12" . . . 30.00
Butter, Reg. . . . 45.00
Butter, Sm. . . . 40.00
Compote, 4" – 6½" . . . 35.00
Compote, 5½", 8½" & 10" . . . 45.00
Creamer, Spooner, or Sugar . . . 25.00
Custard Cup . . . 10.00
Jelly Compote w/Lid . . . 35.00
Nappy . . . 25.00
Orange Bowl w/Base . . . 45.00
Plate, 11" . . . 30.00
Pitcher . . . 85.00
Tumbler . . . 20.00
Punch Bowl w/Base . . . 110.00
Punch Cup . . . 15.00
Rose Bowl, 7" . . . 40.00
Salver, 8" & 12" . . . 50.00
Sherbet . . . 20.00
Toothpick Hldr. . . . 30.00

FEATHER
Banana Bowl, Ftd. . . . 70.00
Green/Blue . . . 185.00
Berry Bowl, Lg. . . . 35.00
Green/Blue . . . 75.00
Amber Stain . . . 95.00
Berry Bowl, Sm. . . . 15.00
Green/Blue . . . 25.00
Butter . . . 55.00
Green/Blue . . . 165.00
Amber Stain . . . 185.00
Cake Stand . . . 50.00
Green/Blue . . . 150.00
Amber Stain . . . 160.00
Celery Vase . . . 30.00
Green/Blue . . . 90.00
Amber Stain . . . 110.00
Compote, Covered, 6" – 8" . . . 85.00 – 135.00
Green/Blue . . . 165.00 – 235.00
Amber Stain . . . 195.00 – 300.00
Compote, Open, 4" – 8" . . . 20.00 – 80.00
Green/Blue . . . 85.00 – 115.00
Amber Stain . . . 100.00 – 140.00
Cordial . . . 100.00
Green/Blue . . . 135.00
Amber Stain . . . 165.00
Creamer or Spooner . . . 35.00
Green/Blue . . . 75.00
Amber Stain . . . 95.00
Cruet . . . 60.00
Green/Blue . . . 275.00
Amber Stain . . . 375.00
Goblet . . . 50.00
Green/Blue . . . 165.00
Amber Stain . . . 225.00
Jelly Compote . . . 65.00
Green/Blue . . . 95.00
Amber Stain . . . 145.00
Milk Pitcher . . . 55.00
Green/Blue . . . 175.00
Amber Stain . . . 235.00
Novelty Bowl . . . 35.00
Green/Blue . . . 75.00
Amber Stain . . . 125.00
Plate, 7" – 8" . . . 35.00
Green/Blue . . . 75.00
Amber Stain . . . 100.00
Plate, 10" . . . 45.00
Green/Blue . . . 80.00
Amber Stain . . . 120.00
Pitcher . . . 85.00
Green/Blue . . . 275.00
Amber Stain . . . 325.00
Tumbler . . . 35.00
Green/Blue . . . 80.00
Relish . . . 20.00
Green/Blue . . . 45.00
Amber Stain . . . 75.00
Shaker, ea. . . . 30.00
Green/Blue . . . 75.00
Amber Stain . . . 110.00
Spooner . . . 25.00
Green/Blue . . . 65.00
Amber Stain . . . 100.00
Square Sauce . . . 15.00
Green/Blue . . . 35.00
Syrup . . . 115.00
Green/Blue . . . 245.00
Amber Stain . . . 325.00
Toothpick Hldr. . . . 75.00
Green/Blue . . . 100.00
Amber Stain . . . 200.00
Wine . . . 45.00
Green/Blue . . . 100.00

FEATHER AND HEART
Pitcher, Very Scarce . . . 375.00
Tumbler, Scarce . . . 75.00

FEATHER BAND
Bowl . . . 30.00
Butter . . . 45.00
Creamer or Spooner . . . 25.00
Pitcher, 2 Sizes . . . 65.00
Tumbler . . . 20.00
Sauce . . . 15.00
Sugar, Flat . . . 25.00
Sugar, Ftd. . . . 30.00

FEATHER DUSTER
Berry Bowl, Sm. . . . 10.00
Green/Blue . . . 20.00
Berry Bowl, Lg. . . . 30.00
Green/Blue . . . 50.00
Butter . . . 65.00
Compote, Covered, 8" . . . 55.00
Covered Bowl, 9" . . . 35.00
Creamer or Spooner . . . 20.00
Egg Cup . . . 15.00
Pickle Dish . . . 10.00
Plate . . . 20.00
Pitcher . . . 60.00
Green/Blue . . . 85.00
Tumbler . . . 15.00
Green/Blue . . . 25.00
Shakers, ea. . . . 10.00
Sugar . . . 25.00
Tray . . . 30.00
Green/Blue . . . 65.00
Waste Bowl . . . 20.00

FEATHERED ARROW
Bowl . . . 50.00
Green/Blue . . . 70.00
Nut Dish . . . 55.00
Rose Bowl, Rare . . . 75.00

FEATHERED OVALS
Butter . . . 65.00
Creamer or Spooner . . . 20.00
Pitcher . . . 85.00
Tumbler . . . 15.00
Sugar . . . 25.00

FEATHERS
Vase . . . 30.00

FEDERAL #1910
Berry Bowl, Sm. . . . 15.00
Berry Bowl, Lg. . . . 35.00
Butter . . . 65.00
Celery Vase . . . 25.00
Creamer or Spooner . . . 20.00
Cup . . . 15.00
Goblet . . . 40.00
Jelly Compote . . . 30.00
Mayonnaise Set . . . 45.00
Pitcher . . . 80.00
Tumbler . . . 20.00
Shakers, ea. . . . 20.00
Sugar . . . 25.00
Vase, 3 Sizes . . . 20.00 – 40.00
Wine . . . 15.00

FEEDING DOG AND DEER
Mug . . . 25.00
Amber . . . 35.00
Vaseline . . . 85.00
Green/Blue . . . 70.00
Lavender . . . 65.00

FENTON GRAPE AND CABLE
Punch Bowl, Very Rare . . . 500.00
Punch Cup, Rare . . . 40.00

FERN BURST (PALM WREATH) (All pieces scarce)
Bowl, 8" – 10" . . . 55.00
Butter . . . 75.00
Carafe . . . 70.00
Creamer, Spooner, or Sugar . . . 40.00
Cruet . . . 65.00

FERNETTE
Berry Bowl, Sm. . . . 10.00
Berry Bowl, Lg. . . . 40.00
Butter . . . 65.00
Creamer or Spooner . . . 20.00
Pitcher . . . 75.00
Tumbler . . . 15.00
Sugar . . . 30.00
Toothpick Hldr. . . . 25.00

FERN GARLAND
Butter . . . 65.00
Celery Tray . . . 30.00
Celery Vase . . . 25.00
Compote, Low . . . 35.00
Compote, Tall . . . 45.00
Creamer or Spooner . . . 20.00
Cup . . . 15.00
Goblet . . . 50.00
Pitcher . . . 95.00
Tumbler . . . 20.00
Shakers, ea. . . . 25.00
Sugar . . . 25.00
Violet Vase . . . 30.00
Wine . . . 15.00

FERRIS WHEEL (AKA: LUCILE)
Butter . . . 65.00
Celery Vase . . . 30.00
Creamer, Spooner, or Sugar . . . 25.00
Jelly Compote . . . 35.00
Goblet . . . 30.00
Pitcher . . . 80.00
Tumbler . . . 25.00
Shakers, ea. . . . 35.00
Wine . . . 25.00

FESTOON
Bowls, Various . . . 30.00
Butter . . . 65.00
Cake Stand . . . 45.00
Compote, Open . . . 75.00
Creamer or Spooner . . . 40.00
Finger Bowl . . . 30.00
Marmalade Jar w/Lid . . . 70.00
Mug . . . 45.00
Pickle Caster . . . 135.00
Pitcher . . . 95.00
Tumbler . . . 25.00
Plate, 7" – 9" . . . 35.00
Relish, Oval . . . 30.00
Sauce . . . 10.00
Sugar . . . 60.00
Water Tray . . . 40.00

Waste Bowl 25.00

FIELD THISTLE

Berry Bowl, Lg. 30.00
Berry Bowl, Sm. 10.00
Butter 45.00
Caster Set 85.00
Chop Plate, 11" 40.00
Compote 30.00
Creamer or Spooner 20.00
Nappy 20.00
Olive Dish 15.00
Plate, 6" & 9" . . . . . 15.00 – 35.00
Pitcher 125.00
Sugar 30.00
Tumbler 40.00

FILE

Banana Dish, 8" 30.00
Berry Bowl, Sm. 10.00
Berry Bowl, Lg. 30.00
Bowl, Shallow, 8½" 25.00
Creamer or Spooner 20.00
Grape Plate 25.00
Oil Bottle 70.00
Plate, 4" – 6" 20.00
Plate, 8" – 10" 35.00
Pitcher 125.00
Tumbler 25.00
Rose Bowl, 5½" – 7" 35.00
Shakers, ea. 25.00
Sugar 25.00
Vase, 7" 25.00

FILIGREE METAL BASE LAMP

Oil Lamp 110.00
Vaseline 225.00

FINECUT

Boat Relish 35.00
Amber 45.00
Vaseline 60.00
Green/Blue 55.00

FINECUT AND BLOCK

Bowl, Hndl. 40.00
Amber 50.00
Green/Blue 50.00
Butter, 2 Styles . . . . . 75.00 – 85.00
Amber 100.00
Green/Blue 125.00
Cake Stand, 2 Sizes . . . . . 40.00 – 45.00
Celery Tray 30.00
Amber 45.00
Green/Blue 50.00
Compote, Covered 40.00
Compote, Open 30.00
Amber 50.00
Green/Blue 45.00
Cordial 25.00
Green/Blue 75.00
Creamer or Spooner 50.00
Amber 75.00
Green/Blue 60.00
Custard Cup 15.00
Amber 40.00
Green/Blue 30.00
Egg Cup 20.00
Amber 50.00
Green/Blue 35.00
Finger Bowl 25.00
Amber 60.00
Green/Blue 60.00
Goblet, 2 Sizes . . . . . 40.00 – 60.00
Amber 70.00
Green/Blue 85.00
Milk Pitcher 50.00
Amber 100.00
Green/Blue 100.00
Perfume Bottle 75.00
Amber 100.00
Green/Blue 100.00
Pickle Jar w/Lid 50.00
Pitcher 80.00
Amber 125.00
Green/Blue 125.00
Tumbler 25.00
Amber 50.00
Green/Blue 50.00
Plate 15.00
Punch Cup 10.00
Green/Blue 25.00
Relish 15.00
Amber 60.00
Green/Blue 50.00
Salt, Master 25.00
Amber 40.00
Salt, Ind. 15.00
Amber 25.00
Sauce, Flat or Ftd. 10.00
Amber 20.00
Green/Blue 20.00
Sugar 55.00
Amber 125.00
Green/Blue 140.00
Tray, Ice Cream 50.00
Tray, Water 45.00
Amber 65.00
Green/Blue 50.00
Wine 25.00
Amber 50.00
Green/Blue 50.00

FINECUT AND FAN

Bowl, Heart Shape 30.00
Butter 60.00
Creamer or Spooner 20.00
Pickle Dish, Oval 20.00
Sauce 10.00
Sugar 25.00
Toy Table Set 90.00

FINECUT AND PANEL

Berry Bowl, Sm. 10.00
Amber 15.00
Vaseline 25.00
Green/Blue 25.00
Berry Bowl, Lg. 25.00
Amber 30.00
Vaseline 40.00
Green/Blue 45.00
Bread Tray 30.00
Amber 35.00
Vaseline 45.00
Green/Blue 50.00
Butter 50.00
Amber 60.00
Vaseline 85.00
Green/Blue 100.00
Cake Stand 35.00
Amber 40.00
Vaseline 60.00
Green/Blue 65.00
Compote, Open 30.00
Amber 35.00
Vaseline 40.00
Green/Blue 45.00
Compote, Covered 45.00
Amber 50.00
Vaseline 65.00
Green/Blue 75.00
Cordial 15.00
Amber 20.00
Vaseline 25.00
Green/Blue 30.00
Creamer or Spooner 25.00
Amber 30.00
Vaseline 40.00
Green/Blue 50.00
Cup 10.00
Amber 15.00
Vaseline 20.00
Green/Blue 25.00
Goblet 35.00
Amber 40.00
Vaseline 50.00
Green/Blue 55.00
Milk Pitcher 45.00
Amber 50.00
Vaseline 65.00
Green/Blue 75.00
Pickle Dish, 7" – 9" 20.00
Amber 25.00
Vaseline 30.00
Green/Blue 35.00
Pitcher 65.00
Amber 70.00
Vaseline 95.00
Green/Blue 110.00
Tumbler 10.00
Amber 15.00
Vaseline 20.00
Green/Blue 25.00
Plate 20.00
Amber 25.00
Vaseline 30.00
Green/Blue 35.00
Platter, Oval 25.00
Amber 30.00
Vaseline 35.00
Green/Blue 45.00
Relish Tray 15.00
Amber 20.00
Vaseline 25.00
Green/Blue 30.00
Sugar 35.00
Amber 40.00
Vaseline 55.00
Green/Blue 65.00
Water Tray 25.00
Amber 30.00
Vaseline 40.00
Green/Blue 45.00

FINECUT FLOWER (PENNSYLVANIA)

Bowl, Lg. 30.00
Bowl, Sm. 15.00
Bowl, Sauce, Rnd. 15.00
Bowl, Sauce, Sq. 20.00
Butter 45.00
Carafe 30.00
Cheese Dish w/Lid 30.00
Creamer, Spooner, or Sugar 25.00
Pitcher 75.00
Tumbler 20.00
Toy Table Set, Complete 85.00
Toy Water Set, Complete 100.00
Toothpick Hldr. 30.00

FINECUT HEART

Bowl, 8" – 9", Rare 425.00

FINECUT OVALS

Bowl, 8" – 9", Rare 450.00

FINECUT SHIELD AND INVERTED THUMBPRINT

Compote, Covered 80.00

FINECUT SQUARE WITH DAISY BUTTON

Butter 75.00
Creamer or Spooner 25.00
Sugar 35.00

FINE PRISMS AND DIAMONDS

Vase, 11" – 15" 45.00

FINE RIB

Vase 20.00

FISH AND SWANS (All pieces rare)

Butter 250.00
Creamer or Spooner 75.00
Sugar 95.00

FISHSCALE

Ashtray (Daisy & Button Slipper on Tray) . 40.00
Butter 65.00
Bowl, Covered, 6" – 7" 40.00
Bowl, Covered, 8" – 9½" 55.00
Bowl, Open, 5" – 7" 35.00
Bowl, Open, 8" – 10" 45.00
Cake Stand, 4 Sizes . . . . . 25.00 – 45.00
Celery Vase 25.00
Compote, Covered, 5" – 7" 40.00
Compote, Covered, 8" – 10" 175.00
Compote, Open, 4" – 7" 35.00
Compote, Open, 8" – 10" 45.00
Condiment Tray 35.00
Creamer or Spooner 20.00
Finger Lamp 70.00
Goblet 40.00
Milk Pitcher 65.00

Mug . . . 25.00
Pickle Scoop, Tapered . . . 20.00
Plate, 7" – 9" . . . 25.00
Plate, 9" – 10" . . . 35.00
Relish . . . 20.00
Sauce, Flat or Ftd. . . . 15.00
Shakers, ea. . . . 20.00
Sugar . . . 25.00
Syrup . . . 65.00
Water Tray, Rnd. . . . 35.00

FLAMINGO

Butter . . . 125.00
Creamer or Spooner . . . 40.00
Goblet . . . 65.00
Pickle Jar . . . 55.00
Sugar . . . 50.00

FLATTENED DIAMOND AND SUNBURST

Butter . . . 45.00
Celery Vase . . . 25.00
Cordial . . . 15.00
Creamer or Spooner . . . 20.00
Pickle Dish . . . 20.00
Sauce . . . 10.00
Sugar . . . 25.00
Toy Table Set . . . 75.00

FLATTENED HOBNAIL

Butter . . . 65.00
Celery Vase . . . 25.00
Creamer or Spooner . . . 25.00
Goblet . . . 40.00
Shakers, ea. . . . 25.00
Sugar . . . 30.00
Toothpick Hldr. . . . 25.00

FLEUR-DE-LIS (THREADED SCRIBE)

Oil Lamp . . . 125.00

FLEUR DE LIS AND DRAPE

Bowl . . . 20.00
Green/Blue . . . 35.00
Butter . . . 60.00
Green/Blue . . . 85.00
Cake Stand . . . 30.00
Green/Blue . . . 60.00
Claret . . . 25.00
Green/Blue . . . 55.00
Compote, High . . . 25.00 – 45.00
Green/Blue . . . 30.00 – 55.00
Compote, Low . . . 30.00 – 55.00
Green/Blue . . . 35.00 – 70.00
Cordial . . . 20.00
Green/Blue . . . 35.00
Creamer or Spooner . . . 25.00
Green/Blue . . . 45.00
Cruet . . . 60.00
Green/Blue . . . 95.00
Cup & Saucer . . . 45.00
Green/Blue . . . 60.00
Finger Bowl . . . 20.00
Green/Blue . . . 35.00
Milk Pitcher . . . 45.00
Green/Blue . . . 60.00
Mustard Jar . . . 40.00
Green/Blue . . . 60.00
Pitcher . . . 65.00
Green/Blue . . . 95.00
Tumbler . . . 20.00
Green/Blue . . . 35.00
Sauces, Flat or Ftd. . . . 15.00
Green/Blue . . . 25.00
Shakers, ea. . . . 30.00
Green/Blue . . . 45.00
Sugar . . . 35.00
Green/Blue . . . 60.00
Tray . . . 35.00
Green/Blue . . . 55.00
Wine . . . 25.00
Green/Blue . . . 50.00

FLOATING SWAN

Pitcher, Rare . . . 425.00

FLORA

Berry Bowl, Lg. . . . 30.00
Green/Blue . . . 40.00
Berry Bowl, Sm. . . . 10.00
Green/Blue . . . 25.00
Bowls, Novelty . . . 20.00 – 40.00
Green/Blue . . . 35.00 – 65.00
Butter . . . 60.00
Green/Blue . . . 85.00
Celery Vase . . . 15.00
Green/Blue . . . 30.00
Compote . . . 30.00
Green/Blue . . . 45.00
Creamer or Spooner . . . 20.00
Green/Blue . . . 30.00
Cruet . . . 80.00
Green/Blue . . . 100.00
Pitcher . . . 110.00
Green/Blue . . . 135.00
Sugar . . . 30.00
Green/Blue . . . 40.00
Toothpick Hldr. . . . 25.00
Green/Blue . . . 35.00
Tumbler . . . 15.00
Green/Blue . . . 25.00

FLORADORA (BOHEMIAN)

Berry Bowl, Lg. . . . 35.00
Green/Blue . . . 45.00
Rose Flash . . . 50.00
Berry Bowl, Sm. . . . 10.00
Green/Blue . . . 15.00
Rose Flash . . . 20.00
Butter . . . 55.00
Green/Blue . . . 70.00
Rose Flash . . . 80.00
Celery Vase . . . 25.00
Green/Blue . . . 30.00
Rose Flash . . . 35.00
Creamer or Spooner . . . 30.00
Green/Blue . . . 35.00
Rose Flash . . . 40.00
Goblet . . . 40.00
Green/Blue . . . 50.00
Rose Flash . . . 60.00
Pickle Dish . . . 15.00
Green/Blue . . . 20.00
Rose Flash . . . 25.00
Pitcher . . . 70.00
Green/Blue . . . 85.00
Rose Flash . . . 100.00
Tumbler . . . 15.00
Green/Blue . . . 20.00
Rose Flash . . . 25.00
Straw Jar . . . 75.00
Green/Blue . . . 90.00
Rose Flash . . . 110.00
Sugar . . . 50.00
Green/Blue . . . 60.00
Rose Flash . . . 65.00
Toothpick Hldr. . . . 35.00
Green/Blue . . . 45.00
Rose Flash . . . 50.00
Wine . . . 20.00
Green/Blue . . . 25.00
Rose Flash . . . 30.00

FLORAL OVAL

Bowl, Rectangular . . . 35.00
Butter . . . 65.00
Creamer or Spooner . . . 25.00
Jelly Compote . . . 35.00
Plate, Sq. . . . 25.00
Pitcher . . . 70.00
Tumbler . . . 20.00
Sugar . . . 30.00
Wine . . . 15.00

FLORAL PEACOCK

Deep Bowl, 10" . . . 40.00

FLORENTINE

Candlesticks, ea. . . . 20.00
Vaseline . . . 55.00
Green/Blue . . . 45.00

FLORIDA

Bowl, Covered, 8" – 9" . . . 35.00
Green/Blue . . . 60.00
Bowl, Open, 8" – 9" . . . 25.00
Green/Blue . . . 35.00
Butter . . . 50.00
Green/Blue . . . 75.00
Cake Stand . . . 35.00
Green/Blue . . . 90.00
Celery Vase . . . 25.00
Green/Blue . . . 60.00
Compote, Sq., Covered or Open . 30.00 – 50.00
Green/Blue . . . 45.00 – 90.00
Cordial . . . 20.00
Green/Blue . . . 90.00
Creamer or Spooner . . . 20.00
Green/Blue . . . 60.00
Cruet . . . 60.00
Green/Blue . . . 225.00
Goblet . . . 45.00
Green/Blue . . . 75.00
Mustard Pot . . . 35.00
Green/Blue . . . 65.00
Pickle Dish . . . 20.00
Green/Blue . . . 35.00
Pitcher . . . 65.00
Green/Blue . . . 110.00
Tumbler . . . 20.00
Green/Blue . . . 40.00
Plate, Sq., 7¼" – 9¼" . . . 35.00
Green/Blue . . . 55.00
Relish Tray, 2 Shapes . . . 15.00
Green/Blue . . . 35.00
Sauce . . . 15.00
Green/Blue . . . 25.00
Shakers, ea. . . . 25.00
Green/Blue . . . 75.00
Sugar . . . 30.00
Green/Blue . . . 55.00
Syrup . . . 60.00
Green/Blue . . . 325.00
Wine . . . 15.00
Green/Blue . . . 75.00

FLOWER AND PANEL

Butter . . . 60.00
Amber . . . 80.00
Slag . . . 125.00
Creamer or Spooner . . . 35.00
Amber . . . 45.00
Slag . . . 65.00
Pitcher . . . 95.00
Amber . . . 135.00
Slag . . . 170.00
Sugar . . . 40.00
Amber . . . 55.00
Slag . . . 80.00

FLOWER AND PLEAT

Butter . . . 55.00
Ruby Stain . . . 70.00
Creamer or Spooner . . . 30.00
Ruby Stain . . . 40.00
Pickle Dish . . . 20.00
Ruby Stain . . . 25.00
Shakers, ea. . . . 20.00
Ruby Stain . . . 30.00
Sugar . . . 40.00
Ruby Stain . . . 50.00
Toothpick Hldr. . . . 35.00
Ruby Stain . . . 45.00

FLOWER BAND

Butter . . . 55.00
Celery Vase . . . 15.00
Compote w/Lid, 2 Shapes . . . 35.00
Creamer or Spooner . . . 20.00
Goblet . . . 40.00
Milk Pitcher . . . 65.00
Pitcher . . . 85.00
Sauce, Flat or Ftd. . . . 10.00
Sugar . . . 25.00

FLOWER BOUQUET

ABC Plate . . . 150.00

FLOWER FAN

Butter . . . 65.00
Cake Stand . . . 35.00
Compote . . . 35.00
Creamer or Spooner . . . 20.00
Cruet . . . 50.00

Pickle Dish. 20.00
Pitcher 85.00
Tumbler 15.00
Shakers, ea. 20.00
Sugar 25.00
Vase. 30.00

FLOWER MEDALLION
Berry Bowl, Sm. 15.00
Berry Bowl, Lg. 40.00
Butter. 65.00
Creamer or Spooner. 20.00
Pitcher 85.00
Tumbler 20.00
Sauce 10.00
Sugar 30.00
Toothpick Hldr. 25.00

FLOWER PANELLED CANE
Bowls, Ftd., Various . . . . . 15.00 – 40.00
Butter. 55.00
Celery Vase 20.00
Creamer or Spooner. 20.00
Goblet 35.00
Ice Bucket 45.00
Pickle Dish. 15.00
Sugar 25.00
Wine 10.00

FLOWER POT
Bread Tray (We Trust in God) 75.00
Butter. 60.00
Cake Stand. 50.00
Compote, Covered 45.00
Compote, Open 30.00
Creamer or Spooner. 30.00
Goblet 45.00
Milk Pitcher. 50.00
Pitcher 80.00
Tumbler 20.00
Sauce 10.00
Shakers, ea. 20.00
Sugar 45.00

FLOWER WITH CANE
Berry Bowl, Sm. 15.00
Berry Bowl, Lg. 30.00
Butter. 45.00
Creamer or Spooner. 20.00
Custard Cup. 10.00
Pitcher 65.00
Tumbler 15.00
Sugar 25.00
Toothpick Hldr., Fancy Base 30.00

FLUTE (MILLERSBURG)
Bonbon, 2 Shapes 175.00
Bowl, Master 150.00
Bowl, Sauce 50.00
Butter, Rare 250.00
Cake Plate, Stemmed. 400.00
Compote, 6" (Wildflower Blank) 275.00
Compote, 9" (Peacock Blank). 400.00
Compote, Round Whimsey 450.00
Creamer or Spooner. 100.00
Milk Pitcher. 150.00
Nappy (Holly Sprig Blank). 200.00
Pitcher 250.00
Punch Bowl w/Base, Rare 625.00
Punch Cup, Scarce. 45.00
Sugar, Very Scarce. 175.00

FLUTE (All Other Companies) (Condensed List)
Berry Bowl, Sm. 15.00
Berry Bowl, Lg. 35.00
Butter. 65.00
Compote. 40.00
Compote, Jelly Size 30.00
Creamer or Spooner. 20.00
Pickle Dish. 20.00
Pitcher 85.00
Tumbler 20.00
Punch Bowl 100.00
Punch Cup 10.00
Shakers, ea. 15.00
Sugar 25.00
Toothpick Hldr. 25.00
Vase. 25.00

FLUTE AND CANE
Berry Bowl, Sm. 10.00
Berry Bowl, Lg. 30.00
Bowl, hndl., 5" – 7". 15.00
Butter. 50.00
Celery Vase 25.00
Champagne 15.00
Compote. 30.00
Cordial. 20.00
Creamer or Spooner. 15.00
Cup 10.00
Goblet 15.00
Milk Pitcher. 45.00
Plate, 6" 20.00
Pitcher 65.00
Tumbler 15.00
Saucer 10.00
Sugar 20.00
Vase. 25.00

FLYING SWAN
Butter. 275.00
Celery Vase 65.00
Creamer or Spooner. 70.00
Jam Jar, Open. 80.00
Pitcher 325.00
Tumbler 50.00
Toothpick Hldr. 65.00
Sugar 95.00

"FOR AULD LANG AYNE"
Plate 55.00

FORGET-ME-NOT BANDS
Berry Bowl, Lg. 35.00
Berry Bowl, Sm. 15.00
Butter. 60.00
Celery Vase 30.00
Creamer, Spooner, or Sugar. 25.00
Jam Jar 25.00
Pitcher 80.00
Tumbler 20.00
Sauce 15.00
Tray 35.00

FORKS (CAMBRIDGE)
Berry Bowl, Sm. 15.00
Berry Bowl, Lg. 40.00
Butter. 70.00
Creamer or Spooner. 20.00
Cruet 50.00
Milk Pitcher. 65.00
Pitcher 80.00
Tumbler 20.00
Sugar 25.00

FORKS (IMPERIAL)
Cracker Jar. 75.00

FOSTORIA CLOCK SET
Candlesticks, Vaseline, ea.. . . . . 65.00
Clock, Vaseline 150.00

FOSTORIA'S #600
Bowl. 20.00
Butter. 45.00
Creamer or Spooner. 20.00
Pickle Dish. 15.00
Rose Bowl 35.00
Shakers, ea. 15.00
Sugar 25.00

FOSTORIA'S DANDELION (#1819)
Berry Bowl, Sm. 15.00
Berry Bowl Lg. 40.00
Toothpick Hldr. 25.00

FOSTORIA'S PRISCILLA
Bowl, 8½". 20.00
Butter. 80.00
Cake Stand. 40.00
Carafe 50.00
Celery Vase 30.00
Compote, Covered 55.00
Compote, Open 35.00
Creamer or Spooner. 30.00
Cruet 75.00
Egg Cup 25.00
Goblet 50.00
Jam Jar 50.00
Oil Lamp 135.00
Pickle Dish. 15.00
Pitcher 65.00
Tumbler 20.00
Salt Dip, 2 Styles 10.00
Sauce 10.00
Shakers, Lg. or Sm. . . . . 15.00 – 25.00
Sherbet Cup 10.00
Sugar 55.00
Syrup 65.00
Toothpick Hldr. 40.00
Vase. 30.00
Water Bottle. 55.00

FOUR PILLARS
Vase, Scarce. 40.00

474 (IMPERIAL)
Bowl, Sq., 9", Rare 65.00
Milk Pitcher. 55.00
Pitcher 75.00
Tumbler 25.00
Punch Bowl w/Base 85.00
Punch Cup 20.00
Vase. 45.00
Vase Whimsey, Very Rare 125.00

474 VARIANT
Bowls, Various . . . . . 10.00 – 30.00
Butter. 40.00
Creamer or Spooner. 20.00
Pitcher 55.00
Tumbler 10.00
Sugar 25.00

FOX AND CROW
Pitcher, Scarce. 275.00

FRAMED JEWEL
Butter. 50.00
  Ruby Stain. 70.00
Creamer or Spooner. 25.00
  Ruby Stain. 35.00
Goblet 40.00
  Ruby Stain. 50.00
Pitcher 70.00
  Ruby Stain. 110.00
Tumbler 20.00
  Ruby Stain. 30.00
Sugar 35.00
  Ruby Stain. 50.00
Toothpick Hldr. 40.00
  Ruby Stain. 60.00
Wine 20.00
  Ruby Stain. 30.00

FRANKLIN CARO
Container w/Advertising. 225.00

FRENCH SELTZER BOTTLE
Seltzer Bottle, Complete. 75.00
  Vaseline. 250.00
  Green/Blue. 185.00

FRINGED DRAPE
Bowl, Deep, 6" 20.00
Bowl, Oval, 5" – 11". . . . . 15.00 – 35.00
Bowl, Rnd., 6" – 9". . . . . 20.00 – 40.00
Butter. 65.00
Celery Tray. 25.00
Celery Vase 20.00
Cordial. 15.00
Creamer or Spooner. 20.00
Cruet 55.00
Cup 10.00
Jelly Compote. 30.00
Pickle Jar 35.00
Pickle Tray. 25.00
Sauce 10.00
Salad Fork Hndl., Unique 55.00
Shakers, ea. 20.00
Sugar 25.00
Syrup 55.00
Vase, Flat, 10" – 14". 45.00
Vase, Ftd., 8" – 9". 35.00

FROG AND LEAF
Match Hldr. 80.00

FROLICKING BEARS
Pitcher, Rare. 3500*
Tumbler, Rare 800.00
Tumbler, Silver Finish, Very Rare. 1500*

FROST CRYSTAL
Berry Bowl, Sm. 15.00
Ruby Stain. 20.00
Berry Bowl, Lg. 35.00
Ruby Stain. 55.00
Butter 70.00
Ruby Stain. 95.00
Celery Boat 30.00
Ruby Stain. 30.00
Celery Vase 35.00
Ruby Stain. 35.00
Creamer or Spooner 25.00
Ruby Stain. 35.00
Custard Cup 15.00
Ruby Stain. 20.00
Plate, 6" 20.00
Ruby Stain. 30.00
Plate, 10" 50.00
Ruby Stain. 40.00
Punch Bowl w/Base 85.00
Ruby Stain. 250.00
Shakers, ea. 30.00
Ruby Stain. 45.00
Sugar 30.00
Ruby Stain. 55.00

FROSTED BLOCK (Condensed List)
Berry Bowl, Sm. 20.00
Berry Bowl, Lg. 45.00
Bowl, Sq. 35.00
Butter 70.00
Compote 40.00
Creamer or Spooner 25.00
Milk Pitcher 65.00
Pickle Dish. 20.00
Plate 30.00
Rose Bowl 40.00
Sugar 30.00
Vase 35.00

FROSTED CHICKEN
Bowl, Covered, Low 80.00
Butter 145.00
Celery Vase 45.00
Compote, Covered 110.00
Creamer or Spooner 50.00
Goblet 65.00
Jam Jar 145.00
Sauce 25.00
Shakers, ea. 35.00
Sugar 65.00

FROSTED CIRCLE
Bowl, Covered, 7" – 8" 65.00
Bowl, Open, 7" – 8" 45.00
Butter 80.00
Cake Stand, 8" – 10". 45.00
Celery Vase 40.00
Compote, Covered 75.00
Creamer or Spooner 30.00
Pitcher 125.00
Tumbler 20.00
Sugar 30.00

FROSTED EAGLE
Bowl, Covered, 6¼" 175.00
Butter 225.00
Celery Vase 45.00
Compote w/Lid, Eagle Finial 190.00
Creamer or Spooner 45.00
Pitcher 165.00
Salt, Master 30.00
Salt, Ind. 15.00
Sugar 60.00

FROSTED FLEUR DE LIS
Butter 45.00
Amber 60.00
Green/Blue. 70.00
Milk Glass 60.00
Cake Stand, Lg. or Sm. . . . . 35.00 – 55.00
Amber . . . . . 45.00 – 70.00
Green/Blue . . . . . 55.00 – 85.00
Milk Glass . . . . . 45.00 – 70.00
Celery Vase 25.00
Amber 35.00
Green/Blue. 50.00
Milk Glass 40.00
Creamer or Spooner 25.00
Amber 35.00
Green/Blue. 50.00
Milk Glass 40.00
Goblet 35.00
Amber 45.00
Green/Blue. 60.00
Milk Glass 50.00
Pickle Dish. 20.00
Amber 30.00
Green/Blue. 40.00
Milk Glass 30.00
Pitcher 85.00
Amber 100.00
Green/Blue. 125.00
Milk Glass 95.00
Sugar 35.00
Amber 40.00
Green/Blue. 55.00
Milk Glass 40.00
Tumbler 15.00
Amber 25.00
Green/Blue. 35.00
Milk Glass 25.00
Wine 10.00
Amber 20.00
Green/Blue. 30.00
Milk Glass 20.00

FROSTED FRUIT
Berry Bowl, Sm. 20.00
Berry Bowl, Lg. 55.00
Butter 165.00
Celery Vase 45.00
Creamer or Spooner 50.00
Pitcher 275.00
Tumbler 50.00
Sugar 65.00

FROSTED HERON
Butter 175.00
Creamer or Spooner 75.00
Pitcher 250.00
Tumbler 65.00
Sugar 100.00

FROSTED LEAF
Butter 165.00
Celery Vase 130.00
Champagne 180.00
Compote, Covered 265.00
Compote, Open 135.00
Cordial 135.00
Creamer 375.00
Decanter 300.00
Egg Cup 115.00
Goblet, 2 Sizes . . . . . 150.00 – 175.00
Lamp, 2 Types 520.00
Milk Glass 385.00
Pitcher 450.00
Tumbler 150.00
Salt, Ind. 65.00
Salt, Master 120.00
Sauce 35.00
Spooner 150.00
Sugar 200.00
Wine 130.00

FROSTED QUAIL (All pieces rare)
Butter 175.00
Compote, Covered 225.00
Creamer or Spooner 65.00
Sugar 90.00

FROSTED RING (Variant of Beaded Mirror)
Compote, Covered 75.00

FROSTED STORK
Bowl, 9" 60.00
Butter 85.00
Creamer or Spooner 55.00
Goblet 70.00
Jam Jar, Covered 130.00
Pickle Caster 130.00
Plate, Hndl., 9". 90.00
Platter, 8¼" – 12" 95.00
Pitcher 225.00
Tumbler 35.00
Sauce 30.00
Sugar 100.00
Waste Bowl 55.00
Water Tray, 11" – 15½" 110.00

FROSTED STORK ABC
Plate, Scarce 55.00

FRUIT BAND
Bowl 35.00
Shakers, ea. 20.00

FUCHSIA
Butter 60.00
Cake Stand 35.00
Celery Vase 20.00
Compote 30.00
Creamer or Spooner 30.00
Goblet 40.00
Mug 35.00
Plate 25.00
Sugar 40.00
Tumbler, 2 Sizes . . . . . 20.00 – 30.00

GALLOWAY (VIRGINIA)
Basket, Hndl. 85.00
Maiden's Blush 150.00
Bowls, 5 Sizes, 2 Shapes . . . . . 20.00 – 55.00
Maiden's Blush . . . . . 65.00 – 95.00
Bowls, Oval or Rect., 2 Sizes . . . . 20.00 – 45.00
Maiden's Blush . . . . . 75.00 – 100.00
Butter 75.00
Maiden's Blush 225.00
Cake Stand, 3 Sizes . . . . . 65.00 – 75.00
Maiden's Blush . . . . . 200.00 – 250.00
Celery Vase 40.00
Maiden's Blush 100.00
Champagne 55.00
Maiden's Blush 95.00
Compote, Covered, 3 Sizes . . . . . 75.00 – 95.00
Maiden's Blush 125.00
Compote, Open, 8 Sizes . . . . . 25.00 – 70.00
Maiden's Blush . . . . . 45.00 – 100.00
Cracker Jar 55.00
Maiden's Blush 125.00
Creamer or Spooner 35.00
Maiden's Blush 75.00
Cruet 55.00
Maiden's Blush 250.00
Custard Cup 20.00
Maiden's Blush 40.00
Decanter 90.00
Maiden's Blush 225.00
Egg Cup 40.00
Maiden's Blush 65.00
Goblet 60.00
Maiden's Blush 125.00
Ice Jug 75.00
Maiden's Blush 150.00
Jelly Compote 35.00
Maiden's Blush 75.00
Milk Pitcher 70.00
Maiden's Blush 200.00
Mug, 2 Sizes . . . . . 45.00 – 60.00
Maiden's Blush 100.00
Olive Dish, Hndl. or Plain 25.00
Maiden's Blush 40.00
Pickle Caster 55.00
Maiden's Blush. 75.00
Pickle Dish. 25.00
Maiden's Blush 40.00
Pickle Jar 35.00
Maiden's Blush 90.00
Plate, 4 Sizes. . . . . 30.00 – 50.00
Maiden's Blush. . . . . 40.00 – 80.00
Pitcher 100.00
Maiden's Blush 350.00
Tumbler 40.00
Maiden's Blush 75.00
Punch Bowl 200.00
Maiden's Blush 625.00
Punch Cup 20.00
Maiden's Blush 35.00
Relish Tray. 30.00
Maiden's Blush 40.00

Ring Hldr. 75.00
Maiden's Blush 200.00
Salt Dip, Ind. 15.00
Maiden's Blush 40.00
Salt Dip, Master. 40.00
Maiden's Blush 75.00
Shakers, 2 Sizes, ea. 40.00
Maiden's Blush 200.00
Sherbet. 25.00
Maiden's Blush 65.00
Sugar 65.00
Maiden's Blush 100.00
Syrup 75.00
Maiden's Blush 350.00
Toothpick Hldr. 40.00
Maiden's Blush 90.00
Vase, 3 Types. 40.00
Maiden's Blush 65.00
Waste Bowl 45.00
Maiden's Blush 70.00
Water Bottle. 65.00
Maiden's Blush 175.00
Water Tray, 2 Sizes. . . . . 35.00 – 50.00
Maiden's Blush 125.00
(Note: Table set pieces come in reg., ind., or hotel size.)
(Add 15% for gold or rose stained pieces.)

GARDEN OF EDEN
Butter. 80.00
Cake Stand. 45.00
Compote, 9" 40.00
Creamer or Spooner. 25.00
Egg Cup 30.00
Goblet, 2 Styles 60.00
Honey Dish 35.00
Mug 25.00
Pickle Dish. 20.00
Plate, Rnd. 40.00
Platter, "Our Daily Bread" 85.00
Pitcher 110.00
Tumbler 25.00
Relish, Oval, 2 Styles 20.00
Salt, Master 20.00
Sauce 10.00
Sugar 30.00

GARDEN PINK
Bowl, Ftd., 4½" – 7½" . . . . . 25.00 – 40.00
Bowl, Oval, 9½" 35.00
Cake Stand. 40.00
Compote, Covered, 8½" 50.00
Dish, Heart Shape 25.00
Goblet 35.00
Jelly Compote. 30.00
Nappy 25.00
Pickle Dish. 25.00
Pitcher 75.00
Tumbler 15.00
Wine 15.00

GAR ENCAMPMENT
Goblet 165.00

GARFIELD ALPHABET
Plate, 7", ABC. 75.00

GARFIELD & LINCOLN MUG
Mug 75.00

GARFIELD DRAPE
Berry Bowl, Sm. 25.00
Berry Bowl, Lg. 50.00
Butter. 90.00
Cake Stand. 45.00
Compote, Covered, High or Low 70.00
Compote, Open 45.00
Creamer or Spooner. 30.00
Goblet, 2 Sizes. 60.00
Honey Dish 30.00
Memorial Bread Plate 75.00
Mourning Plate 80.00
Milk Pitcher. 65.00
Oil Lamp 165.00
Pitcher 145.00
Tumbler 25.00
Pickle Dish. 30.00
Relish. 25.00
Star Center Plate 65.00
Sugar 35.00

GARFIELD MEMORIAL
Plate. 75.00

GARFIELD PLATE WITH 101 BORDER
Plate. 80.00

GARFIELD STAR
Plate. 150.00

GARLAND OF ROSES
Bowl, Ftd. 70.00
Vaseline. 90.00
Butter 110.00
Vaseline. 145.00
Celery Vase 55.00
Vaseline. 65.00
Creamer or Spooner 65.00
Vaseline. 85.00
Egg Cup 40.00
Vaseline. 60.00
Salt, Open, Ftd. 45.00
Vaseline. 65.00
Sugar 80.00
Vaseline. 95.00
Toothpick Hldr. 65.00
Vaseline. 85.00

GEM STAR
Berry Bowl, Lg. 30.00
Berry Bowl, Sm. 10.00
Butter. 45.00
Celery Dish 20.00
Creamer, Spooner, or Sugar 20.00
Cruet 45.00
Pickle Dish. 25.00
Relish Dish 25.00

GERMAN BAND CAP
Novelty Hat 65.00
Amber 75.00
Vaseline. 125.00
Green/Blue. 90.00

GEORGE PEABODY
Cup 40.00
Saucer 30.00

GIANT BULLS-EYE
Berry Bowl, Sm. 20.00
Berry Bowl, Lg. 45.00
Butter. 75.00
Celery Vase 35.00
Compote. 45.00
Creamer or Spooner 25.00
Goblet 45.00
Pitcher 90.00
Tumbler 20.00
Shakers, ea. 25.00
Sugar 30.00

GIBSON CAMEO
Plate, 8½". 75.00

GIBSON GIRL
Butter. 100.00
Creamer or Spooner. 60.00
Plate, 10" 55.00
Pitcher 165.00
Tumbler 35.00
Relish Dish 25.00
Sauce 20.00
Sugar 85.00

GILDED LADY LAMP
Oil Lamp 110.00
Vaseline. 225.00

GIRAFFE
Goblet 95.00

GIRL WITH A FAN
Goblet 90.00

GIRL WITH LADEN APRON
Plate, Rnd., Scarce. 125.00

GIVE US OUR DAILY BREAD
Plate w/Dew Drop Pattern 65.00

GLASSPORT BRAVE
Advertising Tray, Very Scarce 100.00
Amber 125.00
Green/Blue. 115.00

"GLOBE"
Advertising Pie-wedge Shape
on Brazilian Pattern 45.00

GLOBE AND STAR
Butter. 60.00
Cake Stand. 35.00
Celery Vase 20.00
Compote, Covered 50.00
Compote, Open 30.00
Creamer or Spooner. 25.00
Goblet 35.00
Jelly Compote. 30.00
Pickle Dish. 20.00
Sugar 45.00
Wine 20.00

GLOVED HAND
Butter. 65.00
Creamer or Spooner. 30.00
Shakers, ea. 25.00
Sugar 35.00

GOAT'S HEAD (All pieces rare)
Butter. 225.00
Creamer or Spooner. 65.00
Sugar 100.00

GODDESS OF HUNT
Tray, Rectangular w/Hndls. 110.00

GOLDEN MEDALLIONS
Pitcher 110.00
Tumbler 25.00

GOLDEN RULE
Plate, Rnd., Scarce. 65.00

GONTERMAN SWIRL
Berry Bowl, Lg., Amber 40.00
Green/Blue. 50.00
Berry Bowl, Sm., Amber. 20.00
Green/Blue. 30.00
Butter, Amber. 85.00
Green/Blue. 100.00
Celery Vase, Amber 30.00
Green/Blue. 40.00
Cologne Bottle, Amber 75.00
Green/Blue. 85.00
Creamer or Spooner, Amber. 35.00
Green/Blue. 45.00
Cruet, Amber 90.00
Green/Blue. 110.00
Finger Bowl, Amber 30.00
Green/Blue. 45.00
Lamp Shade, Amber. 95.00
Green/Blue. 115.00
Pitcher, Amber 145.00
Green/Blue. 165.00
Shaker, Amber 45.00
Green/Blue. 55.00
Sugar, Amber 50.00
Green/Blue. 60.00
Toothpick Holder, Amber. 45.00
Green/Blue. 55.00
Tumbler, Amber 25.00
Green/Blue. 35.00

"A GOOD BOY"
Mug 45.00

GOOD LUCK (Not part of "Prayer Rug" line)
Relish Dish 35.00

GOOFUS GRAPE
Bowl. 45.00
Plate. 60.00

GOOSEBERRY VARIANT
Mug 35.00
Green/Blue. 40.00

GOOSE BOY
Compote, Open 115.00

GORDON
Compote, Covered 85.00

GOTHIC GRAPE
Dresser Set w/Mirrored Tray 135.00

GOTHIC WINDOWS
Berry Bowl, Sm. 15.00
Berry Bowl, Lg. 40.00
Butter. 65.00
Creamer or Spooner. 20.00
Goblet 45.00
Pickle Dish. 20.00
Pitcher 85.00
Tumbler 20.00

Sugar 30.00

GRAND
Bowl, Covered, Flat or Ftd. 50.00
Bowl, Open, Ftd. 35.00
Butter 65.00
Cake Stand, 8" – 10" 35.00
Celery Vase 25.00
Compote, Covered, High or Low 65.00
Compote, Open, High or Low 40.00
Cordial 15.00
Creamer or Spooner 20.00
Decanter 70.00
Dish, Oval, 7" – 9" 25.00
Goblet 40.00
Mug 25.00
Plate, 10" – 11" 30.00
Relish 20.00
Shakers, ea. 25.00
Sherbet 15.00
Sugar 30.00
Syrup 65.00
Waste Bowl 20.00
Water Tray 25.00
Wine 15.00

GRAPE AND CABLE (NORTHWOOD)
(All pieces scarce)
Banana Bowl 175.00
Orange Bowl 145.00
Sweetmeat, Covered 175.00
Plate, Very Scarce 200.00

GRAPE AND CABLE W/THUMBPRINT
Berry Bowl, Sm. 35.00
Berry Bowl, Lg. 100.00

GRAPE AND FESTOON
Bowl 35.00
Butter 80.00
Celery Vase 30.00
Compote, Covered, High 110.00
Compote, Covered, Low 85.00
Cordial 20.00
Creamer or Spooner 30.00
Egg Cup 25.00
Goblet 60.00
Lamp 7½" 95.00
Milk Pitcher 65.00
Pickle Tray 20.00
Plate 30.00
Pitcher 100.00
Relish Tray 20.00
Salt, Master 25.00
Sauce 10.00
Sugar 40.00
Wine 15.00

GRAPE BAND
Butter 55.00
Celery Vase 25.00
Compote, Covered, High or Low 45.00
Compote, Open 30.00
Cordial 20.00
Creamer or Spooner 25.00
Egg Cup 20.00
Goblet 40.00
Master Salt 15.00
Pickle Dish 20.00
Pitcher 80.00
Tumbler 20.00
Plate, 6" 20.00
Sugar 30.00
Wine 15.00

GRAPE BUNCH
Butter 55.00
Celery Vase 20.00
Creamer or Spooner 20.00
Egg Cup 25.00
Goblet 30.00
Pickle Dish 20.00
Pitcher 80.00
Sugar 30.00
Tumbler 15.00
Wine 10.00

GRAPE ON CRACKLE
Vase, 9" 35.00

GRAPES & ROSES ON BASKETWEAVE
Vase, 10' 35.00

GRAPES WITH OVERLAPPING FOLIAGE
(All pieces have porcelain finish.)
Berry Bowl, Sm. 20.00
Berry Bowl, Lg. 35.00
Butter 120.00
Celery Vase 45.00
Creamer or Spooner 70.00
Nappy, 4" 50.00
Nappy, 8" 65.00
Pitcher, Pedestal-based 250.00
Sugar 85.00

GRAPEVINE AND CHERRY SPRIG
Bowl, Ftd. 125.00
Butter 145.00
Creamer or Spooner 45.00
Pitcher 275.00
Tumbler 30.00
Sugar 60.00

GRAPEVINE BASKET
Basket, Metal Handle 60.00
Green/Blue 80.00

GRAPE WITH OVERLAPPING LEAVES
Butter 65.00
Celery Vase 25.00
Creamer or Spooner 30.00
Nappy, 4" and 8" . . . . . 20.00 – 35.00
Sugar 40.00

GRAPE WITHOUT VINE
Berry Bowl, Sm. 20.00
Berry Bowl, Lg. 45.00
Bowls, 4 Sizes . . . . . 10.00 – 50.00
Bowls, Covered, 4 Sizes . . . . . 15.00 – 60.00
Butter 65.00
Compote, Covered, 4 Sizes . . . . . 35.00 – 85.00
Compote, Open, 4 Sizes . . . . . 20.00 – 60.00
Creamer or Spooner 30.00
Pitcher 110.00
Tumbler 20.00
Sugar 30.00

GRAPE WITH THUMBPRINT
Bowl 30.00
Butter 70.00
Compote, Covered 45.00
Creamer or Spooner 20.00
Cup 10.00
Pitcher 80.00
Tumbler 20.00
Shakers, ea. 20.00
Sugar 30.00
Toothpick Hldr. 25.00

GRAPE WITH VINE
Bowl, Lg. 35.00
Bowl, Sm. 15.00
Butter 45.00
Celery Vase 30.00
Compote 40.00
Creamer, Spooner, or Sugar 25.00
Honey Dish 30.00
Salt Shaker, ea. 25.00

GRASSHOPPER
(Pieces without insect — 50% less.)
Bowl, Covered 45.00
Amber 60.00
Vaseline 125.00
Bowl, Open 25.00
Butter 80.00
Amber 100.00
Celery Vase 45.00
Amber 100.00
Compote, 7" – 8½" . . . . . 55.00 – 75.00
Creamer or Spooner 45.00
Amber 70.00
Vaseline 175.00
Marmalade Jar 150.00
Pickle Dish 25.00
Pitcher 95.00
Amber 165.00
Tumbler 25.00
Plate, 8½" – 10½" 30.00
Amber 100.00

Salt Dip 35.00
Salt Shaker 40.00
Sauce, Flat or Ftd. 15.00
Sugar 75.00
Amber 90.00

GRATED DIAMOND AND SUNBURST
Bowl, Various Sizes . . . . . 15.00 – 35.00
Butter 55.00
Carafe 40.00
Creamer or Spooner 25.00
Punch Bowl 95.00
Punch Cup 15.00
Salt Dip 25.00
Shakers, ea. 25.00
Sugar 30.00
Toothpick Hldr. 30.00

GRATED RIBBON
Bowls, Various . . . . . 15.00 – 35.00
Butter 55.00
Creamer or Spooner 20.00
Goblet 40.00
Pitcher 65.00
Tumbler 15.00
Sugar 25.00

GREEK KEY AND SCALES
Bowl, Dome Ftd. 45.00

GREENTOWN DOLPHIN
Novelty w/Lid 100.00
Amber 125.00
Green/Blue 145.00
Chocolate 300.00

GREENTOWN SQUIRREL
Pitcher, Rare 265.00
Chocolate 600.00

GROGAN
Butter 50.00
Celery Vase 15.00
Creamer or Spooner 20.00
Goblet 30.00
Sugar 25.00
Wine 20.00

GRUMPY WOMAN AND MAN
Mug 60.00
Opaque Blue 90.00

HAIRPIN
Butter 70.00
Champagne 20.00
Compote 40.00
Creamer or Spooner 25.00
Decanter 50.00
Egg Cup 15.00
Goblet 60.00
Sugar, Open 20.00
Wine 15.00

HAND
Bowls, 7" – 10" . . . . . 30.00 – 55.00
Butter 110.00
Cake Stand 35.00
Celery Vase 25.00
Compote, Covered, 7" – 8" . . . . . 45.00 – 65.00
Compote, Open, 8" – 9" . . . . . 30.00 – 50.00
Cordial 20.00
Creamer or Spooner 25.00
Dish, Oval, 7" – 10" . . . . . 20.00 – 35.00
Goblet 75.00
Honey Dish 35.00
Jam Jar 65.00
Mug 55.00
Pickle Tray 25.00
Platter 35.00
Pitcher 150.00
Tumbler 35.00
Sauce, Flat or Ftd. 20.00
Sugar 40.00
Syrup 65.00
Water Tray 45.00
Wine 20.00

HAND AND TORCH
Compote, Open 90.00

HAND VASE
Vase, 5" and 6" 45.00
Amber 65.00

Vaseline . . . 125.00
Green/Blue . . . 100.00

HANOVER
Bowl, 7" – 10" . . . 20.00 – 40.00
Amber . . . 25.00 – 45.00
Green/Blue . . . 30.00 – 50.00
Butter . . . 60.00
Amber . . . 80.00
Green/Blue . . . 100.00
Cake Stand . . . 35.00
Amber . . . 70.00
Green/Blue . . . 90.00
Celery Vase . . . 20.00
Amber . . . 45.00
Vaseline . . . 75.00
Green/Blue . . . 65.00
Cheese Dish, Covered . . . 85.00
Amber . . . 110.00
Green/Blue . . . 130.00
Compote, Covered, 7" – 8" . . . 55.00
Amber . . . 100.00
Green/Blue . . . 135.00
Compote, Open, 7" – 8" . . . 40.00
Amber . . . 55.00
Green/Blue . . . 75.00
Creamer or Spooner . . . 25.00
Cruet . . . 45.00
Amber . . . 65.00
Green/Blue . . . 85.00
Goblet . . . 45.00
Amber . . . 60.00
Green/Blue . . . 75.00
Milk Pitcher . . . 70.00
Amber . . . 90.00
Vaseline . . . 125.00
Green/Blue . . . 110.00
Mug, 2 Sizes . . . 25.00
Amber . . . 50.00
Green/Blue . . . 65.00
Plate, 4" – 10" . . . 20.00 – 30.00
Amber . . . 30.00 – 40.00
Green/Blue . . . 40.00 – 60.00
Platter . . . 45.00
Amber . . . 60.00
Green/Blue . . . 75.00
Puff Box . . . 55.00
Pitcher . . . 75.00
Amber . . . 90.00
Vaseline . . . 175.00
Green/Blue . . . 115.00
Tumbler . . . 20.00
Amber . . . 35.00
Green/Blue . . . 45.00
Sauce . . . 10.00
Amber . . . 15.00
Green/Blue . . . 20.00
Sugar . . . 30.00
Amber . . . 50.00
Green/Blue . . . 70.00
Wine . . . 20.00
Amber . . . 40.00
Green/Blue . . . 55.00

HARP
Double Relish, Scarce . . . 150.00

HARTLEY
Bowl, 6" – 9" . . . 15.00 – 30.00
Amber . . . 20.00 – 35.00
Vaseline . . . 25.00 – 40.00
Green/Blue . . . 25.00 – 40.00
Bread Plate . . . 30.00
Amber . . . 35.00
Vaseline . . . 65.00
Green/Blue . . . 40.00
Butter . . . 65.00
Amber . . . 80.00
Vaseline . . . 140.00
Green/Blue . . . 95.00
Cake Plate . . . 30.00
Amber . . . 80.00
Vaseline . . . 125.00
Green/Blue . . . 100.00
Celery Vase . . . 25.00
Amber . . . 45.00
Vaseline . . . 75.00
Green/Blue . . . 60.00
Compote, Covered, 7" – 8" . . . 50.00
Amber . . . 60.00
Vaseline . . . 125.00
Green/Blue . . . 90.00
Compote, Open, 7" – 8" . . . 35.00
Amber . . . 55.00
Vaseline . . . 80.00
Green/Blue . . . 65.00
Creamer or Spooner . . . 20.00
Amber . . . 35.00
Vaseline . . . 60.00
Green/Blue . . . 50.00
Goblet . . . 35.00
Amber . . . 40.00
Vaseline . . . 50.00
Green/Blue . . . 50.00
Milk Pitcher . . . 60.00
Amber . . . 70.00
Vaseline . . . 125.00
Green/Blue . . . 90.00
Plate . . . 25.00
Amber . . . 30.00
Vaseline . . . 60.00
Green/Blue . . . 45.00
Pitcher . . . 75.00
Amber . . . 95.00
Vaseline . . . 190.00
Green/Blue . . . 110.00
Tumbler . . . 15.00
Amber . . . 20.00
Vaseline . . . 45.00
Green/Blue . . . 30.00
Relish Tray . . . 15.00
Amber . . . 20.00
Vaseline . . . 25.00
Green/Blue . . . 25.00
Sugar . . . 25.00
Amber . . . 45.00
Vaseline . . . 80.00
Green/Blue . . . 65.00
Wine . . . 15.00
Amber . . . 30.00
Vaseline . . . 55.00
Green/Blue . . . 40.00

HATCHET
Novelty Piece . . . 75.00
Ruby Stain . . . 90.00

HAWAIIAN LEI (AKA "Gala")
Basket . . . 55.00
Butter . . . 80.00
Cake Stand . . . 50.00
Celery Tray . . . 30.00
Child's Table Set, Complete . . . 95.00
Compote . . . 40.00
Creamer or Spooner . . . 30.00
Ice Cream, Stemmed . . . 35.00
Jelly Compote, Tall . . . 40.00
Mayonnaise Bowl . . . 30.00
Nappy . . . 25.00
Pickle Dish, Oval . . . 20.00
Pitcher, 3 Sizes . . . 65.00 – 110.00
Plates, Various . . . 20.00 – 50.00
Rose Bowl . . . 30.00
Salver . . . 45.00
Sauce . . . 15.00
Sherbet . . . 20.00
Sugar . . . 40.00
Toothpick Hldr. . . . 40.00
Tumbler . . . 15.00
Twin Relish . . . 30.00
Vase, 2 Sizes . . . 20.00 – 35.00
Wafer Stand . . . 35.00

HEART AND SAND
Bowl, 4½" – 9" . . . 20.00 – 50.00
Butter . . . 75.00
Creamer or Spooner . . . 20.00
Pitcher . . . 90.00
Tumbler . . . 20.00
Sugar . . . 30.00
Toothpick Hldr. . . . 25.00

HEART BAND
Butter . . . 55.00
Ruby Stain . . . 80.00
Celery Vase . . . 25.00
Ruby Stain . . . 35.00
Creamer or Spooner . . . 35.00
Ruby Stain . . . 45.00
Mug . . . 40.00
Ruby Stain . . . 55.00
Shakers, ea. . . . 25.00
Ruby Stain . . . 30.00
Sugar . . . 55.00
Ruby Stain . . . 65.00
Toothpick Hldr. . . . 35.00
Ruby Stain . . . 60.00
Tumbler . . . 20.00
Ruby Stain . . . 30.00

HEART PLUME
Butter . . . 60.00
Compote . . . 35.00
Creamer or Spooner . . . 20.00
Pickle Dish . . . 20.00
Pitcher . . . 75.00
Tumbler . . . 20.00
Relish Tray . . . 20.00
Shakers, ea. . . . 25.00
Sugar . . . 30.00
Syrup . . . 70.00
Wine . . . 15.00

HEART STEM
Berry Bowl, Lg. . . . 75.00
Berry Bowl, Sm. . . . 20.00
Cake Stand . . . 115.00
Celery Vase . . . 85.00
Compote . . . 95.00
Creamer . . . 65.00
Pitcher . . . 175.00
Tumbler . . . 35.00
Salt Shaker . . . 40.00
Tray . . . 85.00

HEART WITH THUMBPRINT
Banana Boat, 2 Sizes . . . 55.00 – 80.00
Ruby Stain . . . 135.00
Barber Bottle . . . 100.00
Berry Bowl, Sm. . . . 25.00
Green/Blue . . . 80.00
Ruby Stain . . . 60.00
Berry Bowl, Lg. . . . 50.00
Green/Blue . . . 125.00
Ruby Stain . . . 85.00
Butter . . . 65.00
Green/Blue . . . 200.00
Ruby Stain . . . 135.00
Cake Stand . . . 35.00
Ruby Stain . . . 185.00
Carafe . . . 50.00
Ruby Stain . . . 165.00
Card Tray . . . 25.00
Green/Blue . . . 60.00
Ruby Stain . . . 90.00
Celery Vase . . . 25.00
Ruby Stain . . . 95.00
Compote, 2 Sizes . . . 45.00 – 75.00
Ruby Stain . . . 180.00
Condiment Tray . . . 50.00
Green/Blue . . . 75.00
Ruby Stain . . . 40.00
Creamer, 2 Sizes . . . 25.00 – 55.00
Green/Blue . . . 50.00 – 100.00
Ruby Stain . . . 65.00 – 165.00
Cruet . . . 65.00
Goblet . . . 65.00
Green/Blue . . . 130.00
Ruby Stain . . . 100.00
Hair Receiver . . . 55.00
Green/Blue . . . 100.00
Ruby Stain . . . 75.00
Ice Bucket . . . 55.00
Mustard Pot . . . 80.00
Green/Blue . . . 125.00
Oil Lamp . . . 95.00

Plate, 6" – 10" 25.00
Green/Blue . . . . 50.00 – 90.00
Ruby Stain . . . . 40.00 – 80.00
Pitcher 165.00
Green/Blue 235.00
Ruby Stain 200.00
Tumbler 20.00
Green/Blue 80.00
Ruby Stain 65.00
Powder Jar 25.00
Punch Bowl 110.00
Punch Cup 10.00
Green/Blue 35.00
Ruby Stain 30.00
Rose Bowl, 2 Sizes . . . . 25.00 – 45.00
Ruby Stain . . . . 75.00 – 100.00
Spooner 45.00
Green/Blue 90.00
Ruby Stain 70.00
Sugar, Sm., Open 30.00
Green/Blue 40.00
Ruby Stain 45.00
Sugar, Lg., Covered 75.00
Green/Blue 85.00
Syrup, 2 Sizes . . . . 50.00 – 70.00
Vase, 2 Sizes . . . . 30.00 – 60.00
Green/Blue . . . . 75.00 – 100.00
Ruby Stain . . . . 60.00 – 85.00
Wine 10.00
Green/Blue 135.00
Ruby Stain 110.00

HEAVY DIAMOND

Bowl, Lg. 30.00
Bowl, Sm. 10.00
Butter 55.00
Compote 35.00
Creamer, Spooner, or Sugar 25.00
Pitcher 70.00
Tumbler 25.00
Vase 25.00

HEAVY FINECUT (#800)

Butter Pat 20.00
Amber 30.00
Vaseline 35.00
Green/Blue 30.00
Celery Boat 20.00
Amber 30.00
Vaseline 35.00
Green/Blue 30.00
Celery Vase 25.00
Amber 35.00
Vaseline 40.00
Green/Blue 35.00
Champagne 15.00
Amber 25.00
Vaseline 30.00
Green/Blue 25.00
Cheese Plate w/Cover 70.00
Amber 85.00
Vaseline 135.00
Green/Blue 95.00
Claret 20.00
Amber 30.00
Vaseline 40.00
Green/Blue 45.00
Cologne, 5 Sizes . . . . 30.00 – 55.00
Amber . . . . 40.00 – 65.00
Vaseline . . . . 60.00 – 90.00
Green/Blue . . . . 70.00 – 95.00
Cordial 15.00
Amber 25.00
Vaseline 35.00
Green/Blue 40.00
Decanter 55.00
Amber 65.00
Vaseline 80.00
Green/Blue 70.00
Finger Bowl, 4 Styles . . . . 20.00 – 40.00
Amber . . . . 30.00 – 50.00
Vaseline . . . . 40.00 – 60.00
Green/Blue . . . . 35.00 – 55.00
Goblet 30.00
Amber 40.00
Vaseline 50.00
Green/Blue 45.00
Lamp 75.00
Amber 85.00
Vaseline 165.00
Green/Blue 145.00
Molasses Can 40.00
Amber 50.00
Vaseline 65.00
Green/Blue 60.00
Mustard Jar 30.00
Amber 40.00
Vaseline 50.00
Green/Blue 40.00
Oil Bottle 50.00
Amber 65.00
Vaseline 85.00
Green/Blue 75.00
Pickle Boat 15.00
Amber 20.00
Vaseline 35.00
Green/Blue 30.00
Pickle Jar 25.00
Amber 30.00
Vaseline 40.00
Green/Blue 35.00
Pitcher 85.00
Amber 95.00
Vaseline 180.00
Green/Blue 145.00
Plate, 3 Sizes . . . . 15.00 – 35.00
Amber . . . . 20.00 – 40.00
Vaseline . . . . 35.00 – 50.00
Green/Blue . . . . 30.00 – 45.00
Salt 15.00
Amber 20.00
Vaseline 30.00
Green/Blue 25.00
Salver, 3 Sizes . . . . 25.00 – 60.00
Amber . . . . 35.00 – 70.00
Vaseline . . . . 60.00 – 100.00
Green/Blue . . . . 55.00 – 85.00
Tray 30.00
Amber 40.00
Vaseline 60.00
Green/Blue 50.00
Tumbler 20.00
Amber 25.00
Vaseline 35.00
Green/Blue 30.00
Water Bottle 45.00
Amber 55.00
Vaseline 70.00
Green/Blue 65.00

HEAVY JEWEL

Bowl, Lg. 40.00
Bowl, Sm. 20.00
Butter 50.00
Celery Vase 35.00
Compote 40.00
Creamer, Spooner, or Sugar 25.00
Tray Oval, 8"x14" 65.00

HEISEY PINEAPPLE AND FAN

See Pineapple and Fan

HEAVY LEAF

Bowl 40.00

HEISEY PINWHEEL AND FAN

See Pinwheel and Fan

HEISEY'S #150

Bowls, Various . . . . 15.00 – 50.00
Butter 85.00
Celery Vase 25.00
Creamer or Spooner 45.00
Pitcher 150.00
Tumbler 30.00
Pickle Dish 30.00
Sugar 55.00

HEISEY'S #300 COLONIAL

Berry Bowl, Sm. 15.00
Berry Bowl, Lg. 50.00
Bowls on Stand, Ftd., 8" – 10" . . . 35.00 – 75.00
Bowls, Oval, 6 Sizes . . . . 20.00 – 50.00
Breakfast Set 55.00
Butter 85.00
Cake Stand 45.00
Celery Tray 30.00
Celery Vase 40.00
Champagne 25.00
Cocktail 25.00
Compotes, 4" – 6" . . . . 25.00 – 45.00
Cordial 30.00
Creamer or Spooner 25.00
Cruet, 5 Sizes . . . . 50.00 – 85.00
Goblet 45.00
Honey Dish, Covered 45.00
Loving Cup w/Spoon 50.00
Milk Pitcher 75.00
Mustard Jar 45.00
Nappy, Hndl. 35.00
Parfait 25.00
Plate, 6" 25.00
Pitcher, 3 Sizes . . . . 85.00 – 125.00
Punch Bowl 225.00
Punch Cup 20.00
Tumbler 25.00
Tumbler Ftd. 30.00
Shakers, 3 Styles, ea. . . . . 20.00 – 35.00
Sherbet, Stemmed, Various . . . . 20.00 – 35.00
Sherbet w/Plate 45.00
Sugar 40.00
Syrup, 3 Sizes . . . . 45.00 – 75.00
Toothpick Hldr. 35.00
Tray, Oval, 4 Sizes . . . . 20.00 – 55.00
Wine 20.00

HEISEY'S #1250

Berry Bowl, Sm. 20.00
Berry Bowl, Lg. 45.00
Bonbon 30.00
Butter 70.00
Celery Vase 30.00
Compote 55.00
Cracker Jar 50.00
Cruet 75.00
Pickle Jar 45.00
Plates, 5" & 6" 35.00
Pitcher 95.00
Tumbler 20.00
Shakers, ea. 25.00
Spoon Tray 35.00
Vase 40.00

HEISEY'S OLD SANDWICH

Ashtray 30.00
Amber 40.00
Green/Blue 50.00
Pink 35.00
Basket 45.00
Amber 60.00
Green/Blue 70.00
Pink 55.00
Bowls . . . . 20.00 – 40.00
Amber . . . . 30.00 – 50.00
Green/Blue . . . . 35.00 – 60.00
Pink . . . . 30.00 – 55.00
Candlesticks, ea. 20.00
Amber 30.00
Green/Blue 40.00
Pink 35.00
Catsup Bottle 35.00
Amber 45.00
Green/Blue 50.00
Pink 45.00
Champagne 25.00
Amber 40.00
Green/Blue 60.00
Pink 45.00
Claret 20.00
Amber 25.00
Green/Blue 35.00
Pink 40.00
Compote 40.00
Amber 50.00
Green/Blue 65.00
Pink 60.00

Cup 10.00
Amber 15.00
Green/Blue. . . . 25.00
Pink. . . . 20.00
Creamer 20.00
Amber 30.00
Green/Blue. . . . 35.00
Pink. . . . 30.00
Cruet 65.00
Amber 80.00
Green/Blue. . . . 95.00
Pink. . . . 70.00
Decanter 55.00
Amber 70.00
Green/Blue. . . . 85.00
Pink. . . . 65.00
Finger Bowl 20.00
Amber 30.00
Green/Blue. . . . 35.00
Pink. . . . 35.00
Goblet 25.00
Amber 35.00
Green/Blue. . . . 40.00
Pink. . . . 30.00
Ice Pitcher 65.00
Amber 80.00
Green/Blue. . . . 90.00
Pink. . . . 70.00
Juice Glass 10.00
Amber 20.00
Green/Blue. . . . 30.00
Pink. . . . 35.00
Mug, 4 Sizes . . . . 20.00 – 30.00
Amber. . . . 25.00 – 40.00
Green/Blue . . . . 30.00 – 50.00
Pink . . . . 25.00 – 35.00
Parfait 15.00
Amber 20.00
Green/Blue. . . . 25.00
Pink. . . . 20.00
Pilsner 20.00
Amber 25.00
Green/Blue. . . . 30.00
Pink. . . . 25.00
Pitcher 70.00
Amber 85.00
Green/Blue. . . . 110.00
Pink. . . . 90.00
Plate, 3 Sizes. . . . 15.00 – 30.00
Amber. . . . 20.00 – 35.00
Green/Blue . . . . 25.00 – 40.00
Pink . . . . 20.00 – 35.00
Shakers 20.00
Amber 35.00
Green/Blue. . . . 40.00
Pink. . . . 30.00
Sherbet. . . . 15.00
Amber 25.00
Green/Blue. . . . 35.00
Pink. . . . 30.00
Sugar 35.00
Amber 45.00
Green/Blue. . . . 60.00
Pink. . . . 50.00
Sundae. . . . 15.00
Amber 35.00
Green/Blue. . . . 40.00
Pink. . . . 30.00
Tumbler 15.00
Amber 25.00
Green/Blue. . . . 35.00
Pink. . . . 30.00
Wine 10.00
Amber 20.00
Green/Blue. . . . 30.00
Pink. . . . 25.00

HEISEY'S SUNBURST

(Condensed List — over 100 items in this pattern)
Bowl, Lg. 40.00
Bowl, Sm.. . . . 20.00
Butter. . . . 60.00
Compotes, Various Sizes. . . . 25.00 – 50.00
Creamer, Spooner, or Sugar. . . . 30.00
Cruet 50.00
Dessert. . . . 30.00
Oval Tray 35.00
Pitcher 70.00
Tumbler 30.00
Punch Bowl w/Base 125.00
Punch Cup 20.00
Salt Shakers, Pr. 60.00

HELMET

Butter/Novelty, Rare. . . . 575.00
Green/Blue. . . . 1250.00*

HENRIETTA

Bonbon 20.00
Bone Dish 20.00
Bowl, Rectangular 30.00
Bowl, Rnd., 7" – 9". . . . 20.00 – 35.00
Bread Plate 25.00
Butter. . . . 80.00
Cake Stand. . . . 40.00
Castor Set. . . . 115.00
Celery Tray. . . . 25.00
Celery Vase 20.00
Compote, Open 25.00
Confection Jar w/Lid. . . . 45.00
Cracker Jar 40.00
Creamer or Spooner. . . . 25.00
Creamer, Ind. 20.00
Cruet 55.00
Cup 10.00
Lamp 90.00
Mustard Jar 35.00
Olive Dish 20.00
Pickle Jar 25.00
Pitcher, 2 Styles . . . . 75.00 – 125.00
Tumbler, 2 Styles . . . . 20.00 – 35.00
Rose Bowl 30.00
Salt, Master 25.00
Salt, Ind. 10.00
Sauce 10.00
Shade, Electric 65.00
Shakers, ea., 2 Styles . . . . 15.00 – 25.00
Sugar 40.00
Sugar, Ind. 30.00
Syrup 60.00
Vase, 5" – 9" . . . . 15.00 – 35.00

HERO

Berry Bowl, Sm. 15.00
Berry Bowl, Lg. 40.00
Butter. . . . 70.00
Cake Stand. . . . 35.00
Celery Vase 25.00
Creamer or Spooner. . . . 20.00
Cruet 50.00
Goblet 35.00
Mustard Pot. . . . 25.00
Shakers, ea. 20.00
Sugar 30.00

HERON

Pickle Castor 85.00

HERON AND PEACOCK

Mug 60.00
Green/Blue. . . . 85.00
Milk Glass. . . . 55.00

HERO'S OF BUNKER HILL

Bread Plate, Oval. . . . 80.00

HERRINGBONE

Berry Bowl, Lg. 35.00
Berry Bowl, Sm. 10.00
Butter. . . . 50.00
Celery Vase 30.00
Compote w/Lid 55.00
Creamer, Spooner, or Sugar. . . . 30.00
Goblet 30.00
Pickle Dish. . . . 25.00
Pitcher 70.00
Tumbler 15.00
Relish. . . . 20.00

HERRINGBONE AND MUMS

Tumbler, Rare 90.00

HEXAGONAL BLOCK BAND

Berry Bowl, Sm. 15.00
Berry Bowl, Lg. 45.00
Butter. . . . 65.00
Celery Vase 25.00
Creamer or Spooner. . . . 25.00
Goblet 50.00
Pickle Dish. . . . 20.00
Pitcher 110.00
Tumbler 20.00
Sugar 30.00
Wine 20.00

HEXAGONAL BULLS-EYE

Butter. . . . 55.00
Celery Vase 30.00
Creamer or Spooner. . . . 20.00
Goblet 35.00
Pitcher 75.00
Tumbler 20.00
Sauce 15.00
Sugar 25.00
Wine 15.00

HEY, DIDDLE DIDDLE

Nursery Rhyme Plate, One in a Series . . . 45.00

HICKMAN

Banana Stand 60.00
Bonbon, Sq. 20.00
Bottle, Pepper 35.00
Bowls, 4" – 8". . . . 15.00 – 40.00
Green/Blue . . . . 20.00 – 60.00
Butter. . . . 45.00
Green/Blue. . . . 75.00
Celery 20.00
Green/Blue. . . . 40.00
Champagne 20.00
Cologne Bottle 40.00
Compote, Covered, 7". . . . 85.00
Compote, Open, 8". . . . 45.00
Cordial. . . . 25.00
Creamer 25.00
Green/Blue. . . . 40.00
Cruet 50.00
Custard Cup. . . . 15.00
Goblet 35.00
Green/Blue. . . . 50.00
Ice Bucket 55.00
Jelly Compote. . . . 35.00
Green/Blue. . . . 45.00
Lemonade 20.00
Mustard Jar w/Underplate 50.00
Nappy 15.00
Olive Dish 10.00
Green/Blue. . . . 15.00
Pickle Dish. . . . 15.00
Green/Blue. . . . 20.00
Plate. . . . 20.00
Pitcher 75.00
Tumbler 30.00
Punch Bowl 200.00
Green/Blue. . . . 425.00
Punch Cup 10.00
Green/Blue. . . . 20.00
Punch Cup, Ftd. 40.00
Relish. . . . 15.00
Green/Blue. . . . 20.00
Rose Bowl 30.00
Green/Blue. . . . 40.00
Salt Dip, Ind. 15.00
Shaker, 3 Styles, Ea. . . . . 20.00 – 35.00
Green/Blue . . . . 25.00 – 60.00
Sauce 10.00
Green/Blue. . . . 15.00
Sugar 45.00
Green/Blue. . . . 65.00
Toothpick Hldr. 40.00
Green/Blue. . . . 80.00
Toy Condiment Set. . . . 95.00
Green/Blue. . . . 150.00
Vase, 10" 15.00
Green/Blue. . . . 40.00
Wine 25.00
Green/Blue. . . . 30.00

HIDALGO

Berry Bowl, Sm. 15.00

Berry Bowl, Lg. 40.00
Bread Plate 25.00
Butter 70.00
Compote, Covered, High or Low . 40.00 – 55.00
Compote, Open, 6" – 11" . . . . 25.00 – 45.00
Creamer or Spooner 20.00
Cruet 55.00
Cup & Saucer 35.00
Finger Bowl 15.00
Goblet 35.00
Milk Pitcher 55.00
Pickle Dish 20.00
Pitcher 85.00
Tumbler 20.00
Salt, Ind. 10.00
Salt, Master 25.00
Sugar 30.00
Syrup 65.00
Water Tray 25.00
Waste Bowl 15.00

HIGBEE FLUTE
Bowls, Various . . . . . 10.00 – 30.00
Butter 45.00
Celery Tray 15.00
Creamer or Spooner 20.00
Goblet 25.00
Pickle Dish 15.00
Stemmed Dessert 10.00
Sugar 25.00
Wine 15.00

HIGBEE MUG
Advertising Mug 70.00

HINTO
Butter 50.00
  Vaseline 110.00
Celery Vase 20.00
  Vaseline 35.00
Champagne 15.00
  Vaseline 25.00
Creamer or Spooner 20.00
  Vaseline 35.00
Egg Cup 25.00
Vaseline 40.00
Goblet 40.00
  Vaseline 65.00
Master Salt, Open 20.00
  Vaseline 30.00
Sugar 35.00
  Vaseline 45.00
Sweetmeat w/Cover 65.00
  Vaseline 100.00
Tumbler, Flat 25.00
  Vaseline 40.00
Whiskey Tumbler 30.00
  Vaseline 50.00

HOBBS BLOCK
Bowl, Oval, 7" – 10" . . . . . 20.00 – 40.00
  Amber Stain . . . . . 35.00 – 70.00
Butter 40.00
  Amber Stain 110.00
Celery Tray, Boat Shape 40.00
  Amber Stain 50.00
Creamer or Spooner 25.00
  Amber Stain 30.00
Cruet 55.00
  Amber Stain 100.00
Finger Bowl 20.00
  Amber Stain 35.00
Goblet 40.00
  Amber Stain 65.00
Pitcher 65.00
  Amber Stain 165.00
Tumbler 20.00
  Amber Stain 30.00
Sauce 15.00
  Amber Stain 25.00
Sugar 35.00
  Amber Stain 50.00
Syrup 50.00
  Amber Stain 125.00
Water Bottle 40.00
  Amber Stain 85.00

HOBBS DEWDROP
Bitters Bottle 75.00
  Amber 95.00
  Vaseline 120.00
  Green/Blue 100.00
  Other 130.00
Bowl, 3 Sizes . . . . . 45.00 – 60.00
  Amber . . . . . 65.00 – 90.00
  Vaseline . . . . . 80.00 – 110.00
  Green/Blue . . . . . 70.00 – 85.00
  Other . . . . . 90.00 – 130.00
Bowl, Oval, 3 Sizes . . . . . 55.00 – 80.00
  Amber . . . . . 70.00 – 95.00
  Vaseline . . . . . 75.00 – 115.00
  Green/Blue . . . . . 65.00 – 90.00
  Other . . . . . 80.00 – 120.00
Butter 110.00
  Amber 135.00
  Vaseline 150.00
  Green/Blue 140.00
  Other 140.00
Celery Vase 35.00
  Amber 50.00
  Vaseline 60.00
  Green/Blue 55.00
  Other 70.00
Creamer or Spooner 30.00
  Amber 50.00
  Vaseline 60.00
  Green/Blue 55.00
  Other 65.00
Cruet, Oil 60.00
  Amber 75.00
  Vaseline 85.00
  Green/Blue 80.00
  Other 90.00
Finger Bowl 25.00
  Amber 40.00
  Vaseline 50.00
  Green/Blue 45.00
  Other 60.00
Pickle Jar 45.00
  Amber 65.00
  Vaseline 75.00
  Green/Blue 70.00
  Other 85.00
Pitcher 120.00
  Amber 155.00
  Vaseline 200.00
  Green/Blue 165.00
  Other 265.00
Sauce 15.00
  Amber 30.00
  Vaseline 45.00
  Green/Blue 40.00
  Other 50.00
Shaker 40.00
  Amber 60.00
  Vaseline 80.00
  Green/Blue 75.00
  Other 85.00
Sugar 45.00
  Amber 65.00
  Vaseline 85.00
  Green/Blue 80.00
  Other 95.00
Toy Tumbler 25.00
  Amber 45.00
  Vaseline 55.00
  Green/Blue 50.00
  Other 65.00
Tumbler 15.00
  Amber 35.00
  Vaseline 45.00
  Green/Blue 40.00
  Other 50.00
Water Bottle 50.00
  Amber 70.00
  Vaseline 90.00
  Green/Blue 80.00
  Other 140.00
Vase 30.00
  Amber 50.00
  Vaseline 65.00
  Green/Blue 60.00
  Other 80.00

HOBBS HOBNAIL
Butter 85.00
Finger Bowl 25.00
Pitcher 145.00
Tumbler 25.00
Toy Water Set 100.00
Tray 40.00
Vase Whimsey, from Pitcher 85.00

HOBBS POLKA DOT
Bar Bottle 65.00
  Amber 80.00
  Vaseline 90.00
  Green/Blue 70.00
  Rubina 95.00
Bowl, Ftd. 55.00
  Amber 65.00
  Vaseline 75.00
  Green/Blue 65.00
  Rubina 80.00
Buttermilk Tumbler 30.00
  Amber 40.00
  Vaseline 65.00
  Green/Blue 55.00
  Rubina 70.00
Celery Vase 25.00
  Amber 35.00
  Vaseline 65.00
  Green/Blue 55.00
  Rubina 70.00
Champagne Glass 20.00
  Amber 40.00
  Vaseline 65.00
  Green/Blue 50.00
  Rubina 60.00
Cheese Dish, Covered 50.00
  Amber 70.00
  Vaseline 100.00
  Green/Blue 85.00
  Rubina 130.00
Cruet 55.00
  Amber 65.00
  Vaseline 85.00
  Green/Blue 70.00
  Rubina 95.00
Custard Cup 20.00
  Amber 30.00
  Vaseline 55.00
  Green/Blue 40.00
  Rubina 60.00
Lemonade Mug 30.00
  Amber 40.00
  Vaseline 70.00
  Green/Blue 60.00
  Rubina 80.00
Mustard Pot 35.00
  Amber 45.00
  Vaseline 80.00
  Green/Blue 70.00
  Rubina 90.00
Oil Bottle 50.00
  Amber 60.00
  Vaseline 90.00
  Green/Blue 75.00
  Rubina 85.00
Pitcher, 5 Sizes . . . . . 75.00 – 115.00
  Amber . . . . . 80.00 – 130.00
  Vaseline . . . . . 125.00 – 250.00
  Green/Blue . . . . . 110.00 – 200.00
  Rubina . . . . . 125.00 – 275.00
Sauce 15.00
  Amber 25.00
  Vaseline 40.00
  Green/Blue 30.00
  Rubina 35.00
Shaker 40.00
  Amber 55.00
  Vaseline 70.00
  Green/Blue 60.00

Rubina....65.00
Sugar, 2 Styles....35.00
Amber....50.00
Vaseline....70.00
Green/Blue....55.00
Rubina....60.00
Tumbler....20.00
Amber....30.00
Vaseline....55.00
Green/Blue....40.00
Rubina....60.00
Water Bottle....50.00
Amber....65.00
Vaseline....90.00
Green/Blue....70.00
Rubina....85.00

HOBNAIL

Bone Dish....15.00
Bowls, Various....10.00 – 45.00
Butter....60.00
Celery Vase....30.00
Creamer or Spooner....25.00
Goblet....40.00
Mugs....15.00 – 50.00
Perfume....65.00
Pitcher....95.00
Tumbler....20.00
Shakers, ea....25.00
Sugar....25.00
Toothpick Hldr....40.00
Tray....35.00
Vase....30.00
Wine....25.00

HOBNAIL BAND

Butter....55.00
Ruby Stain....75.00
Candlesticks, ea....20.00
Ruby Stain....30.00
Celery Tray....20.00
Ruby Stain....25.00
Champagne....15.00
Ruby Stain....30.00
Coaster....10.00
Ruby Stain....25.00
Creamer or Spooner....20.00
Ruby Stain....25.00
Cup & Saucer....35.00
Ruby Stain....40.00
Custard Cup....10.00
Ruby Stain....25.00
Goblet....40.00
Ruby Stain....60.00
Plate....20.00
Ruby Stain....45.00
Pitcher....65.00
Ruby Stain....95.00
Tumbler....10.00
Ruby Stain....25.00
Sauce....10.00
Ruby Stain....15.00
Sugar....30.00
Ruby Stain....45.00
Syrup....55.00
Ruby Stain....85.00
Wine....10.00
Ruby Stain....20.00

HOBNAIL-IN-SQUARE

Bowl, Lg....35.00
Bowl, Sm....15.00
Butter....45.00
Creamer, Spooner, or Sugar....25.00
Cruet, Rare....65.00
Pitcher....80.00
Tumbler....20.00
Shakers, ea....20.00

HOBNAIL WITH BARS

Berry Bowl, Lg....30.00
Berry Bowl, Sm....10.00
Butter....45.00
Cake Stand....45.00
Creamer, Spooner, or Sugar....20.00
Cruet....45.00

HOBNAIL WITH FAN

Butter....45.00
Amber....55.00
Green/Blue....60.00
Creamer or Spooner....20.00
Amber....25.00
Green/Blue....30.00
Dish, Oblong....20.00
Amber....25.00
Green/Blue....30.00
Goblet....35.00
Amber....45.00
Green/Blue....40.00
Pitcher....85.00
Amber....100.00
Green/Blue....90.00
Tumbler....15.00
Amber....25.00
Green/Blue....20.00
Salt Dip, Ind....15.00
Amber....25.00
Green/Blue....20.00
Sauce....10.00
Amber....20.00
Green/Blue....15.00
Sugar....25.00
Amber....35.00
Green/Blue....30.00
Tray....30.00
Amber....40.00
Green/Blue....35.00
Wine....10.00
Amber....20.00
Green/Blue....15.00

HOBSTAR

Berry Bowl, Sm....10.00
Berry Bowl Lg....30.00
Butter....55.00
Celery Vase....30.00
Compote, 10" – 11"....40.00
Cookie Jar w/Lid....40.00
Creamer or Spooner....20.00
Fruit Bowl, 10½"....35.00
Goblet....50.00
Jelly Compote....25.00
Nappy, 5" – 6"....20.00
Milk Jar w/Lid....60.00
Orange Bowl, 11"....35.00
Pitcher....75.00
Tumbler....15.00
Plate, 5"....10.00
Plate, 10½"....25.00
Punch Bowl....75.00
Punch Cup....15.00
Rose Bowl, 5½"....30.00
Rose Bowl, 7" – 9"....40.00
Salver, 13"....45.00
Sherbet....20.00
Sugar....25.00
Sundae....20.00
Syrup....55.00
Water Tray, 13"....25.00
Wine....20.00

HOBSTAR (U.S. #15124)

Butter....50.00
Candy Dish, Covered....35.00
Celery Vase....20.00
Creamer or Spooner....20.00
Pickle Dish....15.00
Pitcher....70.00
Tumbler....15.00
Sugar....25.00

HOBSTAR AND FEATHER (All pieces scarce)

Apple Sauce Dish, 2 Sizes....150.00 – 175.00
Banana Boat, 3 Sizes....60.00 – 75.00
Banana Bowl, Whimsey, from Jelly....350.00
Basket, Hndl., Very Scarce....650.00
Bowl, Master Berry....75.00
Ruby Stain....900.00*
Bowl, Small Berry....35.00
Ruby Stain....350.00*
Bowl, Tri-corner Sauce, Scarce....125.00
Maiden's Blush....150.00
Bowl, Ice Cream, Lg....75.00
Bowl, Ice Cream, Sm....35.00
Maiden's Blush....150.00
Bowl, Lg. Sq., Rare....250.00
Bridge Set, Complete....400.00
Bridge Pieces, ea....95.00
Ruby Stain....550.00
Butter....325.00
Card Tray....60.00
Card Tray Whimsey, from Spooner....400.00
Celery Boat, 10" – 5"....175.00
Compote Whimsey w/Metal Stem....250.00
Compote, Giant Whimsey....2000.00
Cracker Jar....400.00
Creamer or Spooner....80.00
Ruby Stain....550.00
Jelly Compote, 6"....100.00
Master Boat, Lg....85.00
Master Boat, Med....65.00
Master Boat, Sm....45.00
Mint Bowl....350.00
Ruby Stain....600.00
Nut Bowl....250.00
Pickle Dish, Sm....40.00
Pickle Dish, Med....60.00
Sapphire....1250.00
Pickle Dish, Lg....75.00
Pitcher, Standard....450.00
Pitcher, Mammoth, Rare....1000.00
Pitcher w/Metal Top, Rare....1200.00
Pitcher Whimsey, No Spout, Rare....900.00
Tumbler....75.00
Plate, 5"....100.00
Plate, 7"....150.00
Plate, 9"....250.00
Plate, 11" – 12", Rare....500.00
Plate, Diamond Shape, Rare....350.00
Plate, Handgrip, Rare....150.00
Plate, 11", 4 Sides Up, Rare....450.00
Platter, Lg., Rare....650.00
Platter, Sm., Rare....300.00
Rose Bowl, Sm., Flat....200.00
Rose Bowl, Lg., Flat....275.00
Rose Bowl, Stemmed....250.00
Rose Bowl, Giant....1500.00
Rose Bowl Giant ICS Whimsey....2000.00
Punch Bowl w/Base....1425.00
Punch Cup....35.00
Sherbet, Flared Top....75.00
Sherbet, Rose Bowl Shape....150.00
Sherbet, Goblet Shape....100.00
Spittoon Whimsey, Very Rare....3000.00*
Sugar w/Lid....115.00
Ruby Stain....800.00
(*Add 25% for frosted pieces.)

HOBSTAR AND TASSELS

Banana Bowl, 7"....50.00
Berry Bowl, 5"....30.00
Berry Bowl, 7"....35.00
Bowl, Deep, 6"....30.00
Ice Cream, 6½"....30.00
Grape Plate, 7½"....45.00
Plate, 7½"....55.00
Nut Bowl, 5"....35.00
Rose Bowl, 3 Sizes, Rare....75.00

HOBSTAR BAND

Bowls, Various....10.00 – 35.00
Pitcher, Ftd....75.00
Pitcher, Ftd., Advertising, Rare....200.00
Tumbler....35.00

HOBSTAR FLOWER

Compote....40.00
Cruet....60.00

HOLLAND (OAT SPRAY)

Berry Bowl, Sm....20.00
Berry Bowl, Lg....45.00
Butter....80.00
Compote, Covered....60.00
Compote, Open....40.00
Creamer or Spooner....25.00
Goblet....60.00

Pickle Dish....20.00
Pitcher....110.00
Tumbler....20.00
Sugar....30.00
Toothpick Hldr....35.00
Wine....15.00

HOLLIS
Celery Vase....25.00
Pitcher....75.00
Tumbler....20.00

HOLLY
Bowl, Covered, 2 Styles....155.00
Butter....165.00
Cake Stand....140.00
Celery Vase....65.00
Compote, Covered, High....155.00
Compote, Covered, Low....145.00
Creamer or Spooner....120.00
Egg Cup....65.00
Goblet....100.00
Pickle Dish....150.00
Pitcher....185.00
Tumbler, Flat or Ftd....115.00 – 125.00
Salt Dip....45.00
Sauce....15.00
Sugar....130.00
Syrup....150.00
Wine....115.00

HOLLY AMBER (GREENTOWN)
Bowl, 6" – 8½"....100.00 – 125.00
Chocolate....600.00 – 800.00
Bowl, Oval....125.00
Chocolate....425.00
Bowl, Oval, Ftd....200.00
Chocolate....1500.00
Bowl, Rectangular....225.00
Chocolate....1000.00
Butter....325.00
Chocolate....1600.00
Butter, Ftd....900.00
Chocolate....2500.00
Cake Stand....350.00
Chocolate....2200.00
Compote, Covered, 6½" – 8½"....300.00 – 425.00
Chocolate....1500.00 – 2500.00
Creamer or Spooner....175.00
Chocolate....800.00
Cruet....400.00
Chocolate....2800.00
Jelly Compote....350.00
Chocolate....1100.00
Mug....165.00
Chocolate....550.00
Nappy....165.00
Chocolate....625.00
Pickle Dish....90.00
Chocolate....400.00
Pitcher....1000.00
Chocolate....3500.00
Tumbler, Chocolate....950.00
Plate, 2 Styles....225.00
Chocolate....800.00
Shakers, ea....190.00
Chocolate....500.00
Sauce....90.00
Chocolate....325.00
Sugar, 2 Styles....350.00
Chocolate....1000.00 – 3000.00
Syrup....600.00
Chocolate....1350.00
Toothpick Hldr....145.00
Chocolate....725.00
Toothpick Hldr., Ftd....325.00
Chocolate....2300.00
Tray....225.00
Chocolate....1350.00
Vase, 6" – 8"....250.00 – 350.00
Chocolate....900.00 – 2000.00

HONEYCOMB
Bowls, Various....10.00 – 40.00
Butter....60.00
Celery Vase....20.00
Compote....35.00
Creamer or Spooner....30.00
Decanter....55.00
Egg Cup....25.00
Jam Jar, Covered....40.00
Pickle Dish....20.00
Sugar....45.00
Vase....25.00

HONEYCOMB AND HOBSTAR (GLORIA)
(All pieces scarce)
Bowl, 2 Sizes....15.00 – 40.00
Ruby Stain....25.00 – 60.00
Butter....150.00
Ruby Stain....200.00
Carafe....135.00
Ruby Stain....165.00
Compote....70.00
Ruby Stain....90.00
Creamer or Spooner....65.00
Ruby Stain....80.00
Pitcher....250.00
Ruby Stain....300.00
Tumbler....35.00
Ruby Stain....45.00
Sugar....75.00
Ruby Stain....110.00
Vase....350.00

HONEYCOMB WITH STAR
Berry Bowl, Sm....10.00
Berry Bowl, Lg....35.00
Butter....60.00
Cake Stand....35.00
Celery Vase....20.00
Compote....30.00
Creamer or Spooner....20.00
Cruet....50.00
Pickle Dish....15.00
Pitcher....85.00
Tumbler....15.00
Sauce, Flat....10.00
Sugar....25.00

HORSE
Goblet, Engraved....95.00
Tumbler, Engraved....70.00

HORSE AND CART
Match Hldr....100.00

HORSE, CAT, AND RABBIT
Goblet, Rare....265.00

HORSE INKWELL
Double Inkwell, Frosted....250.00

HORSEMINT
Goblet....65.00
Pitcher....150.00
Tumbler....35.00
Wine....25.00

HORSESHOE (AKA: Good Luck or Prayer Rug)
Bowl w/Cover....45.00
Butter....50.00
Cake Stand....40.00
Celery Vase....30.00
Compote w/Lid....50.00
Creamer, Spooner, or Sugar....25.00
Jam Jar....25.00
Master Salt, Rare....65.00
Plate, 8" – 10"....30.00
Plate, Bread Size....20.00
Platter....35.00
Relish....20.00
Wine, Rare....40.00

HORSESHOE DAISEY (NEW MARTINSVILLE)
Bowls, Various....15.00 – 45.00
Butter....90.00
Creamer or Spooner....30.00
Pitcher....125.00
Sugar....45.00
Tumbler....25.00

HOURGLASS
Butter....60.00
Creamer or Spooner....25.00
Goblet....40.00
Pitcher....85.00
Tumbler....15.00
Sauce....10.00
Sugar....30.00

THE HUB (MEMPHIS-NORTHWOOD)
Advertising Bowl, Lg....150.00

HUBER (FALMOUTH)
Bitters Bottle....75.00
Bowl, Covered....45.00
Butter....50.00
Celery Vase....25.00
Compote....35.00
Compote w/Lid, 2 Sizes....45.00
Creamer, Spooner, or Sugar....25.00
Decanter....65.00
Egg Cup, Hndl....30.00
Mug....40.00
Plate....25.00
Pitcher....70.00
Tumbler....15.00
Salt Dip....20.00
Whiskey, Hndl....20.00
Wine....20.00

HUMMINGBIRD
Bowl Covered....55.00
Amber....85.00
Vaseline....95.00
Green/Blue....85.00
Butter....75.00
Amber....95.00
Vaseline....135.00
Green/Blue....85.00
Celery Vase....45.00
Amber....90.00
Vaseline....65.00
Green/Blue....90.00
Cheese Plate....35.00
Amber....55.00
Vaseline....45.00
Green/Blue....55.00
Compote....50.00
Amber....95.00
Vaseline....80.00
Green/Blue....95.00
Creamer or Spooner....40.00
Amber....75.00
Vaseline....65.00
Green/Blue....75.00
Goblet....45.00
Amber....60.00
Vaseline....65.00
Green/Blue....75.00
Milk Pitcher....45.00
Amber....70.00
Green/Blue....95.00
Pickle Dish....30.00
Amber....40.00
Vaseline....35.00
Green/Blue....40.00
Pitcher....95.00
Amber....135.00
Vaseline....180.00
Green/Blue....150.00
Tumbler....30.00
Amber....75.00
Vaseline....50.00
Green/Blue....75.00
Open Salt....25.00
Amber....55.00
Vaseline....45.00
Green/Blue....55.00
Sauce....15.00
Amber....25.00
Vaseline....25.00
Green/Blue....25.00
Sugar....55.00
Amber....100.00
Vaseline....80.00
Green/Blue....100.00
Water Tray....60.00
Amber....145.00
Vaseline....100.00
Green/Blue....125.00

HUMPTY DUMPTY
Mug 55.00
HUNDRED-LEAVED ROSE
Bowl 35.00
Butter 70.00
Creamer or Spooner 30.00
Pitcher 100.00
Tumbler 20.00
Sauce 15.00
Sugar, Open 40.00
Sugar, Covered 50.00
IBEX
Goblet, Rare 155.00
I-H-C
Berry Bowl, Sm. 15.00
Berry Bowl, Lg. 45.00
Butter 70.00
Celery Vase 20.00
Compotes, Various . . . . . 20.00 – 50.00
Creamer or Spooner 20.00
Pickle Dish 20.00
Pitcher 95.00
Tumbler 20.00
Sauce 10.00
Sugar 30.00
Vase, 7" 35.00
I.H.S.
Oval Tray/Platter 45.00
ILLINOIS
Banquet Lamp & Shade 200.00
Basket, Hndl. 40.00
Berry Bowl, Sm. 20.00
Berry Bowl, Lg. 45.00
Bonbon, Stemmed, 5" – 8" 35.00
Bowl, Ice Cream 25.00
Butter 65.00
Breakfast Set, 2 Pcs. 35.00
Cake Stand 40.00
Candlesticks, ea. 30.00
Celery Tray 20.00
Celery Vase 25.00
Cheese Dish, Covered 60.00
Compote, 9" 35.00
Creamer or Spooner 20.00
Cruet 55.00
Finger Bowl 20.00
Ice Cream Tray 20.00
Jam Jar 30.00
Jelly Compote 25.00
Olive Dish 20.00
Pickle Dish 20.00
Green/Blue 40.00
Pickle Jar 30.00
Plate, Rnd. or Sq. 30.00
Pitcher, 2 Sizes . . . . . 75.00 – 100.00
Green/Blue 200.00
Tumbler, 2 Sizes . . . . . 15.00 – 20.00
Green/Blue 45.00
Puff Box 40.00
Relish Tray 20.00
Salt, Ind. 10.00
Salt, Master 25.00
Sauce 10.00
Spoon Tray 20.00
Straw Hldr. 50.00
Green/Blue 350.00
Sugar 25.00
Syrup 70.00
Toothpick Hldr. 30.00
Vase, 2 Sizes . . . . . 30.00 – 40.00
Green/Blue 100.00
Water Jug, Squatty 55.00
IMPERIAL GRAPE
Sandwich Platter, Cntr. Hndl. 25.00
IMPERIAL NU-CUT #91/500
Bowls, 3 Sizes . . . . . 15.00 – 35.00
Breakfast Creamer or Sugar 25.00
Jelly Compote 35.00
Nappy 25.00
Mayonnaise Bowl 25.00
Mayonnaise Plate, Oval 25.00
Vase, 6½" 30.00
IMPERIAL NU-CUT #91/607
Bowls, Various . . . . . 15.00 – 40.00
Pickle Dish, Hndl. 25.00
IMPERIAL SPITTOON
Novelty Spittoon, Lg. 25.00
IMPERIAL'S #262
Olive Dish, Hndl., 5" 35.00
IMPERIAL'S #300
Lemonade Set, Complete 80.00
Pitcher 60.00
Tumbler 20.00
IMPERIAL'S #302
Berry Bowl, Sm. 10.00
Berry Bowl, Lg. 30.00
Bowl, 8½" – 9½" 25.00
Butter 45.00
Creamer or Spooner 20.00
Decanter 40.00
Goblet 30.00
Plate, 6" – 10" 20.00
Sugar 25.00
Sugar Shaker 45.00
Tumbler 15.00
Wine 10.00
IMPERIAL'S #347
Berry Bowl, Sm. 10.00
Berry Bowl, Lg. 30.00
Ice Cream Bowl, Sm. 15.00
Ice Cream Bowl, Lg. 40.00
IMPERIAL'S #370
Salt Shakers, Fancy Tops 60.00
IMPERIAL'S #403½
Pitcher 65.00
Tumbler 15.00
IMPERIAL'S #405
Vase, 11" – 13" 30.00
IMPERIAL'S #737
Salad Bowl 40.00
IMPERIAL'S #750
Stemmed Fruit Bowl 55.00
IMPERIAL'S #3888
Berry Bowl, Lg. 35.00
Berry Bowl, Sm. 15.00
Bowl, Flared, 10" 30.00
Rose Bowl, 7½" 40.00
IMPERIAL'S #4040
Compote, Lg. 60.00
Fruit Bowl, Lg. 60.00
IMPERIAL'S BASKET
Basket, Hndl., 10" 40.00
IMPERIAL'S BELLAIRE
Bowl, 8½", Scarce 65.00
Punch Bowl & Base, Rare 475.00
Punch Cup, Scarce 20.00
IMPERIAL'S PANSY
Bowl, 8" – 9" 40.00
IMPERIAL'S THUNDERBOLT
Bouquet Vase, 13" 35.00
IMPERIAL'S WICKER BASKET (#428½)
Castor Set, 3 Pcs. 50.00
INDEPENDENCE HALL
Mug 50.00
INDIAN SUNSET
Berry Bowl, sm. 10.00
Berry Bowl, Lg. 40.00
Bonbon 25.00
Butter 70.00
Celery Tray 15.00
Creamer or Spooner 20.00
Pickle Dish 15.00
Pitcher 95.00
Tumbler 20.00
Shakers, ea. 20.00
Sugar 25.00
INDIANA
Bowl, 5" – 9" 20.00
Bowl, Oval, 7" – 9" 30.00
Butter 60.00
Carafe 35.00
Catsup Bottle 40.00
Celery Tray 20.00
Celery Vase 25.00
Compote 30.00
Creamer or Spooner 20.00
Cruet 45.00
Finger Bowl 20.00
Ice Tub 45.00
Jelly Dish 20.00
Nappy, 5" and 6" 25.00
Perfume 35.00
Pitcher 85.00
Tumbler 20.00
Sauce 10.00
Shakers, ea. 20.00
Sugar 25.00
Syrup 60.00
Tray, Oblong 30.00
INDIANA'S #115
Berry Bowl, Sm. 20.00
Berry Bowl, Lg. 45.00
Butter 65.00
Creamer or Spooner 20.00
Pitcher 75.00
Tumbler 15.00
Sugar 25.00
INDIANA'S #123
Berry Bowl, Sm. 10.00
Berry Bowl, Lg. 45.00
Bowl, Deep, 8½" 35.00
Butter 65.00
Cabarette Bowl, 11" 35.00
Cake Stand, 2 Sizes . . . . . 25.00 – 40.00
Celery Tray 20.00
Compote, Covered, 4 Sizes . . . . . 30.00 – 70.00
Creamer or Spooner 25.00
Cruet 55.00
Custard Cup 10.00
Goblet 35.00
Jelly Compote 25.00
Orange Bowl, Flat 50.00
Pitcher, 3 Sizes . . . . . 60.00 – 125.00
Tumbler 25.00
Plate, 12" 30.00
Punch Bowl, 4 Shapes 145.00
Punch Cup 10.00
Sugar 40.00
Wine 15.00
INDIANA'S #156
Banana Bowl, Ftd. 45.00
Butter 60.00
Cabarette Bowl 30.00
Celery Tray 20.00
Creamer or Spooner 20.00
Goblet 45.00
Heart Shape Dish 20.00
Nappy 20.00
Nut Bowl 20.00
Pickle Dish 20.00
Plate, 12" 30.00
Pitcher 85.00
Tumbler 20.00
Salad Bowl, Sm. 15.00
Salad Bowl, Lg. 35.00
Sugar 25.00
Vase, Pedestal Ftd. 30.00
INDIANA #165
Berry Bowl, Lg. 35.00
Berry Bowl, Sm. 10.00
Berry Creamer 20.00
Berry Sugar 25.00
Breakfast Set, 2 Pcs. 50.00
Butter 65.00
Celery Dish 15.00
Celery Vase 20.00
Compote, Hndl. 30.00
Compote, Open, 3 Sizes . . . . . 15.00 – 30.00
Creamer or Spooner 30.00
Jelly, Ftd. 25.00
Olive Dish 15.00
Pickle Dish 15.00
Pitcher, 3 Sizes . . . . . 60.00 – 95.00
Tumbler 20.00
Salt, 2 Sizes . . . . . 10.00 – 15.00
Sauce, Ftd. 10.00

Sugar . . . 35.00
Syrup . . . 70.00
Vase . . . 25.00
Water Bottle . . . 40.00

INDIANA SILVER
Berry Bowl, Sm. . . . 15.00
Berry Bowl, Lg. . . . 45.00
Butter . . . 75.00
Creamer or Spooner . . . 25.00
Goblet . . . 55.00
Rose Bowl, Ftd. . . . 35.00
Sherbet . . . 20.00
Sugar . . . 35.00

INNOVATION #407
Basket . . . 40.00
Bonbon . . . 20.00
Bowl, 8" . . . 25.00
Celery Vase . . . 20.00
Compote . . . 40.00
Creamer . . . 25.00
Fernery . . . 45.00
Lamp & Matching Shade . . . 115.00
Nappy . . . 20.00
Rose Bowl, Ftd. . . . 30.00
Sugar, Open . . . 25.00
Vase, Cylinder Shape . . . 30.00

INNOVATION #420
Bowl, 8" & 10" . . . 20.00 – 35.00
Celery Tray . . . 15.00
Compote, Lg., on Stand . . . 55.00
Corset Vase, 12" . . . 60.00
Creamer . . . 20.00
Sugar . . . 30.00
Trumpet Vase . . . 40.00

IN REMEMBRANCE
Platter (Washington, Lincoln, or Garfield) . . 75.00

INSIDE RIBBING
Berry Bowl, Sm. . . . 10.00
Vaseline . . . 20.00
Green/Blue . . . 20.00
Berry Bowl, Lg. . . . 30.00
Vaseline . . . 45.00
Green/Blue . . . 40.00
Butter . . . 50.00
Vaseline . . . 115.00
Green/Blue . . . 70.00
Celery Vase . . . 15.00
Vaseline . . . 25.00
Green/Blue . . . 25.00
Creamer or Spooner . . . 25.00
Vaseline . . . 35.00
Green/Blue . . . 35.00
Cruet . . . 55.00
Vaseline . . . 70.00
Green/Blue . . . 65.00
Pickle Dish . . . 10.00
Vaseline . . . 20.00
Green/Blue . . . 20.00
Sugar . . . 30.00
Vaseline . . . 45.00
Green/Blue . . . 40.00
Syrup . . . 60.00
Vaseline . . . 95.00
Green/Blue . . . 70.00
Toothpick Hldr. . . . 35.00
Vaseline . . . 55.00
Green/Blue . . . 50.00

INTAGLIO BUTTERFLIES
Bowl, 8½" . . . 45.00
Compote, 7½" . . . 55.00
Sauce, 5" . . . 20.00

INTAGLIO DAISY
Berry Bowl, Sm. . . . 15.00
Berry Bowl, Lg. . . . 35.00
Butter . . . 55.00
Cake Stand . . . 30.00
Compote . . . 35.00
Pitcher . . . 80.00
Tumbler . . . 15.00
Sugar . . . 25.00

INTAGLIO SUNFLOWER
Butter . . . 50.00
Creamer or Spooner . . . 20.00
Pitcher . . . 75.00
Tumbler . . . 15.00
Straw Holder w/Cover . . . 65.00
Sugar . . . 30.00
Toothpick Hldr. . . . 25.00

INVERTED EYE
Butter, 2 Styles . . . 85.00
Creamer or Spooner, 2 Styles . . . 45.00
Sugar, 2 Styles . . . 65.00
Toothpick Hldr. . . . 35.00

INVERTED FEATHER
Basket . . . 50.00
Bonbon . . . 35.00
Bowls, Various Shapes & Sizes . . 20.00 – 45.00
Bowl, Berry, Lg. . . . 40.00
Bowl, Berry, Sm. . . . 20.00
Butter . . . 110.00
Cake Stand . . . 45.00
Compote, Lg. . . . 40.00
Compote, Jelly . . . 30.00
Celery Vase . . . 25.00
Creamer, Spooner, or Sugar . . . 30.00
Cruet . . . 80.00
Decanter . . . 100.00
Pickle Tray . . . 35.00
Pitcher . . . 225.00
Tumbler . . . 30.00
Punch Bowl w/Base . . . 425.00
Punch Cup . . . 20.00
Plate . . . 65.00
Salt Shaker, ea. . . . 30.00
Sherbet . . . 20.00
Toothpick Hldr. . . . 75.00
Tray, Rectangular . . . 40.00
Water Bottle . . . 80.00
Whiskey Jug . . . 120.00
Wine . . . 25.00
Vase . . . 65.00

INVERTED FERN
Bowl, Ftd. . . . 30.00
Butter . . . 100.00
Champagne . . . 110.00
Compote, Open . . . 50.00
Creamer or Spooner . . . 100.00
Egg Cup, 2 Styles . . . 45.00
Goblet, 2 Styles . . . 45.00
Honey Dish . . . 15.00
Pitcher . . . 300.00
Tumbler . . . 100.00
Plate . . . 110.00
Salt . . . 40.00
Sauce . . . 10.00
Sugar . . . 85.00
Wine . . . 75.00

INVERTED PEACOCK
Pitcher . . . 425.00
Tumbler . . . 75.00
Water Tray . . . 125.00

INVERTED STRAWBERRY
Basket, Squat w/Handle . . . 55.00
Ruby Stain . . . 75.00
Berry Bowl, Sm. . . . 10.00
Ruby Stain . . . 15.00
Berry Bowl, Lg. . . . 35.00
Ruby Stain . . . 50.00
Bonbon, Ftd. . . . 30.00
Ruby Stain . . . 35.00
Butter . . . 80.00
Ruby Stain . . . 95.00
Candlesticks, ea. . . . 45.00
Ruby Stain . . . 50.00
Celery Vase . . . 20.00
Ruby Stain . . . 25.00
Compote . . . 50.00
Ruby Stain . . . 55.00
Creamer, Ftd. . . . 25.00
Ruby Stain . . . 35.00
Custard Cup . . . 10.00
Ruby Stain . . . 15.00
Fruit Bowl, Ftd. . . . 40.00
Ruby Stain . . . 45.00
Goblet . . . 60.00
Ruby Stain . . . 65.00
Jelly Compote . . . 30.00
Ruby Stain . . . 35.00
Oil Bottle . . . 65.00
Ruby Stain . . . 70.00
Powder Jar w/Lid . . . 75.00
Ruby Stain . . . 85.00
Pitcher . . . 175.00
Ruby Stain . . . 210.00
Tumbler . . . 25.00
Ruby Stain . . . 50.00
Rose Bowl . . . 65.00
Ruby Stain . . . 70.00
Sugar, Ftd. . . . 40.00
Ruby Stain . . . 55.00
Sweet Pea Vase, Stemmed . . . 40.00
Ruby Stain . . . 50.00
Wine . . . 10.00
Ruby Stain . . . 20.00

INVERTED THUMBPRINT AND STAR
Goblet . . . 20.00
Amber . . . 25.00
Vaseline . . . 45.00
Green/Blue . . . 40.00

I.O.U.
Berry Bowl, Sm. . . . 10.00
Vaseline . . . 20.00
Green/Blue . . . 20.00
Berry Bowl, Lg. . . . 30.00
Vaseline . . . 45.00
Green/Blue . . . 40.00
Butter . . . 55.00
Vaseline . . . 95.00
Green/Blue . . . 65.00
Celery Vase . . . 20.00
Vaseline . . . 30.00
Green/Blue . . . 30.00
Creamer or Spooner . . . 25.00
Vaseline . . . 35.00
Green/Blue . . . 35.00
Pickle Dish . . . 20.00
Vaseline . . . 25.00
Green/Blue . . . 25.00
Pitcher . . . 80.00
Vaseline . . . 120.00
Green/Blue . . . 100.00
Tumbler . . . 15.00
Vaseline . . . 40.00
Green/Blue . . . 20.00
Sugar . . . 30.00
Vaseline . . . 40.00
Green/Blue . . . 35.00

IOWA
Berry Bowl, Lg. . . . 40.00
Rose Flash . . . 60.00
Berry Bowl, Sm. . . . 10.00
Rose Flash . . . 20.00
Butter . . . 65.00
Rose Flash . . . 115.00
Cake Stand . . . 50.00
Rose Flash . . . 65.00
Celery Vase . . . 25.00
Rose Flash . . . 35.00
Compote . . . 30.00
Rose Flash . . . 65.00
Creamer or Spooner . . . 25.00
Rose Flash . . . 45.00
Goblet . . . 30.00
Rose Flash . . . 55.00
Pickle Dish . . . 15.00
Rose Flash . . . 30.00
Pitcher . . . 80.00
Rose Flash . . . 165.00
Sugar . . . 30.00
Rose Flash . . . 55.00
Tumbler . . . 15.00
Rose Flash . . . 25.00
Wine . . . 10.00
Rose Flash . . . 20.00

"IT'S GOD'S WAY — HIS WILL BE DONE"
Oval Platter . . . 65.00

IVERNA

Berry Bowl, Sm. 10.00
Berry Bowl, Lg. 30.00
Berry, 6½" 15.00
Biscuit Jar 35.00
Butter 50.00
Celery Tray 25.00
Compote, 6½" 25.00
Creamer or Spooner 20.00
Fruit Bowl, 8½", Ftd. 40.00
Jelly Hndl. 30.00
Pickle Dish 20.00
Punch Bowl 75.00
Punch Cup 10.00
Sherbet 20.00
Spoon Tray 20.00
Sugar 25.00
Vase 25.00

JABOT

Butter 50.00
Creamer or Spooner 20.00
Pitcher 75.00
Tumbler 15.00
Sugar 25.00

JACOB'S LADDER

Bowls, Oblong . . . . . 20.00 – 30.00
Bowl, 9" Ftd., Ornate 145.00
Butter 80.00
Cake Stand, 2 Sizes . . . . . 55.00 – 70.00
Caster Set, Complete 125.00
Celery Vase 50.00
Cologne Bottle 110.00
Compote, Covered, 6" – 9½" . . . 85.00 – 135.00
Compote, Open, 7½" – 10" . . . . . 35.00 – 50.00
Creamer or Spooner 40.00
Cruet 95.00
Goblet 75.00
Honey Dish 15.00
Marmalade Jar 90.00
Mug 125.00
Pitcher 200.00
Tumbler 75.00
Plate, 6¼" 25.00
Relish 20.00
Salt, Master 25.00
Sugar 95.00
Syrup, 2 Style Finials . . . . . 100.00 – 135.00
Wine 40.00

(Double prices for any colored pieces. Some pieces made in amber, vaseline & blue, but not all.)

JAPANESE

Bowl 25.00
Butter 75.00
Celery Vase 20.00
Compote, Covered 45.00
Compote, Open 25.00
Creamer or Spooner 25.00
Goblet 60.00
Pickle Jar w/Lid 35.00
Plate, Fan Shape 30.00
Vaseline 95.00
Pitcher 95.00
Sauce, Flat or Ftd. 15.00
Sugar 40.00

JAPANESE IRIS

Bowl 35.00
Pickle Dish 15.00
Vase, 6½" 30.00
Vase, 10" 45.00

JEFFERSON #271

Berry Bowl, Sm. 10.00
Green/Blue 15.00
Berry Bowl, Lg. 30.00
Green/Blue 35.00
Butter 65.00
Green/Blue 75.00
Celery Vase 25.00
Green/Blue 30.00
Compote 35.00
Green/Blue 40.00
Creamer or Spooner 30.00
Green/Blue 35.00
Pickle Dish 20.00
Green/Blue 25.00
Pitcher 70.00
Green/Blue 85.00
Tumbler 10.00
Green/Blue 15.00
Sugar 40.00
Green/Blue 50.00
Toothpick Hldr. 45.00
Green/Blue 55.00
Wine 20.00
Green/Blue 25.00

JEFFERSON'S WINGED SCROLL

Hair Receiver 30.00
Ruby Stain 45.00
Custard 55.00
Perfume 50.00
Ruby Stain 65.00
Custard 80.00
Puff Box 60.00
Ruby Stain 80.00
Custard 95.00

JEFFERSON WHEEL

Bowl 30.00

JENKINS' DAHLIA

Butter 55.00
Compote 30.00
Creamer or Spooner 20.00
Sugar 25.00
Vase 30.00

JENKINS' SWAN (#460)

Salt Dish 45.00

JENNY LIND (Part of Actress line)

Compote 225.00

JENNY LIND MATCH SAFE

Match Safe 250.00

JERSEY SWIRL

Bowl 25.00
Amber 55.00
Vaseline 45.00
Green/Blue 55.00
Butter 55.00
Amber 65.00
Vaseline 95.00
Green/Blue 75.00
Cake Stand 35.00
Amber 60.00
Vaseline 95.00
Green/Blue 70.00
Candlesticks, ea. 30.00
Amber 35.00
Vaseline 50.00
Green/Blue 40.00
Compote, Covered or Open . . . . . 30.00 – 45.00
Amber . . . . . 40.00 – 60.00
Vaseline . . . . . 35.00 – 55.00
Green/Blue . . . . . 40.00 – 60.00
Creamer or Spooner 20.00
Amber 45.00
Vaseline 40.00
Green/Blue 45.00
Cruet 60.00
Cup 10.00
Vaseline 20.00
Dresser Tray 25.00
Vaseline 50.00
Goblet 30.00
Amber 40.00
Vaseline 45.00
Green/Blue 45.00
Jam Jar 45.00
Pickle Castor 45.00
Amber 70.00
Vaseline 65.00
Green/Blue 70.00
Plate, 6" – 8" 25.00
Amber 40.00
Vaseline 35.00
Green/Blue 40.00
Plate, 10" – 12" 30.00
Amber 50.00
Vaseline 40.00
Green/Blue 50.00
Pitcher 50.00
Amber 95.00
Vaseline 125.00
Green/Blue 100.00
Tumbler 15.00
Amber 25.00
Vaseline 40.00
Green/Blue 30.00
Salt, Ind. 10.00
Amber 25.00
Vaseline 25.00
Green/Blue 25.00
Salt, Master 20.00
Amber 30.00
Vaseline 35.00
Green/Blue 35.00
Sauce 10.00
Amber 20.00
Vaseline 15.00
Green/Blue 20.00
Sugar 25.00
Amber 45.00
Vaseline 65.00
Green/Blue 50.00
Syrup 60.00
Amber 85.00
Vaseline 125.00
Green/Blue 95.00
Wine 10.00
Amber 30.00
Vaseline 50.00
Green/Blue 40.00

JEWELED BUTTERFLIES

Bowls, Various . . . . . 15.00 – 35.00
Butter 40.00
Compote 35.00
Creamer, Spooner, or Sugar 25.00
Plate 30.00

JEWELED HEART

Berry Bowl, Sm. 15.00
Green/Blue 25.00
Berry Bowl, Lg. 35.00
Green/Blue 60.00
Bowl, 9" – 10" 30.00
Green/Blue 50.00
Butter 65.00
Green/Blue 125.00
Creamer or Spooner 30.00
Green/Blue 45.00
Cruet Set (Cruet, Shakers, Toothpick & Tray) 150.00
Green/Blue 225.00
Plate 25.00
Green/Blue 55.00
Pitcher 85.00
Green/Blue 175.00
Tumbler 20.00
Green/Blue 40.00
Rose Bowl, 9" 35.00
Green/Blue 55.00
Shakers, ea. 25.00
Green/Blue 60.00
Sugar 30.00
Green/Blue 55.00
Syrup 75.00
Green/Blue 135.00
Toothpick Hldr. 50.00
Green/Blue 75.00
Tray 30.00
Green/Blue 65.00

JEWELED LOOP

Berry Bowl,Sm. 20.00
Berry Bowl, Lg. 45.00
Butter 65.00
Celery Tray, 11" 35.00
Celery Vase 30.00
Compote, 8" 45.00
Creamer or Spooner 30.00
Goblet 50.00
Jelly Compote, Low 35.00
Pickle Dish, 7" 25.00

Pitcher 90.00
Tumbler 25.00
Sugar 30.00

JEWELED PALM LEAF
Bowl, 10" 45.00

JEWEL WITH DEWDROP
Berry Bowl, Lg. 35.00
Berry Bowl, Sm. 15.00
Bowl, Sauce 20.00
Cake Stand. 55.00
Compote, Lg. 50.00
Compote, Jelly 40.00
Cordial 25.00
Goblet, Rare. 60.00
Plate, Bread Size 35.00
Pitcher 85.00
Tumbler 25.00
Relish. 30.00
Shakers, ea. 30.00
Syrup 60.00
Toothpick Hldr., Rare 65.00
Wine 30.00

JOHN BULL EYE CUP
One Shape, One Size 35.00

JOHNSON'S CHILD'S MUG (KING GLASS #13)
Mug 25.00
Table Set, Complete 75.00

JUBILEE
Butter. 65.00
Celery Tray. 20.00
Compote, High 55.00
Compote, Low 45.00
Creamer or Spooner. 20.00
Dish, Oblong, 8". 20.00
Goblet 45.00
Pickle Dish. 20.00
Plate, 9" 20.00
Pitcher 85.00
Tumbler 20.00
Sugar 30.00
Wine 15.00

JUMBO
Butter, Oblong 650.00
Butter, Rnd., Barnum Head 500.00
Compote, Covered, 7" – 12". . . 450.00 – 900.00
Creamer 275.00
Pitcher 700.00
Sauce 75.00
Spoon Rack 425.00
Spooner, Barnum Head 150.00
Sugar, Barnum Head 475.00

KALEIDOSCOPE
Bowl. 35.00
Rose Bowl 65.00

KATZENJAMMER
Mug, Tall 250.00

KAYAK
Berry Bowl, Lg.. . . . . . 30.00
Berry Bowl, Sm. 15.00
Cake Stand. 40.00
Compote. 35.00
Pitcher 65.00
Tumbler 20.00
Tray 25.00

KEG
Oil Lamp, Scarce 245.00

KENTUCKY
Bowl. 25.00
Butter. 70.00
Cake Stand. 40.00
Creamer or Spooner. 25.00
Cruet 60.00
Cup 10.00
Green/Blue. 35.00
Goblet 30.00
Green/Blue. 85.00
Nappy 15.00
Green/Blue. 25.00
Olive, Hndl. 20.00
Pitcher 75.00
Tumbler 20.00
Green/Blue. 50.00
Plate. 20.00
Punch Cup 10.00
Green/Blue. 25.00
Shakers, ea. 15.00
Sauce 10.00
Green/Blue. 25.00
Sugar 45.00
Toothpick Hldr. 45.00
Green/Blue. 135.00
Wine 20.00
Green/Blue. 45.00

KEYHOLE
Bowl, Dome Ftd. 45.00
Plate, Dome Ftd. 60.00

KING'S BLOCK
Bowls, Oval . . . . . 15.00 – 40.00
Butter. 55.00
Creamer or Spooner. 20.00
Cruet 50.00
Goblet 35.00
Pickle Tray. 20.00
Sugar 35.00
Wine 15.00

KING'S CURTAIN
Bowl. 30.00
Butter. 50.00
Cake Stand. 30.00
Creamer or Spooner. 20.00
Goblet 35.00
Plate, 7" 20.00
Pitcher 65.00
Tumbler 10.00
Sauce 10.00
Shakers, ea. 20.00
Sugar 25.00
Wine 15.00

KING'S CROWN
Banana Stand 75.00
Ruby Stain. 125.00
Bowl, 2 Sizes. . . . . . 35.00 – 45.00
Ruby Stain . . . . . 75.00 – 90.00
Butter. 55.00
Ruby Stain. 100.00
Cake Stand. 40.00
Ruby Stain. 125.00
Caster Bottle 50.00
Ruby Stain. 75.00
Caster Set, Complete 200.00
Ruby Stain. 325.00
Celery Vase 35.00
Ruby Stain. 50.00
Champagne 25.00
Ruby Stain. 30.00
Claret. 30.00
Ruby Stain. 45.00
Compote, Open, 3 Sizes . . . . . 25.00 – 40.00
Ruby Stain . . . . . 50.00 – 95.00
Compote w/Lid, 4 Sizes. . . . . . 45.00 – 65.00
Ruby Stain . . . . . 200.00 – 250.00
Cordial. 40.00
Creamer or Spooner. 20.00
Ruby Stain. 60.00
Cup & Saucer. 50.00
Ruby Stain. 75.00
Custard Cup. 15.00
Ruby Stain. 25.00
Goblet 25.00
Ruby Stain. 50.00
Fruit Basket 45.00
Ruby Stain. 80.00
Honey Dish, Sq.. . . . . . 85.00
Ruby Stain. 165.00
Milk Pitcher. 75.00
Ruby Stain. 100.00
Mustard Pot. 25.00
Ruby Stain. 70.00
Oil Lamp 150.00
Orange Bowl, Ftd. 65.00
Ruby Stain. 85.00
Preserve Dish. 35.00
Ruby Stain. 65.00
Plate. 20.00
Ruby Stain. 45.00
Punch Bowl 250.00
Ruby Stain. 325.00
Punch Cup. 15.00
Ruby Stain. 25.00
Pickle Dish. 20.00
Ruby Stain. 40.00
Pickle Caster 45.00
Pitcher, 2 Styles . . . . . 100.00 – 135.00
Ruby Stain . . . . . 225.00 – 265.00
Tumbler 25.00
Ruby Stain. 35.00
Salt, Ind. 15.00
Ruby Stain. 30.00
Salt, Master 15.00
Ruby Stain. 55.00
Shakers, ea. 25.00
Ruby Stain. 45.00
Sauce, 4" 15.00
Ruby Stain. 25.00
Sugar, 2 Sizes 15.00
Ruby Stain . . . . . 50.00 – 100.00
Toothpick Hldr. 25.00
Ruby Stain. 45.00
Wine 20.00
Ruby Stain. 40.00

KLEAR-CUT #705
Pitcher 80.00
Tumbler 20.00

KLONDIKE
Bowl, Sq., 7" – 11" 85.00
Amber Stain . . . . . 175.00 – 200.00
Butter. 175.00
Amber Stain. 325.00
Cake Stand. 175.00
Amber Stain. 425.00
Celery Tray, Oblong 95.00
Amber Stain. 200.00
Champagne 110.00
Amber Stain. 165.00
Condiment Set, 4 Pcs. 500.00
Amber Stain. 950.00
Creamer or Spooner. 100.00
Amber Stain. 225.00
Cruet 190.00
Amber Stain. 500.00
Cup 55.00
Amber Stain. 110.00
Goblet 100.00
Amber Stain. 375.00
Pitcher, 2 Styles 375.00
Amber Stain. 625.00
Tumbler, 2 Styles. 65.00
Amber Stain. 125.00
Relish Tray. 45.00
Amber Stain. 85.00
Sauce, Flat or Ftd. 45.00
Amber Stain. 75.00
Shakers, Tall or Squat, ea. 75.00
Amber Stain. 125.00
Sugar 110.00
Amber Stain. 225.00
Syrup 200.00
Amber Stain. 600.00
Toothpick Hldr. 150.00
Amber Stain. 325.00
Tray 75.00
Amber Stain. 225.00
Vase, 7" – 10". 115.00
Amber Stain . . . . . 200.00 – 265.00
Wine 225.00
Amber Stain. 350.00

KNIGHTS OF LABOR
Goblet 175.00
Mug 150.00

KNOBBY BULLS-EYE (CROMWELL)
Berry Bowl, Lg.. . . . . . 30.00
Green/Blue. 35.00
Ruby Stain. 50.00
Berry Bowl, Sm. 15.00
Green/Blue. 20.00
Ruby Stain. 35.00

Bowl 10" . . . 35.00
Green/Blue . . . 40.00
Ruby Stain . . . 55.00
Bowl, Deep Oval, 7½" . . . 30.00
Green/Blue . . . 35.00
Ruby Stain . . . 50.00
Bowl, Orange, 10½" . . . 40.00
Green/Blue . . . 45.00
Ruby Stain . . . 55.00
Butter . . . 50.00
Green/Blue . . . 60.00
Ruby Stain . . . 85.00
Celery Tray . . . 20.00
Green/Blue . . . 25.00
Ruby Stain . . . 40.00
Compote, Open . . . 40.00
Green/Blue . . . 45.00
Ruby Stain . . . 60.00
Compote, Covered . . . 50.00
Green/Blue . . . 60.00
Ruby Stain . . . 90.00
Creamer, Spooner, or Sugar . . . 25.00
Green/Blue . . . 30.00
Ruby Stain . . . 45.00
Decanter . . . 55.00
Green/Blue . . . 125.00
Pitcher, 2 Sizes . . . 40.00 – 60.00
Green/Blue . . . 65.00 – 90.00
Ruby Stain . . . 100.00 – 175.00
Tumbler . . . 20.00
Green/Blue . . . 25.00
Ruby Stain . . . 40.00
Plate, 5" & 8" . . . 30.00
Green/Blue . . . 35.00
Ruby Stain . . . 55.00
Punch Bowl . . . 100.00
Green/Blue . . . 125.00
Ruby Stain . . . 165.00
Punch Cup . . . 10.00
Green/Blue . . . 15.00
Ruby Stain . . . 30.00
Salt Shaker, 2 Styles, ea . . . 20.00
Green/Blue . . . 25.00
Ruby Stain . . . 50.00
Toothpick Hldr . . . 30.00
Green/Blue . . . 35.00
Ruby Stain . . . 45.00
Underplate (for Punch Bowl) . . . 50.00
Green/Blue . . . 60.00
Ruby Stain . . . 85.00
Wine . . . 25.00
Green/Blue . . . 30.00
Ruby Stain . . . 45.00

KNOTTED BEADS
Vase . . . 45.00
Red . . . 125.00

KOKOMO
Berry Bowl, Lg . . . 35.00
Berry Bowl, Sm . . . 15.00
Bread Tray . . . 25.00
Ruby Stain . . . 60.00
Butter . . . 50.00
Cake Stand . . . 50.00
Ruby Stain . . . 150.00
Casserole, Covered . . . 55.00
Ruby Stain . . . 100.00
Celery Vase . . . 25.00
Ruby Stain . . . 50.00
Compote, Jelly . . . 35.00
Compote, Covered . . . 70.00
Ruby Stain . . . 175.00
Compote, Open, 5" – 8" . . . 25.00 – 60.00
Condiment Set, 4 Pcs . . . 90.00
Ruby Stain . . . 225.00
Creamer or Spooner . . . 25.00
Ruby Stain . . . 50.00
Decanter . . . 60.00
Ruby Stain . . . 100.00
Goblet . . . 25.00
Ruby Stain . . . 50.00
Hand Lamp . . . 75.00
Ruby Stain . . . 145.00
Jam Jar . . . 25.00
Ruby Stain . . . 125.00
Nappy . . . 25.00
Pickle Dish . . . 20.00
Pitcher . . . 75.00
Ruby Stain . . . 150.00
Tumbler . . . 25.00
Ruby Stain . . . 30.00
Sauce . . . 10.00
Ruby Stain . . . 20.00
Sugar . . . 50.00
Ruby Stain . . . 70.00
Shaker . . . 40.00
Ruby Stain . . . 85.00
Syrup . . . 65.00
Ruby Stain . . . 150.00
Tray . . . 40.00
Ruby Stain . . . 100.00
Wine . . . 15.00
Ruby Stain . . . 40.00

KRYS-TOL COLONIAL
Bowl . . . 35.00
Compote, Lg . . . 60.00
Jelly Compote . . . 45.00
Plate . . . 40.00
Punch Bowl w/Base . . . 120.00
Punch Cup . . . 15.00

LA BELLE ROSE
Bowl, 5" – 9" . . . 10.00 – 25.00
Plate, 6" – 11" . . . 20.00 – 40.00

LACY DAISY
Bowls, 3 Legged . . . 10.00 – 50.00
Butter . . . 75.00
Cake Plate . . . 35.00
Creamer or Spooner . . . 25.00
Cruet . . . 50.00
Jam Jar . . . 35.00
Jelly Compote . . . 20.00
Plates, Various . . . 15.00 – 35.00
Puff Box . . . 35.00
Rose Bowl . . . 25.00
Salt, Ind . . . 15.00
Sugar . . . 40.00
Toy Table Set . . . 95.00

LACY DEWDROP
Berry Bowl, Sm . . . 20.00
Berry Bowl, Lg . . . 40.00
Bowl, Covered, Sm . . . 30.00
Bowl, Covered, Lg . . . 55.00
Butter . . . 65.00
Compote, Covered or Open . . . 25.00 – 50.00
Creamer or Spooner . . . 20.00
Goblet . . . 35.00
Mug . . . 20.00
Pitcher . . . 85.00
Tumbler . . . 20.00
Sauce . . . 10.00
Sugar . . . 25.00

LACY MEDALLION
Mug . . . 40.00
Vaseline . . . 75.00
Green/Blue . . . 50.00
Ruby Stain . . . 60.00
Shakers, Ea . . . 35.00
Vaseline . . . 50.00
Green/Blue . . . 40.00
Ruby Stain . . . 45.00
Toothpick Hldr . . . 45.00
Vaseline . . . 60.00
Green/Blue . . . 45.00
Ruby Stain . . . 55.00
Toy Table Set . . . 115.00
Vaseline . . . 160.00
Green/Blue . . . 135.00
Ruby Stain . . . 145.00
Wine . . . 30.00
Vaseline . . . 45.00
Green/Blue . . . 35.00
Ruby Stain . . . 40.00

LACY ROMAN ROSETTE
Bowl . . . 25.00
Honey Dish . . . 30.00
Plate . . . 35.00

LADDERS (TARENTUM #292)
Berry Bowl, Sm . . . 15.00
Berry Bowl, Lg . . . 45.00
Butter . . . 75.00
Celery Vase . . . 20.00
Creamer or Spooner . . . 20.00
Cruet . . . 45.00
Cup . . . 10.00
Pitcher . . . 85.00
Tumbler . . . 20.00
Sugar . . . 30.00
Vase . . . 25.00

LADDER WITH DIAMONDS
Butter . . . 60.00
Celery Vase . . . 25.00
Creamer or Spooner . . . 25.00
Cruet . . . 70.00
Cup . . . 15.00
Decanter . . . 50.00
Goblet . . . 35.00
Plate, 9¼" . . . 30.00
Pitcher . . . 80.00
Tumbler . . . 20.00
Sugar . . . 30.00
Toothpick Hldr . . . 35.00
Vase . . . 30.00

LADY BUST
Paperweight . . . 250.00

LADY WITH FAN
Celery Vase . . . 85.00

LAMB
Mug . . . 70.00
Green/Blue . . . 95.00
Amber . . . 125.00

LANSBURGH & BROS. ADVERTISING
See Rising Sun

LANTERN
Toy Candy Container . . . 65.00

LAST SUPPER
Plate . . . 55.00

LATE BLOCK (DUNCAN'S #331, U.S. GLASS)
Berry Bowl, Sm . . . 20.00
Berry Bowl, Lg . . . 45.00
Bowls, Sq. & Rect., 4 Sizes . . . 15.00 – 50.00
Butter . . . 95.00
Celery Boat . . . 35.00
Creamer or Spooner . . . 30.00
Cruet . . . 65.00
Horseradish Bottle . . . 50.00
Ice Tub . . . 60.00
Jelly Compote . . . 35.00
Lamp . . . 95.00
Mustard Pot . . . 25.00
Pitcher . . . 150.00
Tumbler . . . 30.00
Pickle Dish . . . 20.00
Punch Bowl . . . 250.00
Punch Cup . . . 20.00
Relish Hndl . . . 25.00
Rose Bowls, Various . . . 20.00 – 45.00
Shakers, ea . . . 25.00
Sugar . . . 35.00
Sugar Shaker . . . 45.00
Syrup . . . 70.00
Water Bottle . . . 55.00

LATE HONEYCOMB
Pitcher . . . 60.00
Tumbler . . . 10.00

LATE TOMATO VINE
Pitcher . . . 55.00
Tumbler . . . 10.00

LATTICE
Butter . . . 65.00
Cake Stand . . . 35.00
Celery Vase . . . 25.00
Cordial . . . 20.00
Creamer or Spooner . . . 25.00
Egg Cup . . . 15.00
Plate . . . 25.00
Platter . . . 35.00
Pitcher . . . 75.00

Tumbler . . . 15.00
Sauce . . . 10.00
Shakers, ea. . . . 20.00
Sugar . . . 30.00
Wine . . . 15.00

LATTICE AND DAISY
Tumbler, Rare . . . 70.00

LATTICE AND NOTCHED PANELS
Bowl . . . 25.00
Goblet . . . 20.00
Sauce . . . 15.00

LATTICE-EDGE
Fruit Bowl, Stemmed, 2 Sizes . . . 45.00 – 70.00

LATTICE LEAF (CO-OP #323)
Berry Bowl, Sm. . . . 10.00
Berry Bowl, Lg. . . . 40.00
Butter . . . 55.00
Creamer or Spooner . . . 20.00
Pickle Dish . . . 15.00
Rose Bowl . . . 30.00
Shakers, ea. . . . 15.00
Sugar . . . 25.00
Toothpick Hldr. . . . 25.00

LATTICE MEDALLION WITH BUDS
Bowl, Ftd. . . . 45.00

LATTICE MEDALLION VARIANT
Bowl, Ftd., Various . . . 15.00 – 45.00

LATTICE THUMBPRINT (CENTRAL #791)
Compote, Covered . . . 75.00
Compote, Open . . . 40.00
(Probably other shapes)

LAVERNE
Bowls, Oval or Rnd. . . . 10.00 – 45.00
Butter . . . 60.00
Cake Stand . . . 40.00
Celery Vase . . . 20.00
Compote, Covered . . . 70.00
Compote, Open . . . 45.00
Creamer or Spooner . . . 20.00
Goblet . . . 50.00
Pickle Tray . . . 25.00
Pitcher . . . 90.00
Tumbler . . . 20.00
Relish Dish . . . 15.00
Sauce . . . 10.00
Sugar . . . 30.00
Wine . . . 15.00

LEAF AND DART
Bowl, Ftd. . . . 25.00
Butter . . . 95.00
Butter Pat . . . 25.00
Celery Vase . . . 35.00
Compote, Covered . . . 70.00
Compote, Open . . . 35.00
Creamer or Spooner . . . 40.00
Cruet . . . 125.00
Egg Cup . . . 25.00
Goblet . . . 40.00
Honey Dish . . . 10.00
Lamp . . . 95.00
Milk Pitcher . . . 80.00
Pitcher . . . 100.00
Tumbler . . . 25.00
Relish Tray . . . 20.00
Salt, Ftd. w/Lid . . . 75.00
Sauce . . . 10.00
Sugar . . . 50.00
Syrup . . . 135.00
Wine . . . 40.00

LEAF AND RIB
Berry Bowl, Lg. . . . 30.00
Amber . . . 35.00
Vaseline . . . 45.00
Green/Blue . . . 40.00
Berry Bowl, Sm. . . . 10.00
Amber . . . 20.00
Vaseline . . . 30.00
Green/Blue . . . 25.00
Butter . . . 65.00
Amber . . . 80.00
Vaseline . . . 110.00
Green/Blue . . . 95.00
Celery Vase . . . 25.00
Amber . . . 30.00
Vaseline . . . 40.00
Green/Blue . . . 35.00
Creamer or Spooner . . . 20.00
Amber . . . 25.00
Vaseline . . . 35.00
Green/Blue . . . 30.00
Pickle Dish . . . 15.00
Amber . . . 20.00
Vaseline . . . 30.00
Green/Blue . . . 25.00
Pitcher . . . 75.00
Amber . . . 80.00
Vaseline . . . 125.00
Green/Blue . . . 100.00
Shakers, ea. . . . 25.00
Amber . . . 35.00
Vaseline . . . 45.00
Green/Blue . . . 40.00
Sugar . . . 30.00
Amber . . . 35.00
Vaseline . . . 50.00
Green/Blue . . . 45.00
Vase . . . 25.00
Amber . . . 30.00
Vaseline . . . 35.00
Green/Blue . . . 30.00

LEAF AND STAR
Banana Boat . . . 40.00
Berry Bowl, Sm. . . . 15.00
Berry Bowl, Lg. . . . 35.00
Butter . . . 65.00
Candy Dish, Ftd. . . . 30.00
Celery Tray . . . 30.00
Celery Vase . . . 25.00
Creamer or Spooner . . . 20.00
Cruet . . . 70.00
Custard Cup . . . 10.00
Dresser Jar . . . 35.00
Fruit Bowl . . . 35.00
Goblet . . . 50.00
Hair Receiver . . . 35.00
Humidor . . . 45.00
Ice Cream Dish . . . 20.00
Jelly Compote . . . 30.00
Nut Bowl . . . 25.00
Plate, 6" – 8" . . . 25.00
Pitcher . . . 85.00
Tumbler . . . 20.00
Relish Dish . . . 20.00
Sauce, Flat or Ftd. . . . 15.00
Toothpick Hldr. . . . 25.00
Vase . . . 30.00
Wine . . . 15.00

LEAF BRACKET
Berry Bowl, Sm. . . . 10.00
Chocolate . . . 35.00
Berry Bowl, Lg. . . . 40.00
Chocolate . . . 100.00
Bowl, Tri-cornered . . . 50.00
Chocolate . . . 120.00
Butter . . . 125.00
Chocolate . . . 245.00
Celery Tray . . . 60.00
Chocolate . . . 125.00
Creamer or Spooner . . . 70.00
Chocolate . . . 115.00
Cruet . . . 155.00
Chocolate . . . 250.00
Jam Jar . . . 145.00
Nappy . . . 50.00
Chocolate . . . 100.00
Pitcher . . . 225.00
Chocolate . . . 500.00
Tumbler . . . 90.00
Chocolate . . . 65.00
Shakers, ea. . . . 100.00
Chocolate . . . 150.00
Sauce . . . 45.00
Chocolate . . . 30.00
Sugar . . . 100.00
Chocolate . . . 175.00
Toothpick Hldr. . . . 125.00
Chocolate . . . 310.00

LEAF MOULD (NORTHWOOD)
Berry Bowl, Sm., Vaseline . . . 90.00
Ruby Glass . . . 70.00
Berry Bowl, Lg., Vaseline . . . 325.00
Ruby Glass . . . 250.00
Butter, Vaseline . . . 575.00
Ruby Glass . . . 475.00
Celery Vase, Vaseline . . . 225.00
Ruby Glass . . . 165.00
Cologne, Vaseline . . . 375.00
Ruby Glass . . . 300.00
Creamer or Spooner, Vaseline . . . 300.00
Ruby Glass . . . 250.00
Cruet, Vaseline . . . 850.00
Ruby Glass . . . 700.00
Fairy Lamp, Vaseline . . . 575.00
Ruby Glass . . . 475.00
Pitcher, Vaseline . . . 900.00
Ruby Glass . . . 675.00
Tumbler, Vaseline . . . 145.00
Ruby Glass . . . 100.00
Salt Shaker, Vaseline . . . 300.00
Ruby Glass . . . 250.00
Sugar Shaker, Vaseline . . . 325.00
Ruby Glass . . . 275.00
Syrup, Vaseline . . . 625.00
Ruby Glass . . . 400.00
Toothpick Hldr., Vaseline . . . 350.00
Ruby Glass . . . 250.00
(Deduct 20% for "Spatterware" colors.)

LEAFY SCROLL
Berry Bowl, Sm. . . . 20.00
Berry Bowl, Lg. . . . 55.00
Butter . . . 85.00
Creamer or Spooner . . . 25.00
Goblet . . . 55.00
Pitcher . . . 90.00
Tumbler . . . 25.00
Sugar . . . 40.00
Toothpick Hldr. . . . 30.00
Wine . . . 20.00

LENOX
Berry Bowl, Sm. . . . 20.00
Berry Bowl, Lg. . . . 45.00
Breakfast Set . . . 50.00
Butter . . . 70.00
Creamer or Spooner . . . 25.00
Cruet . . . 65.00
Jelly Compote . . . 35.00
Mug . . . 25.00
Pitcher . . . 85.00
Tumbler . . . 20.00
Salt Dip, Ind. . . . 20.00
Sugar . . . 30.00
Toothpick Hldr. . . . 25.00

"LET US HAVE PEACE"
U.S. Grant Plate . . . 75.00
Vaseline . . . 150.00

LEVERNE (STAR IN HONEYCOMB)
Berry Bowl, Sm. . . . 20.00
Berry Bowl, Lg. . . . 50.00
Bowl, Oval . . . 35.00
Butter . . . 70.00
Cake Stand . . . 40.00
Celery Vase . . . 25.00
Compote, Covered or Open . . . 35.00 – 60.00
Creamer or Spooner . . . 25.00
Goblet . . . 50.00
Pickle Tray . . . 20.00
Pitcher . . . 90.00
Tumbler . . . 20.00
Relish . . . 20.00
Sauce . . . 15.00
Sugar . . . 30.00
Wine . . . 20.00

LIBERTY
Berry Bowl, Lg. . . . 40.00
Berry Bowl, Sm. . . . 15.00
Butter . . . 65.00

Champagne 25.00
Cordial 20.00
Creamer or Spooner 25.00
Goblet 35.00
Pitcher 85.00
Sugar 35.00
Tumbler 15.00
Water Tray 25.00
Wine 20.00

LIBERTY BELL
Bank 145.00

LIBERTY BELL
Berry Bowl, Sm. 35.00
Berry Bowl, Lg. 110.00
Butter 165.00
Celery Vase 45.00
Compote, 3 Sizes . . . . . 65.00 – 110.00
Creamer or Spooner 100.00
Goblet 50.00
Mug, 2 Styles . . . . . 225.00 – 400.00
Pickle Dish 50.00
Plate, 3 Sizes . . . . . 70.00 – 85.00
Platter, 3 Styles 75.00
Pitcher 900.00
Tumbler 100.00
Salt Dip 40.00
Sauce, Flat or Ftd. 35.00
Shakers, ea. 100.00
Sugar 125.00
Toy Table Set 550.00

LIGHTHOUSE AND SAILBOAT
Mug, 3 Sizes 40.00
Amber 55.00
Green/Blue 65.00

LILY OF THE VALLEY
Berry Bowl, Sm. 15.00
Berry Bowl, Lg. 35.00
Butter 80.00
Cake Stand 45.00
Celery Tray 25.00
Celery Vase 25.00
Compote, Open 35.00
Compote, Covered 55.00
Cordial, Rare 45.00
Creamer or Spooner 30.00
Cruet 65.00
Egg Cup 30.00
Goblet 40.00
Honey Dish 50.00
Milk Pitcher 55.00
Pickle Scoop 25.00
Relish Dish 20.00
Salt, Master, Covered or Open . . 20.00 – 35.00
Sauce, Flat or Ftd. 15.00
Sugar 40.00
Wine, Rare 45.00

LINCOLN DRAPE
Butter 145.00
Celery Vase 80.00
Compote, Covered, 8½" 175.00
Compote, Open, 6" – 7½" 85.00
Creamer or Spooner 100.00
Egg Cup 50.00
Goblet, 2 Sizes . . . . . 125.00 – 165.00
Honey Dish 35.00
Oil Lamp, Various . . . . . 100.00 – 180.00
Pitcher 400.00
Tumbler 60.00
Plate, 6" 100.00
Salt, Master 135.00
Sauce 30.00
Spill 60.00
Sugar 130.00
Syrup 225.00
Wine 150.00

LINCOLN AND GARFIELD
Mug 65.00

LINDBURGH
Berry Bowl, Lg. 30.00
Berry Bowl, Sm. 15.00
Butter 35.00
Cake Plate, 10½" 40.00
Compote, Low Stemmed 35.00
Creamer, Spooner, or Sugar 20.00
Pitcher 60.00
Tumbler 15.00
Rose Bowl, 7" 30.00

LINED HEART
Vase 25.00

LION AND BABOON (All pieces rare)
Butter 325.00
Celery Vase 145.00
Compote, Covered 295.00
Creamer or Spooner 150.00
Lamp, Rare 250.00
Milk Pitcher 250.00
Pitcher 375.00
Sugar 175.00
Toy Table Set (Unconfirmed) 450.00

LION AND CABLE
Bread Plate 75.00
Butter 200.00
Celery Vase 65.00
Compote, Covered, Low, 7" – 9" 95.00
Compote, Covered, High, 7" – 9" 145.00
Creamer or Spooner 45.00
Goblet 120.00
Jam Jar 70.00
Milk Pitcher 90.00
Pitcher 275.00
Tumbler 45.00
Sauce 30.00
Shakers, ea. 45.00
Sugar 60.00

LION AND HONEYCOMB
Compote, Covered 250.00

LION HEAD
Butter 225.00
Compote, Covered, 6" – 9" 125.00
Creamer or Spooner 65.00
Jam Jar 50.00
Sauce, 4" – 5" 35.00
Sugar 75.00
Toy Table Set 300.00

LITTLE BO PEEP
Nursery Rhyme Plate 45.00

LITTLE BO PEEP (DITHRIDGE)
Mug 55.00

LITTLE BUTTERCUP
Mug 45.00

LITTLE FISHES
Bowl, Ftd., 9", Rare 225.00
Bowl, Ftd., 5½", Rare 100.00

LITTLE OWL
Child's Pitcher 80.00

LITTLE SAMUEL
Candlesticks, ea. 45.00
Compote 70.00
Epergne 135.00
Lamp Stem 65.00

LOCKET ON CHAIN
Berry Bowl, Lg. 35.00
Ruby Stain 50.00
Berry Bowl, Sm. 15.00
Ruby Stain 20.00
Butter 80.00
Ruby Stain 95.00
Creamer or Spooner 30.00
Ruby Stain 45.00
Cruet, Rare 135.00
Ruby Stain 175.00
Pickle Dish 15.00
Ruby Stain 30.00
Pitcher 110.00
Ruby Stain 135.00
Sugar 40.00
Ruby Stain 55.00
Toothpick Hldr. 50.00
Ruby Stain 65.00
Tumbler 20.00
Ruby Stain 35.00
Wine 15.00
Ruby Stain 25.00

LOGANBERRY AND GRAPE
Butter 70.00
Celery Vase 20.00
Creamer or Spooner 35.00
Goblet, 2 Types 50.00
Pitcher 95.00
Tumbler 25.00
Sugar 40.00

LOG CABIN
Bowl, Covered 375.00
Butter 325.00
Compote, 10½" 290.00
Creamer or Spooner 125.00
Marmalade Jar w/Lid 325.00
Pitcher 375.00
Sauce 85.00
Sugar 300.00

LONE FISHERMAN, THE (Part of "Actress" line)
Cheese Dish, Covered, with "Two Dromios" Base 400.00

LONG BUTTRESS
Butter 60.00
Celery Vase 20.00
Creamer or Spooner 25.00
Creamer, Ind. 15.00
Pickle Jar 30.00
Pickle Dish 15.00
Pitcher 90.00
Tumbler 20.00
Salt Dip 10.00
Shakers, ea. 15.00
Sugar 30.00
Sugar, Ind. 20.00
Syrup 45.00
Toothpick Hldr. 30.00
Vases, Various Sizes . . . . . 15.00 – 35.00

LONG FAN WITH ACANTHUS LEAF
Berry Bowl, Sm. 20.00
Berry Bowl, Lg. 40.00
Butter 70.00
Creamer or Spooner 25.00
Goblet 35.00
Pickle Dish 15.00
Pitcher 85.00
Tumbler 20.00
Shakers, ea. 15.00
Sugar 30.00

LONG MAPLE LEAF
Bowls, Various . . . . . 15.00 – 30.00
Vaseline . . . . . 25.00 – 55.00
Butter 60.00
Vaseline 85.00
Celery Vase 25.00
Vaseline 35.00
Compote 40.00
Vaseline 55.00
Creamer or Spooner 25.00
Vaseline 35.00
Pickle Dish 20.00
Vaseline 30.00
Pitcher 85.00
Vaseline 145.00
Tumbler 20.00
Vaseline 35.00
Sugar 30.00
Vaseline 50.00

THE LOOKING GLASS
Platter 45.00

LOOP
Bitters Bottle 80.00
Bowl, Covered 35.00
Butter 50.00
Cake Stand 30.00
Carafe 45.00
Celery Vase 20.00
Compote, Covered, 7" – 10" . . . . . 35.00 – 70.00
Compote, Open, 7" – 10" . . . . . 25.00 – 45.00
Creamer or Spooner 25.00
Decanter, Various . . . . . 35.00 – 60.00
Egg Cup 25.00
Goblet, 2 Styles . . . . . 35.00 – 55.00
Milk Pitcher 75.00

Oil Lamp, 10" 185.00
Plate 30.00
Pitcher 110.00
Tumbler 25.00
Salt, Master 20.00
Sugar 30.00
Syrup 90.00
Vase, 10" – 12" . . . . 25.00 – 40.00
Wine 15.00

LOOP AND BLOCK

Berry Bowl, Lg. 35.00
Ruby Stain 45.00
Berry Bowl, Sm. 10.00
Ruby Stain 20.00
Bowl 25.00
Ruby Stain 40.00
Butter 70.00
Ruby Stain 100.00
Celery Vase 30.00
Ruby Stain 40.00
Creamer or Spooner 35.00
Ruby Stain 45.00
Decanter 65.00
Ruby Stain 90.00
Goblet 45.00
Ruby Stain 60.00
Jelly Compote 35.00
Ruby Stain 40.00
Sauce 10.00
Ruby Stain 20.00
Sugar 50.00
Ruby Stain 65.00
Tray 40.00
Ruby Stain 45.00
Tumbler 30.00
Ruby Stain 45.00
Wine 20.00
Ruby Stain 30.00

LOOP AND DART W/DIAMOND ORNAMENT

Bowl, Oval 30.00
Butter 55.00
Celery Vase 20.00
Compote, Covered, High or Low . 40.00 – 60.00
Compote, Open, High or Low . . . 30.00 – 50.00
Cordial 20.00
Creamer or Spooner 20.00
Egg Cup 15.00
Goblet 45.00
Plate, 6" 25.00
Pitcher 85.00
Tumbler 20.00
Relish Tray, Oval 20.00
Salt, Master 15.00
Sauce 10.00
Sugar 25.00
Wine 20.00

LOOP AND JEWEL

Berry Sugar Bowl 35.00
Milk Glass 40.00
Bowls, 6" – 8" . . . . 15.00 – 30.00
Milk Glass . . . . 20.00 – 45.00
Butter 55.00
Milk Glass 65.00
Creamer or Spooner 25.00
Milk Glass 40.00
Dish, 5", Sq. 20.00
Milk Glass 25.00
Goblet 35.00
Milk Glass 40.00
Pickle Dish 15.00
Milk Glass 25.00
Pitcher 85.00
Milk Glass 95.00
Tumbler 15.00
Milk Glass 30.00
Plate, 5½", Sq. 20.00
Milk Glass 25.00
Relish Tray 20.00
Milk Glass 25.00
Sauce, Flat or Ftd. 10.00
Milk Glass 20.00
Salt Dip 25.00
Milk Glass 35.00
Shakers, ea. 30.00
Milk Glass 40.00
Sugar 40.00
Milk Glass 55.00
Syrup 65.00
Milk Glass 80.00
Vase 30.00
Milk Glass 30.00
Wine 15.00
Milk Glass 30.00

LOOP WITH DEWDROP

Bowl 20.00
Butter 65.00
Cake Stand 40.00
Celery Dish 20.00
Compote, Covered, 8" 70.00
Condiment Set, Complete 100.00
Creamer or Spooner 35.00
Cruet 65.00
Cup & Saucer 35.00
Goblet 35.00
Pitcher 80.00
Tumbler 10.00
Shakers, ea. 25.00
Sugar 45.00
Tray, Hndl. 50.00
Wine 20.00

LOOP WITH FISH EYE

Berry Bowl, Sm. 20.00
Berry Bowl, Lg. 45.00
Goblet 55.00

LOOP WITH PRISM BAND

Butter 55.00
Creamer or Spooner 25.00
Goblet 35.00
Pitcher 65.00
Tumbler 10.00
Sugar 30.00

LORNE

Butter 75.00
Vaseline 145.00

LOTUS AND GRAPE VARIANT

Bonbon 65.00

LOUISIANA PURCHASE EXPOSITION

Plate, 7¼" 90.00
Ice Tea Tumbler 35.00

LOZENGES

Bowls, Various . . . . 15.00 – 45.00
Butter 60.00
Compote 40.00
Creamer or Spooner 25.00
Sugar 30.00

LUSTRE ROSE

Fernery 35.00

MAGNA

Berry Bowl, Sm. 15.00
Berry Bowl, Lg. 35.00
Butter 65.00
Celery Vase 20.00
Creamer or Spooner 20.00
Pickle Tray 15.00
Pitcher 85.00
Tumbler 20.00
Shakers, ea. 15.00
Sugar 25.00
Toothpick Hldr. 25.00

MAGNET AND GRAPE

Butter 175.00
Celery Vase 130.00
Champagne 125.00
Compote, Open, Scarce 125.00
Creamer or Spooner 130.00
Egg Cup 25.00
Goblet 65.00
Master Salt 65.00
Sauce 20.00
Sugar 135.00
Wine 125.00

MAIZE

Bowls, Various . . . . 15.00 – 35.00
Custard . . . . 35.00 – 65.00
Bowl, Celery 25.00
Custard 50.00
Bowl, Finger 20.00
Custard 40.00
Butter 65.00
Custard 135.00
Carafe 35.00
Custard 85.00
Condiment Set, Complete 80.00
Custard 175.00
Creamer or Spooner 25.00
Custard 50.00
Decanter 40.00
Custard 80.00
Pitcher 95.00
Custard 225.00
Rose Bowl 35.00
Custard 65.00
Shakers, ea. 25.00
Custard 55.00
Sugar 30.00
Custard 60.00
Sugar Shaker 45.00
Custard 75.00
Tumbler 15.00
Custard 45.00

MALTESE

Basket, 5" . . . . 45.00 – 55.00
Amber 70.00
Vaseline 90.00
Green/Blue 95.00
Bowl, 8" 25.00
Bread Plate . . . . 50.00 – 60.00
Butter 90.00
Celery, Ftd. 55.00
Celery Boat 25.00
Compotes, Covered . . . . 55.00 – 75.00
Compotes, Open . . . . 35.00 – 55.00
Creamer or Spooner 50.00
Custard 15.00
Decanter (Brandy Bottle) 35.00
Finger Bowl 20.00
Goblet 50.00
Nappies . . . . 15.00 – 35.00
Oil Bottle 55.00
Orange Bowl, 7" & 9" . . . . 30.00 – 35.00
Oval Bowls . . . . 25.00 – 35.00
Pickle Boat 25.00
Pickle Jar w/Lid 65.00
Pitcher, 2 Sizes 80.00
Tumbler, 2 Sizes 40.00
Plates, 5" – 7" . . . . 25.00 – 35.00
Sugar 65.00
Tray, 9"x15" 60.00
Water Bottle 55.00
Wine Tray 50.00

MALTESE AND RIBBON

Bowls, 3 Sizes, Oval and Round . 20.00 – 35.00
Amber . . . . 30.00 – 45.00
Vaseline . . . . 45.00 – 70.00
Green/Blue . . . . 40.00 – 60.00
Bowl, Sq. 7" & 8" . . . . 25.00 – 40.00
Amber . . . . 35.00 – 50.00
Vaseline . . . . 50.00 – 75.00
Green/Blue . . . . 40.00 – 65.00
Finger Bowl 25.00
Amber 40.00
Vaseline 60.00
Green/Blue 55.00
Lamp Shade, 2 Sizes . . . . 50.00 – 70.00
Amber . . . . 65.00 – 85.00
Vaseline . . . . 80.00 – 120.00
Green/Blue . . . . 70.00 – 90.00
Master Salt 25.00
Amber 30.00
Vaseline 45.00
Green/Blue 40.00
Pickle Dish 20.00
Amber 25.00
Vaseline 35.00
Green/Blue 30.00
Pitcher, 2 Sizes . . . . 65.00 – 85.00

Amber . . . . . 80.00 – 115.00
Vaseline . . . . . 110.00 – 260.00
Green/Blue . . . . . 90.00 – 185.00
Tumbler 20.00
Amber 25.00
Vaseline 35.00
Green/Blue 30.00

MANHATTAN
Basket 70.00
Maiden's Blush . . . . . 135 .00
Biscuit Jar 55.00
Maiden's Blush . . . . . 100 .00
Berry Bowls (6 Sizes), from 7" – 12½" . 15.00 – 55.00
Maiden's Blush . . . . . 30.00 – 100 .00
Butter or Cheese Dish 65.00
Maiden's Blush . . . . . 135 .00
Cake Stand 45.00
Maiden's Blush . . . . . 75.00 – 115 .00
Celery Vase 30.00
Maiden's Blush . . . . . 75 .00
Compote, 9½" – 10½" 50.00
Maiden's Blush . . . . . 125 .00
Cracker Jar 60.00
Maiden's Blush . . . . . 165 .00
Creamer or Spooner 25.00
Maiden's Blush . . . . . 50 .00
Custard Cup 15.00
Maiden's Blush . . . . . 25 .00
Goblet 30.00
Milk Pitcher 55.00
Maiden's Blush . . . . . 85 .00
Pickle Caster, Complete 15.00
Maiden's Blush . . . . . 165 .00
Pickle Dish 125.00
Maiden's Blush . . . . . 25 .00
Plate, 5" 20.00
Plate, 9½" – 12" 35.00
Maiden's Blush . . . . . 30 .00
Punch Bowl, 2 Styles . . . . . 115.00 – 145.00
Maiden's Blush . . . . . 300.00 – 350 .00
Punch Cup 15.00
Maiden's Blush . . . . . 25 .00
Shakers, ea. 15.00
Maiden's Blush . . . . . 40 .00
Straw Hldr. 60.00
Sugar 30.00
Maiden's Blush . . . . . 60 .00
Syrup 65.00
Maiden's Blush . . . . . 225 .00
Toothpick Hldr. 40.00
Maiden's Blush . . . . . 135 .00
Water Bottle 50.00
Maiden's Blush . . . . . 100 .00
Wine 15.00

MAPLE LEAF
Bowl, Covered, 6" – 11" . . . . . 35.00 – 55.00
Amber . . . . . 45.00 – 85.00
Vaseline . . . . . 85.00 – 150.00
Green/Blue . . . . . 65.00 – 125.00
Butter 60.00
Amber 75.00
Vaseline 180.00
Green/Blue 85.00
Cake Stand 40.00
Amber 65.00
Vaseline 125.00
Green/Blue 85.00
Celery Vase 25.00
Amber 45.00
Vaseline 70.00
Green/Blue 55.00
Compote, Covered, Ftd. 50.00
Amber 75.00
Vaseline 150.00
Green/Blue 100.00
Creamer or Spooner 25.00
Amber 40.00
Vaseline 50.00
Green/Blue 45.00
Cup Plate 20.00
Amber 25.00
Vaseline 35.00
Green/Blue 30.00
Dish, Sq., 10" 30.00
Amber 40.00
Vaseline 75.00
Green/Blue 50.00
Goblet 55.00
Amber 85.00
Vaseline 110.00
Green/Blue 95.00
Milk Pitcher 55.00
Amber 100.00
Vaseline 195.00
Green/Blue 165.00
Plate, 10½" (Diamond Center, Maple Leaf Border) 45.00
Amber 60.00
Vaseline 75.00
Green/Blue 70.00
Platter, Oval (Diamond Center) 50.00
Amber 65.00
Vaseline 80.00
Green/Blue 75.00
Pitcher 90.00
Amber 145.00
Vaseline 250.00
Green/Blue 200.00
Tumbler 20.00
Amber 40.00
Vaseline 65.00
Green/Blue 50.00
Sauce, 3 Ftd. 10.00
Amber 25.00
Vaseline 25.00
Green/Blue 30.00
Sugar 30.00
Amber 50.00
Vaseline 95.00
Green/Blue 110.00
Tray, Oblong 25.00
Amber 40.00
Vaseline 75.00
Green/Blue 55.00
Tray, Oval, Leaf Trim 35.00
Amber 45.00
Vaseline 80.00
Green/Blue 60.00
Twin Relish, Leaf Hndls. 30.00
Amber 35.00
Vaseline 70.00
Green/Blue 50.00

MAPLE LEAF VARIANT
Plate, 10" 45.00
Vaseline 80.00
Platter, 10½" 55.00
Vaseline 100.00

MARBURG LADLE
Punch Ladle, Wood Hndl. 40.00

MARDI GRAS
Banana Bowl 50.00
Ruby Stain 130.00
Bitters Bottle 80.00
Bonbon 35.00
Ruby Stain 70.00
Bowls, Various . . . . . 20.00 – 30.00
Ruby Stain . . . . . 60.00 – 90.00
Butter 55.00
Ruby Stain 165.00
Butter Pat 15.00
Cake Stand, 3 Sizes . . . . . 50.00 – 75.00
Celery Tray 40.00
Champagne 30.00
Claret 35.00
Cocktail 25.00
Compote, Covered 65.00
Ruby Stain 175.00
Compote, Open, 4 Sizes . . . . . 30.00 – 45.00
Ruby Stain . . . . . 50.00 – 70.00
Cordial 30.00
Ruby Stain 60.00
Cracker Jar w/Lid 85.00
Ruby Stain 190.00
Creamer, 2 Sizes . . . . . 25.00 – 35.00
Ruby Stain . . . . . 50.00 – 65.00
Cruet 65.00
Ruby Stain 180.00
Egg Cup 25.00
Epergne 165.00
Goblet 40.00
Ruby Stain 75.00
Lamp Shade 40.00
Ruby Stain 70.00
Milk Pitcher 65.00
Ruby Stain 225.00
Miniature Honey Jug 40.00
Ruby Stain 100.00
Miniature Table Set, Complete 300.00
Ruby Stain 425.00
Mustard Jar 40.00
Nappy, 2 Styles, 2 Sizes 20.00
Ruby Stain 45.00
Olive Dish 20.00
Ruby Stain 40.00
Pickle Dish 15.00
Ruby Stain 35.00
Pitcher, Various Styles, 2 Sizes . . 100.00 – 145.00
Ruby Stain . . . . . 200.00 – 235.00
Tumbler, 4 Sizes . . . . . 20.00 – 35.00
Ruby Stain . . . . . 40.00 – 60.00
Plate, 5" – 8" . . . . . 10.00 – 25.00
Pomade Jar 40.00
Puff Box 35.00
Punch Bowl 100.00
Punch Cup 10.00
Relish 10.00
Salt, Ind. 10.00
Ruby Stain 30.00
Salt, Master 25.00
Ruby Stain 70.00
Salt Shaker, Various 30.00
Ruby Stain 55.00
Sauce, Various . . . . . 10.00 – 15.00
Ruby Stain 25.00
Saucer 10.00
Ruby Stain 20.00
Shade 35.00
Ruby Stain 95.00
Sherry 20.00
Spooner 30.00
Ruby Stain 70.00
Sugar 45.00
Ruby Stain 120.00
Syrup 80.00
Toothpick Hldr. 55.00
Ruby Stain 110.00
Tray 40.00
Vase, Various . . . . . 20.00 – 30.00
Water Bottle 70.00
Ruby Stain 135.00
Wine 25.00
Ruby Stain 70.00
Wine Jug 80.00
Ruby Stain 135.00

MARILYN
Pitcher, Rare 425.00
Tumbler, Rare 85.00

MARJORIE (SWEETHEART)
Berry Bowl, Sm. 15.00
Berry Bowl, Lg. 45.00
Butter 80.00
Card Set 75.00
Carafe 60.00
Cookie Jar, Hndl. 55.00
Cracker Jar, 2 Sizes . . . . . 55.00 – 70.00
Creamer or Spooner 25.00
Cruet 60.00
Knife Rest 25.00
Napkin Ring 25.00
Nappy, 2 Hndl. 30.00
Olive Dish, Hndl. 25.00
Pickle Tray 25.00
Pitcher, Squat 75.00
Pitcher 150.00
Punch Bowl 250.00
Punch Cup 20.00

Tumbler . . . 25.00
Tumbler, Tea . . . 35.00
Punch Bowl . . . 250.00
Punch Cup . . . 20.00
Rose Bowl . . . 50.00
Salt Dip . . . 25.00
Shakers, ea. . . . 25.00
Spittoon Whimsey, Rare . . . 265.00
Sugar . . . 35.00
Syrup . . . 55.00
Toothpick Hldr. . . . 40.00
Tray, Clover Leaf . . . 35.00

MARQUISETTE
Butter . . . 55.00
Celery Vase . . . 20.00
Champagne . . . 25.00
Compote, Covered . . . 50.00
Compote, Open . . . 40.00
Cordial . . . 20.00
Creamer or Spooner . . . 20.00
Goblet . . . 25.00
Pitcher . . . 75.00
Sauce . . . 10.00
Sugar, Open . . . 25.00
Tumbler . . . 15.00
Wine . . . 10.00

MARSH PINK
Bowl, 9" . . . 25.00
Butter . . . 60.00
Cake Stand . . . 45.00
Compote, Covered . . . 60.00
Creamer or Spooner . . . 35.00
Dish w/Lid, 5" . . . 30.00
Honey Dish . . . 65.00
Jelly Compote . . . 35.00
Pickle Castor . . . 115.00
Pitcher . . . 90.00
Plate, 10" . . . 40.00
Salt Shaker . . . 25.00
Sauce, Flat or Ftd. . . . 10.00
Sugar . . . 40.00
Wine . . . 25.00

MARTEC
Berry Bowl, Lg. . . . 30.00
Berry Bowl, Sm. . . . 10.00
Bowl, Deep, 4" & 8" . . . 25.00
Breakfast Set . . . 35.00
Butter . . . 55.00
Celery Tray . . . 15.00
Compote, High Ftd. . . . 35.00
Cruet . . . 55.00
Creamer or Spooner . . . 25.00
Jelly Dish, Oval . . . 20.00
Jelly Compote . . . 35.00
Lemonade Set (Tankard) . . . 95.00
Pickle Tray . . . 25.00
Pitcher . . . 60.00
Plates, 3 Sizes . . . 15.00 – 35.00
Punch Bowl . . . 110.00
Punch Cup . . . 10.00
Shakers, ea. . . . 20.00
Stemmed Dessert . . . 25.00
Sugar . . . 35.00
Syrup . . . 65.00
Water Bottle . . . 40.00

MARY ANN
Vase . . . 50.00
Loving Cup, Rare . . . 140.00

MARYLAND
Banana Dish . . . 35.00
Ruby Stain . . . 150.00
Bowl, 6" – 9" . . . 10.00 – 30.00
Ruby Stain . . . 30.00 – 50.00
Bread Plate . . . 20.00
Ruby Stain . . . 80.00
Butter . . . 70.00
Ruby Stain . . . 190.00
Cake Stand, 8" – 10" . . . 30.00 – 60.00
Ruby Stain . . . 125.00 – 200.00
Celery Tray . . . 30.00
Ruby Stain . . . 40.00
Celery Vase . . . 25.00
Ruby Stain . . . 100.00
Compote, Covered, 6" – 8" . . . 50.00 – 100.00
Ruby Stain . . . 150.00 – 235.00
Compote, Open, 5" – 8" . . . 30.00 – 65.00
Ruby Stain . . . 75.00 – 150.00
Creamer or Spooner . . . 35.00
Ruby Stain . . . 85.00
Cup . . . 10.00
Ruby Stain . . . 30.00
Goblet . . . 45.00
Ruby Stain . . . 165.00
Honey Dish . . . 25.00
Ruby Stain . . . 30.00
Jelly Dish . . . 25.00
Ruby Stain . . . 30.00
Milk Pitcher . . . 50.00
Ruby Stain . . . 200.00
Olive Dish . . . 20.00
Ruby Stain . . . 30.00
Pickle Dish . . . 15.00
Ruby Stain . . . 30.00
Plate, Dinner . . . 25.00
Ruby Stain . . . 100.00
Pitcher . . . 85.00
Ruby Stain . . . 250.00
Tumbler . . . 20.00
Ruby Stain . . . 70.00
Relish . . . 20.00
Ruby Stain . . . 50.00
Shakers, ea. . . . 25.00
Ruby Stain . . . 80.00
Sugar . . . 25.00
Ruby Stain . . . 150.00
Toothpick Hldr, Very Scarce . . . 125.00
Ruby Stain . . . 300.00
Wine . . . 10.00
Ruby Stain . . . 100.00

MASONIC
Bowls, 4" – 9" . . . 15.00 – 50.00
Butter, 2 Styles . . . 50.00 – 65.00
Cake Stand, 9" – 10" . . . 35.00 – 45.00
Celery Vase . . . 20.00
Compote, Covered . . . 55.00
Compote, Open . . . 35.00
Creamer or Spooner . . . 30.00
Cruet . . . 45.00
Custard Cup . . . 10.00
Goblet . . . 35.00
Hndl. Salad Fork . . . 25.00
Honey Dish w/Lid . . . 45.00
Nappy . . . 25.00
Pitcher . . . 90.00
Tumbler . . . 20.00
Relish Dish . . . 15.00
Salt Dip, 2 Styles . . . 20.00
Shakers, ea., 2 Styles . . . 15.00 – 25.00
Sardine Box . . . 35.00
Syrup . . . 85.00
Sugar . . . 50.00
Toothpick Hldr. . . . 35.00
Wine . . . 20.00

MASSACHUSETTS
Butter . . . 60.00
Candy Dish . . . 25.00
Cologne . . . 40.00
Creamer or Spooner . . . 25.00
Cruet, Miniature . . . 60.00
Goblet . . . 40.00
Plate, 8" . . . 30.00
Pitcher . . . 85.00
Tumbler . . . 25.00
Rum Jug . . . 80.00
Shakers, ea. . . . 25.00
Shot Glass . . . 20.00
Sugar . . . 35.00
Table Lamp . . . 650.00
Toothpick Hldr. . . . 30.00
Toy Basket . . . 40.00
Water Bottle . . . 50.00
Vase, 7" – 10" . . . 35.00

MAYFLOWER
Bowl, Rare . . . 450.00

MCHOB
Pitcher, Squat . . . 75.00
Tumblers, 3 Sizes . . . 10.00

MCKEE'S #1004
Vase, 8" (Globe Vase) . . . 50.00

MCKEE'S TAMBOUR ART CLOCK
Clock . . . 85.00
Vaseline . . . 235.00

MEDALLION
Butter . . . 45.00
Amber . . . 55.00
Vaseline . . . 70.00
Green/Blue . . . 85.00
Cake Stand . . . 30.00
Amber . . . 35.00
Vaseline . . . 40.00
Green/Blue . . . 55.00
Castor Bottles . . . 30.00
Amber . . . 35.00
Vaseline . . . 40.00
Green/Blue . . . 55.00
Celery Vase . . . 20.00
Amber . . . 25.00
Vaseline . . . 30.00
Green/Blue . . . 40.00
Compote, Open . . . 35.00
Amber . . . 40.00
Vaseline . . . 45.00
Green/Blue . . . 55.00
Compote, Covered . . . 50.00
Amber . . . 55.00
Vaseline . . . 65.00
Green/Blue . . . 80.00
Egg Cup . . . 20.00
Amber . . . 25.00
Vaseline . . . 30.00
Green/Blue . . . 40.00
Goblet . . . 35.00
Amber . . . 40.00
Vaseline . . . 50.00
Green/Blue . . . 45.00
Pickle Dish . . . 20.00
Amber . . . 25.00
Vaseline . . . 30.00
Green/Blue . . . 30.00
Pitcher . . . 80.00
Amber . . . 90.00
Vaseline . . . 125.00
Green/Blue . . . 165.00
Tumbler . . . 20.00
Amber . . . 25.00
Vaseline . . . 30.00
Green/Blue . . . 35.00
Relish Tray . . . 20.00
Amber . . . 25.00
Vaseline . . . 30.00
Green/Blue . . . 30.00
Sauce, Flat or Ftd. . . . 10.00
Amber . . . 15.00
Vaseline . . . 20.00
Green/Blue . . . 25.00
Sugar . . . 45.00
Amber . . . 50.00
Vaseline . . . 65.00
Green/Blue . . . 75.00
Water Bottle . . . 35.00
Amber . . . 40.00
Vaseline . . . 50.00
Green/Blue . . . 60.00
Waste Bowl . . . 25.00
Amber . . . 30.00
Vaseline . . . 35.00
Green/Blue . . . 40.00
Wine . . . 20.00
Amber . . . 25.00
Vaseline . . . 30.00
Green/Blue . . . 35.00

MEDALLION SUNBURST
Banana Dish, Flat or Stemmed . . . 35.00
Bowl, Rnd. or Sq. . . . 25.00
Butter . . . 65.00
Cake Stand, 9" – 10½" . . . 40.00

Celery Tray . . . 25.00
Celery Vase . . . 20.00
Creamer or Spooner . . . 20.00
Cruet . . . 55.00
Custard Cup . . . 10.00
Jam Jar . . . 25.00
Milk Pitcher . . . 45.00
Mug . . . 25.00
Mustard Jar . . . 20.00
Olive Dish . . . 15.00
Plate, Rnd., 6" – 9" . . . 15.00 – 30.00
Plate, Sq., 7¼" . . . 25.00
Pitcher . . . 85.00
Tumbler . . . 15.00
Relish Tray . . . 20.00
Salt Dip, Ind. . . . 15.00
Shakers, ea. . . . 20.00
Sugar . . . 25.00
Toothpick Hldr. . . . 30.00
Vase, 9½" . . . 25.00
Wine . . . 10.00

MELON WITH LEAF
Novelty Bowl, Covered . . . 55.00
Amber . . . 75.00
Vaseline . . . 120.00
Green/Blue . . . 95.00
Milk Glass . . . 55.00

MELTON
Butter . . . 55.00
Creamer or Spooner . . . 20.00
Goblet . . . 35.00
Sugar . . . 25.00
Wine . . . 10.00

MEMPHIS
Bowl, Berry, Lg. . . . 55.00
Bowl, Berry, Sm. . . . 25.00
Butter . . . 100.00
Vaseline . . . 3000.00*
Creamer, Spooner, or Sugar . . . 40.00
Decanter w/Stopper . . . 175.00
Fruit Bowl, on Metal Base . . . 100.00
Nappy . . . 65.00
Nappy, Adv., Rare . . . 200.00
Pitcher . . . 275.00
Tumbler . . . 35.00
Punch Bowl w/Base, Reg. . . . 375.00
Punch Bowl w/Base, Master . . . 700.00
Punch Cup . . . 30.00
Syrup . . . 90.00
Toothpick Hldr. . . . 95.00

MEPHISTOPHELES
Ale Glass . . . 95.00
Opaque White . . . 110.00
Mug . . . 125.00
Opaque White . . . 140.00
Pitcher . . . 275.00
Opaque White . . . 300.00

MICHIGAN
(AKA: Des Plaines, Loop and Pillar, Panelled Jewel)
Bowls, Various Shapes, 6" – 10" . 10.00 – 55.00
Ruby Stain . . . 35.00 – 85.00
Bride's Basket . . . 85.00
Ruby Stain . . . 165.00
Butter . . . 50.00
Ruby Stain . . . 125.00
Celery Vase . . . 25.00
Ruby Stain . . . 100.00
Creamer or Spooner . . . 25.00
Ruby Stain . . . 85.00
Creamer or Sugar, Ind. . . . 20.00
Ruby Stain . . . 75.00
Cruet . . . 60.00
Ruby Stain . . . 325.00
Goblet . . . 25.00
Ruby Stain . . . 135.00
Lemonade, Hndl. . . . 30.00
Ruby Stain . . . 85.00
Lemon Stain . . . 80.00
Milk Pitcher . . . 75.00
Ruby Stain . . . 150.00
Pickle Dish . . . 20.00
Ruby Stain . . . 30.00
Pitcher, 2 Styles . . . 85.00
Ruby Stain . . . 200.00
Tumbler . . . 30.00
Ruby Stain . . . 60.00
Plate . . . 30.00
Ruby Stain . . . 40.00
Salt Shaker, ea. . . . 20.00
Ruby Stain . . . 100.00
Sauce . . . 15.00
Ruby Stain . . . 35.00
Sugar . . . 75.00
Ruby Stain . . . 135.00
Toothpick Hldr., Rare . . . 85.00
Ruby Stain . . . 250.00
Toy Table Set, Complete, Rare . . . 250.00
Ruby Stain . . . 800.00
Vase, 6" – 17" . . . 25.00 – 100.00
Ruby Stain . . . 40.00 – 165.00
Water Bottle . . . 60.00
Ruby Stain . . . 175.00

MILLARD
Bowl, 7" – 9" . . . 25.00
Ruby Stain . . . 35.00
Butter . . . 50.00
Ruby Stain . . . 75.00
Cake Stand . . . 30.00
Ruby Stain . . . 45.00
Celery Tray . . . 20.00
Ruby Stain . . . 25.00
Celery Vase . . . 25.00
Ruby Stain . . . 35.00
Compote . . . 25.00
Ruby Stain . . . 45.00
Creamer or Spooner . . . 20.00
Ruby Stain . . . 30.00
Cruet . . . 60.00
Ruby Stain . . . 80.00
Cup . . . 10.00
Ruby Stain . . . 25.00
Dish, Oblong . . . 20.00
Ruby Stain . . . 30.00
Goblet . . . 35.00
Ruby Stain . . . 55.00
Plate . . . 20.00
Ruby Stain . . . 30.00
Pitcher . . . 75.00
Ruby Stain . . . 125.00
Tumbler . . . 15.00
Ruby Stain . . . 35.00
Sauce, Flat or Ftd. . . . 10.00
Ruby Stain . . . 25.00
Shakers, ea. . . . 25.00
Ruby Stain . . . 45.00
Sugar . . . 25.00
Ruby Stain . . . 45.00
Syrup . . . 55.00
Ruby Stain . . . 75.00
Toothpick Hldr. . . . 30.00
Ruby Stain . . . 65.00
Wine . . . 15.00
Ruby Stain . . . 25.00

MILLERSBURG CHERRY
Jardiniere Whimsey, Very Rare,
Green/Blue . . . 3000.00
Milk Pitcher, Rare . . . 1200.00
Pitcher, Rare . . . 1400.00

MILLERSBURG TULIP
Compote, Ruffled . . . 500.00
Compote, Goblet Shaped . . . 650.00
Compote, Salver Shaped . . . 650.00

MINERVA
Berry Bowl, Sm. . . . 20.00
Berry Bowl, Lg. . . . 50.00
Bread Plate . . . 35.00
Butter . . . 85.00
Champagne . . . 25.00
Compote, Covered, 7" – 8" . . . 45.00 – 65.00
Compote, Open, 10½" . . . 30.00 – 55.00
Creamer or Spooner . . . 25.00
Goblet . . . 60.00
Honey Dish . . . 35.00
Jam Jar . . . 35.00
Milk Pitcher . . . 65.00
Pickle Dish . . . 25.00
Plate, 8" – 9" . . . 25.00 – 45.00
Platter, Oval . . . 50.00
Pitcher . . . 125.00
Tumbler . . . 25.00
Sauce, Flat or Ftd. . . . 20.00
Sugar . . . 30.00

MILLNER'S
Advertising Ashtray . . . 75.00

MINIATURE LOVING CUP
One Shape, 3 Hndl. . . . 30.00

MINNESOTA
Banana Stand . . . 60.00
Basket . . . 75.00
Berry Bowl, Sm. . . . 20.00
Ruby Stain . . . 50.00
Berry Bowl, Lg. . . . 45.00
Ruby Stain . . . 95.00
Biscuit Jar . . . 50.00
Ruby Stain . . . 165.00
Bonbon . . . 15.00
Bowl, Oval . . . 35.00
Butter . . . 70.00
Carafe . . . 40.00
Celery Tray . . . 25.00
Compote, Rnd. or Sq. . . . 40.00
Creamer or Spooner . . . 25.00
Cruet . . . 50.00
Cup . . . 20.00
Goblet . . . 45.00
Ruby Stain . . . 65.00
Hair Receiver . . . 25.00
Humidor . . . 150.00
Match Hldr. . . . 30.00
Mug . . . 25.00
Plate . . . 25.00
Pomade Jar . . . 40.00
Pitcher . . . 75.00
Ruby Stain . . . 225.00
Tumbler . . . 35.00
Ruby Stain . . . 60.00
Shaker . . . 25.00
Sugar . . . 35.00
Syrup . . . 65.00
Toothpick Hldr. . . . 45.00
Ruby Stain . . . 125.00
Tray . . . 20.00
Vase . . . 25.00
Wine . . . 15.00

MIRROR IMAGE (Possibly other shapes)
Pitcher, 7½" . . . 65.00

MISSOURI
Bowl, Covered, 6" – 8" . . . 40.00 – 65.00
Green/Blue . . . 50.00 – 95.00
Bowl, Open, 6" – 8" . . . 20.00 – 35.00
Green/Blue . . . 40.00 – 70.00
Butter . . . 65.00
Green/Blue . . . 125.00
Cake Stand . . . 35.00
Green/Blue . . . 60.00 – 125.00
Celery Vase . . . 25.00
Green/Blue . . . 80.00
Compote, Covered, 5" – 8" . . . 45.00 – 70.00
Green/Blue . . . 60.00 – 125.00
Compote, Open, 5" – 10" . . . 25.00 – 65.00
Green/Blue . . . 30.00 – 60.00
Cordial . . . 30.00
Green/Blue . . . 135.00
Creamer or Spooner . . . 30.00
Green/Blue . . . 55.00
Cruet . . . 70.00
Green/Blue . . . 250.00
Dish w/Lid, 6" . . . 75.00
Green/Blue . . . 135.00
Doughnut Stand, 6" . . . 50.00
Green/Blue . . . 80.00
Goblet . . . 65.00
Green/Blue . . . 150.00
Milk Pitcher . . . 50.00
Green/Blue . . . 100.00
Mug . . . 40.00

Green/Blue. 75.00
Pickle Dish. 10.00
Green/Blue. 30.00
Pitcher 100.00
Green/Blue. 150.00
Tumbler 20.00
Green/Blue. 65.00
Relish Dish 10.00
Green/Blue. 30.00
Salt Shaker. 45.00
Green/Blue. 100.00
Sauce 10.00
Green/Blue. 25.00
Sugar 60.00
Green/Blue. 80.00
Syrup 95.00
Green/Blue. 325.00
Wine 50.00
Green/Blue. 100.00

MITERED DIAMOND
Berry Bowl, Sm. 10.00
Amber 15.00
Vaseline. 25.00
Green/Blue. 20.00
Berry Bowl, Lg. 30.00
Amber 35.00
Vaseline. 45.00
Green/Blue. 40.00
Butter. 45.00
Amber 50.00
Vaseline. 95.00
Green/Blue. 60.00
Compote. 30.00
Amber 35.00
Vaseline. 45.00
Green/Blue. 40.00
Cordial 20.00
Amber 25.00
Vaseline. 35.00
Green/Blue. 30.00
Creamer or Spooner 25.00
Amber 30.00
Vaseline. 40.00
Green/Blue. 35.00
Platter 30.00
Amber 35.00
Vaseline. 60.00
Green/Blue. 40.00
Sauce 10.00
Amber 15.00
Vaseline. 30.00
Green/Blue. 20.00
Shakers, ea. 25.00
Amber 30.00
Vaseline. 55.00
Green/Blue. 35.00
Sugar 35.00
Amber 40.00
Vaseline. 65.00
Green/Blue. 45.00
Wine 15.00
Amber 20.00
Vaseline. 45.00
Green/Blue. 30.00

MITTED HAND
Bowl, 6" 75.00

MODEL'S GEM
Decanter 65.00
Amber 80.00
Green/Blue. 90.00
Ruby Stain. 100.00
Goblet 35.00
Amber 40.00
Green/Blue. 50.00
Ruby Stain. 55.00
Mug 40.00
Amber 45.00
Green/Blue. 55.00
Ruby Stain. 45.00
Mustard Jar 55.00
Amber 60.00
Green/Blue. 75.00
Ruby Stain. 85.00
Tray 35.00
Amber 40.00
Green/Blue. 50.00
Ruby Stain. 45.00
Tumbler 25.00
Amber 30.00
Green/Blue. 40.00
Ruby Stain. 35.00
Wine 20.00
Amber 25.00
Green/Blue. 35.00
Ruby Stain. 30.00

MONARCH
Bowl, 9" 35.00
Cruet 65.00
Punch Bowl 115.00
Punch Cup 10.00

MOERLEINS
Pilsner, 6", Advertising, 2 Styles Lettering 50.00

MONKEY AND VINES
Mug 60.00

MOON AND STAR
Bowl, Covered, 6" – 10" . . . . . 30.00 – 60.00
Ruby Stain . . . . . 45.00 – 75.00
Bowl, Open, 6" – 10" . . . . . 20.00 – 40.00
Ruby Stain . . . . . 40.00 – 65.00
Bowl, Salad 30.00
Ruby Stain. 40.00
Bowl, Waste. 20.00
Ruby Stain. 35.00
Bread Tray 30.00
Ruby Stain. 40.00
Butter. 65.00
Ruby Stain. 135.00
Cake Stand. 40.00
Carafe 60.00
Celery Vase 25.00
Champagne 45.00
Ruby Stain. 110.00
Cheese Dish. 60.00
Claret 10.00
Compote, w/Lid, 6" – 10", High or Low. . . . . 50.00 – 100.00
Ruby Stain . . . . . 130.00 – 225.00
Compote, Open, 6" – 12", High or Low. . . . . 30.00 – 60.00
Ruby Stain . . . . . 60.00 – 125.00
Creamer or Spooner. 40.00
Ruby Stain. 90.00
Egg Cup 30.00
Ruby Stain. 65.00
Goblet 45.00
Ruby Stain. 75.00
Oil Lamp 165.00
Pickle Tray. 20.00
Ruby Stain. 30.00
Pitcher 185.00
Ruby Stain. 300.00
Tumbler 50.00
Ruby Stain. 75.00
Relish Tray. 15.00
Ruby Stain. 35.00
Sauce 10.00
Ruby Stain. 20.00
Salt Dip 15.00
Ruby Stain. 40.00
Shakers, ea. 30.00
Ruby Stain. 65.00
Sugar 50.00
Ruby Stain. 100.00
Syrup 185.00
Water Bottle. 45.00
Water Tray. 70.00
Wine 10.00
Ruby Stain. 95.00

MORNING GLORY
Butter. 850.00
Champagne 250.00
Creamer or Spooner. 175.00
Dessert, Stemmed 125.00
Egg Cup 95.00
Goblet 1850.00
Pitcher 1200.00
Salt Dip 100.00
Sugar 200.00
Tumbler, Ftd. 95.00
Wine 115.00

MT. VERNON
Bowls, Rectangular . . . . . 15.00 – 40.00
Butter. 50.00
Creamer or Spooner. 20.00
Goblet 35.00
Pickle Dish. 15.00
Relish. 15.00
Sugar 25.00

MULTIPLE SCROLL
Bowls, Various . . . . . 15.00 – 25.00
Amber. . . . . 20.00 – 35.00
Butter. 55.00
Amber 60.00
Green/Blue. 70.00
Celery Vase 20.00
Amber 30.00
Green/Blue. 40.00
Creamer or Spooner. 25.00
Amber 35.00
Green/Blue. 45.00
Mug 40.00
Amber 50.00
Green/Blue. 60.00
Pickle Dish. 15.00
Amber 20.00
Green/Blue. 25.00
Plate, Sq. 20.00
Amber 25.00
Green/Blue. 30.00
Sugar 40.00
Amber 55.00
Green/Blue. 65.00
Wine 20.00
Amber 25.00
Green/Blue. 30.00

MUTT JUG #46
Pitcher, Tankard 95.00

NAIL
Berry Bowl, Sm. 10.00
Berry Bowl, Lg. 35.00
Berry Compote 30.00
Butter. 70.00
Carafe 40.00
Celery Vase 25.00
Claret 15.00
Creamer or Spooner. 20.00
Cruet 65.00
Finger Bowl 15.00
Goblet 55.00
Jelly Compote. 25.00
Mustard Pot 30.00
Pitcher 95.00
Tumbler 20.00
Sauce, Flat or Ftd. 10.00
Shakers, ea. 25.00
Sugar 30.00
Sugar Shaker 75.00
Vase, 7" 25.00
Water Tray. 35.00
Wine 10.00

NAILHEAD
Berry Bowl, Sm. 15.00
Berry Bowl, Lg. 40.00
Butter. 70.00
Cake Stand. 35.00
Celery Vase 25.00
Compote, Covered, 6" – 8" . . . . . 25.00 – 60.00
Compote, Open, 6" – 8" . . . . . 20.00 – 45.00
Cordial 15.00
Creamer or Spooner. 20.00
Goblet 50.00
Plate, Bread 15.00
Plate, Dinner 25.00
Pitcher 90.00
Tumbler 20.00

Sauce 10.00
Sugar 25.00
Wine 15.00

NARCISSUS SPRAY
Berry Bowl, Sm. 20.00
Berry Bowl, Lg. 45.00
Bowl, Rnd. or Oval 30.00
Bowl, Ftd., 7½" 25.00
Butter 60.00
Celery Tray 30.00
Celery Vase, Ftd. 20.00
Creamer or Spooner 20.00
Decanter 65.00
Jelly Compote 25.00
Plate 25.00
Pitcher 85.00
Tumbler 20.00
Sugar 25.00
Wine 15.00

NARROW SWIRL
Pitcher, Small 65.00

NATIONAL
Tray, Shield Shaped, Rare 85.00

NATIONAL STAR
Berry Bowl, Sm. 10.00
Vaseline 20.00
Ruby Stain 15.00
Berry Bowl, Lg. 30.00
Vaseline 50.00
Ruby Stain 45.00
Butter 65.00
Vaseline 110.00
Ruby Stain 80.00
Creamer or Spooner 25.00
Vaseline 40.00
Ruby Stain 35.00
Jelly Compote 30.00
Vaseline 45.00
Ruby Stain 40.00
Pitcher 75.00
Vaseline 160.00
Ruby Stain 125.00
Tumbler 15.00
Vaseline 40.00
Ruby Stain 30.00
Sugar 30.00
Vaseline 65.00
Ruby Stain 45.00

NAVARRE (MCKEE AND BROS-1900)
Butter 85.00
Creamer or Spooner 35.00
Nappy 25.00
Sugar 45.00

NEARCUT #2636
Basket, Hndl. 45.00
Berry Bowl, Sm. 20.00
Berry Bowl, Lg. 45.00
Bowl, Various . . . . 20.00 – 35.00
Butter 65.00
Celery Vase 25.00
Creamer or Spooner 25.00
Cruet 65.00
Pitcher 90.00
Tumbler 20.00
Salt Shakers, ea. 20.00
Sugar 30.00
Vase 30.00
Wine 15.00

NEARCUT #2692
Bowl 35.00
Butter 65.00
Celery Tray 30.00
Creamer, Spooner, or Sugar 30.00
Cruet 55.00
Cup 20.00
Finger Bowl 25.00
Pickle Tray 25.00
Plate, 2 Sizes 40.00
Sauce 20.00
Shakers, Ea. 25.00
Tumbler 25.00
Water Bottle 40.00

NEARCUT DAISY
Bowls, Various . . . . 10.00 – 35.00
Butter 65.00
Creamer or Spooner 25.00
Pickle Dish 20.00
Sugar 40.00
Vases, Various . . . . 15.00 – 35.00

NEAR CUT WREATH (All pieces rare)
Bowl, 8" – 9" 475.00
Rose Bowl 550.00

NELLY
Berry Bowl, Sm. 15.00
Berry Bowl, Lg. 35.00
Butter 55.00
Cake Stand 35.00
Celery Vase 20.00
Compote 30.00
Creamer or Spooner 20.00
Sauce 10.00
Shakers, ea. 15.00
Sugar 25.00

NEW ENGLAND PINEAPPLE
Bowl, 8" 75.00
Butter 275.00
Cake Stand 155.00
Caster Set, Complete 365.00
Champagne 190.00
Compote, Covered, 5" – 8" . . . . 175.00 – 245.00
Compote, Open, 7" – 8½" . . . . 75.00 – 125.00
Cordial 200.00
Creamer 200.00
Cruet 195.00
Decanter 245.00
Egg Cup 45.00
Goblet, 2 Sizes . . . . 75.00 – 125.00
Honey Dish 25.00
Milk Pitcher 550.00
Mug 100.00
Pitcher 400.00
Tumbler, 2 Sizes . . . . 75.00 – 125.00
Plate, 6" 100.00
Salt, Master 50.00
Salt, Ind. 25.00
Sauce, Flat or Ftd. 25.00
Spill 75.00
Spooner 70.00
Sugar 180.00
Sweetmeat 245.00
Whiskey 150.00
Wine 165.00

NEW ERA
Berry Bowl, Sm. 10.00
Berry Bowl, Lg. 35.00
Bowls, Various . . . . 10.00 – 35.00
Bread Plate 20.00
Butter 65.00
Candelabra 55.00
Compotes, Various . . . . 20.00 – 45.00
Creamer or Spooner 20.00
Honey Dish 30.00
Jelly Compote 25.00
Olive Jar, Sq. 25.00
Pickle Tray 15.00
Plate, Sq. 20.00
Pitcher 90.00
Tumbler 20.00
Salt Dip 15.00
Sauce 10.00
Shakers, ea. 15.00
Sugar 25.00
Toothpick Hldr. 25.00
Tray 25.00

NEW HAMPSHIRE
Basket 125.00
Ruby Stain 325.00
Biscuit Jar 45.00
Ruby Stain 150.00
Bowl, Rnd., 6" – 9" . . . . 15.00 – 35.00
Ruby Stain . . . . 25.00 – 75.00
Bowl, Sq., 6" – 9" . . . . 15.00 – 40.00
Ruby Stain . . . . 30.00 – 80.00
Breakfast Set 55.00
Ruby Stain 100.00
Butter 70.00
Ruby Stain 190.00
Cake Stand 45.00
Ruby Stain 200.00
Carafe 55.00
Ruby Stain 135.00
Celery Vase 20.00
Ruby Stain 100.00
Compote, Covered, 6" – 9" . . . . 25.00 – 65.00
Ruby Stain 225.00
Compote, Open, 6" – 9" . . . . 20.00 – 45.00
Ruby Stain 110.00
Creamer or Spooner 25.00
Ruby Stain 80.00
Cruet 55.00
Ruby Stain 235.00
Custard Cup 10.00
Ruby Stain 30.00
Goblet 40.00
Ruby Stain 125.00
Jug, 3 Pt. 125.00
Ruby Stain 250.00
Lemonade Cup 10.00
Ruby Stain 30.00
Mug, 2 Sizes . . . . 20.00 – 35.00
Ruby Stain 85.00
Olive Dish 15.00
Ruby Stain 30.00
Pickle Dish 15.00
Ruby Stain 35.00
Plate, 8" 25.00
Ruby Stain 75.00
Pitcher, 2 Styles 165.00
Ruby Stain 325.00
Tumbler, 2 Styles . . . . 20.00 – 25.00
Ruby Stain 75.00
Relish Tray 20.00
Ruby Stain 40.00
Salt Shaker, 3 Sizes . . . . 25.00 – 50.00
Ruby Stain 100.00
Sauce, Rnd. or Sq. 10.00
Ruby Stain 20.00
Sugar 30.00
Ruby Stain 75.00
Syrup 55.00
Ruby Stain 300.00
Toothpick Hldr. 25.00
Ruby Stain 100.00
Vase, 6" – 9" . . . . 15.00 – 30.00
Ruby Stain 60.00
Wine, 2 Styles 20.00
Ruby Stain 50.00

NEW JERSEY
Bowl, 6" – 10" . . . . 15.00 – 50.00
Ruby Stain 75.00
Bowl, Oval, 6" – 10" . . . . 20.00 – 60.00
Ruby Stain 90.00
Butter 85.00
Ruby Stain 200.00
Cake Stand 65.00
Ruby Stain 225.00
Celery Tray 25.00
Ruby Stain 50.00
Celery Vase 50.00
Ruby Stain 165.00
Compote, Covered, 5" – 8" . . . . 35.00 – 70.00
Ruby Stain 200.00
Compote, Open, 5" – 8" . . . . 25.00 – 50.00
Ruby Stain 100.00
Creamer or Spooner 25.00
Ruby Stain 95.00
Cruet 65.00
Ruby Stain 375.00
Fruit Bowl on Standard, 9½" – 12½" . 40.00 – 65.00
Ruby Stain 135.00
Goblet 50.00
Ruby Stain 245.00
Milk Pitcher 100.00
Ruby Stain 300.00
Olive Dish 10.00
Ruby Stain 35.00

Pickle Tray 20.00
Ruby Stain 45.00
Plate, 8" – 12" . . . . 20.00 – 40.00
Ruby Stain . . . . 75.00 – 150.00
Pitcher, 2 Styles 150.00
Ruby Stain 325.00
Tumbler, 2 Styles . . . . 20.00 – 30.00
Ruby Stain 100.00
Shade, Gas 75.00
Ruby Stain 195.00
Shakers, ea. 55.00
Ruby Stain 125.00
Sugar 55.00
Ruby Stain 150.00
Sweetmeat (High Butter) 100.00
Ruby Stain 300.00
Syrup 100.00
Ruby Stain 325.00
Toothpick Hldr. 60.00
Ruby Stain 225.00
Water Bottle 50.00
Ruby Stain 150.00
Wine 40.00
Ruby Stain 100.00

NEW MARTINSVILLE #169
Candlesticks, 7" 60.00

NIAGARA
Berry Bowl, Sm. 10.00
Berry Bowl, Lg. 35.00
Butter 55.00
Compote 30.00
Cracker Jar 30.00
Creamer or Spooner 20.00
Cruet 50.00
Cup 10.00
Jelly, Hndl. 25.00
Mustard Jar 30.00
Plate 25.00
Sugar 25.00
Syrup 55.00

#9 BOOK
Matchholder 70.00

NOGI
Butter 40.00
Creamer or Spooner 15.00
Fan Tray 20.00
Ruby Stain 50.00
Goblet 30.00
Pickle Dish 10.00
Pitcher 60.00
Tumbler 10.00
Plate 20.00
Sugar 25.00

NONPARIEL
Bowls, Various . . . . 10.00 – 35.00
Butter 45.00
Creamer or Spooner 20.00
Pitcher 65.00
Tumbler 15.00
Sugar 25.00

NORTHERN STAR
Plate, 3 Sizes 55.00
Sauce Bowl 30.00

NORTH STAR
Berry Bowl, Sm. 10.00
Berry Bowl, Lg. 30.00
Butter 55.00
Compote, Stemmed, Ruffled 35.00
Creamer or Spooner 20.00
Pitcher 70.00
Plate 25.00
Punch Bowl w/Base 110.00
Punch Cup 10.00
Tumbler 15.00
Sugar 25.00

NORTHWOOD GOOD LUCK
Bowl, Rare 300.00
Custard 375.00
Plate, Very Rare 525.00
Custard 600.00

NORTHWOOD NEAR-CUT (#12) (Condensed List)
Berry Bowl, Sm. 20.00
Berry Bowl, Lg. 40.00
Butter 70.00
Celery Vase 30.00
Compote 40.00
Creamer or Spooner 25.00
Goblet 35.00
Nappy 25.00
Nappy, Adv., Rare 100.00
Pickle Dish 30.00
Pitcher 125.00
Tumbler 25.00
Shakers, ea. 30.00
Sugar 30.00
Toothpick Hldr. 45.00
Wine 25.00

NORTHWOOD PEACH
Berry Bowl, Sm. 20.00
Berry Bowl, Lg. 45.00
Butter 55.00
Creamer or Spooner 30.00
Pitcher 75.00
Tumbler 15.00
Sugar 30.00

NORTHWOOD STRAWBERRY
Bowl, Very Scarce 200.00
Plate, Rare 325.00

NORTHWOOD THIN RIB
Vase, 9" – 17" . . . . 25.00 – 125.00

NORTHWOOD WILDFLOWER
Compote 25.00
Green/Blue 40.00

NOTCHED PANEL
Berry Bowl, Sm. 10.00
Berry Bowl, Lg. 35.00
Bowl, Sq. 20.00
Butter 45.00
Creamer or Spooner 20.00
Relish 15.00
Shakers, ea. 15.00
Sugar 25.00
Toothpick Hldr. 20.00

NU-CUT #537
Jelly Compote 25.00

NU-CUT STAR
Bowl, Sq., 6" 25.00
Bowl, Rnd., 6½" 20.00
Breakfast Set 50.00
Butter 65.00
Compote, 6" 40.00
Mayonnaise Set 50.00
Nappy 25.00
Pickle Tray 20.00
Sugar 25.00

NURSERY RHYME BOWL
Bowl 45.00

OCTAGON
Berry Bowl, Sm. 10.00
Berry Bowl, Lg. 35.00
Bowl, 11" 40.00
Butter 55.00
Compote, Sm. 35.00
Compote, Lg. 45.00
Cordial 20.00
Creamer or Spooner 25.00
Goblet 30.00
Hndl. Nappy 35.00
Milk Pitcher 45.00
Pitcher, Mid-size 55.00
Pitcher, Standard 70.00
Tumbler 20.00
Punch Bowl 85.00
Punch Cup 10.00
Shakers, ea. 20.00
Sherbet 20.00
Sugar 25.00
Toothpick Hldr. 20.00
Vase, Pedestal 30.00
Wine 15.00
Wine Decanter 45.00

O'HARA'S CRYSTAL WEDDING
Butter 75.00
Cake Stand 45.00
Celery Vase 25.00
Creamer or Spooner 25.00
Pitcher 95.00
Tumbler 25.00
Sugar 35.00

O'HARA'S DIAMOND
Bowl, Covered, 5" – 8" . . . . 25.00 – 45.00
Ruby Stain . . . . 40.00 – 70.00
Bowl, Open, 5" – 8" . . . . 10.00 – 25.00
Ruby Stain . . . . 25.00 – 40.00
Butter 55.00
Ruby Stain 140.00
Cake Stand 65.00
Ruby Stain 135.00
Celery Vase 35.00
Ruby Stain 85.00
Champagne 25.00
Ruby Stain 45.00
Claret 40.00
Ruby Stain 50.00
Compote, Open, 5" – 8" . . . . 40.00 – 70.00
Ruby Stain . . . . 100.00 – 145.00
Condiment Tray 35.00
Ruby Stain 55.00
Creamer or Spooner 25.00
Ruby Stain 65.00
Cruet 50.00
Ruby Stain 150.00
Custard Cup 10.00
Ruby Stain 25.00
Dish, Various . . . . 10.00 – 20.00
Goblet 30.00
Ruby Stain 75.00
Honey Dish 20.00
Ruby Stain 25.00
Lamp 70.00
Pickle Dish 15.00
Ruby Stain 25.00
Pitcher 125.00
Ruby Stain 185.00
Tumbler 25.00
Ruby Stain 50.00
Plate, 7" – 10" . . . . 25.00 – 40.00
Salt Dip 20.00
Ruby Stain 40.00
Salt Shaker 25.00
Ruby Stain 55.00
Sauce . . . . 10.00 – 20.00
Ruby Stain 30.00
Saucer 15.00
Ruby Stain 65.00
Sugar 45.00
Ruby Stain 105.00
Syrup 70.00
Ruby Stain 235.00
Water Tray 40.00
Ruby Stain 80.00
Wine 20.00
Ruby Stain 40.00

OHIO STAR (All pieces rare)
Banana Bowl, 3 Sizes . . . . 55.00 – 90.00
Berry Bowl, Lg. 65.00
Berry Bowl, Sm. 30.00
Bowl, Sq., Deep, 6"x6" 100.00
Bowl, Sq., Lg., Ruffled 150.00
Butter 250.00
Carafe 250.00
Card Tray Whimsey 150.00
Celery Bowl, 2 Sizes . . . . 200.00 – 225.00
Cider Pitcher 165.00
Cider Tumbler 100.00
Cloverleaf Dish, 2 Sizes . . . . 150.00 – 250.00
Compote, Standard 125.00
Sapphire 1700.00
Compote, Standard, Ruffled, Scarce 325.00
Compote, Tall 350.00
Light Amethyst 450.00
Cookie Jar 195.00
Creamer or Spooner 75.00
Cruet 250.00
Milk Pitcher, Very Rare 1500.00
Mint Dish 65.00

Plate, 3 Sizes . . . 75.00 – 175.00
Pitcher, Tankard, 9¼", Rare . . . 800.00
Pitcher, Collar Base, Scarce . . . 450.00
Tumbler . . . 80.00
Plate, Sq., 5" . . . 250.00
Plate, Sq., 7" . . . 275.00
Plate, Sq., 9" . . . 350.00
Plate, Sq., 11" . . . 500.00
Punch Bowl w/Base . . . 1500.00
Punch Cup . . . 45.00
Rose Bowl, Flat, 7" . . . 225.00
Rose Bowl, Flat, 9" . . . 350.00
Rose Bowl Whimsey, Stemmed . . . 300.00
Shakers, ea. . . . 425.00
Sherbet . . . 90.00
Sq. Flat Dish, 5", 7" & 9" . . . 100.00 – 175.00
Sugar . . . 100.00
Syrup . . . 525.00
Toothpick Hldr. . . . 125.00
Vase . . . 325.00
Vase, Sq. Top, Very Rare . . . 1700.00
Vase, J.I.P. Shape, Very Rare . . . 1500.00
Wine . . . 150.00
(Frosted pieces, rare, add 25%)

OKLAHOMA VINEGAR CO.
Advertising Ale Glass . . . 75.00

OLD COLONY
Berry Bowl, SM. . . . 20.00
Berry Bowl, Lg. . . . 45.00
Butter . . . 70.00
Creamer or Spooner . . . 25.00
Pitcher . . . 85.00
Tumbler . . . 20.00
Sugar . . . 30.00

OLD GLORY
Pitcher . . . 75.00
Tumbler . . . 15.00

OLD STATEHOUSE (PHILADELPHIA)
Plate . . . 85.00

OMERO
Berry Bowl, Sm. . . . 10.00
Berry Bowl, Lg. . . . 30.00
Bonbon . . . 20.00
Butter . . . 45.00
Celery Tray, Hndl. . . . 20.00
Celery Vase . . . 20.00
Compote, Hndl. . . . 30.00
Creamer or Spooner . . . 15.00
Nappy . . . 20.00
Pickle Dish, Hndl. . . . 15.00
Plate . . . 15.00
Rose Bowl . . . 30.00
Sherbet . . . 15.00
Sherbet Plate . . . 10.00
Sugar . . . 20.00
Vase, 5" – 12" . . . 15.00 – 30.00

OMNIBUS
Berry Bowl, Sm. . . . 10.00
Berry Bowl, Lg. . . . 35.00
Bowl, Deep, 8" . . . 25.00
Bowl, Shallow, 9" . . . 30.00
Butter . . . 55.00
Celery Tray . . . 25.00
Creamer or Spooner . . . 20.00
Pickle Dish . . . 15.00
Sugar . . . 30.00

ONE-O-ONE
Bread Plate . . . 15.00
Bread Plate, Lettered . . . 40.00
Butter . . . 65.00
Cake Stand . . . 40.00
Celery Vase . . . 25.00
Compote, Covered, 7" – 9" . . . 25.00 – 50.00
Creamer or Spooner . . . 20.00
Goblet . . . 50.00
Hand Lamp, Flat . . . 70.00
Oil Lamp, Standard . . . 85.00
Pickle Dish . . . 15.00
Plate, 6" – 9" . . . 15.00 – 40.00
Pitcher . . . 90.00
Tumbler . . . 20.00
Relish Tray . . . 20.00

Sauce, Flat or Ftd. . . . 10.00
Shakers, ea. . . . 25.00
Sugar . . . 25.00
Vase . . . 25.00
Wine . . . 10.00

OPEN PLAID
Berry Bowl, Sm. . . . 10.00
Berry Bowl, Lg. . . . 35.00
Butter . . . 55.00
Cordial . . . 10.00
Creamer or Spooner . . . 20.00
Plate . . . 20.00
Pitcher . . . 75.00
Tumbler . . . 15.00
Salt . . . 15.00
Shakers, ea. . . . 15.00
Sugar . . . 25.00
Syrup . . . 65.00
Wine . . . 10.00

OPEN ROSE (IMPERIAL)
Bowls, Various . . . 10.00 – 40.00
Rose Bowl . . . 50.00

OPEN ROSE (MOSS ROSE)
Bowls, Oval, Various . . . 15.00 – 30.00
Butter . . . 65.00
Cake Stand . . . 40.00
Celery Vase . . . 25.00
Compote, Covered, 6" – 9" . . . 30.00 – 70.00
Compote, Open, 6" – 9" . . . 15.00 – 30.00
Cordial . . . 20.00
Creamer or Spooner . . . 25.00
Egg Cup . . . 20.00
Goblet, 2 Styles . . . 40.00
Milk Pitcher . . . 60.00
Pickle Dish . . . 15.00
Pitcher . . . 95.00
Tumbler . . . 15.00
Relish Tray . . . 10.00
Salt Dip . . . 20.00
Sauce . . . 10.00
Sugar . . . 50.00

OPPOSING PYRAMIDS
Bowls, Various . . . 10.00 – 30.00
Engraved . . . 20.00 – 45.00
Butter . . . 55.00
Engraved . . . 70.00
Cake Stands, Various . . . 20.00 – 45.00
Engraved . . . 25.00 – 55.00
Celery Vase . . . 20.00
Engraved . . . 35.00
Compotes, Various . . . 25.00 – 45.00
Engraved . . . 35.00 – 60.00
Creamer or Spooner . . . 25.00
Engraved . . . 35.00
Pitcher . . . 85.00
Engraved . . . 110.00
Tumbler . . . 15.00
Engraved . . . 25.00
Shakers, ea. . . . 20.00
Engraved . . . 30.00
Sugar . . . 40.00
Engraved . . . 60.00
Wine . . . 10.00
Engraved . . . 30.00

OPTIC
Salt Dip . . . 20.00

ORANGE PEEL
Bowl . . . 25.00
Desert, Stemmed . . . 30.00
Punch Bowl . . . 100.00
Punch Cup . . . 15.00

ORANGE TREE
Mug, Scarce . . . 55.00
Green/Blue . . . 75.00
Pink . . . 75.00

OREGON
Bowls, Various, 7" – 12" . . . 10.00 – 45.00
Bowl, Covered, 6" – 8" . . . 20.00 – 50.00
Bowl, Open, 6" – 8" . . . 10.00 – 35.00
Bread Plate . . . 15.00
Butter . . . 55.00
Cake Stand, 6" – 10" . . . 25.00 – 45.00

Carafe . . . 45.00
Celery Vase . . . 20.00
Compote, Covered, 5" – 10" . . . 25.00 – 60.00
Creamer or Spooner . . . 20.00
Cruet . . . 60.00
Goblet . . . 40.00
Honey Dish . . . 20.00
Horseradish, Hndl., w/Lid . . . 40.00
Mug . . . 25.00
Olive Dish . . . 15.00
Pickle Dish . . . 15.00
Pitcher . . . 85.00
Tumbler . . . 20.00
Relish Dish . . . 15.00
Salt, Ind. . . . 10.00
Salt, Master . . . 25.00
Sauce . . . 10.00
Sugar . . . 30.00
Syrup . . . 55.00
Toothpick Hldr. . . . 30.00
Vase . . . 25.00
Wine . . . 10.00

ORIENTAL
Bowls, Various . . . 10.00 – 45.00
Butter . . . 65.00
Celery Vase . . . 20.00
Compote, Covered . . . 45.00
Creamer or Spooner . . . 20.00
Goblet . . . 35.00
Pickle Jar . . . 25.00
Pitcher . . . 70.00
Tumbler . . . 15.00
Sugar . . . 25.00
Tray . . . 35.00
Wine . . . 15.00

ORIENTAL POPPY
Pitcher, Squat . . . 350.00
Tumbler . . . 45.00

ORINDA
Berry Bowl, Sm. . . . 10.00
Berry Bowl, Lg. . . . 35.00
Butter . . . 50.00
Celery Vase . . . 20.00
Creamer or Spooner . . . 25.00
Milk Pitcher . . . 50.00
Pickle Dish . . . 20.00
Pitcher . . . 85.00
Shakers, ea. . . . 20.00
Sugar . . . 25.00
Syrup . . . 55.00
Toothpick Hldr. . . . 25.00

ORION THUMBPRINT
Butter . . . 55.00
Celery Vase . . . 25.00
Compote, Covered . . . 45.00
Compote, Open . . . 30.00
Creamer or Spooner . . . 25.00
Goblet . . . 45.00
Platter, Oval (Daisy & Button Center) . . . 40.00
Pitcher . . . 75.00
Tumbler . . . 20.00
Sauce . . . 15.00
Sugar . . . 30.00

ORNATE STAR
Berry Bowl, Sm. . . . 10.00
Ruby Stain . . . 20.00
Berry Bowl, Lg. . . . 35.00
Ruby Stain . . . 40.00
Butter . . . 55.00
Ruby Stain . . . 90.00
Celery Vase . . . 20.00
Ruby Stain . . . 30.00
Cordial . . . 15.00
Ruby Stain . . . 25.00
Creamer or Spooner . . . 20.00
Ruby Stain . . . 30.00
Goblet . . . 40.00
Ruby Stain . . . 60.00
Pickle Tray . . . 15.00
Ruby Stain . . . 25.00
Pitcher . . . 70.00
Ruby Stain . . . 135.00

Tumbler 10.00
Ruby Stain. 25.00
Sugar 30.00
Ruby Stain. 55.00
Wine 10.00
Ruby Stain. 25.00

OUR GIRL/LITTLE BO-PEEP
Mug 50.00
Amber 75.00
Vaseline. 90.00
Green/Blue. 95.00

OVAL DIAMOND PANEL
Goblet 40.00
Vaseline. 85.00

OVAL LOOP
Bowl, Rnd., 7" – 8" 25.00
Bowl, Oval, 5" – 10". . . . . 15.00 – 40.00
Bread Tray 25.00
Butter. 65.00
Candlesticks, ea. 25.00
Celery Vase 20.00
Compote, Covered, 7" – 8" 50.00
Compote, Open, 7" – 8" 35.00
Creamer or Spooner. 20.00
Goblet 40.00
Milk Pitcher, 2 Sizes . . . . . 40.00 – 60.00
Pickle Jar 25.00
Pitcher, 2 Sizes . . . . . 50.00 – 80.00
Tumbler 20.00
Sauce, Flat or Ftd. 10.00
Shakers, ea. 20.00
Sugar 25.00
Sugar Shaker 40.00
Wine 15.00

OVAL MEDALLION
Bowls, Various . . . . . 15.00 – 35.00
Amber. . . . . 20.00 – 40.00
Vaseline . . . . . 25.00 – 50.00
Green/Blue . . . . . 20.00 – 45.00
Amethyst. . . . . 30.00 – 65.00
Butter. 65.00
Amber 80.00
Vaseline. 130.00
Green/Blue. 95.00
Amethyst 110.00
Compotes, Various . . . . . 20.00 – 45.00
Amber. . . . . 25.00 – 50.00
Vaseline . . . . . 30.00 – 60.00
Green/Blue . . . . . 25.00 – 55.00
Amethyst. . . . . 35.00 – 65.00
Creamer or Spooner. 25.00
Amber 30.00
Vaseline. 40.00
Green/Blue. 35.00
Amethyst 45.00
Goblet 35.00
Amber 40.00
Vaseline. 50.00
Green/Blue. 45.00
Amethyst 60.00
Pickle Dish. 20.00
Amber 25.00
Vaseline. 30.00
Green/Blue. 25.00
Amethyst 35.00
Sugar 35.00
Amber 40.00
Vaseline. 45.00
Green/Blue. 40.00
Amethyst 50.00
Wine 20.00
Amber 25.00
Vaseline. 30.00
Green/Blue. 25.00
Amethyst 35.00

OVAL STAR
Toy Water Set 90.00

OVERALL LATTICE
Bowl, Ruffled 25.00
Butter. 50.00
Compote. 30.00
Creamer or Spooner. 20.00
Goblet 35.00
Plate. 25.00
Sugar 25.00
Wine 15.00

OVERSHOT
Bowls, Various . . . . . 15.00 – 45.00
Butter. 70.00
Compotes, Various . . . . . 25.00 – 55.00
Creamer or Spooner. 35.00
Goblet 50.00
Pitcher 115.00
Tumbler 25.00
Plate. 30.00
Sugar 50.00

OWEN COIN BANK LAMP
Oil Lamp 90.00
Vaseline. 235.00

OWL AND POSSUM
Goblet 150.00

OWL AND PUSSYCAT
Cheese Dish, Rare 400.00

OWL IN HORSESHOE
Goblet 135.00

OWL ON A BRANCH
Mug 55.00

PADDLE WHEEL
Butter. 50.00
Celery Tray. 30.00
Celery Vase 25.00
Creamer or Spooner 20.00
Jelly Compote. 25.00
Pickle Dish. 15.00
Pitcher 70.00
Tumbler 15.00
Relish. 20.00
Shakers, ea. 20.00
Sugar 25.00

PADEN CITY #206
Pitcher 125.00

PALISADES (LINED LATTICE)
Vase. 30.00
Green/Blue. 75.00

PALM BEACH
Berry Bowl, Sm. 15.00
Berry Bowl, Lg. 40.00
Butter. 85.00
Celery Vase 25.00
Creamer or Spooner. 25.00
Cruet 60.00
Jelly Compote. 35.00
Plate. 40.00
Pitcher 125.00
Tumbler 20.00
Sauce 15.00
Shakers, ea. 25.00
Sugar 30.00
Wine 20.00

PALMETTE
Butter. 70.00
Cake Stand. 140.00
Caster Set, Complete 135.00
Compote, Open 65.00
Compote, Low Covered 75.00
Creamer or Spooner. 50.00
Cup Plate 50.00
Goblet 40.00
Master Salt Dip 25.00
Milk Pitcher. 140.00
Pitcher 115.00
Tumbler, 2 Sizes . . . . . 35.00 – 60.00
Oil Lamp, 10" 110.00
Relish, Scoop Shape 25.00
Shaker, Lg. 75.00
Sugar 100.00
Syrup 125.00
Wine 125.00

PALM LEAF FAN
Bowls, Lg. . . . . . 25.00 – 55.00
Cake Stand. 40.00
Celery Vase 30.00
Compote. 40.00
Creamer or Spooner. 25.00
Cruet 65.00
Pitcher 90.00
Tumbler 25.00
Sauce 15.00
Shakers, ea. 25.00
Sugar 30.00
Wine 35.00

PANAMA
Berry Bowl, Sm. 15.00
Berry Bowl, Lg. 40.00
Bowls, Various . . . . . 10.00 – 30.00
Butter. 50.00
Celery Tray. 20.00
Celery Vase 25.00
Creamer or Spooner. 25.00
Pitcher 80.00
Tumbler 15.00
Shakers, ea. 15.00
Sugar 30.00
Toothpick Hldr. 30.00

PANELLED 44
Bowls, Various . . . . . 10.00 – 35.00
Bonbon, 3 Legged. 20.00
Butter. 60.00
Candlestick 20.00
Creamer or Spooner. 15.00
Cruet 50.00
Finger Bowl 20.00
Lemonade Set 65.00
Mug 20.00
Olive, Hndl. 15.00
Pitcher 75.00
Tumbler 15.00
Shakers, ea. 15.00
Sugar 20.00
Sugar Shaker 35.00
Toothpick Hldr. 20.00
Vase (Loving Cup) 20.00
Wine 15.00

PANELLED CANE
Berry Bowl, Sm. 15.00
Berry Bowl, Lg. 35.00
Butter. 45.00
Creamer or Spooner. 20.00
Ice Tub. 40.00
Pickle Dish. 15.00
Pitcher 65.00
Tumbler 15.00
Relish. 15.00
Sauce 10.00
Sugar 25.00
Toothpick Hldr. 20.00
Wine 15.00

PANELLED DEWDROP
Butter. 60.00
Celery Boat 20.00
Celery Vase 25.00
Cordial. 15.00
Creamer or Spooner. 25.00
Goblet 35.00
Jam Jar 25.00
Pickle Dish. 15.00
Pickle Jar 20.00
Sauce, Ftd. 10.00
Sugar 35.00
Wine 15.00

PANELLED DIAMOND BLOCKS
Berry Bowl, Sm. 10.00
Berry Bowl, Lg. 35.00
Butter. 50.00
Carafe 30.00
Compote, Covered 45.00
Compote, Open 30.00
Creamer or Spooner. 20.00
Custard Cup. 10.00
Goblet 30.00
Oil Lamp 75.00
Orange Bowl 35.00
Pitcher 70.00
Tumbler 15.00
Sauce 10.00
Sugar 25.00

Syrup 60.00
Toothpick Hldr. 20.00
Vase. 25.00
Wine 10.00

PANELLED DIAMONDS AND BOWS
Vase, Scarce. 45.00
Red 125.00

PANELLED FISHBONE
Bowl. 25.00
Bread Tray 35.00
Shakers, Ea. 20.00

PANELLED FORGET-ME-NOT
Berry Bowl, Lg. 30.00
Amber 35.00
Green/Blue. 40.00
Berry Bowl, Sm. 10.00
Amber 15.00
Green/Blue. 20.00
Bread Tray 20.00
Amber 35.00
Green/Blue. 40.00
Butter. 45.00
Amber 55.00
Green/Blue. 60.00
Cake Stand. 45.00
Amber 70.00
Green/Blue. 75.00
Celery Vase 25.00
Amber 40.00
Green/Blue. 45.00
Creamer or Spooner. 20.00
Amber 40.00
Green/Blue. 45.00
Jam Jar 25.00
Amber 60.00
Green/Blue. 65.00
Sauce, Ftd. 15.00
Amber 20.00
Green/Blue. 25.00
Sauce, Hndl. 20.00
Amber 25.00
Green/Blue. 30.00
Shakers, Ea. 55.00
Amber 65.00
Green/Blue. 70.00
Sugar 35.00
Amber 40.00
Green/Blue. 45.00
Wine 45.00
Amber 65.00
Green/Blue. 70.00

PANELLED HEATHER
Berry Bowl, Sm. 10.00
Berry Bowl, Lg. 35.00
Bowl, Oval, Ftd., 6½" 25.00
Bowl, Salad, Ftd. 30.00
Butter. 55.00
Cake Stand. 30.00
Celery Vase 20.00
Creamer or Spooner. 20.00
Cruet 45.00
Goblet 35.00
Jelly Compote, Covered 40.00
Pitcher 75.00
Tumbler 15.00
Sugar 30.00
Wine 10.00

PANELLED HOBNAIL
Cup 20.00
Green/Blue. 30.00

PANELLED HOLLY
Berry Bowl, Sm. 20.00
Berry Bowl, Lg. 40.00
Bonbon 25.00
Butter. 65.00
Creamer or Spooner. 20.00
Pitcher 150.00
Tumbler 25.00
Sugar 45.00

PANELLED JEWELS
Goblet 55.00
Wine 25.00

Vaseline. 70.00

PANELLED OAK
Berry Bowl, Lg. 45.00
Berry Bowl, Sm. 15.00
Butter. 60.00
Celery Vase 35.00
Creamer, Spooner, or Sugar. 25.00
Pitcher 75.00
Tumbler 20.00

PANELLED OCTAGON
Butter. 55.00
Creamer or Spooner. 25.00
Sugar 30.00

PANELLED PALM
Bowls, Various . . . . . 20.00 – 40.00
Butter. 65.00
Cake Stand. 55.00
Creamer or Spooner. 25.00
Pitcher 125.00
Tumbler 30.00
Salt Shaker. 40.00
Sauce 10.00
Sugar 45.00
Toothpick Hldr. 40.00
Vase. 40.00
Wine 20.00

PANELLED PLEAT
Berry Bowl, Sm. 10.00
Berry Bowl, Lg. 35.00
Butter. 45.00
Creamer or Spooner. 20.00
Goblet 35.00
Pitcher 60.00
Tumbler 15.00
Sugar 25.00

PANELLED STRAWBERRY
Berry Bowl, Sm. 20.00
Berry Bowl, Lg. 45.00
Butter. 60.00
Celery Vase 30.00
Creamer or Spooner. 25.00
Goblet 35.00
Pitcher 65.00
Tumbler 15.00
Sauce, 3 Sizes . . . . . 10.00 – 20.00
Sugar 30.00

PANELLED SUNFLOWER
Basket, 3 Sizes . . . . . 30.00 – 55.00
Butter. 45.00
Cake Stand. 35.00
Celery Vase 20.00
Creamer, Spooner, or Sugar. 25.00
Cruet 45.00
Goblet 25.00
Honey Dish 20.00
Pickle Dish. 20.00
Pitcher 65.00
Tumbler 15.00
Plate, 7½" – 8½". 15.00
Plate, 9½" – 10½". 25.00

PANELLED SWAN
Bowl, Covered 55.00
Compote, Covered 70.00
Goblet 35.00
Wine 20.00

PANELLED THISTLE
Berry Bowl, Lg. 35.00
Berry Bowl, Sm. 10.00
Butter. 45.00
Creamer, Spooner, or Sugar. 25.00
Cup 15.00
Plate. 25.00
Shakers, ea. 15.00
Toothpick Hldr. 35.00

PANEL, RIB AND SHELL
Pitcher, 10½" 130.00
Engraved 150.00

PANEL WITH DIAMOND POINT (#439)
Bowl. 30.00
Cake Stand. 45.00
Cheese Dish, Covered 50.00
Compote. 35.00

Mustard Dish. 30.00
Pitcher 75.00

PANEL WITH DIAMOND POINTS
Butter. 65.00
Celery Vase 20.00
Compote, Covered 45.00
Compote, Open 30.00
Creamer or Spooner. 25.00
Sauce 10.00
Spill Hldr. 25.00
Sugar 30.00

PANTHER
Bowl, 5" – 9½", Rare . . . . . 75.00 – 175.00

PARKER AND WHIPPLE CLOCK FRAME
Clock Frame, 5", Scarce 85.00
Vaseline. 145.00

PARROT (OWL IN FAN)
Goblet 45.00
Wine, Rare. 125.00

PATTEE CROSS
Bowl, Ruffled 25.00
Cake Stand. 45.00
Compote. 35.00
Olive Dish 20.00
Pitcher 75.00
Tumbler 15.00
Relish, 2 Sizes 20.00
Syrup 65.00
Vase. 25.00
Wine 25.00

PAVONIA
Bowl, 5" – 8" . . . . . 15.00 – 30.00
Ruby Stain . . . . . 30.00 – 60.00
Butter, 2 Sizes. . . . . 50.00 – 65.00
Ruby Stain . . . . . 100.00 – 135.00
Cake Plate 25.00
Cake Stand, 8" – 10" . . . . . 40.00 – 60.00
Ruby Stain . . . . . 80.00 – 110.00
Celery Vase 30.00
Ruby Stain. 55.00
Compote, Covered, 5" – 10". . . . . 40.00 – 70.00
Ruby Stain . . . . . 55.00 – 105.00
Compote, Open, 5" – 10" . . . . . 30.00 – 45.00
Ruby Stain . . . . . 65.00 – 95.00
Creamer or Spooner, 2 Sizes 40.00
Ruby Stain. 80.00
Custard Cup. 10.00
Ruby Stain. 25.00
Dish, Oblong, 7" – 9". . . . . 15.00 – 25.00
Ruby Stain . . . . . 35.00 – 45.00
Goblet 40.00
Ruby Stain. 55.00
Mug, Hndl. 30.00
Ruby Stain. 60.00
Pickle Dish. 20.00
Ruby Stain. 30.00
Plate. 15.00
Pitcher, 5 Sizes . . . . . 50.00 – 95.00
Ruby Stain . . . . . 100.00 – 150.00
Tumbler 25.00
Ruby Stain. 35.00
Salt, Ind. 15.00
Ruby Stain. 35.00
Salt, Master 25.00
Ruby Stain. 50.00
Salt Shaker. 30.00
Ruby Stain. 40.00
Sauce, 3 Sizes . . . . . 10.00 – 20.00
Ruby Stain . . . . . 20.00 – 30.00
Sauce, Ftd., 3 Sizes. . . . . 15.00 – 25.00
Ruby Stain . . . . . 25.00 – 35.00
Saucer 15.00
Ruby Stain. 25.00
Sherbet Cup w/Underplate. 25.00
Ruby Stain. 35.00
Sugar, 2 Sizes 50.00
Ruby Stain. 85.00
Tray, 2 Sizes . . . . . 50.00 – 60.00
Ruby Stain . . . . . 85.00 – 100.00
Wine 30.00
Ruby Stain. 40.00

(Add 10% for etched pieces.)

PEABODY
Bowl . . . 95.00
Green/Blue . . . 150.00
Amethyst . . . 165.00
Creamer . . . 85.00
Green/Blue . . . 130.00
Amethyst . . . 140.00
Mug . . . 100.00
Green/Blue . . . 140.00
Amethyst . . . 170.00
Saucer . . . 70.00
Green/Blue . . . 85.00
Amethyst . . . 115.00

PEACOCK
Vase or Lamp Base . . . 50.00

PEACOCK AND URN (NORTHWOOD)
Berry, Master, Custard . . . 250.00
Berry, Sauce, Custard . . . 90.00

PEACOCK AT THE FOUNTAIN
Berry Bowl, Sm., Rare . . . 35.00
Berry Bowl, Lg., Rare . . . 125.00
Pitcher, Rare . . . 450.00
Tumbler, Rare . . . 70.00

PEACOCK FEATHER (GEORGIA)
Berry Bowl, Sm. . . . 15.00
Berry Bowl, Lg. . . . 45.00
Butter . . . 80.00
Cake Stand . . . 35.00
Celery Tray . . . 20.00
Compote, Covered, High, 6" – 8" . 35.00 – 65.00
Compote, Covered, Low, 6" – 8" . . 25.00 – 55.00
Compote, Lg. . . . 45.00
Condiment Set w/Stand . . . 90.00
Creamer or Spooner . . . 25.00
Cruet . . . 50.00
Decanter . . . 50.00
Jelly Compote . . . 35.00
Lamps, 7" – 9" . . . 55.00 – 75.00
Mug . . . 30.00
Pickle Dish . . . 15.00
Plate . . . 20.00
Pitcher . . . 90.00
Tumbler . . . 25.00
Relish Dish . . . 20.00
Sauce . . . 10.00
Shakers, ea. . . . 15.00
Sugar . . . 35.00
Syrup . . . 60.00
Toy Table Set . . . 100.00

PEANUT LAMP
Oil Lamp w/Matching Chimney, Various Styles & Sizes . . . 100.00 – 300.00

PEAS AND PODS
Decanter . . . 45.00
Ruby Stain . . . 65.00
Tray . . . 30.00
Ruby Stain . . . 35.00
Wine . . . 15.00
Ruby Stain . . . 20.00

PEEK-A-BOO
Match Hldr. . . . 45.00
Perfume Bottle . . . 55.00

PEERLESS
Berry Bowl, Sm. . . . 15.00
Berry Bowl Lg. . . . 35.00
Bowl, Sq. . . . 30.00
Butter . . . 55.00
Cake Stand . . . 40.00
Celery Vase . . . 25.00
Cordial . . . 20.00
Cordial Tray . . . 30.00
Cracker Jar w/Lid . . . 50.00
Creamer or Spooner . . . 20.00
Cruet . . . 65.00
Decanter, 2 Sizes . . . 55.00
Olive Dish, Hndl. . . . 25.00
Sugar . . . 25.00
Toothpick Hldr. . . . 40.00
Tray, Rectangular . . . 40.00
Whiskey Glass . . . 25.00
Wine . . . 20.00

PENELOPE
Berry Bowl, Sm. . . . 15.00
Berry Bowl, Lg. . . . 35.00
Butter . . . 55.00
Creamer or Spooner . . . 20.00
Pickle Dish . . . 15.00
Punch Bowl . . . 80.00
Punch Cup . . . 10.00
Pitcher . . . 70.00
Tumbler . . . 15.00
Sugar . . . 25.00

PENNSYLVANIA
Berry Bowl, Sm. . . . 15.00
Berry Bowl, Lg. . . . 45.00
Biscuit Jar . . . 75.00
Bowl, Round, 4" – 9" . . . 10.00 – 50.00
Bowl, Scalloped, Shallow, 4" – 9" 10.00 – 35.00
Bowl, Straight-Sided, 4" – 9" . . . 10.00 – 45.00
Bowl, Sq., 4" – 9" . . . 10.00 – 50.00
Butter, 2 Sizes . . . 50.00 – 90.00
Butter, Child's . . . 125.00
Green/Blue . . . 250.00
Carafe . . . 50.00
Celery Tray . . . 20.00
Champagne, Very Rare . . . 150.00
Cheese Dish, Covered . . . 85.00
Compote, Open . . . 45.00
Creamer . . . 25.00
Creamer, Child's . . . 50.00
Green/Blue . . . 150.00
Cruet . . . 60.00
Custard Cup, Hndl. . . . 15.00
Green/Blue . . . 40.00
Decanter, with & without Hndls. . . 150.00 – 100.00
Goblet . . . 40.00
Green/Blue . . . 75.00
Ice Tub . . . 50.00
Jelly, Hndl. . . . 15.00
Mug . . . 25.00
Green/Blue . . . 60.00
Oil Bottle . . . 45.00
Olive Dish . . . 15.00
Pickle Jar, w/Lid . . . 100.00
Pickle Dish, Oval . . . 15.00
Green/Blue . . . 40.00
Pitcher, Bulbous or Squat . . . 90.00
Green/Blue . . . 250.00
Pitcher, Tankard . . . 135.00
Plate, 7" – 8" . . . 40.00
Platter, Very Rare . . . 135.00
Punch Bowl, Flat . . . 225.00
Tumbler, 3 Sizes . . . 15.00 – 25.00
Green/Blue . . . 25.00 – 60.00
Salt, Ind. . . . 10.00
Salt, Master . . . 40.00
Sauce, Various . . . 10.00
Shaker, 3 Sizes . . . 35.00
Spooner . . . 40.00
Sugar, 2 Sizes . . . 25.00 – 60.00
Sugar, Child's . . . 85.00
Green/Blue . . . 265.00
Syrup, 2 Styles . . . 75.00 – 100.00
Toothpick Hldr. (Toy Spooner) . . . 50.00
Green/Blue . . . 140.00
Water Bottle . . . 65.00
Wine . . . 10.00
Green/Blue . . . 40.00

PENTAGON
Decanter . . . 45.00
Ruby Stain . . . 65.00
Wine . . . 15.00
Ruby Stain . . . 20.00

PEQUOT
Butter . . . 60.00
Castor Set . . . 85.00
Celery Vase . . . 20.00
Champagne . . . 15.00
Compote, Covered . . . 45.00
Compote, Open . . . 30.00
Creamer or Spooner . . . 20.00
Goblet . . . 40.00
Jam Jar . . . 35.00
Pitcher . . . 85.00
Tumbler . . . 25.00
Sugar . . . 30.00
Wine . . . 15.00

PERKINS
Butter . . . 65.00
Cake Plate, Hndl., 12" . . . 40.00
Celery Vase . . . 35.00
Cracker Jar w/Lid . . . 70.00
Creamer or Spooner . . . 25.00
Cruet . . . 50.00
Pitcher . . . 80.00
Sugar . . . 20.00

PERSIAN
Berry Bowl, Sm. . . . 15.00
Berry Bowl, Lg. . . . 45.00
Butter . . . 65.00
Carafe . . . 45.00
Celery Dish . . . 15.00
Celery Vase . . . 20.00
Cheese Dish . . . 65.00
Claret . . . 15.00
Creamer or Spooner . . . 25.00
Cruet . . . 50.00
Cup . . . 10.00
Finger Bowl . . . 20.00
Jelly Compote . . . 30.00
Pitcher . . . 95.00
Tumbler . . . 20.00
Salt Dip . . . 15.00
Sauce . . . 10.00
Shakers, ea. . . . 15.00
Sugar . . . 35.00
Syrup . . . 55.00
Toothpick Hldr. . . . 25.00

PERT
Bowls, Various . . . 15.00 – 30.00
Amber . . . 20.00 – 35.00
Vaseline . . . 25.00 – 40.00
Green/Blue . . . 25.00 – 40.00
Amethyst . . . 20.00 – 45.00
Butter . . . 55.00
Amber . . . 60.00
Vaseline . . . 100.00
Green/Blue . . . 85.00
Amethyst . . . 80.00
Cake Stand, 9" – 11" . . . 30.00 – 40.00
Amber . . . 35.00 – 45.00
Vaseline . . . 40.00 – 50.00
Green/Blue . . . 45.00 – 60.00
Amethyst . . . 40.00 – 55.00
Celery Vase . . . 25.00
Amber . . . 30.00
Vaseline . . . 40.00
Green/Blue . . . 45.00
Amethyst . . . 40.00
Compotes, Covered . . . 30.00 – 55.00
Amber . . . 35.00 – 60.00
Vaseline . . . 50.00 – 85.00
Green/Blue . . . 60.00 – 95.00
Amethyst . . . 50.00 – 85.00
Compotes, Open . . . 25.00 – 40.00
Amber . . . 30.00 – 45.00
Vaseline . . . 35.00 – 55.00
Green/Blue . . . 40.00 – 65.00
Amethyst . . . 35.00 – 60.00
Creamer or Spooner . . . 30.00
Amber . . . 35.00
Vaseline . . . 45.00
Green/Blue . . . 55.00
Amethyst . . . 50.00
Cup & Saucer . . . 25.00
Amber . . . 30.00
Vaseline . . . 40.00
Green/Blue . . . 45.00
Amethyst . . . 40.00
Goblet . . . 35.00
Amber . . . 40.00
Vaseline . . . 50.00
Green/Blue . . . 60.00
Amethyst . . . 55.00
Mustard w/Lid . . . 35.00

Amber . . . 40.00
Vaseline . . . 45.00
Green/Blue . . . 50.00
Amethyst . . . 45.00
Mug . . . 40.00
Amber . . . 45.00
Vaseline . . . 50.00
Green/Blue . . . 55.00
Amethyst . . . 50.00
Plates . . . 15.00 – 25.00
Amber . . . 20.00 – 30.00
Vaseline . . . 25.00 – 40.00
Green/Blue . . . 30.00 – 45.00
Amethyst . . . 25.00 – 40.00
Pitcher . . . 85.00
Amber . . . 95.00
Vaseline . . . 150.00
Green/Blue . . . 165.00
Amethyst . . . 155.00
Tumbler . . . 15.00
Amber . . . 20.00
Vaseline . . . 35.00
Green/Blue . . . 40.00
Amethyst . . . 35.00
Salt, Master . . . 20.00
Amber . . . 25.00
Vaseline . . . 30.00
Green/Blue . . . 35.00
Amethyst . . . 30.00
Sauce . . . 10.00
Amber . . . 15.00
Vaseline . . . 20.00
Green/Blue . . . 25.00
Amethyst . . . 20.00
Sugar . . . 40.00
Amber . . . 45.00
Vaseline . . . 55.00
Green/Blue . . . 65.00
Amethyst . . . 55.00
Toothpick Hldr. . . . 40.00
Amber . . . 50.00
Vaseline . . . 65.00
Green/Blue . . . 75.00
Amethyst . . . 70.00
Toy Table Set, Complete . . . 115.00
Amber . . . 145.00
Vaseline . . . 165.00
Green/Blue . . . 180.00
Amethyst . . . 170.00
Water Tray (Herons, Storks, or Aquatic) . 50.00
Amber . . . 60.00
Vaseline . . . 95.00
Green/Blue . . . 90.00
Amethyst . . . 80.00
Wine . . . 20.00
Amber . . . 25.00
Vaseline . . . 30.00
Green/Blue . . . 35.00
Amethyst . . . 30.00

PETAL AND LOOP
Butter . . . 50.00
Vaseline . . . 105.00
Green/Blue . . . 85.00
Candlesticks, ea. . . . 25.00
Vaseline . . . 45.00
Green/Blue . . . 25.00
Celery Vase . . . 15.00
Vaseline . . . 25.00
Green/Blue . . . 20.00
Champagne . . . 20.00
Vaseline . . . 30.00
Green/Blue . . . 25.00
Cordial . . . 20.00
Vaseline . . . 30.00
Green/Blue . . . 25.00
Creamer or Spooner . . . 25.00
Vaseline . . . 45.00
Green/Blue . . . 40.00
Pickle Dish . . . 15.00
Vaseline . . . 35.00
Green/Blue . . . 30.00
Plate . . . 30.00
Vaseline . . . 45.00
Green/Blue . . . 40.00
Sugar . . . 35.00
Vaseline . . . 50.00
Green/Blue . . . 45.00
Vase . . . 25.00
Vaseline . . . 35.00
Green/Blue . . . 30.00
Wine . . . 15.00
Vaseline . . . 25.00
Green/Blue . . . 20.00

PETALLED MEDALLION
Berry Bowl, Sm. . . . 10.00
Berry Bowl, Lg. . . . 30.00
Butter . . . 45.00
Celery Vase . . . 20.00
Compote, Covered . . . 40.00
Creamer or Spooner . . . 15.00
Goblet . . . 30.00
Pitcher . . . 65.00
Tumbler . . . 10.00
Sauce . . . 10.00
Shakers, ea. . . . 15.00
Sugar . . . 20.00
Syrup . . . 55.00
Toothpick Hldr. . . . 20.00
Wine . . . 10.00

PETER RABBIT
Candy Container . . . 45.00

PETTICOAT (RIVERSIDE)
Berry Bowl, Sm. . . . 15.00
Vaseline . . . 25.00
Berry Bowl, Lg. . . . 35.00
Vaseline . . . 50.00
Butter . . . 70.00
Vaseline . . . 145.00
Compote . . . 50.00
Vaseline . . . 65.00
Creamer or Spooner . . . 30.00
Vaseline . . . 45.00
Cruet . . . 65.00
Vaseline . . . 95.00
Hat Shapes, 3 Shapes . . . 25.00 – 40.00
Vaseline . . . 35.00 – 60.00
Match Hldr. . . . 35.00
Vaseline . . . 45.00
Mug . . . 40.00
Vaseline . . . 50.00
Mustard w/Lid . . . 60.00
Vaseline . . . 75.00
Pitcher . . . 145.00
Vaseline . . . 200.00
Tumbler . . . 25.00
Vaseline . . . 35.00
Salver . . . 45.00
Vaseline . . . 60.00
Shakers, ea. . . . 30.00
Vaseline . . . 40.00
Spoon Tray . . . 40.00
Vaseline . . . 55.00
Sugar . . . 60.00
Vaseline . . . 75.00
Syrup . . . 85.00
Vaseline . . . 125.00
Toothpick Hldr. . . . 55.00
Vaseline . . . 70.00
Vase . . . 40.00
Vaseline . . . 50.00

PHEASANT
Butter . . . 245.00
Compote, Covered, Low . . . 225.00
Creamer or Spooner . . . 80.00
Sugar . . . 100.00

PICKET BAND
Butter . . . 55.00
Green/Blue . . . 80.00
Celery Vase . . . 20.00
Green/Blue . . . 25.00
Compote, Covered . . . 40.00
Green/Blue . . . 60.00
Compote, Open . . . 30.00
Green/Blue . . . 35.00
Creamer or Spooner . . . 25.00
Green/Blue . . . 35.00
Goblet . . . 35.00
Green/Blue . . . 50.00
Pickle Dish . . . 15.00
Green/Blue . . . 20.00
Shakers, ea. . . . 20.00
Green/Blue . . . 30.00
Sugar . . . 35.00
Green/Blue . . . 50.00
Wine . . . 15.00
Green/Blue . . . 25.00

PICKLE VINE
Pickle Jar w/Lid . . . 55.00

PICKERING FURNITURE (MEMPHIS)
Nappy, Adv., Rare . . . 125.00

PIGS IN CORN
Goblet, Rare . . . 500.00

PILGRIM BOTTLE
Butter . . . 65.00
Amber . . . 70.00
Vaseline . . . 125.00
Green/Blue . . . 75.00
Celery Dish . . . 20.00
Amber . . . 25.00
Vaseline . . . 35.00
Green/Blue . . . 30.00
Creamer or Spooner . . . 25.00
Amber . . . 30.00
Vaseline . . . 40.00
Green/Blue . . . 35.00
Cruet . . . 60.00
Amber . . . 65.00
Vaseline . . . 90.00
Green/Blue . . . 75.00
Pickle Dish . . . 20.00
Amber . . . 25.00
Vaseline . . . 35.00
Green/Blue . . . 30.00
Shakers, ea. . . . 30.00
Amber . . . 35.00
Vaseline . . . 45.00
Green/Blue . . . 40.00
Sugar . . . 40.00
Amber . . . 45.00
Vaseline . . . 60.00
Green/Blue . . . 55.00
Syrup . . . 95.00
Amber . . . 110.00
Vaseline . . . 295.00
Green/Blue . . . 195.00

PILLAR BULL'S-EYE
Berry Bowl, Sm. . . . 15.00
Berry Bowl, Lg. . . . 35.00
Butter . . . 50.00
Creamer or Spooner . . . 20.00
Decanter . . . 40.00
Egg Cup . . . 20.00
Goblet . . . 35.00
Pitcher . . . 70.00
Tumbler . . . 15.00
Sugar . . . 25.00
Wine . . . 15.00

PILLOW ENCIRCLED
Bowl, 4" – 8" . . . 20.00 – 35.00
Ruby Stain . . . 25.00 – 40.00
Butter . . . 55.00
Ruby Stain . . . 80.00
Cake Salver . . . 35.00
Ruby Stain . . . 50.00
Celery Vase . . . 20.00
Ruby Stain . . . 30.00
Compote, Covered, 5" – 8" . . . 25.00 – 45.00
Ruby Stain . . . 40.00 – 80.00
Creamer or Spooner . . . 25.00
Ruby Stain . . . 35.00
Nut Bowl . . . 20.00
Ruby Stain . . . 30.00
Pitcher, 2 Sizes . . . 80.00 – 95.00
Ruby Stain . . . 90.00 – 165.00
Tumbler . . . 20.00
Ruby Stain . . . 30.00

Shakers, ea. . . . 20.00
Ruby Stain. . . . 30.00
Sugar 35.00
Ruby Stain. . . . 60.00
Toothpick Hldr. . . . 40.00
Ruby Stain. . . . 55.00
(Add 10% for etched pieces.)

PIMLICO (LOTUS LEAF)
Butter. . . . 50.00
Cake Plate 30.00
Celery Vase 20.00
Creamer or Spooner. . . . 25.00
Goblet 35.00
Pickle Dish. . . . 15.00
Salt Dip 20.00
Sugar 35.00

PINEAPPLE (AND BOWS)
Bowl. . . . 40.00
Azure. . . . 50.00
Butter. . . . 65.00
Azure. . . . 75.00
Creamer 30.00
Azure. . . . 35.00
Sugar 40.00
Azure. . . . 40.00

PINEAPPLE AND FAN (HEISEY)
Berry Bowl, Sm. . . . 10.00
Green/Blue. . . . 15.00
Ruby Stain. . . . 20.00
Berry Bowl, Lg. . . . 35.00
Green/Blue. . . . 40.00
Ruby Stain. . . . 45.00
Butter. . . . 45.00
Green/Blue. . . . 50.00
Ruby Stain. . . . 65.00
Cake Stand. . . . 30.00
Green/Blue. . . . 35.00
Ruby Stain. . . . 40.00
Celery Tray. . . . 20.00
Green/Blue. . . . 25.00
Ruby Stain. . . . 30.00
Creamer or Spooner. . . . 20.00
Green/Blue. . . . 25.00
Ruby Stain. . . . 30.00
Cruet 50.00
Green/Blue. . . . 60.00
Ruby Stain. . . . 75.00
Custard Cup. . . . 10.00
Green/Blue. . . . 15.00
Ruby Stain. . . . 20.00
Decanter 35.00
Green/Blue. . . . 50.00
Ruby Stain. . . . 65.00
Goblet 30.00
Green/Blue. . . . 35.00
Ruby Stain. . . . 40.00
Mug 25.00
Green/Blue. . . . 30.00
Ruby Stain. . . . 35.00
Plate, 6½". . . . 15.00
Green/Blue. . . . 20.00
Ruby Stain. . . . 25.00
Pitcher 75.00
Green/Blue. . . . 95.00
Ruby Stain. . . . 125.00
Tumbler 15.00
Green/Blue. . . . 20.00
Ruby Stain. . . . 30.00
Punch Bowl 85.00
Green/Blue. . . . 125.00
Ruby Stain. . . . 165.00
Punch Cup 10.00
Green/Blue. . . . 15.00
Ruby Stain. . . . 25.00
Relish Jar 20.00
Green/Blue. . . . 25.00
Ruby Stain. . . . 30.00
Rose Bowl 25.00
Green/Blue. . . . 30.00
Ruby Stain. . . . 35.00
Salt Dip 15.00
Green/Blue. . . . 20.00
Ruby Stain. . . . 25.00
Sugar 25.00
Green/Blue. . . . 40.00
Ruby Stain. . . . 50.00
Wine 15.00
Green/Blue. . . . 20.00
Ruby Stain. . . . 25.00

PINWHEEL AND FAN
Bowl, 4" – 5". . . . 25.00
Bowl, 8" 50.00
Creamer 45.00
Jug, 3 Pt. 150.00
Puff Box 80.00
Punch Bowl 200.00
Punch Cup 15.00
Sugar 50.00
Tumbler 25.00

PINWHEEL AND FAN VARIANT
Basket, Rare. . . . 300.00

PIPE MATCH HOLDER
Match/Toothpick Holder, Milk Glass. . . . 65.00

PISTOL
Candy Container 60.00

PITTSBURGH FAN
Butter. . . . 45.00
Cake Stand. . . . 30.00
Creamer or Spooner. . . . 15.00
Goblet 30.00
Pickle Dish. . . . 10.00
Plate. . . . 15.00
Sugar 20.00

PLAIN
Pitcher 45.00
Tumbler 10.00

PLEAT AND PANEL
Bowl, Covered 45.00
Bread Tray 25.00
Butter. . . . 65.00
Cake Stand. . . . 35.00
Candy Jar w/Lid 35.00
Compote. . . . 25.00
Creamer or Spooner. . . . 25.00
Lamp 145.00
Plate, Sq. . . . 20.00
Relish. . . . 15.00
Sauce, Ftd. . . . 10.00
Shakers, ea. . . . 15.00
Sugar 35.00
Water Tray. . . . 25.00

PLEATED BANDS
Goblet 45.00
Pitcher 70.00
Tumbler 20.00

PLEATED MEDALLION
Butter. . . . 45.00
Cake Stand. . . . 25.00
Creamer or Spooner. . . . 15.00
Cruet 40.00
Pickle Dish. . . . 15.00
Plate. . . . 20.00
Sugar 20.00
Toothpick Hldr. . . . 25.00

PLUME (ADAMS)
Bowls, Various, Flat. . . . 10.00 – 50.00
Bowls, Various, Ftd. . . . 20.00 – 65.00
Butter 80.00
Cake Stand 65.00
Celery Vase. . . . 25.00
Creamer or Spooner 35.00
Goblet. . . . 35.00
Lamp 95.00
Sauce 20.00
Sugar 45.00
Add 10% for Ruby Stain.

PLUMS AND CHERRIES (TWO FRUITS)
Bowl, Covered 90.00
Butter. . . . 135.00
Creamer or Spooner. . . . 50.00
Pitcher 225.00
Tumbler 35.00
Sugar 70.00

PLUTEC
Berry Bowl, Sm. . . . 10.00
Berry Bowl, Lg. . . . 35.00
Butter. . . . 60.00
Cake Stand. . . . 40.00
Celery Vase 20.00
Compote. . . . 40.00
Creamer or Spooner. . . . 20.00
Decanter 50.00
Goblet 45.00
Nut Bowl 25.00
Pickle Dish. . . . 15.00
Plate, 11" 25.00
Pitcher 85.00
Tumbler 20.00
Sugar 25.00
Syrup 60.00
Water Tray. . . . 30.00
Wine 15.00

POINTED JEWEL
Bowl. . . . 25.00
Butter. . . . 65.00
Celery Vase 20.00
Compote. . . . 35.00
Creamer or Spooner. . . . 30.00
Cup 10.00
Goblet 30.00
Pickle Dish. . . . 15.00
Shakers, ea. . . . 20.00
Sugar 40.00
Syrup 60.00
Toy Table Set. . . . 90.00
Wine 15.00

POINTING DOG
Mug 40.00
Amber 55.00
Green/Blue. . . . 65.00
Milk Glass. . . . 50.00

POLAR BEAR
Bread Plate 100.00
Creamer 145.00
Goblet 125.00
Ice Bowl. . . . 95.00
Pickle Dish. . . . 60.00
Pitcher 325.00
Sauce 35.00
Sugar 200.00
Tray 155.00
Waste Bowl 75.00

POLKA DOT (DUNCAN)
Butter. . . . 50.00
Amber 55.00
Vaseline. . . . 75.00
Green/Blue. . . . 90.00
Bowls, Ftd. . . . . 20.00 – 35.00
Amber. . . . 25.00 – 40.00
Vaseline . . . . 35.00 – 50.00
Green/Blue . . . . 40.00 – 65.00
Bowl, Finger. . . . 20.00
Amber 25.00
Vaseline. . . . 35.00
Green/Blue. . . . 45.00
Celery Vase 20.00
Amber 25.00
Vaseline. . . . 35.00
Green/Blue. . . . 45.00
Cheese Dish, Covered 65.00
Amber 70.00
Vaseline. . . . 85.00
Green/Blue. . . . 100.00
Champagne 20.00
Amber 25.00
Vaseline. . . . 35.00
Green/Blue. . . . 45.00
Claret. . . . 15.00
Amber 20.00
Vaseline. . . . 25.00
Green/Blue. . . . 35.00
Compote, Covered 45.00
Amber 50.00
Vaseline. . . . 65.00
Green/Blue. . . . 80.00

Creamer or Spooner 30.00
Amber 35.00
Vaseline 45.00
Green/Blue 55.00
Cruet 65.00
Amber 75.00
Vaseline 90.00
Green/Blue 110.00
Goblet 35.00
Amber 40.00
Vaseline 50.00
Green/Blue 60.00
Sauces 15.00
Amber 20.00
Vaseline 25.00
Green/Blue 35.00
Shakers, ea. 25.00
Amber 30.00
Vaseline 35.00
Green/Blue 45.00
Sugar 40.00
Amber 45.00
Vaseline 55.00
Green/Blue 65.00
Syrup 70.00
Amber 80.00
Vaseline 95.00
Green/Blue 115.00
Toothpick Hldr. 35.00
Amber 40.00
Vaseline 50.00
Green/Blue 60.00
Tumbler 25.00
Amber 30.00
Vaseline 35.00
Green/Blue 45.00
Water Bottles, 4 Sizes . . . . . 25.00 – 50.00
Amber . . . . . 35.00 – 65.00
Vaseline . . . . . 40.00 – 70.00
Green/Blue . . . . . 50.00 – 85.00
Wine 20.00
Amber 25.00
Vaseline 30.00
Green/Blue 40.00

POLKA DOT (INVERTED COIN DOT)
Bar Bottle, 2 Sizes, Rubina 240.00
Bitters, Bottle, Rubina 200.00
Bowl, Finger, Rubina 50.00
Bowl, Shell Ftd., Rubina 265.00
Celery, Rubina 80.00
Cheese Dish, Rubina 250.00
Creamer or Spooner, Rubina 85.00
Custard, Rubina 40.00
Decanter, Rubina 100.00
Jug, 6 Sizes, Rubina . . . . . 90.00 – 275.00
Lemonade, Rubina 75.00
Molasses Can, 2 Sizes, Rubina . . 175.00 – 200.00
Mustard w/Glass Top, Rubina 165.00
Nappy, 2 Sizes, Rubina 40.00
Oil Cruet, 3 Sizes, Rubina 150.00
Salt, 2 Sizes, Rubina 80.00
Sugar, Rubina 150.00
Sugar Sifter, Rubina 175.00
Tumbler, 3 Sizes, Rubina . . . . . 45.00 – 60.00
Vase, Rubina 375.00
Water Bottle, Rubina 235.00
(For crystal, vaseline, or Old Gold, deduct 25%; all other colors except rubina add 100%.)

POPCORN (WITHOUT EARS)
Butter 75.00
Cake Stand 35.00
Cordial 20.00
Creamer or Spooner 25.00
Goblet 40.00
Pitcher 110.00
Sauce 15.00
Sugar 40.00
Wine 25.00

POPE LEO XIII
Plate 150.00

POPPY
Puffed Vases, 6" – 10" . . . . . 15.00 – 40.00

POPPY (NORTHWOOD)
Bowl, 7", Scarce 40.00

PORTLAND
Basket, Hndl. 50.00
Butter 65.00
Candlestick, ea. 25.00
Celery Vase 30.00
Compote, Covered 50.00
Creamer, Spooner, or Sugar 30.00
Cruet 65.00
Cup 20.00
Goblet 30.00
Punch Bowl 110.00
Punch Cup 15.00
Pitcher 90.00
Tumbler 20.00
Wine 20.00

PORTLAND BIRCH LEAF
Leaf Shaped Sauce 20.00
Vaseline 70.00
Green/Blue 55.00
Ruby Stain 50.00

POST SCRIPT
Berry Bowl, Sm. 20.00
Berry Bowl, Lg. 45.00
Butter 65.00
Creamer or Spooner 25.00
Creamer or Sugar, Individual 20.00
Cruet 55.00
Goblet 40.00
Olive, Hndl. 30.00
Shakers, ea. 25.00
Sugar 30.00
Wine 30.00

POTPOURRI
Cake Stand 450.00
Compote, Deep Rnd., Rare 100.00
Sapphire 2400.00
Compote (Salver) 75.00
Compote, Goblet Shape 150.00
Milk Pitcher, Rare 600.00
Tumbler, Rare 200.00

POWDER AND SHOT
Butter 145.00
Caster Bottle 40.00
Celery Vase 185.00
Compote, Covered 135.00
Compote, Open 45.00
Creamer or Spooner 65.00
Egg Cup 65.00
Goblet 95.00
Pitcher 250.00
Tumbler 45.00
Salt, Master 50.00
Sauce 25.00
Sugar 100.00

PRAYER RUG
Bonbon, Custard 25.00
Bowl, Custard 30.00
Plate, Custard 35.00

PRESIDENT McKINLEY ASSASSINATION
Pitcher 275.00
Tumbler 40.00

PRESSED DIAMOND
Berry Bowl, Sm. 10.00
Amber 15.00
Vaseline 20.00
Green/Blue 20.00
Berry Bowl, Lg. 30.00
Amber 35.00
Vaseline 45.00
Green/Blue 50.00
Bowl, Finger 20.00
Amber 25.00
Vaseline 30.00
Green/Blue 35.00
Butter 55.00
Amber 60.00
Vaseline 120.00
Green/Blue 80.00
Cake Stand 35.00
Amber 40.00
Vaseline 80.00
Green/Blue 60.00
Celery Vase 20.00
Amber 25.00
Vaseline 35.00
Green/Blue 40.00
Compote, Open 35.00
Amber 40.00
Vaseline 45.00
Green/Blue 50.00
Compote, Covered 55.00
Amber 60.00
Vaseline 100.00
Green/Blue 90.00
Creamer or Spooner 25.00
Amber 30.00
Vaseline 40.00
Green/Blue 45.00
Cruet 50.00
Amber 55.00
Vaseline 80.00
Green/Blue 70.00
Custard Cup 10.00
Amber 15.00
Vaseline 20.00
Green/Blue 25.00
Goblet 30.00
Amber 35.00
Vaseline 45.00
Green/Blue 50.00
Plate, 11" 25.00
Amber 30.00
Vaseline 50.00
Green/Blue 40.00
Pitcher 70.00
Amber 75.00
Vaseline 145.00
Green/Blue 100.00
Tumbler 15.00
Amber 20.00
Vaseline 25.00
Green/Blue 25.00
Salt Dip 20.00
Amber 25.00
Vaseline 30.00
Green/Blue 30.00
Shakers, ea. 25.00
Amber 30.00
Vaseline 35.00
Green/Blue 35.00
Sugar 30.00
Amber 35.00
Vaseline 70.00
Green/Blue 60.00
Wine 15.00
Amber 20.00
Vaseline 35.00
Green/Blue 25.00

PRESSED LEAF
Berry Bowl, Sm. 10.00
Berry Bowl, Lg. 35.00
Butter 45.00
Cake Stand 30.00
Compote 30.00
Cordial 15.00
Creamer or Spooner 25.00
Egg Cup 20.00
Lamp 75.00
Oval Dish 20.00
Sugar 30.00
Syrup 55.00
Wine 15.00

PRIDE
Berry Bowl, Sm. 10.00
Amber 30.00
Vaseline 40.00
Green/Blue 35.00
Berry Bowl, Lg. 25.00
Amber 40.00
Vaseline 55.00
Green/Blue 45.00
Butter 65.00

Amber . . . 85.00
Vaseline . . . 125.00
Green/Blue . . . 100.00
Celery Tray . . . 25.00
Amber . . . 35.00
Vaseline . . . 75.00
Green/Blue . . . 55.00
Compote, Tall, Covered . . . 80.00
Amber . . . 100.00
Vaseline . . . 175.00
Green/Blue . . . 135.00
Creamer or Spooner . . . 25.00
Amber . . . 35.00
Vaseline . . . 55.00
Green/Blue . . . 40.00
Cruet . . . 35.00
Amber . . . 65.00
Vaseline . . . 95.00
Green/Blue . . . 75.00
Salt Shakers, ea. . . . 30.00
Amber . . . 45.00
Vaseline . . . 70.00
Green/Blue . . . 55.00
Sugar . . . 30.00
Amber . . . 45.00
Vaseline . . . 65.00
Green/Blue . . . 50.00

PRIMROSE (CANTON)

Berry Bowl, Lg. . . . 30.00
Amber . . . 35.00
Vaseline . . . 45.00
Green/Blue . . . 55.00
Milk Glass . . . 40.00
Berry Bowl, Sm. . . . 10.00
Amber . . . 15.00
Vaseline . . . 20.00
Green/Blue . . . 30.00
Milk Glass . . . 20.00
Bowl, Flat . . . 15.00
Amber . . . 20.00
Vaseline . . . 30.00
Green/Blue . . . 40.00
Milk Glass . . . 25.00
Butter . . . 50.00
Amber . . . 55.00
Vaseline . . . 115.00
Green/Blue . . . 105.00
Milk Glass . . . 60.00
Cake Stand . . . 40.00
Amber . . . 45.00
Vaseline . . . 60.00
Green/Blue . . . 75.00
Milk Glass . . . 55.00
Cake Plate, Hndl . . . 35.00
Amber . . . 40.00
Vaseline . . . 50.00
Green/Blue . . . 65.00
Milk Glass . . . 40.00
Compote, Covered, 6" – 9" . . . 30.00 – 55.00
Amber . . . 45.00 – 115.00
Vaseline . . . 90.00 – 150.00
Green/Blue . . . 65.00 – 135.00
Milk Glass . . . 40.00 – 65.00
Cordial . . . 15.00
Amber . . . 20.00
Vaseline . . . 25.00
Green/Blue . . . 35.00
Milk Glass . . . 35.00
Creamer or Spooner . . . 25.00
Amber . . . 30.00
Vaseline . . . 40.00
Green/Blue . . . 50.00
Milk Glass . . . 40.00
Egg Cup . . . 20.00
Amber . . . 25.00
Vaseline . . . 30.00
Green/Blue . . . 40.00
Milk Glass . . . 30.00
Goblet . . . 30.00
Amber . . . 35.00
Vaseline . . . 45.00
Green/Blue . . . 55.00
Milk Glass . . . 55.00
Lamp, Finger Size . . . 65.00
Amber . . . 75.00
Vaseline . . . 90.00
Green/Blue . . . 110.00
Milk Glass . . . 80.00
Milk Pitcher . . . 55.00
Amber . . . 65.00
Vaseline . . . 100.00
Green/Blue . . . 90.00
Milk Glass . . . 60.00
Pickle Dish . . . 15.00
Amber . . . 20.00
Vaseline . . . 25.00
Green/Blue . . . 35.00
Milk Glass . . . 25.00
Pitcher . . . 70.00
Amber . . . 95.00
Vaseline . . . 150.00
Green/Blue . . . 160.00
Milk Glass . . . 120.00
Plate, 4½" – 8" . . . 20.00 – 30.00
Amber . . . 25.00 – 35.00
Vaseline . . . 30.00 – 40.00
Green/Blue . . . 40.00 – 55.00
Milk Glass . . . 25.00 – 45.00
Platter, Oval . . . 25.00
Amber . . . 30.00
Vaseline . . . 45.00
Green/Blue . . . 55.00
Milk Glass . . . 35.00
Relish Tray . . . 15.00
Amber . . . 20.00
Vaseline . . . 25.00
Green/Blue . . . 35.00
Milk Glass . . . 25.00
Sauce, 2 Styles . . . 15.00
Amber . . . 20.00
Vaseline . . . 25.00
Green/Blue . . . 35.00
Milk Glass . . . 20.00 – 35.00
Sugar . . . 35.00
Amber . . . 40.00
Vaseline . . . 55.00
Green/Blue . . . 65.00
Milk Glass . . . 55.00
Waste Bowl . . . 25.00
Amber . . . 30.00
Vaseline . . . 35.00
Green/Blue . . . 45.00
Milk Glass . . . 35.00
Water Tray . . . 35.00
Amber . . . 40.00
Vaseline . . . 70.00
Green/Blue . . . 75.00
Milk Glass . . . 45.00
Wine . . . 15.00
Amber . . . 20.00
Vaseline . . . 25.00
Green/Blue . . . 30.00
Milk Glass . . . 30.00

PRINCE OF WALES PLUMES

(Condensed List — over 60 pieces in pattern)

Berry Bowl, Lg. . . . 45.00
Berry Bowl, Sm. . . . 20.00
Butter . . . 100.00
Compote . . . 50.00
Creamer, Spooner, or Sugar . . . 25.00
Jam Jar . . . 35.00
Mustard Pot . . . 40.00
Novelty Bowl . . . 40.00
Pickle Dish . . . 30.00
Pitcher . . . 165.00
Tumbler . . . 30.00
Plate . . . 35.00
Shakers, ea. . . . 30.00
Sauce . . . 20.00
Syrup . . . 95.00
Toothpick Hldr. . . . 40.00

PRISCILLA

Banana Stand . . . 50.00
Biscuit Jar . . . 45.00
Bowl, Covered, 7" – 10" . . . 35.00 – 60.00
Bowl, Sq. . . . 25.00
Cake Stand, 9" – 10" . . . 45.00
Celery Vase . . . 25.00
Compote, Open, 5" – 9" . . . 20.00 – 40.00
Compote, Covered, 7" – 9" . . . 30.00 – 65.00
Condiment Tray . . . 30.00
Cracker Jar . . . 45.00
Creamer or Spooner . . . 20.00
Cruet . . . 65.00
Cup . . . 10.00
Donut Stand . . . 40.00
Goblet . . . 65.00
Jelly Compote, Covered . . . 40.00
Mug . . . 25.00
Pickle Dish . . . 15.00
Plate . . . 20.00
Pitcher, 2 Styles . . . 125.00
Tumbler . . . 25.00
Relish Dish . . . 15.00
Rose Bowl . . . 35.00
Sauce, Rnd. or Sq. . . . 10.00
Shakers, ea. . . . 25.00
Sugar . . . 30.00
Syrup . . . 65.00
Toothpick Hldr. . . . 30.00
Wine . . . 10.00

PRISM

Butter . . . 45.00
Champagne . . . 15.00
Compote . . . 25.00
Creamer or Spooner . . . 15.00
Decanter . . . 40.00
Egg Cup . . . 10.00
Goblet . . . 35.00
Pitcher . . . 65.00
Tumbler . . . 10.00
Sugar . . . 20.00
Wine . . . 10.00

PRISM BARS

Berry Bowl, Sm. . . . 10.00
Berry Bowl, Lg. . . . 30.00
Butter . . . 45.00
Celery Vase . . . 20.00
Creamer or Spooner . . . 15.00
Goblet . . . 30.00
Pickle Jar . . . 20.00
Pitcher . . . 60.00
Tumbler . . . 10.00
Relish . . . 15.00
Sugar . . . 20.00

THE PRIZE

Butter . . . 70.00
Creamer or Spooner . . . 20.00
Cruet . . . 55.00
Goblet . . . 60.00
Pickle Dish . . . 20.00
Pitcher . . . 90.00
Tumbler . . . 25.00
Shakers, ea. . . . 15.00
Sugar . . . 30.00
Syrup . . . 45.00
Toothpick Hldr. . . . 30.00

"PROTECTION AND PLENTY"

Mug . . . 50.00
Plate, 8½" . . . 65.00

PULLED LOOP

Vase, Scarce . . . 35.00

PUNTY AND DIAMOND POINT

Berry Bowl, Sm. . . . 15.00
Berry Bowl, Lg. . . . 45.00
Bitters Bottle . . . 65.00
Butter . . . 75.00
Creamer or Spooner . . . 25.00
Cruet . . . 50.00
Decanter . . . 45.00
Platter . . . 35.00
Pitcher . . . 125.00
Tumbler . . . 20.00
Punch Bowl . . . 165.00
Punch Cup . . . 15.00
Sauce . . . 10.00

Shakers, ea. 15.00
Sugar 35.00
Sugar Shaker 45.00
Toothpick Hldr. 35.00
Water Bottle. 40.00
Vase. 25.00

PUNTY BAND
Butter. 55.00
Cake Basket 40.00
Cake Stand. 35.00
Candy Dish 25.00
Creamer or Spooner. 25.00
Goblet 40.00
Mug 30.00
Pitcher 90.00
Tumbler 20.00
Salt Dip 10.00
Shakers, ea. 15.00
Spoon Tray 20.00
Sugar 35.00
Syrup 45.00
Toothpick Hldr. 25.00
Wine 10.00

PURE PACK MUG
Mug 55.00

PURITAN (MCKEE'S)
Butter. 40.00
Ruby Stain. 80.00
Creamer or Spooner. 20.00
Ruby Stain. 30.00
Pitcher 70.00
Ruby Stain. 105.00
Sugar 25.00
Ruby Stain. 50.00
Toothpick Hldr. 30.00
Ruby Stain. 45.00
Tumbler 15.00
Ruby Stain. 30.00

QUADRUPED
Berry Bowl, Lg. 35.00
Berry Bowl, Sm. 10.00
Bowl, Mid Size. 15.00
Butter. 75.00
Compote, Short-stemmed. 35.00
Creamer or Spooner. 25.00
Hotel Creamer & Sugar 45.00
Jelly Compote. 35.00
Pickle Dish. 15.00
Pitcher 95.00
Relish 15.00
Shakers, ea. 20.00
Sugar 35.00
Sundae Dish 20.00
Tumbler 15.00
Vase. 25.00

QUARTERED BLOCK
Oil Lamp, 4 Sizes . . . . . 75.00 – 150.00

QUATREFOIL
Bowl, Various . . . . . 10.00 – 35.00
Butter. 45.00
Compote, Covered 35.00
Compote, Open 25.00
Creamer or Spooner. 20.00
Goblet, Rare. 85.00
Pitcher 80.00
Tumbler 20.00
Shakers, ea. 15.00
Sugar 25.00

QUEBEC DIAMOND BAND
Goblet 40.00

QUEEN
Bowl, 8½". 30.00
Amber 45.00
Vaseline. 45.00
Green/Blue. 50.00
Butter, 3 Styles. 75.00
Amber. . . . . 60.00 – 115.00
Vaseline . . . . . 100.00 – 155.00
Green/Blue . . . . . 65.00 – 125.00
Cake Stand. 50.00
Amber 60.00
Vaseline. 90.00
Green/Blue. 80.00
Celery Vase 30.00
Amber 40.00
Vaseline. 40.00
Green/Blue. 50.00
Claret 20.00
Amber 40.00
Vaseline. 75.00
Green/Blue. 65.00
Compote, Covered 55.00
Amber 75.00
Vaseline. 95.00
Green/Blue. 110.00
Compote, Open 40.00
Amber 45.00
Vaseline. 60.00
Green/Blue. 55.00
Creamer or Spooner, 3 Styles. 30.00
Amber 35.00
Vaseline. 45.00
Green/Blue. 45.00
Cruet 60.00
Amber 75.00
Green/Blue. 90.00
Goblet 35.00
Amber 40.00
Vaseline. 50.00
Green/Blue. 50.00
Oval Dish, 7" – 9". 20.00
Amber 30.00
Vaseline. 30.00
Green/Blue. 40.00
Pitcher 85.00
Amber 110.00
Vaseline. 150.00
Green/Blue. 125.00
Tumbler 25.00
Amber 30.00
Vaseline. 30.00
Green/Blue. 35.00
Relish Dish 15.00
Amber 20.00
Vaseline. 40.00
Green/Blue. 35.00
Sauce 10.00
Amber 15.00
Vaseline. 25.00
Green/Blue. 20.00
Sugar, 3 Styles 35.00
Amber 45.00
Vaseline. 75.00
Green/Blue. 60.00
Wine 20.00
Amber 30.00
Vaseline. 45.00
Green/Blue. 40.00

QUEEN ANNE
Bowl, Covered, 8" – 9" . . . . . 35.00 – 65.00
Butter. 75.00
Casserole, 7" – 8" 45.00
Celery Vase 20.00
Compote, Covered, High 60.00
Compote, Covered, Low 35.00
Creamer or Spooner. 20.00
Egg Cup 10.00
Milk Pitcher. 45.00
Plate. 20.00
Pitcher 85.00
Tumbler 20.00
Sauce 10.00
Shakers, ea. 15.00
Sugar 25.00
Syrup 40.00

QUEEN'S NECKLACE
Bowl, 10" 30.00
Butter. 70.00
Cake Salver 40.00
Celery Vase 20.00
Cologne Bottle 40.00
Compote, Open 10" 35.00
Creamer or Spooner. 30.00
Cruet 65.00
Lamp 85.00
Oil Bottle 40.00
Pitcher 100.00
Tumbler 20.00
Rose Bowl 25.00
Shakers, ea. 20.00
Sugar 45.00
Syrup 70.00
Vases, 8" – 10". . . . . 20.00 – 35.00
Wine 20.00

RABBIT SITTING
Mug 70.00
Amber 100.00

RABBIT UPRIGHT
Mug 60.00
Amber 80.00
Vaseline. 100.00
Green/Blue. 75.00

RACING DEER
Pitcher, Rare 425.00

RAILROAD
Platter 90.00

RAINBOW
Berry Bowl, Sm. 20.00
Berry Bowl, Lg. 45.00
Carafe 60.00
Cigar Jar. 40.00
Creamer or Spooner. 25.00
Decanter 65.00
Goblet 40.00
Pitcher 85.00
Tumbler 25.00
Salt Dip 30.00
Shakers, ea. 25.00
Sugar 30.00
Wine Tray 35.00

RAINDROP
ABC Plate. 35.00
Amber 40.00
Vaseline. 65.00
Green/Blue. 50.00
Butter. 45.00
Amber 50.00
Vaseline. 95.00
Green/Blue. 70.00
Cake Plate 35.00
Amber 50.00
Vaseline. 95.00
Green/Blue. 70.00
Celery Vase 15.00
Amber 30.00
Vaseline. 55.00
Green/Blue. 35.00
Compote, Covered, High or Low . 35.00 – 50.00
Amber. . . . . 40.00 – 60.00
Vaseline . . . . . 55.00 – 100.00
Green/Blue . . . . . 45.00 – 95.00
Compote, Open, High or Low . . . 25.00 – 45.00
Amber. . . . . 30.00 – 50.00
Vaseline . . . . . 45.00 – 65.00
Green/Blue . . . . . 35.00 – 85.00
Creamer or Spooner. 20.00
Amber 25.00
Vaseline. 50.00
Green/Blue. 35.00
Cup & Saucer. 35.00
Amber 40.00
Vaseline. 50.00
Green/Blue. 45.00
Egg Cup 15.00
Amber 20.00
Vaseline. 45.00
Green/Blue. 35.00
Finger Bowl 15.00
Amber 20.00
Vaseline. 35.00
Green/Blue. 30.00
Miniature Lamp. 45.00
Amber 85.00
Vaseline. 125.00
Green/Blue. 100.00
Pickle Dish. 15.00

Amber . . . 20.00
Vaseline . . . 30.00
Green/Blue . . . 25.00
Plate, Dinner . . . 20.00
Amber . . . 25.00
Vaseline . . . 40.00
Green/Blue . . . 30.00
Pitcher . . . 65.00
Amber . . . 90.00
Vaseline . . . 130.00
Green/Blue . . . 135.00
Tumbler . . . 10.00
Amber . . . 15.00
Vaseline . . . 35.00
Green/Blue . . . 40.00
Relish Tray . . . 15.00
Amber . . . 20.00
Vaseline . . . 30.00
Green/Blue . . . 30.00
Sauce . . . 10.00
Amber . . . 15.00
Vaseline . . . 20.00
Green/Blue . . . 20.00
Sugar . . . 25.00
Amber . . . 45.00
Vaseline . . . 75.00
Green/Blue . . . 65.00
Syrup . . . 65.00
Amber . . . 80.00
Vaseline . . . 125.00
Green/Blue . . . 115.00
Water Tray . . . 30.00
Amber . . . 40.00
Vaseline . . . 60.00
Green/Blue . . . 55.00
Wine . . . 15.00
Amber . . . 25.00
Vaseline . . . 30.00
Green/Blue . . . 35.00

RAMPANT LION (GILLINDER)
Compote, Covered, 7" – 8" . . . 150.00 – 170.00

RAM'S HEAD
Bowl, Covered, 5" – 7" . . . 175.00

RAM'S HEAD
Mug . . . 35.00
Vaseline . . . 75.00

RANSOM
Bowls, Various . . . 15.00 – 30.00
Butter . . . 55.00
Creamer or Spooner . . . 25.00
Cruet . . . 60.00
Sugar . . . 35.00

RAYED FLOWER
Berry Bowl, Sm. . . . 10.00
Berry Bowl, Lg. . . . 30.00
Butter . . . 45.00
Celery Vase . . . 20.00
Creamer or Spooner . . . 20.00
Custard Cup . . . 10.00
Milk Pitcher . . . 45.00
Pickle Dish . . . 15.00
Pitcher . . . 70.00
Tumbler . . . 10.00
Shakers, ea. . . . 10.00
Sugar . . . 25.00
Toothpick Hldr. . . . 30.00

RAYED HEART
Bowl, 8" . . . 35.00
Butter . . . 65.00
Celery . . . 35.00
Compote . . . 40.00
Creamer, Spooner, or Sugar . . . 25.00
Goblet . . . 35.00
Pickle Dish . . . 25.00
Pitcher . . . 75.00
Tumbler . . . 20.00
Sauce, 4" . . . 20.00

REAPER
Oval Platter, Hndl. . . . 70.00

RED BLOCK
Bowl, Rnd., Ruby Stain . . . 75.00
Bowls, Rectangular, Ruby Stain . 50.00 – 80.00
Butter, Ruby Stain . . . 130.00
Creamer or Spooner, Ruby Stain . . . 70.00
Cruet, Ruby Stain . . . 100.00
Cup, Ruby Stain . . . 35.00
Lamp, Ruby Stain . . . 225.00
Mustard Jar w/Saucer, Ruby Stain . . . 75.00
Pitcher, Ruby Stain . . . 225.00
Tumbler, Ruby Stain . . . 45.00
Shakers, Ruby Stain ea. . . . 65.00
Sugar, Ruby Stain . . . 110.00
Syrup, Ruby Stain . . . 125.00

REEDED STAR
Cologne Bottle . . . 50.00
Goblet . . . 30.00
Jelly Compote . . . 20.00
Tumbler, Ice Tea . . . 25.00

REGAL SWAN
Master Salt . . . 125.00

"REMEMBER ME"
Mug . . . 65.00

RETICULATED CORD
Butter . . . 55.00
Vaseline . . . 95.00
Green/Blue . . . 90.00
Cake Stand, Lg. . . . 35.00
Vaseline . . . 45.00
Green/Blue . . . 50.00
Celery Vase . . . 20.00
Vaseline . . . 25.00
Green/Blue . . . 30.00
Creamer or Spooner . . . 25.00
Vaseline . . . 35.00
Green/Blue . . . 45.00
Goblet . . . 35.00
Vaseline . . . 125.00
Green/Blue . . . 135.00
Plate . . . 30.00
Vaseline . . . 40.00
Green/Blue . . . 50.00
Relish . . . 20.00
Vaseline . . . 25.00
Green/Blue . . . 35.00
Pitcher . . . 85.00
Vaseline . . . 150.00
Green/Blue . . . 165.00
Tumbler . . . 15.00
Vaseline . . . 35.00
Green/Blue . . . 35.00
Sauce . . . 10.00
Vaseline . . . 20.00
Green/Blue . . . 25.00
Sugar . . . 35.00
Vaseline . . . 45.00
Green/Blue . . . 55.00

REVERSE DRAPERY
Bowl . . . 25.00
Plate . . . 55.00
Vase . . . 30.00

REVERSE FAN AND DIAMOND
Pitcher . . . 85.00
Tumbler . . . 20.00

REVERSE TORPEDO
Banana Dish . . . 35.00
Berry Bowl, Sm. . . . 20.00
Berry Bowl, Lg. . . . 45.00
Butter . . . 70.00
Cake Stand . . . 40.00
Celery Vase . . . 30.00
Compote, 8 Sizes . . . 40.00 – 110.00
Creamer or Spooner . . . 30.00
Fruit Basket . . . 50.00
Plate . . . 25.00
Shakers, ea. . . . 30.00
Sugar . . . 30.00

REVERSE TWIST
Child's Cup . . . 30.00

REXFORD
Butter . . . 65.00
Cake Stand . . . 45.00
Celery Vase . . . 30.00
Compote . . . 40.00
Creamer or Spooner . . . 25.00
Goblet . . . 50.00
Honey Jar . . . 45.00
Plate, 7", Sq. . . . 30.00
Pitcher . . . 90.00
Tumbler . . . 20.00
Sugar . . . 30.00
Toothpick Hldr. . . . 40.00
Toy Table Set, Complete . . . 110.00
Wine . . . 20.00

RHINE STAR
Vase, 6½", Very Scarce . . . 70.00

RIB AND FLUTE
Vase . . . 20.00

RIB BAND
Butter . . . 55.00
Creamer or Spooner . . . 25.00
Pitcher . . . 80.00
Tumbler . . . 10.00
Sugar . . . 30.00

RIBBED ELLIPSE (ADMIRAL)
Berry Bowl, Sm. . . . 15.00
Berry Bowl, Lg. . . . 45.00
Butter . . . 65.00
Cake Plate . . . 35.00
Compote . . . 30.00
Creamer or Spooner . . . 20.00
Mug, Hndl. . . . 40.00
Plate . . . 20.00
Pitcher . . . 85.00
Tumbler . . . 20.00
Sugar . . . 30.00

RIBBED FORGET-ME-NOT
Creamer, Ind. . . . 25.00
Amber . . . 30.00
Vaseline . . . 35.00
Green/Blue . . . 30.00
Cup . . . 15.00
Amber . . . 20.00
Vaseline . . . 25.00
Green/Blue . . . 20.00
Mustard, Hndl. . . . 40.00
Amber . . . 50.00
Vaseline . . . 60.00
Green/Blue . . . 55.00
Toy Table Set, Complete . . . 110.00
Amber . . . 140.00
Vaseline . . . 175.00
Green/Blue . . . 155.00

RIBBED LEAVES VARIANT
Mug . . . 45.00

RIBBED PALM
Butter . . . 110.00
Celery Vase . . . 70.00
Champagne . . . 100.00
Compote, Covered, 6" . . . 130.00
Compote, Open, 7" . . . 85.00
Creamer . . . 145.00
Egg Cup . . . 30.00
Goblet . . . 45.00
Lamp . . . 125.00
Plate, 6" . . . 40.00
Pitcher . . . 245.00
Tumbler . . . 65.00
Salt, Master . . . 35.00
Sauce . . . 15.00
Spooner . . . 45.00
Sugar . . . 85.00
Wine . . . 60.00

RIBBED WINDOW
Vase (For Shelf Supports) . . . 25.00

RIBBON
Berry Bowl, Sm. . . . 20.00
Berry Bowl, Lg. . . . 60.00
Butter . . . 85.00
Cake Stand . . . 60.00
Celery Vase . . . 40.00
Champagne . . . 80.00
Cheese Dish, Covered . . . 110.00
Cologne Bottle . . . 70.00
Compote, Covered, 6" – 8" . . . 70.00
Compote, Open, Dolphin, Round, 10½". 275.00
Compote, Open, Rebecca

at the Well, Oval 300.00
Creamer or Spooner 85.00
Goblet 35.00
Milk Pitcher 75.00
Pickle Jar 100.00
Plate 45.00
Platter 70.00
Pitcher 90.00
Tumbler 30.00
Sauce 20.00
Shakers, ea. 35.00
Sugar 70.00
Waste Bowl 50.00
Water Tray 110.00
Wine, Rare 140.00

RIB OVER DRAPE
Butter 85.00
Creamer or Spooner 40.00
Pitcher 135.00
Tumbler 20.00
Sugar 55.00

RICHARD WALLACE
Compote 250.00

RING NECK
Oil Bottle 45.00

RIPPLE
Vase, Squat 35.00
Vase, Standard 30.00
Vase, Funeral 75.00

RISING SUN
Bonbon, Ftd. 15.00
Green Stain 25.00
Berry Bowl, Lg. 35.00
Green Stain 40.00
Berry Bowl, Sm. 15.00
Green Stain 20.00
Butter, 3 Sizes 60.00
Green Stain . . . . 45.00 – 65.00
Cake Stand 35.00
Green Stain 50.00
Celery Vase 25.00
Green Stain 35.00
Champagne 20.00
Green Stain 25.00
Compote 45.00
Green Stain 65.00
Creamer Or Spooner, 3 Shapes 30.00
Green Stain 45.00
Cruet 55.00
Green Stain 75.00
Custard Cup 10.00
Green Stain 25.00
Goblet 25.00
Green Stain 35.00
Milk Pitcher 40.00
Green Stain 60.00
Pickle Dish 15.00
Green Stain 25.00
Pitcher 75.00
Green Stain 135.00
Tumbler 20.00
Green Stain 25.00
Sauce 10.00
Green Stain 15.00
Shakers, ea. 20.00
Green Stain 35.00
Toothpick 30.00
Green Stain 50.00
Tray, for Water Set 35.00
Green Stain 45.00
Sugar, 3 Shapes . . . . 30.00 – 45.00
Green Stain . . . . 35.00 – 60.00
Vase 20.00
Green Stain 30.00
Wine 30.00
Green Stain 40.00

RISING SUN ADVERTISING
Sweetmeat, 3 Hndl. 70.00

RIVERGLASS FLUTE
Bowl, 5" – 9" 50.00

RIVERSIDE COLONIAL
Table Lamp, Hndl., 3 Sizes . . . 225.00 – 300.00

RIVERSIDE ELK (DEER)
Goblet 85.00
Pickle Jar 65.00

RIVERSIDE'S DERBY
Berry Bowl, Lg. 35.00
Vaseline 60.00
Berry Bowl, Sm. 10.00
Vaseline 30.00
Bowls, Sq. or Octagon 25.00
Vaseline 40.00
Breakfast Set 45.00
Vaseline 65.00
Butter 75.00
Vaseline 165.00
Compote, Covered, 3 Sizes . . . . . 40.00 – 80.00
Vaseline . . . . 90.00 – 165.00
Compote, Open, 2 Sizes . . . . 30.00 – 65.00
Vaseline . . . . 65.00 – 120.00
Creamer or Spooner 25.00
Vaseline 45.00
Cruet 80.00
Vaseline 120.00
Individual Creamer or Sugar, ea. 30.00
Vaseline 50.00
Jelly Compote 35.00
Vaseline 60.00
Pickle Dish 15.00
Vaseline 30.00
Pitcher 115.00
Vaseline 185.00
Sugar 35.00
Vaseline 60.00
Tumbler 15.00
Vaseline 30.00
Water Goblet 40.00
Vaseline 65.00
Wine Goblet 30.00
Vaseline 40.00

ROARING LION
Goblet, Rare, Vaseline 250.00

ROBIN HOOD
Butter 55.00
Green/Blue 65.00
Celery Vase 20.00
Green/Blue 25.00
Compote 35.00
Green/Blue 45.00
Creamer or Spooner 20.00
Green/Blue 30.00
Goblet 40.00
Green/Blue 45.00
Jelly Compote 35.00
Green/Blue 40.00
Milk Pitcher 60.00
Green/Blue 70.00
Pickle Dish 15.00
Green/Blue 20.00
Pitcher 85.00
Green/Blue 100.00
Tumbler 20.00
Green/Blue 25.00
Shakers, ea. 20.00
Green/Blue 35.00
Sugar 30.00
Green/Blue 45.00
Syrup, Scarce 80.00
Green/Blue 95.00

ROBIN IN A TREE
Mug 40.00
Amber 50.00
Vaseline 80.00
Light Amethyst 80.00

ROCK CRYSTAL
Butter 65.00
Cake Stand 40.00
Celery Tray 25.00
Creamer or Spooner 25.00
Custard Cup 20.00
Goblet 35.00
Pitcher 85.00
Tumbler 25.00
Shakers, ea. 30.00
Sugar 30.00
Sundae Glass 25.00

ROCKET
Berry Bowl, Sm. 15.00
Berry Bowl, Lg. 40.00
Butter 65.00
Cake Stand 40.00
Compote 35.00
Creamer or Spooner 20.00
Pitcher 70.00
Tumbler 15.00
Sugar 30.00

ROMAN KEY
Bowl, 8" – 10" . . . . 30.00 – 45.00
Butter 70.00
Caster Set 110.00
Celery Vase 20.00
Champagne 15.00
Compote, 8" – 10" 50.00
Cordial 10.00
Creamer or Spooner 25.00
Custard Cup 15.00
Decanter, 2 Sizes 55.00
Egg Cup 20.00
Goblet 40.00
Jam Dish 25.00
Milk Pitcher 60.00
Mustard Jar 30.00
Oil Lamp 250.00
Pitcher 90.00
Tumbler 20.00
Plate, 6½" 20.00
Relish Dish 15.00
Salt, Master 20.00
Sugar 30.00
Wine 15.00

ROMAN KEY WITH RIBS
Berry Bowl, Sm. 20.00
Berry Bowl, Lg. 45.00
Butter 80.00
Caster Set 95.00
Celery Vase 25.00
Compote, Covered 55.00
Compote, Open 30.00
Creamer or Spooner 25.00
Goblet 55.00
Pitcher 145.00
Tumbler 25.00
Sugar 40.00
Wine 15.00

ROMAN ROSETTE
Bowl, 5" – 8" . . . . 20.00 – 45.00
Ruby Stain 55.00
Bread Plate, Oval 45.00
Ruby Stain 80.00
Butter 65.00
Ruby Stain 125.00
Cake Stand, 2 Sizes . . . . 35.00 – 45.00
Caster Set, 3 Bottles 75.00
Celery Vase 45.00
Ruby Stain 85.00
Compotes, Covered, 5" – 8" . . . . . 25.00 – 55.00
Creamer or Spooner 25.00
Ruby Stain 50.00
Goblet 45.00
Milk Pitcher 45.00
Ruby Stain 165.00
Mug, 2 Sizes . . . . 30.00 – 35.00
Ruby Stain 145.00
Plate 35.00
Ruby Stain 60.00
Pickle Dish 25.00
Ruby Stain 35.00
Pitcher 85.00
Tumbler 20.00
Ruby Stain 40.00
Shakers, ea. 30.00
Ruby Stain 55.00
Sugar 35.00
Ruby Stain 65.00
Syrup 75.00
Ruby Stain 135.00

Wine 25.00
Ruby Stain. 55.00

ROMEO (BLOCK AND FAN)

Berry Bowl, Sm. 15.00
Berry Bowl, Lg.. . . . . 40.00
Biscuit Jar 50.00
Ruby Stain. 150.00
Bowl, Rectangular 30.00
Butter. 65.00
Ruby Stain. 125.00
Cake Stand. 35.00
Carafe 40.00
Ruby Stain. 100.00
Caster Set w/Tray. 120.00
Celery Tray. 25.00
Celery Vase 20.00
Ruby Stain. 80.00
Compote, Covered, 7" – 8" 50.00
Ruby Stain. 225.00
Compote, Open, 4" – 8" 35.00
Ruby Stain. 150.00
Condiment Set, 4 Pcs. 75.00
Cracker Jar. 55.00
Creamer, 4 Sizes . . . . 25.00 – 35.00
Ruby Stain . . . . 35.00 – 100.00
Cruet 60.00
Decanter 45.00
Finger Bowl 20.00
Goblet 50.00
Ruby Stain. 130.00
Ice Bucket 45.00
Ruby Stain. 70.00
Ice Cream Dish, Oblong. 20.00
Lamp 125.00
Milk Pitcher. 50.00
Pickle Dish. 15.00
Plate, 6" – 10" . . . . 15.00 – 35.00
Pitcher. 85.00
Ruby Stain. 165.00
Tumbler. 20.00
Ruby Stain. 50.00
Relish Tray. 20.00
Rose Bowl 25.00
Sauce, Flat or Ftd. 10.00
Ruby Stain. 35.00
Shakers, ea. 25.00
Spooner 30.00
Sugar 30.00
Sugar Shaker 40.00
Syrup 70.00
Ruby Stain. 100.00
Waste Bowl 20.00
Wine 35.00
Ruby Stain. 75.00

ROOSTER ABC

Plate. 175.00

ROSE

Cake Plate, Hndl. 50.00
Vaseline. 70.00
Green/Blue. 85.00
Candlesticks, ea. 40.00
Vaseline. 55.00
Green/Blue. 65.00
Cologne 55.00
Vaseline. 65.00
Green/Blue. 75.00
Compote. 45.00
Vaseline. 55.00
Green/Blue. 65.00
Console Bowl. 35.00
Vaseline. 40.00
Green/Blue. 50.00
Dresser Tray 40.00
Vaseline. 45.00
Green/Blue. 55.00
Trinket Box 60.00
Vaseline. 75.00
Green/Blue. 85.00
Trinket Tray. 35.00
Vaseline. 45.00
Green/Blue. 55.00

ROSE AND OTHER FLOWERS

Berry Bowl, Sm., Vaseline 30.00
Berry Bowl, Lg., Vaseline 70.00

ROSE IN SNOW

Bitters Bottle 65.00
Amber 85.00
Vaseline. 85.00
Green/Blue. 100.00
Bowl, Covered, 8" – 9" 50.00
Amber 75.00
Vaseline. 75.00
Green/Blue. 85.00
Bowl, Open, 8" – 9" 30.00
Amber 40.00
Vaseline. 40.00
Green/Blue. 55.00
Butter, 2 Styles. 60.00
Amber 75.00
Vaseline. 135.00
Green/Blue. 125.00
Cake Stand. 85.00
Amber 90.00
Vaseline. 110.00
Green/Blue. 165.00
Compote w/Lid, High or Low. . . 75.00 – 100.00
Amber. . . . . 85.00 – 125.00
Vaseline . . . . 100.00 – 150.00
Green/Blue . . . . 95.00 – 135.00
Creamer or Spooner. 50.00
Amber 60.00
Vaseline. 75.00
Green/Blue. 65.00
Dish, Oval 15.00
Amber 20.00
Vaseline. 30.00
Green/Blue. 30.00
Mug 35.00
Amber 45.00
Vaseline. 60.00
Green/Blue. 95.00
Pickle Dish. 20.00
Amber 25.00
Vaseline. 40.00
Green/Blue. 30.00
Plate, 5" – 9" . . . . 20.00 – 35.00
Amber. . . . . 25.00 – 30.00
Vaseline . . . . 40.00 – 65.00
Green/Blue . . . . 30.00 – 40.00
Platter, Oval. 40.00
Amber 45.00
Vaseline. 45.00
Green/Blue. 60.00
Pitcher 145.00
Amber 165.00
Vaseline. 250.00
Green/Blue. 225.00
Tumbler, Scarce 65.00
Amber 85.00
Vaseline. 90.00
Green/Blue. 100.00
Relish Dish, Oval. 25.00
Amber 30.00
Vaseline. 30.00
Green/Blue. 40.00
Sauce, Flat or Ftd. 10.00
Amber 15.00
Vaseline. 20.00
Green/Blue. 25.00
Sugar 55.00
Amber 70.00
Vaseline. 95.00
Green/Blue. 110.00
Sweetmeat w/Lid 85.00
Amber 95.00
Vaseline. 135.00
Green/Blue. 120.00
Toddy Jar w/Lid & Underplate 150.00
Amber 165.00
Vaseline. 225.00
Green/Blue. 200.00

ROSELAND (LATE)

Berry Bowl, Sm. 10.00
Berry Bowl, Lg.. . . . . 30.00
Pitcher. 45.00
Tumbler 10.00

ROSE POINT BAND

Berry Bowl, Sm. 10.00
Berry Bowl, Lg.. . . . . 30.00
Bowl, Ftd.. . . . . 25.00
Butter. 45.00
Celery Vase 15.00
Compote. 30.00
Creamer or Spooner. 20.00
Pitcher 70.00
Tumbler 15.00
Sauce 10.00
Sugar 25.00

ROSES IN THE SNOW

Bowl, 9" 35.00
Plate, 11" 45.00
Oil Lamp, 10". 90.00

ROSE SPRIG

Biscuit Jar 95.00
Amber 185.00
Vaseline. 200.00
Green/Blue. 235.00
Bowl, Sietz Shape 30.00
Amber 45.00
Vaseline. 50.00
Green/Blue. 60.00
Cake Stand. 65.00
Amber 80.00
Vaseline. 85.00
Green/Blue. 100.00
Celery Vase 40.00
Amber 55.00
Vaseline. 60.00
Green/Blue. 70.00
Compote, Covered, 7" – 8" . . . . . . 70.00 – 85.00
Amber. . . . . 90.00 – 135.00
Vaseline . . . . 95.00 – 140.00
Green/Blue . . . . 100.00 – 150.00
Compote, Open, 7" – 8" . . . . 35.00 – 45.00
Amber. . . . . 50.00 – 65.00
Vaseline . . . . 55.00 – 70.00
Green/Blue . . . . 60.00 – 75.00
Creamer or Spooner. 50.00
Amber 60.00
Vaseline. 65.00
Green/Blue. 70.00
Dish, Oblong 20.00
Amber 25.00
Vaseline. 30.00
Green/Blue. 35.00
Goblet 50.00
Amber 55.00
Vaseline. 60.00
Green/Blue. 70.00
Milk Pitcher. 60.00
Amber 70.00
Vaseline. 80.00
Green/Blue. 90.00
Mug 45.00
Amber 55.00
Vaseline. 60.00
Green/Blue. 65.00
Nappy 20.00
Amber 30.00
Vaseline. 35.00
Green/Blue. 40.00
Pickle Dish. 20.00
Amber 25.00
Vaseline. 30.00
Green/Blue. 35.00
Pitcher 75.00
Amber 95.00
Vaseline. 135.00
Green/Blue. 140.00
Tumbler 20.00
Amber 30.00
Vaseline. 40.00
Green/Blue. 45.00
Plate, 6" – 10" . . . . 30.00 – 40.00
Amber. . . . . 35.00 – 45.00

Vaseline . . . 40.00 – 50.00
Green/Blue . . . 50.00 – 70.00
Punch Bowl, Ftd. . . . 115.00
Amber . . . 175.00
Vaseline. . . . 245.00
Green/Blue. . . . 265.00
Relish. . . . 20.00
Amber . . . 25.00
Vaseline. . . . 30.00
Green/Blue. . . . 35.00
Salt (Sleigh Shape). . . . 50.00
Amber . . . 70.00
Vaseline. . . . 75.00
Green/Blue. . . . 80.00
Sugar . . . 55.00
Amber . . . 65.00
Vaseline. . . . 70.00
Green/Blue. . . . 75.00
Tray . . . 45.00
Amber . . . 50.00
Vaseline. . . . 55.00
Green/Blue. . . . 60.00
Wine . . . 25.00
Amber . . . 30.00
Vaseline. . . . 35.00
Green/Blue. . . . 40.00

ROSETTE (MAGIC)
Bowl, Covered . . . 50.00
Butter. . . . 70.00
Celery Vase . . . 20.00
Creamer or Spooner. . . . 20.00
Fish Relish. . . . 35.00
Jelly Compote. . . . 25.00
Plate. . . . 25.00
Plate, Hndl. . . . 35.00
Pitcher. . . . 100.00
Tumbler. . . . 20.00
Shakers, ea. . . . 25.00
Sugar . . . 25.00
Tray . . . 30.00

ROSETTE AND PALMS
Banana Stand . . . 45.00
Butter. . . . 75.00
Cake Stand. . . . 35.00
Celery Vase . . . 20.00
Creamer or Spooner. . . . 25.00
Goblet . . . 50.00
Plate, 9" . . . 25.00
Pitcher . . . 85.00
Tumbler . . . 15.00
Relish Dish . . . 20.00
Sauce . . . 10.00
Shakers, ea. . . . 15.00
Sugar . . . 35.00
Wine . . . 10.00

ROSETTE BAND
Bowl, 8", Covered. . . . 50.00
Ruby Stain. . . . 80.00
Engraved . . . 70.00
Butter. . . . 75.00
Ruby Stain. . . . 110.00
Engraved . . . 90.00
Compote, Rare . . . 120.00
Ruby Stain. . . . 165.00
Engraved . . . 135.00
Creamer or Spooner. . . . 20.00
Ruby Stain. . . . 45.00
Engraved . . . 35.00
Shakers, ea. . . . 25.00
Ruby Stain. . . . 30.00
Engraved . . . 25.00
Sugar . . . 30.00
Ruby Stain. . . . 60.00
Engraved . . . 50.00
Toothpick Hldr. . . . 35.00
Ruby Stain. . . . 55.00
Engraved . . . 45.00

ROSETTE WITH PINWHEELS
Bowl, Ftd.. . . . 35.00
Butter. . . . 70.00
Celery Vase . . . 25.00
Creamer or Spooner. . . . 25.00

Cup, Ftd. . . . 20.00
Honey Dish, Sq.. . . . 25.00
Jelly Compote. . . . 30.00
Pitcher . . . 85.00
Tumbler . . . 25.00
Sugar . . . 30.00

ROTEC
Bowls, Various . . . 10.00 – 40.00
Butter. . . . 65.00
Celery Tray. . . . 20.00
Creamer or Spooner. . . . 25.00
Pitcher . . . 75.00
Tumbler . . . 15.00
Sugar . . . 30.00

ROYAL CRYSTAL
Bowls, 5" – 8", 3 Shapes . . . 15.00 – 35.00
Ruby Stain . . . 30.00 – 65.00
Butter. . . . 60.00
Ruby Stain. . . . 90.00
Cake Stands, Various . . . 25.00 – 45.00
Ruby Stain . . . 40.00 – 60.00
Candy Jar. . . . 45.00
Ruby Stain. . . . 65.00
Celery Vase . . . 20.00
Ruby Stain. . . . 30.00
Cologne . . . 45.00
Ruby Stain. . . . 85.00
Compote, 6" and 7" . . . 50.00
Ruby Stain. . . . 55.00
Cracker Jar. . . . 65.00
Ruby Stain. . . . 70.00
Creamer or Spooner. . . . 30.00
Ruby Stain. . . . 40.00
Cruet, 2 Sizes. . . . 80.00
Ruby Stain. . . . 110.00
Goblet . . . 40.00
Ruby Stain. . . . 60.00
Milk Pitcher. . . . 65.00
Ruby Stain. . . . 80.00
Plate, 2 Styles . . . 35.00
Ruby Stain. . . . 40.00
Pitcher, 2 Styles. . . . 165.00
Ruby Stain. . . . 145.00
Tumbler . . . 20.00
Ruby Stain. . . . 30.00
Sauce, Flat or Ftd. . . . 15.00
Ruby Stain. . . . 25.00
Shakers, ea. . . . 25.00
Ruby Stain. . . . 45.00
Sugar . . . 40.00
Ruby Stain. . . . 60.00
Syrup . . . 80.00
Ruby Stain. . . . 85.00
Toothpick Hldr. . . . 45.00
Ruby Stain. . . . 65.00
Water Bottle. . . . 35.00
Ruby Stain. . . . 60.00
Wine . . . 20.00
Ruby Stain. . . . 40.00

ROYAL IVY
Berry Bowl, Sm. . . . 30.00
Rubina. . . . 40.00
Berry Bowl, Lg. . . . 65.00
Rubina. . . . 85.00
Butter. . . . 125.00
Rubina. . . . 225.00
Creamer or Spooner. . . . 60.00
Rubina. . . . 165.00
Jam Jar, Covered . . . 100.00
Lamp, Rubina . . . 375.00
Pickle Caster . . . 110.00
Rubina. . . . 350.00
Pitcher . . . 175.00
Rubina. . . . 300.00
Tumbler . . . 40.00
Rubina. . . . 85.00
Shakers, ea. . . . 35.00
Rubina. . . . 75.00
Sugar . . . 100.00
Rubina. . . . 175.00
Syrup . . . 110.00
Rubina. . . . 250.00

Toothpick Hldr. . . . 60.00
Rubina. . . . 125.00

ROYAL JUBILEE
Basket, Ftd., Vaseline . . . 95.00
Green/Blue. . . . 75.00

ROYAL KING
Shot Glass . . . 40.00
Ruby Stain. . . . 50.00

ROYAL LADY (ROYAL)
Bread Plate, Crying Baby . . . 70.00
Butter. . . . 165.00
Celery Vase . . . 85.00
Cheese Dish. . . . 175.00
Compote, Covered, 9". . . . 175.00
Creamer or Spooner. . . . 100.00
Dish, Oval w/Lid . . . 125.00
Salt, Master . . . 35.00
Sugar . . . 110.00
Tray . . . 150.00

ROYAL LILY
Toothpick Hldr. . . . 40.00

RUBY DIAMOND
Butter. . . . 75.00
Creamer or Spooner. . . . 30.00
Goblet . . . 50.00
Pitcher . . . 125.00
Tumbler . . . 20.00
Sauce . . . 10.00
Sugar . . . 40.00
Toothpick Hldr. . . . 50.00
Wine . . . 15.00

RUBY THUMBPRINT (KING'S CROWN)
Banana Bowl, Ftd. . . . 75.00
Bowl, 2 Styles . . . 40.00
Butter. . . . 65.00
Cake Stand, 2 Sizes . . . 70.00
Caster Set, Complete . . . 155.00
Celery Vase . . . 30.00
Champagne . . . 20.00
Claret . . . 25.00
Compote, Covered, 8" – 12" . . . 75.00
Compote, Open, 5¼" – 8¼". . . . 55.00
Cordial. . . . 40.00
Creamer, Reg.. . . . 40.00
Creamer, Ind.. . . . 20.00
Cup & Saucer. . . . 60.00
Goblet . . . 30.00
Honey Dish . . . 90.00
Milk Pitcher. . . . 70.00
Mustard Jar w/Lid . . . 35.00
Oil Lamp . . . 150.00
Olive Dish . . . 20.00
Preserve Dish. . . . 30.00
Pickle Dish. . . . 15.00
Pitcher, 2 Styles. . . . 125.00
Tumbler . . . 25.00
Plate, 7" . . . 15.00
Punch Bowl . . . 250.00
Punch Cup . . . 10.00
Punch Bowl Underplate. . . . 75.00
Salt, Master . . . 20.00
Salt, Ind. . . . 10.00
Shakers, ea. . . . 30.00
Sauce . . . 10.00
Spooner . . . 35.00
Sugar, Reg. . . . 45.00
Sugar, Ind. . . . 30.00
Toothpick Hldr. . . . 25.00
Wine . . . 20.00

RUFFLED EYE
Pitcher . . . 90.00
Amber . . . 125.00
Vaseline. . . . 300.00
Green/Blue. . . . 215.00
Chocolate . . . 350.00

SADDLE
Match Hldr. . . . 45.00
Amber . . . 80.00

SAILING SHIP
Plate, 8" . . . 10.00

SAINT BERNARD
Berry Bowl, Sm. . . . 15.00

Berry Bowl, Lg. 45.00
Butter 65.00
Cake Stand 35.00
Celery Vase 15.00
Compote, Covered, High, 7" – 8" . 45.00 – 65.00
Compote, Covered, Low 50.00
Compote, Open, Low, 6" – 8" . . . . 30.00 – 55.00
Creamer or Spooner 25.00
Cruet 45.00
Goblet 35.00
Jam Jar 25.00
Pickle Dish 20.00
Pitcher 85.00
Tumbler 20.00
Sauce 10.00
Shakers, ea. 20.00
Sugar 30.00

SALAMANDER
Vase, 10", Rare 350.00
Amber 375.00
Green/Blue 400.00

SALT LAKE TEMPLE PLATTER
See Egyptian

SANDWICH CURTAIN TIEBACKS
Curtain Tiebacks, ea. 30.00
Amber 50.00
Vaseline 70.00
Green/Blue 60.00
Pink 50.00

SANDWICH DOLPHIN CANDLESTICKS
Candlesticks, ea. 85.00
Vaseline 150.00

SANDWICH SCROLL SALT DIP
Salt Dip 25.00
Amber 35.00
Vaseline 50.00
Green/Blue 40.00

SANDWICH STAR (All pieces very rare)
Butter 900.00
Vaseline 1650.00*
Amethyst 1300.00*
Champagne 250.00
Vaseline 400.00
Amethyst 325.00
Compote, Dolphin Base 400.00
Vaseline 650.00
Amethyst 425.00
Cordial 275.00
Vaseline 375.00
Amethyst 450.00
Creamer or Spooner 175.00
Vaseline 250.00
Amethyst 375.00
Decanter 300.00
Vaseline 425.00
Amethyst 550.00
Goblet, Very Rare 1500.00
Vaseline 2000.00*
Amethyst 1200.00*
Spillholder, Stemmed 225.00
Vaseline 300.00
Amethyst 375.00
Sugar 250.00
Vaseline 325.00
Amethyst 525.00
Wine 350.00
Vaseline 425.00
Amethyst 450.00

SANTA IN CHIMNEY
Novelty Container, Sq. 75.00

SAWTOOTH
Bowl, Covered, 6" and 7" 50.00
Bowl, Open, 6" – 10" . . . . . . 15.00 – 60.00
Butter 80.00
Cake Stand, 9" – 14" . . . . . . 40.00 – 85.00
Carafe 55.00
Celery Vase 55.00
Champagne 60.00
Child's Table Set 125.00
Compote, Covered, 6" – 10" . . . . 35.00 – 90.00
Compote, Open, 6" – 10" . . . . . . 20.00 – 50.00
Cordial 45.00
Creamer or Spooner 75.00
Cruet 110.00
Decanter 70.00
Dish, Oval, 5" – 7" 35.00
Egg Cup 50.00
Fruit Bowl, Rnd., 6" – 11" . . . . . . 30.00 – 65.00
Gas Shade 60.00
Goblet 60.00
Honey Dish 30.00
Milk Pitcher 100.00
Oil Lamp, 4 Sizes . . . . . . 100.00 – 165.00
Plate, 6½" 50.00
Pomade Jar 55.00
Pitcher 165.00
Tumbler 55.00
Salt, Master, Covered or Open 65.00
Sauce 25.00
Spillholder 20.00
Water Tray, 10" – 14" 75.00
Wine 35.00

SAWTOOTHED HONEYCOMB
Bonbon 20.00
Ruby Stain 35.00
Bowl 15.00
Ruby Stain 40.00
Butter 50.00
Ruby Stain 125.00
Celery Vase 30.00
Ruby Stain 70.00
Compote, Open 35.00
Ruby Stain 55.00
Creamer or Spooner 25.00
Ruby Stain 45.00
Cruet 45.00
Ruby Stain 135.00
Goblet 30.00
Ruby Stain 65.00
Nappy 30.00
Ruby Stain 40.00
Nappy, Adv., Rare 125.00
Pitcher 65.00
Ruby Stain 165.00
Tumbler 20.00
Ruby Stain 30.00
Punch Bowl w/base 140.00
Ruby Stain 235.00
Punch Cup 15.00
Ruby Stain 30.00
Sauce 10.00
Ruby Stain 25.00
Shakers, Ea. 25.00
Ruby Stain 50.00
Sugar 40.00
Ruby Stain 65.00
Toothpick Hldr. 30.00
Ruby Stain 135.00

SCALLOPED FLANGE
Tumbler, 5 Styles . . . . . . 15.00 – 40.00

SCALLOPED SIX-POINT
Berry Bowl, Sm. 20.00
Berry Bowl, Lg. 35.00
Butter 65.00
Carafe 45.00
Creamer or Spooner 25.00
Cup 15.00
Pitcher 70.00
Tumbler 20.00
Shakers, ea. 25.00
Sugar 30.00
Toothpick Hldr. 40.00
Wine 20.00

SCALLOPED SKIRT
Berry Bowl, Lg. 30.00
Green/Blue 45.00
Amethyst 50.00
Berry Bowl, Sm. 10.00
Green/Blue 20.00
Amethyst 35.00
Butter 60.00
Green/Blue 80.00
Amethyst 95.00
Creamer or Spooner 25.00
Green/Blue 40.00
Amethyst 50.00
Jelly Compote 35.00
Green/Blue 50.00
Amethyst 65.00
Novelty Bowls . . . . . . 15.00 – 35.00
Green/Blue . . . . . . 25.00 – 60.00
Amethyst . . . . . . 30.00 – 70.00
Pickle Dish 15.00
Green/Blue 25.00
Amethyst 35.00
Sugar 30.00
Green/Blue 45.00
Amethyst 55.00
Toothpick Hldr. 40.00
Green/Blue 55.00
Amethyst 65.00
Vase 35.00
Green/Blue 45.00
Amethyst 55.00

SCALLOPED SWIRL
Berry Bowl 25.00
Green/Blue 45.00
Ruby Stain 40.00
Butter 55.00
Green/Blue 90.00
Ruby Stain 80.00
Cake Plate 35.00
Green/Blue 50.00
Ruby Stain 40.00
Celery Vase 25.00
Green/Blue 40.00
Ruby Stain 30.00
Compote 30.00
Green/Blue 45.00
Ruby Stain 40.00
Creamer or Spooner 25.00
Green/Blue 40.00
Ruby Stain 35.00
Goblet 40.00
Green/Blue 60.00
Ruby Stain 50.00
Plate 25.00
Green/Blue 40.00
Ruby Stain 35.00
Pitcher 75.00
Green/Blue 165.00
Ruby Stain 135.00
Tumbler 15.00
Green/Blue 40.00
Ruby Stain 30.00
Sugar 40.00
Green/Blue 65.00
Ruby Stain 60.00
Toothpick Hldr. 30.00
Green/Blue 60.00
Ruby Stain 55.00
Vase 25.00
Green/Blue 50.00
Ruby Stain 40.00

SCALLOPED SWIRL (YORK HERRINGBONE)
Bowl 20.00
Ruby Stain 30.00
Butter 55.00
Ruby Stain 75.00
Cake Plate 35.00
Ruby Stain 45.00
Compote 40.00
Ruby Stain 50.00
Creamer or Spooner 25.00
Ruby Stain 35.00
Pitcher 80.00
Ruby Stain 120.00
Tumbler 15.00
Ruby Stain 30.00
Toothpick Hldr., Ruby Stain 65.00
Shakers, ea. 20.00
Ruby Stain 45.00
Sugar 35.00
Ruby Stain 55.00
Wine 25.00
Ruby Stain 35.00

SCHEREZADE
Bowls, Various . . . . 20.00 – 35.00
SCHRAFFT'S CHOCOLATE
Advertising Plate 85.00
SCROLL WITH CANE BAND
Butter 45.00
Celery Vase 15.00
Compotes, Various . . . . 20.00 – 45.00
Creamer or Spooner 15.00
Cruet 45.00
Pitcher 75.00
Tumbler 15.00
Shakers, ea. 15.00
Sugar 20.00
Toothpick Hldr. 30.00
SCROLL WITH FLOWERS
Butter 55.00
Cake Plate, Hndl. 40.00
Cordial 25.00
Creamer or Spooner 20.00
Egg Cup, Hndl. 25.00
Goblet 50.00
Mustard, Covered 35.00
Plate 40.00
Pitcher 70.00
Tumbler 20.00
Relish 25.00
Salt Dip, Hndl. 25.00
Sugar 30.00
Wine 25.00
SEDAN
Berry Bowl, Lg. 35.00
Berry Bowl, Sm. 10.00
Butter 70.00
Celery Tray 20.00
Celery Vase 25.00
Compote, Covered 55.00
Compote, Open 35.00
Creamer or Spooner 25.00
Goblet 30.00
Mug 40.00
Pickle Tray w/Double Hndl. 30.00
Pitcher 85.00
Relish Tray 20.00
Shaker 40.00
Sugar 30.00
Tumbler 10.00
Wine 10.00
SENSBUSH INK WELL
One Shape 35.00
SEQUOIA
Berry Bowl, Sm. 10.00
Berry Bowl, Lg. 35.00
Bowl, Canoe Shape 45.00
Brandy Tray 20.00
Butter 60.00
Butter Pat 10.00
Celery Boat 30.00
Celery Vase 20.00
Cheese Plate 25.00
Compote, Covered or Open 55.00
Cordial 10.00
Creamer or Spooner 20.00
Cruet 50.00
Decanter 45.00
Finger Bowl 20.00
Goblet 30.00
Nappy 20.00
Pickle Boat 20.00
Pickle Jar 35.00
Plate 20.00
Pitcher 85.00
Tumbler 20.00
Relish 15.00
Salt Dip 10.00
Shakers, ea. 20.00
Sugar 30.00
Syrup 45.00
Tray 35.00
Wine 10.00
SERRATED FLUTE
Vase, Scarce 25.00
SERRATED RIB
Butter 45.00
Creamer or Spooner 15.00
Pitcher 70.00
Tumbler 10.00
Shakers, ea. 10.00
Sugar 20.00
SEXTEC
Berry Bowl, Sm. 15.00
Berry Bowl, Lg. 40.00
Berry Creamer 25.00
Butter 70.00
Celery Tray 25.00
Compote, Tall 45.00
Creamer or Spooner 20.00
Cruet 50.00
Goblet 35.00
Nut Bowl, Hndl. 25.00
Orange Bowl 45.00
Pickle Jar 35.00
Plate 25.00
Punch Bowl 85.00
Punch Cup 10.00
Pitcher 65.00
Tumbler 15.00
Relish Dish 15.00
Shakers, ea. 20.00
Sugar 30.00
Syrup 45.00
Wine 10.00
SHASTA DAISY
Bowls, Various, Green/Blue . . . . . 40.00 – 95.00
Amethyst . . . . 35.00 – 90.00
Compotes, Various, Green/Blue 60.00 – 125.00
Amethyst . . . . 50.00 – 110.00
Nappy, Green/Blue 60.00
Amethyst 50.00
Plate, Lg. or Sm., Green/Blue . . . 65.00 – 95.00
Amethyst . . . . 55.00 – 85.00
SHEAF AND BLOCK
Berry Bowl, Sm. 20.00
Berry Bowl, Lg. 45.00
Butter 65.00
Celery Vase 20.00
Creamer or Spooner 25.00
Goblet 50.00
Pickle Dish 25.00
Pitcher 90.00
Tumbler 20.00
Shakers, ea. 25.00
Sugar 30.00
Wine 15.00
SHEAF AND DIAMOND
Bowl 30.00
Butter 70.00
Cake Plate 45.00
Creamer or Spooner 30.00
Pickle Dish 25.00
Sugar 35.00
SHEEP MUG
Child's Mug 75.00
SHELL AND JEWEL
Banana Stand 60.00
Bowl 25.00
Amber 45.00
Butter 65.00
Cake Stand 50.00
Compote 45.00
Creamer or Spooner 25.00
Pitcher 75.00
Amber 165.00
Green/Blue 165.00
Tumbler 25.00
Amber 45.00
Green/Blue 45.00
Shakers, ea. 30.00
Sugar 35.00
SHELL AND TASSEL
Berry Bowl, Sm. 15.00
Berry Bowl, Lg. 45.00
Vaseline 125.00
Bowl, Covered, 3 Sizes . . . . 25.00 – 65.00
Butter 85.00
Cake Stand, 7 Sizes . . . . 25.00 – 80.00
Celery Vase 20.00
Compote, Covered, 8 Sizes . . . . 30.00 – 100.00
Creamer or Spooner 25.00
Dish, Rect., 4 Sizes . . . . 20.00 – 45.00
Vaseline 85.00
Goblet 60.00
Ice Cream Tray 25.00
Oyster Plate 30.00
Pickle Jar 40.00
Pitcher, 2 Styles . . . . 115.00 – 165.00
Tumbler, Soda, 3 Sizes . . . . 25.00 – 45.00
Plate 30.00
Plate, Fruit 40.00
Plate, Tart 25.00
Platter, Sq. or Oblong 45.00
Sauce, Flat of Ftd., 3 Sizes . . . . . 10.00 – 20.00
Shakers, ea., Rare 115.00
Sugar 35.00
Vase 50.00
SHELTON STAR
Butter 50.00
Creamer or Spooner 15.00
Pitcher 70.00
Tumbler 15.00
Shakers, ea. 20.00
Sugar 25.00
SHERATON
Berry Bowl, Sm. 10.00
Amber 15.00
Green/Blue 15.00
Berry Bowl, Lg. 30.00
Amber 40.00
Green/Blue 40.00
Bread Plate, Oval 25.00
Amber 40.00
Green/Blue 40.00
Butter 45.00
Amber 65.00
Green/Blue 125.00
Creamer or Spooner 20.00
Amber 35.00
Vaseline 125.00
Green/Blue 75.00
Dish, 8 Sided or Rnd. 30.00
Amber 40.00
Green/Blue 40.00
Goblet 40.00
Amber 55.00
Green/Blue 55.00
Milk Pitcher 55.00
Amber 75.00
Green/Blue 75.00
Platter, Oblong, 8 Panels 35.00
Amber 45.00
Green/Blue 45.00
Pitcher 65.00
Amber 95.00
Green/Blue 145.00
Tumbler 20.00
Amber 25.00
Green/Blue 25.00
Relish Tray 15.00
Amber 20.00
Green/Blue 20.00
Sauce 10.00
Amber 15.00
Green/Blue 15.00
Sugar 30.00
Amber 55.00
Green/Blue 55.00
Wine 15.00
Amber 25.00
Green/Blue 25.00
SHIELD
Bowl, Sauce, 5" 10.00
Butter 60.00
Celery Vase 25.00
Creamer or Spooner 25.00
Flower Vase, 3 Sizes . . . . 20.00 – 35.00
Goblet 25.00

Knife Rest . . . 15.00
Pitcher . . . 85.00
Sugar . . . 30.00
Tumbler . . . 15.00

SHIMMERING STAR
Berry Bowl, Lg. . . . 30.00
Berry Bowl, Sm. . . . 10.00
Butter . . . 50.00
Creamer or Spooner . . . 25.00
Pitcher . . . 65.00
Tumbler . . . 10.00
Shakers, Ea. . . . 20.00
Sugar . . . 30.00

SHRINE
Berry Bowl, Lg. . . . 40.00
Berry Bowl, Sm. . . . 15.00
Butter . . . 60.00
Compote, Jelly . . . 35.00
Creamer, Spooner or Sugar . . . 25.00
Pickle Tray . . . 35.00
Pitcher . . . 80.00
Rose Bowl, Scarce . . . 65.00
Tumbler . . . 20.00
Sauces . . . 20.00
Shaker, 2 Sizes, ea. . . . 30.00

SHUTTLE
Berry Bowl, Sm. . . . 15.00
Berry Bowl, Lg. . . . 45.00
Butter . . . 55.00
Celery Vase . . . 20.00
Cordial . . . 15.00
Creamer or Spooner . . . 20.00
Cruet . . . 45.00
Custard Cup . . . 10.00
Goblet . . . 35.00
Mug . . . 20.00
Pitcher . . . 70.00
Tumbler . . . 15.00
Sauce . . . 10.00
Shakers, ea. . . . 15.00
Sugar . . . 25.00
Wine . . . 10.00

SIETZ BATH
Novelty Bowl . . . 80.00
Amber . . . 200.00
Vaseline . . . 325.00
Green/Blue . . . 285.00

SINGING BIRDS
Berry Bowl, Sm. . . . 15.00
Berry Bowl, Lg. . . . 55.00
Butter . . . 95.00
Creamer or Spooner . . . 30.00
Goblet, Rare . . . 550.00
Mug . . . 100.00
Pitcher . . . 250.00
Tumbler . . . 50.00
Sherbet . . . 45.00
Sugar . . . 50.00

SIX PANEL FINECUT
Bowls, Various . . . 10.00 – 45.00
Butter . . . 65.00
Compote . . . 35.00
Creamer or Spooner . . . 20.00
Cruet . . . 45.00
Goblet . . . 35.00
Pitcher . . . 75.00
Tumbler . . . 15.00
Sugar . . . 30.00
Sugar Shaker . . . 40.00
Syrup . . . 65.00

SIX-SIDED CANDLESTICKS
One Shape, ea. . . . 20.00

SKILTON (EARLY OREGON)
Bowls, 5" – 8", 2 Styles . . . 20.00 – 40.00
Ruby Stain . . . 40.00 – 55.00
Butter . . . 45.00
Ruby Stain . . . 125.00
Cake Stand . . . 50.00
Celery Vase . . . 40.00
Ruby Stain . . . 85.00
Compote, Covered . . . 55.00
Compote, Open . . . 30.00
Ruby Stain . . . 45.00
Creamer or Spooner . . . 35.00
Ruby Stain . . . 60.00
Dish, Oblong, 3 Sizes . . . 10.00 – 20.00
Goblet . . . 40.00
Ruby Stain . . . 60.00
Milk Pitcher . . . 50.00
Ruby Stain . . . 110.00
Pickle Tray . . . 20.00
Pitcher, 2 Styles . . . 65.00 – 70.00
Ruby Stain . . . 145.00
Tumbler . . . 25.00
Ruby Stain . . . 45.00
Shakers, ea. . . . 25.00
Ruby Stain . . . 40.00
Sauce . . . 10.00
Ruby Stain . . . 25.00
Sugar . . . 45.00
Ruby Stain . . . 75.00
Tray . . . 40.00
Wine . . . 35.00
Ruby Stain . . . 50.00

SLEWED HORSESHOE
Berry Bowl, Lg. . . . 40.00
Berry Bowl, Sm. . . . 20.00
Butter . . . 65.00
Compote . . . 45.00
Creamer, Spooner, or Sugar . . . 25.00
Cup . . . 15.00
Goblet . . . 35.00
Ice Cream Tray . . . 25.00
Novelty Bowl . . . 40.00
Pickle Dish . . . 25.00
Punch Bowl . . . 165.00
Punch Cup . . . 15.00
Under Plate, 32" . . . 85.00
Wine . . . 25.00

SLICK WILLIE
Vase . . . 25.00

SNAIL
Banana Stand . . . 160.00
Ruby Stain . . . 250.00
Butter . . . 80.00
Ruby Stain . . . 175.00
Bowl, Covered, 7" – 8" . . . 35.00 – 60.00
Ruby Stain . . . 50.00 – 95.00
Bowl, Open, 7" – 10" . . . 40.00
Ruby Stain . . . 40.00 – 75.00
Cake Basket, 10" . . . 100.00
Cake Stand, 9" – 10" . . . 90.00
Celery Tray . . . 35.00
Celery Vase . . . 40.00
Ruby Stain . . . 90.00
Cheese Dish, Covered . . . 110.00
Compote, Covered 6" – 10" . . . 45.00 – 120.00
Ruby Stain . . . 100.00 – 165.00
Compote, Open, 6" – 10" . . . 30.00 – 75.00
Creamer, 2 Sizes . . . 60.00
Ruby Stain . . . 80.00
Cruet . . . 125.00
Ruby Stain . . . 265.00
Custard Cup . . . 35.00
Finger Bowl . . . 55.00
Goblet . . . 75.00
Ruby Stain . . . 100.00
Jam Jar . . . 45.00
Ruby Stain . . . 135.00
Jug, 4 Sizes . . . 35.00 – 85.00
Ruby Stain . . . 45.00 – 110.00
Milk Pitcher . . . 110.00
Ruby Stain . . . 200.00
Plate, 5" – 7" . . . 35.00
Pitcher, 2 Styles . . . 125.00 – 150.00
Ruby Stain . . . 250.00
Tumbler . . . 45.00
Ruby Stain . . . 65.00
Relish . . . 25.00
Rose Bowl, 3" – 7" . . . 50.00
Salt, Ind. . . . 25.00
Ruby Stain . . . 45.00
Salt, Master . . . 35.00
Ruby Stain . . . 80.00
Sauce, Flat or Ftd. . . . 20.00
Ruby Stain . . . 40.00
Shakers, ea. . . . 65.00
Ruby Stain . . . 100.00
Spooner . . . 40.00
Ruby Stain . . . 70.00
Sugar . . . 55.00
Ruby Stain . . . 100.00
Sugar Shaker . . . 65.00
Ruby Stain . . . 175.00
Syrup . . . 135.00
Ruby Stain . . . 250.00
Vase . . . 50.00
Ruby Stain . . . 100.00

SNAKE DRAPE
Goblet . . . 85.00

SNOW FANCY
Berry Bowl, Sm. . . . 20.00
Berry Bowl, Lg. . . . 45.00
Butter . . . 75.00
Creamer or Spooner . . . 20.00
Rose Bowl, 7½" . . . 45.00
Sugar . . . 30.00

SNOW FLAKE
Bread Plate . . . 15.00
Butter . . . 65.00
Celery Tray . . . 25.00
Celery Vase . . . 30.00
Condiment Set, Complete . . . 80.00
Compote, Sm. . . . 30.00
Compote, Med, 2 Sizes . . . 45.00
Compote, Lg, 2 Sizes . . . 55.00
Creamer or Spooner . . . 25.00
Nappy, Sm. 2 Sizes . . . 25.00
Nappy, Med, 2 Sizes . . . 35.00
Oil Bottle . . . 55.00
Pickle Dish . . . 25.00
Pitcher . . . 110.00
Tumbler . . . 20.00
Toothpick Hldr. . . . 45.00
Shakers, ea. . . . 20.00
Sugar . . . 35.00
Vase, 6" – 8¼" . . . 35.00

SNOWFLAKE AND SUNBURST
Milk Pitcher . . . 45.00
Pitcher . . . 75.00
Tumbler, Scarce . . . 35.00
Vase . . . 40.00

SNOW STAR
Bowls, Various . . . 10.00 – 30.00
Butter . . . 50.00
Celery Vase . . . 20.00
Creamer or Spooner . . . 20.00
Sugar . . . 30.00

SOLAR
Bowls, Sm. . . . 20.00
Bowls, Lg. . . . 45.00
Cake Stand, 2 Types . . . 65.00
Celery Tray . . . 40.00
Celery Vase . . . 35.00
Compote w/Lid . . . 75.00
Cruet . . . 85.00
Custard Cup . . . 15.00
Goblet . . . 45.00
Jelly Compote . . . 30.00
Milk Pitcher . . . 55.00
Pickle Dish . . . 25.00
Pitcher . . . 125.00
Tumbler . . . 20.00
Relish . . . 25.00
Shakers, ea. . . . 25.00
Syrup . . . 80.00
Water Tray . . . 40.00
Vase . . . 50.00
Wine . . . 25.00

SOWERBY BERRY BOAT
Handled Boat Shape Bowl . . . 70.00
Vaseline . . . 125.00

SOWERBY HOBNAIL
Handled Basket . . . 65.00
Vaseline . . . 110.00

SPANGLED
- Bowl, Finger, Mica Plated 250.00
- Creamer, Mica Plated 265.00
- Globes, Mica Plated. 300.00
- Pitcher, 5 Various Shapes & Sizes, Mica Plated . . . . 265.00 – 600.00
- Salt, Mica Plated 225.00
- Tumbler, Mica Plated. 250.00
- Vase, 3 Various, Mica Plated . 250.00 – 425.00

SPANISH AMERICAN
- Dewey Pitcher w/Cannonballs 85.00
- Tumbler 45.00
- Dewey Pitcher w/Bullets . . . . . 150.00 – 190.00
  - Green/Blue. 300.00
- Tumbler 100.00

SPANISH MOSS
- Hatpin Hldr.. . . . . 50.00

SPARKLING GEM
- Butter. 65.00
- Creamer or Spooner. 20.00
- Sugar 35.00

SPECIALTY'S #100
- Butter. 45.00
  - Ruby Stain. 75.00
- Creamer or Spooner. 25.00
  - Ruby Stain. 35.00
- Goblet 35.00
  - Ruby Stain. 55.00
- Sugar 40.00
  - Ruby Stain. 45.00
- Toothpick Hldr. 45.00
  - Ruby Stain. 60.00

SPILLS (Various Makers)
- Spills, Various Shapes and Sizes. 20.00 – 65.00
  - Vaseline . . . . 40.00 – 85.00

SPIRAL DIAMOND POINT
- Vase or Jar 45.00

SPIRALLED IVY
- Butter. 50.00
- Creamer or Spooner. 15.00
- Pitcher 65.00
- Tumbler 15.00
- Sauce 10.00
- Sugar 20.00

SPIREA BAND
- Butter. 40.00
  - Amber 50.00
  - Vaseline. 95.00
  - Green/Blue. 65.00
- Cake Stand. 45.00
  - Amber 55.00
  - Vaseline. 95.00
  - Green/Blue. 70.00
- Celery Vase 30.00
  - Amber 35.00
  - Vaseline. 65.00
  - Green/Blue. 40.00
- Compote, Covered 55.00
  - Amber 65.00
  - Vaseline. 125.00
  - Green/Blue. 75.00
- Compote, Open 40.00
  - Amber 45.00
  - Vaseline. 75.00
  - Green/Blue. 55.00
- Creamer or Spooner. 25.00
  - Amber 40.00
  - Vaseline. 50.00
  - Green/Blue. 40.00
- Goblet 30.00
  - Amber 40.00
  - Vaseline. 50.00
  - Green/Blue. 40.00
- Platter, Oval. 35.00
  - Amber 45.00
  - Vaseline. 45.00
  - Green/Blue. 60.00
- Pitcher 70.00
  - Amber 85.00
  - Vaseline. 150.00
  - Green/Blue. 110.00
- Tumbler 20.00
  - Amber 25.00
  - Vaseline. 40.00
  - Green/Blue. 30.00
- Shakers, ea. 30.00
  - Amber 40.00
  - Vaseline. 45.00
  - Green/Blue. 40.00
- Sugar 35.00
  - Amber 45.00
  - Vaseline. 65.00
  - Green/Blue. 40.00
- Sugar Shaker 45.00
  - Amber 60.00
  - Vaseline. 75.00
  - Green/Blue. 70.00
- Wine 15.00
  - Amber 20.00
  - Vaseline. 40.00
  - Green/Blue. 30.00

SPITTOON
- Spittoon Shape. 50.00
  - Vaseline. 95.00
  - Green/Blue. 70.00

SPRIG (AKA: Royal)
- Berry Bowl 25.00
- Butter. 60.00
- Cake Stand. 40.00
- Celery Vase 30.00
- Compote. 35.00
- Creamer, Spooner, or Sugar. 20.00
- Pitcher 70.00
- Tumbler 15.00
- Sauce 15.00
- Wine, Scarce 40.00

SQUARE HANDLED HOBNAIL
- Child's Mug 40.00

SQUAT PINEAPPLE
- Berry Bowl, Sm. 15.00
  - Green/Blue. 20.00
- Berry Bowl Lg. 30.00
  - Green/Blue. 45.00
- Butter. 55.00
  - Green/Blue. 85.00
- Creamer or Spooner. 25.00
  - Green/Blue. 40.00
- Cruet 65.00
  - Green/Blue. 90.00
- Pickle Dish. 20.00
  - Green/Blue. 30.00
- Pitcher 75.00
  - Green/Blue. 100.00
- Tumbler 15.00
  - Green/Blue. 25.00
- Shakers, ea. 20.00
  - Green/Blue. 30.00
- Sugar 25.00
  - Green/Blue. 35.00

SQUIRREL
- Mug 50.00
  - Green/Blue. 130.00
  - Opaque Blue 175.00

SQUIRREL AND STUMP
- Match Hldr. 85.00

SQUIRREL IN BOWER
- Butter. 300.00
- Creamer or Spooner. 50.00
- Goblet, Rare. 375.00
- Oil Lamp 475.00
- Pitcher 400.00
  - Chocolate 900.00
- Sauce 50.00
- Sugar 75.00

SQUIRREL WITH NUT
- Pitcher, Scarce 350.00

S-REPEAT
- Butter. 85.00
- Celery Vase 25.00
- Compotes . . . . 25.00 – 50.00
- Creamer or Spooner. 35.00
- Cruet 70.00
- Decanter 100.00
- Jelly Compote. 35.00
- Pitcher 175.00
- Tumbler 35.00
- Punch Bowl 200.00
- Punch Cup 15.00
- Shakers, ea., Scarce 40.00
- Sugar 45.00
- Toothpick Hldr. 45.00
- Tray 50.00
- Wine 25.00

STAR AND CRESCENT
- Berry Bowl, Sm. 10.00
- Berry Bowl, Lg.. 35.00
- Butter. 50.00
- Creamer or Spooner. 20.00
- Cruet 55.00
- Pickle Dish. 15.00
- Pitcher 65.00
- Tumbler 10.00
- Shakers, ea. 15.00
- Sugar 25.00

STAR AND DIAMOND
- Bottle w/Stopper, 6", Vaseline 100.00

STAR AND FILE
- Bowl, 7" 20.00
- Bowl, Square 20.00
- Butter. 65.00
- Celery Vase 35.00
- Compote. 40.00
- Cordial 25.00
- Creamer or Sugar. 25.00
- Custard Cup. 15.00
- Decanter 55.00
- Ice Cream, Stemmed 20.00
- Juice Tumbler. 15.00
- Milk Pitcher. 75.00
- Pitcher 95.00
- Tumbler 20.00
- Relish, Hndl. 25.00
- Rose Bowl 50.00
- Saucer 20.00
- Wine 25.00

STAR AND IVY
- Cup 10.00
  - Amber 15.00
  - Green/Blue. 20.00
- Plate, Lg. 25.00
  - Amber 30.00
  - Green/Blue. 40.00
- Saucer 10.00
  - Amber 15.00
  - Green/Blue. 20.00

STAR AND NOTCHED RIB
- Butter. 50.00
- Creamer or Spooner. 20.00
- Cruet 55.00
- Pitcher 75.00
- Tumbler 20.00
- Shakers, ea. 15.00
- Sugar 25.00

STAR AND PUNTY
- Cologne Bottle 60.00
- Creamer 25.00
- Lamp 95.00
- Pitcher 85.00
- Sugar 35.00

STAR AND RIB
- Butter 45.00
- Creamer or Spooner. 20.00
- Pitcher 80.00
- Tumbler 20.00
- Shakers, ea. 15.00
- Sugar 25.00

STAR AND THUMBPRINT (All pieces rare)
- Bowls, Various . . . . 35.00 – 65.00
- Butter. 85.00
- Creamer or Spooner. 35.00
- Lamp 165.00
- Pitcher 125.00
- Tumbler 30.00
- Spill Hldr. 40.00
- Sugar 45.00

STAR BAND
Berry Bowl, Lg. 30.00
Berry Bowl, Sm. 10.00
Butter 60.00
Celery Vase 25.00
Creamer, Spooner, or Sugar 20.00
Pitcher 70.00
Tumbler 20.00

STARFLAKE AND FAN
Bowl, 8½" 50.00
Compote 65.00

STAR GLOW
Berry Bowl, Sm. 10.00
Berry Bowl, Lg. 35.00
Butter 45.00
Cake Stand 30.00
Caster Set 65.00
Celery Vase 20.00
Compote 30.00
Creamer or Spooner 20.00
Cruet 55.00
Pickle Dish 15.00
Plate 25.00
Pitcher 75.00
Tumbler 20.00
Sugar 25.00
Syrup 50.00
Wine 15.00
Vase 25.00

STAR IN BULL'S-EYE
Berry Bowl, Sm. 10.00
Berry Bowl, Lg. 35.00
Butter 50.00
Cake Stand 30.00
Celery Vase 25.00
Compote, Covered 45.00
Compote, Open, Low 25.00
Creamer or Spooner 20.00
Cruet 45.00
Dish 15.00
Goblet 35.00
Nappy w/Advertising 40.00
Pitcher 65.00
Tumbler 10.00
Sugar 25.00
Toothpick Hldr., Double or Single . . . . . 35.00 – 55.00
Wine 10.00

STAR MEDALLION
Bowls, Rnd. or Sq. . . . . . 10.00 – 30.00
Butter 65.00
Celery Vase, Hndl. 20.00
Claret 15.00
Compote 35.00
Creamer or Spooner 20.00
Custard Cup 15.00
Lemonade Set 125.00
Milk Pitcher 65.00
Plate, 2 Sizes . . . . . 20.00 – 30.00
Pitcher 85.00
Tumbler 15.00
Rose Bowl, 2 Sizes . . . . . 20.00 – 35.00
Shakers, ea. 20.00
Wine 15.00

STAR OF DAVID
Berry Bowl, Sm. 15.00
Berry Bowl, Lg. 40.00
Butter 60.00
Compote 35.00
Creamer or Spooner 20.00
Cruet 45.00
Goblet 35.00
Hair Receiver 30.00
Pickle Tray 20.00
Pitcher 85.00
Tumbler 20.00
Sugar 25.00

STARRED HORSESHOE
Tumbler 25.00

STARRED HORSESHOE BAND
Tumbler 30.00

STARRED LOOP
Bowl 30.00
Cup 15.00
Pickle Tray 25.00
Pitcher 60.00
Tumbler 15.00
Shakers, ea. 20.00
Wine 20.00

STARRED SCROLL
Bowl 35.00
Butter 65.00
Celery Vase 20.00
Creamer or Spooner 30.00
Cruet 45.00
Goblet 35.00
Pitcher 85.00
Tumbler 20.00
Rose Bowl 30.00
Shakers, ea. 15.00
Sugar 35.00
Syrup 65.00

STAR ROSETTED
Bowl, 7" – 9", 2 Styles . . . . . 15.00 – 25.00
Amber . . . . . 20.00 – 30.00
Vaseline . . . . . 25.00 – 40.00
Green/Blue . . . . . 35.00 – 60.00
Bread Plate 35.00
Amber 40.00
Vaseline 45.00
Green/Blue 55.00
Butter 45.00
Amber 55.00
Vaseline 75.00
Green/Blue 85.00
Compote, Covered . . . . . 50.00 – 70.00
Amber . . . . . 55.00 – 80.00
Vaseline . . . . . 65.00 – 85.00
Green/Blue . . . . . 75.00 – 95.00
Compote, Open . . . . . 30.00 – 45.00
Amber . . . . . 35.00 – 50.00
Vaseline . . . . . 40.00 – 55.00
Green/Blue . . . . . 45.00 – 65.00
Creamer or Spooner 35.00
Amber 40.00
Vaseline 45.00
Green/Blue 50.00
Goblet 40.00
Amber 50.00
Vaseline 60.00
Green/Blue 65.00
Pickle Dish 15.00
Amber 20.00
Vaseline 25.00
Green/Blue 30.00
Pitcher 85.00
Amber 100.00
Vaseline 160.00
Green/Blue 175.00
Plate 25.00
Amber 30.00
Vaseline 35.00
Green/Blue 40.00
Relish Tray 15.00
Amber 20.00
Vaseline 25.00
Green/Blue 30.00
Sauce 15.00
Amber 20.00
Vaseline 25.00
Green/Blue 30.00
Sugar 55.00
Amber 60.00
Vaseline 65.00
Green/Blue 70.00
Wine 40.00
Amber 45.00
Vaseline 50.00
Green/Blue 60.00

STARS AND STRIPES (BRILLIANT)
Berry Bowl, Lg. 20.00
Berry Bowl, Sm. 45.00
Butter 65.00
Creamer or Spooner 20.00
Cup 10.00
Pitcher 85.00
Tumbler 20.00
Toy Table Service 100.00
Sauce 10.00
Shakers, ea. 25.00
Sugar 25.00
Vase 20.00

STAR SPRAY
Bowl 20.00
Bride's Basket 40.00

STARTEC
Butter 45.00
Ruby Stain 80.00
Creamer or Spooner 20.00
Ruby Stain 35.00
Cruet 55.00
Ruby Stain 90.00
Goblet, Moose Etched on Side 60.00
Ruby Stain 75.00
Pitcher 80.00
Ruby Stain 150.00
Tumbler 20.00
Ruby Stain 35.00
Sauce 15.00
Ruby Stain 30.00
Sugar 30.00
Ruby Stain 70.00
Syrup 50.00
Ruby Stain 90.00

THE STATES
Butter 70.00
Compote 40.00
Creamer or Spooner 30.00
Cup 15.00
Nappy, 3 Hndl. 25.00
Plate 30.00
Punch Bowl 85.00
Relish 25.00
Shakers, ea. 20.00
Sugar 35.00
Syrup 65.00
Toothpick Hldr., 2 Kinds 35.00

STELLAR (SQUARED SUNBURST)
Berry Bowl, Lg. 35.00
Berry Bowl, Sm. 15.00
Butter 60.00
Compote 35.00
Creamer, Spooner, or Sugar 25.00
Pitcher 75.00
Tumbler 20.00

STERLING
Butter 60.00
Compote 35.00
Creamer or Spooner 20.00
Goblet 50.00
Pitcher 85.00
Tumbler 20.00
Punch Bowl 150.00
Punch Cup 15.00
Sugar 40.00
Toy Table Set 85.00
Wine 15.00

STIPPLED BAR
Butter 55.00
Creamer or Spooner 20.00
Plate 25.00
Pitcher 80.00
Tumbler 15.00
Sugar 30.00

STIPPLED CHAIN
Berry Bowl, Sm. 20.00
Berry Bowl, Lg. 45.00
Butter 55.00
Cake Stand 35.00
Celery Vase 25.00
Creamer or Spooner 25.00
Dish, Oval 20.00
Egg Cup 15.00
Goblet 50.00
Pickle Tray 25.00

Pitcher 85.00
Tumbler 20.00
Relish Dish 15.00
Salt Dip, Master 20.00
Sugar 30.00

STIPPLED CHAIN VARIANT (WITH CAT HANDLE)
Butter, Rare 325.00
Creamer or Spooner, Rare 100.00
Sugar, Rare 175.00

STIPPLED CHERRY
Berry Bowl, Sm. 20.00
Berry Bowl, Lg. 50.00
Bread Plate, 9" 35.00
Butter 75.00
Creamer or Spooner 25.00
Plate, 6" 25.00
Pitcher 90.00
Tumbler 25.00
Sugar 35.00

STIPPLED DAISY (Either clear or stippled)
Butter, Covered 65.00
Celery Vase 25.00
Compote, Open 35.00
Creamer or Spooner 20.00
Pitcher 75.00
Tumbler 20.00
Relish 20.00
Sauce 15.00
Sugar, Open 20.00
Sugar w/Lid 25.00
Wine 15.00

STIPPLED FORGET-ME-NOT
Berry Bowl, Sm. 20.00
Berry Bowl, Lg. 45.00
Butter 80.00
Cake Stand, 9" – 12" 30.00 – 50.00
Celery Vase 20.00
Compote, Covered, 6" – 8" 45.00
Compote, Open, 6" – 8" 35.00
Cordial 20.00
Creamer or Spooner 25.00
Cup 10.00
Dish, Oblong 20.00
Goblet 45.00
Milk Pitcher 65.00
Mug, Toy 35.00
Mug, Lg. 40.00
Plate, 6" and 7", Baby Face or Star Center 60.00
Plate, 8" and 9", Kitten or Star Center 70.00
Pitcher 85.00
Tumbler 20.00
Relish, Oval 15.00
Salt, Master 15.00
Sauce, Flat or Ftd. 10.00
Sugar 30.00
Syrup 50.00
Toothpick Hldr. 130.00
Toy Table Set 200.00
Waste Bowl 20.00
Water Tray 35.00
Wine 15.00

STIPPLED FORGET-ME-NOT WITH KITTEN
Plate, Scarce 75.00

STIPPLED LEAF
Syrup 85.00

STIPPLED MEDALLION
Butter 55.00
Cake Plate 30.00
Compote, Low 35.00
Creamer or Spooner 15.00
Egg Cup 15.00
Goblet 40.00
Plate 20.00
Sauce 10.00
Sugar 25.00

STIPPLED PEPPERS
Butter 65.00
Creamer or Spooner 25.00
Egg Cup 20.00
Pitcher 85.00
Tumbler, Ftd. 15.00
Salt, Ftd. 20.00
Sauce 10.00
Sugar 35.00

STIPPLED SANDBUR
Berry Bowl, Sm. 10.00
Berry Bowl, Lg. 35.00
Butter 45.00
Celery Vase 20.00
Compote, Covered 40.00
Creamer or Spooner 20.00
Goblet 35.00
Pickle Jar 25.00
Pitcher 70.00
Tumbler 15.00
Sugar 25.00
Toothpick Hldr. 15.00
Wine 10.00

ST. LOUIS ENCAMPMENT
Goblet, Very Scarce 250.00

ST LOUIS WORLD'S FAIR
Washington Hatchet, Ruby Stain 95.00

STORK AND RUSHES
Basket, Hndl. 45.00
Pitcher 225.00
Tumbler 50.00
Punch Bowl 375.00
Punch Cup 25.00

STRAWBERRY AND CABLE
Berry Bowl, Sm. 20.00
Berry Bowl, Lg. 40.00
Butter 65.00
Creamer or Spooner 25.00
Goblet 25.00
Pitcher 80.00
Tumbler 20.00
Shakers, ea. 25.00
Sugar 30.00
Sweetmeat w/Lid, 2 Styles 95.00
Wine 15.00

STRAWBERRY AND CURRANT
Butter 70.00
Celery Vase 20.00
Cheese Dish w/Lid 85.00
Compote, Covered 55.00
Compote, Open 35.00
Creamer or Spooner 25.00
Goblet 60.00
Milk Pitcher 65.00
Mug 35.00
Pitcher 110.00
Tumbler 25.00
Sauce, Ftd. 10.00
Sugar 45.00
Syrup 150.00

STRAWBERRY AND PEAR
Mug 15.00
Amber 25.00
Vaseline 50.00
Green/Blue 35.00

STRIGEL
Berry Bowl, Sm. 10.00
Berry Bowl, Lg. 30.00
Butter 45.00
Celery Vase 15.00
Compote 30.00
Creamer or Spooner 15.00
Egg Cup 20.00
Goblet 35.00
Pitcher 65.00
Tumbler 10.00
Sugar 20.00
Wine 15.00

STUDIO
Butter 65.00
Creamer or Spooner 25.00
Hair Receiver 40.00
Sugar 35.00

STUMP
Toothpick Hldr. 75.00
Amber 110.00
Green/Blue 155.00

SUMMIT (X-BULL'S-EYE)
Berry Bowl, Sm. 15.00
Berry Bowl, Lg. 40.00
Butter 55.00
Compote 30.00
Creamer or Spooner 20.00
Pitcher 75.00
Tumbler 20.00
Shakers, ea. 20.00
Sugar 25.00
Wine 15.00

SUNBEAM
Berry Bowl, Sm. 20.00
Berry Bowl, Lg. 45.00
Butter 65.00
Carafe 35.00
Celery Vase 25.00
Creamer or Spooner 25.00
Cruet 60.00
Jelly Compote 30.00
Pickle Dish 20.00
Pitcher 95.00
Tumbler 20.00
Sauce 15.00
Shakers, ea. 20.00
Sugar 30.00
Syrup 55.00
Toothpick Hldr. 20.00

SUNBURST
Butter 55.00
Cake Stand 30.00
Celery Vase 20.00
Compotes, Various 20.00 – 55.00
Cordial 15.00
Creamer or Spooner 20.00
Egg Cup 15.00
Plates, Various 15.00 – 35.00
Pitcher 75.00
Tumbler 20.00
Shakers, ea. 15.00
Sugar 25.00
Wine 15.00

SUNBURST ON SHIELD (DIADEM)
Breakfast Set 45.00
Butter 60.00
Celery Tray 25.00
Creamer or Spooner 20.00
Cruet 70.00
Pickle Tray 20.00
Pitcher 85.00
Tumbler 20.00
Shakers, ea. 20.00
Sugar 35.00

SUNFLOWER
Berry Bowl, Sm. 20.00
Amber 25.00
Milk Glass 40.00
Berry Bowl, Lg. 45.00
Amber 55.00
Milk Glass 65.00
Butter 55.00
Amber 75.00
Milk Glass 125.00
Creamer or Spooner 25.00
Amber 35.00
Milk Glass 60.00
Pitcher 85.00
Amber 100.00
Milk Glass 150.00
Tumbler 20.00
Amber 30.00
Milk Glass 50.00
Sugar 30.00
Amber 45.00
Milk Glass 70.00

SUNK DAISY
Butter 60.00
Carafe 35.00
Compote 40.00
Cracker Jar 45.00
Creamer or Spooner 20.00
Goblet 40.00

Pitcher . . . 75.00
Tumbler . . . 20.00
Shakers, ea. . . . 15.00
Sugar . . . 30.00
Toothpick Hldr. . . . 20.00
Wine . . . 15.00

SUNKEN BULLSEYE
Butter . . . 60.00
Creamer or Spooner . . . 25.00
Goblet. . . . 45.00
Pitcher . . . 90.00
Tumber. . . . 20.00
Sugar . . . 40.00

SUNKEN PRIMROSE
Banana Bowl . . . 35.00
Green/Blue. . . . 45.00
Ruby Stain. . . . 65.00
Berry Bowl, Sm. . . . 10.00
Green/Blue. . . . 15.00
Ruby Stain. . . . 20.00
Berry Bowl, Lg.. . . . 30.00
Green/Blue. . . . 35.00
Ruby Stain. . . . 45.00
Butter. . . . 65.00
Green/Blue. . . . 75.00
Ruby Stain. . . . 85.00
Compote. . . . 40.00
Green/Blue. . . . 45.00
Ruby Stain. . . . 55.00
Creamer or Spooner . . . 30.00
Green/Blue. . . . 35.00
Ruby Stain. . . . 40.00
Lamp . . . 70.00
Green/Blue. . . . 80.00
Ruby Stain. . . . 95.00
Pitcher . . . 100.00
Green/Blue. . . . 120.00
Ruby Stain. . . . 145.00
Tumbler . . . 20.00
Green/Blue. . . . 30.00
Ruby Stain. . . . 35.00
Relish. . . . 20.00
Green/Blue. . . . 25.00
Ruby Stain. . . . 30.00
Salt Shaker. . . . 35.00
Green/Blue. . . . 40.00
Ruby Stain. . . . 50.00
Sugar . . . 45.00
Green/Blue. . . . 50.00
Ruby Stain. . . . 60.00
Toothpick. . . . 45.00
Green/Blue. . . . 50.00
Ruby Stain. . . . 60.00
(Condensed List, many shapes)

SUNKEN TEARDROP
Berry Bowl, Sm. . . . 20.00
Berry Bowl, Lg. . . . 45.00
Butter. . . . 75.00
Creamer or Spooner . . . 25.00
Goblet . . . 60.00
Pickle Dish. . . . 20.00
Pitcher . . . 95.00
Tumbler . . . 20.00
Shakers, ea. . . . 20.00
Sugar . . . 30.00
Wine . . . 20.00

SUNK HONEYCOMB
Berry Bowl, Lg. . . . 30.00
Ruby Stain. . . . 45.00
Berry Bowl, Sm. . . . 10.00
Ruby Stain. . . . 15.00
Butter. . . . 50.00
Ruby Stain. . . . 80.00
Creamer or Spooner . . . 25.00
Ruby Stain. . . . 35.00
Cruet . . . 60.00
Ruby Stain. . . . 85.00
Decanter . . . 45.00
Ruby Stain. . . . 60.00
Ind. Creamer or Sugar . . . 20.00
Ruby Stain. . . . 35.00
Jelly Compote. . . . 25.00
Ruby Stain. . . . 45.00
Mug . . . 35.00
Ruby Stain. . . . 60.00
Shakers, ea. . . . 20.00
Ruby Stain. . . . 30.00
Sugar . . . 35.00
Ruby Stain. . . . 50.00
Toothpick Hldr. . . . 35.00
Ruby Stain. . . . 65.00
Wine . . . 25.00
Ruby Stain. . . . 35.00

SUNK JEWEL
Nappy . . . 25.00
Pitcher . . . 70.00
Tumbler . . . 15.00

SWAG WITH BRACKETS
Butter. . . . 165.00
Compote. . . . 55.00
Creamer or Spooner . . . 90.00
Cruet . . . 165.00
Pitcher . . . 225.00
Tumbler . . . 55.00
Salt Shaker. . . . 65.00
Sugar . . . 150.00
Toothpick Hldr. (Age ?) . . . 100.00

SWAN (BRYCE BROTHERS)
Mug . . . 45.00
Amber . . . 55.00
Milk Glass . . . 60.00

SWAN (ETCHED)
Compote, Covered . . . 150.00

SWAN AND EGRET
Mug . . . 50.00

SWAN NAPPY
One Shape, 4½" . . . 75.00

SWAN ON POND
Butter. . . . 60.00
Amber . . . 70.00
Green/Blue. . . . 90.00
Creamer or Spooner. . . . 25.00
Amber . . . 35.00
Green/Blue. . . . 45.00
Goblet . . . 35.00
Amber . . . 45.00
Green/Blue. . . . 60.00
Pitcher . . . 85.00
Amber . . . 100.00
Green/Blue. . . . 145.00
Tumbler . . . 20.00
Amber . . . 30.00
Green/Blue. . . . 40.00
Sugar . . . 35.00
Amber . . . 45.00
Green/Blue. . . . 60.00

SWAN WITH MESH
Butter . . . 150.00
Vaseline. . . . 250.00
Compote, Covered . . . 110.00
Vaseline. . . . 250.00
Creamer or Spooner. . . . 70.00
Vaseline. . . . 125.00
Goblet . . . 85.00
Vaseline. . . . 150.00
Pitcher . . . 280.00
Vaseline. . . . 400.00
Tumbler . . . 85.00
Sauce . . . 25.00
Vaseline. . . . 45.00
Sugar . . . 165.00
Vaseline. . . . 225.00
Wine . . . 90.00
Vaseline. . . . 125.00

SWAN WITH RING HANDLE
Mug . . . 35.00
Amber . . . 45.00
Green/Blue. . . . 65.00
Black . . . 80.00

SWAN WITH TREE
Goblet . . . 90.00
Pitcher . . . 235.00

SWIRL AND BALL
Butter. . . . 75.00
Cake Stand. . . . 40.00
Candlesticks, ea. . . . 30.00
Celery Vase . . . 20.00
Child's Mug . . . 30.00
Cordial Set . . . 95.00
Creamer or Spooner. . . . 20.00
Jelly, Ftd. . . . 25.00
Plate, 6" . . . 20.00
Shakers, ea. . . . 20.00
Sugar . . . 30.00
Syrup . . . 65.00

SWIRL AND CABLE
Creamer . . . 25.00
Pitcher . . . 85.00

SWIRL AND DIAMOND
Bowl, Sm. . . . 15.00
Bowl, Lg. . . . 45.00
Butter. . . . 60.00
Carafe . . . 50.00
Creamer or Spooner. . . . 20.00
Pickle Tray. . . . 20.00
Pitcher . . . 80.00
Tumbler . . . 15.00
Shakers, ea. . . . 15.00
Sugar, Open . . . 20.00
Sugar w/Lid . . . 25.00

SWIRLED COLUMN
Bowl, Covered, Ftd., 5" – 9". . . . 25.00 – 45.00
Bowls, Flat or Ftd., 5" – 9" . . . 15.00 – 35.00
Butter. . . . 55.00
Cake Stand. . . . 35.00
Celery Vase . . . 25.00
Creamer or Spooner. . . . 20.00
Cruet . . . 50.00
Cup . . . 10.00
Egg Cup . . . 15.00
Goblet . . . 40.00
Mug . . . 20.00
Plate. . . . 20.00
Pitcher . . . 85.00
Tumbler . . . 20.00
Sauce . . . 10.00
Shakers, ea. . . . 15.00
Sugar . . . 25.00
Sugar Shaker . . . 35.00
Syrup . . . 40.00
Wine . . . 15.00

SWIRLED STAR
Butter. . . . 55.00
Creamer or Spooner. . . . 20.00
Sugar . . . 25.00

SWIRL HOBNAIL (MILLERSBURG)
Spittoon, Very Rare . . . 2000.00*
Amethyst . . . 2500.00

SWIRL-STEM HOBSTAR
Vase, 11" . . . 45.00

SWORD
Novelty Pickle Dish . . . 95.00

SWORD AND CIRCLE
Berry Bowl, Sm. . . . 15.00
Custard Dish . . . 15.00
Tumbler . . . 25.00
Tumbler, Juice . . . 20.00

SYDNEY
Bowl, 6" – 8". . . . 25.00
Butter. . . . 70.00
Celery Vase . . . 35.00
Compote, Open . . . 40.00
Compote w/Lid . . . 50.00
Creamer or Spooner. . . . 20.00
Pickle Dish, 6" – 9". . . . 15.00
Pitcher . . . 80.00
Tumbler . . . 15.00
Shakers, ea. . . . 15.00
Sugar . . . 20.00

TACOMA
Banana Dish . . . 40.00
Ruby Stain. . . . 80.00
Bowls, Various . . . 20.00 – 90.00
Ruby Stain . . . 35.00 – 100.00
Butter. . . . 50.00
Ruby Stain. . . . 130.00

Cake Stand. 40.00
Ruby Stain. 150.00
Carafe 35.00
Ruby Stain. 170.00
Celery Tray. 20.00
Ruby Stain. 55.00
Celery Vase 20.00
Ruby Stain. 85.00
Compote, Open 55.00
Ruby Stain. 165.00
Cracker Jar 55.00
Creamer or Spooner 35.00
Ruby Stain. 70.00
Cruet, 2 Sizes 40.00
Ruby Stain. 130.00
Decanter 60.00
Ruby Stain. 140.00
Dish, Oblong 15.00
Goblet 35.00
Ruby Stain. 70.00
Pickle Jar w/Lid 45.00
Ruby Stain. 125.00
Pitcher, 2 Styles 65.00
Ruby Stain. 200.00
Tumbler 20.00
Ruby Stain. 35.00
Plate. 20.00
Salt, Ind. 10.00
Ruby Stain. 30.00
Salt, Master 20.00
Ruby Stain. 60.00
Shaker, 2 Styles 25.00
Ruby Stain. 40.00
Sauce 10.00
Ruby Stain. 20.00
Sugar 40.00
Ruby Stain. 115.00
Syrup 55.00
Ruby Stain. 225.00
Toothpick Hldr. 30.00
Ruby Stain. 200.00
Vase, 2 Styles . . . . . 30.00 – 40.00
Wine 25.00
Ruby Stain. 50.00

TANDEM DIAMONDS AND THUMBPRINT

Butter. 75.00
Creamer or Spooner 25.00
Goblet 50.00
Pitcher 95.00
Tumbler 20.00
Sugar 35.00

TAPE MEASURE

Butter. 70.00
Creamer or Spooner 20.00
Goblet 50.00
Pitcher 80.00
Tumbler 20.00
Sauce 10.00
Sugar 30.00

TARA'S HARP

Art Nouveau Tray 100.00

TARENTUM'S MANHATTAN

Berry Bowl, Lg. 30.00
Berry Bowl, Sm. 10.00
Butter. 65.00
Cake Stand. 35.00
Compote, Open 35.00
Creamer or Spooner 25.00
Cruet 70.00
Goblet 25.00
Oval Dish. 20.00
Plates, 6" & 8" 20.00
Shaker 40.00
Sugar 30.00
Syrup 65.00
Tumbler 15.00

TARENTUM'S VIRGINIA (Condensed List)

Berry Bowl, Sm. 10.00
Berry Bowl, Lg. 35.00
Butter. 50.00
Celery Tray. 20.00
Celery Vase 25.00
Compote. 35.00
Cordial 15.00
Creamer or Spooner 20.00
Cruet 60.00
Egg Cup 15.00
Goblet 35.00
Jam Jar 25.00
Mustard Pot 25.00
Pickle Tray 15.00
Pitcher 70.00
Tumbler 15.00
Shakers, ea. 15.00
Sugar 25.00
Syrup 40.00
Wine 10.00

TARGET

Vase. 30.00

TEARDROP

Bowls, Rectangular . . . . . 15.00 – 40.00
Bowls, Sq. . . . . . 20.00 – 45.00
Butter. 55.00
Candlesticks, ea. 25.00
Compote. 35.00
Creamer or Spooner 20.00
Cruet 45.00
Goblet 50.00
Pickle Dish. 15.00
Pitcher 65.00
Tumbler 10.00
Sugar 25.00
Wine 10.00

TEARDROP AND TASSEL

Bowl. 35.00
Green/Blue. 55.00
Nile Green 75.00
Butter. 85.00
Green/Blue. 130.00
Nile Green 300.00
Celery Vase 45.00
Compote, Open 70.00
Green/Blue. 85.00
Nile Green 125.00
Compote, Covered 35.00
Green/Blue. 45.00
Nile Green 75.00
Creamer or Spooner 40.00
Green/Blue. 75.00
Nile Green 90.00
Goblet 90.00
Green/Blue. 150.00
Nile Green 100.00
Pitcher 175.00
Green/Blue. 165.00
Nile Green 800.00
Tumbler 35.00
Green/Blue. 60.00
Nile Green 80.00
Sugar 65.00
Green/Blue. 120.00
Nile Green 100.00
Wine (2 Varieties from Greentown). 45.00 – 70.00
Green/Blue. 75.00
Nile Green 125.00

TEASEL

Berry Bowl, Sm. 20.00
Berry Bowl, Lg. 45.00
Bowl, Pedestal, 2 Sizes . . . . . 30.00 – 45.00
Butter. 75.00
Cake Stand. 35.00
Celery Vase 30.00
Compote. 40.00
Creamer or Spooner 25.00
Cracker Jar 40.00
Cruet 65.00
Goblet, 3 Types . . . . . 40.00 – 60.00
Honey Jar, Covered 55.00
Plate, 7" – 9". 35.00
Pitcher 100.00
Tumbler 25.00
Shakers, ea. 30.00
Sugar 35.00
Toothpick Hldr. 40.00

TEEPEE

Berry Bowl, Sm. 20.00
Berry Bowl, Lg. 50.00
Butter. 60.00
Cheese Dish w/Lid 85.00
Creamer or Spooner 25.00
Cup 15.00
Jelly Compote 35.00
Jelly Hndl. 30.00
Plate. 25.00
Shakers, ea. 20.00
Sugar 35.00
Syrup 65.00
Toothpick Hldr., Rare (Green) 75.00
Wine 20.00

TEN POINTED STAR

Berry Bowl, Sm. 10.00
Berry Bowl, Lg. 45.00
Bowls, Ice Cream Shape . . . . . 10.00 – 45.00
Butter. 70.00
Cake Salver, Stemmed 40.00
Compotes, 2 Sizes . . . . . 30.00 – 45.00
Compotier, 8". 55.00
Creamer or Spooner 25.00
Cruet 60.00
Milk Pitcher 65.00
Pickle Dish, Rnd. or Sq. 15.00
Plate. 20.00
Plate, Sq., 7½" 15.00
Pitcher 100.00
Tumbler 20.00
Sugar 30.00
Vase, 12" 25.00

TERRAPIN

Novelty Dish 85.00

TEXAS

Bowl, Covered, 6" – 8" 100.00
Ruby Stain. 200.00
Bowl, Open, 6" – 9" 60.00
Ruby Stain. 100.00
Bread Tray 25.00
Ruby Stain. 75.00
Butter. 50.00
Ruby Stain. 285.00
Cake Stand, 9" – 11". 40.00
Ruby Stain . . . . . 250.00 – 400.00
Celery Tray. 25.00
Ruby Stain. 70.00
Celery Vase 85.00
Ruby Stain. 200.00
Compote, Covered, 6" – 8" 225.00
Ruby Stain. 275.00
Compote, Open, 7½" – 9½". 100.00
Ruby Stain. 200.00
Creamer . . . . . 20.00 – 95.00
Ruby Stain . . . . . 50.00 – 225.00
Cruet 150.00
Ruby Stain. 350.00
Goblet 100.00
Ruby Stain. 200.00
Horseradish, Covered 100.00
Ruby Stain. 285.00
Olive Dish 20.00
Ruby Stain. 40.00
Pickle Tray. 35.00
Ruby Stain. 90.00
Plate. 65.00
Ruby Stain. 150.00
Pitcher, 2 Styles 275.00
Ruby Stain. 525.00
Tumbler 75.00
Ruby Stain. 125.00
Relish Tray. 15.00
Ruby Stain. 50.00
Salt Dip, Master. 100.00
Ruby Stain. 200.00
Sauce, Flat or Ftd. 15.00
Ruby Stain. 35.00
Shakers, ea. 100.00
Ruby Stain. 225.00
Shaker, Hotel 100.00
Ruby Stain. 225.00

Spooner, Ruby Stain 200.00
Sugar 25.00
Ruby Stain 225.00
Syrup 200.00
Ruby Stain 500.00
Toothpick Hldr. 30.00
Ruby Stain 150.00
Vase, 6½" – 10" 50.00
Ruby Stain 80.00
Water Bottle 125.00
Ruby Stain 225.00
Wine 60.00
Ruby Stain 125.00

TEXAS STAR
Berry Bowl, Sm. 10.00
Berry Bowl, Lg. 45.00
Pitcher 75.00
Tumbler 15.00
Shakers, ea. 20.00

TEXAS STAR (SNOWFLAKE BASE)
Butter 60.00
Creamer or Spooner 20.00
Pitcher 80.00
Tumbler 20.00
Sauce 10.00
Shakers, ea. 20.00
Sugar 40.00

THEODORE ROOSEVELT
Platter 185.00

THIS LITTLE PIG WENT TO MARKET
Nursery Rhyme Plate 45.00

THISTLE
Berry Bowl, Sm. 10.00
Berry Bowl, Lg. 30.00
Butter 55.00
Cake Stand 35.00
Compote, Covered, 6" – 8" 60.00
Compote, Open, 6" – 8" 35.00
Cordial 20.00
Creamer or Spooner 25.00
Dish, Oval 20.00
Egg Cup 25.00
Goblet 30.00
Milk Pitcher 55.00
Pickle Dish 20.00
Pitcher 90.00
Tumbler 20.00
Plate, Lg. 25.00
Relish Tray 20.00
Salt, Master 25.00
Sugar 40.00
Syrup 65.00
Wine 20.00

THONGED STAR (IMPERIAL)
Olive Dish 25.00
Oval Dish, Handled 30.00

THOUSAND EYE
ABC Plate 45.00
Amber 60.00
Vaseline 75.00
Green/Blue 60.00
Bowl, 5" – 8" . . . . 50.00 – 65.00
Amber 70.00
Vaseline 80.00
Green/Blue 70.00
Butter 60.00
Amber 95.00
Vaseline 165.00
Green/Blue 125.00
Cake Stand 40.00
Amber 60.00
Vaseline 125.00
Green/Blue 100.00
Celery Vase, 2 Shapes 40.00
Amber 50.00
Vaseline 75.00
Green/Blue 50.00
Christmas Light 35.00
Amber 40.00
Vaseline 65.00
Green/Blue 45.00
Cologne 30.00
Amber 40.00
Vaseline 60.00
Green/Blue 45.00
Compote, High, 6" – 10" . . . . 45.00 – 65.00
Amber . . . . 50.00 – 80.00
Vaseline . . . . 65.00 – 90.00
Green/Blue . . . . 65.00 – 80.00
Compote, Low, 8" 35.00
Green/Blue 135.00
Creamer or Spooner 30.00
Amber 40.00
Vaseline 70.00
Green/Blue 40.00
Cruet 45.00
Amber 95.00
Vaseline 175.00
Green/Blue 125.00
Dish, Sq., 5" – 10" . . . . 30.00 – 55.00
Amber . . . . 35.00 – 60.00
Vaseline . . . . 40.00 – 75.00
Green/Blue . . . . 35.00 – 60.00
Egg Cup 50.00
Amber 60.00
Vaseline 100.00
Green/Blue 80.00
Goblet 45.00
Amber 55.00
Vaseline 75.00
Green/Blue 60.00
Honey Dish 75.00
Amber 80.00
Vaseline 100.00
Green/Blue 85.00
Ink Well 35.00
Amber 70.00
Vaseline 125.00
Green/Blue 90.00
Jelly Glass 20.00
Amber 30.00
Vaseline 45.00
Green/Blue 30.00
Lamp, 12" – 15" . . . . 100.00 – 135.00
Amber . . . . 110.00 – 150.00
Vaseline . . . . 225.00 – 275.00
Green/Blue . . . . 200.00 – 245.00
Milk Pitcher 65.00
Amber 95.00
Vaseline 120.00
Green/Blue 100.00
Mug, 2 Sizes 25.00
Amber 40.00
Vaseline 65.00
Green/Blue 45.00
Pickle Dish 20.00
Amber 25.00
Vaseline 40.00
Green/Blue 30.00
Plate, 6" – 10" 30.00
Amber 35.00
Vaseline 50.00
Green/Blue 35.00
Platter 40.00
Amber 45.00
Vaseline 65.00
Green/Blue 45.00
Pitcher, 4 Sizes . . . . 75.00 – 110.00
Amber . . . . 85.00 – 125.00
Vaseline . . . . 135.00 – 225.00
Green/Blue . . . . 95.00 – 165.00
Tumbler 25.00
Amber 50.00
Vaseline 70.00
Green/Blue 60.00
Salt Dip, Master 60.00
Amber 50.00
Vaseline 95.00
Green/Blue 75.00
Salt Dip, Ind. 40.00
Amber 50.00
Vaseline 95.00
Green/Blue 75.00
Sauce 10.00
Amber 15.00
Vaseline 25.00
Green/Blue 20.00
String Hldr. 35.00
Amber 45.00
Vaseline 75.00
Green/Blue 55.00
Sugar 50.00
Amber 55.00
Vaseline 85.00
Green/Blue 75.00
Syrup 60.00
Amber 95.00
Vaseline 150.00
Green/Blue 135.00
Toothpick, Hldr., 3 Types . . . . 20.00 – 35.00
Amber . . . . 35.00 – 55.00
Vaseline . . . . 75.00 – 95.00
Green/Blue . . . . 70.00 – 90.00
Water Tray 60.00
Amber 75.00
Vaseline 95.00
Green/Blue 70.00
Wine 25.00
Amber 30.00
Vaseline 40.00
Green/Blue 35.00

THOUSAND EYE VARIANT
Lamp 95.00
Amber 120.00
Vaseline 235.00
Green/Blue 190.00

THOUSAND EYE WITH FAN
Compote, Stemmed, Vaseline 110.00

THREADING
Butter 45.00
Celery Vase 20.00
Compote 35.00
Creamer or Spooner 20.00
Goblet 30.00
Pitcher 60.00
Tumbler 15.00
Sauce 10.00
Sugar 25.00
Wine 10.00

THREE BIRDS
Pitcher, Scarce 275.00

THREE DOLPHINS
Match Hldr. 60.00
Amber 80.00
Green/Blue 95.00

THREE FACE
Biscuit Jar 350.00
Bowl, High or Low 100.00
Butter 165.00
Cake Stand, 9" – 11" 175.00
Celery Vase, 2 Styles 110.00
Champagne 95.00
Compote, Covered, Low, 6" – 10" 175.00
Compote, Covered, High, 6" – 10" 225.00
Compote, Open, High, 7" – 9" 150.00
Compote, Open, Low, 6" 100.00
Cordial 110.00
Creamer or Spooner 150.00
Goblet 125.00
Jam Jar 250.00
Milk Pitcher 225.00
Oil Lamps, Several Sizes & Styles 250.00
Pitcher 400.00
Tumbler 75.00
Salt Dip, Ind. 45.00
Sauce 35.00
Sugar 140.00
Wine 165.00

THREE FRUITS (NORTHWOOD)
Bowl 75.00
Plate 125.00

THREE-IN-ONE
Berry Bowl, Lg. 30.00
Ruby Stain 65.00
Berry Bowl, Sm. 15.00
Ruby Stain 25.00

Bowl, Ftd., 6" – 7" . . . 35.00
Bowl, Ftd., 8" – 9" . . . 20.00
Biscuit Jar . . . 60.00
Butter . . . 80.00
Ruby Stain . . . 110.00
Cake Stand . . . 55.00
Candlesticks, ea. . . . 40.00
Carafe . . . 60.00
Catsup Cruet . . . 90.00
Celery Vase . . . 35.00
Ruby Stain . . . 45.00
Compote, Covered, 3 Sizes . . . 40.00
Creamer, Spooner, or Sugar . . . 25.00
Ruby Stain . . . 40.00
Cruet . . . 75.00
Fruit Compote . . . 45.00
Goblet . . . 25.00
Jelly Compote . . . 30.00
Milk Jar, Covered . . . 85.00
Ruby Stain . . . 95.00
Nappy . . . 25.00
Pickle Dish, 7", 8", and 9" . . . 25.00
Pickle Jar . . . 35.00
Ruby Stain . . . 60.00
Pitcher . . . 165.00
Tumbler . . . 25.00
Punch Bowl . . . 325.00
Punch Cup . . . 20.00
Shakers, ea. . . . 30.00
Shot Glass . . . 25.00
Syrup . . . 65.00
Toothpick Hldr. . . . 40.00
Vase, Stemmed, 3 Sizes . . . 40.00
Whiskey Decanter . . . 100.00
Wine Decanter . . . 85.00
Wine Goblet . . . 15.00

THREE PANEL
Bowl, 8½" – 10" . . . 20.00 – 30.00
Amber . . . 25.00 – 35.00
Vaseline . . . 35.00 – 50.00
Green/Blue . . . 30.00 – 45.00
Butter . . . 55.00
Amber . . . 65.00
Vaseline . . . 100.00
Green/Blue . . . 65.00
Celery Vase, 2 Styles . . . 20.00
Amber . . . 25.00
Vaseline . . . 35.00
Green/Blue . . . 25.00
Compote, Open, 7" – 10" . . . 25.00 – 40.00
Amber . . . 30.00 – 45.00
Vaseline . . . 40.00 – 60.00
Green/Blue . . . 35.00 – 55.00
Creamer or Spooner . . . 25.00
Amber . . . 35.00
Vaseline . . . 50.00
Green/Blue . . . 35.00
Cruet . . . 75.00
Amber . . . 225.00
Vaseline . . . 325.00
Goblet . . . 35.00
Amber . . . 40.00
Vaseline . . . 60.00
Green/Blue . . . 45.00
Milk Pitcher . . . 40.00
Amber . . . 55.00
Vaseline . . . 90.00
Green/Blue . . . 65.00
Mug, 2 Sizes . . . 20.00 – 30.00
Amber . . . 25.00 – 35.00
Vaseline . . . 35.00 – 50.00
Green/Blue . . . 30.00 – 40.00
Pitcher . . . 80.00
Amber . . . 120.00
Vaseline . . . 150.00
Green/Blue . . . 135.00
Tumbler . . . 20.00
Amber . . . 30.00
Vaseline . . . 55.00
Green/Blue . . . 50.00
Sauce . . . 10.00
Amber . . . 15.00
Vaseline . . . 20.00
Green/Blue . . . 25.00
Sugar . . . 25.00
Amber . . . 35.00
Vaseline . . . 75.00
Green/Blue . . . 65.00

THUMBPRINT (ARGUS THUMBPRINT)
Ale Glass . . . 35.00
Banana Boat . . . 40.00
Berry Bowl, Sm. . . . 20.00
Berry Bowl, Lg. . . . 45.00
Bitters Bottle . . . 140.00
Bone Dish . . . 15.00
Butter . . . 65.00
Cake Stand . . . 40.00
Caster Bottles . . . 25.00
Celery Vase . . . 20.00
Champagne . . . 15.00
Claret . . . 20.00
Cologne . . . 35.00
Compote, Covered, 4" – 13" . . . 75.00 – 175.00
Compote, Open (High or Low) . 60.00 – 125.00
Cordial . . . 20.00
Creamer or Spooner . . . 20.00
Egg Cup . . . 20.00
Goblet . . . 50.00
Jelly Dish . . . 30.00
Mug (Beer) . . . 30.00
Pickle Dish . . . 15.00
Plate 8" . . . 20.00
Pitcher . . . 100.00
Tumbler . . . 20.00
Punch Bowl . . . 150.00
Punch Cup . . . 15.00
Relish Dish . . . 20.00
Salt Dip, Master . . . 20.00
Sauce . . . 10.00
Sugar . . . 30.00
Syrup . . . 150.00
Whiskey . . . 20.00
Wine . . . 75.00

TIDY
Butter . . . 65.00
Celery Vase . . . 25.00
Compote . . . 40.00
Creamer or Spooner . . . 25.00
Goblet . . . 55.00
Pitcher . . . 95.00
Tumbler . . . 20.00
Sugar . . . 35.00
Wine . . . 15.00

TILE (OPTICAL CUBE) (Condensed List)
Bread Tray . . . 30.00
Butter . . . 60.00
Cake Stand . . . 35.00
Celery Vase . . . 20.00
Celery Tray . . . 25.00
Compote, Covered . . . 45.00
Compote, Open . . . 30.00
Cordial . . . 15.00
Creamer or Spooner . . . 20.00
Cruet . . . 50.00
Decanter . . . 40.00
Goblet . . . 45.00
Olive Dish . . . 15.00
Pickle Dish . . . 20.00
Pickle Jar . . . 35.00
Pitcher . . . 75.00
Tumbler . . . 15.00
Shakers, ea. . . . 15.00
Sugar . . . 25.00
Wine . . . 15.00

TIPTOE (RAMONA)
Berry Bowl, Sm. . . . 10.00
Berry Bowl, Lg. . . . 30.00
Butter . . . 45.00
Celery Vase . . . 20.00
Compote . . . 30.00
Creamer or Spooner . . . 15.00
Pickle Dish . . . 15.00
Shakers, ea. . . . 15.00
Sugar . . . 20.00
Toothpick Hldr. . . . 25.00

TOGO
Berry Bowl, Sm. . . . 10.00
Ruby Stain . . . 20.00
Berry Bowl, Lg. . . . 35.00
Ruby Stain . . . 45.00
Bowl, Ftd., 7" . . . 25.00
Ruby Stain . . . 35.00
Bowl, Ftd., 9" . . . 30.00
Ruby Stain . . . 40.00
Breakfast Set, 2 Pcs. . . . 40.00
Ruby Stain . . . 60.00
Butter . . . 60.00
Ruby Stain . . . 90.00
Creamer or Spooner . . . 20.00
Ruby Stain . . . 35.00
Cruet . . . 55.00
Ruby Stain . . . 85.00
Jelly Compote . . . 25.00
Ruby Stain . . . 35.00
Olive Dish, Leaf Shape . . . 20.00
Ruby Stain . . . 30.00
Plate, Sq., 5" . . . 15.00
Ruby Stain . . . 30.00
Pitcher, 2 Styles . . . 85.00
Ruby Stain . . . 145.00
Tumbler . . . 15.00
Ruby Stain . . . 30.00
Sugar . . . 25.00
Ruby Stain . . . 45.00

TOKYO
Berry Bowl, Lg. . . . 25.00
Vaseline . . . 35.00
Green/Blue . . . 40.00
Berry Bowl, Sm. . . . 10.00
Vaseline . . . 15.00
Green/Blue . . . 20.00
Butter . . . 45.00
Vaseline . . . 75.00
Green/Blue . . . 90.00
Compote . . . 25.00
Vaseline . . . 40.00
Green/Blue . . . 50.00
Creamer or Spooner . . . 20.00
Vaseline . . . 30.00
Green/Blue . . . 35.00
Donut Stand . . . 35.00
Vaseline . . . 60.00
Green/Blue . . . 75.00
Plate . . . 25.00
Vaseline . . . 30.00
Green/Blue . . . 35.00
Pitcher . . . 75.00
Vaseline . . . 110.00
Green/Blue . . . 135.00
Tumbler . . . 15.00
Vaseline . . . 25.00
Green/Blue . . . 30.00
Shakers, ea. . . . 20.00
Vaseline . . . 25.00
Green/Blue . . . 30.00
Sugar . . . 35.00
Vaseline . . . 45.00
Green/Blue . . . 60.00
Syrup . . . 45.00
Vaseline . . . 70.00
Green/Blue . . . 85.00
Toothpick Hldr. . . . 35.00
Vaseline . . . 50.00
Green/Blue . . . 60.00
Vase . . . 20.00
Vaseline . . . 35.00
Green/Blue . . . 40.00

TOLTEC
Berry Bowl, Sm. . . . 10.00
Ruby Stain . . . 20.00
Berry Bowl, Lg. . . . 35.00
Ruby Stain . . . 50.00
Butter . . . 65.00
Ruby Stain . . . 95.00
Celery Vase . . . 20.00
Ruby Stain . . . 30.00

Compote 35.00
Ruby Stain 50.00
Claret 15.00
Ruby Stain 20.00
Creamer or Spooner 25.00
Ruby Stain 30.00
Cruet, 3 Styles . . . . . 30.00 – 55.00
Ruby Stain . . . . . 40.00 – 65.00
Cup 10.00
Ruby Stain 15.00
Finger Bowl 15.00
Ruby Stain 20.00
Jelly Compote 25.00
Ruby Stain 35.00
Plate, 9" – 10" 35.00
Ruby Stain 45.00
Pitcher 90.00
Ruby Stain 135.00
Tumbler 20.00
Ruby Stain 30.00
Sherbet, Ftd. 20.00
Ruby Stain 25.00
Spoon Tray 20.00
Ruby Stain 30.00
Sugar 30.00
Ruby Stain 70.00
Syrup, 3 Styles . . . . . 35.00 – 70.00
Ruby Stain . . . . . 65.00 – 100.00
Toothpick Hldr. 35.00
Ruby Stain 50.00
Wine 15.00
Ruby Stain 30.00

TONG
Berry Bowl, Sm. 15.00
Berry Bowl, Lg. 35.00
Butter 45.00
Celery Vase 25.00
Creamer or Spooner 25.00
Goblet 40.00
Pickle Dish 15.00
Pickle Jar 30.00
Pitcher 75.00
Tumbler 20.00
Sugar 30.00

TORPEDO
Banana Stand 40.00
Bowl, Covered, 4" – 10" . . . . . 25.00 – 55.00
Ruby Stain . . . . . 65.00 – 95.00
Bowl, Open, 4" – 10" . . . . . 15.00 – 35.00
Ruby Stain . . . . . 20.00 – 50.00
Butter 65.00
Ruby Stain 120.00
Cake Stand 35.00
Celery Vase 20.00
Ruby Stain 80.00
Compote, Covered 95.00
Creamer or Spooner 20.00
Ruby Stain 80.00
Cruet 40.00
Cup & Saucer 25.00
Decanter 40.00
Ruby Stain 145.00
Finger Bowl 25.00
Goblet 50.00
Ruby Stain 90.00
Jelly Compote, Covered 35.00
Jelly Compote, Open 20.00
Jam Jar 50.00
Ruby Stain 110.00
Lamp, 2 Styles . . . . . 65.00 – 95.00
Milk Pitcher 55.00
Ruby Stain 135.00
Pickle Caster 140.00
Ruby Stain 250.00
Pitcher 90.00
Ruby Stain 210.00
Tumbler 20.00
Ruby Stain 50.00
Salt, Master 25.00
Ruby Stain 60.00
Salt, Ind. 15.00
Ruby Stain 35.00

Sauce 15.00
Ruby Stain 30.00
Shakers, ea. 35.00
Ruby Stain 65.00
Sugar 50.00
Ruby Stain 100.00
Syrup 100.00
Ruby Stain 200.00
Tray, 10" – 12" . . . . . 25.00 – 35.00
Wine 50.00
Ruby Stain 95.00

TOURING CAR
Candy Container 35.00

TREE
Butter 75.00
Creamer or Spooner 30.00
Pitcher 125.00
Tumbler 25.00
Sugar 35.00
Toothpick Hldr. 30.00

TREE BARK
Berry Bowl, Sm. 10.00
Berry Bowl, Lg. 25.00
Butter 40.00
Creamer or Spooner 20.00
Pitcher 45.00
Tumbler 10.00
Sugar 25.00

TREE OF LIFE
Bowls, Oval or Rnd. . . . . . 15.00 – 45.00
Butter 75.00
Celery Vase 20.00
Champagne 15.00
Compote, Covered, High or Low . 65.00 – 175.00
Compote, Open, High or Low . . 45.00 – 110.00
Creamer or Spooner 25.00
Epergne 175.00
Goblet 55.00
Honey Plate 25.00
Milk Pitcher 65.00
Mug 35.00
Plate, Rnd. 20.00
Pitcher 125.00
Tumbler 30.00
Salt, Master 20.00
Sauce 15.00
Sauce, Leaf Shape 35.00
Sugar 40.00
Toothpick Hldr. 35.00
Water Tray 35.00
Wine 20.00
Vases, Several Sizes . . . . . 15.00 – 55.00

TREE OF LIFE WITH HAND (HOBBS)
Bouquet Vase 350.00
Vaseline 500.00
Green/Blue 695.00
Butter 110.00
Vaseline 165.00
Green/Blue 225.00
Cake Stand 150.00
Vaseline 215.00
Green/Blue 285.00
Compote, 4" – 10" . . . . . 40.00 – 85.00
Vaseline . . . . . 60.00 – 110.00
Green/Blue . . . . . 100.00 – 200.00
Creamer or Spooner 70.00
Vaseline 110.00
Green/Blue 150.00
Lamp, 3 Sizes . . . . . 135.00 – 295.00
Vaseline . . . . . 150.00 – 315.00
Green/Blue . . . . . 250.00 – 575.00
Sugar 90.00
Vaseline 125.00
Green/Blue 195.00

TREE OF LOVE
Bowl 25.00
Butter or Cheese Dish 75.00
Compote 40.00
Creamer or Spooner 25.00
Cup 20.00
Plate, Ruffled 30.00
Sugar 35.00

TREE STUMP
Bowl, Covered, Ftd. 65.00
Compote, Covered, Stemmed 90.00
Sauce, Ftd. 20.00

TREE TRUNK
Vase, Standard 30.00
Vase, Mid Size Funeral 125.00

TREFOIL FINECUT
Bowl, Ruffled, Rare 500.00
Bowl, Ice Cream Shape, Very Rare 800.00
Bowl, Rnd., Flared, Very Rare 750.00
Plate, Very Rare 1500*

TRIPLE THUMBPRINTS
Berry Bowl, Sm. 15.00
Berry Bowl, Lg. 45.00
Butter 85.00
Creamer or Spooner 25.00
Pitcher 125.00
Tumbler 30.00
Shakers, ea. 25.00
Sugar 40.00

TRIPLE TRIANGLE (DOYLE & U.S. GLASS)
Bowl, 6" – 10" . . . . . 10.00 – 25.00
Ruby Stain . . . . . 15.00 – 40.00
Bread Plate 35.00
Ruby Stain 80.00
Butter 55.00
Ruby Stain 75.00
Creamer or Spooner 20.00
Ruby Stain 55.00
Cup 10.00
Ruby Stain 25.00
Goblet 25.00
Ruby Stain 50.00
Mug 30.00
Ruby Stain 40.00
Pitcher 75.00
Ruby Stain 150.00
Tumbler 15.00
Ruby Stain 35.00
Sugar 25.00
Ruby Stain 80.00
Wine 10.00
Ruby Stain 40.00

TRIPOD STEM (ARCHED TRIPOD)
Butter 75.00
Celery Vase 25.00
Creamer or Spooner 30.00
Goblet 60.00
Pitcher 135.00
Tumbler 30.00
Sugar 40.00
Wine 20.00

TROPICAL VILLA
Compote, Covered 165.00

TROUT AND FLY (MILLERSBURG)
Bowl, Rare 600*
Plate, Very Rare 1200*

TRUNCATED CUBE
Berry Bowl, Sm. 15.00
Ruby Stain 20.00
Berry Bowl, Lg. 45.00
Ruby Stain 50.00
Butter 80.00
Ruby Stain 100.00
Celery Vase 20.00
Ruby Stain 25.00
Creamer or Spooner 25.00
Ruby Stain 35.00
Cruet 65.00
Ruby Stain 80.00
Decanter 70.00
Ruby Stain 90.00
Goblet 50.00
Ruby Stain 60.00
Milk Pitcher 65.00
Ruby Stain 85.00
Pitcher 100.00
Ruby Stain 140.00
Tumbler 25.00
Ruby Stain 35.00
Sauce 15.00

Ruby Stain. 25.00
Shakers, ea. 20.00
Ruby Stain. 30.00
Sugar 45.00
Ruby Stain. 55.00
Syrup, 2 Sizes . . . . . 40.00 – 60.00
Ruby Stain . . . . . 50.00 – 75.00
Toothpick Hldr. 30.00
Ruby Stain. 70.00
Water Tray. 35.00
Ruby Stain. 45.00
Wine 15.00
Ruby Stain. 35.00

TULIP

Butter. 60.00
Celery Vase 25.00
Compote, High or Low . . . . . 30.00 – 50.00
Creamer or Spooner. 20.00
Decanter 50.00
Goblet 45.00
Jug, Pint. 35.00
Jug, Quart. 50.00
Pitcher. 85.00
Tumbler. 20.00
Sugar 25.00
Wine 15.00

TULIP WITH SAWTOOTH

Barber Bottle 55.00
Butter. 110.00
Celery Vase 20.00
Champagne 15.00
Compote, Covered, 6" – 8". . . . . 90.00 – 110.00
Compote, Open, 6" – 9" . . . . . 60.00 – 85.00
Creamer or Spooner. 20.00
Cruet 50.00
Decanter 135.00
Egg Cup 20.00
Goblet 50.00
Honey Dish 30.00
Mug 85.00
Plate, 6" 20.00
Pomade Jar 40.00
Pitcher. 185.00
Tumbler. 50.00
Salt, Master, Either Edge 20.00
Sugar 30.00
Whiskey Tumbler. 30.00
Wine 45.00

TWIGS (BEAUTY BUD)

Vase. 25.00

TWIN CORNUCOPIA

Vase. 100.00
Amber 175.00
Vaseline. 200.00
Engraved 135.00

TWIN CRESCENTS

Butter. 50.00
Creamer or Spooner. 20.00
Pomade Jar 30.00
Sugar 25.00

TWINKLE STAR (UTAH)

Bowl, Covered, 6" – 8". . . . . 25.00 – 50.00
Bowl, Open, 6" – 8" . . . . . 15.00 – 35.00
Butter, 2 Sizes. . . . . 40.00 – 55.00
Cake Plate 25.00
Cake Stand, 8" – 10". 35.00
Celery Vase 20.00
Compote, Covered 45.00
Compote, Open 35.00
Condiment Set, 3 Pcs. 75.00
Creamer or Spooner. 20.00
Cruet 60.00
Goblet 45.00
Pickle Tray. 15.00
Pitcher. 80.00
Tumbler. 20.00
Sauce 10.00
Shakers, ea. 15.00
Sugar 25.00
Syrup 60.00
Wine 10.00

TWINS (HORSESHOE CURVE)

Berry Bowl, Lg.. . . . . 30.00
Berry Bowl, Sm. 10.00
Bowl, 6½". 15.00
Bowl, 10" 35.00
Plate, 7½". 35.00
Pitcher. 65.00
Tumbler 15.00
Rose Bowl, 7". 40.00

TWIN SNOWSHOES

Butter. 65.00
Cake Stand. 35.00
Celery Vase 20.00
Compotes, Various . . . . . 20.00 – 55.00
Creamer or Spooner. 20.00
Cruet 60.00
Cup 10.00
Pitcher. 100.00
Tumbler. 25.00
Relish. 15.00
Relish, Hndl. 20.00
Sugar 30.00
Toothpick Hldr. 25.00
Toy Table Set. 125.00
Wine 10.00

TWIN TEARDROPS

Banana Plate 30.00
Bowl, 6" 15.00
Celery. 25.00
Compote. 45.00
Cruet 65.00
Goblet 40.00
Plate, Sq, 8" 35.00
Plate, Rnd, 10". 35.00
Sauce 15.00
Sugar 25.00

TWISTED RIB

Vase. 30.00

TWO BAND

Butter. 45.00
Celery Vase 20.00
Compote. 30.00
Compote, Low, Covered w/Hndls. 45.00
Creamer or Spooner. 20.00
Pickle Dish. 15.00
Plate, Hndl. 25.00
Pitcher 75.00
Tumbler 15.00
Shakers, ea. 15.00
Sugar 25.00
Toy Table Set, Complete 85.00

TWO OWLS

Compote, Covered, Lg. 250.00

TWO PANEL

Bowls, 7" – 9". . . . . 20.00 – 45.00
Amber. . . . . 25.00 – 50.00
Vaseline . . . . . 30.00 – 55.00
Green/Blue . . . . . 35.00 – 60.00
Butter. 65.00
Amber 70.00
Vaseline. 100.00
Green/Blue. 100.00
Celery Vase 30.00
Amber 55.00
Vaseline. 75.00
Green/Blue. 65.00
Compote, Covered 55.00
Amber 70.00
Vaseline. 125.00
Green/Blue. 100.00
Compote, Open 40.00
Amber 65.00
Vaseline. 85.00
Green/Blue. 75.00
Creamer or Spooner. 25.00
Amber 30.00
Vaseline. 45.00
Green/Blue. 40.00
Goblet 40.00
Amber 45.00
Vaseline. 60.00
Green/Blue. 55.00
Mug 30.00
Amber 40.00
Vaseline. 50.00
Green/Blue. 55.00
Oil Lamp, Tall 100.00
Amber 200.00
Vaseline. 375.00
Green/Blue. 295.00
Pitcher 85.00
Amber 100.00
Vaseline. 150.00
Green/Blue. 135.00
Tumbler 25.00
Amber 30.00
Vaseline. 40.00
Green/Blue. 35.00
Salt, Ind. 15.00
Amber 20.00
Vaseline. 25.00
Green/Blue. 25.00
Salt, Master 25.00
Amber 30.00
Vaseline. 35.00
Green/Blue. 30.00
Shakers, ea. 30.00
Amber 40.00
Vaseline. 50.00
Green/Blue. 45.00
Tray Hndl. 35.00
Amber 55.00
Vaseline. 75.00
Green/Blue. 60.00
Wine 20.00
Amber 25.00
Vaseline. 35.00
Green/Blue. 40.00

TWO POST

Oil Lamp, 2 Variations . . . . . 175.00 – 225.00

U.S. COMET (DOYLE'S COMET)

Bowls, Various . . . . . 15.00 – 35.00
Amber. . . . . 25.00 – 45.00
Vaseline . . . . . 50.00 – 70.00
Butter. 70.00
Amber 90.00
Vaseline. 145.00
Celery Vase 25.00
Amber 35.00
Vaseline. 50.00
Creamer or Spooner. 25.00
Amber 35.00
Vaseline. 50.00
Goblet 45.00
Amber 55.00
Vaseline. 70.00
Pickle Dish. 15.00
Amber 25.00
Vaseline. 50.00
Pitcher 85.00
Amber 100.00
Vaseline. 165.00
Sugar 35.00
Amber 45.00
Vaseline. 65.00
Tumbler 20.00
Amber 30.00
Vaseline. 45.00
Wine 15.00
Amber 25.00
Vaseline. 40.00

U.S. #16046

Vase. 50.00

U.S. GLASS #25 (AKA: Late Crystal)

Berry Bowl, Lg.. . . . . 35.00
Berry Bowl, Sm. 15.00
Butter. 60.00
Celery. 20.00
Compote, Tall. 45.00
Compote, Short 40.00
Creamer, Spooner, or Sugar. 25.00
Egg Cup 30.00
Pitcher. 75.00
Tumbler 20.00

Sauce 15.00
Shakers, ea. 25.00
Vase 30.00

U.S. GLASS LATE BLOCK

See Late Block (Duncan's #331, U.S. Glass)

U.S. GRANT (PATRIOT AND SOLDIER)

Plate, 11", Sq. 85.00

U.S. HOBSTAR

Bowls, Various . . . . . 15.00 – 40.00
Butter 60.00
Candy Dish, Covered 40.00
Celery Vase 25.00
Creamer or Spooner 20.00
Pickle Dish 20.00
Pitcher 80.00
Tumbler 20.00
Shakers, ea. 20.00
Sugar 25.00

U.S. NURSERY RHYME

Butter 65.00
Creamer or Spooner 25.00
Pitcher 70.00
Tumbler 20.00
Sugar 35.00

U.S. RIB #15061

Berry Bowl, Lg. 30.00
Berry Bowl, Sm. 15.00
Butter 65.00
Cake Stand 40.00
Celery Tray 20.00
Celery Vase 25.00
Compote 35.00
Creamer, Spooner, or Sugar 20.00
Desert 15.00
Goblet 25.00
Pickle Dish 20.00
Pitcher 75.00
Tumbler 20.00
Wine 20.00

U.S. SHERATON

Berry Bowl, Sm. 20.00
Berry Bowl, Lg. 45.00
Bowls, Ftd. . . . . . 20.00 – 40.00
Butter 65.00
Creamer or Spooner 25.00
Cruet 45.00
Dresser Set, 3 Pcs. 70.00
Jam Jar 30.00
Mayonnaise Plate 25.00
Miniature Lamp 65.00
Mustard Jar 25.00
Pintray 20.00
Plate, Sq. 20.00
Pitcher, 2 Styles . . . . . 70.00 – 95.00
Tumbler 25.00
Ring Stand 30.00
Sardine Tray 25.00
Shakers, ea. 20.00
Sugar 30.00
Sundae Dish 20.00
Syrup 55.00
Tea Tumbler 20.00
Toothpick Hldr. 20.00
Trinket Tray 30.00

U.S. WICKER EDGE

Compote 40.00
Fruit Bowl 35.00

VALENCIA WAFFLE

Berry Bowl, Sm. 15.00
Amber 20.00
Vaseline 25.00
Green/Blue 30.00
Berry Bowl, Lg. 35.00
Amber 40.00
Vaseline 45.00
Green/Blue 55.00
Bread Plate 30.00
Amber 35.00
Vaseline 60.00
Green/Blue 55.00
Butter 65.00
Amber 75.00
Vaseline 95.00
Green/Blue 100.00
Cake Stand 40.00
Amber 70.00
Vaseline 95.00
Green/Blue 95.00
Caster Set 95.00
Amber 150.00
Vaseline 250.00
Green/Blue 235.00
Celery Vase 25.00
Amber 45.00
Vaseline 65.00
Green/Blue 55.00
Compote, High or Low . . . . . 30.00 – 45.00
Amber . . . . . 35.00 – 70.00
Vaseline . . . . . 60.00 – 95.00
Green/Blue . . . . . 60.00 – 95.00
Dish, Oblong, 7" – 9" . . . . . 20.00 – 35.00
Amber . . . . . 25.00 – 40.00
Vaseline . . . . . 25.00 – 50.00
Green/Blue . . . . . 30.00 – 60.00
Goblet 40.00
Amber 50.00
Vaseline 55.00
Green/Blue 60.00
Milk Pitcher 55.00
Amber 60.00
Vaseline 95.00
Green/Blue 95.00
Pickle Dish 20.00
Amber 25.00
Vaseline 30.00
Green/Blue 35.00
Pickle Jar 25.00
Amber 45.00
Vaseline 60.00
Green/Blue 50.00
Pitcher 95.00
Amber 100.00
Vaseline 145.00
Green/Blue 165.00
Tumbler 20.00
Amber 25.00
Vaseline 25.00
Green/Blue 30.00
Relish Dish 20.00
Amber 25.00
Vaseline 25.00
Green/Blue 30.00
Salt Dip 15.00
Amber 20.00
Vaseline 25.00
Green/Blue 25.00
Sauce, Flat or Ftd. 10.00
Amber 15.00
Vaseline 20.00
Green/Blue 20.00
Shakers, ea. 15.00
Amber 20.00
Vaseline 25.00
Green/Blue 25.00
Sugar 40.00
Amber 50.00
Vaseline 60.00
Green/Blue 65.00
Syrup 55.00
Amber 80.00
Vaseline 150.00
Green/Blue 135.00
Water Tray 30.00
Amber 50.00
Vaseline 65.00
Green/Blue 60.00

VALENTINE

Berry Bowl, Lg. 45.00
Berry Bowl, Sm. 15.00
Bowl, 10" 50.00
Plate, 11" 85.00

VEGETABLES

Relish Tray 40.00

VENETIAN

Berry Bowl, Lg. 50.00
Berry Bowl, Sm. 20.00
Breakfast Creamer & Sugar . . . . . 25.00 – 30.00
Butter 125.00
Compote, 6" 100.00
Compote, 9", Squat 75.00
Creamer or Spooner 55.00
Lamp w/Shade 400.00
Giant Vase (Rose Bowl) 300.00
Pickle Dish, Deep 40.00
Pitcher 250.00
Punch Bowl & Base, Rare 500.00
Punch Cup, Stemmed 50.00
Rose Bowl, 6" 125.00
Sherbet, Hndl. 75.00
Spittoon Whimsey 150.00
Sugar 65.00
Tumbler 40.00
Vase, 6" 60.00
Vase, 9" 95.00
Vase, Cylinder Shape, Scarce 110.00

VENICE

Berry Bowl, Sm. 15.00
Amber 20.00
Vaseline 25.00
Berry Bowl, Lg. 40.00
Amber 45.00
Vaseline 55.00
Butter 55.00
Amber 65.00
Vaseline 135.00
Creamer or Spooner 20.00
Amber 25.00
Vaseline 45.00
Goblet 45.00
Amber 55.00
Vaseline 65.00
Pickle Jar 25.00
Amber 30.00
Vaseline 35.00
Pitcher 75.00
Amber 200.00
Vaseline 250.00
Tumbler 20.00
Amber 25.00
Vaseline 45.00
Sugar 30.00
Amber 35.00
Vaseline 60.00

VENUS

Butter 85.00
Celery Vase 20.00
Compote, Covered, 8" 65.00
Creamer or Spooner 35.00
Plate, Crying Baby 70.00
Pitcher 125.00
Tumbler 35.00
Shakers, ea. 25.00
Sugar 40.00

VICTORIA (RIVERSIDE)

Berry Bowl, Sm. 15.00
Ruby Stain 25.00
Amber Stain 35.00
Berry Bowl, Lg. 30.00
Ruby Stain 50.00
Amber Stain 70.00
Butter 65.00
Ruby Stain 110.00
Amber Stain 145.00
Celery Dish 20.00
Ruby Stain 30.00
Amber Stain 40.00
Celery Vase 25.00
Ruby Stain 40.00
Amber Stain 45.00
Compote, 2 Sizes . . . . . 25.00 – 45.00
Ruby Stain . . . . . 35.00 – 65.00
Amber Stain . . . . . 50.00 – 85.00
Creamer or Spooner 30.00
Ruby Stain 45.00
Amber Stain 60.00

Creamer, Ind. 20.00
Ruby Stain. 30.00
Amber Stain. 40.00
Cruet 70.00
Ruby Stain. 85.00
Amber Stain. 125.00
Jelly 25.00
Ruby Stain. 40.00
Amber Stain. 400.00
Pickle Dish. 15.00
Ruby Stain. 30.00
Amber Stain. 40.00
Pickle Jar 40.00
Ruby Stain. 60.00
Amber Stain. 80.00
Pitcher 90.00
Ruby Stain. 165.00
Amber Stain. 210.00
Tumbler 20.00
Ruby Stain. 30.00
Amber Stain. 40.00
Sauce 10.00
Ruby Stain. 25.00
Amber Stain. 35.00
Sugar 45.00
Ruby Stain. 65.00
Amber Stain. 80.00
Syrup 70.00
Ruby Stain. 95.00
Amber Stain. 135.00
Toothpick Hldr. 50.00
Ruby Stain. 70.00
Amber Stain. 90.00

VIKING
Apothecary Jar 75.00
Bowl, Covered, 8" – 9" . . . . . 55.00 – 65.00
Bread Platter 65.00
Butter. 85.00
Casserole w/Lid 55.00
Celery Vase 25.00
Compote, Covered, High, 7" – 9" . 45.00 – 85.00
Compote, Covered, Low, 9" 65.00
Compote, Open, High 50.00
Creamer or Spooner. 45.00
Cup, Ftd. 25.00
Egg Cup 35.00
Jam Jar. 75.00
Mug 55.00
Pickle Dish. 20.00
Pitcher 145.00
Relish Tray. 25.00
Salt, Master, Ftd. 50.00
Sugar 75.00

VINEGAR AND OIL CRUET
One Shape 60.00

V-IN-HEART
Pitcher. 125.00

WADING HERON
Pickle Jar w/Lid 95.00
Green/Blue. 115.00
Pitcher 250.00
Green/Blue. 335.00
Tumbler 55.00
Green/Blue. 85.00

WAFFLE AND FINECUT
Banana Boat, 12" 45.00
Bowl. 20.00
Butter. 65.00
Creamer or Spooner. 25.00
Pitcher 95.00
Tumbler 15.00
Sugar 25.00
Wine 20.00

WAFFLE AND STAR BAND
Butter. 50.00
Compote. 30.00
Creamer or Spooner. 20.00
Nappy 25.00
Pickle Dish. 20.00
Punch Bowl 80.00
Punch Cup 15.00
Rose Bowl 35.00
Sugar 25.00
Toothpick Hldr. 40.00

WAFFLE BLOCK (IMPERIALS #698)
(Condensed List — over 40 pieces in pattern)
Basket, Hndl. 25.00
Bowl, 7" – 9" 20.00
Butter. 55.00
Celery Tray. 20.00
Compote. 35.00
Creamer, Spooner, or Sugar 20.00
Cruet 65.00
Fruit Bowl w/Stand. 55.00
Parfait, Stemmed 20.00
Pickle Dish. 20.00
Plate. 25.00
Pitcher 85.00
Tumbler 20.00
Punch Bowl 110.00
Punch Cup 15.00
Rose Bowl 35.00
Shakers, ea. 20.00
Syrup 55.00
Vase. 25.00

WAFFLE VARIANT
Berry Bowl, Sm. 20.00
Berry Bowl, Lg. 40.00
Butter. 55.00
Carafe 30.00
Celery Vase, Flat or Ftd. 25.00
Cheese Dish, Covered 60.00
Creamer or Spooner. 20.00
Cruet 45.00
Ice Cream Tray. 25.00
Sugar 25.00
Sugar Shaker 35.00
Tray, 7" – 8" 25.00

WAFFLE WINDOW
Shakers, ea. 45.00

WASHINGTON CENTENNIAL
Bowl, Rnd., 7" – 9" 35.00
Bowl, Oval, 7" – 9" 40.00
Butter. 90.00
Cake Stand, 8½"x10" 65.00
Celery. 30.00
Champagne 55.00
Compote, Covered, 7" – 8" 85.00
Compote, Open, 7" – 8" 45.00
Creamer or Spooner. 70.00
Egg Cup, Ftd. 30.00
Milk Pitcher. 125.00
Pickle Dish, Fish Shape 35.00
Pitcher 155.00
Tumbler 50.00
Platter, Lettered 125.00
Salt, Master 40.00
Salt, Ind. 20.00
Sauce 15.00
Shakers, ea. 55.00
Sugar 85.00
Syrup 165.00
Wine 45.00

WASHINGTON (EARLY)
Ale Glass 125.00
Bitters Bottle 85.00
Bowl, Covered, 5" – 8" . . . . . 25.00 – 55.00
Bowl, Open, 5" – 8" . . . . . 15.00 – 40.00
Bowl, Oval, 7" – 10" . . . . . 25.00 – 50.00
Butter. 175.00
Celery Vase 90.00
Champagne 125.00
Claret 25.00
Compote, Covered. . . . . 125.00 – 175.00
Compote, Open . . . . . 50.00 – 85.00
Cordial 125.00
Creamer or Spooner. 200.00
Decanter, 2 Sizes . . . . . 100.00 – 125.00
Egg Cup 75.00
Goblet, 2 Sizes . . . . . 30.00 – 55.00
Honey Dish 30.00
Jelly Tumbler 30.00
Lamp 150.00
Mug, 2 Sizes . . . . . 55.00 – 85.00
Plate, 6" – 7" 25.00
Pitcher 300.00
Tumbler 65.00
Salt Dip, Ind. 20.00
Salt Dip, Master. 55.00
Sauce 15.00
Sugar 125.00
Syrup 175.00
Wine 100.00

WASHINGTON HATCHET (LIBBEY)
Novelty 65.00
Ruby Stain. 95.00

WATERFORD
Butter. 70.00
Celery Vase 30.00
Creamer or Spooner. 25.00
Double Relish 30.00
Goblet 45.00
Pickle Dish. 25.00
Sugar 45.00

WEDDING RING
Butter. 65.00
Champagne 25.00
Creamer or Spooner. 20.00
Decanter 125.00
Finger Lamp 85.00
Lamp, Tall 80.00
Pitcher 75.00
Tumbler 20.00
Sugar 100.00
Syrup 65.00
Wine 20.00

WELLINGTON
Berry Bowl, Lg. 30.00
Ruby Stain. 35.00
Berry Bowl, Sm. 10.00
Ruby Stain. 15.00
Butter. 70.00
Ruby Stain. 90.00
Creamer or Spooner. 20.00
Ruby Stain. 30.00
Goblet 25.00
Ruby Stain. 45.00
Pickle Dish. 15.00
Ruby Stain. 25.00
Pitcher 80.00
Ruby Stain. 130.00
Sugar 25.00
Ruby Stain. 45.00
Tumbler 15.00
Ruby Stain. 25.00
Wine 15.00
Ruby Stain. 25.00

WESTMORELAND'S #98 (Condensed List)
Bowls, Various . . . . . 10.00 – 55.00
Butter. 55.00
Celery. 25.00
Creamer or Spooner. 20.00
Pitcher 65.00
Tumbler 10.00
Pickle Dish. 15.00
Sugar 20.00
Wine 15.00

WESTMORELAND'S #750
Basket, 3" – 8" . . . . . 20.00 – 65.00

WESTMORELAND'S #777
Berry Bowl, Sm. 15.00
Berry Bowl, Sm. 45.00
Butter. 65.00
Creamer or Spooner. 20.00
Nappy 25.00
Sugar 25.00

WESTMORELAND'S DIMPLED DIAMOND
Child's Condiment Set, 4 Pcs. 85.00

WESTON
Bowls, Various . . . . . 15.00 – 50.00
Butter. 65.00
Cake Stand. 35.00
Creamer or Spooner. 20.00
Plate. 30.00
Pitcher 75.00
Tumbler 20.00

Sugar 25.00

WESTWARD HO

Bread Plate 200.00
Butter 225.00
Celery Vase 100.00
Compote, Covered, 5" – 9" . . . . 150.00 – 300.00
Compote, Open, 5" – 8" 165.00
Creamer or Spooner 100.00
Goblet 100.00
Marmalade Jar 250.00
Milk Pitcher 175.00
Mug, 2 Sizes . . . . . 175.00 – 250.00
Pickle Dish 85.00
Platter, Oval 150.00
Pitcher 275.00
Tumbler 100.00
Sauce, 3" – 5" . . . . . 95.00 – 125.00
Sugar 225.00
Wine 225.00

WHEAT AND BARLEY

Berry Bowl, Sm. 15.00
  Amber 20.00
  Vaseline 25.00
  Green/Blue 30.00
Berry Bowl, Lg. 35.00
  Amber 40.00
  Vaseline 50.00
  Green/Blue 50.00
Butter 70.00
  Amber 80.00
  Vaseline 95.00
  Green/Blue 95.00
Cake Stand 35.00
  Amber 45.00
  Vaseline 95.00
  Green/Blue 65.00
Compote, Open 35.00
  Amber 45.00
  Vaseline 65.00
  Green/Blue 75.00
Compote w/Lid 45.00
  Amber 50.00
  Vaseline 75.00
  Green/Blue 85.00
Creamer or Spooner 25.00
  Amber 35.00
  Vaseline 45.00
  Green/Blue 50.00
Goblet 40.00
  Amber 50.00
  Vaseline 60.00
  Green/Blue 65.00
Mug 30.00
  Amber 35.00
  Vaseline 55.00
  Green/Blue 50.00
Plate, 7" – 9" 30.00
  Amber 35.00
  Vaseline 45.00
  Green/Blue 40.00
Pitcher 80.00
  Amber 95.00
  Vaseline 135.00
  Green/Blue 145.00
Tumbler 15.00
  Amber 20.00
  Vaseline 30.00
  Green/Blue 35.00
Shakers, ea. 20.00
  Amber 30.00
  Vaseline 45.00
  Green/Blue 50.00
Sugar 25.00
  Amber 40.00
  Vaseline 65.00
  Green/Blue 60.00
Syrup 90.00
  Amber 165.00
  Vaseline 200.00
  Green/Blue 225.00

WHEAT SHEAF (All pieces rare)

Basket, Hndl. 65.00
Compote, 5½" 50.00
Compote, 8" – 9" 70.00
Celery Vase 30.00
Cruet, Double Hndl. 65.00
Decanter w/Stopper 150.00
Milk Pitcher 95.00
Pitcher, 3 Sizes . . . . . 95.00 – 145.00
Rose Bowl 65.00
Tray 40.00
Tumbler 35.00
Punch Bowl 200.00
Punch Cup 15.00
Sweetmeat w/Lid 85.00
Wine 25.00
Vase, 8", Stemmed 45.00

WHEEL OF FORTUNE

Butter 45.00
Creamer or Spooner 15.00
Shakers, ea. 15.00
Sugar 20.00

WHEELS

Berry Bowl, Sm. 10.00
Berry Bowl, Lg. 40.00
Fruit Bowl, 10" 50.00
Rose Bowl, 7½" 60.00
Tumbler 25.00

WHIRLED SUNBURST IN CIRCLE

Bowl 30.00
Butter 70.00
Creamer or Spooner 20.00
Pitcher 90.00
Tumbler 20.00
Sugar 30.00

WHIRLWIND

Bowls, Various . . . . . 20.00 – 40.00
Compote, Lg., Open 35.00
Pitcher 85.00
Shakers, ea. 25.00
Tumbler 15.00

WHISK BROOM

Pickle Dish 40.00
  Amber 55.00
  Vaseline 95.00
  Green/Blue 65.00

WIDE AND NARROW

Butter 55.00
Creamer or Spooner 25.00
Oil Lamp 95.00
Pitcher 65.00
Tumbler 15.00
Sugar 20.00

WIDE RIB (NORTHWOOD)

Vase, 7" – 13" . . . . . 25.00 – 80.00

WILDFLOWER

Bowl, Rnd., 6½" 20.00
  Amber 25.00
  Vaseline 25.00
  Green/Blue 30.00
Bowl, Sq., 6" – 9" . . . . . 20.00 – 40.00
  Amber . . . . . 25.00 – 45.00
  Vaseline . . . . . 25.00 – 45.00
  Green/Blue . . . . . 30.00 – 50.00
Bread Plate, Oval 30.00
  Amber 35.00
  Vaseline 40.00
  Green/Blue 45.00
Butter 65.00
  Amber 70.00
  Vaseline 95.00
  Green/Blue 95.00
Cake Basket, Oval 45.00
  Amber 70.00
  Vaseline 95.00
  Green/Blue 95.00
Cake Plate 35.00
  Amber 40.00
  Vaseline 45.00
  Green/Blue 50.00
Cake Stand 40.00
  Amber 85.00
  Vaseline 95.00
  Green/Blue 95.00
Celery Vase 20.00
  Amber 50.00
  Vaseline 65.00
  Green/Blue 60.00
Champagne 15.00
  Amber 40.00
  Vaseline 50.00
  Green/Blue 45.00
Compote, Covered, 7" – 8",
  High or Low, 3 Styles . . . . . 35.00 – 60.00
  Amber . . . . . 40.00 – 65.00
  Vaseline . . . . . 65.00 – 95.00
  Green/Blue . . . . . 60.00 – 90.00
Creamer or Spooner 20.00
  Amber 35.00
  Vaseline 50.00
  Green/Blue 50.00
Dish, Sq., 6" – 8" . . . . . 15.00 – 30.00
  Amber . . . . . 20.00 – 35.00
  Vaseline . . . . . 20.00 – 35.00
  Green/Blue . . . . . 25.00 – 40.00
Goblet 40.00
  Amber 50.00
  Vaseline 60.00
  Green/Blue 70.00
Platter, 8"x11" 35.00
  Amber 40.00
  Vaseline 55.00
  Green/Blue 60.00
Pitcher 80.00
  Amber 90.00
  Vaseline 125.00
  Green/Blue 145.00
Tumbler 20.00
  Amber 25.00
  Vaseline 35.00
  Green/Blue 40.00
Relish 15.00
  Amber 20.00
  Vaseline 25.00
  Green/Blue 30.00
Salt Dip 10.00
  Amber 20.00
  Vaseline 35.00
  Green/Blue 40.00
Sauce, Flat or Ftd. 10.00
  Amber 15.00
  Vaseline 25.00
  Green/Blue 30.00
Shakers, ea. 20.00
  Amber 35.00
  Vaseline 50.00
  Green/Blue 50.00
Sugar 30.00
  Amber 35.00
  Vaseline 65.00
  Green/Blue 65.00
Syrup 100.00
  Amber 175.00
  Vaseline 275.00
  Green/Blue 265.00
Water Tray 35.00
  Amber 60.00
  Vaseline 75.00
  Green/Blue 70.00
Wine 20.00
  Amber 35.00
  Vaseline 50.00
  Green/Blue 55.00

WILD ROSE LADY'S MEDALLION (RIVERSIDE GLASS CO.)

Oil Lamp, 4 Sizes . . . . . 400.00 – 675.00

WILD ROSE LAMP

Lamp, 4 Sizes . . . . . 300.00 – 550.00

WILD ROSE WITH BOW KNOT

Berry Bowl, Sm. 15.00
Berry Bowl, Lg. 50.00
Butter 85.00
Creamer or Spooner 20.00
Pitcher 125.00
Tumbler 25.00
Sauce 15.00

Shakers, ea. . . . 20.00
Smoke Set on Tray 100.00
Sugar 30.00
Toothpick Hldr. 30.00
Tray, Rect. 35.00

WILD ROSE WREATH
Mini Compote, Gilded 50.00

WILLOW OAK
Berry Bowl, Sm. 15.00
Amber 20.00
Vaseline. 30.00
Green/Blue. 25.00
Berry Bowl, Lg. 35.00
Amber 40.00
Vaseline. 55.00
Green/Blue. 45.00
Butter 60.00
Amber 85.00
Vaseline. 125.00
Green/Blue. 125.00
Cake Stand. 50.00
Amber 80.00
Vaseline. 125.00
Green/Blue. 125.00
Celery Vase 30.00
Amber 60.00
Vaseline. 80.00
Green/Blue. 75.00
Creamer or Spooner 30.00
Amber 35.00
Vaseline. 55.00
Green/Blue. 50.00
Milk Pitcher 65.00
Amber 85.00
Vaseline. 125.00
Green/Blue. 125.00
Mug 45.00
Amber 50.00
Vaseline. 65.00
Green/Blue. 55.00
Plate. 30.00
Amber 50.00
Vaseline. 65.00
Green/Blue. 60.00
Pitcher. 75.00
Amber 100.00
Vaseline. 150.00
Green/Blue. 145.00
Tumbler 20.00
Amber 25.00
Vaseline. 40.00
Green/Blue. 45.00
Sauce 15.00
Amber 20.00
Vaseline. 30.00
Green/Blue. 25.00
Shakers, ea. 25.00
Amber 40.00
Vaseline. 60.00
Green/Blue. 55.00
Sugar 45.00
Amber 55.00
Vaseline. 80.00
Green/Blue. 70.00
Tray 45.00
Amber 65.00
Vaseline. 95.00
Green/Blue. 85.00
Waste Bowl 25.00
Amber 45.00
Vaseline. 60.00
Green/Blue. 50.00

WILTEC
Bonbon 30.00
Ruby Stain. 45.00
Butter. 65.00
Ruby Stain. 95.00
Cigar Jar. 50.00
Ruby Stain. 65.00
Creamer or Spooner. 25.00
Ruby Stain. 30.00
Custard Cup. 15.00
Ruby Stain. 20.00
Flower Pot, Scarce 60.00
Ruby Stain. 85.00
Plate, 6" – 8". 25.00
Ruby Stain. 30.00
Plate, 10" – 12". 35.00
Ruby Stain. 40.00
Pitcher 85.00
Ruby Stain. 150.00
Tumbler 15.00
Ruby Stain. 25.00
Punch Bowl 100.00
Ruby Stain. 195.00
Punch Cup 15.00
Ruby Stain. 20.00
Sugar 25.00
Ruby Stain. 55.00

WILTED FLOWERS
Basket 65.00
Bowl. 40.00

WINDFLOWER (All pieces rare)
Bowl. 75.00
Black 90.00
Nappy, Hndl. 90.00
Plate. 125.00

WINDMILL SERVER
Dispenser & Glass in Nickel-plated Frame, Rare. 125.00
Vaseline. 325.00

WINDOW TRIM VASE
Vase for Shelf Supports 15.00

WINDSOR ANVIL
Paperweight. 55.00
Amber 80.00
Green/Blue. 95.00

WINGED SCROLL
Berry Bowl, Lg.. . . . . 35.00
Green/Blue. 45.00
Custard 60.00
Berry Bowl, Sm. 15.00
Green/Blue. 25.00
Custard 35.00
Bonbon 20.00
Green/Blue. 30.00
Custard 40.00
Butter. 80.00
Green/Blue. 95.00
Custard 135.00
Cake Stand. 45.00
Green/Blue. 55.00
Custard 65.00
Celery Vase 25.00
Green/Blue. 30.00
Custard 45.00
Cologne 60.00
Green/Blue. 75.00
Custard 90.00
Compote, High Standard 45.00
Green/Blue. 50.00
Custard 75.00
Cup 10.00
Green/Blue. 20.00
Custard 30.00
Creamer or Spooner. 20.00
Green/Blue. 30.00
Custard 45.00
Cruet 70.00
Green/Blue. 85.00
Custard 120.00
Humidor 65.00
Green/Blue. 80.00
Custard 140.00
Olive Dish 20.00
Green/Blue. 30.00
Custard 45.00
Pickle Dish. 20.00
Green/Blue. 30.00
Custard 45.00
Saucer 10.00
Green/Blue. 20.00
Custard 35.00
Smoker's Set 75.00
Green/Blue. 90.00
Custard 125.00
Sugar 35.00
Green/Blue. 45.00
Custard 65.00
Syrup 85.00
Green/Blue. 110.00
Custard 165.00
Toothpick Hldr. 35.00
Green/Blue. 45.00
Custard 75.00
Trinket Box 40.00
Green/Blue. 50.00
Custard 80.00

WINTER CABBAGE
Bowl, Ftd.. . . . . 35.00

WISCONSIN
Banana Stand 40.00
Bonbon 20.00
Bowl, Covered, 6" – 8", 2 Shapes. 25.00 – 60.00
Bowl, Open, 6" – 8" . . . . 15.00 – 40.00
Butter. 55.00
Cake Stand, 6½" – 11½" . . . . 25.00 – 45.00
Celery Tray. 30.00
Celery Vase 20.00
Compote, Covered, 5" – 8". . . . . 25.00 – 60.00
Compote, Open, 6" – 8" . . . . 20.00 – 45.00
Condiment Set, 5 Pcs. 75.00
Creamer or Spooner. 20.00
Cruet 125.00
Cup & Saucer. 35.00
Custard Cup. 10.00
Goblet 40.00
Jelly Dish, Covered or Open . . . . 25.00 – 35.00
Jam Jar 125.00
Milk Pitcher. 60.00
Mug 25.00
Mustard Jar 30.00
Oil Bottle 40.00
Pickle Dish. 15.00
Pickle Jar 30.00
Plate, 5" – 7". 20.00
Preserve Dish, 6" – 8". 25.00
Pitcher 80.00
Tumbler 20.00
Relish Tray. 15.00
Saucer, Stemmed 15.00
Shakers, ea., 2 Shapes. 25.00
Sherbet Cup 10.00
Sugar 30.00
Sugar Shaker 45.00
Syrup 65.00
Toothpick Hldr. 25.00
Vase, 6", Rnd. 25.00
Wine 10.00

WM. J. BRYAN
Tumbler 95.00

WOLF
Mug 75.00
Amber 85.00
Vaseline. 130.00
Green/Blue. 110.00

WOODEN PAIL
Butter. 85.00
Amber 110.00
Vaseline. 110.00
Green/Blue. 125.00
Amethyst 250.00
Creamer or Spooner. 40.00
Amber 60.00
Vaseline. 60.00
Green/Blue. 80.00
Amethyst 125.00
Ice Bucket 65.00
Amber 85.00
Vaseline. 85.00
Green/Blue. 110.00
Amethyst 165.00
Jelly Bucket 30.00
Amber 60.00
Vaseline. 60.00
Green/Blue. 75.00

Amethyst . . . 90.00
Pitcher . . . 100.00
Amber . . . 125.00
Vaseline . . . 185.00
Green/Blue . . . 200.00
Amethyst . . . 250.00
Tumbler . . . 25.00
Amber . . . 35.00
Vaseline . . . 35.00
Green/Blue . . . 45.00
Amethyst . . . 75.00
Sugar . . . 40.00
Amber . . . 65.00
Vaseline . . . 65.00
Green/Blue . . . 80.00
Amethyst . . . 95.00
Sugar Pail, Open . . . 30.00
Amber . . . 50.00
Vaseline . . . 50.00
Green/Blue . . . 70.00
Amethyst . . . 80.00
Toothpick Hldr., 3 Sizes . . . 20.00 – 45.00
Amber . . . 25.00 – 50.00
Vaseline . . . 25.00 – 50.00
Green/Blue . . . 30.00 – 65.00
Amethyst . . . 40.00 – 75.00
Toy Table Set . . . 175.00

WYOMING
Bowl . . . 30.00
Butter . . . 85.00
Cake Stand . . . 45.00
Compote, Open . . . 35.00
Compote w/Lid . . . 50.00
Creamer . . . 25.00
Pitcher . . . 150.00
Tumbler . . . 60.00
Sauce . . . 20.00
Shaker . . . 50.00
Sugar, Open . . . 25.00
Sugar w/Lid . . . 35.00
Wine . . . 40.00

X-LOGS
Bowl, Oval . . . 25.00
Butter . . . 55.00
Cake Stand . . . 35.00
Creamer or Spooner . . . 20.00
Goblet . . . 40.00
Mug . . . 25.00
Pickle Dish . . . 15.00
Sauce . . . 10.00
Shakers, ea . . . 25.00
Sugar . . . 25.00
Wine . . . 20.00

X-RAY
Berry Bowl, Sm . . . 15.00
Green/Blue . . . 20.00
Berry Bowl, Lg . . . 45.00
Green/Blue . . . 55.00
Butter . . . 70.00
Green/Blue . . . 95.00
Celery Vase . . . 20.00
Green/Blue . . . 30.00
Compote . . . 40.00
Green/Blue . . . 50.00
Creamer or Spooner . . . 25.00
Green/Blue . . . 35.00
Cruet . . . 65.00
Green/Blue . . . 145.00
Cruet Set, Complete . . . 100.00
Green/Blue . . . 325.00
Jelly Compote . . . 30.00
Green/Blue . . . 40.00
Shakers, ea . . . 25.00
Green/Blue . . . 35.00
Sugar . . . 40.00
Green/Blue . . . 65.00
Syrup, Rare . . . 100.00
Green/Blue . . . 250.00
Toothpick Hldr . . . 40.00
Green/Blue . . . 75.00
Tray, Clover Leaf . . . 45.00
Green/Blue . . . 90.00

YALE
Berry Bowl, Sm . . . 15.00
Berry Bowl, Lg . . . 30.00
Butter . . . 45.00
Cake Stand . . . 30.00
Celery Vase . . . 20.00
Compote, Covered . . . 35.00
Compote, Open . . . 25.00
Creamer or Spooner . . . 20.00
Goblet . . . 35.00
Pitcher . . . 85.00
Tumbler . . . 20.00
Relish, Oval . . . 15.00
Sauce, Flat or Ftd . . . 10.00
Shakers, ea . . . 20.00
Sugar . . . 25.00
Syrup . . . 65.00

YOKE AND CIRCLE
Berry Bowl, Sm . . . 15.00
Berry Bowl, Lg . . . 45.00
Butter . . . 65.00
Celery Dish . . . 20.00
Creamer or Spooner . . . 25.00
Goblet . . . 50.00
Milk Pitcher . . . 60.00
Mustard Jar . . . 35.00
Pickle Dish . . . 20.00
Pitcher . . . 90.00
Tumbler . . . 20.00
Shakers, ea . . . 20.00
Sugar . . . 30.00

YORK
Banana Bowl . . . 35.00
Bowl, Sm . . . 15.00
Plate . . . 20.00
Rose Bowl, Rare . . . 100.00

YUTEC
Berry Bowl, Lg . . . 30.00
Berry Bowl, Sm . . . 10.00
Butter . . . 60.00
Cordial . . . 15.00
Creamer or Spooner . . . 20.00
Pickle Dish . . . 15.00
Pitcher . . . 75.00
Punch Bowl . . . 95.00
Punch Cup . . . 10.00
Relish Tray . . . 15.00
Sugar . . . 25.00
Tumbler . . . 15.00
Wine . . . 10.00

ZENITH
Candlesticks, ea . . . 45.00
Cruet . . . 50.00
Shakers, ea . . . 20.00

ZIG-ZAG BAND
Bowl, Covered, 7" with Squirrel Finial . . 125.00
Creamer . . . 40.00
Sugar . . . 65.00

ZIPPER
Bowl, 7" . . . 20.00
Butter . . . 60.00
Celery Vase . . . 20.00
Cheese Dish, Covered . . . 65.00
Compote, Covered . . . 55.00
Compote, Open . . . 35.00
Creamer or Spooner . . . 25.00
Cruet . . . 45.00
Dish, Oblong . . . 25.00
Goblet . . . 50.00
Jam Jar . . . 45.00
Milk Pitcher . . . 65.00
Pitcher . . . 90.00
Tumbler . . . 20.00
Relish Tray . . . 20.00
Salt Dip . . . 15.00
Sauce, Flat or Ftd . . . 10.00
Sugar . . . 30.00
Vase, Stemmed . . . 30.00

ZIPPER CROSS
Butter . . . 45.00
Compote . . . 30.00
Creamer or Spooner . . . 20.00
Mug . . . 35.00
Sugar . . . 25.00

ZIPPERED CORNER
Bowl . . . 35.00
Butter . . . 60.00
Creamer or Spooner . . . 25.00
Pickle Dish . . . 15.00
Sugar . . . 35.00
Syrup . . . 55.00

ZIPPERED HEART
Berry Bowl, Sm . . . 10.00
Berry Bowl, Lg . . . 25.00
Bowl, Sq . . . 35.00
Butter . . . 75.00
Candleholder from Punch Cup . . . 75.00
Celery Vase . . . 45.00
Creamer or Spooner . . . 25.00
Creamer or Sugar, Sm . . . 20.00
Custard Cup . . . 10.00
Finger Bowl & Plate . . . 40.00
Fruit Bowl, 12" . . . 85.00
Jelly Compote . . . 30.00
Mayonnaise & Plate . . . 40.00
Nappy . . . 25.00
Nut Bowl, 2 Sizes . . . 30.00
Orange Bowl, 12" . . . 85.00
Pitcher, Sm . . . 75.00
Pitcher . . . 225.00
Tumbler . . . 30.00
Punch Bowl . . . 165.00
Punch Cup . . . 10.00
Rose Bowl, 2 Sizes . . . 65.00 – 125.00
Rose Bowl Whimsey, Rare . . . 100.00
Sherbet . . . 15.00
Spoon Tray, Hndl . . . 25.00
Sugar . . . 30.00

ZIPPERED WINDOWS
Wine . . . 20.00

ZIPPER LOOP
Hand Lamp . . . 75.00
Lamp, Sm . . . 145.00
Lamp, Med . . . 125.00
Lamp, Lg . . . 165.00

ZIPPER SLASH
Banana Dish . . . 30.00
Berry Bowl, Sm . . . 10.00
Berry Bowl, Lg . . . 30.00
Butter . . . 65.00
Celery Vase . . . 20.00
Compote, Covered . . . 45.00
Compote, Open . . . 30.00
Creamer or Spooner . . . 20.00
Cup . . . 10.00
Jelly Compote . . . 25.00
Pitcher . . . 85.00
Tumbler . . . 20.00
Sauce, Ftd . . . 10.00
Sherbet . . . 15.00
Sugar . . . 30.00
Toothpick Hldr . . . 25.00
Wine . . . 10.00